JAMAICA
Talk

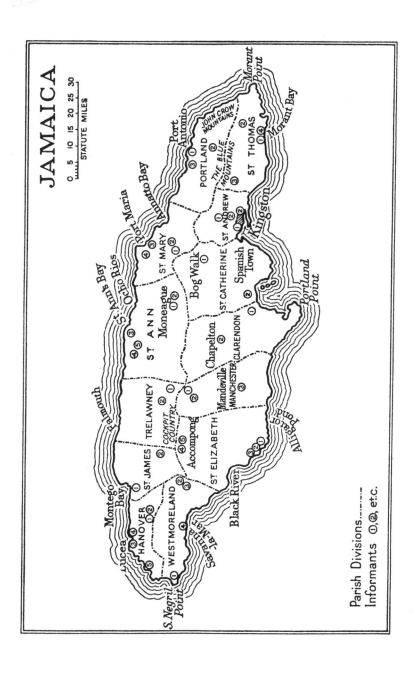

JAMAICA

0 5 10 15 20 25 30
STATUTE MILES

Parish Divisions ....
Informants ①,②, et.c.

JAMAICA *Talk*

THREE HUNDRED YEARS
OF THE ENGLISH
LANGUAGE IN JAMAICA

Frederic G. Cassidy

University of the West Indies Press
Jamaica • Barbados • Trinidad and Tobago

University of the West Indies Press
7A Gibraltar Hall Road   Mona
Kingston 7   Jamaica
www.uwipress.com

11 10 09 08 07   5 4 3 2 1

Cassidy, Frederic G., 1907–2000
Jamaica talk: three hundred years of the English language in Jamaica /
Frederic G. Cassidy.

p. cm.

Previously published: Kingston, Jamaica: Macmillan/Sangsters
Bookstores, 1982.

Includes bibliographical references.

ISBN: 978-976-640-170-2

1. English language – Provincialisms – Jamaica. 2. English language –
Dialects – Jamaica. 3. Creole dialects, English – Jamaica. I. Title.

PM7874.J3 C32 2007 427.972 92

Cover design by Robert Harris.
Printed in the United States of America.

To the memory of my Mother,
to whom Jamaica was home,
and to my Father,
whose second home it became.

CONTENTS

I. HISTORY, PRONUNCIATION AND GRAMMAR

II. JAMAICAN VOCABULARY

PREFACE TO THE FIRST EDITION
AND ACKNOWLEDGEMENTS

THIS BOOK is for anyone interested in Jamaica or in language. Though written especially for the layman, it should hold some interest for the linguist too. The reader who likes to read without interruption may ignore the reference numbers in the text; anyone who wants more detail will find among the notes at the back dates, sources, etymologies, names of fauna and flora, and so on. These are condensed to save space, yet may be read (see the directions) with reasonable ease. There is a word-finding list at the end.

This book seeks to give an account of the language, both past and present, of Jamaicans of all ranks. To avoid possible misconceptions I use a few linguistic terms in preference to the popular ones. 'Standard' here means what it does in England: the language of the educated, accepted for public use and superseding local or regional differences. 'Folk' language here refers to the usages of the Jamaican commonalty of country and city: cultivators, labourers, small artisans, domestic servants, and so on, with little formal education beyond the 'three R's'; 'folk speech' is that which they use among themselves. I employ the established term 'Informant' for anyone who answered my questions or gave me information. A list of informants, their home parishes, ages, occupations, and other facts necessary to a judgement of their contribution, precedes the notes. There is a list of the books, periodicals, and manuscripts from which citation is made.

Though the folk materials derive from many sources, the greatest share by far are from my own collections, made in 1951–2 (completed 1955) when I travelled for several months throughout the island, questioned in detail some thirty-eight local inhabitants, and recorded on tapes the voices of more than a score of others. Whatever is claimed as a Jamaicanism is attested, and has been checked against the great historical dictionaries: the *Oxford* or *New English Dictionary*, its *Supplement*,

vii

the *Dictionary of American English*, and the *Dictionary of Americanisms*. If other parts of the Caribbean had been adequately studied, it might have been possible to make an even better check. 'Jamaicanisms' will no doubt be found elsewhere in the area too; at least we are certain of them for this island.

For the help of many kinds both great and small that I have received in writing this book I am most grateful. Specific acknowledgements are made in the notes; the numerous references are my thanks to those authors whose books have proved the most valuable. But the following must have special mention: The United States Government Fulbright programme (Research Fellowship at University College of the West Indies, 1951–2); the Carnegie Corporation (research aid at UCWI, 1955); the University of Wisconsin (Graduate School research aid, 1951–2, 1955). The UCWI was my 'host' institution in 1951–2, when Prof. Sandmann took a generous interest in the work; and again in 1955, when Dr Le Page arranged for my visit, let me use the UCWI collections, and gave much personal help. The director of the Institute of Jamaica, Mr Bernard Lewis, on both occasions opened all its facilities to me: the indispensable West India Reference Library, where Miss Phyllis O. B. Caws was ever helpful, and later the Scientific library and collections, which Messrs R. P. Bengry and G. R. Proctor put at my disposal, including the unpublished file of fish names made recently by Miss Victoria Smith, and *Natural History Notes*. For bird names I have found very useful Lady Taylor's charming *Introduction to the Birds of Jamaica*, published by the Institute with Macmillan. Prof. Asprey and Mrs Thornton of UCWI made available their valuable articles on *Medicinal Plants of Jamaica*. I have seen (too briefly) the notebooks of Mr H. P. Jacobs, on loan to the UCWI; and I have had the use of the personal collections and publications of the late Mr J. L. Pietersz, kindly given me by his sisters. Of the many writers of 'dialect' literature, Mr E. N. Burke ('Uncle Newton') and Miss Louise Bennett seem to me truest to both the spirit and the letter of the folk speech; they have my congratulations.

I am quite aware — no one better — that this book is neither complete nor perfect. I have not included all my collections nor collected all that exists. Many problems remain to be solved; some of my proposals will certainly prove wrong. However, I hope that publication now may encourage others to further work by giving them some idea of the abundance and interest of the materials. Studies in progress at the University College will deal with all aspects of it in greater detail. Meantime, I invite any interested reader to correct or add what he can.

F. G. C.

PREFACE TO THE SECOND EDITION

IN THIS second edition of *Jamaica Talk* I have made such typographical corrections as were necessary. Other changes are in the nature of updating. Since 1961 the *Dictionary of Jamaican English* has appeared (Cambridge University Press, 1967). In the course of completing that book, Dr Le Page and I were able to improve or expand on a number of details, chiefly etymological. I have also published four articles in the *American Speech* magazine ('Some footnotes on the "Junjo" Question', 36.101–3; 'Hipsaw and John Canoe,' 41.45–51; 'Multiple Etymologies in Jamaican Creole', 41.211–5; 'Some New Light on Old Jamaicanisms', 42.190–201) which treat matters more fully than space permitted in the two books. What is new in these sources has been used in preparing this second edition.

The reception given to *Jamaica Talk* has been gratifying. My hope in writing it was that a semi-popular treatment would reach readers outside academic circles, and present the subject not in the traditional disdaining and imperceptive manner, but show, on the contrary, that it is a fit subject for scientific observation. An accurate examination of the language throws much light on the history and development of the life of Jamaica, and here, in a folk creation, are found plentiful evidences of imagination, poetry, a lively humour, and a real feeling for the multiform capacity of a language to communicate and to express.

That a wider public than was anticipated has found interest in *Jamaica Talk* is a pleasure for which I here express my gratitude.

Madison, Wis., USA   F.G.C.
June, 1971.

I

HISTORY, PRONUNCIATION AND GRAMMAR

Chapter One

JAMAICANISMS

WHAT LANGUAGE do Jamaicans talk? The question is asked not only by strangers to the Caribbean but also by English and American visitors who have heard Jamaicans speaking what they did not at first recognize as a type of their own tongue. It is a question raised as well by students of language, and they mean, How is Jamaica Talk to be classified — as a type of English, or as something quite different, though obviously related? A real question, this, which deserves a sound answer — one, however, that cannot be given until we have carefully examined the language as Jamaicans use it.

Another and equally interesting question is, How did Jamaicans come to talk as they do? The musical lilt and staccato rhythms, the mingling of strange words, the vowel sounds that go sliding off into diphthongs, the cheerful defiance of many niceties of traditional English grammar, the salty idioms, the wonderfully compressed proverbs, the pungent imagery of nicknames and epithets in the bestowal of which these islanders appear to be peculiarly adept — where do all these hail from, and how did they come to be?

It is now three hundred years since the English language, which has found its way to every corner of the earth, took root in Jamaica. There it has flourished and developed its own local forms and flavour, as transplanted languages do everywhere. For language — let us never forget — is infinitely multiform, highly variable, ever on the change so long as it is alive. Only dead languages lie still. What was 'right' in a living language a century ago was not the same as what is 'right' today. If we could hear Shakespeare or Milton, Wordsworth or Lord Tennyson conversing or reading their poetry, they would sound at worst foreign, at best old-fashioned. And that, even if they were on their best behaviour so to speak; for if they spoke as men from Stratford, London, Cumberland and Lincoln, admitting the local flavour of their native shires, they would sound still more peculiar. Even today, with all the effects of standardized schooling, Englishmen (to say nothing of Welshmen, Irishmen, and Scots) speak their language in countless variations. Considering the history of the British Isles, this is in no way surprising. Nor should one be disturbed to find yet other variations where people of many kinds in a new colony have pooled their home differences, seasoned them with the tropical spices of Arawak and Carib Indians, Africans, Spaniards, Frenchmen, and assorted others, until a strong and tasty pepperpot of language is concocted. This, of course, is what has happened in Jamaica.

But even if we are able to name the ingredients of our mixture, and perhaps the proportion of each, this is not all. Some like it hot, some like it cold; some strain it, some serve it thick and rich; and everyone has a right to eat as he pleases if he is prepared to take the consequences. That is — if we may move from the kitchen to the schoolroom — Jamaica Talk is not by any means of the same kind on all Jamaicans' lips. It exists in two main forms, which may be imagined as lying at opposite ends of a scale, with every sort of variation between, but each variant inclining in some degree toward the right or the left. At one end is the type of Jamaica Talk that aims toward the London 'standard' or educated model, and, in many Jamaicans' usage, reaches it extremely well — certainly as well as the speech of many a Britisher living outside the 'home counties' around London. At the other end of the scale is the inherited talk of peasant and labourer, largely unaffected by education and its standards. This is what the linguist calls 'creolised' English, that is, an English learned incompletely in slave days, with a strong infusion of African influences, and continued traditionally in much the same form down to the present.

These are at the ends of the scale. Moving toward the middle from the educated end, one finds an increasing inclusion of local elements — of Jamaican rhythm and intonation, of words that the Londoner would have no reason or need to know, of turns of phrase that have grown up in this island — what may be called 'Jamaicanisms'. Or, moving toward the middle from the uneducated end, one finds more and more adoption of the elements of standard English — the acquisition of grammatical features that were entirely lacking in the old creolised speech, a gradual tendency to pronounce in the standard way, at least when one is on guard or in a formal situation. And, unfortunately, pride of education often brings with it scorn of the homely, or at least a tendency to hide the homely.

At the middle of the scale are the 'bilinguals' — those who can use the speech of either end. Some live comfortably in this position, employing the folk talk in private or informal life, but switching to something closer to standard English in business or public life. Others — 'old-time Jamaicans' — though brought up with standard English, can also handle the folk talk as they heard it from their *nanas* or nurses and the country folk in their childhood. The only painful group is that of the *parvenu* in education who, having crossed the middle of the scale, now feel that the folk speech is beneath them and scornfully reject it. This happens all over the world, of course, when people 'go up' in the social scale, but the results are no less uncomfortable in Jamaica than in Birmingham or Chicago. The nervous conformity, the hard-won 'correctness', are inevitably flat and flavourless. When pepperpot is made in a factory and sold in tins, it will taste like this and be equally lacking in nourishment.

What, then, are the ingredients of Jamaica Talk? What constitutes a 'Jamaicanism'? Most obviously this term would include any word, meaning, or feature of grammar, idiom, or pronunciation that has originated in Jamaica, or has been adopted here from a foreign source. It should also include any similar element that has survived in this island after dying elsewhere, or which has received a decidedly higher degree of use in Jamaica than elsewhere.

Putting this into a more rational order, we may classify Jamaicanisms as belonging to five main types: preservations, borrowings, new formations, transferred meanings, and special preferences. Let us have some examples — first, of preservations. The Oxford English Dictionary (hereafter referred to as the OED) comments that *moonshine* is 'now rare or poetic' — yet it is more current among the Jamaican folk than *moonlight*. The latest citation given for *tinnen* (made of tin) in the OED is from 1653 — yet the word may be heard any day in Jamaica (and Barbados too). The latest citation for *roguing* is 1672; for *hold (one's) road*, 1795; for *catch (to)* (arrive at), 1393; yet all of these are flourishing still in Jamaica, where they were undoubtedly brought by early English settlers and preserved among the common folk. Surprising numbers of such words survive — words which one has met, if at all, only in books before, and which therefore fall upon the ear with a distinct shock. I shall never forget hearing a cultivator in Mandeville drop the word *paraventure* — Shakespearean pronunciation and all — in a casual sentence as we walked along; nor the ginger-grower in Christiana who spoke of the *quitter* (pus) in a wound — a word I had first met in the medieval encyclopedia of Bartholomaeus Anglicus, *De Proprietatibus Rerum*, and which the OED traces no later than 1689 in this sense. Such sudden echoes from the past are a daily occurrence in the Jamaican countryside.

Next come borrowings — words of non-English origin which entered the English language via Jamaica, though many of them have ceased to be only Jamaican. An example is *cashew* (*Anacardium occidentale*), which came into English from French *acajou* (from Portuguese *acaju*, from Tupí Indian *acajú*). The OED first cites the word from 1703, but it was borrowed at least forty-five years before that time. In *The State of Jamaica* (dated post 1660), we find 'Cashues' in a list of fruits along with 'supotillia, advocatas, custard apples' and others, and in 1662 Stubbe denies to 'the fruits of Jamaica call'd Cushu' the quality of an aphrodisiac. In 1679 Trapham also mentions 'Cushewes', and in 1696 Sir Hans Sloane writes of having seen the 'Cashew or Acaju Tree' growing in gardens and fields in Jamaica. Not only is this a Jamaicanism in origin — though spread since to the English language generally — but its beheading appears to be a part of the original adoption. The standard pronunciation now accents the second syllable, but the Jamaican folk accent the first: /kyáshu/. And the spelling of Stubbe suggests that the pronunciation /kúshu/, which schoolboys use when playing a game similar to marbles with the nuts, was already in existence from the start.

The third kind of Jamaicanisms — new formations — has three subdivisions: alterations, compositions, and creations. A simple alteration of pronunciation may produce essentially a new word. For example, the vegetable known elsewhere as *scallion*, is *skellion* in Jamaica. In this word only one sound is changed, but far more complex changes have taken place in others, as when *Spanish elm* becomes, among the folk, *panchalam* or *panchalang*. (The origin of these formations is discussed in the chapter on pronunciation.) Another sort of alteration is beheading, or aphetism, which may be illustrated in such standard words as *lone* from *alone*, or *fence* from *defence*, and has already been noted in *cashew*. Another Jamaicanism of this sort is *jesta*, an iron cooking pot with a long handle, derived from *digester*. Metathesis has produced such a word as *cruffy*, probably from *scurfy*, with *sk-* regularly reduced to *k-*; on the other hand it may be a blend or 'portmanteau word' based on *rough* and *scurfy*.

By far the largest number of new formations are made by composition of existing elements, whether native or foreign or both. *Garden egg* is an example of the first. Though not recorded in any of the historical dictionaries, it has been in use in Jamaica since at least 1811,[1] and is now the accepted term throughout the island and among all classes. In the Kingston area the presence of English and Americans in some numbers has introduced *egg-plant* to the market women, but its usage is recent and restricted. *Macca-fat* which we shall come to in a moment, is a combination of foreign and native, and *macca yam* of two foreign elements to form Jamaicanisms. 'Blend' words are one type of composition: *cruffy* has already been mentioned as a possible example. Reduplications might be put here too — such words as *tief-tief* (thieving), *fenky-fenky* (finicking), *kas-kas* (using strong language, quarrelling), but this is so large a group that it must receive special attention later on.

Among creations a few are the result of back-formation — such a word as *reduck*, for example, a verb meaning to reduce, back-formed in all probability from *reduction*. Similarly formed is the interesting verb *devel* (with accent on second syllable) as in a fisherman's remark that the 'breeze is develin' up', which would seem to come from the interpretation of *develop* as a verb-plus adverb phrase, *devel up*. Malapropisms are represented by *strive* for *thrive* (though over-correction may be at work here) and *ignorant* for *indignant*.

Onomatopoeia or echoism accounts for a number of Jamaicanisms, as the name for a large ant which makes a loud gnashing with its mandibles, and is therefore called *kap-kap*. Then there is the bird named *pechary* (pichíeri) in imitation of its cry; but this word may be ultimately Indian since it is paralleled in Cuba and Puerto Rico in the form *pitirre*. Every Jamaican child knows what a *fee-fee* is (a whistle); and another bird is well known as the *gimme-me-bit*, a name partly echoic, partly formed by folk-etymology. This last process is very common. One's first attempts to say an unfamiliar word are likely to be imperfect. But one attempt sounds 'better' or 'more familiar' than the others — it seems to 'make sense'. And so eventually this form survives as the 'right' one. No bird actually says *gimme-me-bit*, but these words, taken as the imitation of the cry, seem preferable to a mere series of senseless syllables. On the same pattern, the name of the plant *sempervivum* has produced, by folk etymology, *simple-bible* and *single-bible*, as well as other forms; and the tree *Poinciana*, whose flowers are a blaze of scarlet and yellow, becomes, far more meaningfully and appropriately, *Fancy-Anna*.

The fourth type of Jamaicanism is that of the transferred meaning — a common type, of course, in all new lands, where it is easier to use a familiar word in a new way than to adopt or invent an unfamiliar one. The European dandelion is *Taraxacum officinale*; in Jamaica the name has been transferred to several different plants: *Cassia ligustrina* or *Cassia occidentalis* are 'man dandelion' — having thicker stalks and coarser leaves, while *Cassia tora* is 'woman dandelion' — with finer stalks and leaves. Incidentally, the English folk name of the dandelion, *pissabed*, has also found its way to Jamaica: *Cassia occidentalis* is also known as *pissibed*. Before these transfers of meaning can occur, of course, the users of the language must see or imagine some similarity between the old object and the new, to which the transfer of meaning is anchored.

The last type of Jamaicanism is that in which the word, though not exclusively Jamaican, is the preferred term in the island — the one said more frequently than the word that is standard elsewhere. As good an example as any is *puss*, the usual word for *cat*. The native Jamaican would of course understand *cat*, yet it would not come first to his lips. Similarly, *vine* is understood, but the normal word is *wis* (from *withe*), which is vastly commoner and has entered into at least twenty combinations.

Many a foreign word has come in without much change; others have followed a rough road before settling into their present form or usage. The OED lists *caveach* as a method of preparing fish with vinegar (from Spanish *escabeche*), the verb from 1750–88, the noun with only one citation, 1822. Here the entire first syllable has been aphetised. The present Jamaican form of this word is *scaveech*, with only the initial vowel dropped, and it has been so since at least 1893,[2] though the OED fails to list this form.

A thoroughly Jamaican word (though also found in the Taki-taki patois of Surinam) is *macca*, which now means any kind of prickle, thorn, bur, or sharp spine on plants or animals — on cactus, sea-eggs, and hundreds of other things. It is used in many combinations too, like *macca breadfruit*, *macca yam*, *macca fern*, *pingwing macca*. And what a curious history it has had! No dictionary lists the word — it is presumably too local — and despite its indispensability in Jamaica I have seen no explanation offered for it. We can now show, however, that it is American Indian, that it goes back by an interesting road to the *macaw tree* (genus *Acrocomia*), also called the *macca-fat palm* in Jamaica, and is connected with the name of the *macaw* bird. This tree gets its name from Arawak *macoya*, which probably came into English through Spanish *macoya*. The earliest Jamaican reference to it (missed by the OED, which begins its citations at 1699) is in Sir Hans Sloane's list of Jamaican plants of 1696. He identifies this palm as the 'Macow' mentioned by Ligon, in his *History of Barbados*, and describes them as 'High Date-trees, and full of Thorns'. One variety he has seen growing along the road to Guanaboa (in Jamaica): 'the great Macaw-tree'. In his description he has put his finger on the two most prominent features of these trees — the fruits (not dates, but a similar nut-like berry with an edible rind, the *macca-fat* of today) and the thorns. These latter are long, sharp, and incredibly numerous, and cover both the bark and leaf-ribs of the tree. They fall to the ground all about the tree, a menace to anyone going barefoot. It is not surprising that the name *macca-tree* should have been reinterpreted as meaning 'the tree characterised by macca';

B

thus *macca* acquired the meaning *prickle* or *prickles*, which sense was then generalised to any kind of prickles. The tree appears also to have given its name to the large parrot, now extinct in Jamaica though formerly plentiful, whose favourite food was the fruit of the *macaw-tree*. Long (1774) remarks that the Great Macaw Tree yields palm-oil, and that the seeds are 'covered over with a yellow pulp, of which the macaw bird is excessively fond'. Barham mistakenly attributes the name of the tree to the bird: the development, as we have seen, went just the other way.

Macca, then, entered the English language in Barbados before the English ever came to Jamaica. It got into the common speech and has remained in Taki-taki and in Jamaican. Indeed, in the latter it has in the course of time become by far the commonest folk word; it has developed new meanings and entered new combinations. *Thorn* and *prickle* are both known but less often used. What the ordinary Jamaican says when he has run a thorn or prickle into himself is, 'Macca jook me!'

Anything called a 'Jamaicanism' in this book may be put into one of these five classes, but it should be evident that some could fit in more than one place. Many a foreign word, having entered the language and having been reformed to suit the sounds and the accentual patterns of Jamaican, may then become indistinguishable from native words and combine freely with them without any sense of hybridism. So it often is in standard English, of course. Nobody thinks of *law*, *part*, *face*, or *cook* as foreign words, though in origin they are; nobody thinks of *first-class* and *second-hand* as hybrids, though in origin they are. Once a word is naturalised in any language it may do whatever any native word of the same sort may. So with Jamaican words.

But it is not by peculiarities of vocabulary alone that Jamaica talk is characterised. The pronunciation differs in some striking ways from that of standard English, and in the grammar of the common folk we find the widest differences of all. The first time that an outsider hears spoken Jamaican he will be struck by unfamiliar sounds and rhythms; some words he will recognise fairly soon, others will be new; but hardest to grasp will be the phrases in which — to him — some words are unexpectedly missing and others unexpectedly present. If he concludes that this is a chaotic babble he will be wrong. The rules are different, but he may be assured that there *are* rules.

From the point of view of the standard language, these changes are usually thought of as 'corruptions'. The fact is that they do not pretend to be standard, and therefore the criteria of comparison are not the same. But a greater mistake comes when all sorts of unwarranted conclusions are drawn about the kind of people who could perpetrate such 'corruptions', that they are at best simple children of nature, at worst ignorant, lazy, willful, or stupid. Such conclusions show a woefully unhistorical and uninformed view, unless one is to throw all people learning a foreign and imposed speech into the same limbo. The English, in this case, were also, from the Norman conquerors' point of view, barbaric, ignorant, lazy, and stupid in learning the upper-class language no better than they did. They corrupted French in horrible ways, and they clung willfully to their corruptions. The point is, of course, that the African slave trying to learn English was in much the same position as the Anglo-Saxon commoner having to learn Norman — and the Jamaican has done no worse on the whole. The changes he has made have followed the same sorts of linguistic laws as those which governed the adoption of French words in eleventh-century England, and with no more outlandish results. An automatic belief in the superiority or purity of the English language may prove no more than that one has never truly observed it.

In the following chapters we shall examine in turn all the components of Jamaica Talk, beginning with pronunciation. But before coming to this it is necessary to run over briefly the story of the settlement of the island, and so anticipate the kinds of influences that may have gone into the production of its speech.

Chapter Two

SOURCES OF JAMAICA TALK

'XAYMACA' — land of springs. If this is not the certain meaning of the name, at least it is clearly an Arawak word, and these Indians were the natives when Columbus discovered Jamaica. The Arawak family ranged through the western islands of the central American archipelago and occupied much of what is now Venezuela, the Guiana coast, and other parts as far as the Amazon delta. The Eastern islands and inner area of the present Guianas were inhabited by Carib Indians, and east and south of them, in what is now northern and much of eastern and southern Brazil, were the Tupí and Guaraní.

Cultural connections between these major tribes and many minor ones diffused foodstuffs and artifacts of each among the others; and with the things often went the names. The Spanish and Portuguese, when they settled this huge coastal area of Central and South America and the Caribbean islands, continued and enlarged the process, borrowing the Indian words and spreading them to other Europeans — the French, English, Dutch. We have already seen how *cashew*, a typical word, came from Tupí to Portuguese to French to English. And Arawak *macaw* came through Spanish to Barbadian to Jamaican and Surinam Taki-taki.

Direct Arawak influence in Jamaican English is unlikely because these Indians had been exterminated by the Spaniards long before 1655. If some Indians had submitted to the Spaniards and survived with their Negro slaves, or even intermingled with them, it is still unlikely that under such conditions they could have preserved their language. Arawak words that had entered Spanish are probably the only ones which could come to the English here.

It is true that some Indians came to Jamaica (1671–5) with the settlers from Surinam. There were only thirty-one, and the language they spoke is not mentioned, but coming from Surinam they were probably Arawaks. Besides these, the Mosquito Indians (speakers of Misumalpan) in 1687 placed themselves under the protection of the English Crown — and their shore, in present Nicaragua, continued under this protection till 1856. They were employed by the English to help in hunting down the Maroons, and some settled in Jamaica after that war was over. These two small groups may have brought direct influences, but they cannot have been great in any case.

The Spanish influence was another matter. Spanish words have been entering Jamaican English directly from the very first and still continue to do so, especially at the folk level. Some of the earliest — *hato, barcadero, palenque* — have since virtually died out; but with the general importance of the Spanish language throughout this area, with Jamaicans going to Panama to help build the canal and to Cuba to work on sugar estates, the Spanish words have never ceased to trickle in.

The possibility of French and Dutch influence has always been small, since contacts with the colonies speaking these languages has been much less than with the Spanish ones. There were some French in Jamaica from the seventeenth century — Lewis Galdy, who was swallowed up in Port Royal during the earthquake of 1692 and flung up again into the sea — was a Frenchman. *The Importance of Jamaica*, of 1740, mentions 'English, Scots, Irish, and French' as among the 'Planters, Merchants, or Factors'. And a number of French families came over from Haiti in the first years of the next century when the revolts began. Any influence from these sources, however, must have been scattered and therefore slight; at any rate, few now survive. French words continued, of course, to come into English generally, and thus into Jamaican use as everywhere else.

The two main early components of Jamaica talk were, then, English of various kinds and African of various kinds. It is impossible today to know about these in detail, since no proper record was kept of the origin of the settlers. We must do the best we can to piece out the general story from incidental information. Repeated attempts were made from the first to stock the island with English-speaking colonists. In 1655 great encouragement was given to the New Haven (Connecticut) group, planning to move to Delaware Bay, to come instead to Jamaica;

they were promised free land, assured that they would be pro-
tected, and their transportation was provided for. In the same
year orders were given for 1,000 Irish girls and young men to be
sent to the new colony. There is no evidence that either of these
schemes came to anything,[1] but another planned at the same
time did succeed, as in 1656 Governor Stoke of Nevis came with
1,600 men, women, and children, servants, and Negro slaves,
and settled in St Thomas in the East. And between 1671 and
1675 at least three shiploads of settlers were transplanted from
Surinam to St Elizabeth and Westmoreland, a few coming as
far east as Old Harbour bay. This colony totalled 1,231, of whom
there were, in the words of the early account, '250 Christians,
31 Indians, and 950 negroes.' Cundall has reprinted the list of
names, and though we cannot with any certainty know from
mere names where these people came from and what varieties
of English they may have spoken, there is clear evidence that
the group was mixed. Probably Spanish or Portuguese were
de Silva, de Solis, Solvadore; *Matemara* or *Mekmemare* (McNa-
mara?), *Norris* and *Ohane* very likely Irish and *Dunn* and *Davidson*
Scottish; *Vaughan, Jennison, Jones* and *Phillips* look to be Welsh,
and *Gheste*, Dutch; *Westhorpe, Hudson* and *Haxby* are north-
country English names, but the rest are indeterminate and
might have come from many parts of the British Isles. Even so,
the English formed a clear majority.

The same conclusion must be drawn from the other lists of
settlers that survive. Livingstone has published one from 1670
that includes all the known white inhabitants. Of these names
80 per cent are clearly English, at most 13 per cent may be
Welsh and the remaining 7 per cent Irish, Scots and others. A
list of the militia also survives from 1700 in the Public Record
Office in London: 'All His Majesty's Forces both Horse and
Foot,'[2] which shows that among able-bodied men (including a
few free Negroes) the names are in a not very different ratio, the
English always predominating. This is no guarantee, but it
makes it distinctly improbable that there should have been any
noticeably un-English cast to the language of the class that set
the pattern at this time.

It is true that many of the white settlers were people of little
education — the servants, artisans and adventurers of all sorts
who came to try their chance in the new colony. The lists often

refer to a floating population of soldiers, sailors and privateers who could not be properly included on a par with the settlers, and were in any case impossible to count exactly. There is no doubt, however, that this group furnished a number of settlers; and conversely, some who did not thrive as settlers were easily drawn into privateering. Their language must have been a thorough mixture both geographic and social.

Servants were always much in demand. Long has written of the prices paid in 1703 to the captains of vessels that brought them in: 'Every servant, English, Scotch, Welsh, or of Jersey, Guernsey, or Man: in time of war, £18; in time of peace, £14; Irish servants, in time of war, £15; in time of peace, £12,' and adds, 'The cause of this depreciation of the Irish I am not informed of; but possibly they were more turbulent, or less skillful in work than the others.' He might have mentioned the religious reason too. The most able of these servants who survived their years of indenture set themselves up as 'planters, merchants, or factors', the last term signifying something like wholesale agents. Their speech was no doubt different in many respects from that of the 'plantocracy'; with that of the adventurers it would probably account for the provincial element in Jamaica talk.

As time went on the number of Scots increased noticeably. Long wrote in 1774:

> Jamaica, indeed is greatly indebted to North-Britain, as very near one third of the [white] inhabitants are either natives of that country, or descendants from those who were. Many have come from the same quarter every year, . . . To say the truth, they are so clever and prudent in general, as by an obliging behaviour, good sense, and zealous services, to gain esteem.

Somewhat later, Lady Nugent remarked similarly of the overseer of Hope estate:

> They say he is a good overseer; so at least his brother Scotchman told me, and there is no one here to contradict him, as almost all the agents, attorneys, merchants and shop-keepers, are of that country, and really do deserve to thrive in this, they are so industrious.

New settlements of Europeans were made after emancipation

of the slaves in 1834, but unless they had thriven enormously
they could not be looked to, at so late a date, as sources of more
than a local influence on the language, for by that time Jamaican
English had already been long established. It is perhaps worth
quoting, nevertheless, the remarks of Sturge and Harvey:

> It is the intention of the Legislature to form a colony of
> white immigrants in each of the three grand division of the
> island. . . . The one in Cornwall has already been formed,
> and is called Seaford-Town. We did not visit it but heard a
> very unfavourable account of its progress. The Middlesex
> colony is not yet in existence. This, of Altamont in Surrey,
> has probably the best promise of success, as considerable
> attention has been paid to the selection of the families. While,
> however, we have thus expressed the agreeable impressions
> we received from our visit to Altamont, we cannot but con-
> sider the artificial system upon which the settlement has been
> formed as most unlikely to produce good results of a per-
> manent nature. In addition to the formation of the settle-
> ments, European colonisation has been encouraged, by grant
> of an indiscriminate bounty of £15 a-head, to the importers
> of immigrants; a plan which could promote no other end than
> the introduction of the European vices of drunkenness and
> housebreaking; so that, in some of the parishes, a further
> expense has been incurred in order to deport them. Europeans
> have also been settled by individual proprietors on many of
> the estates, almost uniformly with an unfavourable result.
> Notwithstanding, however, the experience of the past, the
> mania for immigration still continues, as if there were a
> charm in a European birth and white complexion. These
> attempts may be traced to the boasted knowledge, but real
> ignorance, of the colonists, of the Negro character. The
> present condition of the low white population of Barbadoes
> has been forgotten or disregarded, as well as the fact that the
> introduction of Europeans, as labourers, must in the first
> instance be attended with an enormous waste of life, and when
> this difficulty is overcome, they can never compete with the
> superior adaptation of the Negroes to a tropical climate.[3]

This prediction has proved well founded. The immigration
of European settlers in the past century or so has been of no sort
to affect the established speech of Jamaicans. A far more potent
force has been the increasing power of American influence,
through commercial ties with the United States, the large in-

flow of tourists to Jamaica, the numbers of Jamaicans who have
been to America for long or short periods, and in recent years
the long voice of radio, phonograph records, moving pictures,
magazines and the like. A number of new Jamaicanisms are
based on Americanisms, and some older ones are now being
displaced by the United States' words.

Returning to the English speech of the early years — from
the capture of Jamaica in 1655 till the end of the seventeenth
century, the very time when the slaves were first adopting the
language of their new home — we may expect that the kind of
English they had to imitate was 'colonial' — that is, a speech
mostly of middle-class origin but with some admixture of both
upper- and lower-class features, and drawn from every part of
the British Isles and the previously established colonies of North
America and the Caribbean. For the white population the ideals
of England would no doubt have prevailed, though they were
by no means always attained, and sometimes not even actively
sought (as we shall see from some descriptions of Creole speech).
For the slaves the models must have been the speech of those
whites with whom they had direct contact: the book-keepers,
attorneys, overseers and white servants. The amount of English
that they would have needed to acquire in order to perform
field labour would be rudimentary; the English they learned
would largely depend on the intelligence and attitude of each
individual, and the situation in which he chanced to find himself. But before considering this matter further we must ask
about the African languages of the slaves.

The chief obstacle to a clear knowledge of this is the fact that
slaves were seldom listed by their speech but usually according
to the port of shipment from Africa; and since traders got their
slaves through many channels from a vast and unknown hinter-
land, we remain with all kinds of possibilities and few certainties.
It is certain, however, that the Spaniards, being unable to
enslave the Arawaks, were already bringing in Negroes by 1515.
When the English attacked one hundred and forty years later,
the Spaniards freed their Negroes, who took refuge in the hills
and became the nucleus of the Maroons. Some Spanish Negroes
submitted to the English, and no doubt formed a link with the
free Maroons for a time. But the English began importing fresh
slaves very soon, not only with the Nevis and Surinam settlers,

and with Governor Modiford's group from Barbados, but directly. In 1662 a charter was granted to the African Company to supply 3,000 slaves per annum, and such records as we have show a steady increase in their numbers down through the years.

Long's figures, which are generally accepted, give the number of Whites in 1658 as 4,500 and of Negroes as 1,400, a ratio of 76 per cent to 24 per cent. But by 1673 the ratio had turned the other way: Whites 8,564 (47 per cent), Negroes 9,504 (53 per cent). Thereafter the number of Negroes rapidly increased — by 1690 there were 40,000 — while the number of Whites remained much the same or even decreased. In 1734 there were 7,644 Whites (8 per cent) and 86,546 Negroes (92 per cent). In 1740 the Negroes were said to be 'so numerous, as to be reckoned about 15 to one White; therefore every Person is obliged to keep one white Servant to thirty Negroes'.[4] Though the numbers of both black and white continued to increase in the succeeding years this ratio has not been altered greatly since.

In his *New and Exact Account of Jamaica* (1739), Charles Leslie has declared that the slave traders 'trade from *Sierra Leona* to *Cape Negroe*, a vast territory on the Coasts, near 1,500 miles in length, in which are a great multitude of petty Kingdoms, where the Kings sell their Subjects and Prisoners of War, some mean Men their Children, and sometimes their Wives'.

We also find, in *The New Act of Assembly of Jamaica*, 1789, the figures on the importation of slaves by four companies over the periods from 1764–74 and 1779–88, with the numbers brought from each place. The totals, arranged in descending order, are:

Annamaboe	8,550	(Gold Coast)
Bonny	8,203	(Niger Delta)
Gold Coast	5,724	(Gold Coast)
Calabar	2,688	(South Nigeria
Windward Coast	2,679	(Liberia)
Whydah	2,438	(Dahomey)
Angola	1,894	(Angola)
Old Calabar	1,667	(South Nigeria)
Benin	1,319	(South Nigeria)
Papaw	131	(Dahomey)
Gambia	95	(Gambia)
(Unidentified	6,039)	

It is evident that the smallest numbers come from the northern extreme (Gambia) and the southern extreme (Angola); the vast majority come from the Gold Coast (14,274) and Southern Nigeria (13,877), the rest from the westward equatorial coast. It is true that the first slaves brought in by the English had come a century before; besides, these figures show the importations of only four companies for only twenty-one years. Neverthless, as the trade was a solidly established one, they are probably typical, and we may derive from them a general idea of the chief origins of the Jamaican Negroes.

Somewhat later than Leslie, Long discussed the various tribes.[5] From his account we may add the names 'Arada, Bongo, Concha, Congo, Coromantim (including Akim, Ashantee, Fantim), Ebo, Minnah, Quamboo and Quaqua' — presumably all represented in Jamaica. And from yet other sources we can add Chamba, Crongoe, Hittoe, Madagascar, Moco, Mundingo, Mungola, Nago, Nanga, Sumino, Wakee and Wawee.[6]

The information afforded by these names is incomplete, yet it points much the same way: we may safely conclude that at the time when the basis of Jamaican folk speech was laid, the largest number of slaves came from the area of the Gold Coast and Nigeria, and were therefore speakers of the Niger-Congo or West Sudanese languages.[7] We may expect that while elements from any of the individual languages or dialects may have remained in the language of the slaves, the largest number would be from the dominant group — whether dominant numerically or in some other way — and further, that the more fundamental elements of grammar and intonation would be those possessed in common by the Niger-Congo languages.

One must also ask, What of the survival of the African languages once transplanted? The situation was largely against their survival. The slaves of different tribes, often traditional enemies, were indiscriminately mixed together on the plantations. As Leslie wrote in 1739: 'The Slaves are brought from several places in Guiney, which are different from one another in Language, and consequently they can't converse freely; or, if they could, they hate one another so mortally, that some of them would rather die by the Hands of the *English* than join

with other *Africans* in an Attempt to shake off their Yoke. . . .
'Tis true the Creolian Negroes are not of this Number: They all
speak English.'

Tribal consciousness and separateness were kept up throughout the time when slaves were being imported. So late as 1838
we find the following description of the Christmas celebration
on a coffee plantation: 'The Mongolas, the Mandingoes, the
Eboes, the Congoes, &c. &c., formed into exclusive groups, and
each strove to be loudest in the music and songs, or rather yells,
peculiar to their country; and their dance, if dance I must call
it, was a display of unseemly gestures.'[8]

Once the immigration of Africans had ceased, however, the
forces of adaptation, always at work, were accelerated. The
situation twenty-four years after emancipation may be judged
by Chambre's account:

> When negroes were captured in slave-vessels and brought
> to Jamaica, there was considerable difficulty experienced in
> communicating with them, or understanding what they said.
> Here and there a few old men were to be met with who had
> been brought from the coast of Guinea in their youth; and
> even they had almost forgotten their native tongue. They
> knew enough of it, however, to serve as interpreters.

It had always been to a slave's advantage to learn English.
Without it he could not hope to improve his condition or get the
more desirable employments. Prestige was attached to English
by the Jamaican-born Negroes, who naturally spoke it. In the
words of Long, 'The Creole Blacks . . . hold the Africans in the
utmost contempt, stiling them "salt-water Negroes", and
"Guinea birds". Even those who happened to be born at sea on
the voyage across and were therefore not full natives of Jamaica,
were called "salt-water Creoles".' To this day there is a strong
awareness, even among those at the bottom of the social scale,
of the difference between the speech of city and country, especially the remoter hill settlements. The old-fashioned expressions and turns of phrase are denominated 'Bungo talk';
and part of the humour connected with Anancy, hero of the
folk tales, is that he talks this way. It is usually explained that
'him tongue tie', but the sounds by which he is characterised
are, as we shall see, often African ones.

When Russell wrote in 1868, he remarked that the inter-jection *babwa* (expressing wonder) 'is used only on estates and their vicinity, and is of African origin. Settlers in the mountain-ous parts would consider it disgraceful to be heard using such a word'. This should remind us that the larger number of new-come slaves would normally have remained in the lowlands, and further, that even after emancipation a considerable number of free, indentured African agricultural workers con-tinued to be brought in for a time.

In sum it may be said that all Jamaican-born Negroes learned English, whether or not they kept up some part of African; that there were always great numbers of new-come Africans who, however, had good reason to learn English as well as the situation permitted; that their first models were not upper-class English, and that the chief models after the seven-teenth century must have been the native Negroes rather than the whites.

Two other factors should not be forgotten. For the first hundred years of the colony no real effort was made to Christian-ise the slaves, and of course education was not even thought of. The established church was in an even greater state of decay in the colonies than at home, the ministries a sinecure within the granting of the plantocracy; Lady Nugent's remarks as late as 1800 are painfully revealing. The first active missionaries were the Moravians, who began their work in the early eighteenth century; the Wesleyans' mission began in 1789; individual Presbyterian and Baptist ministers were at work at about the same time, though the mission of the latter was not actually founded till 1814. All these sects played a large part in the fight for emancipation. But during more than a century before, nothing was done actively to civilise the slaves, who, left to their own resources, kept up many African customs: music and dancing on their rare holidays, burial customs and games, obeah, myalism. These activities naturally tended to preserve some African words and patterns of speech, if no actual African language as such.

The second factor is the possibility of direct survival of African speech among the Maroons. As we have seen, the nucleus of this group was Spanish-speaking. They established themselves in the mountain fastnesses and were joined over the years by runaway slaves, among whom there must have been speakers of English. As Bryan Edwards described the Maroons in 1796, 'Their language was a barbarous dissonance of the African dialects, with a mixture of Spanish and broken English.' But 'was' is significant; for Dallas, who knew the Maroons intimately, wrote only seven years later:

> The Maroons, in general, speak, like most of the other negroes in the island, a peculiar dialect of English, corrupted with African words; and certainly understand our language well enough to have received [religious] instruction in it.

Indeed, the Maroons can not have kept up their Spanish long, and it is doubtful how much African they preserved as an articulate speech. Dallas reports a conversation that has striking resemblances to the Maroons' language of today — or, for that matter, to Jamaican folk speech in general. The Governor has told a Maroon who has two wives that he may keep no more than one. The man argues the point:

> 'Top, Massa Governor,' said he, 'top lilly bit — you say me mus forsake my wife.'
> 'Only one of them.'
> 'Which dat one? Jesus Christ say so? Gar a'mighty say so? No, no, massa; Gar a'mighty good; he no tell somebody he mus forsake him wife and children. Somebody no wicked for forsake him wife! No, massa, dis here talk no do for we.'

On the other hand, according to Dallas, the Coromantee or Kromanty Negroes, who had a reputation for fierceness, came in time to dominate the Maroons, and it is possible that that dominance may have kept African language alive. It would certainly have had its uses for secret communication. Reports of this tenor continue to be heard from time to time — they have become traditional. There is no real evidence, however, that any articulate African speech survives in any community in the island today, and it is very doubtful whether any has been spoken at all within the twentieth century. A few snatches of African or African-like words are preserved in some songs, and some of the revivalist cults keep up a terminology among themselves that has African elements, but these are all vestiges in a structure that is not genuinely African, but Jamaican (though paralleled in other parts of the Caribbean). Jamaican folk

speech in general, not in the Maroon settlements alone, preserves some 250 words of African origin, a number of which are
common property throughout the island, others restricted to the
conservative localities. Even the Maroon communities of Moore
Town and Accompong are, today, no longer isolated; to all
intents they take part intrinsically in the life around them, and
their speech differs only in minor ways from that of the neigh-
bouring areas.

Chiefly out of African and English, then, there emerged a
blended language, that of native or 'creole' Jamaicans, which
may be called for the moment 'Creole English'. The term
creole, so often misunderstood, meant, to the many travellers and
writers who used it, simply 'island born'. It was applied equally
at first, and down into the nineteenth century, to whites,
Negroes, or People of Colour. Thus the 'creole' speech which
was so often a subject of comment (usually unfavourable) referred to the usage of both slave and master, in so far as that
differed from English usage. That the Negroes should have
learned English incompletely was only to be expected under the
circumstances; that a large influence from their native African
should be felt in such English as they learned, goes almost without saying. That the resulting blend should also become to a
greater or less degree the speech of the creole whites was the
result of conditions of life on the plantations.

As early as 1739 we find Leslie deploring the situation. He
thinks it is out of the question to expect that Jamaica may produce 'a *Homer*, or a *Virgil*, . . . a *Tully*, or a *Demosthenes*', considering the way young gentlemen are reared; 'and it cannot be
otherwise, for a Boy till the Age of Seven or Eight diverts himself
with the Negroes, acquires their broken Way of talking, their
Manner of Behaviour, and all the Vices these unthinking
Creatures can teach; then perhaps he goes to School, but young
Master must not be whipt; if he learns, 'tis well, if not, it can't
be helped.'

The situation was as bad, if not worse, for the young women.
Long has an elaborate description of these unfortunate creatures:

> Those, who have been bred up entirely in the sequestered
> country parts, and had no opportunity of forming themselves
> either by example or tuition, are truly to be pitied. We may
> see, in some of these places, a very fine young woman

awkwardly dangling her arms with the air of a Negroe-servant, lolling almost the whole day upon beds or settees, her head muffled up with two or three handkerchiefs, her dress loose, and without stays. At noon, we find her employed in gobbling pepper-pot seated on the floor, with her sable hand-maids around her. In the afternoon, she takes her *siesto* as usual; while two of these damsels refresh her face with the gentle breathings of the fan; and a third provokes the drowsy powers of Morpheus by delicious scratchings on the sole of either foot. When she rouzes from slumber, her speech is whining, languid, and childish. When arrived at maturer years, the consciousness of her ignorance makes her abscond from the sight or conversation of every rational creature. Her ideas are narrowed to the ordinary subjects that pass before her, the business of the plantation, the tittle-tattle of the parish; the tricks, superstitions, diversions and profligate discourses, of black servants, equally illiterate and unpolished.

They have little hope, he says, of escaping these influences, 'even after an English education, unless sent away extremely young.'

Another writer, not long after, gives examples of creole talk which, both in pronunciation and in diction, are anything but elegant. A young gentleman, at dinner in a sumptuous plantation greathouse, speaks to a young creole 'lady':

'Pray, miss Louisa, will you permit me to help you to a bit of turkey; it is very fine!'
'Tank you, sir, *wid* all my *haut*.'
'Pray miss, what part do you like best?'
'Sir, Ise don't love turkey rump — Ise love turkey bubby.'[9]

These manners, and the accompanying language, did not escape the lively observation of Lady Nugent, who comments on them in several places. 'Mrs C. (a Major's wife) is a perfect Creole, says little, and drawls out that little, and has not an idea beyond her own Penn.' 'Mrs S. is a fat, good-humoured Creole woman, saying dis, dat, and toder. . . .' 'The Creole language is not confined to the negroes. Many of the ladies, who have not been educated in England, speak a sort of broken English, with an indolent drawling out of their words, that is very tiresome if not disgusting. I stood next to a lady one night, near a window, and, by way of saying something, remarked that the air was much cooler than usual; to which she answered, "Yes, ma-am, *him rail-y too fra-ish.*" '

More than fifty years later, after conditions for schooling in the island had begun to improve, one still finds these strictures:

> There is scarcely a black in a hundred who speaks pure English, and the white people take no pains to correct them. Sometimes they even adopt the barbarous idiom of the negro, thinking to make themselves understood. The consequence is, their pronunciation is abominable, and the rising generation, notwithstanding the pains taken to educate them, retain the villainous *patois* of their parents.[10]

If there is any consolation in it, Jamaicans may reflect that similar strictures were frequently expressed by Englishmen upon the contemporary speech of ordinary Americans, whose differences from standard English, though not the same, were yet numerous and striking. The Americans, too, were charged with ill manners, awkwardness, bad grammar and all the rest — and not without good reason. The conditions of colonial society cannot reasonably be expected to compare with those in the home land, and certainly not with the top of the scale. Such comparisons, in short, are unequal and have a foregone conclusion. Ideals of 'purity' and 'elegance' were at their height in the eighteenth century, while snobbism in language came to its peak in the nineteenth. Small wonder, then, that the Creole, whether master or slave, for whom purity and elegance of language were a practical impossibility, should have received such constant abuse. From the scientist's point of view it is unfortunate, since this low opinion led to neglect, and no careful observation of the language was made.

The best we have is a small, now rare, book called *The Etymology of Jamaican Grammar*, 1868, thought to have been written by Thomas Russell. Russell is both marked by his time, and ahead of it; for while he subscribes to the eighteenth-century tenets that 'Grammar is the art of speaking correctly, according to certain rules sanctioned by old and proper usage', that the system of language is a product of rational control, and that the English tongue was or could be in some sense 'pure' — positions which no linguist today would attempt to uphold — he nevertheless is aware that out of the confusions incident to the

c

formation of Creole speech must emerge some principle of order;
in other words, he recognises the fact that this new speech is not
merely chaotic:

> Although it is evident that this, as every other corrupted
> form of language, is spoken by no previously well-planned
> system, yet, as in course of time, every corruption resolves
> itself into certain fixed rules, so shall we find that this has
> settled into certain very plain and distinct ones, which are, in
> not a few instances, in direct opposition to those of the pure
> parent language.

Russell then goes on to describe the Jamaican folk speech in
some detail, with honest observation, and without the attitude
of superiority or scorn (still to be found today) that marks the
unscientific approach and usually disqualifies the observer as
biased and unobjective. Russell's book is therefore a valuable
one; we have cited it already and shall return to it often. If
more like it had been undertaken we would be able to trace
with greater accuracy the development of Jamaica talk. As it is,
we must piece together scanty remains and guess at the probable
consequences of settlement, correcting our guesses as best we
may by what has survived to the present time.

It remains only to mention two other groups which have
latterly settled in Jamaica, though their contribution to the
speech has been small. Beginning in 1834, but especially in 1845
and 1847, and later (1883–5, and from 1890 to about 1913)[11]
indentured labourers were brought in from India. These
'Coolies', as they have always been called in the island, worked
at first on sugar estates, and some continue to do so; others are
now independent cultivators. Some are urban dwellers, but the
majority have remained on the land. In some communities they
keep their separateness, but the process of their absorption into
the common life of the island is well started. They have contributed no more than a score of words to general usage.

Some Chinese also — Cantonese, chiefly speakers of the
Hokka dialect — have come in, especially after 1865.[12] Their
contribution to Jamaican language has been very small: it is
limited almost wholly to words connected with gambling.

While the purpose of the foregoing sketch has been to give a
basis for anticipating the various components of Jamaica talk,

there is only one way to know really what those components are: to examine the language as it has been and as it is. The influences, to put it another way, cannot be known by foresight but only by hindsight. Let us turn at once, then, to this examination, beginning with the pronunciation.

Chapter Three

JAMAICAN PRONUNCIATION

THE EDUCATED Jamaican pronounces Standard English as well as the educated man anywhere — that is to say, according to his personal lights and attitudes, his interests, and the impression of himself that he may seek to establish. Like everybody else he will have his local differences, yet no more of those necessarily than the educated Irishman, Welshman, or Scot — or, for that matter, than the educated Englishman who is not from the 'home counties'. These local differences are heard in Jamaica in individual words and turns of phrase, but perhaps most strikingly as a pattern of intonation and accentuation that is often very different from the levelness of many Americans, on the one hand, or the hilliness of many Englishmen on the other. Jamaican speech is more accidented: it goes up and down more frequently, and by sharper rises and falls. In short, it has a decided and characteristic lilt, the origin of which we shall discuss in a moment.

As for the intonation of the folk, their patterns show even greater variation — they swoop and tumble, up and down, seldom remaining level for more than a few syllables together, frequently alternating the levels from syllable to syllable. It is this that gives the sing-song effect for which Jamaica talk is known.

Such a description, however, is merely impressionistic. To have an accurate picture of these patterns of intonation we shall have to call in mechanical aids, to catch the speech with a recording device and afterwards take it apart laboriously — in short, this is a job for the phonetician, the details of which do not belong in this book. Nevertheless we must give a real sample to show how the folk speech differs from Standard English in its patterns of stress, pause, and pitch. Let us take the opening sentences from a story told by a cane-field labourer which I recorded by the roadside near Morant Bay in 1952. The story was unrehearsed and is typical — I have recorded similar ones in many other parts of the island. It represents the folk speech well, with some dramatic heightening, a feature which is very often present in even the informal conversation of the common man in Jamaica. The words are put upon 'staircases' to show the levels of the voice, first as told in the folk speech, then as told (also on a tape recording) by a speaker of Standard English.

As spoken by informant 7 :

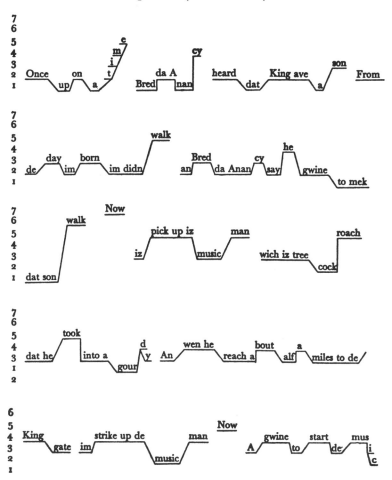

As spoken in Standard English :

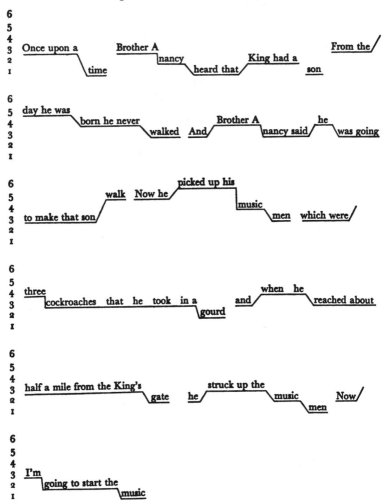

A comparison of these two versions will show at once that the folk speech changes up or down (not considering the degree of change) 61 times in 88 syllables (69 per cent), while the Standard speech changes level only 31 times in 89 syllables (35 per cent). Thus the folk intonation is almost twice as accidented as the Standard. The degree of change is also greater in the first: the changes average 1·61 steps, as against 1·23 steps in the Standard.

These are the extremes, of course; they do not represent the many kinds of variation that exist between. Indeed, the folk story already shows some of the influence of Standard: such forms as 'heard', 'he', 'took' (instead of *hear, him, tek*) are borrowed from it; and conversely, the accidentation of the folk speech often carries over to the pronunciation of educated Jamaicans — somewhat softened and smoothed, to be sure, but definitely present — furnishing much of the characteristic local flavour.

A secondary effect of this accidentation is to make the syllabic divisions prominent, which gives, along with the sing-song, something of a pattering effect. Yet this is present even without the changes of pitch, as one can hear when the speaker becomes excited, for then his voice jumps to the top level and stays there, clattering away like a drumbeat, sharp, percussive. When Jamaicans become angry and indulge in a *kas-kas*, the lilt is quite lost and the imprecations come pelting in a high-pitched volley.

In Standard English, intonation is not tied to the meaning of every word, as it is, for example, in Chinese, Indo-Chinese, and West African languages. We use it, however, at the end of sentences, dropping the pitch decidedly in exclamations and turning it upward if we are asking a question that requires a yes-or-no answer. Jamaican practice is much the same for such questions and exclamations, but the declarative sentences — which are of course by far the most numerous — do not correspond. It is chiefly in these that one hears the unexpected upturn at the end which, in Standard English, might indicate a question. Though this upturn is never as great as it is for questions, it is a feature which gives to Jamaican conversation, when heard by an outsider, a peculiarly tentative or inconclusive effect, as if the speakers were perpetually in doubt about something.

Occasionally one finds that homonymous words or phrases depend on the contrast of intonation to distinguish their meanings. In the folk pronunciation the words *can* and *can't* may become homonyms, both being pronounced [kjã:]: in such a case the affirmative may be spoken in the declarative pattern, while the more emphatic negative is spoken in the exclamatory pattern. The sentence /it kyaang hiit/, for example, may mean *it can eat* or *it can't eat* — that is, it is edible or inedible. The difference is heard and understood at once, however, from the intonation:

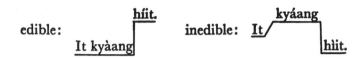

edible: It kyàang híit.   inedible: It kyáang hìit.

In Standard English the main contrast is between the sounds of *can* and *can't*, quite apart from pitch; in Jamaican the contrast is in the pitch (with some accentual difference).

The origin of the Jamaican lilt, naturally enough, has been a subject of speculation. So far as I am aware, however, there has been no real study of the question — a difficult one, in which angels well might fear to tread. The prevailing 'theory', if it can be called so, holds that this is an influence from the Welsh. At first glance this seems possible enough since there are some similarities; an Englishman hearing Jamaican intonations for the first time will naturally enough recall the other lilt that is closest to his experience and wonder whether there may not be a connection. This kind of surmise, however, is very far from anything like a proof. To make the theory plausible, one would have to demonstrate that just at the time when African slaves were learning English, or shortly after, a powerful influence was exerted upon them by Welshmen. And there is no way to show this — indeed, the evidence is against it. We have no record of any solid or dominant Welsh settlement in Jamaica within which the patterns of intonation could have been transferred in this way. The lists of names that survive[1] show a rather small proportion of Welsh settlers (at most 13 per cent in 1670) and these were generally distributed among other speakers, very largely English.

Jamaican folk English was established, in its early form, before the end of the seventeenth century; but if one were even to look for some later Welsh influence — for example, from the end of the eighteenth century till emancipation, when the missionaries were so powerfully evangelising the slaves — the facts would favour the theory no more. In *Udgorn Jubili* (Trumpet of the

Jubilee), a book in Welsh printed in 1844, describing the work of the Baptist Church in Jamaica, there is a list of the twenty-two ministers of this sect then in the island. But of these names only three are at all likely to be Welsh — Francies, Merrick, and Williams. The rest — more than eighty-six per cent — are clearly English. Under the circumstances the 'Welsh theory' becomes most implausible. At least, anyone who espouses it must undertake the burden of the proof.

There was undoubtedly a mixture of local types in the English spoken early in Jamaica; Welshmen and Irishmen were present from the first, and later many Scots. The Englishmen who came were of all ranks of life with their differences of language. We may expect to see reflections of this variety lasting in Jamaican speech to this day, but they appear in terms of words and phrases rather than of something so fundamental as intonation.

The only possible alternative source for the characteristic Jamaican intonation is the African languages that the slaves spoke when they came. We have already seen that many travellers and visitors to the island in the eighteenth and nine-teenth centuries commented upon the differences they noticed: how the slaves' habits of speech worked their way upward from the servants to the young creole masters and mistresses and established themselves so firmly as to defy complete eradication. Nor were these observed merely in the pronunciation of par-ticular sounds or in the choice of words; there were remarks on 'whining, languid, childish, and drawling' speech,[2] which imply differences not only of tempo but of intonation as well.

What precisely these were it is impossible to tell from such scanty evidence, but it may be noted that the Niger-Congo languages are characterised by differences of meaning which depend upon pitch — or 'tone' — and stress. Twi, for example, a typical one, has five different tones: high, middle, low, rising, and falling. Every syllable of every word is said in one of these tones, and a different tonal pattern may change the meaning even though the individual sounds are the same. To give only one example, *adidí* (last syllable in high tone) means *feasting* or a *meal*, but *adídí* (second syllable high, third syllable middle tone) means *Turkey-red thread*. There is nothing corresponding to this in English, of course.

In English, stress and pitch are normally associated: greater stress, higher pitch. In $\overset{\text{PA}}{\underset{\lfloor \text{per}}{}}$ the first syllable is emphasised and the tone is higher; in $\underset{\text{op}}{\overset{\text{POSE}}{}}$ it is the second syllable that has more stress and higher pitch. In Twi nouns, however, the stress may fall either on the first high-toned syllable or on the low-toned syllable before it. Those of the first type would sound much like English words: $\overset{\text{PA}}{\underset{\lfloor \text{per,}}{}}$ $\underset{\text{op}}{\overset{\text{PO}}{}}\underset{\text{nent}}{}$ — but the others would be most un-English. Suppose *opponent* had high pitch on the third syllable; *po* would take the stress and *then* the voice level would rise. To the ears of speakers of Standard English this would be topsy-turvy, since stress usually precedes a lower pitch, while here it precedes a higher. Yet that is precisely what one hears so often from Jamaicans: $\underset{\text{opPO}}{\overset{\text{nent,}}{}}$ $\underset{\text{PA}}{\overset{\text{per,}}{}}$ $\underset{\text{NA}}{\overset{\text{tion.}}{}}$

Thus the very feature in which Jamaican intonation differs strikingly from that of Standard English is found in a typical language of the West African coast. All that we know about the way in which languages in contact behave makes it plausible that as the Africans in Jamaica learned English they carried over into it some of the accidentation of pitch to which they were accustomed. Somewhere along the line of assimilation it lost its power to distinguish meaning but remained as a secondary feature of the folk speech, one that has lasted to some extent until the present time. In short, they did not need to imitate the Welsh, even if the latter had been in a dominant position.

As to the languidness and the drawl which annoyed Lady Nugent and others it is hard to be sure. Some people still complain that Jamaicans drawl, yet others find their speech too rapid — Jekyll, for example, who was surely a competent judge, has written:

And above all, speed. When the stranger lands in Jamaica and hears the rapid rush of words, and the soft, open vowels, he often says: 'Why, I thought they talked English here, but it sounds like Spanish or Italian.'

In short, one can hear from individuals both slow and rapid tempos; it would require some careful experimentation to show that the 'average' Jamaican speaks at a notably slower rate than the 'average' Englishman; we have no trustworthy evidence either way. These matters depend at present on impressions, and impressions are often due to a misreading of the facts. Our habits of listening have a very powerful and quite unconscious effect upon what we think we hear. The fact is that Jamaican speech does tend to make some vowels longer than those of Standard English, and this may be what gives the impression of a drawl. Besides, in emphatic or emotional speech, Jamaicans (especially the folk, but others too at all social levels) lengthen the vowels very strikingly: 'it's *reaaaly* a shame!' On the other hand it makes some vowels shorter, which is perhaps responsible for the effect of rapidity noted by Jekyll. Probably the longer vowels and the shorter compensate to some degree for each other. In any case, whatever 'impression' one may arrive at, it is certainly not proved that it takes a Jamaican more time to say a sentence than it does an Englishman or American. These matters must be carefully studied before anyone's opinion or impression can carry much weight, and for the present the question must remain suspended.

We now come to the individual sounds of Jamaica talk. And since at one end of the scale there is a close approach to Standard English pronunciation, it is to the other extreme that one must look for the characteristic differences.

The vowels and diphthongs of Standard English are sixteen, and may be illustrated by the sample words *beat, bit, bet, Bert, bat, boot, book, bought, bot, but,* and *Bart,* for the vowels, and *bait, bite, boat, bout, boil* for the diphthongs. These are the distinctive phonemes because the difference in meaning of the words depends on the contrast of sound between them: all the words begin and end alike,[3] but their nuclei are different.

Jamaican folk speech has phonemes corresponding to all of these except *Bert, bought, bot,* among the vowels, and *boil* among the diphthongs: in pronunciation these fall in respectively with *but, Bart, bat,* and *bile* (like *bite*). Thus *bird, word,* and others like them are regularly *bud, wud; bought* would not be used, since the verb is *buy* for all tenses and other forms, but *lawn, corn,* become *laan, kaan;* and so for the rest. (See further Appendix I.)

Speaking technically for a moment, the low-mid back vowel of Standard is not present, and the low back and high mid vowels take their place. This kind of change leads, of course, to situations where words that are distinct in Standard are not distinct in Jamaican, and where meaning must therefore depend on the broader context. In such a sentence as /di lag ful a rat/ one would not know whether the *log* was full of *rot* or of *rats.* Other words too become homonyms: *haughty* and *hearty, lawn* and *learn, pot* and *pat, thought* and *tart* (also the *thwart* of a boat), and so on. (As the reader may guess, *r* is kept, as in Standard, only before vowels, and *t* is said for *th.*) It is unlikely that these homonyms, though identical in sound, would get in each other's way very often: the difference of context would almost always make the meaning evident. That is why the example of *rat* and *rot* had to be contrived. Every language seems to be able to tolerate a number of homonyms, and those that result from the smaller number of vowel phonemes in Jamaican folk speech do not appear to cause any strain.

This pronunciation was considered characteristic of Jamaica before the end of the eighteenth century. Moreton tells of a young Creole lady asking for a drink of *mobby,* 'Do, momma, get me some mauby, *mine* head no *'tand* good'. Here the vowel is lengthened (is this the 'drawl'?) and may represent either *aa* or *aw.* And *Tom Cringle* depicts, a little later, an old woman in the Kingston streets selling spruce beer to sailors, and saying, 'Dozen *battle* of pruce,' instead of *bottles.* So also in the Slave's Diary (1837) we find *Garge* for *George* and *clak* for *clock.*

As for the missing diphthong *oi* that has fallen in with *ai,* its absence produces the homonymous pairs *toil* and *tile, loiter* and *lighter, oil* and *isle* (also *aisle*), and so on. From the last pair Louise Bennett gets some fun in the verses:

> Den dem ax de po' pickney all 'bout British Isles
> W'en is ongle t'ree ile she know good,
> Kerosene ile fe de lamp, Castarile wen we sick
> An' cokenat ile wey we trow 'pon we food.

This particular pronunciation is not only Jamaican, of course; it was in cultivated use in the eighteenth century in England — as witness Pope's rhymes of *join* with *line*, *designs* with *coins*, and many such. It is now an archaic or dialectal feature in many places, but still the established thing in Jamaican folk speech.

The lack of these three vowels and the diphthong is quite regular, yet there is a curious effect that shows the influence of Standard persisting behind. Compare:

Standard	*Jamaican folk*
cot, cat	/kat, kyat/
corn, can't	/kaan, kyaan/
got, gat	/gat, gyat/
Gordon, garden	/gaadn, gyaadn/

If *cot* and *cat* behaved like *pot* and *pat*, they would become complete homonyms, and so would *got* and *gat*. But these consonants *k* and *g*, when they precede Standard *a* become *ky* and *gy* in Jamaican, and so a distinction is still preserved from the words with Standard *o*. So strong is this pattern that there is even a parallel development after *f* in the word *fern*, sometimes pronounced /fyaan/.

Standard	*Jamaican folk*
bile, boil	/bail, bwail/
pile, spoil	/pail, pwail/

Here *p* and *b*, when they precede Standard *oi*, become *pw* and *bw* in Jamaican; and so, though the Standard diphthong is lost, a distinction is preserved and homonymy is avoided.

Jamaican folk diphthongs have a clear system, then, which closely parallels that of Standard English though four sounds have fallen in with others quite similar to them. It might be remarked in passing that the same thing has happened in some parts of Canada and the United States (western Pennsylvania, northern Michigan, and parts of Ontario) and for the same reason: in these places a colonial pronunciation has survived among the populace despite the competition of pronunciations from other regions that carry greater prestige. Jamaica has some differences, nevertheless, in vowels and diphthongs. The tense vowels tend to be longer in duration than the corresponding Standard ones (as in *beat*, *boot*, *Bart*). And two diphthongs, those

of *bait* and *boat*, are quite unexpected. Whereas in Standard
these glide from a mid position up to a high position, in Jamaican folk speech they start high and glide down to the mid
position. This makes *bait* sound a good deal like *BE-et*, and *boat*
a good deal like *BU-ot*. Local variations may be found throughout the island and, as always, those who seek to acquire Standard
pronunciation normalise them somewhat; but among the commonalty they are usual, no doubt being responsible, among
other things, for the strange effects of Jamaica Talk on the outsider's ear.

Still another source of this strangeness is the fact that Jamaican words can end with the vowels of *bet*, *bat*, *book*, and *but*,
though this is impossible in Standard. Jamaican examples are
often words of African origin, such as *senseh* fowl, *bankra* basket,
patu, the goatsucker, and *conga-so*, a cunning person.[4] In addition
to not knowing what these words mean, the stranger hears combinations that seem to him clipped or incomplete, yet the first
and third sounds are the same as in Standard, and the second
and fourth are not much different (*bat* is made somewhat
farther back in the mouth, and *but* somewhat closer to *bot*, with
the lips a little rounded).

Except for the absence of the two sounds of *th* (as in *thin* and
then), which have fallen in respectively with *t* and *d*, the consonants of Jamaican folk speech are the same as those of Standard
English. They cannot, however, come in all the combinations of
Standard — consonant clusters are frequently simplified, as we
shall see. And one consonant [ʒ], the sound of the *g* in *rouge*,
cannot come at the end of a word, though it can come in the
middle, as in *measure*, *pleasure*. This is one of the newest consonants to be added to the English language. In Standard it cannot
start a word; it is even unstable in final position, the tendency
being to make it *j*, converting *rouge* into *rouje*. It is hardly surprising, then, that this Anglicising tendency should affect
French words in Jamaica. It even applies, sometimes, *within*
words, as in /akíejanali, divíjan/ *occasionally*, *division*, which I
have heard in the Jamaican countryside.

One other consonant, *h*, behaves in a non-Standard way. It is,
as often as not, prefixed to stressed vowels or diphthongs, as in
heggs and *hice*, and dropped irregularly from other words —
'*ow*, '*igh*, '*ouse*. This is very much like Cockney usage — indeed,

some historical connection is not at all impossible; yet the Jamaican and Cockney confusions with *h* may merely result from the same conditions: loss of the sound, followed by an attempt to replace it that goes awry and puts it in the un-Standard places.

Jamaican folk words undergo many transformations owing to sound-changes. We shall look first at the sounds that are lost, next at those altered in various ways, and finally at those added. Aphetism (which has produced such Standard English words as *mend* from *amend*, or *sport* from *disport*) is responsible for *cashew* (already cited): others found among the folk are *nuff, pon, weh, bout, long*, from *enough, upon, away, about, along*. But these would be found in familiar speech anywhere. More specifically Jamaican are *shorance* from *assurance, flecta* from *reflector* (a lamp); and Russell almost a hundred years ago recorded *pecta* for *inspector* — which would probably not be used today. Yet aphetism is always with us. From educated speakers in England one might hear any day the colloquial '*Pon* my word!' or 'I'll come '*long* '*bout* eight'.

Far more characteristic of the island speech are the reductions of consonant groups, regularly made. At the beginning of words *s* is lost before *p*, *t*, or *k*; I have recorded the phrases *plit* wood, kill *pider, peckle* colour, and wash *pawn*; *tuff* mattress, and *trip* aloes; *queeze* out milk, *crape* root, *quint* eye, *corpion* bite, and *crawny* man. This kind of simplification must have been made from the first. Moreton (1790) spells *corpion* in a passage of creole talk; Scott has *cratch*, in Tom Cringle's Log, as well as *pruce*, mentioned above; in the Slave's Diary we find *tocks* (stocks), *tap* (stop), *treat* (straight); Russell lists *ky* (sky), *pangshalla* (Spanish elm), *chupit* (stupid), *ticky* (sticky), *tout* (stout), and for *sterling*: 'I boughted a horse for ten pounds '*talin* money.' In another place, however, he goes astray:

> All words which begin with *s* and end without, the *s* from the first part of the word is transferred to the last part of it; thus; De walking ticks.

This statement is obviously mistaken: Russell's own examples, just cited, do not bear it out. An *s*, true enough, is added to some words, but quite independently of the lost initial *s*. It is a result of 'overcorrection', as we shall see farther on.

Consonant clusters become simplified at the ends of words,

too. If the second sound in any cluster is *p, t, k, d, g, s*, or *z*, that sound and everything following it in the same syllable is regularly lost: /kris/ *crisp*, /baptis/ *Baptist*, /taas/ *task*, /hos/ *husk*, /saaf/ *soft*, /kalek/ *collect*, /bag/ *bagged*, /kuol/ *cold*, /uol/ *old*, /san/ *sand*, /kyaan/ *can't*, /laisn/ *license*, /fif/ *fifths*. This sometimes even affects words internally, as when *fistula* becomes /fisla/. Were these combinations of consonants difficult for speakers of African languages to pronounce? Discussion of this question must be postponed to Chapter XVII. One must note here, however, another way in which clusters are dealt with: When the combination is *sm-* or *sn-* the *s* is not lost but a vowel is inserted to make it a separate syllable (never accented), and the result is /sunúk/ *snook*, /siníek/ *snake*, /sumúud/ *smooth*, /sinórin/ *snoring*. /sumáal/ *small*, and so on. Similarly, when the *r* is not lost from the combination *-rm*, a vowel may be inserted to form an added syllable. A common pronunciation of *worm* is /wom/, but there is also the form /wórom/, and for the *rust* on orange trees I have heard /rósit/.

Even when they are not in clusters, final consonants are in danger of disappearing. So the *-z* of *because* often goes, the *-t* of *what, it*, etc., and the *-l* of *will*. McKay records *little* as being reduced to *lee*, with both the *t* and *l* lost, and Bennett repeatedly spells it *li'*, both of which spellings represent /li/. Final nasals may remain or may disappear, or they may be reduced to a nasal quality on the preceding vowel: *from* often becomes [frã], *can't* becomes [kjã:], *him* becomes [ĩ], and so on. (This nasalisation is here treated as a variation of /m/, /n/, or /ng/ as the case may be, and the words are therefore written /fran, kyaan, in/, etc., the nasal phoneme depending on the following consonant — for example, /im baal se ing kyaang go fran dem/.) The most striking instance of this, one which all recent writers in the dialect attempt to represent, occurs when /ng/ follows /ou/ as in *town, brown*, and the like. Thus Jekyll, who has observed it well:

> It is difficult to convey the exact value of *do'n* (down), *groun'* (ground). There is a faint trace of *ng* at the end of these words, and they rhyme to *tongue* pronounced very shortly and with a dumber vowel sound.

The *ng*, of course, is reduced to nasality and the preceding diphthong to /o/; we write it /ong/. As long ago as 1868 Russell noted this feature; in recent years it has also been recorded (by Bennett and others) in the spellings *tung* (town), *dung* (down), *roung* (round). And I have heard /nong/ for *now*, formed, no doubt, on this same pattern, despite there being no final nasal in the Standard word.

Other processes by which sounds are lost may be illustrated with Jamaican words: *l* is assimilated to *r* in *ar-ready, ar-right*, and *d* to *n* in *brennut* (breadnut); *d* is vocalised out of *mel* (meddle) and *b* out of *s'm'ady* (somebody).

In common with southern England and the eastern and southern United States, Jamaican speech at all levels loses *r* before consonants and at the ends of words. Examples from the folk speech are: /bied/ *beard*; /sho, po/ *shore, poor*; /banikl, ya/ *barnacle, here*; /ton, bon, bod, wot/ *turn, burn, bird, worth*, and so on. This loss dates from the eighteenth century at least: Moreton spells *fia* (fire), *nebba* (never), and *gran-coppa* (grand copper), the Slave's diary spells *chouch* (church), and McKay rhymes *hard* with *Gahd* (God). Sometimes *r* is lost even before a vowel, as in the American local pronunciation of *Ca'lina* (Carolina): in Jamaica *carry* regularly becomes /kya/ or /kyai/ among the folk, and Williams wrote in 1826 of a creole girl:

> Miss Harriot, or, according to her pronunciation, Haiot; — 'Miss Haiot,' she said, . . .

A curious reduction similar to this is *wat'melon* (watermelon), mentioned by Russell in 1868 and still widely current. Some *r*'s, however, are retained, or are coming back, after /ie/: *pear, bear, chair* for example now end in *r*.

The reduction of the present participial ending *-ing* to *-in* — what is popularly but mistakenly called 'dropping one's g's', though it is really the substitution of a front nasal for a back one — is found regularly in Jamaican folk speech, as everywhere else in the English speaking world. This is an archaism; it was Shakespeare's normal usage: he would have read his line

> Full of sound and fury, *signifyin nothin.*

Today it is preserved at the bottom of the social scale (and sometimes, in England, at the very top) though condemned at the levels between. The *-en* found in the occasional form *becausen* is probably added on this analogy.

D

Another archaism is the pronunciation '*oman* for *woman*, which came into English in the fifteenth century, was one of the acceptable upper-class forms down into the nineteenth century, but has fallen to dialectal status since, in Jamaica as elsewhere.

As to substitutions of sounds, Jamaican folk speech has its full share, though the majority are phonetic commonplaces. The fact that among consonants the *th* sounds are lacking, and that *t* and *d* are regularly substituted for them, has been noted. This surely dates back to the beginnings: Moreton records *dere* and *dat* in 1790; the Slave's diary of 1837 has *wit* for *with*, *adder* for *other*.

Less regular substitutions, however, are such as that of the stop sounds *k* for *t* and *g* for *d*. The first is heard in /sekl/ *settle*, /wakl/ *wattle*, /likl/ *little*, /brikl/ *brittle*, /wiklo/ *whitlow*; also, Jamaican cows and goats do not *butt*, they *buck*. The second is heard in /figl/ *fiddle*, /rigl/ *riddle*, /niigl/ *needle*, /egvaantij/ *advantage*; and when the *d* comes after *n*, the *n* also changes to *ng*: /bringgl/ *brindle*, /hanggl/ *handle*, /kyanggl/ *candle*, /dwinggl/ *dwindle*, and so on. One may note that this substitution takes place usually before *l*, and that it is found in dialect speech elsewhere. The common verb /finggl/, to *finger*, may be partly due to analogy with this pattern, partly to the *l/r* variation. These substitutions of *k* for *t* and *g* for *d* are fairly common; but occasionally one even finds *p* substituted for *k*: /plaba/ for *clabber*, and /plaa/ apparently representing the verb *claw*.

Another substitution (this time of a stop sound for a fricative) is that of *b* for *v*: /beks/ *vexed*, /bitl, bikl/ *victuals*, /shub/ *shove*, and so on. Moreton again furnishes eighteenth-century examples, *libba* and *nebba* for *liver* and *never*, while Russell records for the nineteenth century *cobring*, *guaba*, *balinsteer* (*covering*, *guava*, and *volunteer*), the last also exhibiting an intrusive *s*. McKay rhymes *hab* (have) with *sob*. The opposite substitution is also made, though far less often: Russell has noted *savat* for *Sabbath*, and Bennett *truvel* for *trouble*. I have not heard it myself. Other labials are interchanged in a few individual words: *been*, usually /ben/ sometimes becomes *min*, sometimes *wen*.

As is well known, *l* and *r* are frequently substituted for each other — the history of *pilgrim*, *colonel*, and other words of Standard English show the same phenomenon. One Jamaican example has just been given: *fingle*; others are /braial/ *briar*,

/talabred/ *thoroughbred*, and /brufil/ *Bluefields* cedar. In these there is probably dissimilation as well.

Minor substitutions of many sorts, affecting individual words, may be heard. Since at least 1823, *s* has been used for *th* in /pass/, a *path*; it is still current — in *cross-pass* too.[5] In *ferm* for *fern*, *m* replaces *n*. Metathesis occurs frequently, as in /aks/ for *ask*, /hoks/ for *husk* (which otherwise becomes /hos/). *Countra* is recorded for *counter*, the common herb *basil* regularly becomes /baazli/, and I have heard two fishermen change the word *porcupine* (the less common name for the soursop fish) into /pakrapain/ and /prakapain/; similarly one gets /slandaz/ for *sandals*, and /kromuujin/ evidently for *curmudgeon*, /terenggl/ for the musical *triangle*, and /flim/ for a *film*. The name of the tree *lignum vitae* very often becomes /nìngkambáiti/ with *n* for initial *l* and internal metathesis.

The *l* in *always* sometimes becomes *z*: /aazwiez/ — here assimilation may be at work; very likely too when *goblet* becomes /gaglit/. Simple voicing may be seen when *coop* becomes /kub/, both for noun and verb: 'Coob up dat fowl in de coob,' I heard a St Mary planter say. The voicing of *t* between vowels until it almost becomes *d* — a common feature of American pronunciation today — may be heard occasionally in Jamaica: Russell has recorded *pedita* for potato — it is still current. The 'flapped *r*' which substitutes for *d* has been recorded, and may yet be heard, in a few Jamaican words: *impurence, brara, casara, tarra*, and *warra* for *impudence, brother, cassada, t'other*, and *what-a*.

What is known sometimes as 'Vellerism' in honour of Mr Pickwick's famous manservant — the use of *v* for *w* — is apparently an archaic feature in Jamaica. I had read about it but found no one using it until I visited Accompong in 1955, where I heard it regularly in the usage of at least one important inhabitant in such words as *vell, valk, vater*.

What looks like a substitution of *h* for *w* in such words as *wood, wouldn't* — recorded by Louise Bennett and others as *hood, hood'n* — I interpret as two unrelated changes: loss of initial *w* (compare *woman*), and then the addition of 'cockney *h*.'

The last consonants are the curious group that perhaps reflect an African habit behind. The combination of *tr-* (or *str-* or *thr-*, both of which would normally be reduced by the folk to *tr-*) and of *dr-* appear to cause trouble for many speakers, especially those whose speech is in other ways old-fashioned. They substitute /ch/ and /j/ respectively: *tree* therefore becomes /chii/ (or /tyii/), *through* becomes /chruu/, *stringhalt* becomes /chinghaalt/, and *drink* becomes /jink/ (or /dyink/), *draw* and *dry* become /jaa/ and /jai/. Now this is just the kind of substitution that Anancy the spider makes when that hero of the folk tales speaks: Jekyll has him saying *yeddy, fooyish, byute, yitty,* for *ready, foolish, brute, little* In explanation he is said to be tongue-tied, but it is really something else: 'Bungo talk'. When we consider that in the Twi language, for example, there is no *r* sound, but that the other two sounds are common enough, it seems very likely that this feature is a relic of Africanism.

Even without the *r*, *t* sometimes becomes /ch/. This may be observed in *cheeny* for *teeny*, very small, and in the name of one kind of banana, the Martinique, which becomes *Manchinic* according to McKay (1912), and is today abbreviated and familiarised to *mancha*. Along with the loss of *r*, and the change of *t* to *ch*, there is an intrusive *n*.

Finally there is another 'Anancyism', *y* for *l*, as in /yikl/ for *little*, which I have heard in the Trelawny cockpit country, and *ny* for *y*, as in /nyong/ for *young*, at Quickstep, St Elizabeth. Though in Standard English initial /ny-/ comes only before *u* (*new, numerous,* etc.), it is very common in the Niger-Congo languages, and one finds it in other Jamaican words of African origin: *nyam, nyaka-nyaka*, and so on.

Many substitutions take place among vowels as well. We shall consider first the front series, then the back, then diphthongs. For the lax *i*-sound of *bit* we hear the closer, tense vowel of *beet*. In St Mary I was told that when children have /hiich/ (*itch*) they should be bathed with the plant called *snake-cap*; and in Hanover also that 'land pussley good fe kratch-kratch — or *hiich* — on baby skin'. Perhaps the most conspicious example of this pattern is the alteration of *in* to /iin/ or /iina/, *into*. Another remarkable example is in the common pronunciation /dwiit/ for *do it*, the /u/ of *do* becoming /w/ as the two words are reduced to a single syllable. Uncle Newton tells of a mischievous schoolboy pleading, 'Do Teacher! A won't dweet again.' This is the same kind of reduction that occurs when *go on* becomes *gwaan* and *going* becomes *gwine*.

In common with some English and American local dialects,

Jamaican folk speech may substitute the lax *i* of *bit* for lax *e* of *bet*: /trimbl/ *tremble*, /chis/ *chest*, /krisent/ *crescent*. Jekyll records the opposite of this too in the word *sperit* for *spirit* — but this can hardly be considered dialectal; it is merely archaism. As late as the middle of the past century Matthew Arnold, in *Requiescat*, rhymed *spirit* with *inherit*. Jamaicans still often say /henda, tel, ef/ for *hinder, till, if*; and the word 'yedda' probably renders *hither*.

The same lax *e* of *bet* is itself very often used instead of the tense *e* (or diphthong *ei*) of Standard. A St Thomas man, telling of a bush which multiplied too rapidly, said, 'It come to a /pleg/' (*plague*). Whereas such words as *sake, cake*, and *snake* have the regular Jamaican diphthong /ie/ already described, the verbs *make* and *take* are always /mek/ and /tek/ among the folk; and *where* and *there* become reduced to /we/ and /de/. On the other hand this *e* may appear instead of the vowel of *but*, as in *brother*, spelled *breder* as early as 1837, *anedda* for *another*, and *keiba* for *cover*.

Historically this lax *e* had a dual development when it came before *r* in accented syllables in early Modern English. It became *a* in some words (*dark, farm*), but remained *e* in others (*verse, virtue*), or else it retained both forms with some difference of usage (*person, parson*; English *clark, darby*, U.S. *clerk, derby*). In Jamaica one still occasionally finds the archaic form /masi/ for *mercy*, /saatin/ for *certain* and so on. One of the most interesting words of this kind is *fern*, which has undergone many changes. The form *farne* is found in Scotland in the sixteenth century, and McKay records it in Jamaica in 1912 as *fyahn*. Its present form is usually *ferm* (St Mary, Trelawny, Hanover, St Catherine), which reintroduces the *r* and alters the nasal unaccountably; but I have also heard /faam/ (St Elizabeth) and the curious dissyllabic /fierin/. The vowel before *n*, which makes the second syllable, is reminiscent of the extra syllable at the end of /panchalam/ for *Spanish elm* (paralleled in dialect elsewhere, where *elm* becomes *ellum*, and so on).

Finally this *e* my be used for the *a* of *bat*, as in /heng/ *hang*, /tenk/ *thank*, /rengkin/ *rank*, /gelop/ *gallop*. And I have even heard one instance of the contrary of this: /mash/ for the *mesh* of a fishing net.

A recent advertisement in the Kingston *Gleaner* (21 January,

1952) offers to teach music 'by air' — meaning, of course, 'by ear'. This testifies to the preservation of an older pronunciation of /ee/ that has moved up in its position of articulation to /ii/ in Standard. The folk pronunciation of *ears* (which is both singular and plural) is often rendered in print as *aise* and pronounced /iez/, which indicates the same tendency. Another example is the common use of *rale* (pronounced /riel/) for *real*.

As we have seen, there are two *a* sounds in Jamaican folk pronunciation, one in mid position, as in *bat* (Standard makes this farther front), and the other in back position, as in *Bart* — respectively /a/ and /aa/. In individual words these are sometimes interchanged. The back one used for the Standard *o* or front *a* was noticed by Scott in *Tom Cringle's Log* (1833), when some children are made to ask, 'Cousin Taam, what you bring we?' It appears again in 1905 in Smith's *Chim-Chim* stories: 'Annancy . . . hab' a God-mamma an' God-pappa call Raabit,' and I have heard it regularly in /kraab/ *crab*, /raamuun/ the *ramoon* tree, and so on. On the other hand, we find *barnacle* pronounced with the short, mid *a*, /banikl/, and *harsh* as /hash/.

Coming now to the back series of vowels we find the /u/ of *book* used for the /o/ of *but*: /shub aaf im kunu/ *shove off his canoe*, and /kum/ and /humoch/ for *come* and *how much*. Contrariwise, however, *conch*, which might be expected to be /kangk/, is /kongk/ in Jamaica.

The diphthong of *boat*, in Jamaican folk pronunciation /uo/, is found for the vowel of *bought* in /tuoch/ *torch* and /tuochwud/ *torchwood*; it is found for the vowel of *but* in /uonyan/ *onion* and /huovn/ *oven*. The first of these appears to be an archaic pronunciation; an electric torch, rather than one made of torchwood, is the normal /taach/; and so also *torture* is /taacha/, *horse* /haas/, and so on. A curious substitution is found in the word /hat/, used for Standard *hurt*. On the analogy of *bird* we should expect this to be /hot/; instead it becomes homonymous with Standard *hot*, as if some heat were involved. Yet '/mi hed hat mi fi truu/' has nothing to do with my head being heated; it merely *hurts*. There is no evidence as to the way this substitution came about.

Apart from the usual differences between the folk and Standard diphthongs, there are occasional tendencies to substitute. So for *raging* we get /raijin/ and /raigin/, and for *prayer* /praia/. *Hag* and *bag*, too, often turn up as /haig/ and /baig/. Sometimes a vowel has failed to diphthongise in the regular way (as *u* did in English, for example, during the sixteenth century, becoming *au*). A fisherman told me that 'porpoise /spuut/ water' (*spout*) — a pronunciation parallel to that of English and American dialect areas, where one hears (and finds in print) *snoot* for *snout*, *cooch* for *couch*, *pooch* for *pouch*, and the like.

In contrast with Standard, Jamaican folk speech does not centralise or neutralise the unstressed vowels. In Standard, such words as *circus*, *parrot*, *Cuba*, despite the spelling, all have the same vowel in the second syllable ([ə] in the International Phonetic Alphabet). In the latter, even the 'unstressed' syllables have some noticeable accentuation. The vowels of these syllables divide between /a/ and /i/. Accordingly, the three words above would have /a/, while *coral* becomes /koril/, *sorrel* /saril/, *ebony* /hebini/, and *for* /fi/.

Change of the vowel quality to show emphasis — known as a dialect feature, as when *little* becomes *leetle* — is also heard in Jamaica. In the description of a tiny fly: /a liikl wan/; also /huogly/ instead of the usual /hogli/ (ugly), /kraap/ instead of /kriep/ (scrape).

In addition to lost and altered sounds there are a number of added sounds, most of them simple phonetic intrusives. Thus *d* intrudes in /uondli/ (*only*) and 'liard' (liar); *t* in /diistant/ (*decent*), /wist/ (*withe*, usually simply /wis/), and formerly in /saatintli/ (*certainly*); *n* regularly enters /kanchaniil/ (*cochineal*), Jekyll records 'concentina' for a *concertina*, and Louise Bennett bears witness to 'repatrilate' and 'bunks' (*bounce*), showing intrusion of *l* and *k*. Since *r* is not pronounced after vowels, it intrudes only after consonants: /puoltris/ (*poultice*), /shaatrij/ (*shortage*), /primenta/ (*pimento*). After *s*, *w* occasionally intrudes: /swagi/ *soggy*, /swinj/ *singe*, /swipl/ *supple*, usually pronounced /sipl/.

An interesting intrusive *n* may be found in present participles or nouns formed from them, which comes before the final -*in*: /hontnin/ *hunting*, /fishnin/ *fishing*, or the /aisnin/ on a cake. Just what this represents is difficult to say. Is it due to simple assimilation or to some analogy (as with *lightning*), or may it possibly be a dialectal preservation of the Anglo-Saxon forms *huntnunge*, *fiscnunge*? Because these two activities are such basic and traditional ones, kept up over the centuries, there is a real possibility that these words may have continued too from ancient times. Analogy with them would account for other words — such as the 'icening' on the cake.

The word *eye* appears in two non-Standárd forms: /hai/, with the 'cockney *h*', and /yai/, which parallels the formerly widespread pronunciation in England of *ears* as 'years' (whence comes the pun on the length of 'donkey's years'). In Jamaica the verb *hear* has lost initial *h*- and, like *eye*, prefixed *y*-. This must have happened early, for in the traditional tales and songs it has an archaic form 'yerry':

> /yu no yeri wat de uol man se
> yu no tai yu dangki dong de/

— and so in many others. If 'yedda' is from *hither*, it is yet another example.

In addition to simple intrusives there are sounds that come in when the speaker begins to adapt his speech to Standard patterns. The first phoneme to be added seems to be the vowel of Standard *Bert*, a fronted, mid-central sound. One hears it in *dirt*, *bird*, *first*, and so on, instead of the older folk forms /doti, bod, fos/. Speakers who have achieved some literacy are putting in the *r*, too — an effect of 'spelling-pronunciation', perhaps reinforced by American pronunciation heard from tourists, moving pictures, and radio.

But the striking effects come from the mistakes made by the speaker who attempts to imitate Standard by 'restoring' the sounds that the folk speech had dispensed with. All too easily this attempt leads to what is called 'over-correction', for he puts sounds into places where they do not belong in Standard. This frequently happens with *s*, which as we have seen, is regularly lost in the folk speech before *p*, *t*, and *k*. Russell noticed it as long ago as 1868 in 'balinsteer', used for *volunteer*; it is very common today, as in /sprikl/ *prickle*, /sprangs/ *prongs*, /skil/ *kiln*, /stanjariin/ *tangerine*, and probably also in /instral/ *entrails*.

Russell also said that the *s* of 'ticks' (*stick*) was always moved from the beginning of the word to the end, but as we have seen, this is not so. The *s* comes into a number of words, true enough — we may add *a shoes* (one shoe), *a charges*, *half a miles*; but this is much more likely owing to over-correction, partly in the sound pattern, partly in the grammar: an attempt to restore inflection which the folk speech entirely lacks, though in this case plurality is inappropriate.

Another over-correction may be seen when *lungs* is rendered as /lounz/: the speaker, in an effort to avoid /-ong/, which is known as a dialect feature, 'restores' /-oun/. Similarly the use of *d* or *t* for the *th* sounds, recognised as an error by those who are trying to acquire Standard pronunciation, may lead to the false use of *th* for *d* or *t*. This would explain the careful pronunciation of /maaths/ for *moss*, and the common form *filther* used in Kingston for *filter*. Folk etymology is probably present also in the latter.

The older stages of Jamaican folk English had a feature that has almost disappeared today: the tendency to add /-i/ or /-a/ to words that would otherwise end with a consonant. Examples of the first are seen in /yeri/ *hear*, /dedi/ *death*, /taaki/ *talk*, /doti/ *dirt*, /grandi/ *grand*; of the second in /rata/ *rat*, /uona/ *own*. Claude McKay has written concerning this last word: 'There is a delicious caressing sound about this intrusive "a",' and he uses it in the lines 'Fe me own *a* dear,' and 'When you were me own *a* true sweetheart.' As here, these sounds sometimes have a linking function; so also in /rakatuon/ *rock-stone*, /disaya/ *this-here*, /sochilaik/ *such-like*. In some places it is impossible to say that this -*i* is not influenced by the English diminutive suffix -*y*, which also has a familiarising function — as in names: Janey, Charlie. No doubt the two sometimes coincide and reinforce each other, for this suffix is a favourite with Jamaicans. On the other hand, since words of the Niger-Congo languages almost never end in consonants, these vowels may have been added to English words to satisfy the African pattern. They are certainly more numerous in the earlier texts, and rather old-fashioned today. Focke's dictionary of the 'talky-talky' of Surinam, related to Jamaican folk English, shows the words having a very large proportion of these forms with -*a* or -*i* added.

The pronunciations we have been discussing represent, in Jamaica, the 'folk' end of the scale, the other end of which is Standard English. It would be impossible here to describe all the gradations between. Yet one must not forget that there are many 'bilinguals' who can talk on either side, and that very few people at either side can remain unaffected by features of the other side. The best educated Jamaican must use some local words (and why not?), and will fall into some local rhythms of intonation and accentuation (again, why not?), giving his speech a music that may be as pleasant to the ear, or as harsh, as human speech can be anywhere. The least educated Jamaican is exposed to some features of the Standard language and is likely to adopt some unconsciously even if he makes no special effort to imitate. The movement of rapprochement has increased rapidly in this century with the spread of schooling and the social rise of many individuals. There is no danger, however, that Jamaican English will soon be mistaken for West-end Londonese. Nor would that be a consummation at all to be wished. In the human sphere, at least, uniformity is not desirable. Vive la différence!

Chapter Four

JAMAICAN GRAMMAR

THE MOST striking differences between the folk speech of Jamaica and the educated speech are not in the sounds, still less in the vocabulary — they are in the grammar, the functional patterns into which the words fall. It is also in this respect that the most fundamental influence from African backgrounds is to be seen, and that is why Jamaican folk speech is not a dialect in the same sense that the rural speech of Devonshire or Lanca-shire, say, are dialects of English. Those who would hold that Jamaican folk speech is not to be considered a type of English at all, but a new and different language, will find their strongest arguments here — but of that later.

As we have seen, the slaves were brought speaking African languages and dialects, and had to pick up as best they could, without the least possibility of instruction, the particular type of English which was spoken by the master and the other slaves amongst whom they happened to fall. Was the master from the north or south of England, a man of much education or none at all — perhaps not an Englishman but a Welshman, an Irish-man, a Scot? His kind of English, whatever it was, probably (in the nature of the case) not of the best, was yet the model. Thus the folk speech came into being as an often uneasy compromise between the African speech which the slave already knew and the English which he might be able to pick up. How much he picked up depended in part, no doubt, upon the individual, but pro-bably even more on his situation. The field hand needed a limited knowledge of English; the domestic would have far better oppor-tunities to learn. And there is no doubt that the kind of English a slave spoke had a direct relation to the kind of job he might be given. In Jamaica, as everywhere else, language has been and is a recognised social criterion.

The structure of the West African languages, as we know today, was quite as complex as that of the European, though of

49

course in many ways very different. As might be expected, when English and the Niger-Congo languages had some feature in common, that had a good chance of surviving in the new compromise speech. Features that differed markedly in English and African would be harder for the learner to acquire or to preserve. Thus, not only was a lot of English grammar ungained, but a lot of African grammar was unkept: such were the inevitable terms of the compromise.

Jamaican folk grammar deserves a full description, and there is hope that one will be made before long. But this is not the place for it. Our approach will be, as before, to see both ends of the scale as they exist in Jamaica, and some of the features between. In other words, we shall look primarily at those respects in which the grammar of the folk differs from Standard English.

Nouns

Unlike those in other European languages, the English noun has no grammatical gender but only 'natural gender' — that is, differences are based on the nature of the thing named, whether it is animate or inanimate, male or female. Actually, with the English noun today the question 'what gender' arises only when a pronoun must be made to agree; the nouns themselves function precisely the same way at all times regardless of 'gender'. Grammatical gender was lost in English some six or seven hundred years ago; accordingly, in seventeenth-century Jamaica there was one complication less for the slave to face than for his brethren in Haiti or Cuba who were learning French or Spanish.

But though he did not have to struggle with grammatical gender, he still found possession and plurality expressed in English generally by inflectional suffixes. The Niger-Congo languages do not inflect for possession, and though some do inflect for plurality it is the beginning, rather than the end of the word, that they change. In Twi, for example, we find *akyené*, drum, *ŋkyené*, drums; *ehíŋ*, edge, *ahíŋ*, edges.[1] This conflict between the structures of African and English was resolved in an effective if somewhat drastic way: inflection was dispensed with altogether. In the traditional folk speech of Jamaica this method of pluralisation does not exist. Each noun has but one form, taken almost always from the Standard English singular: *head, foot, tree, river* — but sometimes from the plural: *teeth, lice* (probably because these words are irregular in Standard itself: compare the confusion of many educated speakers with *dice* and their reluctance to use the supposedly 'correct' singular *die*). *Peas* is the invariable form for both singular and plural but in this case the first is probably an archaism, for *peas* was once singular in Standard English. Whereas Standard falls into a grammatical quandary with such two-in-one objects as *trousers* and *scissors*, escaping it not too gracefully by resort to 'a pair', Jamaican folk speech rejects the subterfuge: it knows only a *trousers* and a *scissors*. Kingston tailors and shop assistants follow their English opposite numbers by speaking of 'a nice *trouser*', and they have treated the Americanism *pants* to the same reduction: 'a nice *pant*' — but theirs is not folk speech; it is many cuts closer to the Standard.

The folk speech does show plurality, however, in two ways. The first is by the mention of a numeral or similar word, as Standard does with the 'invariable' plurals: *six swine, many deer*. So in Jamaica, 'Him lif' up de *two hamper*. . . . *Nuff cow* pass ya. . . . Dem hab *plenty yam*. . . . *Puss an Rat* was good *frien'*.' In the absence of any such pluralising word a second device is employed: *dem* (i.e. *them*) is added to the noun, not with the strong stress that demonstratives normally have, but with reduced stress so that it combines with the noun: 'De *wass-wass-dem*,' the wasps; 'Wasp was very proud a him *teet' dem*' — *teet'* is invariable, meaning both *tooth* and *teeth*.

This curious device has been explained as coming out of a relative use of the demonstrative pronoun, as in 'De cow, dem run 'way.' But this would hardly apply to the many situations in which the pluralised noun concludes the statement, as in 'him teet' dem' above. Russell remarked that in his time (1868) *dem* 'in most cases' was added with the conjunction *an*: 'De horse an dem hard fe ketch' — but 'sometimes *an* is omitted'. This would suggest that possibly 'the horse' was pluralised by the addition of 'and those [other horses]' — an explanation which carries not much more conviction than the first. But when one discovers that some of the Niger-Congo languages place a demonstrative or similar word after the noun to pluralise it, exactly as here, one has found at last a plausible source for this Jamaicanism.[2]

Two other uses of *dem* are reported by Bailey: *Jan-dem*, or *Jan an dem*, mean 'John and his bunch' (which testifies to the survival of Russell's form) and *dem pikni*, meaning 'children in whom the speaker has some special interest', which, in its word-order, seems to show adaptation toward Standard English though in sense it is very close to *Jan-dem*.

Speakers of the folk language, increasingly aware of plural-isation as a feature of educated speech, make some attempts to adopt it that produce unorthodox results. They get into the same kind of confusions that Cockneys have with their 'haitches'. They may add the plural inflection to a singular noun — it has almost become idiomatic in some phrases: 'a garden flowers', 'it have a green looks', 'big as a ticks', 'to put a spokes to dem wheel', and especially 'a lots a trouble'.³ Or the noun may be doubly pluralised: 'Anancy . . . tek way de whole a Dog lickle bone and *scrapses* meat.' (The same thing has happened, of course, in such Standard English words as *bodices* and *cherubins* — and John Milton was using the regular form of his day when he wrote *Chineses*.)⁴ One even finds a back-formation resulting when a supposed plural is singularised: from *species* is made /spiish/: as a fisherman explained, '/juna/ is a smaller speesh of wipry' (whip-ray). Or when the Standard pluralising suffix is added to a folk word, the new form may not be Standard: *nest* is reduced to *nes*, then pluralised as /nesiz/.

As for possession, the folk speech again shows a compromise. Standard English marks possession in nouns by inflection and position: the noun adds the morpheme *s* and is put in adjective word order — that is, before another noun or its modifiers, or in final position after a copula: *John's* (red) book; the book is *John's*. One may also use periphrasis with *of*, which must then come after the noun it modifies: the tail *of the cat*. Jamaican folk speech traditionally ignores inflection altogether but follows adjective word order; if it uses periphrasis, /fi/ (*for*) takes the place of *of*. Thus one finds 'one ol' *'oman* yard . . . de *bwoy* bes' fren . . . *Mary* go-a-town hat', and, less often, 'de knife a *fi John*' (the knife is *John's*). Because *fi* has become a regular prefix of possession in pronouns, as we shall see shortly, one even finds this periphrasis occasionally used, by analogy, *before* the modified noun: 'Pass me fe Leah tumpa knife.'⁵

English nouns have been losing their inflections for a thousand years. The last surviving case inflection, the possessive, is itself slowly waning: it may hardly be used with neuters any more — one uses the uninflected noun or perphrasis instead: not 'the table's leg' but 'the table leg' or 'the leg of the table'. Jamaican folk usage, then, has merely anticipated the development of Standard English in this respect. Inflection for plurality, however, is by no means waning; the lack of it is therefore one feature in which the folk speech differs strikingly from the Standard.

Personal Pronouns

The Standard English personal pronouns have kept up differences since Anglo-Saxon times better than other parts of speech, with special forms for person, number, gender and case. But the distinctive forms are by no means as numerous as they appear when displayed in some grammars: since *thou, thy, thee,* and *thine* are mere relics, *her, it,* and *you* are used for two cases each, while *you, your, yours* serve for both numbers. Furthermore — a thing which grammars almost never point out — even the distinctive forms have not the freedom they once knew: the patterns of word order are the same for them, and just as stringent, as for the nouns. Thus the fact that these pronouns have different forms for subject and object is of no grammatical value; their respective functions would be perfectly clear from their position in the sentence even if the forms were identical.

Jamaican folk speech does not have even this reduced array of personal pronouns; it has forms chiefly for person and number, only one each for case and gender. Why the case distinctions were dispensed with is readily understood: once the Standard word order had been adopted, case forms were grammatically unnecessary. It is not so easy to account for the lack of gender distinction; possibly the pronoun's reference to the noun was felt to furnish identification enough. The traditional scheme is as follows:

Singular:

Person
1. *me* (all cases), *I* (subjective),
2. *you* (all cases),
3. *him* (all cases and genders), *it* (all cases, neuter)

Plural:

Person
1. *we* (all cases),
2. *you* (all cases), *unu* (all cases)
3. *dem* (all cases), (*him*).

Examples are:

Me (pronounced /mi/): '*Me* a try fi remember.' 'Im tief all *me* money run 'way lef *me*.'

I (pronounced /a/): Usually for Standard *I*, sometimes for *me*: '*A* tink so, sah,' 'Mek *a* si' (let me see). This is less common than *me*, probably a later acquisition. The fact that in Twi (and some related languages) its equivalent is *me* (me, my) was surely a factor in the preference for *me* over *I* in Jamaican folk speech.

you (pronounced /yu/): 'Mine *you* no mash me, man!,' 'Tek, 'way *you* foot,' 'Dem a call *you*.'

him (pronounced /him, im, ing, ng/): 'You no work *him* [the hips] like a-me,'[6] '*Him* [a wife] gone so lef' me,'[7] 'Miss Matty cum from Kingston town/ *Him* come back to *him* mammy gown,'[8] 'De one dat lef *him* gie *him* wife.'[9]

it (pronounced /hit, it, i/): '*It* naa go so,' 'T'row *i* out.' Dialect writers sometimes render this erroneously as 'he', no doubt thinking that /i/ is a 'Cockney' form. Russell records it as being used for all genders but it appears to be limited to neuter today.

we (pronounced /wi/): 'It surprise ebery one of *we*,' 'All a *we* fren a come.'

unu (pronounced /unu/): 'You t'ink judge don't know *unno* well?'[10] 'Tek *unu* basket galang!' This is based on some African word — probably Ibo *unu* which has the same meaning.[11] Since *you* can be either singular or plural, *unu* serves in Jamaica the same purpose as other English dialect forms (Irish *youse*, southern U.S. *you-all, you-uns*) which supply the deficiency of a clear second person plural in Standard English. *Unu*, nevertheless, now thought to be countrified, is growing less common.

dem (pronounced /dem/): '*Dem* no come yet,' '*Dem* house blow down pon *dem*.' (Plural *him* is illustrated with the singular.)

In addition to these forms there is the very interesting usage of *fi-* (reduced from *for*), prefixed to the pronoun, to form an adjectival possessive or a possessive pronoun in the predicate: 'Hi! Da *for me* bible book,' 'She is a sista to *femme* sista Lize,' 'Disya a *fi-me* an dat-de a *fi-him*.' This usage still flourishes.

Russell reported in 1868 as a device 'for emphasis', the use of *him* immediately after a singular noun: 'Dis teacher *him* bery cross.' But this interpretation is doubtful. If there is any emphasis in the example it is rhetorical, not grammatical, and is due to the setting off of the subject. One can hardly call this a Jamaicanism; the same effect would be gained in Standard English in the same way: 'This teacher, he's very cross!'

As one moves from the folk end of the scale toward the Standard end, the paradigm of pronouns is gradually amplified: *he* and *she* are among the first to be added, then *her*; the rest come decidedly later. Again there are many confusions, as in 'No flyin fis can beat *she*', or in the 'correction' of the line in 'Big Big Sambo Gal', when 'tek *im* back to *im* mumma' is changed to 'tek *she* back to *she* mumma' — which gets the gender right but still misses the case. Russell offers an extreme and probably made-up example: 'Me good sista, me tell *she* bout *e*, but him tink *fe her* own way better than fe we. You see *she* pass we gate yet?'

Demonstratives

Jamaican demonstratives are generally as in Standard English elsewhere, but the folk speech often adds *ya* (here) — compare *this-here* and *them-there* of substandard English and American. They may be used adjectivally or pronominally. No doubt these combinations were at first emphatic but later became generalised: '*Dish-ya* one ya,' 'Put *dis-ya* rope 'pon you,' meaning simply *this*; '*Dem-ya* a hog plum,' meaning *these* are hog plums; so *dat-de* and *dem-de* for *that* and *those*. Russell warrants the latter; they are pronounced /ya, de/. All forms are also used without *ya* or *de*, except when contrasted.

Russell records as 'now nearly obsolete' (1868) a form which has since died: *dari*. It shows, of course, the final unstressed vowel that was once added to a great many words (see Chapter 3) as well as *r* substituted for *t* — in short, it was simply a form of *that*.

E

Interrogatives

Interrogative pronouns are *who, which, what,* pronounced /huu, hu; we, wich; wat, wa, we/: 'Is *who* a come?,' '*Who* dem a call?', '*Who* grasspiece light afire?', '*Wich* kine a yam?', '*Wa* im a do?' The other interrogative words, *when, where, why, how,* pronounced /wen, we, wai, hou/, have also been adopted. Thus, except that *who* is uninflected and word order of subject and verb is not inverted, interrogation of this kind is close to the Standard.

It should be noted, however, that Twi and other Niger-Congo languages have an interrogative particle *à,* which probably survives to some extent in Jamaica in such questions as '*A* who sen you?' It is impossible, of course, to show that this is not the verb *a* meaning *is,* since the two are identical in form and fit such a context equally well.

It might be remarked in passing that Standard English has three more ways of asking questions: by inverting the word order, by beginning with some form of *do,* and (for yes-or-no questions) by turning up the pitch of the voice sharply at the end of the sentence. Standard might have, 'Have you some food?', 'Do you have some food?' or (with rise of pitch) 'You have some food?' Jamaican folk speech has only the last of these. An early example of failure to invert the subject and verb even with an introductory interrogative word comes from the Slave's Diary of 1837: 'How you will do to drink it?'

Such a question as 'Is wat?' — What is it, What is this? — seems at first glance to have inversion of subject and verb, but it is rather another result of the absence of expletives from the folk speech. In other words, 'It is what?' is adopted without *it.* The other expletive, *there,* is also wanting: 'Is two speesh a wipri,' there are two species of whip-ray. Louise Bennett has the line, 'Riggle me guess is wat' — Answer my riddle, guess what this is.

Russell recorded, with *dari,* another archaic form *wara,* meaning *what,* 'nearly obsolete' in 1864. It is still alive, however, though not common:

> me hear de bull frog A halla,
> me ask de Watchman, A warra?

Relative Pronouns

The folk speech usually dispenses with the relative pronouns of Standard English; like the Niger-Congo languages it gets along with paratactic constructions: 'De man im a hire no good' — The man (whom) he is hiring is no good; 'De man owe me money gone a Cuba' — The man (who) owes me money has gone to Cuba; 'Is dis tree dem chop' — It is this tree (that/ which) they chopped. The relative does sometimes come in, however: 'Me no know *who* tief de spoon-dem' — I don't know who stole the spoons; and 'You no cya *who* (possibly *fe-who*) house blow down' — You don't care whose house blows (or blew) down. *Which, what, why, when, where, how,* pronounced like the interrogatives, are used like *who.* Inflected forms do not appear until one reaches the Standard end of the scale; but since parataxis is very common in colloquial English, and since *whom* today is largely literary, there is much less pressure toward adoption of these than of many other features.

Indefinite Pronouns

Standard *something* (pronounced /sinting, snting/) is frequently converted to a noun meaning simply *thing*: 'Wat a strange sinting!', 'Dat not de sinting im want'. Similarly, *somebody* (usually /smady/), becomes a noun merely meaning *person*, human being: 'Im is a haad smady!', 'Smady can heat it' — Human beings can eat it.

Reflexive and Intensive Pronouns

The folk speech, like the Standard, forms reflexive pronouns by adding *-self* to the personals: *meself, weself,* and the rest: 'A wen im ben hat imself?' — When did he hurt himself? The same forms are used intensively, but the most characteristic intensive is simply *self* used after the noun or pronoun: 'Gravel self cyaan harder' — Gravel itself can't be harder; 'Me self do it' — I myself did it.

Verbs

Those of us who were brought up on Latin Grammar sometimes do not realise that the Standard English verb today has only three living inflectional suffixes: (*e*)s of the third person singular (go*es*, sing*s*), (*e*)*d* (or *t*) of the weak past (tast*ed*, swep*t*), and *ing* of the present participle (com*ing*). One cannot even include the (*e*)*n* of such verbs as brok*en*, since it is never added to new verbs, and survives in a decreasing number of old ones. In the course of its history the English verb has been discarding inflection more and more, and this kind of structure is quite absent from the Niger-Congo verbs. Thus it should be no surprise that Jamaican traditional folk speech has simply failed to adopt it.

The verb accordingly has a single form. This is usually taken from the Standard present or infinitive: *go, sing, walk, taste,* but in a few instances from the past tense form: *broke, left, lost* — 'Lef' me alone, Bredda Anancy!' In still other instances a related adjective serves for the verb: not *fill* but *full* — 'Him *full* him long bag wid cane'; not *die,* but *dead* — 'Anancy da *dead* wid laugh'; and, a similar thing, 'Rum *drunk* you very quick.'

Attempts by the folk to adopt inflection bring in the usual confusions and over-corrections: 'I *boughted* a horse', 'De bulbs is *dugged* out', '*Dug* de eart' an put in de vial', 'Dry and parch and *ground* de seeds', 'Me never will *fegat* de night', 'I have no money *giving* you', 'Ah swear dat ah mus fine a way/ *Fe wounded* cousin Rose',[12] that is, to wound cousin Rose. There is also the peculiar idiom in which a predicate adjective is followed by an infinitive: 'De man who was *usual to worry* me life', and 'When we were *tired to bawl* we watched the fire'.[13]

In the absence of inflection, expression of time differences must depend on other factors (as to some extent it does in Standard, especially with such invariable verbs as *put, cut, set*). Simple present and past are expressed by adverbs or adverbial phrases in the context: 'Mary come *ebry Sunday*', '*Yesterday* me buy salt fish', '*From im born* im nebber like okro'. The present is usually (and the past occasionally) in the 'progressive' aspect, using one of the auxiliary verbs *de, da,* or *a*: 'Him see her gran pickney . . . *dah read* one story book' — (*was*) *reading*; 'You *dah play* so nice wid Rat' — *are playing*; 'Me *a try* fe remember' — *am trying*; 'Brer Nancy *ah dead* fe put on one long black gown' — *was dying*. In short, *de, da,* or *a* before a verb has the same function as the Standard *be* followed by a present participle. Attempts to show more complex concepts of time introduce other auxiliaries, but this construction, early and firmly established it would seem, remains: 'Anancy *wasa pass* one ole oman yard' — *was passing*.

As folk speakers begin to adapt the verb toward Standard patterns the first feature that is acquired is present participial *ing*, pronounced /in/. The oldest way of saying 'I am coming' would be *A come* or *Me a come*; somewhat later, *Me comin* or *A comin*. But with at least one verb this may become confused: *gone* sometimes takes the place of *going*, as in the following:

Me kean [can't] stop Jane, me gone next door. . . .

'*Be*' and Similar Verbs

De, *da*, and *a* are used like *be* in other constructions too. A Kingston policeman in Sutton Street court (1952) was asked by a man how he would know when his turn for trial came. The reply was, 'Anywe' you *de*, we call you' — Wherever you *are*. . . . And a man explaining why the galliwasp is called 'snake waitin'-boy': 'Anywe' im *de*, snake don' lef' far' — Wherever he *is*, a snake is not far off. So also in Standard sentences beginning with the expletives *it* or *there*, the Jamaican folk speaker omits the expletive but retains *be* or uses *a* (or *da*) in its place: '*Is* accident!'; 'Hi! *da* for me bible book'; a ginger planter speaking of ganja smoking, '*Is* coolie bring it in', and another describing hog plums, '*A* two quality of dem', or the proverb, 'You care mauger cow, *a* you im buck [butt]'. Here, as elsewhere, adaptation brings mixed forms. A man speaking of needle-cases (dragonflies): '*It is* two sort of dem.'

One finds current the explanation that *a* is from the older English *a-* as in *a-coming*, *a-going*, or *aflame*, *afloat*, which goes back to Anglo-Saxon *on*. I question this. Jamaican *a* is used not only in the present participle construction (to show the progressive aspect of the verb) but in several others, always[14] as the equivalent of the verb *be*, and virtually interchangeably (though there may be geographical preferences) with *de* or *da*. It seems to be clearly verbal, not prepositional, and to be either a phonetic reduction of *is* or, far more likely, an African loan-word. I take it to represent Twi *à* (or some related form), an 'emphatic particle' which, following a noun or adjective, means *it is*, *they are*. In Jamaica the word order has been reversed: *a* comes before the noun or adjective, following the English pattern; yet it has exactly the force of *it is* or *there are*, or the English expletive and verb. From this use I suspect it gained the other uses of the verb *to be*.

De is quite certainly African; it is found in most Ewe dialects, in the Ibo language, and others, as a 'verb of incomplete predication' meaning *to be.*[15] *Da* is either a simple phonetic variant of *de* or a combination of *de* and *a*: one occasionally finds them together but uncombined: 'Mary de a come.' (Similarly, *no a* combines into /naa/ 'It naa go so!') Or else *da* also is African: there is in Twi, for example, an extremely common verb *da* meaning to *lie, be situated, live, remain, rest,* and so on. Obviously these all involve the idea of *being* in a place; thus *da* could easily have been converted to uses equivalent to those of English *be.* (Compare the Jamaican folk use of *stan', stay,* and other such verbs for *be.*)

The folk speech boasts several other auxiliaries used in more or less regular constructions, as *ben* and *wen* for expression of past time: 'A *ben* go las week' — I went last week; 'A wha' me *ben* wan'' — It is what I have wanted or have been wanting; 'Ribber *ben* come dung' — The river has come down; 'me *wen* know 'ow much i-come to' — I knew how much it came to; 'Ef she *wen* good' — If she had been good. *Ben* clearly derives from *been,* and *wen* appears to be merely a phonetic variant, the *b* semi-vocalised with its labial quality kept.

There is also *waan* (from *want*) meaning *does,* but used unemphatically: it merely forms a present tense. A fisherman speaking of whelks: 'Dem *waan* favor soldier' — They look like the soldier-crab; and a small-settler: 'Chiny yam *waan* bear like pinda' — China yam bears like peanuts. *Come* acts like the auxiliary *become* in such a clause as 'Wen de baby come baan' — when the baby was born.

The auxiliary *do,* used in Standard English to introduce questions (*Do* you do it?) or to emphasise statements (I *did* do it) has neither of these uses with the Jamaican folk. They use *don't* as a general negative (like their *no*): 'Postman don't come yet' — meaning *hasn't*; 'It don't cook' — It *isn't* cooked; 'Him don't do nuttn' — He *doesn't, didn't* do, *hasn't* or *hadn't* done anything. When forms of *do* are adopted in imitation of Standard, they are not emphatic but simply indicate past time: 'Anancy ax her wat fruit Dora *did* like' — what fruit Dora *liked.* This usage probably reflects the period of its adoption, for the unemphatic use of *do,* now an archaism, flourished in early Modern English.

The word *will,* reduced to *wi,* is the general auxiliary of the future. Russell stated in 1868 that *wi* was not used in negative expressions: 'never A we not go, but I sha'n go.' This has since become obsolete, following, no doubt, the decay of *shan't* in Standard. The present-day folk version would be 'Me *no a* go', (often pronounced /naa/): 'I *am not* going, I *won't* go. As in Standard, thus, the continuing or progressive present is often used with future force. Similarly, and frequently, *gwine*: 'Him gwine dead' — He *is going to* die, *will* die.

The modal auxiliaries of Standard English are sporadically adopted on a par with other verbs. *Must, can, need* are common, *would* (or /hud/), *should*, and *could* fairly frequent, *shall, may, might, dare, ought* very seldom used. The verbal phrase *to be able* is hardly heard; *can* is used in its stead: 'A *should can* find some' — I *should be able* to find some; 'Him *mus' can* do it' — he *must be able* to do it. Other attempts to produce complex verbal expressions end in strange ways. A garage workman in Port Maria: 'Come back! You *had was to* repair de coil,' and a fisherman: 'A *had was to* tell him.' Both were trying for *had to*, but *was* evidently stepped in to aid the expression of past time. Possibly these represent a blend of 'had to' and 'was (or were) to', combining the virtues of both.

The Passive

Completely lacking from folk use, and apparently one of the last acquisitions on the road to Standard English, is the passive voice. Such sentences as 'The property was sold,' 'The food is bought' become simply 'De property sell,' 'De food buy.' These are clearer even so than statements with animate subjects: 'Him gwine ketch' — He will be caught; 'Shark can eat' — Shark can be eaten; 'How de pickney fe feed?' — How are the children to be fed? In these one might expect an object: catch *what*? eat *what*? feed *whom*? But since they are complete as they stand yet clearly not transitive, they must be something else — usually passive. In short, the only certain distinction of this kind that the folk speech makes in verbs is between active-transitive (verb with expressed object: De gimlet *bore de wood*) and others. The latter group may include active-intransitive (verb with unexpressed object: De gimlet *bore*) and passive (De wood *bore*). But neither of these is unambiguous: gimlets may be bored, and wood may be used for boring. The meaning intended in each case must be determined from the context, verbal or material, since it is not indicated grammatically.

There is one other result, a semantic one: every transitive verb now has twice as many senses, its regular active ones and the added passive ones. Things are never broken — they break; never fastened — they fasten; never caught — they catch. A fisherman, describing how soft jellyfish are, said, 'As you touch it it bore' — almost as if the fish itself took a part in its piercing. To a person used to Standard English this feature of the folk speech gives an effect of activeness or vitalism even with inanimate things.

Time distinctions in the passive are analgous to those of the active verb. 'De bread t'row in-a de wata' might mean *is thrown* in one context, *was thrown* in another; in the song 'Dip Him Mr Bedward' it happens to be the latter. Or in the Anancy story, 'Tiger woulda like all him fren and neighbour fe come when him *gwine bury*' — when he was going to be buried. In short, such distinctions are not made grammatically.

These constructions are due, of course, to the absence of an inflected participle, and the usual absence of the auxiliary *be* (or its equivalent) from the folk speech. *Be* is also omitted in other places where Standard would have it: 'Coconut leaf mek bood (booths) and arch when someone going to married,' 'De King. . . sey him hooda like fe get her married to', 'Me an Lize nat wan mada, yuh know?', 'Yes Bredda 'Nancy me wi tenkful', and the proverb, 'When a man belly full him broke pot.'

One very striking feature of the folk speech is that verbs are used in sequences without connectives. Standard English does this occasionally, especially with *come* and *go*: Shakespeare's 'Then *come kiss* me, sweet and twenty' or 'I'll *go tell* him', joining the verbs closely. We also find simple contiguity and pause taking the place of logical connectives: Milton's 'I *woke*, she *fled*'. But such uses as these would not furnish models enough to account for the extremely frequent expressions of the Jamaican folk: 'Policeman *a come* fe *go mek* a row', 'Let me *kyar* de basket *come show* you', 'Anancy *run* over Dog yard *go tell* him *say* dat Bredda Puss have it . . .', 'You *'queeze* i', wata *run* outa i'', 'So him *siddung res* himself tell [till] him wife *call* him *tell* him *say* the plantain dem *roas*, him *mus come*'. And a fisherman speaking of black sea-eggs: '*Bait* pot, *tek* it *ketch* fish.' The paratactic piling up of verbs, such as we see here, is a characteristic feature of the Niger-Congo languages.

Clearly enough, some of these verbs form natural sense-groups, the second reinforcing the first (as in the case of *done*, already mentioned): *bring-come, carry-come, walk-go, send-go, run-gone, tell-say* are the most common. These are sometimes compounded further: 'You *carry* any more *bring come*?'

The verb *say* is a special case: it follows any verb of speaking, thinking, wondering, and the like: 'She *think say*, that I run away', 'Anancy . . . *tek a oat* (oath) *seh* him mus put himself eena Story Book', 'You no *know sey* Rat is nice meat?', 'It *look like sey* de people do fe purpose . . .'. Two things are to be noted about this use of *say*. The first is that it does not necessarily have the full significance of saying. The next-to-last example above may be translated, 'Don't you know *they say* or *it is said* Rat is nice meat?', but it is just as well rendered, 'Don't you know *that* Rat is nice meat?' In short, *say* loses full verb function and becomes tantamount to a conjunctive relative pronoun. The second and more important fact is that it is regularly pronounced /se/, which the spellings *seh* and *sey* represent more truly than *say*. Indeed, if it came from English *say* we should expect it to be pronounced /sie/ in Jamaican folk speech. The probability is, therefore, that at the root of this expression is an African verb such as Akan *se*, which after a previous verb means saying, telling, commanding, and introduces the words spoken; but it 'is often not to be translated' — it means no more than *namely*, or 'serves as a mere quotation mark'.[16] The African verb has no doubt been reinforced by the coincidence in form and meaning of English *say*.

Another peculiar expression is one which usually begins with an impersonal construction, then, apparently for emphasis, anticipates the verb with itself, so to speak. In the song 'Sammy Dead Oh' we find, 'A no *lie* Sammy *lie* meck im dead oh A no *tief* Sammy *tief* meck dem kill him.' A mat-seller in Kingston: 'Is *dye* dem *dye* it.' A boy speaking of an escaped donkey: 'Is *chaw* im *chaw* de rope.' A woman who lost a parcel on a Kingston bus: 'Is not *leave* I *leave* it in the bus — is *drive* the man *drive* away with it.'[17] The earliest printed example found of this is from 1929: 'A don' mind the *wet* a *wet*, but de '*prain* a '*prain* me foot!'[18] Standard English would simply have, 'It's not that Sammy *lied* that made him die; it's not that Sammy *thieved* that made them kill him,' and so on. To call this anticipating word simply a 'verb', however, is not to tell the whole story; for in some instances it looks very much like a noun. The nearest thing to it in Standard is perhaps the present participle, which is clearly verbal while approaching a noun in function.

A very similar idiom with repeated verb is one beginning with 'All the —' and meaning 'No matter how (much) —': 'All the *call* his wife can *call* to him to leave off, no use' (from 1837); 'An all de *draw* me dah *draw* me kean get im out'; 'But all de *tun* de pickney *tun*, an all de *look* Anancy *look*, . . .; 'But all de *strain* me *strain* me aise/ Me couldn' ketch a wud him sey'. In Standard these would be, No matter how much his wife *called*, No matter how I *drew*, and so on. Here again the first of the two words, to a speaker of Standard English, appears like a noun without losing its verbal force; to the dialect speaker it is expressive of the repeated action — it is even one type of that iteration which, as we shall see shortly, is a characteristic inheritance from Niger-Congo language structure.

Other Parts of Speech

There is little to be noted of the remaining parts of speech. The adjective is occasionally placed *after* the noun it modifies, but not with any difference of syntax: 'You can get a *raise good* [good price] for conch'; 'Him *grampa dead* [dead grandpa's] watch'. Occasionally too — and it would seem by analogy with the verbal idiom — one finds adjectives repeated. A man talking about a certain kind of timber: 'A don' know if a *tough* it *tough* wood — it bruck de ax.' Adjectives (and adverbs) have taken over the inflections for degree of comparison, -*er* and -*est*, and preserve also the multiple comparatives and superlatives that were acceptable through the seventeenth century but have since been condemned as redundant: *most unkindest, more stronger*; also /wósara/ — *worserer* — actually a triple comparative!

The definite article follows that of Standard English, though it is frequently omitted altogether; the indefinite article is *one*, traditionally, but *a* is also well established: 'Anancy wasa pass *one* ole oman . . . dah read *one* story book.'

Almost any adjective or participle seems to be usable in the folk speech as an adverb. Thus *heavy, strong, moist* and so on do not need -*ly* to make them adverbs: 'Im walk strong . . . im sleep heavy . . . de fog fall moist.' This has the effect — and may be the result — of preserving and extending an older Standard pattern that still flourished when the slaves were first learning English, though it is much weakened today. The use of -*ly*, when attempted, may lead to over-correction: 'Anancy ah tek him casually walk . . .' — his casual walk.

The participle *done* enters into a peculiar adverbial idiom. Placed after verbs it shows completion of the action, becoming equivalent to *entirely* or *altogether*. This usage has been in existence certainly for more than a century: 'We pray to God to take poor nega before Buckra *kill* him *done*'[19]; 'Me *feed* him *dun* dis long time'; 'De bush *cut done*'; 'Wen she *sell* me *done*'; 'Teng Gad we *sell* off *dun*.' It is true that one finds the verb *do* used in similar ways, usually dialectally, elsewhere: 'I've done finished it. . . . He's done bought it'; what is peculiarly Jamaican is the placement *after* the verb. This idiom may result from ellipsis: 'The bush is cut *and* (*is*) done', or simply from the African predilection for heaping verbs up. In any case, *done* loses verbal force and becomes a modifier of the other verb.

But some adverbs are not usable as adjectives. *Not* is usually /no/ (sometimes /nat/) and has been so for a long time: 'English Bacceroes no know one another' (1740); 'No use me ill, Obisha!' (1790); and today, /mi no nuo/ — I don't know.

Conjunctions, Prepositions, Adverbs

Jamaicans have developed some conjunctions, prepositions, and adverbs of their own either by adding new meanings to English words, or by forming phrases. Conjunctions include *after* (since, because), *before* (instead of), *so* (even as), *so* (and thus).

The first may be seen from examples out of two Anancy stories: 'Is who yuh dah tell fe quiat, no sh-sh me, afta me no fowl,' and 'Jackass sey, "But how you mean?" Hear Anancy, "Afta yuh so handsome!"' Another instance is in a poem of Louise Bennett's:

> But me blame yuh Bredda Nancy
> After yuh no got no right . . .
> Fe go start up any fight.

Before, in the sense of 'instead of' or 'rather than', may be seen in the following: 'Before yuh tank me fe carry yuh pon me head yuh dah shake-up shake-up yuhself, and come back-answa me.'

So means, first, 'even as':

> For so we moul' it up, he root it do'on.

That is, as we mould up the earth, the pig roots it down. And second, *so* is almost the equivalent of 'and' or 'and thus'. Anancy, to make trouble, is advising the cat that rat's meat is very good to eat. He says, 'Nex' time unoo meet up you ketch him an tase him so see.' Another example: 'Him climb up one ah dem big shade tree so drap ah sleep tell ah marnin.' Now though there are English senses of *so* from which these might derive, one must note that in Twi *sò* means 'after the manner of'. It is surely the African word which is added in such combinations as *conga-so*, *ya-so*; it probably also coincides with English *so* in the expressions just discussed.

Prepositions and prepositional phrases include *sake of* and *fe*, both meaning 'because of' or 'on account of':

> Sake a dah big mout' police-man
> Me nearly miss de train.

Or,   De bank dem . . . caan' 'tan
       Sake o' we naybor pig.

And *fe* (which is from *for*): 'To hender de pickney dem fram frighten fe you.'

Adverbs and adverb phrases are more numerous, and particularly interesting is *no*, used in comparisons. With the positive degree of the adjective today it means 'as'; 'Hot no pepper' — or in the proverbial phrase referring to the star-apple tree, which does not drop its fruits even when they are ripe: 'Cubbitch no star-apple,' mean as the star-apple. This word comes from *nor*, meaning 'than' used with the comparative degree; we have an example from as early as 1826: 'more no 9 and tirty;' also the proverb, 'Jamaica long more no rope.'[20] This was then reduced to the positive degree, 'hotter no pepper' becoming 'hot no pepper.' — and so *no* acquired the sense of 'as'.

Another expression of comparison is *same like*: 'Cane have flag same like corn,' 'Abbay shape same like coconut.'

Same time usually means 'immediately': 'Same time im step outa door me hole im'; but it can also mean 'all the same, nevertheless': 'Ah might ah risk it, and try mek ah fool dem same time.'

Same way means 'as usual':

Me eatin' jus as usual an⁻
Me big an fat same way.

So long is the abbreviated form taken by 'so long as': 'He had a puppy which could tell the time by going outside (so long the day was sunny) looking at the sun. . . .'

After is still used in Jamaica, though obsolescent elsewhere, to mean 'in imitation of', as in the proverb 'Young cock crow after old'.

Kya (from 'I don't *care*') frequently means 'no matter', in such phrases as 'Kya how you try, she don't please'.

Fe purpose means 'on purpose, intentionally': 'It look lika sey de people do fe purpose an lef cane j'int dem eena Anancy way.'

Finally, the expression *fe true* — very frequent and of long standing — is the usual intensive, meaning 'truly, really'. From 1790: 'A man, for true;'[21] and from 1950: 'Fe-you chewstick sweet fe true, me frien.'

Most of the Standard English prepositions have been adopted, with the usual changes of form and some alterations of meaning. *A* from *at*, and meaning *to* has already been mentioned; so has *a* from *of* (compare Standard: five o'clock, lots o' luck). There is another use of *de*, also clearly African,[22] to mean *to, toward*: 'Go de Long Pond fe wata . . .' in the words of the song. *Fe* (/fi/) has the usual senses of *for*, but it is also used for *to* of the infinitive. This is either an abbreviation of *for to*, common in earlier English: 'I've come *for to* see you,' which the present-day Jamaican folk would render 'Me come *fe* see you', or it is from an African verb such as Twi or Yoruba *fa* which, used before another verb, has the effect of English infinitive *to*,[23] Jamaican *fe*. It is perfectly possible, of course, that the two expressions have reinforced each other.

Ya and *de* (here, there) have been mentioned in passing. There is also the peculiar *di-de*: 'Him fine say cow no *did-deh*' — He found that cow was not *there*. Despite the spelling, this is not a use of *did*, but a reduplication of *de*, there, on the pattern of many another African-like form.

Jamaicans particularly like to tag adverbial particles on to verbs. The favourites are *up* and *off*: 'Ketch up him hen', 'Kiss up de gal dem'; 'Puss pose off eena book', 'Anancy . . . baptize off all of dem', 'Him nyam dem off clean', and, with the new verb *to foreign* (to make something seem foreign):

> Den me sey me want fe learn it to,
> Me haffe buckle dung,
> Screw up me mout an roll me y'eye
> An foreign up me tongue.[24]

The contrary tendency is also present: to leave off adverbial particles that Standard requires — for example, to *look* instead of *look for*. (See 'Physical Actions' in a later chapter.)

Conjunctions, as we have seen, are often suppressed between clauses, but *and* joins nouns regularly, and is one of the first features to be adopted from the Standard side of the scale. Other conjunctions are discussed among Relational Words. Conjunctive force may be obtained by repetition of the verb: 'Yuh haffe *goh* wid me tonight *goh* prove it.' This too is carried over from the Niger-Congo languages — for example Ewe, Fante, Twi, Efik.[25]

Another remarkable feature of Modern English which grammars do not often point out is the easy convertibility of our parts of speech. Just because English has lost so much of the inflection that characterised its early stages, nouns and verbs particularly, and other parts of speech to a lesser degree, can take on each other's functions without change of form. This power of conversion was exploited to the full by Shakespeare and Milton, to name only two writers, but it is used at all levels of the language: 'The dark *backward* and abysm of time' converts an adverb to a noun; 'Spirits . . . that *syllable* men's names' makes a noun into a verb. The forester does not *fell* a tree today, but *falls* it. In Jamaica, as we have seen, *dead* and *full* become verbs; *shine* becomes an adjective meaning *shiny*; and so on. The almost total absence of inflection from the folk speech has made conversion easy — has, in fact, even blurred some of the syntactic distinctions between parts of speech which the Standard preserves. 'De basket full up,' for example; is *full* a predicate adjective or a simple intransitive verb? Are we to understand 'The basket is/was full up' or 'the basket fills/filled up'? There is no way to know without going to the broader context. The part of speech, then, less and less fixed in Standard English, is certainly as flexible in Jamaican folk usage, though this does not necessarily follow Standard on all occasions.

As to word order, the folk speech has only the declarative pattern of Standard: it lacks the inverted and transposed orders.

Word Formation

New words are formed in the folk speech by compounding, derivation, back formation, and the like, much as in Standard English. But one device is strikingly characteristic and different; the use of iteration or reduplication of form. In Standard English one finds three kinds of these iteratives: the simple ones like *hush-hush*, *tinkle-tinkle*, *goody-goody*; those with vowel gradation like *ding-dong*, *tick-tock*, *skimble-skamble*; and the rhyming ones like *handy-dandy*, *hocus-pocus*, *hoity-toity*. Jamaican examples of the second and third types are relatively few: *pitchy-patchy* (covered with patches), *raw-chaw* (coarse, vulgar), *pingwing* (the pinguin plant) — and these are the commoner types in Standard. But the simple iterated form, least common is Standard, is over-whelmingly the most numerous in Jamaican folk speech. One might well say that it is the only lively pattern of the three, for it may be called upon at any time to produce new words, or, put-ting it another way, almost any word or phrase may be iterated at will (with close juncture of the parts and reduced stress on the second), producing certain definite shades of meaning.

These folk iteratives fall into four types: those directly trace-able to African sources; those which, though not traced, seem at least quasi-African; some that look like local onomatopoetic creations; and (the largest number) those in which English words, adapted regularly to the folk speech, are then iterated. I have collected close to two hundred — none of them Standard — of which nearly one-half are nouns, one-third adjectives, one-sixth verbs; there are a few adverbs too, but only one preposition. (However one must bear in mind the ease with which the parts of speech may be converted.) The full list is too long to be given here, but we may illustrate each of the parts of speech and the four types. In the first, forms from Twi are given for comparison.

Of African origin:

Nouns: *fufu*, mashed starch-vegetables (yam, etc.) — Twi
   fufuú, same.
   tum-tum, same — Twi *túm tum*, sound of fufu being
      pounded.
   shum-shum, corn and sugar pulverised — Twi *o-stãm*,
      parched, ground corn.
   nyam-nyam, food — Twi *ɛ-nãm*, flesh, meat.
   mumu, a mute person, idiot — Twi *e-múmu*, deaf-
      mute.
   bobo, a foolish person — Twi *bɔ́ɔ-bɔɔ*, phlegmatic, dull.
   kas-kas, contention — Twi *kasákàsa*, to dispute.
   putta-putta, mud — Twi *pɔtɔpɔtɔ*, muddy.
Verbs: *pra-pra*, gather up — Twi *prápra*, gather up.
   susu, whisper — Twi *susúw*, utter a suspicion.
   sese, gossip — Twi *sisé*, talk a lot.
   saka-saka, cut roughly — *sàkasàka*, disordered, irregular.
Adjec: *buffro-buffro*, clumsy — Twi *o-bò-fúro*, lazy, good-for-
      nothing.
   nyaka-nyaka, untidy, slovenly — Twi *nyãnkãnyãnkã*, cut
      into pieces.
   chaka-chaka, disorderly — Twi *tàkatàka*, muddy,
      miry.
Advrb: *krakra*, weakly, nervously — Twi *kràkra*, restless, de-
      ranged.

Quasi-African forms:

Nouns: *grang-grang*, *krang-krang*, and similar forms, small bits of
      wood or sticks, usable for kindling.
   toto, round ginger-flavoured biscuit.
   chi-chi, wood ants and their fecal dust.
   jeh-jeh, bottle-fish.
   fini-fini, and *jeng-jeng*, materials connected with Obeah
      (witchcraft).
Verbs: *fum-fum*, to beat with a switch.
   mala-mala, to beat.
   shi-shi, to drive away.
Adjec: *mini-mini*, tiny and shining.
   ruku-ruku, shaky, tumbledown.

Onomatopoetic creations, probably Jamaican:

Nouns: *kap-kap*, an ant which makes a clacking noise with its
    mandibles.
    fee-fee, a whistle.
    pee-pee, a turkey chick.
    pooka-pooka, sound of a kettle on the boil.
Adjec: *kwee-kwee*, squeaking.
    chi-chi, hissing.

Based on English words:

Nouns: *wass-wass*, wasps.
    wiss-wiss, withes, vines.
    tun-tun, turned cornmeal.
    sprickle-sprickle, prickles, spines.
    dibidibi, the libidibi tree.
    matta-matta, matter, pus.
    moos-moos, mouse, mice.
    lobby-lobby, loblolly.
    shaky-shaky, earthquake.
Verbs: *talky-talky*, talk a lot.
    wiggle-wiggle, wriggle quickly.
    batta-batta, beat repeatedly.
    pop-pop, to break all over.
    winjy-winjy, twist and turn.
    hinka-hinka, to hanker.
Adjec: *fool-fool*, foolish.
    preachy-preachy, preaching too much.
    checky-checky, covered with spots.
    tief-tief, thieving.
    wee-wee, very small.
    mouty-mouty, mouthy, impertinent.
Advrb: *flat-flat*, very flatly.
    lickle-lickle, in little quantities, by degrees.
    plenty-plenty, plentifully.
Prepn: *bout-bout*, round about.

It is clear that the basic meaning expressed in these forms is
repetition, which, however, takes on a variety of nuances depending on the meaning of the element repeated. If it expresses
a completed action, when iterated it may express simple

F

repetition — *beg-beg*, *kill-kill*, repeated acts of begging or killing; but if it expresses an action that may be continued, when iterated it may also express continuation — *look-look*, to keep on looking, *galang-galang*, to keep on going along. Repetition forms habits, so a *cry-cry* child is not merely one who cries continually, but perhaps habitually.

If the basic element expresses a thing, when iterated it may express accumulation or multiplicity — *bit-bit*, many bits, bit after bit, *feed-feed*, many things to feed on. (I once asked a small boy whether the trumpet tree produced any fruit. He replied, 'No sah, only lickle feed-feed fe bird.') By reducing the importance of the individual components of an accumulation one makes them seem smaller, even miscellaneous — *wass-wass*, a swarm of wasps, or wasps in general. There may be an accumulation of mass, rather than individual things — *mud-mud*, a lot of mud, *ragga-ragga*, covered with rags, very ragged. Sometimes emphasis goes not on accumulation but distribution — *one-one*, one at a time, one here and one there, *lickle-lickle*, a little here and a little there, a little now and a little then.

If the basic element expresses a quality or property, when iterated it usually expresses intensification — *pretty-pretty*, *plenty-plenty*, *flat-flat*, *fast-fast*, mean very pretty, plentiful, flat, fast; *tear-up-tear-up*, extremely torn up; *fus-fus*, the very first, first of all. Occasionally it may express just the opposite: a lessened degree of the quality — *yalla-yalla*, somewhat yellow, yellowish.

Finally, the iterative pattern seems to have the function of making things seem more familiar, closer to one — *tun-tun* is suggestive of the repeated action of turning corn meal as it cooks, but it also has the familiarity of a nickname; and one finds this kind of effect in the most familiar talk of all, baby talk, with such a hypocoristic form as *chim-chim*, a chamber pot.

This word-forming device seems completely natural to the folk in Jamaica, and may appear in their speech at any moment to produce expressions that they have never heard before. An old man, explaining to me how to cure the earache with a substance he called *god-cotton*, said, 'It have lickle-lickle hole-hole, an' you strawn-it-up-strawn-it-up [pull it into strands], dip in ile from doctor-shop, an' put it eena you ears — mek corruption run out.'

What is to be noted, then, is that whereas this first type of iteration is the least common in Standard English, it is the most common and vital in the folk speech; it may be recognised clearly as another of the inheritances which this speech preserves from its African backgrounds.

II

JAMAICAN VOCABULARY

Chapter Five

WORK AND OCCUPATIONS

JAMAICANISMS have already been defined and classified according to their types. We now present them by topics — the aspects of life with which they deal. No words will be included unless they fall under our definition. 'Thank-you-Ma'am,' for example, which some think of as a peculiarly Jamaican expression, is quite as well known in the United States. 'Kittereen' was once widely used in this island for a small carriage, yet the word neither originated here nor was especially characteristic, nor is there any evidence of its having lasted longer in use here than elsewhere. Such words as these are excluded. If the reader's favourite examples of 'Jamaican words' are omitted it will probably not be because they have not been considered, but because they are of these kinds.

Boats, Vehicles, Roads, etc.

In the eighteenth and nineteenth centuries a dugout boat known as a *bongo* was widely used in the Caribbean area — in Jamaica too, though here the name was somewhat different. From as early as 1788 Marsden wrote of 'a large boat called a *bungay*, made out of the cotton tree, and capable of carrying five or six hogsheads', and in 1835 Senior mentioned *bungays* on the Black River. The word, pronounced /bonggi/, is still known in Hanover and Westmoreland, but *lighter* is displacing it and the boats so named are no longer dugouts. The DA derives *bongo* from an African source via American Spanish; *bungay* is no doubt a local variant, probably reflected also in the form *bonque*, used in Peru.[1]

In fishermen's canoes and other Jamaican boats the *thwart* (or cross-support) becomes a /taat/. This is a preservation of the English dialectal form *thought* with the normal changes into Jamaican folk speech (*t* for *th*, *aa* for *aw*). In these canoes the 'ribbon board' fastened outside the upper edge below the gun-wale is called the *bends* (Old Harbour), a word thought to have been obsolete after the sixteenth century[a] but still very much alive in Jamaica.

Instead of rowlocks the canoes have blocks of wood with thole pins which are fastened to the gunwales. Each such block is called a *balad plate* or *balyad plate* (from *bollard*). Another arrangement is to hold the oars to the gunwales with straps of rope, called *brags*, perhaps from Spanish *braga*, a lashing rope.

Though *dinghy* usually means a boat, it (or *ginghy*) may mean a two-wheeled, horse-drawn cart for carrying people. Another name for the same vehicle is *parry-cart*; a donkey cart is a *tegrey*. (None of these is in the dictionaries, nor has any clue to their origin been found.)

In former days, buggies for hire were common in Kingston under the name of *bus*. By the 1920's automobiles had begun to take their place, and in the 1930's motor omnibuses (called buses too) appeared in competition with electric tramcars. Since the second World War the trams are gone and the buggies have almost disappeared, taking the old Jamaican sense of *bus* with them. Recent motor buses have been nicknamed *chi-chi bus*, the adjective imitating the hissing of the compressed air that operates the doors. Louise Bennett has the lines,

> Me wi haffe stop car-drivin
> An go sponge pon chi-chi bus.

An early Jamaicanism is *pass* for 'path', with the combination *cross-pass* for a crossing of paths. This has nothing to do with the meaning of passing; it simply exhibits a substitution of *s* for *th*, since the latter sound is lacking from the folk repertory.

The common limestone used in making roads, called *bruck stone* (broken stone), is dug out of the hillsides from *marl holes*. As Senior wrote in 1835: 'In a deep cavity of a somewhat crumbling rock, near the road-side, which they term a "marl-hole", are seen, probably, from ten to twenty men' digging. In road-making a foundation of this *bruck stone* is laid, then rolled with a steam roller (which is called *pressing* the road) in preparation for an asphalt surface. A sharp turn in a road is called a *deep curve*.

The common word for the sleepers (US 'ties') of a railway track is *poleen* — an importation of Cuban Spanish *polin*. It has no connection, despite the likeness, with *polink* (from Spanish *palenque*, a palisade, paling), current in Jamaica from the seventeenth century for an enclosure containing poultry and small stock, and also applied to similar arrangements, for example one used in fishing (see below, pages 94–5).

Said to have been current in 1921 are two terms for which no other evidence has come to hand: 'The train continues through numerous "tubes", as Jamaicans call a tunnel.' and 'In the island dialect a local train is a "walkin' train" (because it is slow and stops often?), and all Jamaican trains fall into this category.'[3]

Buildings, Furnishings, Constructions, etc.

A Jamaicanism very common a century and a half ago, though now almost dead, is *barquadier*, from the Spanish *embarcadero*, wharf. The English spelling suggests a French source, yet no such form exists in French: it must have been supplied by Englishmen. The word goes back at least to 1774, when Long wrote: 'The barquadier . . . is built of timber, and projected to a considerable distance into the sea, for better conveniency of shipping goods.' Beckford also alluded to 'the distant wharves, or barquadiers'. Once borrowed in Jamaica, however, this word developed a second meaning — a shipping port: 'Savanna la Mar, though it is the principal barquadier, has nevertheless but a very indifferent harbour,' and Passage Fort 'is a barquadier for Spanish Town'; also, 'The barquedia, or shipping place'. The word is unrecorded in the dictionaries. Another early Jamaicanism — though never common — was *rap-house*. In 1683 we read that there are 'at the East by Port St Thomas, Port Morant, several Houses called Rapp-Houses, which serve for Store-Houses and Ale-Houses for the Neighbourhood, and such Vessels as use that Port'.[4] This word is a puzzle, occurring only here. Is it to be connected with *rap* (OED vb.[4]) meaning to exchange or barter?

On the plantations of the past an owner might refer to his dwelling as the 'greathouse'; the servants' name for it was the *buckra-hall* or *buckra-house* — that is, white-man's house. A wind-mill such as those formerly used to furnish power for sugar estates was called a *breeze-mill*. Though these are now in ruins the word is still current for a children's toy and for small wind-mills used to frighten birds away.

Cook-house or *cook-room* were terms early applied to a separate building used as a kitchen. Sloane writes: 'The Kitchens, or Cook-Rooms here, are always at a small distance from their Houses.' 'The Cook-Room, this term is used to signifie their Kitchen, and is a Sea word, as many others of that Country.' More recently we find a special application: 'the cook-house, where an obeahman mixes his medicines and potions.'[5]

What is evidently an African survival among the Jamaican folk is *padda*, or *patta*, which has two related meanings: first, a peasant's hut, thatched kitchen, or temporary shelter; second, a frail barbecue of sticks, a stand for drying things, or a kitchen table or shelf. One may compare the Twi word *pata*, meaning a scaffold made of sticks, a shed, a hut. A similar word, though English, is *kitchen-dresser* — a cupboard or shelf — probably best known in the proverb, 'When kitchen-dresser fall down, mauga [thin] dog laugh.'

The coping of a roof has developed a local name: 'Black man call it a saddle.' One current riddle likens a house with a bad roof to a beast of burden: its back is sore because it needs a new saddle.

A former term, *back jamb*, for the wing of a house is mentioned in *Tom Cringle's Log*: 'A very handsome diningroom, situated in what I believe is called a back jamb, a sort of outrigger to the house, fitted all round with movable blinds, or *jealousies*, and open like a lantern to all the winds of heaven except the west.'

Jealousies is not a Jamaicanism, of course, but *cooler* is: a slatted wooden shutter hinged above a window, or built around outside it. The first type may be closed tight over the window or pushed out at an angle in manner of an awning. An *upstairs* (as in Barbados) is a two-storey house.

A very common folk word is *door-mouth*, meaning doorway, 'and also the whole space just outside the door.'[6] It has the sound of a loan-translation from some African tongue. The standard word in Jamaica for the land around a dwelling is *yard* (usually fenced in). It enters into many combinations, of which one now obsolete was *guinea-yard* — an enclosure where new slaves were put after debarkation.[7]

Many Jamaican peasant cottages are of *wattle-and-daub* — that is, walls wattled with bamboo or some other wood and daubed with red clay. When a partition within the house is made of un-plastered wattle, it is called a *wattle-pane*: 'The torchlight glistens through the wattle-pane,' as McKay writes.

There are various terms for beds — usually simple or roughly made ones. A *bedja* or *bedwa* means an old-time wooden bed of any size — perhaps of mahogany — but without springs. This word is probably of African origin: compare Twi *mpa-dùd*, a bedstead, and *mpatia*, a short-legged bedstead. In Jamaican speech, the *m-* in such un-English combinations as *mp-* was lost; the remaining *pad-* or *pat-* may have become assimilated to the English *bed*. Another word for a bed may also be African: *kitty-up* is probably to be connected with Twi *kɛtɛ̃*, the usual bed of the Niger Coast natives. On the other hand, *catya* or *catawiah*, a roughly made bed may well be from *khat* (the Hindi source of English *cot*) brought to Jamaica by East Indians. Finally there is *marosh*, which basically means 'marsh' — here a type of bulrush growing in marshes, and the bed-pads made from these rushes. The word was still in use among the Accompong Maroons in 1946 for 'a mat of river reeds on which a mattress is laid'. To some it also means *moss*.

Also made from river rushes, or the central ribs of banana or plantain leaves, are coarse mats humorously called *lick-an'-'tan-up*, which are hung on verandas and get their name because they are stiff enough to stand leaning against a wall.

Ordinary roller-shades are usually called 'blinds' or 'curtains'; sometimes also *Holland blinds* since they were formerly made of Holland cloth.

In Jamaica there are not only lime-kilns but coal-kilns (or *coal-skill*) for the burning of charcoal, which is called *fire-coal*. Jamaicans also make a kind of water-tank or cistern that goes by the quaint name of *kick-an'-buck*, referring to the mode of construction: a hole is dug in clay earth, and its inner sides are 'kicked and bucked' — that is, rammed with mallets — to form hard walls that hold water. This method of construction is referred to repeatedly by Baillie in 1821, but the folk name has not been found in print before 1905.

Spanish wall is the type made of 'bruck stone' — lumps of lime-stone — with red clay as mortar, or 'a filling of stone covered with lime and earth neatly plastered and whitewashed'. This term must be quite old; evidently this method of making walls is associated with the Spanish occupation.

Jar pipe is sewer pipe, from its being made of the clay commonly used for making jars.

A *funda* is a fireside. The word is perhaps to be connected with *fondo*, which in Cuba and Porto Rico means a small caldron used in a sugar-mill. Such caldrons are fixed in place on stone foundations and the fire to boil the cane juice is put beneath — hence the transfer to the fireplace itself.

Finally, Jamaicans have a number of jocular terms for ill-kept dwellings. An old house, tumbledown and perhaps full of idlers, is likely to be called a *ratta castle* (rat castle); and a slum house is a *wappen-bappen* — the sound of which is sufficient description. Also applied to an old house, an old bed — almost anything ill-shaped or badly made — is *roocoondang*. The latter two terms, of unknown origin, probably involve some sort of sound-symbolism intended to suggest something thrown or clapped together, shaky and in danger of collapse.

Tools, Utensils

The universal tool in Jamaica, essential to the agricultural worker and to many another, is the *cutlass* or *machete*. The Jamaican digs and cultivates with it, chops wood, peels his cane or breadfruit, opens coconuts, cuts grass — he may even use it to pick his teeth or scratch his head. Hardly ever without it, he sometimes gives it the name *combolo*, which ordinarily means companion or friend.

As general terms, cutlass and machete are virtually inter-changeable and of about equal currency. The first came in with the seafaring English; the second was borrowed from the Spanish, now anglicised in pronunciation to /mashet/ or /mashiet/ — never three syllables. *Cutlass* became a Jamaicanism when it was applied to an agricultural tool rather than a weapon: Marsden writes of it in 1788 as being used for clearing brush. Our first Jamaican citations for *machete* are somewhat later, in descriptions of the Maroons: 'On the left side he [Cudjoe] wore a

mushat, or couteau, three inches broad, in a leather sheath . . .
his men . . . all had guns and cutlasses.'

This shows, in fact, that there was still in 1803 a distinction
between a *machete* (broader and sometimes double-edged) and a
cutlass, and that the pronunciation of the word had already
become as it is today (not *matchet* with first syllable accented as
the OED records it from other places). It therefore seems probable that the Spanish origin of the word continued to be felt in
Jamaica. Other citations bear this out: '[The Maroons'] arms
were a light fusee and powderhorn, a *machetto*, or short sabre,
sometimes a lance.'

Just when the distinction between *cutlass* and *machete* began to
be lost is unknown, but apparently before 1826: 'a machet, or
cutlass, made by one of his own blacksmiths.' The old distinction
is still alluded to in the proverb, 'Pannya [Spanish] machate cut
two side,' which warns the hearer to expect a counter-blow.
Also in the comparison, Sharp as a Spanish machete, and in the
transferred application to a clever or tricky person: 'Soh Anancy
bein' a 'panish machette goh to Ma Kayke an ax her. . . .'

One other implement referred to repeatedly in early accounts
is the bill, a double-edged knife used in cutting sugar cane. This
was soon identified with the machete, so that today we may hear
of a *Spanish bill*. *Bill* has also been converted into a verb: to cut
with a bill (or similar knife). Grass in Jamaica is quite as often
billed as mowed.

Today there are three main types of machetes in use: the
turn-bill, *turn-point*, *hook-point*, or *hooky machete*, with a hooked tip
useful in pulling toward one the thing to be cut; the *open-guard
machete*, which broadens toward the tip; and the *wampara*, or
sword, or *sow*, which is the same width throughout. The term
'open-guard' appears to refer to the lack of any protection for
the fingers grasping the handle, such as a military cutlass would
have needed — unnecessary in an agricultural tool. The
Mother Thomas (/mada tamas/) and *Rozlin* (/razlin/) are two
types of open-guard machete. *Sword* is reported to be the St
Thomas word for what is a *sow* in Vere and elsewhere. The first
is pronounced /suod/, and the second /sou/; thus the latter may
well be derived from the former. *Wampara* (/wámpara/) is clearly
from the Cuban *guámpara*, of like meaning.

Still remembered, though not in widespread use, is *afini* or *afana* (accented on the second syllable) for a bush knife or cut-lass. These are certainly African, though from what exact form we cannot be sure. Twi has *afõa*, Akan *afǎnǎ*, meaning sword; Twi *ɔfãnnya* (with the plural *afãnnya*) means 'a bill-hook without a nose'. It is quite possible that all these and others were brought over, and were combined in Jamaica.

A folk word for a pocket-knife, or any small knife, is /pun-yaak/. One type commonly sold had a red wood handle and single blade. The word very probably comes from *poniard*. *Adze* has been repronounced by workmen in Jamaica as /aj/ or /haj/. *Dundu* has been reported as meaning a razor.

After cutting-tools, the next most essential utensils must be baskets, if one may judge by the number of words current for them. They range all the way from the large *ground basket*, which one takes to one's 'ground' to bring back produce, to the *lady-basket*, pretty ones made in many designs of palm straw, grass, sisal, and other materials — 'made for a girl's trips to the city' — to say nothing of the curio-seeking tourist.

The two best known baskets have African names. The *bankra* is of woven thatch-palm, square, with a cover, and with a plaited handle that goes down two sides and under the bottom to support it. Thus it may be carried by hand or on the head. Our earliest citation is from 1868, 'bankra — A hand-basket'.[8] The word may be compared with Twi *bõnkǎrǎ*, a travelling-basket; but the Jamaican pronunciation is /bángkra/. The other is the *cutacoo*, pronounced /kòtokú/, which strikingly reflects the Twi word *kotokú*, 'bag, sack, pouch, pocket; purse, money-bag; wrapper or cover in form of bag; etc.' Obviously, a word of wide usage in its homeland, and in Jamaica it has preserved the basic senses and added at least one more. Williams describes, in 1826, the equipment of a guide to Blue Mountain Peak: 'A machet, . . . and a cutacoo (a small basket) which contained his pipe, some tobacco, a flint, steel, and touchwood, not forgetting a bunch of plantains.' The cutacoo is often made of palm thatch and has a cover, and it is usually slung by a strap over the shoulder and hangs at one's side. However the word is also applied to 'a flat fish basket', 'a small bag or sack . . . which is associated with the Obeah-man,' 'a *big* basket; ship things to Kingston in them,' and 'a thatch basket used in pressing cassada for bammy'.

Two other containers of a very similar kind are the *heng-pon-*

me and the *side-bag*. 'The "hang-'pon-me", also of thatch, is a square pocket hung from the neck'; 'flat "han-pon-mes" which are thrown over the right shoulder to carry food.'[9] The *side-basket* or *side-bag* is identified with a *namsack* — which introduces another curious word, also found in the forms *nambu* and *nambo*.

Whereas the *cutacoo* and *heng-pon-me* are made of palm thatch, the *namsack* is made of cloth. The word appears to be a blend of *knapsack* with *nyam* (food, eat), for as we have seen, all these are used to carry food. *Nambu* and *nambo* look like nicknames, reduced familiarly as so often in Jamaica from the full form of the word — compare the pronunciation /báasi/ sometimes used for *basket*. Another word reported once for a knapsack is *buzuyako*. And finally there is the 'bag carried on the shoulders to stow away pilfered things' which is known as a *roguin' Joe*, as is also the man who carries one. It must surely bear some kinship to the Australian 'Waltzing Matilda'!

An arrangement for hanging meats and fish over the fire to smoke and preserve them is called a *hankra* (Westmoreland) or *hangra* (Manchester). This is a puzzling word. Folk-etymology may be responsible for the second form by association with *hang*, or possibly with *hanger*, one sense of which is a 'chain or rod to which a pot-hook is hung over the fire'. But probably a better connection is to be seen with Akyem *haŋkárá*, a fireplace, hearth. Sometimes the *hankra* is only a hook — compare Twi *hãnkáre*, a hoop or circle of iron, etc; sometimes it is a basketlike vessel — which suggests the possibility of an echo from *bankra*. Another name reported for the same device is *kekrikè* or *kreng-kreng*, the latter evidently being a local reduplication.

Largest of all the baskets are the panniers slung at the sides of a donkey or mule, and called *hampers* in Jamaica.

Similar to the baskets is a kind of bundle that is made when one has to travel carrying ground provisions — a *tanna* (or *tenna*). This is described as something 'tie up in trash with wiss [withes] — like string-bag' — which makes it virtually certain that we have here another African loan-word, for Twi *tănã, tĕnã, atĕnã* means 'a travelling-net'.

A common word for string is *te-tie* (pronounced /titái/) which has been in use since at least 1868.[10] It is perhaps a Jamaican reduplication of the English *tie*. Both words are found together in the proverb, 'When bull old, dem tek hog-meat ti-tie fe tie him' — that is, when a bull is old, they can tether him with a convolvulus vine.

One of the most familiar devices in Jamaica is the *cotta*, whose uses were first described by Long (1774): 'The Negroes use their heads instead of their shoulders, or backs, for carrying all sorts of burthens; with a dried plantain leaf they plait a circular pad, which they call a *cotta*; upon this, the load rests, and preserves their wool from being rubbed off. . . . The cotta serves likewise for another purpose; on the voluntary divorce of man and wife, it is cut in two and each party takes half.' Nowadays the cotta is often made of a cloth, but it is essential to balance a load. I have heard the word put to figurative use in the description of a 'jumping dick' bird, which was said to have a 'cotta-like, brush-top' — that is, a crest on its head. The source of *cotta* is uncertain, but since the object itself is from Africa the word probably originates there too. Twi has a verb *katá* meaning to cover, overspread, protect, etc., and a noun *ŋkata-hó*, cover, covering, with which our word may well be connected.

Jamaica shares with the southern United States the word *crocus* as a coarse material from which bags are now made. But whereas *crocus-bag*, *crocus-sack*, *croker-bag*, and *croker-sack* are all to be heard in the U.S.,[11] the only term in Jamaica is the first, pronounced /krokos-bag/. Our earliest citation refers to the material, which was used for slaves' clothing: 'Both men and women are also provided with great coats (or crookas, as they call them) of blue woolen stuff.'[12] Nowadays the material is brown, coarse, and not of wool but hemp — 'the "cruckuss bag", or bag of sack-cloth'[13] — nor is it cut for clothing, though often used to shed rain or for warmth on the road.

An old pronunciation of *bag* was /baig/. One finds it in proverbs such as 'Empty bige cyan 'tan' up,' and in folk tales — where also one finds *hige* for *hag*. However, only /bag/ would ordinarily be heard today.

Jekyll mentions a *barrel-bag* as one having the capacity of a flour-barrel. A common type of money purse is the *thread bag*, a small cloth bag tied with a thread or string, and used by higglers and others — often hung around the neck.

A natural container greatly favoured in Jamaica is the calabash, different varieties of which may remain as small as an ordinary drinking glass or become twice as large as a football.

The small size is a *packy*, first found in *Tom Cringle's Log*: 'They [Negro children] had all their little packies, or calabashes, on their heads, full of provisions.' Despite its appearance, the word has nothing to do with English *pack*, but comes rather from Africa: Twi *apǎkyi*, Akan *apǎkyie*, 'a broad calabash with a cover'. Another name is *gourdy* (pronounced /guodi/), a familiarised form of *gourd*. The *took-took* is medium sized, halfway between calabash and packy, and gets its name echoically from the sound it makes when water is poured from it. One other name that has been reported for a small calabash is *coobla*, which looks very much like another familiarising pronunciation.

An unusual container is the *jug*, that is, a six or eight-foot length of bamboo with the joint-partitions broken through so that a single tube is formed. I have seen many a Jamaican countryman walking with such a 'jug' full of water balanced over his shoulder, the ends preceding and following him by several feet each way.

From the Spaniards in early days at least two containers were borrowed. The first are still to be found in a few places; Moreton refers to them as early as 1790: 'Filtering stones are used, which not only purify but cool the water amazingly.' The filtering stone is porous; it is cut out in the shape of a flower pot, about two feet high, with sides and bottom about three inches thick and a square flange at the top which supports it in a wooden frame. Water poured into it seeps slowly through and drips into a receptacle. The Spaniards also used for storage huge earthenware jars, some holding two or three bushels. These, and later ones like them, are called '*panya jaws* . . . These are believed to have been buried in the earth, or placed in caves by the Spaniards when they were leaving the country'. Old ones have been dug up from time to time, and legend has made them almost objects of superstition.

A container for salt provisions, or salt keg, is known as a *saalchung*, pronounced /saalchong/. While the first element is obviously *salt*, the second is obscure. Could it be from *trunk*? Or is the whole word somehow related to *salt-junk*?

A Jamaican creation seems to be *tin-case* — a metal trunk. I have known it since at least 1915 but do not find it in print before 1947: 'Here I was . . . stuck into the "Kingston Train" with my tin case, a basket . . . and the little bag.'

Metal containers have displaced others more and more, bringing in new names. Beckwith mentions two in 1929: 'The gasoline drum lately introduced is locally distinguished from the kerosene as the "jo pan" or "drum pan".' For a metal pail, *bucket pan*, a redundant formation, is sometimes used.

Heavy, glazed earthenware bowls and pots of many shapes and sizes are made in Jamaica and known as *yabbas* (pronounced /yaba/, sometimes /yabo/). Though the exact source of this word has not been found, it is surely African. The Twi word for 'earthen vessel or dish' is *ayawá*; when such words were borrowed the initial vowels were often dropped; *w*, too, is phonetically very close to *b*.

One curious usage is *cistern*, a 'wash-hand basin', along with *goblet* (sometimes pronounced /gaglit/), a water-jug or ewer:

> Me two pung goblet an' cistan me chile
> Mash up, mash up, . . . (Bennett)

'Chamber-pot' has been abbreviated to *chamber*, and that in baby-talk to *chimmy*, also reduplicated as *chim-chim*. Another name for this valuable utensil is a *bed-glass*, and still another is *po*, also applied to a clay pot or yabba.

The commonest small stove is a *coal-pot*, in which *fire-coal* (charcoal) is burned; it is of cast iron with a six-inch circular base and a bowl-like top with a grate.

Cooking vessels range from the simple yabba used over an open fire to the aluminium pots of modern kitchens. A heavy black iron cooking-pot with round bottom, flaring top, and three legs is commonly called a *negro-pot*. A particularly large pot 'used in cooking for gatherings' is a *met-pot* (a *met* is a meeting), or, jocularly, a *bella-gut*, which also means a 'pot-belly' and thus reverses the common metaphor.

A heavy iron or enamelled pot with a cover and long, straight handle is a *jesta* — a form reduced from *digester*. It is ambiguously identified in the following: 'Anancy get one iron jesta dutch pot an bore out two hole.' Properly speaking, a 'Dutch oven [pronounced /uovn/] have t'ree foot, and cover' while a 'Dutch pot don' got no cover'. The Dutch pot is also a *Dutchy maid* or *Dutchy*. A pan with a big handle is said to be called a /pani/ or /paani/ in St Mary, but in St James this word means a *pan-tub* or *tub-pan*, that is, a tub.

Of lighter weight is the well-known *bun-pan* (burnt-pan) —
'a tall saucepan', as McKay describes it. Stafford writes:

> In a burnt-pan she is cooking
> „ Hafoo-yam and sweet potato.

And Beckwith explains the name: 'The pail-shaped tin which
constitutes the ordinary cooking vessel is called a "bu'n pan"
from the black look it gets after being over the fire.'

Pone pan (/puon pan/) and *pudding pan* (/pudn pan/ or /pun
pan/) were already synonymous in 1868: 'Poun pan, pudding
pan'.[14] Sullivan describes one: 'Put it in a "pudding pan", as
they call the little round baking tins, and bake until firm.'

A pan for keeping food, with a cover that can be closed
tight, is a *shut* or *shet pan*;

> Wan day, Cousin Sue keiba up li bickle (victual)
> Eena wan lickle shet pan,
> De sort wey dem use fe ketch duppy yuh know. . . .'[15]

Also: 'So I opened the sugarpan, the shut-pan we call it in the
country.'[16]

Men working along the roads usually have a woman to cook
their food, but if they cook their own, the pot, suspended on a
stick, is called a *ooman-be-dyam* (woman-be-damned).

To stir cooking food one uses a *pot-stick* or *turn-stick* (/tontik/).
To scrape it out of the pot one may use a *pot-spoon* (/patpuun/)
made by slicing a packy in two. The sound of meal frying in
water is *shwuwa* or /shuwa/ — which may be African and is
certainly onomatopoeic.

A mortar is sometimes called a *denky*, and a tin baking-sheet a
larta (laata)—the second word apparently from Spanish *lata*.
Pannicle and *cannicle* for a drinking can, however, though neither
is listed in the dictionaries, probably come from *pannikin* and
cannikin. *Bickla*, a scrubbing board, is of unknown source.[17]

Chunta, fire tongs, is clearly a borrowing from Hindustani
chimtā or *synnthā*, tongs. *Fro-fro* means fire, or matches: 'Gi me a
light of fro-fro'; it is probably African — compare Twi *fràm-
fràm*, blazing, flaming, and *fràfrafra*, (burning) brightly. *Pre-pra*
is fire too — apparently a variant form of the same word. In
parts of Jamaica where there is no electricity, the common lamp
burns kerosene, called 'lamp oil' — and sometimes, realistically

enough, *stinkin' oil*. The lamp itself is also a *flecta* (from *reflector*), and the lamp chimney a *chimblet*, a variation on the English dialect *chimbley*. In emergencies a kind of crude lamp is devised by putting oil in a bottle, corking it with paper, and lighting the paper. This arrangement bears the imaginative name of *sore toe*.

The Jamaican of any social level does not buy thread on spools, as Americans do, but on *reels*. The wooden cylinder is a *cotton-reel*. Eyeglasses that pinch the nose (pince-nez) are called *squeezers*, and crutches are *arm-sticks* to some. A kind of walking stick or cudgel famed for its hardness is the coco-macca (pronounced /koko-/ or /kuku-maka/), originally made, to judge by its name, from macaw palm or macca-fat wood. It is put to a characteristic use in the song *Sweetie Charlie*:

> Sweetie Charlie a go bus' Matty head
> Wid im coco-macca.

A stick used by fishermen to kill fish is a *mantle-stick*, from *mortar-stick*.

Candy vendors may be seen carrying and displaying their wares in wooden boxes (about 24 × 16 × 8 inches on the average) with glass sides, which are known as *candy-bowls*. Today they have no resemblance to a bowl, but no doubt a bowl was formerly used for the purpose, whence the name.

Whistles, horns, and other signals have figured in the Jamaican vocabulary from the first. Writing of plantation life in 1707, Sloane says that the slaves 'are rais'd to work as soon as the day is light, or someti[m]es two hours before by the sound of a *Conche-Shell*, and their Overseers noise, or in better Plantations by a Bell'. Beckford remarks that some 'loiter away the time in useless inactivity until the shell prepares them for a renovation of toil'. This led to time-telling by 'shell-blow' (see above). Today a warning blow of the shell, of a factory whistle telling the time, or of a train whistle, is known as *cauchie* (pronounced /káachi/). One may hear any day the question, 'Cauchie blow yet?' This is doubtless from American Spanish *cacho*, a conch shell, with the familiarising suffix *-y* that the folk add to so many words.

Sugar Making

With temporary lapses, sugar has been from the beginning one of the most important crops, and a considerable vocabulary

G

has grown up about it. The knowledge of sugar planting and manufacture, and the distilling of rum, came to Jamaica from Barbados. If we can trust Ligon, the Barbadians learned it from the Portuguese of Pernambuco. Ligon gives a good account of the early machinery and methods, with the terms already in use. But processes changed continually over the years, and a number of Jamaicanisms — borrowings and new creations — have followed. Some of these, in turn, have been rendered obsolete by scientific agriculture and industrial techniques.

It is surprising to find that so common a word as *cane-piece* remained unrecorded so long. I have not found it before 1801, when Lady Nugent wrote, 'We took a cross road, through a sugar plantation, or rather cane-piece, as it is called.' The word was surely in existence long before this! Yet *cane-hole* is also lacking in the dictionaries. Our earliest citation is from Marsden, who tells how the canes are planted 'in the deep furrows made with the negroes' hoes; these furrows or cane-holes are remarkably strait and exact'. Into these were put the cane 'germs', or pieces of cane that would sprout — also called 'junks', which led to the formation of the verb to *junk*, meaning to cut into pieces or cut off short. Both these words are still current in Jamaica, though the form in England or the United States would be 'chunk'.

The best part of the cane for planting was considered to be the *cane-top*. *Plant-canes* were those being started, to be transplanted later. A *stool* or *stole* was another name for the root of the sugar-cane plant, both first recorded in Jamaica.[18]

The fields were, and still are, manured partly by *penning over*. Stewart explained in 1823: 'A still more effectual mode of enriching the fields to be planted is what is called penning them over — that is, penning or folding the cattle on successive divisions of the land until the whole field is gone over.' Because these pens were temporary or movable, they were called *flying pens*, today abbreviated to *fly pens*, and the process is *fly-penning*.

In slave days the workers on a plantation were divided into various 'gangs', according to their capacity and the types of work to be done. The most important was the *big gang* or *great gang*, which did the heaviest work of digging and planting. Next was the *second gang* 'composed of people who are thought to be of rather weakly habits'. Third, there was 'a small gang called the *pickeniny gang* — these were the most numerous' and 'consisted of the children'.[19] Alternative terms were *light-work people*, the *grass gang* composed of 'the young boys and girls', who were usually engaged in *picking grass* — that is, bringing in fodder for the cattle — but might also be used to put the junks in the furrows, or as a *weeding gang*. A *holing gang* dug the cane holes together. *Jobbing gangs* were 'gangs of negroes belonging to men who have just land enough to raise provisions for their slaves and themselves. . . . These gangs (generally from twenty to forty stout male and female Negroes) are hired out, by proprietors and managers to do the heaviest parts of labour on sugar estates, and to repair roads, &c'.[20]

The gangs did not work by shifts, as one might say today, but by *spells*. In 'spell keeping' each gang would be 'expected to take spell' at certain times. The word became transferred to the gang itself: 'One spell was called *John Crow Spell*, and the other *Quality Spell*.' According to Sloane, 'When a Plantation has many Men or Women, 'tis said to be well handed, or in case of few, it is said to be bad handed, or to want Hands. This expression comes, as some others, from the Planters of Jamaica, coming a long Voyage at Sea, whereby they get some of the Sea Phrases.'

The fields of cane were divided by roads or pathways, called *intervals*, which allowed access to them. This word was in use by 1790 and is current still, though not in the dictionaries.

As the canes grew, they would have to be *trashed* — to have the dried leaves pulled off. One planter warned against *trashing high*, 'that is, of stripping the trash and redundant leaves too indiscriminately from his canes at an early period of their growth,' which would make them 'bleed', or lose juice. There was another sense of the verb: 'The canes in those places (sloping grounds) should be well trashed, or bolstered with trash, to keep them from lodging'[21] — that is, lying on the ground. But the chief use of the trash was for fuel, and it was usually kept in a *trash house* until wanted.

When the canes were getting ripe they were said to be '*in arrow* (or full blossom)' because 'from the center . . . shoots up an arrow, like a silver wand, . . . from the summits of which grows out a plume of white feathers'. Another name for this arrow is the *flag*, found first applied to sugar cane in 1739, but it has become the usual term today.[22] *In arrow* is probably a loan

translation of the French *en flèche*. If the canes were left uncut too
long they would become overripe; thus *arrowed* came to mean
spoiled, and *arrowing* spoilage. According to Roughley, 'The
arrowed top is a pithy, almost hollow, sapless trunk, with little
life, few eyes, and those mostly blind ones;' the cane tops should
not be allowed to become 'a prey to arrowing'. Thus the best
canes for either grinding or planting were *unarrowed*.

The chief disease to which canes were subject was the *black
blast*. Beckford wrote, 'the black blast attaches itself to the stem,
and the leaves of the canes; is . . . an accumulation of insects;
and . . . they will . . . in a great measure suppress their vegetation.' The other great enemy, of course, was rats, against which
traps, 'springs', fire, other rats, ants and the mongoose were all
employed. On each estate there was a *rat-book* 'in which account
was kept of the rats killed'.

The word that became the most inclusive for the sugar-
making season was 'crop'. Different fields were (and are) planted
so as to ripen successively, and *crop* or *crop time*, when the canes
were *in crop*, became the busy time of the year, *crop-over* the end
of this period, and *out of crop* the slack season. All of these may be
considered Jamaicanisms, as they are recorded earliest from
Jamaica when recorded at all, or because they are still current
here though obsolete elsewhere. *Crop time* first appeared in 1782.
Beckford used *out of crop*; McNeill wrote, 'During Crop, every
Negro is allowed to eat as much of the *cane* and drink as much of
the *hot liquor* from the coppers, as he chuses;' and in 1826, we
read, 'The day on which the last of the canes are cut down upon
a sugar plantation, flags are displayed in the field, and all is
merriment. A quart of sugar and a quart of rum are allowed to
each negro on the occasion, to hold what is called crop-over, or
harvest home.'[23]

When the time came to *take off crop*, the canes would be cut in
the fields, bundled up with *cane bands*, and taken to the mill. At
this time it was necessary to separate the good canes for sugar
from the bad ones — those which were 'arrowed, bored, or rat-
eaten'; the latter, used only to make rum, were therefore known
as *rum-canes*. The first process was the grinding of the canes, and
to start this process was called *putting the mill about* — which
alludes to the fact that early mills were turned by cattle-drawn
sweeps. This phrase was still in use in 1825 though the steam

engine was just coming in. Barclay wrote, the following year: 'I was much struck with their [the Negroes'] admiration of the first "steam-engine", or "smoke-mill", as they called it, that was set to work in the neighbourhood where I resided and which they came from all quarters to see. The common exclamation was, "Massa-nigger! wharra dem Buckra no savi? Wharra dem no can do?"'

The essentials of a sugar factory were the mill, the series of boilers for evaporating the juice, the arrangements for potting the sugar, and the distillery. The mill stood in the *cockpit*, so called from the circle described by the rotating sweeps. At first the rollers were vertical — a set of three working together with cogs. The canes were put through between the first two rollers, and back between the second and third, the juice running below and draining off into a cistern. Moreton writes that 'these rollers [are] . . . supported on the mill bed . . . on small pieces of metal about the size and shape of whipping-tops, called *capouses*'. As the source of this word I am inclined to look to Portuguese (or Spanish) *capuz*, meaning a cowl, and referring perhaps to the shape of these bearings.

Roughley remarked that 'The head boiler and *boatswain of the mill* are the leading, ostensible, and confidential persons about the works in crop time.'[24]

The cane juice was evaporated in 'coppers' of different sizes — originally a series or 'battery' of five, later of seven — each smaller than the preceding. These were heated from below by fires of *copperwood* — brushwood and branches of trees that had to be gathered continually. Largest was the *great copper*, *grand copper*, or *grand boiler*. Marsden refers to the first two coppers together as *St Hild's coppers*, and implies that they were the same size. The smallest was the *tach*, later *teach* (also spelled *tache*, *tatch*, *tetch*, *tack*, *taitch*, *teache*). This is an interesting word, a borrowing of Spanish *tacho*. Its first pronunciation must have rhymed with 'match' — the earliest known use in English is in 1657 in the forms *tach* and *tatch*; by 1756 it was *tetch*, and by the end of the century it rhymed with 'H'.[25] But changes in the methods of evaporation have done away with the old batteries, and this word is unknown today.

The early coppers were cylindrical with their bottoms rivetted on; later a new type was introduced, the *shell copper* and *shell teach*. Higgins explained: 'Shell teaches, being hemispherical, are preferable to those formerly used, because their bottoms are sufficiently concave for the purpose of ladling.' Another improvement was the *clarifier*, which took the place of the grand copper. To bring about the crystallisation there was put into the cane liquor a quantity of 'temper' — usually lye or lime. *Temper lime* was burned locally in kilns — their like may still be seen, today preparing lime for mortar. Long mentioned the 'conical or *French kiln*' as being in use. 'Most of the planters who use the Jamaica lime, burn it in circular, conical piles, ranging the strata of stone and wood alternately from the bottom to the top, which they bring to a point.' The term, however, is not mentioned elsewhere and now disused.

As the liquor became heated in the coppers it was said to *yaw*, which meant that it began to look blistered or frothy like the skin of a person with the disease of *yaws*. This liquor or syrup, while evaporating in the coppers, had to be constantly stirred to avoid *burning to* or sticking to the inside of the copper. This and other difficulties attending the evaporation led to experiments such as that described by Mathison:

> A different method has been lately practiced . . . which is principally experienced in the improved quality of the sugar. . . . This process is distinguished by the term '*Cold tempering*', according to which the lime is administered to the cane-liquor in a cold state in a vessel, contrived for that purpose, called the *receiver*; to which no fire is applied during any part of this early process. . . . At the expiration of fifteen or twenty minutes the clear saccharine liquor is fit to be drawn off by cocks suitably placed in the receiver.

At first the evaporating liquid was also ladled by hand from each copper to the next smaller, a process called *striking*, and later *skipping*. It required experience to know when it was *skipping time* or time for a *skip*. Later, instead of ladling, the liquor was brought forward through a *skipping trough* or *skipping gutter*. The term *skip* became transferred from the single step to the whole process and to the quantity of syrup in a vessel which received the sugar at the end. Senior wrote,

> The juice from the mill is carried in gutterings into the boiler, and after having gone sufficiently through its fiery ordeal,

passes into the taitch, where it receives the temper lime, &c., and being removed into flat vessels, called 'skips', proceeds gradually through the process of granulation. This completed, the skips are emptied into casks.

These skips superseded the earlier cooler, a container where the sugar was kept until ready for potting. As the hot sugar came into the cooler it had to be stirred with 'a *stirring stick*, a long, stout rod, made flat for eighteen inches at one end, and three inches broad where it is flat' — also called a *turn stick*.

At first the cooled sugar was put into hogsheads, later on into wooden molds called pots, while the molasses drained out. Marsden described this in 1788:

> Holes are made in the hogsheads with plantain suckers stuck through, from whence the molasses drain into a cistern like the hold of a ship, the hogsheads standing upon beams about a foot from each other. This process is called *potting the sugar*.

Instead of plantain suckers Beckford speaks of '*curers*, or *thatch sticks*' used in this way, but says they have proved a failure and are being discontinued. The small *sugar-pots* were square and 'wide at the Top and taper downwards, where a Hole is left for the Molasses to drain'. At the bottom the pots were 'stopt with a Twig till they are set upon the *Dripps*' — that is, on racks; and the molasses fell into gutters that led to the *molasses-cistern*.

Rum was made from everything not fit for sugar — the rum canes already mentioned, the skimmings from the coppers. This was all sent on to the still-house to ferment. The first distillation was performed in the *liquor still* and produced 'low wines'; these were put through a second distillation in the *rum still*, which produced rum. What remained in the first still after distillation was called 'dunder' (from Spanish *redondo*, the sphere of the retort), some of which was kept to start fermentation in the next 'set' of rum. After the second distillation some low wines would remain — which Baillie called *lowes*. The stills were also called *worms* from the spiral shape of their tubes. Roughley warned that 'Stills should never be filled quite; six or eight inches should be left empty at the top, to prevent accidents by *blowing*, or sending the liquor or low wine down the worms instead of low wine from the liquor still, and rum from the low wine still',

The surplus dunder was kept in a *dunder-cistern*, and the low wine in a *low-wine butt* until they were ready to be used again. Most of these words about distilling continue in current use.

The names for different kinds of canes are included among the plants (below) and the kinds of sugar with foods. Only one other expression remains to be mentioned, and that is obsolete. It was the jocular 'Calibash estate', which 'comprehends the whole island of Jamaica'; and which referred to the slaves' practice of stealing sugar from the curing-house in calabashes. When caught, they pleaded that they were 'carrying sugar to Calibash estate'.[26]

Other Crops, Cultivation, etc.

In settlement days Jamaicans borrowed a number of terms for estates and plantations from the Spanish and developed others from English elements. The former have nearly disappeared. Perhaps the earliest was *hato*, never full anglicised though found in place names. Gardner took it to mean simply 'a plantation' but it was more properly a grazing area. Long wrote, 'The savannahs were by the Spaniards formed into what they called hatos. . . . Hato signifies a flock.' This term cannot have survived long; nor did *stancha*. Blome, in 1672, mentioned 'the Spaniards that were in the Isle at the Landing of the English, keeping their slaves at their several small Plantations, or Stanchas'. This is from *estancia*, in which full form the word was later to be reborrowed in the southwestern United States.

Palenque, on the other hand, was early anglicised in the form *polink*; it remained so in place names, and as *palenka* is still a fishing term. In American Spanish it meant an enclosure for raising stock or for protection, hence a farm. Sloane was first to record it for Jamaica: 'A Palenque is here a place for bringing up poultry.' Leslie's *History* has a map which shows, in St James parish, 'Negro Palink' and 'Old Palink'; and White's *Inquiry* lists '360 Polinks and provision plantations'. Long used this spelling several times, as did Bedford, though the OED records only *palenque*. As these polinks were relatively small enclosures, the word may have kept alive also the sense of palings or posts; even so, and despite a tempting similarity of form, it cannot be connected with *poleen*, a railway 'sleeper' or 'tie'. *Palenka* was used in one other connection: Rampini distinguishes two methods of fishing, one the 'palenka' or long line fishing with 1,650 hooks attached to a single line, the other 'bateau' fishing. Here the sense connection seems to be through the long series of hooks joined together, like the posts of an enclosure.

Another early word is *crawl*, apparently the Jamaican version of Afrikaans *kraal* (which is cognate with Spanish *corral*); in this case the animals being kept were hogs. As Hickeringill wrote in 1661;

> They build two or three little Houses, or more; by them called a Crawle, and in these, they first inclose these tame Hogs, with which they begin their stock, and there feed them; that after (being let out) they will come to the haunt, at the sound of a Horn.

The *Acts and Laws* of ca. 1695 provided that 'None shall hunt any Gang of Dogs within 4 Mile of any Crawl or Settlement, except on his own land'. Sloane also said, 'These Crawles, or Houses and Sties built for feeding and breeding Hogs, are kept by some Whites, *Indians* or Blacks,' and Long, 'the word Craal being commonly used in the West-Indies to signify a place where provisions are planted, and hogs bred.' Though *sty* is more common, *crawl* is still used today, pronounced in the same way: /pig kraal/.

The penning of animals was so important a part of the Jamaican settler's and planter's life that *pen*, commonly in the form *penn*, has become the usual word for a property or farm. It appeared before the end of the seventeenth century in the *Acts and Laws*: 'All Owners of Neat Cattle shall keep one white Man at each Pen, and 2 white Men at every Pen whereunto belongs above 200 Head of Cattle.' Marsden wrote, 'At these pens or country-houses . . . they breed plenty of hogs, sheep, goats, and poultry.' Lady Nugent used the word regularly, as: 'We drove to Lord R's Penn,' and it is very much alive today. Long used the combinations *breeding-pen* and *lowland-penns*; also *grass-penn*: 'A number of little grass-penns, with good houses on them, are dispersed about the neighbourhood [of Halfway-Tree]' and 'a small grass-penn stocked with sheep and goats'. These three terms are no longer in use.

Another interesting Jamaicanism of the past is *coffee mountain*, that is, a coffee plantation — a term current in the early nineteenth century and alluding to the practice of planting coffee on mountainsides. Though this term is not in the dictionaries it was in general acceptance for fully fifty years. Lady Nugent wrote in 1801, 'Intend to drive to Mr Lewis's Coffee Mountain;' Bickell employed it repeatedly, 'I was walking out with a Mr Jackson . . . who had a coffee mountain near. . . . Sometimes, coffee mountains are bought well established, in full bearing.' So also Marly and McMahon; but it is now apparently disused, the more prosaic 'plantation' or 'property' having taken its place.

In the high times of sugar planting during the eighteenth century some land was 'vulgarly called *ready-money land*; which gives a present return in good sugar almost as soon as it is opened, but will soon fall off'.[27] The practice of overusing and abandoning such land produced another word: *ruinate*, 'lands worn out by agriculture'. It was used first as an adjective but soon became a noun, as in the following: 'We would advise parents never to allow their little ones to wander about near woods, or ruinates by themselves;'[28] and so it is still. Since such abandoned lands soon grow up in 'bush', the word now also implies 'woodland'. It is pronounced /ruunit/ or /runit/.

In Jamaica *piece* is certainly the most common term applied to a cultivated field. *Cane-piece* has already been mentioned; we find *grass-piece* as early as 1756[29] and today one may also hear *coffee piece, potato piece, yam piece*, and so on. When, however, the reference is not to a particular field but to a general cultivation, the word is *ground* (pronounced /grong/ or /groun/ by the folk) or *provision ground*, which recalls a custom of slave days to which McNeill has referred: 'There is a portion of land belonging to every estate, denominated *Negro-Grounds*, of which each slave is allowed as much as he can cultivate, for his own use.' The OED considers this sense of *ground* obsolete, yet it is still the everyday word in Jamaica. Less common words that have been reported are *benjy*, a field, *bubaka*, bad bush land now in cultivation, and *barampa*, fallow land.[30]

The word 'orchard' would seldom be heard in this island, and no more would 'grove'. What one hears for a group of trees planted or naturally growing together is *walk*, and one hears it in a great many combinations. Perhaps the earliest is *plantain walk*, found from 1661. As Hickeringill wrote:

Cacao-trees . . . especially in their Infancy must be pro-
tected from the scorching Sun by the favourable interposition
of some shady Trees; and therefore the Plantane-Walks are
usually made choice of for such Nurseries.

Cocoa-walk is found in the same work. *Orange-walk* appears in
1707, *coffee-walk* in 1756, and *Pimento-walk* in 1774.[31] Others not
mentioned in the dictionaries are *logwood walk, gungu walk, banana
walk, chocolate walk, peas walk* and *citrus walk.* All of these refer to
some kind of bearing plant but the meaning may be transferred
— a testimony to its currency. I heard a garage helper who was
examining a badly punctured tyre remark to the owner, 'You
mus' a drive in a *prickle walk*!'

Names for fences vary a great deal from place to place, and
Jamaica has a few of its own. *Bush-fence* does not mean what it
once did in the United States; it means a live or quick hedge,
such as one of pinguin (*pingwing macka*), cactus, or the like. A
fulling-up fence is one made by stacking logwood hearts between
posts until they 'full up' the space solidly, while a *pigsty fence* has
stakes criss-crossed at a forty-five degree angle to the ground so
that they overlap each other. Miss Beckwith also mentioned a
takada or wattled fence 'of close-set bamboo or of some other
wood, carrying five rails' which is built around a peasant's
house and yard. She interpreted the name as meaning 'take care
there!' but it is clearly from Spanish *estacada*, stockade. It also
appears without the final *a*.[32]

Though the vocabulary connected with sugar is the most
extensive, other crops have produced Jamaicanisms. Coffee, for
example, is picked when the berries are *cherry ripe* — a term that
goes back certainly to 1835[33] and has the echo of Shakespearean
song. Also from 1835 comes *pulper*, the name of a machine by
which the coffee berries 'are divested of the outside skin and
glutinous substance between the skin and berry'. 'The first fruit
which ripens in August is called "Burn Side", because only one
side shows red, and is harvested for home consumption.' Unfit
for marketing too is *rat-cut*, that is, the berries which have fallen
to the ground because rats have bitten or 'cut' the skins. There
is a similar term used about fruit: 'Then I would pick the fruits,
praying that some would burst or that some would be "bird
mouth" (that is picked by birds).'[34]

Coffee berries and several other crops are dried on platforms, usually of stone or cement, with a raised edge, known as *barbecues*. The earliest OED citation (sense 5) is from 1855, but the word may be found in Ligon's *History of the Barbados* almost two centuries earlier: 'The place where they unload [the canes], is a little platform of ground, which is contiguous to the Mill-house, which they call a *Barbycu*; about 30 foot long and 10 foot broad.' It must have come early to Jamaica but does not appear in print till 1756: 'Such as have large coffee-walks, should be provided with a convenient *barbakue*, or platform, to dry these seeds more commodiously upon.'[35] It is still in universal use.

In connection with coffee there is, finally, a word which probably combines /basi/, basket, with *cut*: 'At night each barbicueful is safely pushed up into a centre compartment of the barbicue, called a "bassecott", and covered with a tarpaulin. Next morning the contents of the bassecott are spread abroad on the barbicue.' It was still known in 1943.[36]

Another crop which has produced a number of Jamaicanisms is 'corn' (maize). By assimilation to sugar-cane, an *arrow* is said to shoot out of the top of the stalk, but the word for this is more commonly *flag*, which even becomes a verb, as in the statement, 'Dat corn soon flag.' Still another name for this is the *blossom* (pronounced /blaasam/ or /blousam/). What would be called an 'ear of corn' in the United States is simply a *corn* in Jamaica; a recent cookery-book directs: 'Choose young, tender corns, and plunge into boiling water.' McKay also recorded *pod* for this, though I have not found it otherwise:

> Lilly, lilly, t'rough de corn
> Till de pod dem shed.

(Incidentally, the OED last records the word *shed* in this sense — that the ears are formed and separate themselves from the stalk — in 1659!)

One elderly man referred to the ear as the *corn-head*, which metaphor is echoed in such other terms as *corn-mouth* for the top of the ear, and *corn-beard* or simply *beard* for the 'silks'. 'The corn-beard come out of the corn-mouth.' One man also called this the *brush*. The corn 'cob' is, in Jamaica generally, the *corn stick*.

The metaphor of the head is by no means limited to corn; if anything it is more commonly applied to *coco* and *yam*: 'Some good, ripe, dry cocoa heads, with good vegetating eyes,' and 'a sufficiency of yam heads, or plants ready to be put in the ground'.[37] A similar figure is used when the roots of ginger are referred to as *toes*: 'Ginger has to be handled toe by toe.' Cocos, like human beings, may get *yaw-bumps* — soft, scaly bumps 'that come if the coco is planted in May.'

The phrase generally used about harvesting corn (and other crops) is to *break* or *break in*. Beckford wrote in 1790: 'The Indian corn . . . is ripe, and requires to be gathered, or, as it is called in Jamaica, to be broken in.' Or, in a contemporary example, 'Kling-kling [a bird] eat off peas or corn that's ready to *bruck in*.' So also McKay: 'Her pa an' ma about de fiel'

Are brukin' sugar-pine.'

What is harvested is the *first breaking*, *second breaking*, and so on. When a root, such as coco, is getting fit to plant, it becomes *chowy* (/chaui/) and is said to *tek spring*.

The general folk term for what is borne by a plant is the *bearing* — it may be a fruit, a pod, a tuber, anything. For example, 'The bearing of aribeka is mos' like ginger.' The bearing of a peanut is called a *boot* or *nit* when it just begins to form, that is, when the plant begins to *peg*. Seeds planted in a garden are said to *hatch* (germinate).

Three-quarter bananas or plantains are those which are not quite filled out; when filled out but still green they are called *full*, and this term has been in use for over a century and a half. Beckford wrote: 'I have known the plantain shoot forth, and the fruit become full, according to the term adopted by the negroes, and which expresses the first state in which it is fit for use, in less than eleven . . . months.' Incidentally, the word *fit*, used by itself, is also a Jamaicanism: 'Dem cut de pine before it fit.' And there is the word *turn*, too, referring to the colour of fruit. Sullivan wrote of plantains, ' "Turned" is when they are between green and ripe.' These three terms may apply to any fruit.

A single banana or plantain (a 'finger' of the hand) is often called a *seed*: The Robusta banana has a 'larger number of seeds to each hand' than Gros Michel; and 'Horse plantain has few seeds but very stout'. The fruits that grow together in a group form a 'hand', and in the terminology of the banana trade, nine hands or more make a *stem*, *bunch*, or *count bunch*, eight hands a *three-quarter bunch*, seven hands a *half bunch*, six a *quarter bunch*, and less than six are not accepted for export. This is alluded to in one of the best Jamaican folk songs, the song of the banana-loaders:

> Come, Missa Tally-man, Come tally me banana —
> Day dah light an' me wan' go home . . .
> Six han', seven han', eight han', Bunch! . . .

The word *trash*, though not by any means limited to Jamaica, has essentially Jamaican uses which cannot be ignored. It means the dried leaves, stems, pods, or fibers of a plant — the part left over from the fruit or crop. It is regularly applied to sugar cane, bananas, plantains, and many other things. Thus you must 'bake chocolate berries (i.e. cocoa beans) and get off the trash'; after squeezing coconut milk out of the nut you 'trow way trash; fowl eat it'. As a verb, *trash* means to separate the trash from the plant or fruit; thus you 'trash coffee out de trash' — beat off the outer skin of coffee berries. Plantain trash 'can mek matrass'. Of dry beans: 'Tek it up an' trash it out' — though *shell* is the commoner verb in this case.

An agricultural labourer in Jamaica lays claim to an area in which he is later going to work by chopping about it — this is called *marking work*. When afterwards the busha or head man measures how much he has done, to know how much to pay him, this is called *taking up work*. One cultivator reports that in St James and Westmoreland one speaks of a *yam field*, while in Hanover it is called a *yam ground*; the heap of earth in which the yams grow is a *yam bank* in St Elizabeth, Manchester, and Westmoreland, but a *yam hill* generally. The last term has been in use since at least 1823, when Roughley wrote: 'The gang must be set in with hoes to dig yam holes, or as it is termed, to raise yam hills.'

The centre rib or main stem of a long composite leaf (as fern, coconut, etc.) is called sometimes the *staff* but more often the *bone*: 'Bone of leaf mek basket.' 'Fern bones' are used to make mats for drying ginger; Napier grass has a 'bone like cane'. The leaf sheath of the cabbage and other palms, which wraps most of the tree before it falls, is cut off the fallen leaf and used as a rough mat — called a /buba mat/ — or as a kind of sleigh on which children slide down grassy hills.

The unwanted shoot or 'sucker' on a plant (such as tomato) goes by the wonderful name of a *gormandiser*, which must be from French *gourmand*, that has this meaning among others.

A place where ropes are twisted (from native sisal) is a *rope lay*, and the grooved block of wood used to keep the three strands apart while they are being twisted is a *frog* — perhaps from its resemblance to the railway switch-plate so called. The simplest way of making rope, however, is by braiding three strands of bark. 'When the rope is finished the looped end is called the *nose*.'

A *pillung* is a tobacco factory; the source is Cuban *pilón*, a pile of tobacco stalks. Tobacco tied up in bunches for sale it is said to be *handed up* and a bunch of herbs prepared for the market is a *tie*.

When indigo was grown and manufactured, in early days, it was passed through a series of three vats, the first called a *steeper*, the latter two *beaters*, *beating-vats*, or *batteries*, because the liquid or 'mud' was beaten up in them. According to Sloane, 'If the Mud be put on Cloath [instead of in boxes] stretch'd and dried in the Sun, 'tis call'd *Fig-Indigo*.' These words have since disappeared with abandonment of the indigo trade.

We may conclude 'cultivation' words with a series that vary much in their sounds but have strikingly similar meanings, along with reduplication of form. *Grang-grang, cran-cran, crang-crang, brang-brang, bram-bram, pran-pran, jeng-jeng, jen-jen, jan-jan*, have all been reported from various parts of the island as meaning small sticks or pieces of wood, dry branches or brambles, often those gathered for kindling; thus also, more generally, rubbish. Of these forms, *grang-grang* and *crang-crang* (which are merely phonetic variants) are the most common. Coupled with their reduplicative form, this suggests some African source. Perhaps they are to be connected with Twi *krann*, 'wild, confused, entangled,' etc. *Bram-bram* and *brang-brang* are perhaps to be connected with English *bramble* or *brame* (see EDD). One finds a familiarised form *grangi-grangi*, and on the same pattern has been formed out of an English word, and meaning much the same, *brush-brush*.

Domestic Animals

Though they are not numerous, several Jamaicanisms for domestic animals are quite characteristic. A horse, mule, or donkey (and sometimes a cow or ox) is still commonly called a *beast*, though the term has generally fallen into disuse elsewhere.

An earlier and now obsolete term for a small donkey was *asinego* (from Spanish), which the OED traces as late as 1685. However it still appears in the laws of Jamaica in 1739, and it also acquired an erroneous form — *assnegroes* or *asnegroes*[38] — the Spanish word being corrupted, perhaps by some peculiar folk-etymology.

Two unrecorded local creations are *barble-jack*, for a large male donkey, and *mule-rial*, the small mule that is the offspring of a horse (the father) and a donkey (the mother). This term *rial* enters other combinations in Jamaica for which the dictionaries mark no precedent — *turkey-rial*, for example, and *Chinee-rial* — the meaning in each case being 'hybrid' and somewhat unfavourable. In this case the mule is smaller than the offspring of a mare and a jackass. One informant also calls the mule-rial a *nanny* — perhaps a mistake for *hinny*. As to *barble-jack*, one is reminded of a *barble-dove*, the local name for a Barbary dove; some association with Barbary horses no doubt lies behind.

Jabby has also been recorded as a word for 'donkey'. A *paha* or *namprel* is a horse or mare too old or sick to work. None of these words is of known source.

Horses were of course imported to the tropics, where the climate produced diseases such as the *pant*. Lady Nugent wrote: 'The horse, which drew the gig the whole way, died of the complaint they call the pant, which is very common with horses not bred in the West Indies.' From the past comes another term, noticed by Roughley:

> A disorder, which breaks out in mules, called in that country the pox, so termed by the negroes, and considered as such by white people. Whether through ignorance, or by giving facility to such a term, to make the complaint or disorder better understood, is a thing I cannot determine. This disorder . . . being neither more nor less than a blood spavin.

Today, another disease is known as *black water*, which refers to the fluid that gathers in the frog of the horse's hoof — for example, after a blacksmith has pricked it.

As to words for cattle: a polled cow becomes to the Jamaican countryman a *poll-head* — one which either never had horns or has had the horn points clipped. In earlier days a brand on cattle was known as a *burn-mark*, apparently with official sanction: the *Acts and Laws* of about 1695 state that 'Ear markt, or burn-markt Cattle shall belong to the right Owners, if claimed at any time'. Draught animals, as on a sugar estate, are called *road cattle*; those first in front of the waggon are *tongue-cattle*, or *tongue-steers*, and if three yokes are drawing together, the first is known as the *leading cattle* and the second as the *middle cattle*. Most of these terms, still current, were first recorded by Roughley in 1823. He also noted an interesting local phrase: 'when the cow happens to calve . . . or *brings* (as they say in that country) *her calf out*.' I have not found this, but it may well be in use still. A current term, however, used throughout Jamaica but apparently not elsewhere is *breast* for the cow's udder. Three words have been reported once but without confirmation: *buaw* for bullock, *abukani* for bull, and *abukress* for cow;[39] their origin is unknown.

The Jamaican term *small-stock* has been in use for over 150 years without having been put in the dictionaries. Moreton first recorded it: 'the sheep, goats, swine, and poultry (called the small stock)'; and it is also found in the *Ordinances* of 1828. As in other parts of the world, there are in Jamaica nicknames for the smallest pig in a litter. It may be called /winji/, which perhaps reflects the English dialect word *winge*, meaning 'to shrivel, as fruit kept too long'; or a *pampy pig* — an unexplained term, unless it represents the verb *pompey*, meaning to pamper, and referring to the extra care the small pig requires; or it may be called the *water-fetcher*, with reference to the task which even a very small Jamaican country child is expected to perform. *Bran*, a boar, is a north-of-England dialect word still found in Jamaica. Cundall wrote that *bracho* means a pig in the 'Coromantyn of Accompong'; no certain source has been found, but it may represent Portuguese *porco*, borrowed into African languages.

The goat, an important animal in this island, has acquired its share of names. McKay records *taffy goat* as meaning a ram — or *ram-goat* as Jamaicans would more often say. This term is believed to be an allusion to the Welsh pronunciation of David, but the evidence is scanty and the term appears to be less known than formerly. The term *Taggoram*, in the recent song 'Nobody's Business', is explained by Murray as 'an old ram goat';

> Ef me even old like Taggoram
> An' me wan' fe pose as twenty-one,
> Nobody's bus'ness but me own.

H

Yet this looks as if it might be a personal name, perhaps *Methuselah*, passing through such a form as *Tusalum*. Another word reported for a goat is *gumbesh* but verification is lacking.

Words relating to poultry are more numerous. For example there is the bantam chicken with thick feathers just above the feet, therefore named /fedafut/ (*feather-foot*) or *booty-foot* — as if it wore boots on its feet. The same or a similar variety of hen is a *ducky hen* or *duggy fowl*: its short legs, so they say, make it look like a duck. This may, however, be folk-etymology; at least it should be noticed that there is a Bambara word *dogo*, small, short, and a Twi word *atɛkɛ́*, a short-legged fowl.

Another kind of chicken is distinguished by having no feathers on its neck and very few on its head — therefore called a *peel-head* fowl or more often a *peel-neck*. Because the turkey's neck is also featherless and red, this chicken is associated with it in the name *turkey-rial*, as if the peel-neck were an inferior sort of turkey. Still another name for this chicken is the /jak-panya/ (Jack-Spaniard); while young it has a small tuft on the head, a few feathers on the wings, and is bare otherwise. None of these names is in the dictionaries except the last, but that only in the sense of a large West Indian wasp.

Most interesting of all is the name /sense/, spelt *senseh* or *sensay*, applied to a fowl with untidy feathers sticking out in many directions. The word is clearly African — compare Twi 'asɛnsɛ, a hen without a tail (a fowl with curled ruffled feathers)'. I have not found it in print before 1929, but heard it at least fifteen years before. It is surely a word brought in by the slaves, with its superstitious associations. There is a saying, 'Keep sensay fowl fe pick obeah,' which means that if someone 'plants' obeah in your yard to do you harm, this fowl will dig it out.

A quaint Jamaicanism is the term *maiden pullet*, one of long standing. Moreton, writing in 1790 of a feast of which he partook, says, 'four capons, two maiden pullets (as they call them), twenty-four pigeons ... lost their lives.' The term is still current and means 'a fowl of one to one-and-a-half years, that don't lay'. Young fowl, usually turkeys, are called *pee-pees* and ducklings *dills*, or *dill-dills*. The disease of *yaws* (/yaaz/), once very prevalent in Jamaica, has given its name to a swelling or scab around the eyes and beaks of poultry. Moreton mentions it, speaking of turkeys, and Thomson, speaking of 'fowls, as well as pigeons'. 'Negroes call it the yaws' he continues; 'I have examined several . . . it was nothing else but *chigoes* which caused it.' Sullivan attributes it to cashew nuts, which have a very strong oil in the husk. The term is still current, though dictionaries do not record it in this sense.

It has already been remarked that Jamaican usage greatly prefers *puss* to *cat*. Evidently this has been so for a considerable time, since Long tells of a doctor who, though seriously wounded, continued to move, whereupon a Negro standing near exclaimed that 'he had as many lives as a puss'. The male cat is not called a Tom but a *ram puss*, occasionally a *ram cat*— by parallel, no doubt, with goats. *Ram* is nearly equivalent to *male*; I have heard it applied even to lizards! It may be worth remarking that in Cornwall today cats are either 'ram' or 'ewe'. The usual reputation of cats is reflected in Jamaica in the word *pussery*, which means trickery. A *corn-puss* is a tricky, thieving cat.

The only local phrase found for a dog is *bruck-kitchen*, either as adjective or noun, for a thieving one.

Traps

The earliest new word for a trap of which we have a record is the *calaban*. This is a square pyramid of sticks held in place by two pieces of 'wiss' fastened crosswise over the top. This 'box' is set on one edge, and the opposite edge is held up by a *setting stick* from which strings run to the back corners. The bird goes under for the bait, trips the string and the setting stick, and the cage falls over it. I have found this in none of the dictionaries, though recorded by Sloane from as early as 1707:

> Ground-Doves . . . are taken with Clavannes, and wild Cassada seed for Bait.

In his 1725 edition, Sloane made this *Clavanies*. Russell spelt *calibean*, 'A basket snare for birds. African.' The modern spelling is first used by Smith (1905): 'Anancy try to ketch Chim-Chim, by springes, an' Calaban, an' lime.'[40]

Despite Russell, this appears to be not African but an English dialect word, *Callyvan*, much better attested in Jamaican use, indeed, than in its shire of origin, Somerset. The word was adopted early enough to have found its way to Cuba in the form *caravana*.[41]

Other names for bird-snares are the *chokie*, *breakneck*, or *haulie*, which work by means of a noose, and a *tambo* (stand-bow?) — 'a bow-shaped trap' or springe.

Chapter Six

SEASONS AND PLACES: MEASUREMENTS

Time

EXPRESSIONS for times and seasons, both concrete and abstract, have grown up in some numbers in Jamaica. To refer to the past, for example, there is the word *from*, which means 'from the time when', or 'since'. In a letter to the *Gleaner* a sugar estate worker declares, 'I have been paying taxes from I was a young man,' or, as a less educated workman put it, 'fram me a lickle bwoy'. It turns up in a lively, almost proverbial expression, 'I've been handling cats from my eyes were at my knees' — from the time when my eyes were as high as my knees are now. Abbreviated otherwise it becomes *from time*: 'It had been the custom "from time" (as the saying is in Jamaica) for the Governor... to be entertained.'[1]

Several similar phrases are in common use. *Long time* means long ago ('Him gone long time') but may also be used adjectivally to mean 'from long ago'; thus a 'long-time cassada' would be a variety of cassava introduced long ago. *First time* means much the same — formerly or long ago — as when in a poem of McKay's, a woman reminds a countryman who has joined the police force that his uniform does not disguise his origin:

> You t'ink say you's de only man,
> Yet fus' time ko how you be'n 'tan.[2]

This is still current: 'Custard apple and cherrymayas used to be plenty, firs' time.' (On the other hand, the Standard English *first time* becomes merely *first*: 'Is de fus Tom look soh clean.' This is common also in the United States.)

Another word referring to the past is *aback*, which is unrecorded as dealing with time: 'About five weeks aback' — that is, ago; but this is less common than *again* in negative expressions which may be heard every day, not in the standard sense of failure to repeat, but meaning failure to continue. An educated Jamaican lady said, 'They don't sell those again' — that is, any more. The OED has citations for this locution only from Shakespeare (1602) and the Bible (1611), yet it has remained in Jamaican use. Over a hundred years ago Belisario wrote: 'On being asked if he were a married man, he replied, "Yes, Massa; but me wife no tay wid me again — him gone, so lef me." '

If something must be done fast, the saying is *quick time*: 'Him run quick time an tell him mumma,' or, farther up the social scale, 'You better come here quick time!' Very common for 'immediately' is *same time*: 'Im see me a come, same time im shut de door,' or 'Same time me call im, im run gone'. Very similar in the negative sense is a use of the word *never* to mean hardly, scarcely, or no sooner: 'De word nevah drop outa Puss mout' before Anancy run ovah Dog yard go tell him.'

Take time has the standard neutral meaning: go slowly, therefore carefully, cautiously, even gently. As the proverb has it, 'Tek time get deh today; mek has'e get deh tomorrow.' But in other tones the phrase may be a plea, 'tek time how you hole me Corpy' — said to a policeman, or a threat if the same thing were said to a person one did not fear.

From over-correction or some other cause one often hears not simply *while* but *during the while*. *Bigens* means 'by the time': 'Bigens you done deh, me wi ready.' This is perhaps connected with the obsolete sense of *against*, in preparation — indeed, it may represent a combination of *by* and *'gainst*.

Expressions for the time of day reveal some customs of the past and present. The naval and military custom of firing a gun to mark certain hours is of long standing, yet interestingly enough the word *gunfire* is not found by the OED before 1823. Lady Nugent used it repeatedly in 1801, however — to her it was commonplace: 'Oct. 30. Up at gunfire' — that is, at 5 a.m.; or: 'Nov. 6th. Drive to the Penn at gunfire.' These guns, fired by naval vessels standing off Port Royal, were heard at Spanish Town. A gun was fired also at 6 p.m., and a third at 8 p.m. warning ships to lie outside the harbour thereafter.

Another expression, the old *cockcrow*, was elaborated in Jamaican use, if we may trust Barclay's account: 'They [the Negroes] designate the hours of the night by the crowing of the cocks — "before cock crow", signifies before two o'clock; then follows "second cock-crow" — then "cock crow fast" — and, lastly, "day cut", or dawn.' *Day-cut*, at least, is still current: it means sunrise, and *day da cut* means the sun is rising. Parallel to this verbal expression is the other, perhaps better known, which has already been cited in the refrain of the banana-loaders' song: 'Day dah light, an' me wan' go home.' Occasionally heard for 'daybreak', too, are *day-morning* and twilight.[3]

In slave days a conch shell used to be blown on plantations to mark the times for starting and stopping work. To this custom are due several phrases: 'Many overseers have the first shell-blow, for dinner, at half past twelve o'clock, and the second at two, to go to the field again.' 'At shell-blow numbers of the negroes are seen making traps or examining those they have got in the water.' 'The heavy fall of rain . . . continued untill shell turn-out'[4] — which appears to mean noon. (The OED also records *shell-blowing* from 1869.)

The word *noon* is not much used by the folk; they prefer 'twelve o'clock' or *middleday*. But the oldest, and still current expression is *sun hot*. Banbury recorded it in 1895 and Dodd in 1905 as meaning 'noon', and there is the well known proverb referring to the white man who does not know how fortunate he is by comparison with the Negro: 'Rock-'tone a ribber bottom nebber feel sun hot,' where it appears to mean 'the heat of the sun' as much as 'the time when the sun is hot'.

No nicknames for the days of the week have developed except the now obsolete *Negro day* for Saturday. The reason for this was that on Saturdays slaves were released from plantation labour to work their own provision-grounds. Marly used the term: 'Saturday being negro day, the two book-keepers . . . rode to the mountain,' and 'At last negro-day came'. For times of the year there is one well-established current expression: *tamarind season*, /tambran siizn/ — the period from about January to March, when crops are scanty and only tamarinds are 'in'. Thus, the more generalised meaning of 'hard times'.

The OED records with two quotations (1748, 1823) the expression 'banian day' — meaning one on which one eats no meat, and referring, of course, to the Banians of India. From the practice on many ships of serving meat on alternate days (or less often!), this became chiefly a nautical expression. Its last known occurrence is in a book about Jamaica: 'I should have had a banyan day but for half a dozen eggs that Miss Louisa had the humanity to offer me.'[5] While this is not a Jamaicanism it may be the source of one, the phrase *Ben Johnson day*, which now means the day before pay-day, but, according to H. P. Jacobs, originally referred to shortage of food. Jacobs cites the popular saying, 'Every Friday Ben Johnson trial and Saturday him heng' — a typical way of suggesting the 'trial' of food shortage and the execution that comes when the shortage is over.[6] *Banian day* was one of the considerable number of nautical expressions that were current in Jamaica in an earlier day; *Ben Johnson day* may well be *banian day* — a meatless day — in disguise, personified perhaps by reference to some real man, though no evidence for the existe~~ce of such a person has been found.

Weather

Various kinds of wind have, naturally, been of great importance to Jamaicans, first at sea, then for their effect upon health and cultivation. *Land breeze* and *sea breeze* are two early phrases both in use here before the end of the seventeenth century. The OED records *sea breeze* first from 1697, but we find it from 1693 in *The Truest and Largest Account* of the earthquake at Port Royal (1692). Much later, Long identified it as 'the trade, or as it is called here, the sea-breeze'. Though one would expect *land breeze* to have been coined to complement *sea breeze*, it is actually recorded sooner. OED has it from 1667, but it may be found earlier in *The State of Jamaica*: 'From Eight at night till nine it the morning it frequently blowes westerly wch they call Land breezes; wth this wind the vessels git out of the Harbours.' Both these terms, of course, are still in use.

Another of importance to sailors was called the *rock wind*. As Long wrote: 'At certain times of the year, when the sea-breeze, or trade, is veering either towards the Northern points, or returning from them to the South-east, a wind blows, known here by the name of the rock-wind, and so called from its sweeping close along shore from East to West.' The term is still used by Jamaican fishermen, though in a less specific sense; it seems not much different from 'land breeze'. They say, 'Rock win' is a blow-and-stop win' — blow high; come on with a little cloudiness — good weather for a while. Fisherman watch it — have time to turn back; [it's a wind] bringing *strong weather.*'

The breeze most famous for health, of course — the sea breeze — has been nicknamed *the doctor*. Though later adopted elsewhere, this phrase was apparently created in Jamaica.[7] In a poem of 1777 we find the apostrophising line, 'Sweet doctor! waft me to some purling rill,' with the footnote, 'The sea breeze, so called for its salubrious effects.'[8] With less justification the land breeze has more recently been jocularly dubbed the *undertaker* or *undertaker's wind*.

The chilling winds from the north have been mentioned also from the seventeenth century as *norths*, a term now being challenged by its cousin *northers*. Trapham remarked, 'These norths are smart winds and cold;' and Beckford, 'The north winds (or the Norths, as they are indiscriminately called in Jamaica) may sometimes be . . . prejudicial to the canes.' That they did harm to the cacao trees was early recognised in the term *chocolate north*,[9] which is paralleled nowadays by the term *banana breeze* — that is, one of about forty miles per hour, hard enough to blow down the bananas. *North* is still in use but *norther* has begun to compete with it within the past fifty years, coming in from the United States where it has been used since at least 1820. The first Jamaican record of it I have found is from 1912, but today, as the meteorologist's choice, it is usurping the place of *north*, the Spanish word yielding to the Yankee one.[10]

Though 'hurricane' originates in the Caribbean it is not specifically Jamaican. Nor has it been generally adopted by the folk, who prefer to use the simpler term *the blow* or *the breeze* — an understatement with a smack of irony. The last winds of a hurricane, however, have been referred to as the *tail* from as early as 1828.

The word *storm* is equally neglected by the Jamaican fishermen and others, who use instead, in a specific sense, *weather*. OED labels this 'now *dial.* and *naut.*' and considers the specific use obsolete. Yet one may hear any day, 'When we get a weather' — when a storm comes; or 'It look weathery' — that is, threatening. 'When wedda time,' another man told me, 'ants shake dem wing loose — full up de whole place when wedda gwine set in' — that is, when the rainy season is about to begin. Incidentally this brings in the verb *set* in reference to clouds and rain, which is still current in Jamaica. Banbury quotes the proverb illustrating improvidence: 'Jancro say him da go mek house when rain set.'

A similar phrase is *it buil' a squall* or *it buildin' up a squall* — it's getting ready for a squall. Though the only OED quotation for *white squall* is from 1801, it has continued in use in this island: 'They had not proceeded far before a white squall upset the boat, and many of the guests . . . were drowned.'[11] This means a sharp storm of rain and wind at sea or coming off the sea, and 'white' refers to the effect of the breaking waves with the rain beating on them. *White squall* has also acquired the transferred meaning of 'hunger', and *squally* of 'hungry'.

In *white rain*, 'white' alludes to the absence of dark clouds and the lightness of the air, but a white rain lasts longer than a heavy rainstorm would. A long, steady rain that 'no wan' stop' is an *old woman rain*, and a light rain that falls and stops is an *overhead rain*. The Shakespearean 'water-gall' is remembered in Jamaica as simply a *gall*, described as being like the short part of a rainbow; it is considered 'a sign of weather'.

The use of *season* to mean a heavy seasonal rainfall evidently began in Jamaica, though it is now also found in the southern United States. The first known instance is that of Sloane, 1707:

> In those rainy Seasons, I was forc'd to ride on Horseback, . . . And these Seasons, as they are call'd, from their being fit to Plant in, are generally so over the whole Island. . . . In the month of January is likewise expected a Season or Rain, but this is not so constant nor violent as are the other two (in May and October).

Williamson also wrote,

> We had frequent and heavy rains during the month, as are usually expected under the name of October seasons; weather much cooler; norths more prevalent.

Today one hears reference too to a *season rain*, and a weather saying has grown up: 'Rain and sun is good season.' An equivalent phrase formerly used was *fall rains* (now common in the United States) which seems to have been first recorded in

Jamaica. In 1823 Stewart wrote, 'The autumnal or fall rains, as they are called by the planters, fall in October and November.' A flash of lightning is called a *gash* — probably by malapropism. A drought is a *water-dry*.

The continued use of *moonshine* in Jamaica has already been noticed. Another phrase is *moon-full* for the full of the moon. A countryman, speaking of 'full-mouth' beans, said, 'Plant it on moon-full and it grow well.' There does not seem to be much astronomical lore current among the folk, but Beckwith writes of a constellation of seven stars called the *clot of blood*. These are said to 'come out in May and scatter in June', and it is they that reputedly cause the heat.

Finally, the earthquake. Kelley stated in 1838, 'The Negroes call the earthquake "ground shake".' From 1907 Jekyll reported *groun' shakin'*, and I have heard it irreverently called *shaky-shaky*. It might be noticed that *shake* has been a name for an earthquake in English since at least 1622.

Clothing

Specifically Jamaican words for clothing appear to run chiefly to the two extremes of the creature — to shoes and to hats. From the past comes the term *mosquito boot*. As Long wrote, 'The usual guard for the legs is the muskeeto-boot, or a kind of half-trouzer, made of linen, tied above the knee, and reaching to the shoes.' This is no longer in use. Obsolete for the same reason — that the garment no longer exists — is the *buck-toe* boot or shoe, which had a high toe that stuck up (like a 'buck' forehead). These were in use before 1915, to the best of my recollection, but the name has not been found recorded.

What seems to be an old term, *blue boots*, apparently meaning black rather than blue — one's best pair — remains in the phrase, 'Me ha' fe wear me blue boot, go up eleven steps' — that is, to go to the Court House.

For rough wear, Jamaicans have long used *board slippers* — simple pieces of board cut to the shape of the foot and held on with a plain leather strap across the vamp. Another name for these is *sand-patta*, or *samplatta*, which goes back well over a century, for Roughley recorded it in 1823: 'His foot clothed with a kind of sandal, (called in Jamaica a sand-patta).' McKay had two spellings: *samplatta* and *sandplatter* and said the material was leather; he also used the word attributively to refer to 'anything that is flat and broad' — in one case, to a man's nose:

'Ko 'pon you' jam [damn] samplatta nose!'

These forms are evidently folk-etymologies by association with *platter* and (the first) with *sand* (and perhaps also with the verb *pat*). The original form that lies behind is probably represented by the current pronunciations /sampata/ and /shampata/; and I suspect this source to be *zapata* (pronounced /sapáta/), which in Cuba and Porto Rico is the name of a wooden-soled cloth shoe. An intrusive nasal before the *p* would produce the Jamaican word. A form showing yet another alteration is *shoe-patta*.

Somewhat better than these, though home-made too or of local production, are 'auto-tyre shoes', also called *Hitler boot*, *dadjaka*, *masha*, and *power shoes*. The first term is, of course, from the Second World War, but the shoes themselves go back at least to the first war when *sampatta* may have been applied to them. *Dadjaka* is said to be the East Indian name. *Power* is apparently a fairly recent term, now favoured over the others; it refers to the strength of these sandals and perhaps also with ironic intent to their style. *Masha* most likely represents *masher*, from the shoes or the tyres mashing things. The most recent nickname is *jump-and-jive*. McKay wrote in 1912 of *bulldog boots* as rope-soled slippers — named for the same reason as power shoes; but this seems now to be out of use.

A word certainly introduced by East Indians is *juta*, applied to shoes in general. Coarse, heavy shoes are called *plunkas* — apparently from the way they sound.

Tennis shoes with rubber soles and canvas tops are widely known in Jamaica as *puss boots* or *puss shoes*. No reference is intended to Puss in Boots, but simply to the quietness they permit — just as Americans call them 'sneakers'. Similar to these but with thin crepe soles (the distinction is not always clearly made) are *hard-socks*. The state of poverty is scornfully suggested in Louise Bennett's line about a woman who 'Kean even buy one hard-socks fe har foot'. And finally, one trade name, *G.B.*, has become current. It is popularly interpreted as meaning, in pungent Cockney, 'Gaw Blimey!' — also, by euphemism, *dog-bline-me*.

Another kind of shoe is a *grambay* in St James and elsewhere, but the word has not been traced. *Shrip-shrap* or *slip-slop*, heard occasionally for old shoes, is probably the general American colonial word surviving in Jamaica. Long boots have evoked the grotesque metaphor of *foot post-hole.*

The best known Jamaican-made hat is the *jipi-japa*, also called *yipi-yapa* and *ipi-apa*, which comes from the name of the town Jipijapa, in Ecuador. It refers primarily to the 'straw' of fine strips of palm leaf, and by transference, to the hats made from this. The word is found elsewhere in the Antilles and the mainland but has developed Jamaican forms. A hat made from a similar or the same palm leaf, but made more coarsely for local use, is variously called a *trash hat*, a *thatch hat*, and a *we-fi-du* (what to do?), the last term implying humourously that this is the best hat one can afford. A similar name is *shall-I*, meaning cheap material, and implying that despite the poor quality one has no choice — it's buy this or go naked!

The cooking vessel called a *burn-pan* (because it is put directly on the fire and becomes quite black) has been applied to headgear: a *bu'n-pan hat* is a silk hat or top hat. (Americans, by a similar image, call it a 'stove-pipe'.) This term also includes the bowler or *bowl-hat*. One kind of felt hat is called a *coon* or *coon-hat* for its shape: low in front, high behind. (This could be from *cone*.)

Other articles of clothing that have acquired special names, now obsolete, are the *back-tie*, *crookas*, and *tanky-massa*. The first was used in slave days by nursing mothers to carry their babies while they worked. As Kelly wrote, 'There was a midwife on every estate, who . . . brought the children to the overseer when a month old. She then received . . . certain clothing for the baby, always including a few yards of Osnaburg linen for the back-tie.'

Crookas appears to be nothing but a special application of the very common word *crocus*, the coarse cloth of which *crocus bags* are made. 'Both men and women slaves are also provided with great coats (or crookas, as they call them) of blue woolen stuff,' Stewart wrote in 1808 and 1823. The Jamaican pronunciation of this word /krókos/, is suggested by the spelling 'cruckuss bag' — it does not sound like the name of the flower.

A *tenky-massa* appears to have been a neckerchief (or something similar) given as a gift. It is found in the song *Quaco Sam*:

Hankicher tie me head, tenky-massa tie me troat.

A *cutta-frock* is a short frock — which recalls the Scots *cutty sark*. The old word *pane* seems to have found its way to the island though it was never widely used: 'a country cotton paen or petticoat'[12] was worn by slave children. *Shift*, for the same article, has not yet disappeared. In Jamaica a new sense of *merino* has developed: it has come to mean knitted underwear, especially that of children, and not necessarily made of merino wool. A parent may tell a child, 'I've bought you a new merino.'

An old-fashioned word for a child's dress is *jerkin*, and *streela* means 'the sash worn around a lady's waist,' — evidently from the Irish *streel*, to trail on the ground, stream, float at length. Ready-made clothes are called *heng-'pon-nail* — which suggests how they are treated in the shop, and their shapelessness.

A dress, new or old, may be called a *lawma* (/laama/) from the exclamation it evokes: 'Law, Ma!' A pair of trousers, as often as not, is a *pant*, and long trousers are called by envious small boys *gun foot*, from the long tubes. A shirt or a peasant woman's skirt folded round the waist is a /braga/ — which could well be from Spanish *braga*, a rope that holds the load on an animal.

A shirt without a collar is a *dandan*, and since, as a verb, this also means to 'dress pretty', it very likely comes from *dandy*, fitted into the reduplicative pattern.

Jamaicans have a variety of terms meaning old clothes, rags, rubbish, or rubbishy adornments, most of which depend on some element of sound-symbolism. Some may have African connections. *Rullucks* and *lurrucks* (which correspond by metathesis) are old clothes. *Reg-jegs* is clearer: it is surely from *rags* and *jags*. A phonetic variant of 'rag-rag' is *yeg-yeg*; and *yagga-yagga* is evidently an extension of the same. *Para-para* and *were-were* (rags, torn garments, bits of rubbish) begin to sound African, though sources have not been satisfactorily traced. *Jeng-jeng* (compare *yeg-yeg*) means any old, rubbishy stuff, or *ruggage*[13] as it is also called.

From rags and rubbish one moves to the sense of gew-gaws with such words as *fandangus*, *bangarang*, and *parangles* — each with some element of echoism. The first is no doubt from *fandangle*, the second is based on *bang* (it means noise as well as rubbish), and the third is very similar, referring to the *trinklets* with which an overdressed person is behung.

In recent years several words for men's styles of hair cutting have become current. The *wig* is supposed to simulate the judicial look; the *sab* is modelled on the longish locks of Sabu, the Indian Boy, hero of a popular motion picture; and the *victory* has a V cut at the back of the head — a Second World War style. *Lay-him-straight* is the nickname of a dressing that straightens the hair. Louise Bennett writes of a woman who wanted to do a thorough job: 'She get one big horsemane comb, one bristle-comb brush an a jar of lay-him-straight hair dressin.' And Uncle Newton reveals other beauty secrets and their esoteric terminology:

> Then comes the First Dress . . . that's the process whereby a heated iron comb is applied to the African kinks, producing nearly straight Indian Hair. That is why we girls say, 'We are going to visit our Indian Cousins' instead of 'Going to the Hairdresser'.

Direction, Position, Location

In Jamaica one finds the word *after* frequently used when Standard English may have *at* or *to*. Thus, to hit a dog, a garden boy would throw a rock-stone *after* it; and if he wanted to attract someone's attention, he would call *after* him.

Instead of 'backwards' Jamaicans generally say *backways* (among the folk also *backway*). Uncle Newton writes 'I fell off the chair backways', and a man explaining why a certain kind of very tough sugar candy is called 'stagger-back', said, 'You stagger backway when you bite it.'

The old verb *to cross-pile* is still alive in Jamaica in an altered form: it has produced an adverb, 'We walked zigzag or as we used to say "cross and pile" down the hill,' and a preposition, 'I rested for a few moments before walking "cross-and-pile" the hill.'[14]

There is a common phrase *this side* meaning here, in this locality or neighbourhood, which Russell noticed as long ago as 1868: 'De people dem dis side lib well fe true.' And from an Anancy story: 'Darg! You see Breda Tiger go dis side?' Its natural complement is *that side*: 'Me never travel dat side.' Nor are these phrases alone, for one hears 'topside' for 'up above' — on a hill, for example; and the island is normally thought of as having a north side and a south side. 'Topside,' while not a Jamaicanism, is worth mention as one of the numerous nautical usages that have taken root; 'windward' is another, used for the eastern part of the island — it is even used attributively in such a phrase as the 'Windward Maroons' for those whose centres were Moore Town and Nanny Town.

Ya-so is a combination made out of *here* and *so*, and means 'right here';[15] and similarly *deh-so* means 'right there': 'For a right deh so you deh!'[16] — For you are right there!

Foreign becomes in Jamaica an adverb or quasi-substantive, used after *from*, to mean 'a foreign land', or 'abroad'. A country man, describing the large cockroach called a 'drummer', said, 'It come from foreign.' Another said that 'Jigger fleas is a ting come from foreign come here'.

A place where, for any reason, you cannot go again, is called a *go-no-mo*, which reminds one of the equally imaginative place name that once so eloquently suggested the mountain retreats of the western Maroons: 'You no sen, we no come.'

Which part is often used in the sense of where, both as the relative and interrogative pronoun. Louise Bennett furnishes examples of both:

> Wen me look pon dem road wich part
> Ole tram car line use fe lie!

And, Sometime me want ask a question
> Wich part, wa meck, why or who.

Land Terms

In the United States it is a matter of geography whether one throws a 'rock' or a 'stone' at a stray dog; in Jamaica there is no problem — the missile is a *rock-stone* or *rock-a-stone*. Jamaica preserves this term later than other places; it may even be an independent creation in this island — at least, there are others of the same pattern. A stone, such as one lying in a field, is also called a /grónggàd/ (*ground-god*) — a curious term which suggests some forgotten folk belief lying behind.

In slave days the disease of geophagy, or earth-eating, was widespread. The earth that was eaten was called *aboo earth*. As Long wrote, 'this is chiefly found in marley beds, running in veins of various colours. . . . Some Negroes get such a habit of eating it in excess, that it often proves mortal to them.' *Aboo* is surely of African origin — compare Twi *a-bó*, stones, rocks. *Abu stone* is still known though no longer eaten. There is a kind of stony clay soil called /brogadu/ — a word which may be connected with *bragadap*. Sloane also mentioned a kind of rock found widely through the island: 'Honey Comb Rock. The greatest part of all the Rocks I have seen in this Island, are of this Stone, many Hills are mostly made up of it. It is whitish and soft like Alabaster.'

Among the Jamaican folk the word 'dirt' is little used; the common noun is *dutty*, which most people take to be merely an alteration of *dirt* or *dirty*. But it is more likely to be of African source — from such a word as Twi *dɔté*, meaning soil, earth, clay, mud. There may yet, of course, be some assimilation to 'dirty' despite the difference in part of speech. *Dutty*, as dirt once did in Standard English, also means dung.

The small offshore islets that abound throughout the Caribbean area, called 'keys' off Florida, are also so called by Jamaicans, but the favoured spelling is 'cay'. The earliest English examples reported in the dictionaries are from 1697 (*key*) and 1707 (*cay*) but the map added to the *Laws of Jamaica*, many years earlier than this (1684), shows *Sand Coi, Brasilett Coi, Gun Coi, Easternmost Cois*, etc., and *The Truest and Largest Account* (1693) of the great earthquake at Port Royal tells of the multitude of corpses which 'floated a great many days after from one side of the Harbor to the other . . . till at last some were sunk, others dispers'd . . . upon the Keys to the Leeward of the place'. The *Acts and Laws* of ca. 1695 spells *Kays*, and *Vice-Admiral Nevill's Journal*, 1697, spells *Kees*. Thus the word was in use in Jamaican English in several forms before being adopted elsewhere. It is well known to come from Arawak *cayo* through Spanish. *Coi*, of course, represents the Spanish word 'Englished' by abbreviation to one syllable and pronounced /kai/ or /kei/. Since 'key' in its usual sense had these same pronunciations in the seventeenth and eighteenth centuries, this new word became identified with it and thereafter both changed to the present pronunciation, though Jamaican usage retains the older spelling *cay*.

An interesting and puzzling word is the one which remains today in the name of the *Bogue* Islands of Montego Bay. The dictionaries give us little help in explaining it, except the DA, which lists *boca* from 1832 meaning 'the mouth of a river, gorge

I

etc.' — from the Spanish of the Southwest U.S., and *bogue* from 1832, which it traces through American French to Choctaw *bok*, *bouk*, reduced forms of *bayuk*, from which comes the Louisiana *bayou*.

These American citations are relatively late: there is earlier evidence from Jamaica. The map attached to the *Laws* of 1683 shows *Boga Creek* coming into the sea just north of 'Cabaritto Pt', and *Bog Walk*, one of the earliest Jamaican place names, is understood to be from *Boca de Agua*, referring to the deep gorge of the river. These meanings and forms correspond very closely to those in the Southwestern U.S., and suggest the same Spanish source. On the other hand, Browne, in 1756, mentions 'Mendsy's Bogue, in St Anne's' and later 'Mendzey's-Bog' — which might suggest the French word, as do the Montego Bay islands. Since the French never held any part of Jamaica, while the Spanish held it all for over a century and a half — *Montego Bay* itself is from Spanish *manteca*, referring to the lard once shipped from that port — the likelihood is that the word *bogue* is ultimately from *boca*, but that (like *cayo*) it was first reduced to one syllable, and then respelled as if it had been French (compare *barquadier*). When one thinks of the many distortions to which Spanish place names were subjected, there is little difficulty in accepting *bogue* (or *bog*) as coming from *boca*. On the other hand, there may be a connection with the Louisiana-French word of Choctaw origin. (The ordinary English *bog* is also possible, of course.)

The OED records *salina* from 1697 meaning 'salt pond' and 1748 meaning 'salt pan', both now obsolete; the word is from Spanish: a salt-mine or other source of salt. In Jamaica it has acquired two other senses: 'level grounds adjacent to the sea,' as Long defines it, and salt marsh: 'if there are salinas or marshes in the vicinity.'[17] The word is still current in the first of these senses — an example of a preservation in Jamaica.

A curious form of the word *morass* — influenced no doubt by Spanish, though the word is Dutch — was found early in Jamaica. In *The Present State* (1683) we are told of settlers taking up 'ill chosen Seats when they Plant in low Valleys, ... or by Mountains or Morossos, and have too much Rain'. The form *morass* /morás/ or /marósh/ is favoured today for what would be called more often a *marsh* elsewhere. A term of the same sort, *mecky-mecky*, swampy or watery, is probably based on *mucky*.

Gully, like salina, has acquired new uses in Jamaica. In McKay's line 'De gully ripples 'cross de glade,' it means a 'brook', and, as he went on to say, 'The word is more generally used in the sense of precipice.' Roughley also had it in a curious adjectival use: 'Steep places . . . are generally poor and *gully*, and disfigure a cane piece.' Evidently the meaning here is 'like a gully — washed out'.

Another Jamaican 'first' is *sand-gall*, which Long remarks on. 'The savannah lands are for the most part clayey, or intermixed with sandy spaces, some of which are of great extent or depth. These are called sand-galls, and are wholly unproductive of trees, or any other vegetable than a small wire-grass.'

In as mountainous a place as Jamaica it is not surprising to find a number of words for land that comes loose and slides down. 'Landslide' is hardly used; 'landslip' would be the regular term among the educated. One also hears the generally colonial words 'water-wash' and 'washaway'. But there are four specifically Jamaican terms. In the place name Newington *Breakaway* we find the first; country people call it /brokwe/, and it is applied also to the spot on the mountain-side from which the earth broke away. Synonyms are *cutaway* (/kotwe/), *runaway*, and *rundown*. *Come down* is the phrase used generally when a river floods, as in the song 'Ribber Ben Come Dung'.

One folk name for a cave is *stone hole*. The sink-holes that develop in limestone regions are *sinkets*. *Benkin* (from *banking*) is an alternative word for a bank — for example, along a river. And one jocular name for a steep hill is *bruck-tummick* (break-stomach) — evidently referring to the effort required to go up it.

Size, Quantity, Number, Degree

Words of measurement, specific and general, have come into popular use in Jamaica mostly by the usual processes of semantic change — by extension or restriction of meaning, transfer, conversion, and so on. Most are from English words, but a few may be from African. The most specific, perhaps, are the pair *big gill* (the standard gill, one-eighth quart) and *little gill* (half this quantity). It is difficult to imagine which of these terms came into being first. Louise Bennett has the lines,

> 'An yuh kean get gill a ackee
> Till yuh call fe big-gill ile.'

This suggests that *gill* was first misapplied to half a gill's quantity, that *big-gill* was then used in contrast to it for the full gill's quantity, and finally that *little-gill* was formed to complement *big-gill*. Though the earliest citation found is from 1942 it is certain the terms were in use long before.

Weight, in reference to fish, has a specific meaning at Calabash Bay and on the Pedro Plains. Like the well-known 'baker's dozen' it means thirteen pounds furnished by a fisherman to a dealer, and paid for as twelve pounds. This appears to be the preservation of an old measurement current also in St Elizabeth; in St Thomas, however, a weight of fish is six and a half pounds.[18]

Tall is favoured by the Jamaican folk where *long* would be the standard word. Okro is 'tall like finger'; the cutlass fish is 'taller dan snapper'; a woman may put on her 'tall' dress for a special occasion.

Words of quantity are: *bands*, a great many; a *gross*, a drove; *'nough*, a good many; *kench, kemps, chenks*, a small quantity; *bresheh* and several others, plenty; but they have certain restrictions of application. The standard word *bands* (e.g., of people) is apparently first altered to mean a great many, and then applied to things or actions: cameras, food rationing, and so on. 'Grouper [fish] run in a gross,' according to one fisherman — that is, they swim habitually in schools. In an Anancy story we find, 'You got nuff smaddy [people] deh ah you yard?' and a small planter described the blood-berry: 'tall tree — nuff branches.'

The noun /breshe/ refers to a time when foodstuffs are plentiful, therefore abstractly also to 'plenty'. There are several similar expressions: *culu-culu* (or *cunu-cunu*), plentiful: 'Yam is *culu-culu*'; so *dugolow, leggeh-leggeh* or /logologo/, *pasa-pasa*, and *wagga-wagga*.

> 'Dem nagwine get a kemps more a
> Me wagga-wagga bickle [food].'[19]

The Spanish *tanto* also has some currency, meaning plenty; and *all and all* is sometimes used for 'everything':

> 'An dis
> Is all an all me do.'[20]

In Louise Bennett's poem *An Food*, a servant describes with indignation the fussy and insubstantial way in which the mistress feeds her guests:

> 'Li kench a dis, li kemps a dat
> Li chenks a warra-warra
> Bans a different-different knife and fork
> An spoon and tarra-tarra.'

The third line illustrates the words *bands*, just mentioned; in the first two lines are our three words for a small quantity or little piece. *Kench* may be from the Scots *kinch*, ordinarily applied to rope but here transferred (as it is also in 'she no got a kench a hair pon her head'; which appears too as *skench* by over-correction). *Kemps* may possibly be connected with *skimp*; and *chenks* probably represents *chunk* (though *junk* is the usual Jamaican form) — compare, 'Anancy nyam off everyting an nevah gi Cockroach a "chenks".'

In Russell we find *chin-chilly* said to mean small, with the example 'Gie me chinchilly bit', and labeled 'African'. This looks like one of Russell's very few misinterpretations. *Chinchilly* should probably be analysed as *chinchy li*, tiny little; for *chinchy* is a preservation of the old word meaning niggardly, sparing, miserly — related to the Chaucerian noun *chinch*, a stingy person. *Chinchy*, in this sense, is still very much alive in the American south (Georgia and other states), therefore not a Jamaicanism; but neither is it an Africanism.

One word which does mean small or tiny is *beeny*, which is used both separately and in combination, as *beeny bird*, one name of the banana quit (or a small variety thereof) also called *beeny quit* or *little beeny*. One wonders whether there can be any connection with *mini-mini*, which also means tiny, or with *menya-menya*, reported by Russell as meaning slender.

Mini-mini is not only an adjective or attributive, as in 'a little mini-mini fly', but also a noun with at least three senses: first, the little shining figures which are said to be seen by a person smoking the narcotic ganja; second, visible particles of water vapour; and third, 'spots before the eyes' seen when one's head is struck: 'If they knock you, you see mini-mini.' The common element is tiny, shining appearances.

Other words for a small quantity are *tep* and *tweh*, the first perhaps a form of *tup* (a penny-halfpenny), the second unidentified. *Nubbin,* as an adjective applied to bits of bread, cane, or the like, means small too. From little size one moves to little value in /perepere/—small worthless things. So *pettifogging,* which normally applies to persons, is applied in Jamaica to things 'of little consequence'; and *poco-tempo* (from Spanish *pocotiempo*) — temporary, provisional, therefore not valuable. Finally, /tufe/ or /tefe/ means 'worth nothing'; it imitates the sound of spitting.

The opposite idea — that of largeness — is suggested by *dickens* used as an adjective: 'A dickance big tree.' In standard meaning, of course, *dickens* is a euphemism for *devil,* thus the Jamaican adjective has the force of standard colloquial 'devilish'.

Both *mickle* and *muckle,* in British dialectal use, mean large. Among the Jamaican folk they have come to be opposites, *mickle* meaning small, which may have come about through analogy with *lickle,* the common pronunciation of *little.* Thus *mickle-muckle* means little and big. And in St James an old woman quoted to me a Scots proverb ('Many a little makes a mickle') in the form 'Many a mickle makes a muckle'.

The adverbs *well* and *too* have acquired special Jamaican senses. *Well* ordinarily refers to quality ('I well remember,' 'well made') but in this island it may also refer to degree: very much — 'Him well tired;' 'Yuh well want i.' *Too* is used to mean too much, and is placed before its verb: 'You too lub chat' — you excessively enjoy gossipping.

The phrase *can't done* has acquired too a special adverbial use, meaning without end, illimitably: 'Spirit weed smell very strong — can't done!'; 'Nice can't done', extremely nice; 'Dem enjoy demself kean done'. This locution is strikingly similar to the English colloquial phrase 'no end'. *To pieces* has also become an intensifying adverb: 'handsome to pieces', extremely handsome.

A number of phrases have developed by ellipsis in the same way: *how much* (pronounced /hómoch/) means however much, as much as: 'You can have how much you can eat.' *Care how* means I don't care how, no matter how:

> A man can't eben ketch a mac,
> Care how him 'train him neck. (McKay)

All may mean despite all, no matter how much: 'But all Bra Cockroach try, . . . not a soun' coulda come from him troat.'

By a curious kind of inversion, *much more* comes to mean 'much less':

> Dere is no star fe light de way,
> Much more de white roun' moon. (McKay)

Here the negative of the first line is perhaps expected to carry over to the second. Yet another example gets no aid from a negative: 'We were so glad and frightened to be in the car that we could hardly *breathe*, much more, *touch*'[21] — unless *hardly* is to be thought of as a sort of negative.

Another peculiar reversal due to ellipsis makes *no* mean any, as in the cry of the higgler who buys used bottles: 'No wine pin'! no ale pin'! No soda water bottle!' — probably reduced from such a question as 'Have you no wine pints?'

For the better means all the more: 'An him [*sc*. Cow] go on ah fan him tail fe de better.' *Little most* means almost: 'De gal did like de way Anancy dress up an lickle mos' she say "yes".' Here we probably have a combination of 'a little more' with 'almost'.

Another expression with very similar meaning is *just left*, followed by the infinitive, which means 'just short of' doing whatever the verb expresses: "Im heat heat [eat, eat] till 'im belly jus' lef' fe bus'; 'An me heart dis leff fe bruck up'.

Down to means 'even including', as if one were at the bottom of a long list:

> she always carry
> Plenty tings fe eat . . .
> . . . dung to ice deh ya.

The phrase *so tell* appears to be another ellipsis, as if one began a comparison, '— so, till —', but, not finding anything comparable, left the words hanging in the air. The meaning, in effect, is 'extremely, excessively': 'I hate him so till!', "Im cubbitch [greedy] so tell', 'him frighten so tell'. This is a widely current folk usage.

The word *next* in standard English can be used after *the* but not after *a* because it is specific in meaning. In Jamaica it has been generalised and is therefore used among the folk, and well up the scale, to mean 'other'; "Im gwine buy a nex' one' — another one. *Namo*, no more, which we associate with Chaucer, remained in use (so far as the OED has traced it) only into the early nineteenth century. The last citations give *na ma* (1809) and *no mo* (1813). Yet it may still be heard in Jamaica as a unitary adjectival phrase meaning 'only' or '(and) nobody else': 'But it was ongle she an Dora no mo did know de song,' or 'mere': 'One no mo' farden bump she buy!'

Another preservation is *one* in the sense of 'alone'. This is OED sense 27, 'as predicate or complement following sb. or pron.', and the latest citation is from 1551. Yet we find a Jamaican example in 1826: 'The girls ... told him he wanted them all for himself one,'[22] and it may be heard currently today: 'Is him one lif' it' — He lifted it alone, by himself. 'Den me one wi have de road.'

The word *self* may be used as an adjectival modifier meaning 'even': 'No wut gill self' — not worth even a gill (three-farthings) — where it is perhaps an abbreviation of the emphatic *itself*. It may also mean 'very, same': 'Is de self man do it' — the very (same) man did it — where the emphatic pronoun is converted into a modifier. *Same one* is another form of the emphatic, equivalent to 'myself' in Louise Bennett's lines,

> Eee-Hee Missis, is me same one
> Sidung yah all de time.

And the word *said*, borrowed from legal parlance, is commonly employed to mean 'very same'.

Deggeh means 'sole, only': 'De one deggeh goat me have you teck grudgeful kill him.' The word sounds African (it is sometimes reduplicated as *deggeh-deggeh*) but no source has been found.

The OED gives the adjective *so-so* as meaning 'mediocre ... neither very good nor very bad, but usually inclining toward bad'. It has been eagerly adopted in Jamaica where it has developed local senses and a new pronunciation: the chief accent is clearly on the first syllable, the second taking little or none: /súoso/. It usually precedes its noun. The standard sense is seen in the name of the mango 'Big-an'-so-so', which has size at the expense of quality. But there are the new senses also: 'plain, single, only, nothing but'. To have 'so-so water' would imply that something might have been added — sugar or rum, say. 'Wa you ha' fe eat?' — 'So-so yam' would not mean that the yam was mediocre but that it was alone, there was nothing else.

A particularly good example may be found in the banana-loaders' song, already mentioned. The loader complains that he has been given nothing but full bunches to carry — the heaviest:

> Noh gimme so-soh bunch
> Me no horse wid bridle.

These latter senses, however, may not have developed simply from the English word; there may be a mingling of African influence — from such a word as Yoruba *sho-sho*, which means 'only'. *Chooka-chooka*, or *chaka-chaka* mean something like so-so, though they refer not so much to quality as to degree of action: not well done, half-done — for example half washed — and so on.

The English colloquialism 'chock', as in 'chock full', may lie behind the Jamaican uses of /chak/ to mean quite, all the way. Thus 'chack to St Ann' would be a long distance from Kingston. The words *chaka* and *chuku*, meaning far away, distant, may be from the same source. There is also the curious expression *chack an' belay* which means entirely full, just right, as in the sentence 'The market is chack an' belay with things' — fully provided. This phrase has a nautical ring to it but has not been found in any of the dictionaries. Perhaps it is to be connected with 'chock-a-block', which began as a sea term but has gone ashore.

Finally, the phrase *what a way* often serves in place of the exclamatory *how* of standard English: 'Wat a way dem musa shame!' — How ashamed they must have been! Though this is exclamatory rather than interrogative it perhaps comes from *what way*, meaning 'how?' in Scotland and the north of England.

Chapter Seven

PARTS OF THE BODY: BODILY CONDITIONS

Diseases and Remedies

IN THE DAYS before modern medicine, a number of diseases and unhealthy conditions afflicted dwellers in the tropics. Some affected the Whites, who did not know how to live in a warm climate, ate or drank to excess, or contracted infections and died with shocking suddenness. Others affected the Negroes — some which they themselves brought from Africa, some of the Caribbean, some caught from the Europeans. Whites and Blacks alike were thought of as passing through a period of *seasoning*; those who survived were considered to be acclimatised. This word appears first in Jamaican sources, as follows: 'Almost half the new imported Negroes die in the seasoning'; 'The dread of seasoning, as it is called, has, I think, a visible effect upon the spirits of every stranger who visits the country.' And as a verb: 'Unless . . . he [a newly arrived person] has no means of *seasoning* in the cooler part of the island.'[1]

Among the early diseases that earned the most fearful reputation was the *dry belly-ache* or *dry colic*. As Trapham wrote in 1769,

> If any thing hath dismal aspect in the Indies, it is this Disease of the dry Belliach. . . . Even there where the Sun showers his most plentiful heat . . . cold taken between the hot Tropicks if seated in the region of the Belly, &c., Cramps the Muscles of the Abdomen and tender Fibres of the Guts with the contractings of the torturing Bellyach.

And Ward:

> That Fatal and Intolerable Distemper, The Dry Belly-Ach; which in a Fortnight, or Three Weeks, takes away the use of their limbs, that they are forc'd to be led about.

By 1740 we find:

> The dry Belly-ach . . . does not prevail now so much as it did formerly . . . which is attributed to their not drinking their Punch so strong or sweet as before, nor made with Brandy; Rum, by Experience, being found a more wholesome Liquor.

Dry colic was a later term, from the end of the eighteenth century, never as widely used.[2]

The term *country disease* acquired here two unrecorded senses. The OED defines it only as 'homesickness', but in Jamaica it meant any disease endemic to or characteristic of a country, and, specifically, 'the dropsy'. In one of the earliest descriptions we find: 'There is no Countrey Disease (as at Virginia and Surinam) endemically raging throughout the Isle; nor any new and unheard of distempers that want a name.'[3] But very shortly after, one was apparently acquired: 'the . . . epidemick, called the Dropsie or Country Disease, to which many Servants and neglected persons especially are obnoxious.' A hundred years later Long was happily able to write: 'The *dropsy* was formerly so common in Jamaica, that it went by the name of the *country disease*; . . . It is now grown uncommon.'

Bilious fever, another name for *yellow fever*, seems to have been first used in Jamaica:

> That no one hath yet endeavoured to explain to the Public the Nature and Causes of this fatal bilious, or yellow Fever of Jamaica, is somewhat Strange; . . . The bilious, or yellow Fever, so called from the yellow appearance of the Skin.[4]

Most of the other names that may claim to be Jamaican refer to diseases of the Negroes. The word *yaws* is thought to come from American Indian (W2 gives Calinago *yáya*, Galibi *iaïa* as etyma), but since the disease itself was almost certainly brought to the Caribbean from Africa by Portuguese slaves, it is very likely that the name came with it. Behind the Indian may well lie some such word as Twi *gyàtɔ*, the yaws. Trapham is the first to use it in English (1679), the plural as a noun (on the pattern of *measles, pox*), the singular as an adjective, and in the form *yawy*: 'In the most radicated and polluting Yaws, rest three daies and take away blood. . . . And so successively dress the

Yawe sore with this Unguent. . . . And opening . . . the Body . . .
of the Yawy Patients, which thereby is more ·balsamically
tinctured.'

This disease, now well under control, was once a scourge. It
was said that white men could not contract it; their freedom
from it, however, was probably chiefly owing to their wearing
more clothes and so being less exposed to the infection. On the
sugar estates there was often a building where yaws patients
could be isolated: the *yaws-house, yaw-house,* or *yaw-hospital.* The
manifestation of the disease on the skin was described by Dancer:
'There is generally one pustule larger than the rest, called the
Master or *Mamma* Yaw.' Thomson elaborated, giving several
additional terms and phrases:

> The negroes call this ulcer affected with the yaws the
> *mamma-yaw*; it must, however, be carefully distinguished from
> the *common master* yaw, a name they also give to one or more
> large fungi that appear on the body during the course of the
> eruption, and remain much longer than the others, leaving a
> broad scar behind. . . . There are several varieties in appear-
> ance of the eruption for which the negroes have distinct
> names, as the *watery yaws, ring-worm yaws, Guinea corn yaws.* . . .
> The natives say the *skin is bitter for the disease,* and they regard
> the patient as liable to constitutional symptoms at a future
> period of life. . . . In what is termed the ring-worm yaws the
> number of eruptions is great, and at the most irregular inter-
> vals. . . . If symptoms, called the dregs of the yaws, or some
> hereditary tendency, should be called into action, they may
> be sent to a practitioner. . . . Old and sensible negro women
> will tell you, that the skin of such infants [having yawy
> mothers] is forever after rendered *bitter* for the disease.

This last term clearly means 'peculiarly susceptible'; the others
are descriptive of appearance — as *Guinea-corn,* which usually
suggest mottled dark and light. *Mamma-yaw* probably translates the French *maman-pian*; the name is appropriate because
about this large pustule cluster several small ones. Trapham also
mentioned 'the Yaw teint found especially in the Children';
Mathison called these *yaws-children.*

One particular kind, *crab-yaws,* has been recorded since 1739:
"'Tis long before they can be cured [of Yaws], two years is the
soonest; and that which they call the Crab-Yaws is never re-

moved.' Moreton has made from this the adjective *crab-yaw'd*. Thomson, again, gives the fullest account:

Crab-yaws. There are two distinct diseases included under this name. The one is a painful affection, resulting from the fungus of the yaw finding difficulty in penetrating the hardened cuticle on the soles of the feet or hands; the other is a disease of the cuticle itself, and in no way connected with any previous disease.

Two present-day descriptions say that it is 'on foot-bottom — make you toe pop-pop' and 'cut-up-cut-up under foot-bottom'. A *yawsy-kenge* is a person who has yaws, and therefore walks on his heels. (A *kenge* is a 'sore on the foot'.)

A similar ailment, very common among those who go barefoot (also with animals) is the *ground-itch*: 'Mules ... with soft pervious hoofs, which often split, and contain deep-seated crab-yaws and ground-itch,' and 'Little trash should be permitted to lie about in the mill-yard ... to make swampy, spungy foot-passages, impeding the carriers, and giving them tender and ground-itched feet'.

A type of elephantiasis has been known in the island from at least 1820 under the names *big leg* or *big foot* — the latter still current. From the way it swells, it is also called *jackfruit foot*. Louise Bennett writes of a woman using obeah to cause one:

But she goh wey fe him, an me hear sey
Him ha' wan big jackfruit foot.

Or it may be a *tumbozoo* — which suggests again a supernatural cause, since *buzu* is an obeah word. To this may well be related *timbim*, a sore foot 'hard to be better', *bimma*, a boil, ulcer 'on foot — hard to heal', and *dimmo*, 'a lame foot'. A *sabbat-foot* is a lame or deformed one — presumably because it can do no work, as on the Sabbath. A *George* /jaaj/ is a sore toe or other sore place; one might say 'You have a George to keep' — meaning that it is difficult to cure.

A type of leprosy with an African name is the *cocobay* (Twi *kokobé*). OED enters it under the spelling *cocoa-bay*, but this is hard to justify. In Jamaican sources it appears as: 1788–9 *Cocaby*; 1801 *Coco-Bay*; 1807 *cacabay*; 1820 *Coco-bay*; 1895 *cocoaba*.[5] The last identifies it as the 'king's evil'; it was also called the *joint-evil* and the *Red Disease of Guiana*.⁶ A *cocobay-man* is a leper. Since the bullfrog is believed to cause this disease by spitting, it is said to 'spit cocobay'.

Other diseases that manifest themselves most strikingly on the skin include the *craw-craw*, reported first from 1790 as *cockcraws*, and in 1801 as *Craw-Craws*: 'Negroes are liable also to a peculiar species of Itch, called Craw-Craws.' In the same source it is also called the *negro itch* — today simply the *itch*, pronounced /híich/ among the folk. According to Thomson, 'KRA-KRA is a corrupted Eboe word,' but the OED considers it 'apparently a Dutch Negro name from Du. *kraauw*, scratch'. Today this, or a similar roughness on the skin is Englished as *kratch-kratch* or *scratch-scratch*. It is said to be 'finer than eczema', which is known as *Cudjo-rubba* (pronounced /kòjorúba/). Another skin disease, rash, or itch is *Cuffy-routen* (pronounced /kòfiróutn/). Both of these seem to be connected with African day-names, Cudjo and Cuffy, now used in a depreciatory way by the folk, in this case suggesting the kind of condition that only backward or less civilised people would tolerate.

A disease brought over from Africa, and for a time very serious, was geophagy, locally known as *dirt-eating*, *earth-eating*, *mal d'estomac*, or *stomach evil*. As Dancer wrote, 'Angola negroes . . . are more particularly addicted to Dirt-Eating than any others.'⁷ And Stewart (1808):

> The negroes are subject to a strange craving of the stomach for earth: earth-eaters are common upon almost every plantation. . . . An elderly negro . . . considered a *mud-cake* as preferable to any [other provisions].

Williamson too: 'What is known by the name of *mal d'estomac* among the French; among the British, the stomach evil, or dirt-eating.' A few years later we find the French term partly translated as *mal de stomach*; and *stomach evil* is a full translation. This disease is fortunately a thing of the past. So, apparently, is 'the *bastard pleurisy*, as it is called . . . peripneumonia notha. . . . Unfortunately for the patient, it is generally confounded with pleurisy, to which, at the very commencement, it bears some resemblance'.⁸

Diseases of small children included, at one time, the *jaw-fall* or *jaw-falling*: 'The tetanus or locked-jaw; a disorder which the negroes call the jaw-fall.... Immediately before death, a general relaxation comes on, and the lower jaw falls on the breast.' 'Though the terms Jaw-Fall and Locked-Jaw are used synonimously, the Jaw-Fall proper signifies that state of the Disease, where the mouth either remains open ... or else where the Chin falls down on the Sternum.' 'The retension of this excrement [the *meconium* in new-born infants] has been fatal to multitudes, by bringing on mortal convulsions, generally known here by the name of *jaw-falling*.'⁹ Nowadays one hears more often of *mirasmy* or a *mirasmy baby* (i.e., one having *marasme* or *marasmus*). When a child's hair turns red, this is considered a symptom; trumpet leaf and other plants are 'good for baby mirasmy'. Louise Bennett uses the phrase for humourous purposes:

> Se' de marga man wat hol'in' han'
> Wid de nice fat lady,
> She musa feel like she dah hol'
> A mirasmi baby!

Pot-belly, as a medical term referring to a condition common still among children, seems to have been used here very early — perhaps first.

Pregnancy and birth-giving have had a local vocabulary among the folk, beginning in at least 1820 (Thomson): 'Some [Negro women] do not show belly, as they call it, till a few months before they are delivered.... The midwife on every estate should have a house built for her.... To these apartments the pregnant woman is to be removed ... and placed under the sole direction of the *grandee*, as they call her.' This term is still current for a midwife, pronounced /graandi/; it may be compared with the United States dialectal *granny-woman*, now becoming archaic. Kerr writes of the diet considered desirable during pregnancy: 'The mother must not drink too much water ... ; she must not eat eggs because they cause "minglin" pains.' The varicose veins that often accompany pregnancy are called *breedin' veins*. A danger after the birth, writes Kerr, may be avoided thus: 'Sometimes a yard stick or sticks from bitter cassava are put across the doorway. Anyone entering would have to step over them and this prevents the mother catching a bad belly.' The afterbirth is called the *bed*, as

Beckwith reported in 1929 — a sense of the word recorded by the OED only from 1611!

On the estates in slave days the hospital was called the *hot-house*,[10] because it was kept warm. (But note that *hurt* is pronounced by the folk identically with *hot*.) Beckford has referred to 'the nurse or hot-house woman' who attended in this establishment; James referred to this person as a *doctor woman*, and the term *doctress* was also current.

Other older names for conditions attending sickness include 'a discharge of mucus [in dysentery] which they [the Negroes] call *white flux*'; and *come down*, a verb phrase used about inflammation and enlargement of the soft palate (and nearby areas) which caused it to fall, or *come down*.

Scars caused by tattooing before the slaves left Africa were usually called, in Jamaica, *country marks*, occasionally *country scars* — those, that is, from his home country. They often showed what tribe he belonged to, and therefore served to identify runaways. Very common was the following type of advertisement: 'Brown, a Nago, 4 ft. 11 in ... has country marks on his temples.' 'An ill-made African negro ... much marked on the face with country scars.' A negro who had had most of the skin of his forehead removed in Africa, apparently as a caste mark, was a *brichy* or *bruchy*. *Chamba*, meaning cut or disfigured, appears in Bennet's line, 'De whole a him face chamba up.'

Present-day folk words for miscellaneous ailments are numerous. *Bad feelin'* means a rather vague malaise, or psychosomatic condition. Uncle Newton writes of 'Guinea pepper for pain in the stomach ... and assafoetida ... for bad feeling', and he recalls the song about the prophet of August Town in which were the lines,

> Dip im, dim im Mr Bedward,
> Dip im fe cure bad feelin.

There is the noun *bilious*, meaning biliousness. *Brice* means 'constipate'; *hard-bound* means to constipate, as in the proverb suggesting endurance, 'Is not one day hard-boun' old daag [dog].' Fatal constipation is *knot-gut*. To *operate* is to purge; one must be sure to 'cut off the point' of the jokotu plant before eating 'or it will operate you'.

Some words still in use here though long dead elsewhere are

quitter, for pus, which the OED considers obsolete; *fleam*, an old form of *phlegm*: 'Ganja takes off fleam from the chest;' *fassy* (for Standard *farcy*), a sore, eczema on man or beast; and *wring*, a wrench or sprain. Russell recorded *sicky* meaning sickly.

Dead-flesh is the granulation tissue in a sore or wound — called 'proud flesh' in English and United States dialects. When a swelling diminishes it is said to *draw down*. A *coco* is a swelling on the head caused by a blow, as Uncle Newton has it, 'That breadfruit gave me a "coco" (don't you know the sudden swelling called a "coco") on my head.' *Kaffir pox* is a name for a mild form of smallpox — a term neglected by the dictionaries. Gonorrhea goes by the elegant name of *gentleman's complaint*.

A peculiar word is *fennay*, pronounced /féne/, recorded first as meaning to 'have a hard time', but much more specifically to 'suffer, fret, swoon, vomit'. It might be used in such a sentence as 'I frighten so till I nearly fenneh'. It is clearly of African origin, and may have been retained partly out of euphemism to avoid the crudity of its specific meaning.[11]

Two words for abnormal conditions may be mentioned here: *andrin*, which means queer, odd, very thin; and *baffan* or *baffany* (also *baffong* and *bafwam*) which has several related senses: a disfigured or crippled child, puny, backward, slow to walk. This, too, is African. Twi *bafáŋ*, Akyan *bafané* means 'a child who did not learn to walk the first 2–7 years; rachitis, the rickets; sluggard, lazy-bones'; and Ewe *bafa*, 'lame from birth'. The verb *baf*, to lag behind, be slow, looks like a Jamaican back-formation from this.

Most of the remedies with specifically Jamaican names are simply herbs, and are treated among plants (Chapter XVI). Others involve obeah, myal, and other 'magic' and are therefore treated with superstitions (Chapter XI). But there are some others. An early remedy for gallstones was mentioned by Sloane as *manatee stones*: 'The *Manati* Stones are ... taken from behind the Ears of that Animal, each Ear having one,' and 'They have Stones in their Heads, good for the Diseases of the Liver burnt and powder'd, taken in a Morning with white Wine, it takes away the Pain in the Kidneys, breaks the Stone, and brings away with Urine the Sand, which is also done with other Fish Stones.' And an early remedy for the fever was the *bark jacket*: a covering of *quinquina* bark sprinkled upon a patient till it covered him like

K

a jacket.[12] Today, among the folk, weeds and herbs used to treat fevers are known by the general term *fever bush*: 'But of all de medicine and fever bush I know, none cure you so quick as dis.'

In the country a *doctor shop* is a chemist's or 'drug store'. It has not been found in print before 1893. Here one may buy, among other things, various kinds of 'healing oil' (whose fantastic names are discussed under superstitions, below); and *anisow* (/anisou/) — a cough medicine made from 'aniseed' and rum, also 'good for fever'.[13] The word *vial* is still preferred by the folk for a medicine or perfume bottle. Castor oil is known as *press-oil* from the oil being pressed out of the beans. A long established disinfectant, Jeyes' fluid, has become simply *jeyes*, virtually a generic term. Uncle Newton gives a hint at one of its many applications: 'In vain the tooth was stuffed with healing oil, jeyes, creosote. . . .' It is even used in medicines against fever.

Physical Peculiarities

Terms of this group are all from the folk, but some have come up into wider usage. One redundant combination refers to the cerebrum: 'We boys called that area the *head skull*, and it was great fun to us to kunk . . . one another on the head skulls.' A *peel-head* is a bald one: we find the word used attributively in the song 'Wheel an Tun Me', referring to a turkey-buzzard, 'One unconscionable peel-head johncrow.'

One word preserved since the seventeenth century with slightly changed meaning is *baby*, in the sense of the small image reflected in the eye. Jamaicans use it of the pupil itself[14] and transfer it simply enough to mean the centre of a target. A misunderstanding that occurs while some boys are at play is amusingly reported by Uncle Newton:

He has hit the baby? Whose baby? The baby of the Bull's Eye? Oh I see . . . the dead centre of it, eh?

Full eyes or *pulp eyes* are those that bulge out. In fact, *pulp* is quite as often a verb: 'Dem y'eye dah pulp wid fright!' and 'Mango bug have two big eye an' pulp out'. Or it may refer to other things than eyes: a countryman, telling how to get rid of chiggers in the skin, said, 'Pick it and they pulp up' — that is, the eggs are extruded.

An expression that appeals to the imagination is, to *make four eyes*, meaning that two people look at or see each other: 'Is long time sence you an' me meck four eyes.'

A *cast eye* is the same as a 'cock-eye' — one that does not focus. *Eye-water* (tears) is an archaism elsewhere, but not in Jamaica: 'De door open an ongle her daughta y'eye wata was een de room.' Similarly, *mouth-water* is saliva. It may well be, however, that both these expressions are loan-translations from African languages: Ibo and Mandingo have just these combinations. Mouth-water is not the only word for saliva: a common phrase is to *swallow one's spit* — that is, to keep silence, not to speak when one could:

> Well me hear him talk 'bout him cattles . . .
> Me dis swallow me spit for all him 'ave
> Is wan big head maga cow.

Mack-eye is said to mean very dark eyes, and *montompy* 'the refuse of the eye'.[15] The mucus from the nose is *bubu* or *bagabu*.[16] A *cut-eye* is the action of 'cutting' the eye at someone by way of insult — that is, catching the person's eye, then deliberately turning one's own away. Or one may *suck* one's *teeth* or one's *tongue* to make a disrespectful or disdainful sound: 'No bada suck yuh teet',' and 'May still dah suck her tongue'. Uncle Newton, describing a school feud, writes: 'That evening at private class, the Lopez group exchanged many cut-eyes and suck-teeths with the Stephensons.' In the same spirit, children also *long out* their *tongues* or their *mouths* (pouting): 'How I "long out my mouth" when Mami was not looking!' On the other hand, to smile (sometimes artificially) is to *skin one's teeth*, and to *skin up one's lip* is to raise it disdainfully:

> Wid dem nose an mout-lip kin-up
> Like pet dog a view pig-sty.

A *'kin-teet'* man is one whose teeth are always exposed.

A curious word used about the teeth is to *nedge*, meaning to hurt: 'Me teet' a nedge me.' A medicinal plant used against this is accordingly known as *nedge weed*. This word is nothing but a reduced form of *on edge*, and therefore reflects the same process of formation that accounts for the English word 'newt', from 'an ewt'.

Teeth that stick out are *buff teeth*, and a tongue-tied person has a *tie-tongue* — a condition usually attributed to Anancy the spider.

A frequent word for grimaces is *monkey-faces*:

> For when she laugh it like she
> Dah meck up monkey face.

If the grimace is a set one, expressing displeasure or anger, one says that the person's face *tie-up*, or simply *meck-up*:

> She stare pon me, her face meck up
> Like she was eena pain.

The depression at the back of the head and neck, which is believed to indicate by its size how greedy one is, is known as the *cubbitch hole* (from *covetous*). It is at the *neck-back*. The strong muscles at the front of the neck are the *neck-strings*:

> An she start blow hard fe breat' an
> Her neck tring dem start fe swell.

The *ears-corner* is the part of the head around the ear, which gives such trouble when the hair has to be cut.

The palm or hollow of the hand is frequently called the *hand-middle*. 'If you han'-middle cratch, you get money.' 'Crab-yaw come on footsole or han' middle.' The thumb is usually known as the *big-finger* but also as *tumpy* (stumpy), while the little finger is nicknamed *chi-chi-mus* (little mouse), and the tip of the finger is sometimes the *finger-head*.

Bang-belly means a protruding stomach — for example, that of an ill-nourished child; and the word *bang* used separately means to swell. 'I saw a long procession of ghosts of all types, (long, short, . . . with one or two bang-bellied ones).' Another name for an enlarged abdomen is a *ten-penny*. *Belly-cork* is reported from Kingston for the navel; for the stomach, *bem-bem*.

A puny person (or the smallest pig in a litter) may be called *windgy* (/winji/); but one who is merely thin is *mauger* (/maaga/). This word must have been condemned as 'uneducated' in recent years; at least, the folk seem to feel uncomfortable with it, and one hears them say it and then 'correct' it to *meager*, as if that were the 'better' word. *Maugre* is attested from as long ago as 1826.[17] A countryman recently described a mosquito as a 'long, mauga lickle trashy ting wid long leg', — that is, slender; but the word may imply hunger (or *hungry* as the folk say): 'Lawd Bra Nancy, me dah dead fe hungry.'

A curious word is *kimbo*, used of the hip:

> Ah put me han' pon me kimbo
> Ah meck a sudden movement
> Ah tun me rydim full gi her.

This must come from *akimbo*, understood first as meaning 'at the hip' (which is the position of the hands when the arms are akimbo), and so *kimbo* alone would mean hip. In the same passage the phrase '*tun me rydim*' means 'turn my rhythm'— swing my hips — hard against someone. The most widely used word for the buttocks, however, is *batty* (/bati/) — a baby-talk form (though by no means used only by children) probably based on *bottom*. It is applied also to the abdomen of insects: 'Red wasp have big head and batty'; 'Duck-ants head-part hard, batty sof', white'. Another children's term forty years ago (though I cannot vouch for its continuance today) was *dumby*, euphemistically *dumbarton*, neither of which is to be found in the dictionaries. It is surprising that the OED should have missed it, as Urquhart's translation of Rabelais' *Gargantua* was one of the books read, and it appears there in the spelling *dounby*.[18]

Still another Jamaican word for the buttocks is *rass*, in school-boy slang and current vulgar use. It has been in Jamaica since at least 1790, when Moreton puts it into an amusing but un-quotable song, in the spelling *rassa*, which represents the pro-nunciation of a creole woman and makes the rhyme with *Massa*.[19]

The word *leg* is hardly used in the folk speech, not for any reasons of prudery, but because *foot* serves for all purposes. An amputated leg is thus a *tumpa-foot* (from *stump*); the artificial substitute is a *wooden-foot*, and its wearer a *wooden-foot man*. Jamaicans have their own proverb that enjoins doing as the Romans do: 'If you go a tump-a-foot dance, you must dance tump-a-foot.'

An amusing word is *juck-cum-peng*, meaning (and seeming to symbolise in its sound) 'the walking of a wooden-legged man'. It has a striking similarity to the Twi *a dwòŋkú-beŋ*, pains in the hip, coxalgia; and *adwòŋkù-tɔ*, hobbling.

Bow-legged becomes *bow-foot*, *buckle-foot* means knock-kneed, and a *K-foot* is a leg bowed in at the knee against the other to form a 'capital K'. The English (though not common) word *pommel-foot* or *pummel-foot*, a club foot, survives in Jamaica in the form *pumble-foot*, meaning clumsy in walking:

> De pumble foot gal wey work wid me
> Teck careless so drop i' dung stairs.

Pumble-foot is also a disease of chickens.

The hind foot often becomes the *back-foot*, as in the proverbial simile, 'Proud as any puss back foot.' And the sole is usually the *foot-bottom*. Like *tumpa-foot*, there is *tumpa-toe*, which however does not necessarily mean amputated. In McKay's line,

> An' chigger nyam you' tumpa toe,

it seems to refer rather to the stumpy shape that the toes assume when the countryman goes barefoot constantly.

Bluefoot, finally, does not seem to have a very specific meaning, but is an insult, as in the lines,

> Lick him with a stick,
> Get up, you brute, blue-foot brute!

Also reported as current in St Thomas about 1940 was the expression 'a bluefoot man', applied to an outsider who had come in to live, and who was not yet accepted.

Physical Actions

By far the largest number of verbs expressing physical action in Jamaica have been adopted from English, very few from African or other sources; yet the striking thing is how often in the folk speech they have acquired quite different meanings, by transfer, metaphor, or some other means, from those of Standard speech.

It has already been pointed out that where *to be* would be required in the Standard, the popular syntax either omits it altogether or uses *a* or *de*. Two other verbs that normally express action, *stand* and *stay*, also preserve the older sense of 'be'. As long ago as 1790 Moreton wrote, 'I often laughed heartily at hearing a Creole master or miss say, "Do, momma, get me some mauby [mobby], *mine* head no *'tand* good" ' — that is, is not well. Similarly, 'Red an pretty dem tan.' And *stay*: 'You know dat man stay same way lak me an' you,' and 'When kreng-kreng calalu boil, stay like okro.'

Instead of Standard 'allow, let, permit', the universal folk word is *make*, pronounced /mek/: 'Mek a see' — let me see; 'Eric make haste daub your skin make me bathe' — allow me to bathe. 'Look after the coffee; don't make rain wet it.' The word is also used in its standard senses of 'do, construct, force', and the somewhat archaic 'cause': 'Is Anancy mek it.' Reduplilicated as a noun, /mekmek/, it may either show hesitation and lingering, as when a person *makes* tentative movements without completing any, or it may mean confusion or quarrelling, as when people *make* contrary or opposed actions.

Walk, run, and the other standard words for movement on foot are used by everybody; the folk also have *lep* (from *leap* — probably a Scots inheritance), to walk briskly, and *gander*,[20] to walk or run. The fanciful word to *trampooze*, walk about from place to place, for example when on holiday, is recorded in the OED from 1798 to 1850. It apparently survived longer in America than in England, and longer still in Jamaica, being current yet. A special type of walking, the consciously swaying walk of a woman — almost a dance step — is *yanga*. This is doubtless from *yanga*, a form of *ñanga* used in Spanish America. *A la yanga*, *ñanga*, or *ñanga-ñanga* means carelessly, in an ill manner, but it has apparently gained a more favourable sense in Jamaica. The ultimate source is African.[21]

Another expression for the same kind of movement is to *cut Grecian*, or simply to *Grecian* — that is, to put on stylish airs (to do a Grecian bend). One stanza of the song 'Fan me, Soldier Man' goes, 'What's de use of you Grecian? . . . Gal, you character gone!' (This peculiar sense of *cut* will be discussed shortly.)

An old phrase that survives in Jamaica is to *pull foot* — walk fast, run. We find it in *Tom Cringle's Log*: 'The whole crew pulled foot as if Old Nick had held them in chase,' and currently:

> Me peep an se' one wite oman
> Dah pull foot fe May shop.

Similar are *catter-foot* (probably from *scatter*) and *put you foot in order*, to run away. Also referring to rapid movement on one's feet is *lif'-up*:

> Dem done nyam off me big-big lunch
> An lif up gawn dem ways!

Lif-up has come to refer not only to walking but to driving a car fast; so much does *mash-flat*, which may describe what one does with the accelerator, or, more likely, to anything in one's way on the road.

Contrary to this is the long established expression *tek time*, go slowly, be careful, as in the proverb, 'Tek time, get deh teday; mek-has'e, get deh tomorrow;' or in the warning phrase, 'Tek time how you hol' me!'

If taking time is not a matter of carefulness but of delay, perhaps deliberate, there is the expression to *roast coco* — a lengthy process: 'Mr X . . the Member of the House of Representatives, him gone sleep. Him a roast coco. We caan hear a thing 'bout him.'[22] The hint is that he is planning trouble for someone.

To move over and make room for someone else is expressed commonly with the soldier phrase to *dress down*: 'I can jus' dress dung lickle more.'

Several phrases have to do with travelling: to *hold* one's *road* for a place — go toward; *catch* or *catch to*, or *reach* — arrive (at): 'The two ah dem hol' dem road fe Brer Nancy yard,' 'Tengad we ketch home safe,' 'When him reach him fine say cow no diddeh.' The American colloquial phrase to *meet up with* is parallelled by the Jamaican *meet up*: 'Nex' time unoo meet up you ketch him.'

A number of words or phrases mean to 'take hold' in various ways. To catch someone suddenly and firmly against his will is expressed by to *buckle* or *buckle-hold*, to *hold*, or to *collar on* (*upon*); and they may be extended to refer to things as well as to people: 'A bokle de chap sa'; 'Missus de bwoys was gran! Fe buckle hole *two* century Pon *one* six wicket stan!'; 'Ah wish . . . ah could hole de man dat tief me fowl'; 'De pain hol' her dat way'; 'Anancy colla awn pon Jackass'.[23]

Another very common word meaning to pick up — used almost always about things — is to *pawn* (pronounced /paan/) or *pawn up*. Its origin is uncertain. It can hardly be connected with the standard senses of *pawn*; one guess is Jekyll's, who records it as *palm* (to take in the palm of the hand): 'Dog . . . run in de ring an' palm puss an begin to fight him'; But perhaps a better one is to derive it from *span*.[24] 'You . . . pawn you books an' went away'; 'De po' gal open de door an Anancy pawn her up an carry her go gi de king.'

Illustrating the substitution of *l* for *r* is *fingle*, which means to finger or *feel up* something — a form perhaps also affected by the analogy of such others as *handle* or *fondle*. 'Duppy fingle a man food — mek im sick.' And a word in which onomatopoeia and analogy combine is *swips*, to slip quickly or easily:

> An she jus sidung deh wutless
> Meck him swips outa her han.

Words for lifting include the African-derived *massu*, which was recorded as long ago as 1833, when Tom Cringle tells how a Creole master speaks to his servant: 'Here, Pilfer, Pilfer, . . . give me my stick, and massu the chair, and run home.' The word is said to be still in use among dock workers and others. A similar word is *luggo-luggo*, to move a heavy weight which you can scarcely manage; it is probably based on English *lug* but has the iterative form common in African words.

Many Jamaicans carry loads on their heads which they can hardly raise there by themselves. To *help up* and to *help down* mean to help someone to get the burden safely on or off the head: 'We [wood gatherers] were getting ready to "help up" and leave when we felt drops of rain'; 'An be de time me help dung, Everybody deh pon spot'. This is also called *lif' up*, and the phrases are used as exclamations at the moment of lifting, and as nouns, as in 'Gi me lif'-up!'

Words for throwing include *hib* or *heb*, very likely from *heave* (as *shove* often becomes /shub/); they may even be English dialectal forms preserved in Jamaica. Like *heave*, these words may mean to toss, to throw, or to throw away. *Throw* itself is not used only in the standard way, but also to mean throw out, or empty: 'Come on, now, and we throw the water and the first one that is dry, that is the winner.'

Similarly, standard 'drive away' becomes simply *drive*, with a slightly grotesque effect: 'Cow . . . busy ah drive de gingy-fly dem wid him tail'; 'Row [noise] enough to "Dribe de Debbil!"' *Wile* apparently has the same sense in:

> All de vender dem
> Dah sell scissors an' fine teet' comb
> Till police wile dem weh.

The verb *run*, normally intransitive, has become causative among the Jamaican folk: to make someone run, therefore drive him away, as in the well known song,

> Come we go down a Unity
> Fe see duppy run Miss Martin.

An old word meaning to beat (people or things) is *fum*, as in the slave-girl's song, 'Then misses fum me wid long switch,' or 'His wife in the kitchen "fumming tum tum"' — pounding yams to swallow with soup.[25] This word, like *tum-tum*, is obviously onomatopoetic. No African source has been found for it, but it might well have been formed by analogy with *drum, thrum, thump*, and the like.

To strike with the head, in Jamaica, is not to butt but *buck* (by substitution of *k* for *t* — a common occurrence). This is said not only of cows and goats but of people striking some part of their body. 'If you buck you left foot — bad luck.' It may also be used intransitively: 'Same way Tom forrid buck' — that is, his forehead protrudes (compare 'buck teeth'). *Buck toes* stick up (or 'cock up'); there once were 'buck-toe shoes' which had a high point. But the most characteristic phrase is to *buck-up*, meaning to meet or happen upon someone or something. A Falmouth fisherman, asked about a certain kind of shellfish, said, 'I never buck-up dat,' and a Lucea painter, speaking of the ghost called the 'three-foot horse', said, 'If im buck you up a night im blow bad breeze pon you.'

The most general word for striking is to *lick*, which no doubt comes from whipping: to lick a child, a donkey, and so on; in fact, a *lick* is a blow, and a *beast-lick* a particularly hard one. Though the basic sense is whipping, the word now means any kind of beating, and the verb is often used with adverbs that make it more specific — *up, down*, etc.: 'He raise up his stick . . . I said, you can't lick me down, Sir, the law does not allow that'; 'De big backra car dem A lick up de dus' in a we face'.

Beating or pounding is expressed by *mala-mala* — a word of unknown source. On the other hand, *pung* is nothing but a folk pronunciation of *to pound*. *Clate* has been reported from St Elizabeth for knock, beat.

The word *chum* perhaps belongs here, though its primary meaning appears to lie not in the beating but in its result: separation of a vegetable product into the useful part and the 'trash'. Thus you *chum* coffee berries (in a mortar or with a pulper) to get the beans free of the skin, or you *chum* cucumber: take the seeds out. A countryman who used the word said it meant to *churn*, but this makes a doubtful explanation. It seems more plausible to look to Scots *chun* — to nip off the shoots from the eyes of potatoes.[26] Even in Jamaica, *chum* is considered a countrified word.

An interesting verb is *bill*, to cut (grass, or the like) with a bill or agricultural knife. The latest OED citation is 1833, from *Tom Cringle*, 'a small path that had been billed in the bush.' The word was in use in Jamaica before this, however; Roughley has it repeatedly in 1823, as, 'All grass . . . should be billed down . . . so that rats will not have an asylum close to the plant canes.' And it is still current both in country and city.

Other words for cutting are *saca-saca* and *chamba*, the first probably African, the second certainly so. *Saca-saca* is evidently in part imitative of a sawing action, but apparently a rough one that spoils the thing being cut. It is first reported in 1868 by Russell: 'To cut as with a saw; thus, Dis knife jis da saca-saca de meat,' and now 'to cut badly, spoil, waste, destroy'. A possible source is Twi or Gã *sàkasàka*, which may be noun, adjective, or adverb, meaning disorder, confusion; irregular, tangled, etc. Also possible is Kongo (Angola) *saka*, to cut off, if this were iterated, as it so easily could be.

Chamba means 'to cut with a dull tool, channel or furrow', and in such an expression as 'him face all chamba up' — furrowed, creased, scratched. This interesting word (also iterated as *chamma-chamma*) comes from the name of an African tribe who scarred their faces in a striking way. As Bryan Edwards wrote, 'Some of the Negroes of the Gold Coast . . . (the *Chamba* Negroes for instance) appear to me to use the same, or nearly the same, marks as the savages of New Zealand; *viz.* deep incisions on each cheek drawn circularly from the ear to the mouth.' (1793 II 125). These 'country marks' must have been impressive indeed to convert *Chamba* into a verb of general meaning. The word also appears in the name of a bird with conspicuously striped cheeks: the *Chamba Beezer* (see Chapter XIV).

A word that combines the senses of striking and cutting is *malahack*, 'to manhandle, treat roughly' — as when an animal is cruelly beaten. This dialect word from East Anglia came also to New England and is now preserved in Jamaica. The same sense is expressed by *mammick* — of unknown origin.

One of the most characteristic Jamaicanisms is *jook* (/juk/), to jab, prick, pierce — a word of such common usage that one would expect its source to be easily found. Yet this is anything but the case. The pronunciation is very close to Scots *jouk*, but the meaning is hardly to be connected. The Scots verb means to hide oneself; if this were done by 'a sudden jerking or dodging motion downward or aside' (one sense of the noun), this might approach a jabbing action. Beyond this the meaning would have to be strained. To derive *jook* from *jerk* also strains meaning; it is not merely a sudden movement but the act of jabbing, usually piercing: 'Poison-grouper jook you'; 'After numb-fish jook you it cramp you'; 'An him teck him long fork juck me'. The word *juke*, as in the American *juke box* (coin-in-the-slot record-player) and *juke-house* (a disorderly house, such as those in which juke music was first played) has been traced by Turner to Wolof *jug*, to misconduct oneself, with which he compares Bambara *jugu*, wicked, violent.[27] But again, the meaning cannot well be connected with Jamaican *jook*. The one plausible source that I have found is Fulani *jukka*, 'to spur, poke, knock down, as fruit'. The form is close, the meaning very close; the Fulani were among the West African tribes who might well have contributed to the Jamaican folk speech; and perhaps there were similar, reinforcing forms in related dialects which have not yet been brought to notice.

To *jam* is also used in the sense of jab, and may, in fact, be influenced by its similarity of both sound and sense; on the other hand, this may simply be a newly developed meaning of standard English *jam*, squeeze, cram.

The common term in Jamaica for burst, or break in two, is *pop*, whether or not there is any noise involved. One pops a string, a shoelace, the leg of a chair, or someone's neck: 'Den ah wi get ah chance fe pop him neck.' By transference, even news or gossip may be popped:

> Pop 'tory gimme wey dat yuh sey?

and
> Pop-tory gimme Dela, all
> De labrish from yuh yard. (Bennett)

Similarly, the common word for break in the sense of crush or smash is *mash* or *mash up*. It has been used from at least 1837: 'She was mashed up . . . her shins were mashed up.' Today anything that is dropped heavily, run into or over, or struck violently, is likely to be *mashed*. The pedestrian who has a close brush with an automobile will shout, 'You wan' mash me?'

Various kinds of bending have their special words. One version of the song 'Hill and Gully Rider' has:

An' a ben dung low dung, Hill an' gully,
An' a low dung bessy dung, Hill an' gully,

in which *bessy* means bend. *Bussu, butty, butu* have also been reported: these four are probably variants. *Jocoto* and *junkuto*, another variant pair meaning to stoop down, probably are African in origin. But *tip-dung* is more likely some alteration of the English words *stoop down*.

The manner of sitting on the heels with soles flat and one's back resting against a wall is known as /sángkuku/; it has been reported in the forms *sankoko, sankutu* (stoop), and *sanchocho* (sit). No clue as to source has been found.

The English verb *lap*, meaning wrap, has gradually gone out of general into rather specific or technical uses — yet in Jamaica one may still hear it in the older sense: 'Sea-cat is cousin to octopus — it claw you and lap you.'

To *pull* often has the sense of loosen — to *pull a knot*, for example. And one does not fill things, but *full* them: 'Full i' up!' may be heard in any market when produce is being measured.

The word *catch* has in Jamaican folk use the usual English dialect pronunciation *ketch* (the result of the raising of [æ] to [ɛ].) *Ketch-up* has ordinary senses of catching, as in the children's counting-out rhyme:

Waterman Trinity very good man,
Ketch up 'im hen an put dem in pen. . . .

Or a woman tying her hair in a cloth:

Me ketch up me head an' goh look 'bout har.

It also means to kindle or rebuild: 'Ketch up de fire.'

But from the verb *scotch* also comes *cotch*, to hold, or fasten, or support something for the time being: 'Cotch de door' — to

keep it open; 'Cotch de bed' — wedge the legs to make it firm
To *walk an cotch* means to lean on things for support as one goes:

> But Bra Nancy get a bad kick
> For him still a walk an cotch.

The sense of temporariness carries over to a visit or the like:

> So me cotchin' wid Miss U . . . an Cousin B.,

— that is, staying for a short while. The sense of fastening
carries over farther to something stubborn: 'Cotch Donkey . . .
him always cotch' — that is, the donkey refuses to move.

Quinge-up, meaning squeeze, probably represents *squinch*
(screw or distort) which OED traces down to 1840, after which
DA shows it as an Americanism (compress or squeeze together)
coming down to 1909. The Jamaican word could be connected
with either, as the sense of the following shows:

> Se har quinge up eena corner deh,
> Ah so she shamey-shame.

An exactly parallel case is *crunge* (from *crunch* or *scrunge*?), meaning crush, squeeze.

A very common usage makes *look* into a transitive verb meaning look for, gather: 'Arthur and I joined a group of boys to
"look wood".'

One interesting Jamaican distinction that goes far back into
the past is that between *thieving* and *taking*. Examples may be
found from the eighteenth century forward. The idea seems to be
that when a person sets out with the purpose of appropriating
another's property, that is thieving; but if he comes across —
perhaps by the grace of the gods — something that has no ap-
parent owner, and he supplies an owner for it, that is merely
taking. A real distinction, no doubt, though unrecognised by the
law. From 1788 comes the following:

> Finding a pair of shoes . . . , he took and converted them to
> his own use . . . he was ordered to be flogged . . . the negro all
> the time of his punishment cried out, *Massa me no teevee, me takee.*

A similar justification is made (1828) when a slave argues that
since he is his master's property, whatever he 'takes' is still his
master's — 'him no tief from Massa, him take from Massa.'[28]

This euphemistic use of *take* is still current. But there is also an

African word meaning to gather up and appropriate: *pra-pra* (see Twi *prap'ra*, to gather, sweep). One woman complained of some greedy neighbours, 'Me say "tek a lickle", but dem pra-pra de whole of it, tek it way.'

The English word *hanker* has evidently been metamorphosed to *hinka* or *hinka-hinka*: 'Hanging after for the purpose of getting something; thus; Don't hinka-hinka after de backra massa so.'[29] A similar idea is expressed in *moochu*, to beg, which strongly suggests *mooch*, to loiter, sponge; and in *shoolah*, to loaf, suggestive of *shool*, to skulk, beg, sponge. Both of these have the flavour of cant words. On the other hand, *fadge*, to manage, contrive, as in 'Fadge for yourself', is a preservation of a quite respectable word which died out of standard use in the eighteenth century, though it is well preserved in Jamaican folk speech.

One very characteristic usage, early established in this island and very much alive still, is the word *cut* in the sense of to handle language vigourously or impressively. Thus to *cut English* means to speak it in a high-flown way, polysyllabically, and with the unorthodoxies of over-correction. Russell describes it amusingly in 1868:

> In trying to 'cut English,' the most elegant form of the verb is the past tense of the verb to be, and the past participle used together, or with another verb, thus, A was ben told you of it. A was ben da go wen de boy come.

English is cut, he tells us, when things are going well, and he gives part of a self-appointed 'preacher's' sermon in which all the devices of awesome verbalism are paraded.

Used neutrally, this word may merely mean to pronounce or express; thus when a country woman was asked the meaning of 'Mozella' yam, she replied, 'They jus' cut it that way.' But *cut* usually implies some special ability with language: 'Yuh want hear har cut Spanish' — that is, she speaks it with enviable or admirable style. This may, of course, be too much for the hearer to follow, as when, in Louise Bennett's poem, the Jamaican women visiting Paris cannot make themselves understood:

> Den bans a more man gather roun
> Start cut language pon we,
> An sometime me get bex an sey
> 'Me naw go stan fe i'.

Cutting language gets a special sense from its use by the less orthodox religious cults. When 'possessed' by spirits, the practitioner begins to babble, and is said to be 'cutting an unknown tongue'. The Biblical source is obvious. Some believe that the unknown tongue is African when they are possessed by 'ancestral spirits'. Kerr tells of an encounter with a woman revivalist:

> I tried a Latin tag from the *Æneid* on Mother Evangeline as an experiment. She replied 'cutting nine'. I asked what this meant. She said she realised I was talking spirit language and her spirit told her to answer with these words.

Louise Bennett makes a humourous picture of a woman who is trying to work Obeah magic:

> Every mawnin . . .
> Ah keas me y'eye an' stap me breath
> An' cut some unknown tongue.
>
> Wen me deh pon haste me cut it shart
> An' sey 'skarash ni-toe'
> But wen me ha' mo' time me sey
> 'Ski bam bam chinka po'.

The sense of *cut* in regard to language goes back to English thieves' cant, now obsolete (see OED).

It is difficult not to see some connection with *cut capoose*, which means to move oneself up and down, bending the knees, as when riding a horse. Or, in Uncle Newton's description, 'Hold on to something before you, then rise from and fall gracefully and rhythmically to your seat.' I have heard this phrase explained as a rendering of 'cut capers', but this sounds unlikely, as the accentual pattern is wrong, since *capoose* is stressed on the second syllable. Perhaps it should be connected with the bearing of the roller in the old sugar mills, called a *capouse* (see above). Whatever the correct derivation, it would seem to involve, for *cut*, the sense of vigorous, bouncing action.

A quaint Jamaicanism is the verb *back-answer*, which means the same as answer back, or 'talk back' to someone. Anancy, on one occasion, pretends to be indignant with Puss because, as he says, 'yuh . . . a come back-answa me.'

Jamaican children do not usually cry, they *bawl* — that is, weep: 'Den all de pickney dem start fe bawl, "No, pappie!" '

On the other hand, Jamaican shoes do not squeak, they *cry*: 'The sun was pleased with our shining appearance, if not with our "crying" shoes.' To grieve over something is to *ceremone* — which appears to be a back-formation from *ceremony*, blended perhaps with *moan*.

To *call* is used in the special sense of to name, as when a man was trying to name a series of vegetables, and a bystander asked, 'You no call cabbage yet?' And to *curse* is used with a double object (not found in standard English):

> You . . . put you' back agains' de wall
> An' cuss our teacher fool.

And in the proverb: 'Don't cuss alligator long-mout' till you cross river done.' This could have come about by analogy with the standard sense of *call*.

Instead of the verb *splash*, *flash* is widely used among the folk. When one has to carry water in a bucket one should put leaves — or *water-bush* — on top of the water to 'henda de wata from flash out'. This is probably a simple substitution of words, but since in any case *splash* would normally be reduced to *plash*, it is but a short step further to *flash*.

Words for scratching are *crab*, *plaw*, and *hough*. The first and third look like simple conversions of noun into verb: *crab* (usually pronounced /kraab/) thus means to claw as a crab does, and *hough* to scratch with the hoof. *Plaw* is probably a phonetic alteration of the verb *claw* (compare *plabba* for *clabber*).

Similar formations may be seen in *sipple*, to make supple, and *fan* (transitive), to wave like a fan: 'An' a pigeon meat im a sipple you jin',' (supples your joints), and 'Cow ah fan him tail'.

One distinction made in early days, which holds no longer, is described by Sloane (1707):

> *Indians* and *Negros* lie on the Floors, most generally on Mats . . . with very little or no coverings, and a small Fire near them in their Cottages. Hence they and ordinary white Servants, who lie not in Beds, are not said to go to Bed, but to go and Sleep: and this phrase has generally obtain'd all over the Plantations.

The nursery word *do-do*, to sleep, evidently a borrowing of the French word, may be heard in Jamaica. One might hear a mother say to a small child, 'Come do-do.' Jocular terms for yawning and snoring are to *draw bungy* and to *cut cedar board*. The sense of the first is hardly clear; the second alludes to the sawing of cedar logs, still laboriously done by hand in the Jamaican hills.

To *drunk* or to *drunken* seems to show in some uses a confusion with the word *drown*. Thus, in an account of a method of catching crabs: 'He returns, and his prisoners [crabs] being by this time "drunkened" (half drowned), they tumble out . . . and are caught.'[30] But *drunk* also is the simple verb: 'Cow neck [cheap rum] drunk you very quick.'

Another verb converted from an adjective is *dead*, to die, which has been so used in the folk speech probably from the beginning: Williams wrote in 1826 of the Negroes 'When they were old and "ready to dead" ', and James, in 1837, 'When she faint . . . all her fellow apprentice set up crying, and ask if she going to dead left them.' This results from omission of *be*.

Though the verb *grate* is found in kitchen use, *grater*, converted from the noun, is common too: You 'grater coconut' to get the milk, and 'grater green banana' to make porridge.

An interesting extension of grammar and meaning may be seen in the verb *quail*, which becomes transitive and means to wilt a leaf, by holding it over the fire till it becomes limp. Thus, to make duckunoo, you 'quail green banana leaf', and 'boil duckunoo in a quailed green banana leaf'. Another sense of *quail* is to drink or drink up: 'It sweet him so tell him quail off de whole ah de bottle full.' But this may be a separate word. To drink at a quick draught is to *swips* (*off*), which sounds onomatopoeic: 'Him tek up de battle an swips it off.'

Two other words of the same kind are *gwat* and *gwap*, to drink and to swallow food hastily. Not found in either English or African sources, these are probably local creations.

The common word for eating — now somewhat countrified — is to *nyam*, clearly African.[31] It was frequently noticed in the past in several forms and both as verb and noun: 'The negroes say, the black parroquets are good for yam, i.e. good to eat.'[32] Moreton spelt it *knaum*. Dancer wrote that the '*Geophagi* [dirt-eaters] . . . display as much curiosity and nicety in their choice of the earth they *yam*, as snuff-takers or smokers in the kind of tobacco they make use of'. And as a noun: 'Eh! mosquitoes, hab grandy nyamn on dat new buckra!' And with an adverb: 'Anancy . . . nyam off de whole a de cane dem.'

To *mumble*, meaning to crush with the gums, is still alive in Jamaica, and some also use /muka/ in the same sense.

An expression in St Thomas is to *drink Yallahs water* — meaning, to be an outsider. The implication is that the stranger would have had to cross the Yallahs River to enter the parish. The phrase has overtones of suspicion and unwelcome.

To *pran* means to clean, tidy, put in order:

> Dis 'oman scrub de floor,
> She lick an' pran de dutty room.

This comes by abbreviation from the phrase 'to give a lick and a promise,' which usually means 'to clean superficially' but here evidently means 'to clean thoroughly.' Probably from *primp* is *prims* or *prims off*, to pose or display oneself; as when Anancy indignantly inquires, 'A wen since Puss get so high dat him can primse off himself eena backra book?' In the same sense, a few lines before, we find *pose off*.

A word now out of use, but which we have found earliest in Jamaica, is to *creolise* — that is, to lounge easily and elegantly, as Lady Nugent learned to do after she had been in the island for a time: 'After breakfast, the usual routine; writing, reading, and creolising.' This word, obviously, would be used by outsiders, not by creoles, in explanation of the informal dress and relaxed habits that they adopted because of the climate.

The verbs discussed above relate to actions by human beings. A few others describe actions by plants and other things. For example, flowers in Jamaica do not bloom, but *blow* — a word which elsewhere was preserved only by the poets until a century ago (the latest OED citation is from Lord Tennyson, 1855), yet the word is current still in the speech of this island. When I asked in Mandeville about certain plants, I was told, 'Dem don' blow yet.' Though the dictionaries do not record it, the verb has also been used transitively of plants since at least 1788, when Marsden wrote, 'Ocro . . . blows a yellow flower.' And so it is today.

When a tree sheds its leaves, it is said to *throw off*, and a bare tree that gets new leaves is said to *feather up*. Quite a number of Jamaican plants or fruits *scratch*, that is, they irritate the skin or the tongue, by acidity or some corrosive quality. Beckford called attention to this as a property of eddos in 1790, and Barham in 1794. The fruit of pinguin will also *scratch* the tongue. Cowitch will *scratch* the skin, making it itch violently; it was taken internally as a vermifuge in slave days.

Finally, *fat* has become a verb, meaning to exude oil. Cacao seeds are pounded in a mortar until they 'begin to fat'. *Fly* has become a transitive (causative) verb meaning to make something fly, to blow out (e.g., a cork from a bottle): 'Just like how yeas' get strong an' sometimes fly de cark.' And *draw*, used of a liquid, means to ferment. Thus Jamaican folk speakers have done as others speakers of English: they have extended meanings, converted parts of speech to new functions, borrowed and invented; but they have their own ways of doing, which give the creolised talk a lively savour.

Chapter Eight

PEOPLE: RACES AND TYPES

THOUGH it is by no means limited to Jamaica, one very common and characteristic word is /bakra/ or /bokra/, variously spelled *backra* or *buckra* today and in other ways in the past, and meaning a white man. It is obviously African, from Ibo, Efik, or some related language (probably brought in variant forms) which have *mbakara* in this sense, or, more literally, 'he who surrounds or governs.' The earliest known use is from Antigua in 1736, but it is found only four years later in a description of Jamaica:

> 'They (the Negroes) say ... *England* must be a large Place, and *Scotland* a small one; for *Scots Baccaroes* (which they call all white Men) all know one another, but *English Bacceroes no know one another.*'[1]

Williams writes in 1826, 'Buckra, I fear, is derived from Buccaneer' — which is not offered as serious etymology, yet testifies to the second pronunciation.

The word began to acquire new uses very soon. Attributively, in *buckra yam* (1774), *buckra pine* (1788), *buckra calalu*, and so on, it meant the best variety or highest quality. As Russell shows, it referred less to colour than to social station:

> Backra or buckra ... is not used exclusively in referring to the white man, a brown or black gentleman is also called so in acknowledgment of his gentility, or genteel appearance; but this little 'privilege' (?) is only given him with his good morning or good evening, or when he is asked a favour, otherwise he is only 'gentleman' or 'smart fella'. Should he however, by his education and position, or money, move much in the upper class society, then he is said to turn 'pure-pure backra'.

Another evidence of the social meaning is seen in the term *walking buckra*:

Marly, not having yet procured a horse, he in consequence could not accompany them; no disgrace being considered so great in the island, as that of a white man being seen walking on foot when away from his home. No person does it, but such as have forfeited their character and situation, and who, in consequence, are styled walking buckras, a name, synonimous to beggar, coupled with that of vagabond.

Nevertheless, the association with colour has never been forgotten: one name today for an albino negro is *backra*.

No simple division between master and servant or white and black was ever made. From the beginning of English settlement there were indentured white servants whose condition was very close to slavery; on the other hand, many blacks earned or were granted their freedom. The position of the individual in the scheme of things, then, was more important than his colour; and those negroes who were born in the island, spoke English, and had better kinds of employment considered themselves almost a different order of beings from the newcome Africans. As Long wrote:

The Creole Blacks differ much from the Africans, not only in manners, but in beauty of shape, feature, and complexion. They hold the Africans in the utmost contempt, stiling them 'salt-water Negroes', and 'Guiney birds'; but value themselves on their own pedigree.

A sort of half-way condition between the creole Negro and the salt-water Negro was the *salt-water Creole* — one born during the voyage to Jamaica. For the slaves a special bond was forged through their passage to the new land on the same ship: such fellow-slaves knew each other as *shipmates*. A person born in the island is now called among the folk a /baanya/ (born-here); *creole* is hardly used any more.

This feeling of the Jamaican Negro that he was far above the African is reflected still in many expressions. The word /níega/, which the OED enters under *neger* but which is usually spelled *nayga* or *naygur* in the dialect literature, is used by black people to condemn those of their own colour. In the song 'Sammy Dead Oh' there is the line, almost a proverb, 'Nayga kean [can't] bear fe see Nayga flourish,' which Louise Bennett echoes in the poem 'Oonoo Lie!' as, 'Nayga won' meck nayga prospa.'

Naygur is often tantamount to 'good-for-nothing', and *neegrish* is 'mean or despicable'.

The same feeling is reflected through the present uses of the old African day-names, which survive mostly in derisive or depreciatory applications. Long wrote, in 1774:

> Many of the plantation Blacks call their children by the African name for the day of the week on which they are born; and these names are of two genders, male and female, as for instance:

Male	Female	Day
Cudjoe,	Juba,	Monday.
Cubbenah,	Beneba,	Tuesday.
Quaco,	Cuba,	Wednesday.
Quao,	Abba,	Thursday.
Cuffee,	Pheba,	Friday.
Quamin,	Mimba,	Saturday.
Quashee,	Quasheba,	Sunday.

Quashie was already taken as a typical name for a negro, as Long indicates in another place when he describes the fate of the educated children of a white planter and a negro mother:

> He is soon, perhaps, left to herd among his black kindred, and converse with Quashee and Mingo, instead of his school-fellows, *Sir George*, or *My Lord*; while mademoiselle, instead of modish French, must learn to prattle gibberish with her cousins *Mimba* and *Chloe*.

So in *Tom Cringle's Log* and still today, *Quashie* simply means a peasant, but one also finds it glossed as 'fool'.

By Long's day *Quasheba* already meant the coloured mistress of a white man:

> Europeans . . . are too easily led aside to give a loose to every kind of sensual delight: on this account some black or yellow *quasheba* is sought for, by whom a tawney breed is produced.

Moreton's couplet shows the same:

> When pepper-pot and wine his blood alarms,
> He takes a quashiba unto his arms.

And Stewart, not much later:

> To use an expression in common use here, many of them [creole women] (who have not had the advantage of a judicious education, and introduction into polite company) exhibit much of the Quashiba.

Russell, in 1868, remarked:

> An ugly stupid looking man with grey eyes, is called a 'Quaw' by way of derision.

Today this means a mountain person or an albino Negro. It has also a familiar form *Quawy*.

Quaco and *Quamin* have suffered the same fate: the first means a Maroon or country boy, the second a stupid person or an eel. Perhaps by association of sound, *queng* signifies a weird creature. Finally, *Cooba* came to mean a casual woman servant, and now a womanish man. If such a one meddles in women's affairs he is very likely to be addressed as *Miss Cooba*. And *Cuffee* (/kofi/) means several things, all uncomplimentary: a stupid person, one who 'don't have much speech', one who is easily fooled, or a shrimp.

McKay noted in 1912 that 'Sun is the regular nickname for James.' but I have found no confirmation; perhaps it has gone the way of the old day-names.

The tribal names of the Negroes brought to Jamaica have been discussed in an earlier chapter. Some have remained in popular legend with much the same overtones as the day-names. As Beckwith wrote in 1929, 'even today the term "Congo" refers to one who is the butt of his fellows,' and though this may be decreasing, as she suggests elsewhere, it has by no means disappeared. *Moco* is probably to be seen in /mòkojíi/, a countryman, 'not clever', and in the name of the tree *Moco John* (*Bauhinia divaricata*).

In his soldier poem *Flat Foot Drill*, McKay has the line, 'Right tu'n, you damn' bungo brut'!' and explains *bungo* as meaning a 'black African'. The insulting connotation is evident, as it is also in Bennett's lines,

> Me always get out cross w'en uncle
> Cuss me bungo fool.

With the recrudescence of the cumina revivalist cult one finds the word again: 'The dancers are supposed to be "Bongo Men" or Africans. They sing songs during the dance which they say are in Bongo language.' *Bungo* okro is a coarse variety of *Hibiscus esculentus*. All these evidently refer to the Bongo tribe of the Chari-Wadai area of Africa, or to some other of similar name. But the Hausa word *bunga*, an article of poor quality, or its like, may have had a reinforcing effect.

The *Nanga* (from the Ivory Coast) are still said to be a distinctive type in St Catherine's parish; they are known by a decided depression in the centre of the forehead. *Crongoe* yam recalls another tribal name, now reduced to *crunjo*.

In Gardner's *History of Jamaica* we find,

> The term Madagass is still applied to certain light-complexioned negroes, especially to those whose hair is less woolly than common. These are found in families where there is a very slight mingling of European blood, and the name therefore only indicates that there was a period when people light in complexion and possessing rather straight hair were known in the colony by that term.

Madagass obviously comes from *Madagascar*, and we may trace back the tradition behind this word through Dallas's description of the origin of the Maroons:

> Cudjoe was joined, but at what period is unknown, though certainly after he had become formidable, by another tribe of negroes, distinct in every respect; . . . They were called Madagascars, but why I do not know, never having heard that any slaves were brought from the island of Madagascar. . . . They said that they ran away from the settlements about Lacovia, in the parish of St Elizabeth, soon after the planters had bought them. It does not appear that their number was great, but they were remarkably prolific. Some of the older people remember that their parents spoke . . . a language entirely different from that spoken by the rest of the negroes with whom they had incorporated. . . . The Coromantee language, however, superseded the others, and became in time the general one in use.

Other names for particular groups of Negroes that sprang up

in the island were the *Accompongs, Cottawoods, Kencuffees, Paratees.*
Again Dallas is our chief source:

> Those of Accompong are in every respect the same as the
> people of Trelawney town, being only a part of them who had
> followed Accompong, the brother of Cudjoe, to settle in the
> town called after him. But neither the Accompongs, nor any
> other of the Maroon bodies, could be induced to join in the
> rebellion.

Also:

> Previous to the year 1730 a part of them [Maroons]
> separated from the others, and distinguished themselves by
> the name of the Cottawoods; having, it is supposed, originally
> come from a place so called, near the present Maroon
> Charlestown, in the parish of St George's. . . . The name of
> Cottawood was preserved among the descendants of that
> tribe, and the original body of negroes under Cudjoe were
> distinguished by the appellation of Kencuffees.

Accompong is still the name of the chief village of the western
Maroons, in St Elizabeth, and *Cottawood Spring*, a tributary of the
Rio Grande river in Portland, preserves the second name. Of
Kencuffee no trace seems to remain.

The term *Paratee* is used repeatedly by Williams, as in his
account of someone 'who had been shot at by a Paratee brown
man', 'the conversation I had had with the Paratee,' 'the Paratee was going to shoot.'[2] Presumably this referred to the people
from Pedro Plains, in St Elizabeth, near Parottee Point and
Bay, who are generally light complexioned.

Though it has been used elsewhere, the word *Maroon* is
another which gained a special significance in Jamaica. There
can be little doubt that it comes ultimately from Spanish *cimarron*, a Negro slave who has escaped and taken refuge in the hills,
and that it reached English through French *marron*. The development of its specifically Jamaican sense is noted by Dallas:

> The term Maroon had been hitherto confined to the body
> of original fugitives, and it was not till about the year 1730,
> when Cudjoe had become formidable, . . . that he and his
> people were included in the appellation.

In short, it was applied originally to the bands of slaves escaped
from the Spanish, later of those escaped from the English, who

succeeded in preserving their freedom in the mountains for many years until at last they gained autonomy in 1738 by treaty with the English government.

Because these people won self-rule, the word *Maroon* today has more favourable connotations than any tribal or other African name. Several plants are associated with them: *Maroon blister*, used medicinally, *Maroon wiss*, with which they camouflaged themselves when fighting, *Maroon lance*, and for less obvious reasons, *Maroon pimento*, *Maroon weed*.

The vocabulary of racial mixture in the Caribbean is generally derived from Spanish. Some special forms and senses, developed in Jamaica, are: *Cast*, a general term for a person of mixed blood, used by Long as the equivalent of 'person of colour' and 'coloured person', which came in somewhat later. Another general term was *creolian*, which is found very early:

> The island is exceeding healthful, the Children which are Borne in it thriue exceedingly, so that the Croyoliens and natives will in a few yeares make a great People.

It was, of course, equivalent to the more common *creole*, and like it at first meant simply 'born in the island', rather than in Europe or Africa. Long wrote of 'the native white men, or Creoles of Jamaica', and also of 'the Creole Blacks'. The first attributive use is found in 1740:

> The *Creol* Negroes greatly value themselves as much, superior on that account, as an ancient *Britain* would himself to a *Norman*, and are afraid of the wild Negroes.

Yet by the following century the word had become so firmly attached to the matter of colour that writers felt they must correct it:

> Many people are impressed with the idea, that a *creole* must have been born of black or coloured parents. Such a notion is ridiculous. The meaning of creole is precisely this: *an individual born in the West Indies, of white parents*!

Also:

> The term 'Creole' has no reference to colour, as is commonly supposed by Europeans, but merely means 'native'. We speak of a Creole horse, or of any vegetable or esculent not common

to the country, as the Irish potato, which, when cultivated on the mountains, are called Creole potatoes.

But the attempt was hopeless; the new colour-conscious meaning spoiled the old, and today the word is little used.

Mulatto has undergone a curious change in the folk speech: it has not stopped with /maláta/, the expected form, but has gone further to /maránta/, with substitution of *r* for *l* and intrusion of *n*.[3] Strictly speaking, it means the first generation of mixture between black and white, but by Long's day it was already used 'in common parlance' for all casts.

The next degree of mixture — of white with mulatto — was originally *Terceron*, but this term had little currency in Jamaica; its equivalent seems to have been *Mustee* (from Spanish *mestizo*); and the equivalent of *Quarteron*, *Castee* (from *cast*, by analogy with *mustee*):

> There are also Mulattoes and Mustees; the first are from a Negroe and a white Man; the other is from the second Generation; and the third are called Castees.[4]

But as Long pointed out, the terms were early confused:

> These distinctions, however, [those of the Spaniards] do not prevail in Jamaica; for here the Terceron is confounded with the Quateron; and the laws permit all, that are above three degrees removed in lineal descent from the Negro ancestor, to vote at elections and enjoy all the privileges and immunities of his majesty's white subjects of the island.

Yet another term existed, *Mustifino*, which the dictionaries do not record:

> The nearest to a Negro is a Sambo, the next a Mulatto, next a Quadroon, next a Mustee, and next a Mustiphino; after which the shade is lost, for the children of a Mustiphino, by a white man, are accounted white by law, and have higher privileges than the others.[5]

Others spell it *Mustiphini* and *Maestifino*.[6] It is evidently made up from *Mustee* or *Mestee* with Spanish *fino* (fine) added.

The increasing complexity of racial mixture, the end of slavery, and equality of all colours under the law, have contributed to the disuse of most of these terms. The survivors have anything but precise meanings. A police description of an escaped criminal in the *Gleaner* (1951) made him a *dark-sambo*, and *sambo* is elsewhere explained as 'between black and brown'. A mulatto is derisively referred to by the blacks as *white-a-middle*, and those with mottled skin are *liver-spot* or *liver* (/liba/). Particularly insulting also is the term *red Eboe* for a mulatto, the word 'red' being used by the Jamaican folk in many places where standard English would have yellow or orange. So also in Bennett's line, 'Wat a red kin 'oman mean!' — What a mean red-skinned woman!

Other races in Jamaica are East Indians and Chinese. The former (never the latter) are commonly *coolies*, and a *wrapper coolie* is one who uses the East Indian loin cloth instead of trousers — an old-fashioned type. These also used to be called *salaam babu*. A little East Indian girl (sometimes a boy) is commonly called *Betty* — obviously from Hindustani *beti*, daughter; and an East Indian woman is called *Mawy* (/maai/) — from Hindustani *ma*, a mother, apparently with the familiarising suffix -*y* added.

For the Chinese the old form *Chinee*, pronounced /cháini/, is the commonest; also *chinee-man*. A nickname is *squeeze-eye*, as in the line,

'Queeze Yeye hooden sell me wan small tin. (Bennett)

The offspring of Chinese and Negro is a *Chinee-rial*. These terms, once neutral, are now considered uncomplimentary or insulting.

Trades and Occupations

In the first years of settlement when the woods and savannahs were open and many animals ran wild, there was at least one occupation which later ceased to be — that of the *driver*, or *horse-catcher*, who rounded up wild horses for sale. We find in Leslie's *Account* (1739) the following:

No common Driver or Horse-catcher shall sell, or barter any Horse, Mare or other Cattle, without bringing two sufficient Evidences to vouch for him. . . . If any Driver or Horse-catcher shall fraudulently or designedly put any false Mark, or deface any old Mark, he shall for such Offence be guilty of Felony. No common Horse-catcher shall ride or drive in any *Savannah*, without giving 100 l. Bond.

A similar term was *hog-hunter*, an early alternative of 'maroon' or 'buccaneer' before the latter terms gained their present specific senses; for the earliest 'marooners' were simply men who hunted wild hogs in the islands, cured the meat by 'boucaning' and sold it to passing ships. By 1803 the word 'maroon' had already become specific, but was still identified with the occupation of hog-hunting: 'fugitive negroes, now designated by the appellation of Maroons, or hog-hunters.'

Other adventurers lived by cutting dyewoods: Beckford wrote of 'the logwood-chippers, whose axes are heard to resound from the depths of the wood. . . . Some are felling the heavy timber, and some with their bills are lopping the branches; while others, sitting upon the roots or stumps, are chipping off the bark'. And so their successors may be heard and seen today.

The term *black-shot*, on the other hand, lasted only during the first quarter of the nineteenth century. We find it first in 1803 (Dallas):

> To this force [of regular soldiers and militia] was attached a number of confidential negroes, called Black-shot, Mulattoes and Indians. . . . The Black-shot and Musquito Indians proved of great service.

Again, in 1825, in *An Account of a Shooting Excursion*: 'a party of eleven whites, . . . accompanied by about twelve black shots.'

Two thorough Jamaicanisms are *penn* and *penn-keeper*. The OED's earliest citation for the latter is from 1840, but it was in use over a hundred years before in this island:

> If any Person whatsoever shall refuse, either by himself, Overseer, or Pen-keeper, to discover, upon Oath, the true number of their Slaves, Horses, &c. it shall be lawful for the Justices and Vestry to tax such Person.[7]

The practice of absentee ownership also led to the development of a special sense for the word *attorney*. As Beckford explained it: 'An Attorney is a man who has a delegated power to act for principals in England; but is essentially different in practice from an Attorney at law.' In short, the attorney was the owner's deputy, the man on the spot with the real authority.

Book-keeper similarly gained an entirely new significance on the sugar estates: it meant the assistant to the Overseer. Again Beckford has explained:

Book-keepers are in subordinate command to the Overseers, they attend the still-house in crop, and out of crop the the [sic] field. There are many so little deserving the name they bear, that so far from being able to calculate accounts they cannot many of them even read: and yet from this situation, from being frequently indented servants they become overseers, and have the conduct of a plantation.

Moreton furnishes further distinctions in the usage which the dictionaries do not record:

He who is chief in the superintendency of a plantation in Jamaica, is called an Overseer; and in the Windward Islands, a Manager; and the Overseer's Deputies are called Book-keepers; and in the Windward Islands Overseer's or Negro-Drivers.

The slaves in Jamaica developed the entirely new word *busha*, whose metamorphosis from *overseer* may be seen in a series of quotations from 1790 to 1828: 'Hecta *nebba* will make puncheon for you, Obisha . . .', 'No use me ill, Obisha!'; 'Overseer, first corrupted to Oberseer, is now Bersheer or Busha'; 'The Busha, as the people call him'.[8] This word is in full, current usage still.

The manager of an estate was sometimes nicknamed a *cowskin hero*, in allusion to his power to wield the whip. As Moreton wrote, 'When they become cowskin heroes, or managers, [they] are totally ignorant of instructing their overseers or negroes . . . (if they know nothing about distilling).'

In Jamaica, as elsewhere, *driver* was the usual title for the man in charge of a gang of slaves. An alternate term, *head-man*, also came into use:

He himself has been domineered over by a driver or head-man; it is now his turn to domineer over others. . . . The poor boys perform their task . . . but they console themselves with the hope that they will one day be head-men themselves.[9]

The feminine form *driveress* was created too; Roughley wrote:

Negro children, after they pass five or six years, if . . . healthy, should be taken from the nurse in the negro houses, and put under the tuition of the driveress, who has the conducting of the weeding gang.

These feminine forms are favoured in Jamaica. Though *driveress* is obsolete, one finds *butleress* commonly for the servant who, among other things, waits at table; and *teacheress* for a woman teacher. The hospital on the slave-days sugar estate was also attended, often, by a *doctoress* or *doctress*.

An obsolete institution of over a century ago was the train of servant women following a lady, jocularly referred to as the *trunk fleet*. One visitor has given his impression thus:

> A string of about nine or ten negro girls, walking along the road, and sweating under the load of huge trunks and enormous bandboxes; . . . I was told very gravely that it was the *trunk fleet*, the interpretation of which is neither more nor less than a company of waiting maids, to a visiting party of ladies, who thus transport the wardrope of their mistresses from place to place.[10]

Among the Maroons an important person was the *hornman*, who gave signals with a horn or conch. Dallas mentioned them repeatedly, as in his account of the conclusion of their treaty with the English:

> Captain Adair made a halt, and ordered his guide to blow his horn. The Maroons knowing by the information given by the sounds that they proceeded from the missing hornman, returned an answer with one of their horns.

And in 1929, Beckwith: 'In Accompong the "horn man" calls out the name of the dead through a conch, and everyone listens to the signal.'

Though the word *waiting-boy* may not have been invented in Jamaica it was first recorded there in 1798: 'He attended me as a waiting-boy, and he is about 15 years of age.' This servant lad, dancing attendance on his master, must have been a familiar sight in former days — indeed, two kinds of small fish that always follow bigger fish have acquired the names *barracouta waitin'-boy* and *shark waitin'-boy*.

Nana, which in the Twi language means a grandparent of either sex, means in Jamaica a grandmother, an old woman, and therefore also a midwife (compare dialectal 'granny-woman' in the United States). But the most usual sense in the cities is probably nursemaid: Jamaican children refer to the servant who takes care of them as *Nana*. Though in recent years the English 'Nanny' has been coming in, and the ODS gives *nanna* as a variant form of *nanny*, those are quite different words, and they are far from displacing the African one.

The term *housekeeper* was early used as a euphemism for the coloured mistress of a white planter. Stewart, carefully italicising, referred to those women 'who, being the *housekeepers* of men of fortune, were enabled to dress finely.' Women of the same profession but less elevation are referred to today as *pinks* or *sporters*. The first word may have developed from *pink* in the sense of 'slightly vulgar, indecent, or violent'; the second is clearly connected with the American word *sporting-house*, a brothel.

In a note to one of his songs, McKay explained the word *come-around* as follows: 'Day-labourers, men and women, in Kingston streets and wharves, famous for the heavy weights they carry, are called come-arounds.' This is a rather more favourable sense than that prevailing now: a loiterer, a petty thief. The word is probably from Spanish *camarón*, a beggar or parasite. One may be fairly sure, too, of the source of /ba-u/ or /ba-ul/, current in Kingston for a handcart-man (or other labourer) 'of a disreptuable or suspicious kind'; it is probably from French *bahut*, possibly with concurrent influence of Spanish *baul*,[11] though one may note, also, that *barrow* is sometimes pronounced /ba-u/.

Reported once from St James parish is *mantry-maker*, a dressmaker. This is clearly the preservation of the obsolete *mantua-maker*, once very common.

There are various names for itinerant vendors, the commonest being *higgler* — a Jamaicanism only because the word is so frequent. Beckwith has written: 'The street vendors of Kingston, the "higglers" or "cadgers" as they are called, have each their own musical cry which rises and falls with a peculiar inflection, generally with an upward turn at the end.' *Cadger* is hardly used any more, and was never common. Another vendor is the *ball-pan man*, so called because he carries his wares, including balls of meat, in a pan. The vendors of other foods — pindas, jelly-coconuts, booby eggs, snow-balls — have no special names; the names of their wares are discussed below.

Physical Characteristics

Physical characteristics of people and things are not always kept apart; a number of words are applicable to either. We begin with those chiefly used of people.

M

Somebody, usually pronounced /smadi/, has become a noun meaning a human being. It is in common use and has been since at least 1826, when Williams recorded 'You wicked somebody' for 'You are a wicked person'. In 1955 I heard the remark about a fruit: 'S'mady can eat it' — that is, it is edible by human beings. This development is parallel, of course, to the common use of *something* as a noun meaning simply *thing*: 'What dat sunting you hab day?' Instead of Standard *adult* or *grown-up* the folk say *big-s'mady* or *big-people*, which are in contrast with *pickny*, the Jamaican version of pickaninny.

This word did appear here in the longer form first, and with the generally accepted explanation: 'Their Children call'd Piganinnies or rather Pequenos Ninnos.'[12] The shorter form made its first appearance in 1790, as *pickinnies*; in 1868 also *pickini*; in 1927 *pickines*;[13] and one still occasionally hears it with three syllables: /pikini/. But the two-syllable form was also recorded in 1868: *pickni*. While it may well be a condensation of *pickaninny* it quite conceivably comes by independent adoption of Spanish *pequèno*, a child. *Pickny* is transferred half humourously to young animals — as, *duck pickny*. It is common in the phrase *pickny mumma*, a nursing mother, therefore a symbol of plenty or of good fostering. In an account of 1838, we read: 'The pickaninny mothers [mothers with small children], as they are called, on coming into the field, gave the children to a nurse.' *Pickny mumma* is also a nickname for the white coco, and some other plants.

A very tall, overgrown person may be derisively called a *langulala*. The first part of this is, of course, *long*; the latter seems to be a symbolic extension by repetition of the *l*'s. This is the only word we have found remarking on tallness, but there are many for shortness. *Duggy*, used of short legged chickens, is also used of people: a *duggy* man. A *timiny* — from the *Temne* tribe name? —is a short man; but sound symbolism may be involved too, as in *teeny* or *tiny*. A *tuku*, on the other hand, though short, is thickly built. *Tumpa*, from *stump*, ordinarily used of things — a knife, an amputated leg, and so on — may be applied to a person; *puchin* and *kunchin* both mean short — even dwarfed.

A word for strong, firm, is *samba* (perhaps from *sambo*); the opposite is *pianji*, slight: 'a lickle pianji-pianji pig' would be a thin, runtish or undernourished one — also called a /winji/.

Russell reported as 'African' the very similar phrase *wenya-wenya*: 'Meagre, not fat. Dat wenya-wenya boy 'trong.' Favourable senses of slenderness are suggested by *limba* (evidently Standard *limber* with some change of sense), and *slimmy-like*. *Tutty* means 'of stunted growth'; *shekrey* is 'thin, light, meagre'. Both may be applied to people.

As for largeness, a *pawnzo* is a 'big-belly boy' — the word obviously based on *paunch*; so is /paanz-beli/. A *fattoon* is a very fat man, and *asono*, which originally meant an elephant, is applied to a large, clumsy, greedy person. Another of Russell's 'African' words in use by Jamaicans was *buffro-buffro*, meaning 'clumsy, stout. What a buffro-buffro man!' This is easily traced to Twi *'o-bò-fùro*, a lazy, good-for-nothing fellow'. Other closely similar words are: *bufu* or *bufu-bufu*, 'big, clumsy, stout'; *bobo*, 'ugly, fat, oafish, stupid' — also applied to earthworms — compare the *bubu* of Grenada. (These carry over from the physical conditions to associated traits of character, discussed below.) *Bubu* as a verb means to disfigure, and a frightful or disfigured person is a *bubuafu*, which clearly comes from Twi *'o-búbuafo*, a man lamed by sickness or palsy' — or some related form.

There are a few words for prettiness, a great many for different kinds of ugliness or ill looks. French *beau* is probably the source of *bow-bo* (the reduplication is made in French too). *Sauly*, nice, attractive, is undoubtedly connected with the phrase *to be in one's salt* (discussed below among foods) — well off, on top of the world. And of course the iterated form *pretty-pretty* is very common. The owl-like bird called *patu* has become a symbol of ugliness throughout the island:. 'Ugly no patu!' An ugly person is therefore a *patu-dowdow*, the latter part probably being a term of endearment used ironically. *Monkey-Jesus* and *muckumdash* are other words for the same. *Funnyakın* (funny of skin) puts the emphasis on ugliness probably due to some disease.

The ugliness that comes from being ill clothed, ragged, untidy, dirty, with its associated ideas of poverty or illness, is expressed by *wera-ke-te*, *jangra*, *pitchy-patchy*, *ragga-ragga*, *raggity*, *reggid and saacy*, and *harrigan*. The last suggests a possible connection with *harridan*; the next to last recalls the United States dialectal phrase 'fat, ragged, and sassy', which, however, implied a cheerful or insouciant state of mind.

Quite a number of words mean rough, coarse — of both

persons and things. *Carra-carra*, for example, would apply to a stony road. But *raw-chaw* is uncouth, the same as *cruff*. Russell recorded *cruffy*. Since this is often said of people's skins, it may be a blend of *rough* and *scurfy*; but perhaps *cra-cra* (an itching disease) and *rough* are the elements combined. Applied to a person, *cruff* may mean 'worthless — has no intention of uplifting [himself]'. Another of Russell's 'African' forms is *bogro-bogro*: 'Coarse. Wa me fe do wid dis bogro-bogro ting?' This is still to be found in use: coarse salt is sometimes *bogro-salt*.

Russell also lists *chaka-chaka*: 'Disorderly ... De boy clothes so chaka-chaka'; *nyaka-nyaka*: 'Filthy-looking ... De yard look so nyaka-nyaka'; and *takro-takro*: 'Ugly, ill-proportioned. Dat is a takro-takro man'. The second of these may be connected with Twi *nyaka*, to cut in pieces; all are no doubt, as Russell thought, of African origin.

Jing-bang means a crowd of noisy, dirty people, usually, but may refer to one disreputable person. *Crawny* is 'nasty-looking, unclean-looking', but also has the same sense as Standard *scrawny*, from which it appears to come. *Let-go*, as an adjective pronounced /légo/, means without control, unkempt. It applies to people, but I have heard it used of a cabbage that did not form a proper head because the leaves were not tied up. *Bru-bru* also means untidy; apparently in the sense of unorganised it is applied to a 'scratch race' which anyone can enter. *Paka, puka,* or *puka-puka* all seem to suggest something uncontrolled, disorderly, a spoilt piece of work, and it merges imperceptibly into *pyaka-pyaka*, muddled, untidy, dirty.

Another fairly common word with a number of associated meanings is *bugu-yaga*, an 'unkempt, untidy person'. Bennett uses it with heavy scorn: 'Yuh an' yuh buggo-yagga fren'.' It has a secondary form *bugu-waga*, which means 'a fat, shapeless woman' — also 'a chrysalis', and *bugu-yanga* has been reported for gonorrhea.

Words meaning weak, worthless, in various shades of application, include *freketeh, chekre*, a much worn and broken basket, *reke-reke*, weak, rickety, and when applied to a person, weak from sickness. Similar is *rukuruku*, rough, rickety, shaky; and *rukuto*, rough, is no doubt connected. Many of these words seem to be best explained as onomatopoetic or formed by some kind of sound symbolism.

Frenkeh, reported to mean delicate, is probably a by-form of *fenky*, weak, or *fenky-fenky*, fussy, fault-finding, which seem to come from *finicky*. A strange adjective is *waang-fu*, want-food, therefore hankering after food, undernourished, 'mauger', as in the saying 'waang-fu boy always hang about'.

An extremely poor person who barely manages to get on is *puckro*. *Mafeena* means 'refined, effeminate; a poor person' — especially the latter: one who is much reduced. There is a characteristic saying, 'Me is poor Mafino — don' business wid trouble.'[14] *Duffidia* (pronounced /dufidáia/) is one who goes about carelessly, as if stunned.

The Standard word *albino* seems to have entered the language through a Jamaican source: 'The offspring of two Negroe-parents, if born with a white or light-coloured *reticulum*, is called an Albinoe.'[15] The folk have their own words, however. Most common is *quaw* or *quawy* (/kwaa, kwaau, kwaai/); others are *dundus* (/dundus/), *moodoo* (/mudu/), *payrin*, and *white-man*. *Dundus* means 'a freak of nature; undersized', but surprisingly is also used as a term of affection for a child or sweetheart.

A number of words apply to the physical characteristics of things, far more than of people, but sometimes there may be a transfer. *Bamboo ashes* is the symbol of something negligible. Some plants are *swipple* — that is, slippery, exuding a mucilaginous juice. This has another form, *sipple*, and both probably come from *supple*. *Switchy* means pliant — an okro plant was described as 'a tall, switchy one'. A fruit that is not ripe is *fluxy* — that is, it will cause the 'flux' if eaten. A fruit picked green and forced to ripen so is *force-ripe* — a word often used of precocious people; the fruit is *fubba* when force-ripe and withered. A *scratchy* plant is one that *scratches*, or irritates the tongue by its pungency or astringency. *Scratch* may also be used as an adjective in this sense — and all three words are quite common, apparently Jamaican creations.

A *stain* in a fruit or plant is a strong tartness; it refers to the effect on the taste, not the sight, *stain* being both adjective and noun, and *stainy* an adjective. We read of jimblings, in 1893, 'These are very stainy to the taste;' and of plantain we are told you can 'eat it ripe or boil out the stain'. A similar sense is found in *clammish*, said of the macca-fat fruit, which is puckering and astringent. Another word for the latter is *strawny* — that is, 'strandy' — it pulls into sticky strands.

Russell reported *makla-makla* as 'Bad taste from too many mixtures. Dis is a makla-makla drink'. *Shine* becomes an adjective instead of *shiny*: 'It have a shine look.' The cutlass fish is 'flat, shine, good for frying'; the satin fish is 'longer, rounder, shiner' than the silk fish.

A plant that exudes gum or other liquid is called *fat*, and one that 'don't show fat' is /tosty/ — which apparently represents *thirsty*. A vegetable root that is getting ready to spring is said to become *chowy* (pronounced /choui/) — that is, sticky, gluey, and not good to eat. This is no doubt based on the north-English and Scots variant of chew, *chow*. Wood that does not form splinters is *barky*, and may therefore be made into rope. *Paly*, somewhat pale, considered 'chiefly poetic' in Standard, is a common type of folk word in this island.

Something that is 'inside out' is *wrong-side*. *Tinnen*, made of tin, which was last recorded by the OED from 1653, is still to be heard in everyday use: 'A bucket is a tinnen thing,' an excellent example of a 'preservation'.

Finally, there are a number of words for something worthless, rubbishy, fit only to throw away: *corojungo, caroachy, cruchument, bangarang, bangarance,* or *banganance, floolooloops,* and *screbbey.* The last may be applied to a person — a good-for-nothing, a dunce. *Cruchument* is reduced from *accoutrement* and *caroachy* from Spanish *ċorotos*; none of the rest have been traced to any clear source; like others above, they no doubt depend for their meaning largely upon sound-symbolism.

Attributes of Character

The regular association between physical characteristics and mental or emotional traits makes the division between them somewhat arbitrary. Indeed, in many cases the words literally describe something physical while implying the further meaning. The trait may be expressed with a descriptive adjective or with an abstract noun. There are also concrete nouns classifying people by their traits.

The simple verb *nyam*, to eat, leads for example to the word *nyami-nyami*, which may mean either greedy or a greedy person. Similarly, from the noun *ninyam*, food, comes *ninyam Surrey*, a person who eats a lot but is never satisfied.[16] Other words referring to greediness are *craven* (a form of *craving*) as:

Po Anancy couldn' tan de temptation as him did bawn craven, him nyam aff de whole a de cane dem.

Or, as a countryman told me, ganja smoking adds to one's appetite — 'make you craven, call for something sweet.' A synonym is *gravilitious*, or *grabalicious*, perhaps a blend of *grab* and *delicious*.

Another such word is *hoganeer* or *hoganeerin*. In Bennett's line, 'Hear dah hoganeer man deh dah blow!' This is obviously based on *hog*, perhaps extended by analogy with *buccaneer*, *domineer*, and so on — especially as one additional sense of *hoganeerin* is *rough*. *Bella* and *bella-gut* mean a greedy person, one who 'has a long belly-gut':

> Doah me no got long bella-gut
> An me no licky-licky,
> Me can put weh a hearty meal,
> Me kean nyam picky-picky. (Bennett).

A large cooking-pot, used for cooking down the entrails of slaughtered animals, was also, by obvious transfer, a *bella-gut*.

Picky-picky, in the verse just cited, means finicking, taking a little here and a little there; *licky-licky* is very much the same as greedy but implies the epicurean approach, tasting different things not so much out of hunger as in sensuality. There is a proverb, 'Licky-licky fly follow coffin go a hole' — which hints at the danger of following too far the pleasures of the palate.

The same proverb appears in another form: 'Sweet-mout' fly follow coffin go a' hole.' But this is the less common meaning of *sweet-mouth*; more often it has the sense of a persuasive or flattering manner of speech. Russell recorded it in 1868: 'Henry wossa sweet-mout dan William.' Uncle Newton gives a description of a sweet-mouth person in action:

> He is a newspaper vendor. He has what they call a 'sweet mouth'. 'Lady, buy a paper for your husband. But what a pretty lady. Your son, mam? What a lovely little gentleman!' The poor woman 'falls' for the flattery and spends her valuable quattie.

Returning to greed, we find another aspect of it, covetousness, expressed in a number of words. Again Russell has recorded it: 'Greedy, covetous, selfish. Big-eye people nebber is fe satisfy in dis wol.' This appears to be a loan translation from African: the Ibo expression 'eye big' means just this.

From the word *covetous* itself has also developed *cubbitch*, avaricious, stingy. Jekyll has written, 'Cubbitch is used only in the sense of close-fisted' . . . a cubbitch man 'will not part with what he has'. ('Only' overstates the case.) The depression at the back of the neck is popularly known as the *cubbitch-hole* and indicates by its depth how grasping one is. Uncle Newton describes the tortures of a boy being barbered: 'Then he pushes that pair of scissors, one end of which is broken, DOWN INTO MY TENDER HOLE OF CUBBITCHNESS.' In the proverbial comparison, 'Cubbitch no starapple' the allusion is to the starapple tree, which holds on to its fruits and never lets them fall.

Cramoojin (which surely comes from *curmudgeon*) is used as an adjective meaning 'sly, underhand, deceitful' and as a noun to mean stinginess, tight-fistedness; and for some it means shirking, worthlessness:

Annotto can't sell, the price is unfair,
Pimento a blossom and drop
Hard time, hard time,
Hard time a carry the day.
Hard time, hard time,
For they won't put cramouchin' away.

Geechy, a term which in Florida refers to certain negroes considered wilder than others, in Jamaica simply means stingy: 'Him han' tight.' If a person holds on to his money not out of avarice but because he is clever, wise in spending, he is more likely to be called *cave-headed* or *cavy*. One man said that this was the same as *cagy*; what it might be otherwise is anybody's guess.

According to Jekyll, *strong-yeye* means covetousness; perhaps this is connected with big-eye, already mentioned. Russell, however, recorded '*Trong-eye* — Domineering, not easily browbeaten. If Jim no bin trong-eye him wouldn't get de money'. Very similar is *strong-mouth* (both adjective and noun). Again from Russell, '*Trong-mout* — Boisterous, brow-beating. De lawyer gain de case by trong-mout.'

Obstinacy or stubbornness is *hard-eye*, as in the proverb 'Hard eye pickney nebber go good', or, much more commonly, *hard-ears*, which carries over to unwillingness: 'Hard-aze — Disobedient, wilful. Hard-aze people nubba prasper'[17], and the proverb 'Hard-aize pickney walk two time'. The similar idea, that of being determined or headstrong, is found in the adjective *purpose*:

> If you said: 'Kindly pick two breadfruits,' he would pick twenty; while if you asked him to pick a few dozen he would most surely pick four or six. He was what you and I would call *a very purpose man.*

I take this to be a malaprop form of *perverse.*[18]

A Scottish word which survives in wide use in Jamaica but with somewhat altered meaning is *crabbit* — rough, greedy, ferocious. *Bringle*, fierce, is a normal local form of *brindle* though the connection of this word with anger is not clear. Since it is also used as a verb, it may possibly be a form of *bridle*, but more plausible is some connection with *brindle* (through dogs or cows?).

The curious word /raatid/ is used both as adjective and interjection to show anger, and has been for at least forty years. I knew it as schoolboy slang, but it is more widely heard today. It would appear to be a form of *wroth* or *wrothed*, probably Biblical in origin. The latter, in folk pronunciation, would be exactly that just given. As an exclamation it shows sudden surprise, anger, or objection. Louise Bennett has it in an unusual form, but the usual meaning, in the line,

> Lawd me no righted, me mad! me mad!

Rygin, pronounced /raigin/, has both favourable and unfavourable senses. The first might be rendered as vigorous, spirited, wholehearted — a jockey who gives himself completely to the race is 'a rygin rider'. The other meaning is cross, wild, raging. From its sound this word ought to represent Standard *ragging* (compare *hag, bag, lag*), and it probably does: I take it to be a shortening of *bully-ragging*. But not so many years ago there was a local desperado named Rygin — is his name at the basis of this word, or did *he* acquire the name from the word?

Strong-physic has become an adjective. As Russell recorded it, '*Trong-physic* — Hot tempered, bad. Creole pickni too trong-physic sista.' *Flighty* has the curiously changed sense of fiery, brazen. *Hoodias*, reported to mean terrible, may represent *odious* or *hideous*, or perhaps even the addition of *-ous* to such an African form as Twi *ahú-de*, a fearful thing, terrible things.

Trespass may become an adjective: 'And I said, "Some of these sheep are very trespass." '[19] One who is *bad-minded* is evil-minded, interpreting things in a derogatory way, as in the song,

> I don' know, I don' know
> Why some people bad-minded so.

Unconscionable, 'with depreciatory terms, as an intensive,' is last cited in OED from 1755; yet in the same sense it is still quite alive in Jamaica. In the song 'Wheel an Tun Me' are the lines,

> One unconscionable peel-head johncrow
> Come tief it away.

Grudgeful is another adjective widely used as an abstract noun. It signifies envy or spite: 'Same time grudgeful start grow eena Anancy an him study a way how fe mash up Wasp life.' In the song 'Sammy Dead Oh!' it is an adjective, in a thoroughly Jamaican context: 'But a grudgeful dem grudgeful kill Sammy' — it was because they were envious that Sammy was killed.

'Ceitful does not mean merely deceitful but has acquired the new sense of speaking evil of someone or calling his honesty into question. So in the Anancy story, 'If yuh ketch anybody dah 'ceitful pon yuh, yuh got right fe teck wey everyting dem got.'

Trickiness is expressed in different shades. *Trickify*, an adjective, means mischievous more than anything else. Beckwith alludes to 'the belief that every man is accompanied by two duppies, a good and a bad, or a trickify one, as Wilfred says'. Actual dishonesty, however, is *hood-i-up*, and a person who was 'crooked' or not straightforward would be told, 'You is hood-i-up!' The source would seem to be 'hood-it-up', symbolic of the concealment practiced by a dishonest person.

Cunning, both as noun and adjective, has been reduced to *cunny*: 'Bredda Nancy, wid him usual cunny;' and in the Maroons' song:

> Docta bud a cunny bud,
> Hard bud fe dead!

— the doctor-bird is a cunning bird, a hard bird to kill. *Suna* has been reported as meaning smart. If this is the comparative form of *soon*, it may be connected with Uncle Remus's remark, 'Now Br'er Rabbit was a mighty soon man!' — and perhaps also with the nickname of the settlers of Oklahoma, *Sooners*; but the evidence is scanty.

Worthlessness is expressed in the phrase *no wut*. From 1826 we find, 'Quamina . . . began to . . . curse the preacher's religion, since it was "no worth";'[20] and today, 'Me deh tell you say de Jackass no wut.' The abstract noun is also reduced: 'All because o' you, wid you' wuthless now.'

A similar, widely used word, that appears in many associated forms, is *pyaa-pyaa*, which means careless, weak, feeble, insignificant. Bennett writes of a Governor and the impression he makes:

> . . . wen him show
> Sey dat him no peaw-peaw,
> Dat nobody couldn' bribe him,
> An wat him sey is law.

Other recorded forms are *pyaw-pyaw*, *pea-piu*, and the nasalised *pean-pean* and /pyaang-pyaang/.

A person who will not take the trouble to look refined has no *ambition* (self-respect), and is therefore worthless, or *chapunko*. Carelessness of a different kind is *don't-care*; again, it may be an adjective meaning 'inattentive' or a noun meaning 'nonchalance, indifference'.

Ignorant is a frequent folk malapropism for *indignant*. Pride of manner is expressed by /buosi/ — evidently representing 'boasty'. As one man described a bird named *Bessy Shake-up*, it is a 'small, yellow-looking bird — shakes itself as it walks, like dem boasy lady shake up dem hip'. *Boasify* similarly means boastful, proud. Ostentation is well called *oba-do* (overdoing). A boastful person is a *big-na-do*, and pride may be /kris/ — evidently from English *crisp*, in reference to the manner of a proud person, a *nyanga*, from an African word which describes a dance (the *yanga*) or a manner of walking self-importantly.

Pretentiousness is *geow*, pronounced /gyou/. *Quality* continues in the folk speech as an adjective or adverb meaning 'high class'. As one man remarked, you 'have to curse some quality bad words to get rid of a ghost'. Another word for high class or 'classy' is *stoshus*, which seems to end like other words in *-ocious*, though I have no clue to the first part.

A number of degrees of impertinence are expressed, from mild to violent. *Prusy*, reported as meaning 'pert, womanish', no doubt represents the Americanism *prissy*. A much commoner word, meaning impudent, 'nervy', officious, and the like is /faas/ — evidently a development from *fast*. McKay spelt it *fass*; another example is: 'Bra 'Nancy, fas' as usual, fine himself a King yard.'

A word of very similar force is /fiesti/, impertinent, rude. In Louise Bennett's lines:

> Ah hooden stan' har facetiness
> Far we wasen company.

This word is met with in print in the form *facey* — for example, in Beckwith's account: 'Although good spirits also come back to earth "to make holiday", as some say, only a bad spirit is "facey" enough to show himself to you.' Also in McKay, 'facey: brisk, forward'. But this seems to me to imply a misinterpretation, as if the word were connected with *face*. This is not at all impossible, if they have heard it aright; but I have heard it only in the form with *t*, as in Bennett's lines just cited, and I take it rather to be connected with *feisty*, which flourished in seventeenth-century England in just such senses and is still vigourously alive in the southern United States.

Russell recorded *mannish* in the same sense (1868): 'Ga lang yanda sa, you too mannish. (Go away from me sir, you are too froward.)' This may also be applied to a woman. Some sharper terms are: *funkify*, precocious, rude (which would seem to be a Scots legacy with Jamaican alteration of the ending);[21] *renk*, fierce, impertinent: 'You is renk!' — a development from *rank*, referring to a bad smell. What looks like a euphemism (or an understatement) is the use of *untidy* to mean indecent, vulgar. As one man put it, 'Bubby is the untidy word; bus', breas' are decent.' Another word that surprisingly means indecent is *outlaw*: 'Her song it was outlaw (fine folks say improper).'

A word of similar meaning is *tallawah*, pronounced /tálawa/, which seems to have the basic sense of strong, tough, but goes beyond the physical to mean dangerous, even bad, or if applied to a woman, immoral. The proverbial phrase, 'Me lickle but me talawa,' may mean any of these things: Don't underestimate me; I may be small but I'm dangerous! This has also been reported in the form *tallaban*, and in the song 'Matty Walla',

> Matty run, Matty run, Matty tumble dung,
> Matty run a mile an' a half fe go tallala,

the last word is probably a disguised form of *talawa*.

Louise Bennett gives us the terms *mannersable* and *unmannersable*:

> She mannasable, wen we meet
> She allways bow an' smile.

and, referring to men who won't offer their seats to women in the tramcar,

> Dem man gwan unmannasable.

A generally disagreeable person may be called a *wack-a-tack*; one who is rough-mannered or 'crusty' is *bugobugo* (probably related to *bugubugu*, met with above). *Fenky-fenky* means (among other things) fussy, fault-finding, and is both adjective and noun. Very typical is the following, with two phrasal adjectives placed before their noun:

> Once upon a time dere was a very fine-fault an pick an choose gal livin' in dis country.

'Unusually fault-finding' is the meaning of *mekam-fekam*, which has a very Scottish ring but has not been traced. A nagging, railing old woman is an *old surrasy* — from the plant *cerasee* (pronounced /sórasi/) which makes a very bitter tea. A fretful, peevish person is a *sucko-bolo*[22] — of unknown origin. Much the same is meant by *cry-cry*, in which the iterated form suggests continuation to the point of habit. There is a proverb, 'Cry-cry pickney neber hab him right.'

The word *labrish*, gossip, will be discussed shortly; one given to gossip, or a chatterbox, is a *labrisher*, or a *laba-laba*. *Lebbey-lebbey* is 'bad talking', 'to make a lot of noise', and *bra-bra* means loud talking, brawling, outrageous or disrespectful talk. All of these have obviously an echoic element in their formation. Humourously condemnatory terms for a chatterbox are *mouty-mouty* (mouthy), *mout-a-massy* (mouth have mercy), *mout-have-*

nutt'n-fe-do, and, by analogy to *telegram* (perhaps also a pun on *tell*) *mout-a-gram*, one who spreads false news.

A *cobell* (/kobél/) is a confusion or quarrel, 'a quarrel actually leading to a fight,' according to H. P. Jacobs, who plausibly derives the word from *cabal*.[23] For a troublesome, teasing person, Russell has recorded *pick-mout*: 'A pick-mout boy come again fe make quarrel.' A *teggereg* is the same, or a bully. As Bennett has it, 'Gwan gal you favah teggereg,' which suggests some of the other shades of meaning implicit in the source of the word — for it would seem to come from *tag-rag*, a 'low, despicable person'.

Derisive names for bullying or belligerent people are *duppy-conqueror* and *Champung-Nanny*; the second is said to mean *champion* (though this is probably folk-etymology) and perhaps *Nanny* alludes to the Maroon leader of Nanny Town — 'man or woman like to fight.' The same meaning is expressed by *rowasam* (pronounced /róuasam/), the first part of which is probably *rower*, one who makes a row. The second is probably *-some*, on such an analogy as *quarrelsome*. *Kas-kas*, quarrelling — an African word[24] — is often interpreted as if it had to do with cursing, as in the proverb, 'Cuss-cuss neber bore hole in a you 'kin,' but this is folk etymology.

Crampify means unfriendly; *shabers* (apparently connected with *shabby*) is 'not good company'. On the other hand, both *bolo* and *combolo* mean a friend, companion. Jekyll quotes the expression 'Combolow is comrade oh!' and H. P. Jacobs speaks of the line 'We all a combolo' in 'a well known song'. This word has a Spanish sound, but has not been found.[25] Another word for friend, *pasayro*, is certainly Spanish, from *pasajero*, passenger.

Opinions differ about the word *tetes*: some say 'a friend', some 'a bully' — which seem too far apart to be reconciled. *Quabs* means companions, equals: 'I and he is not quabs.' One who spends freely among friends is *racial*, but what the connection may be with the usual meanings of the word is hard to imagine. *Libwell*, reckless, is the extreme of this kind of generosity. *Jokify* is merry, jolly, humourous. *Playing*, as an adjective, means not serious — the negative of it is illustrated in the following:

Henry said he was taught not to tell lies. . . . He was flogged for doing it. His mother is not a 'playing woman'; she is very serious when she is vexed and 'will lash your head off' during this time.[26]

Gallantin, with second-syllable stress, signifies frivolous, and describes one who goes 'fooling around, instead of doing duties'. This is from the preservation of the verb *to gallant*, which itself means in Jamaica to 'skylark, flirt, roam about aimlessly'. The word *sad* also lasts in an old-fashioned sense, that of stability, firmness, therefore used for example to compliment a cricketer: a 'sad man' is a steady, dependable one. A word once used to mean good, fine, esteemed, was *macky*, which had an unusual development. It began in the phrase *Macky Massa*, 'Good day, Master,' evidently from Twi *makyέ*, Good morning! But evidently it became detached, and Moreton recorded it as an adjective: a slave-girl sings as she dances, 'A little more, my macky massa!' and in another reference to women dancing, they 'Twist, wind and wriggle with the mackey beaux'. Today it survives, apparently, disguised in the term of address *bucky massa* (which see below).

A number of words mean 'fool' in various keys. A *brinjah* is a comical person; to *banja* is to play the fool. *Fool* can be an adjective meaning foolish: 'Cho, man! You too fool!' — or as the abstract noun, foolishness: 'De whol a de nex week Wasp wid him fool fly up an dung.' *Fool-fool*, or *foo-fool* have the same two uses. 'Wich one a we more foo-fooler?' A credulous kind of fool is a *precky* (/preke/), which is no doubt connected with other senses of this word discussed later — a wonderful happening, cause for admiration — by way of the fool's gaping wonder, or his being foolishly impressed.

An unintelligent person, idiot, may be a *bobo* (discussed above); a *mumu* is a stupid, clownish, backward person; both words appear to be from Africa.[27] *Buffuto* is 'big and worthless' or clumsy and stupid. In Louise Bennett's lines:

> Dem dah halla an dah sing, an
> Dah got big pleasuration
> Becausen Clem buffooto daughter
> Pass examination!

This has the appearance of a tribal name; perhaps it is to be identified with *Mafutu* (as in *Mafutu wiss*). Other words reported for a foolish person are *busquine*, *jegge*, and *hanya-huo*; also, by simple metaphor, a *coco-head*. The old word *gawky*, which OED defines as 'an awkward, foolish person; a lout, a simpleton' —

chiefly a Scots and north-country word — is still to be heard in Jamaica for an idiot.

Finally, the names for some miscellaneous types of people. A *follow-line* is a stranger who has come into one's district along the railway track — and is clearly unwelcome! An *allibutton* is a person who works for nothing: to *mek allibutton* is to work and not be paid. The word is condemnatory; one is a fool to do this and spoils the trade for others. This word has been reported chiefly from the central part of the island; perhaps it is to be traced to a local person named Halliburton — one who worked for nothing, or possibly an estate owner who did not pay after people had worked for him. A *property pony* is a person who does everything for everybody — like a pony belonging to a 'property' or estate, which anyone may load with work.

For people who have gone up in the world there are two amusing expressions, both implying the disapproval of those left behind. *Since-when* comes out of such a question as, 'Since when they get so fussy?' It may be used as a name for the person, or merely as an exclamation when the person appears. The other is *hurry-come-up*. In the words of Claude McKay:

> Tack was in peasant parlance, a hurry-come-up. That was the native word for *nouveau riche*, only more inclusive, as it meant not merely a have-nothing who had risen to be a have-something, but also one of bad reputation.

A person who attends weddings frequently is a *wedd'n-bessy*.[28] A *kitchen-key* is a man who loves the kitchen. A *mama* or *mama-man* is one who does women's work, is woman-like or mean, worthless as a man. The word said to be the highest possible insult among the Jamaican folk is /mampáalo/, which may be spelt *mampalo*. It means a man who is unmanly, abusive to women; also one who indulges abnormal sexual relations of any kind. (Cf. Colombian *mampolón*, a cock without fighting spirit.)

Mental and Emotional Actions

Not only physical actions, but mental and emotional relationships between people have produced a number of verbs and abstract nouns. For example, to please very much would be to *sweet*, which has been current for well over a century and a half; from 1790 we find, in a song, 'You sweet me, mackey massa!'[29]

Much later it appeared in *Blackwell's Magazine,* in a letter from Jamaica, 'You will hear of something that will sweet you greatly.' Today it would be heard mostly among the folk, as in the Anancy story, when Brother Jackass is laughing, and Anancy asks, 'What sweet yuh Bredda Jackass?'

However, to *sweet-up* is to be pleasant to, or play up to someone: 'Go sweet-up Joe, an' treat him nice,' and to *rub* or *scrub dry yaws* carries the purpose a step farther — to curry favour, ingratiate oneself; it apparently refers to the soothing effect of rubbing 'where it itches'. A similar idea is found in the phrase, to *baba-lad* — to 'soft soap' or humour a person — since the phrase suggests calling him by a pet name (*baba* means brother).

Exactly the opposite feeling is found in such a threatening phrase as to *make (one) know*: 'I will mek you know!' It would seem to be the abbreviation of something like 'I'll make you know what trouble is', or 'I'll show you what's what'; McKay glosses it himself as, 'give you beans'! On the same order is to *raise a kite*, to 'grumble, complain'.

To *mash* someone's *sore toe* means to cause him pain or embarrassment:

> Beggin you pardon Jane,
> Me gwine mash oonoo sore-toe,
> But me haffe talk out plain.

Mine (mind), used with an affirmative verb, is equivalent to 'be careful' used with a negative verb — in other words, 'be careful lest'. Thus, 'Mine you mek police arres' me' means 'be careful that you don't make police arrest me'.

To *wrap up* is to associate with equals, and to *neutral-up* is to equalise:

> Ef you kean do Good, no do no Bad,
> Try neutral-up yuh deal.

To *keep malice* is to refuse to get on with others, or to bear a grudge:

> Ef you heel dem dah kip malice, . . .
> dem we haffe curb dem tempa.

Quite a number of verbs mean to annoy or hurt in different

N

degrees: *sheg, fatigue, udge, mell, rax, hige, hackle.* The first is considered rather slangy; it may be a new creation or a preservation of *shag*, 'to toss about, to shake'. *Fatigue* and *udge* (from *urge*) mean, in the folk speech, to provoke or tease — thus they are extensions of meaning. *Mell* is to interfere or meddle — indeed, it is from the latter word, a Scots or North-country form, as *rax* is too, meaning to abuse, as in 'You rax de chile!' *Hige* and *hackle* apparently involve the added element of annoyance by spirits. *Hige* is an older pronunciation of *hag* (compare *bige*, for *bag*), which OED records as a verb 'now dialectal'; and *hackle* is found in Moore's account of an 'African' cult's method of curing 'a sick' with goat's blood and rum: 'Meantime, the drums knock you and hackle you, and probably by daylight, you come back a strong man.'

To *shooks* is to deceive or disappoint, and thus to hurt another's feelings: one person waiting for another who did not come as he had promised, might say, 'Him shooks me.' To *sherrif* is to renege, but the origin of this word is a blank. When people break off relations and one ceases to speak to the other, it may be expressed as Anancy puts it: 'Ah did sorry fe true when Brer Tiger did tek way him speech from me.'

There are several related expressions meaning to think hard or deeply, to devise a plan or scheme: to *work, study,* or *consider* one's *head*: 'Same time Anancy start work him head pon Jackass, for him did bex bout how Jackass laugh after him.' 'She tudy her head an sey she gwine fe lock up Dora.' 'Him consider him head long time fe fine a way fe ketch him.'

The usual Jamaican meaning of *throw words* is, to use bad language, as in Bennett's lines:

> Takooma sey dat Nancy wasa
> T'row wud an dah cuss.

Two curious phrases that describe similar actions are to *throw sarcasm*, and to *throw words at the moon*. The first is a kind of vituperation by proxy, in which a person relieves himself verbally of a sense of injury. The second is described as 'the practice still in vogue in Jamaica' (in 1934) whereby 'You may tell the moon the most insulting things about a party within his hearing without being liable for libel, as you would be if you addressed the same words to your victim or to another person. Thus you in turn may be called "a tief" or "a liar fee true", every word reaching you and those who are standing about, and yet if you ask the vilifier what he is saying, the answer will be: "Not you, sah, Him moon talk." '30

Several verbs may be noticed here because they have been formed by conversion from nouns. Thus *choice* (choose), *business* (have business with), *custom* (be accustomed to), *advantage* (take advantage of), and *neighbour* (be the next thing to, be very much like): 'But you choice your way' — choose, have chosen; 'Ah gwine ch'ice De one in de bes' position'; 'Ah doan custam fe talk bad wud It dis fly outa me mout'; 'Don' mek 'im advantage you!' 'We naybor pig' — we are much like the pig. Another word meaning resemble is 'favour', found in many other places than Jamaica. It becomes a Jamaicanism, however, in the phrase *favour say*, meaning 'it looks as if, it seems as though'.

After resemblance comes imitation, for which idea there are several Jamaicanisms. One may 'copy' or 'pattern' somebody else. A slavish imitator is said to be 'too follow-fashion', (adjective), and there is the proverb 'Follow-fashion mek monkey cut 'im tail' (noun). But most characteristic is the verb *form*, which carries the suggestion of pretending: 'Ah don't mean ah really gwine dead, ah only gwine form dead.' Uncle Newton recounts the effect of his first attempt to speak educated English to villagers: 'One day I tried to use the new "High English" at Burrell Run. Sam started the crew laughing by asking: "A [is] what Newsy a form?" So I had to use one language at school and another at Burrell Run.'

Some nouns that show conditions or relationships between people are the expressions for gossip or mischievous talk. *Lie-an'-story* is an obvious one; *labrish* less so:

> Me 'ave a lot a labrish fe tell yuh —
> Gimme Dela, all De labrish from yuh yard.

The origin of this word is a puzzle. The -*ish* is English enough, but it is harder to tell whence *labr-* can come. My guess is that this word is from the base of *laba-laba* (already discussed) with English suffixes -*er* and -*ish*. As an adjective *labrish* would then basically mean wordy, talkative, even gossiping, from which the actual meaning of the noun would normally follow.

Seh-sa has been reported as meaning 'mischievous chat,

quarrel', but it recalls another word, *su-su*, to whisper. All these words meet in the following lines of Louise Bennett's:

> Dem su-su and dem sey-sey, an
> Dem labrish an disgrace.

Seh-sa, or *sey-sey*, look to be no more than reduplications of English *say*, but behind the iterated particle more probably lies an African word: Twi has *sè*, to say, tell; mention, speak of, etc.; and its reduplicated form is *sise* (two syllables). *Su-su* itself may be iterated as *su-su-su-su*. Tale-bearing is expressed too in the eloquent phrase *carry-go-bring-come*, in which English words run to African syntax.

Yet another African word is certainly *cong-con-se*, or *congo-se*, flattery — compare Twi *ŋkoŋkonsá*, falsehood, duplicity, double-dealing. The Jamaican word is sometimes spelled *come-come-say*, which shows the naturalisation of folk etymology. *Conga-so*, meaning tricky, may be influenced by this (though it is possible to analyse it otherwise).

Nyaams means nonsense, as in /yu taakin nyaams/. It is also used about people: 'He's a nyaams' — a worthless, weak sort.[31] Nonsense in the sense of irrelevance is expressed effectively by *caca-nabu*. A series of seemingly variant forms perhaps related to this — *caranapu*, *cararapum*, *cononapu* and *canana* (with heavy accent on the last syllable) — mean 'nothing at all, no answer, silence' in such a sentence as, 'I speak to him but he don't even say caranapu!' None of these words has been traced to its source; no doubt sound-symbolism enters into their composition.

Expressions for a quandary, predicament, trouble in general are *dog corn-piece* and *precke* (or *pricke*). To be caught trespassing in a corn-field means trouble; but if the field is owned by a dog, one is really in a predicament. Many an instance of praedial larceny must lie behind this expression! The other word, /preke/, may possibly be connected with *predicament* itself, but there is no firm evidence. It also means 'an amazing occurrence', as in Bennett's lines:

> Wat a precky wen dem fine out
> Is me sidung front dem yah.

Another word for trouble, upset, distress is *pooroo*, reported several times, but no source is known.[32] *Chakum-peckle* is said to mean confusion.[33] Jekyll reported *frettenation* but was uncertain whether the suffix was added to *frighten* or to *fretting*. He preferred the first; I prefer the second, since *fretting* would normally become /fretn/ in the folk speech, and they would never confuse this with /fraitn/. The meaning of *frettenation* is worry, emotional upset. On the other hand, Louise Bennett bears witness to words with both these bases, the first meaning *fright*, the second *fret*:

> De 'ole Districk got frightration
> On dis ceremonial day.

and,
> Me never se car run so fas'
> Or so much street so broad,
> Me life eena fretration
> Wen me cross a Boulevard.

Ugly, as a noun meaning *evil*, is either converted from the adjective or abbreviated from *ugliness*: ' "Massa," said one of them [Maroons], . . . "Gar A'mighty no love ugly (that is wickedness) and if we do something for curse us, he will punish us." '[34] One finds, too, the curious phrase *do-fe-do* (do for do) — literally, tit for tat. Quite often it implies the same threat, but it may also mean do-as-you-would-be-done-by, or the return of a favour. There is an ambiguous proverb, 'Do-fe-do mek nayger come a Jamaica,' of which several variants have sprung up, substituting other things — mongoose, guinea grass, etc. — for *nayger*.

Finally, there are words which probably aim at extra expressiveness by their unorthodox addition of suffixes: *pleasuration*, *pleasureness*, and *sympathisement* — and no doubt others which did not chance to come our way.

Chapter Nine

DOMESTIC AND SOCIAL LIFE I

Foods and Cookery

JAMAICA is justly known for its cookery. The foods of all kinds and methods of preparation have produced a varied vocabulary, exotic, jocular, or imaginatively descriptive. Some words — the names of meals, and of foods in general — still echo the old plantation customs, in the country parts especially. Among the peasants the first food of the day is called *tea*, though it seldom includes that luxury. As McKay has written, *tea* is the 'generic name for any non-alcoholic hot drink', and so it has been since at least 1740: 'They make several *Infusions* or *Teas* (as they call them) in Fevers without Mixtures.'[1] Besides medicinal decoctions *tea* includes coffee or cocoa (which I have heard called *coffee tea* and *cocoa tea*), fish broth (*fish tea*), and often simply hot *sugar-and-water* with lime leaves (*sugar tea*).

Taken first thing in the morning, *tea* is a meal: 'You tek you tea yet?' In many places this first meal may be called /chakláta/, but some make a distinction: *tea* is at half past six, *chaklata* at half past seven or eight. The latter usually includes a little boiled food, perhaps some from the day before, bread or bammy. Russell described it as 'a light meal before work or school' and thought it 'African', but it is clearly a reminiscence of the Spanish *chocolate*.[2] Uncle Newton writes: 'Then we had our early morning breakfast ("choclata" to be correct), each of us boys getting a whole tin of "whatever you want".' Morning *tea* is also jocularly called *wash-mout'*.

Traditionally, *breakfast* came at eleven o'clock or somewhat after, and this usage continues in many country parts among the peasants. But customs are changing; as one man said, 'breakfast is the better-off people's name for the early meal; for the poorer people it is the 12 o'clock meal.' From Uncle Newton again, 'And come back here before breakfast time (the Chapelton way of saying "lunch-time").'

A hundred and fifty years ago the meal taken at midday was called *second breakfast*, but this term has disappeared. Lady Nugent noted in her diary (1802): 'Had fruit for the children at 10; then second breakfast a little after 11. — Dined at 3.' And Stewart (1808):

> The ladies here . . . sit down to breakfast about nine, or past it, have what they call second breakfast at twelve, dine at three or four, and drink tea at eight; but seldom eat much, if any supper. . . .
> The meal called second breakfast is the most favourite of all their meals. . . . This meal has something peculiar in it. It must consist of certain favourite viands. . . . This must be eaten with the assistance of the fingers alone; for knives and forks are on this occasion proscribed! In short, so fond are the ladies in general of this second breakfast, that they would . . . relinquish all the other three, rather than part with this one.

In the country today *dinner* may be from three o'clock to five or six — usually from 'four to five o'clock, when people come from grung' (the fields) and it is the 'biggest meal'.[3]

A light, quick meal eaten between times may be a *cotch-up* (/káchop/) — that is, one that supports you temporarily; or it may be a *rash*, *rashy*, or *rashin*. Russell thought this 'African', but it is simply the word *ration* variously reduced. It may apply also to a regular, full meal, and is then equivalent to *victuals*, which usually takes the form /bikl/ or /bitl/, though this word is now considered old-fashioned or countrified. A curious word is /watlef/, which Uncle Newton describes as 'food put aside for *bambi* (by and by) i.e., later in the day'. And elsewhere, 'After we had eaten our "what-left" and a bit of potato pudding. . . .'

An African word for food is still to be heard: /ninyam/ — evidently the reduplicated form of /nyam/, to eat greedily. Related words appear in most of the Niger-Congo languages, usually meaning meat; but one may also note such a form as Twi *ànyinam*, a species of yam. The first record I have found is from 1912 (McKay): 'buccra . . . Hab 'nuff nenyam fe waste;' and more recently in Bennett:

> Dem dah married de ninyam!
> Yuh kean get onion widout yuh buy
> Tomatis now me child!

The English word 'bread-kind' has been in use since the seventeenth century, and in Jamaica since at least 1756: 'The root [of Coco] is more valuable, and supply many of the poorer Sort of people with what they call *Bread-kind*, in those parts of the world.' To McKay it was the 'general name for the staple vegetables and fruits' — all of the starchy kind. But if this word is not specifically Jamaican it has produced others by analogy: *meat-kind* (beef, pork, mutton, etc.) and *fish-kind* (herring, mackerel, 'salting'). Bennett also writes *food-kind*, which may be a general term, or perhaps an alternative to bread-kind:

> Me teck har een, buy some food kine,
> An' load wan baskit well.

Probably synonymous also is *ground-fruit*, recorded from only one source (1788): 'They . . . raise more ground-fruit, bread-fruit and vegetables.'⁴ Here *bread-fruit* must mean bread-kind, for the breadfruit tree was not introduced to Jamaica till four years later.

A word with special Jamaican meanings is *salt*, reduced to /saal/. In slave days it was required that each slave be given at stated times an 'allowance' of salt meat or fish. In one account from 1825 we find:

> At Christmas . . . they have an extra allowance of salt cod-fish, which they use in like manner; it generally goes with them under the name of salt, and they take a small portion of it at most of their meals, and put it in the pot to boil with the vegetables.⁵

And again in 1837, 'Massa give we no salt allowance, and no allowance at Christmas.' The list of slaves, with the number of herrings given out to each was called the *herring roll*.⁶

From this has come the general word /saalting/ (salt-things), which today covers 'salt fish, pickled herring, mackerel, shad, corn pork', etc. When a person was well stocked with these provisions he was said to be 'in his salt', which expression has become extended: as McKay explains, 'So de young man was in dem sall' — 'So the young men had a fine time of it,' and 'in mi saal: having a good time'. At least one present-day nickname for a herring comes from this too: *long-saal*, because it is 'tall and straight'. Probably a personification of a Spanish word for mullet is behind the nickname *Liza*;⁷ and another personifying name is *one-eye Cuffee*.

The most famous soup is *pepperpot*, a name used elsewhere, but apparently having entered the language in Jamaica. The earliest OED citation is dated a1704, but there is in 1698 an account by one who found it too hot for his taste:

> They make a rare *Soop* they call *Pepper-pot*; it is an excellent Breakfast for a *Salamander*, or a good preparative for a *Mountebanks Agent*, who Eats Fire one day, that he may get better Victuals the next.[8]

When made in the traditional way the basis of pepperpot was the pot-liquor in which cassava roots had been boiled to free them of their poison, known to the Carib Indians as *casiripo* — what Gardner called *casareep*. This word, though never widely used in Jamaica, is still known in Montego Bay.

Another exotic soup — this time Spanish — is *sancocho*, a 'soup of meat, yuca [cassava], plantain and other ingredients. It is the "olla podrida" of these countries [Ecuador and Puerto Rico]'.[9] It has been reported in the form *sangkochie* 'to feast surreptitiously at night after a funeral', but this seems a far too limited 'definition'. *Macooche* has also been reported as meaning 'soup' — it is probably another altered form of *sancocho*.

Thin soup is sometimes derisively *chew-water*; pot liquor is *potwater*. As one man put it, if you 'cook banana and lean pork, drink de pot-water, you "trong like a cow".'

Porridge or gruel of various kinds have been much used, from the loblolly of sailors, which became among the slaves *loblob* or *lobby-lobby*, to others brought from Africa. Loblolly was a pap made of maize, as Ligon saw it in Barbados: 'This we call Loblollie. But the Negroes, when they come to be fed with this, are much discontented, and cry out, *O! O! no more Lob-lob.*' It must have been much the same in Jamaica. Today a pap made of grated green corn, cooked with a little water and with milk added, is jocularly called *wash-pap*. *Loblob* and *lobby-lobby* became the symbol of softness and remain today in the names of softwood trees.

From Africa came 'couscous' — ultimately an Arabic word — which Russell described as 'Gruel of any kind whatsoever', but today it seems to refer to something less liquid. To make it you 'parch, beat, and sieve corn, put in a pot with hot water, turn [stir] till it comes hard, put in a pan and smooth it. Slice like pone, and eat with pear, saltfish, or mackerel'. In short, it is essentially the same as *turned cornmeal*, except that the latter usually has coconut milk added. A familiarised name for this is *tun-tun*, since it requires much stirring.

Also from Africa is *fungee* (/fonjii/), a porridge which may be made of corn meal, cassava, or green-banana flour. The word has been in Jamaica since at least 1790: Moreton refers to one use, 'for the pains in their stomachs, to eat plenty of homony and fungee;' and into a poem he puts a slave who, deserted by his wife, exclaims anapestically, 'My fungee, alas! is unboil'd. . . .' Russell and Beckwith have also mentioned it, and Turner connects it with 'Kimbundu (Angola) *funzi*, cassava mush'. Russell also recorded 'Qua-qua — Cassava in the form of a thick paste. African', which is no doubt the same as Sullivan's 'Quaco' — cassava flour. This looks very much like an extended use of the day-name, familiarising the dish and implying that it is favoured by the humbler people.

Similar too are *green-plantain porridge* and /kòngkònté/ or /kònggoté/ — the latter from Twi '*kokònté*, pl. *ŋkoŋkònté*, cassada or plantains cut in pieces and dried; a kind of food prepared of it, looking like country soap'.[10] The pieces of banana or plantain are dried, pounded, sifted to a flour, and made into porridge or dumplings.

Not a porridge but a kind of paste or sticky dough is made from these and similar ingredients under the names *fufu* or (less commonly) *tumtum*. The earliest dictionary citation of this is from 1851 — yet it was used in Jamaica over a hundred years before (1739): 'Boil it with beat Maiz or *Indian* Corn, (which they call Fu Fu).'[11] Barclay wrote too (1826), 'a negro . . . would greatly prefer his own good substantial dish of foo-foo, composed of eddoes, ochras, and mashed plantains, made savoury with rich crabs, and pungent with Cayenne pepper.' The word is African, of course: in Twi, *fufuú* is the same food, yam, plantains, cassada, etc., cut, boiled, and pounded to a 'tough, doughy mass'. The word refers to the whiteness of the substance once prepared: *fu* means white, and *e-fúfu*, any white thing.[12] In Jamaica, as in Africa, it is served in soft lumps and eaten with soup, but is not made as often now as formerly. The softness had at least one advantage, to which Louise Bennett alludes in her *Food Alphabet*:

F is fe fufu, when yuh lose you teeth.

Tumtum is an onomatopoetic name for the same food: in Twi *tumtum* is 'imitative of the sound of pounding "fufuu" in a wooden mortar' — which Banbury called a *tumtum mortar*. The earliest record of the word appears in Jamaica (1790): 'Plantain,' wrote Beckford, is 'beaten up into a kind of paste, which the white people, as well as the negroes, are accustomed to eat with pepper pot, under the vulgar name of tum-tum'. This word was never as common as *fufu* and is hardly used today.

An older name for essentially the same dish was *buff-jacket*. Sloane wrote in 1725: 'Plantains . . . are likewise boil'd in the Skins, peel'd and beat to a Paste, form'd like a Dumplin, and call'd, *Buff-Jacket*.' But this was probably an Englishman's name applied to the colonial dish.

Favourites among Jamaican folk foods are dumplings and their like, and most famous the *duckunoo* (pronounced /dúkunu/ or /dókunu/), another African delicacy: compare Twi ɔ-dɔ́kóno, boiled maize bread. This has been frequently referred to; first in 1740: 'The fruit [of the Plantain] . . . when boil'd in its Leaves it is called Duckano (*i.e.* Pudding or Dumpling).' 'Duckonoo — Corn boiled in balls, and then toasted.' 'Cornmeal Duckoonoo. . . . A cupful of cornmeal boiled thick with some butter . . . sugar . . . flour and a little spice. Let it cool. Then roll up in bits of plantain leaf and bake.' The dokunu may be made with green banana, sweet potato, yellow yam, coco — but it is always wrapped in plantain or banana leaf, which fact is responsible for two other names: *tie-a-leaf* or *tie-leaf*, and *blue-drawers* (pronounced /bluu-draaz/), from the bluish-green cast of the leaf. Nowadays the dokunu is more often boiled than baked and has become more like a pudding than a dumpling. The last name is /bóya/, probably from Spanish, and less common than the others.[13]

More truly a dumpling is the Jamaican version of *johnny-cake*, which, among the folk, is of cornmeal (or plantain flour) mixed with water and salt and rolled into a lump or ball; it is usually boiled, sometimes fried. Only in this special sense is the word Jamaican; in the United States johnnycake is flat corn-bread (maize). Something closer to this sense — presumably more sophisticated — is found in Jamaican cook-books: 'Flour . . . soda . . . lard . . . butter . . . mix into a dough . . . roll about ½ an inch thick, cut in rounds with a small tumbler . . . bake on the gridiron. Open, butter, cover again and serve.' Or it may be made with crushed cocos in the same form. This is very much like a *bammy*, to which we shall come shortly.

Small dumplings, rolled in the hands, are /spinaz/ — evidently *spinners*; *munjay* has been reported for a large dumpling.[14]

The *bammy* is a flat cake of cassava flour or meal, made by the country folk; it is usually round because formed in a griddle or pot (*pot bammy*) and may be from ½ to 1½ inches thick. Beckwith describes it well.[15] Though the first record of the word found is from 1893, it surely came in very much earlier, for this was the native bread of the Arawak Indians from whom the first African slaves learned how to make it. The word itself is probably indigenous: Friederici lists a dozen variant forms — among them Tupí *mbeiyú*, Guaraní *mbeyu*, and Mainland Carib *meiú* — for 'a kind of cake made of manioc'.[16] Gardner mentioned *carribi* as 'cakes made from cassava' but gave no source; the word has not been found elsewhere. Of the same substance, but very thin, are *cassava lace-cakes* — the commercial name. In St Elizabeth these are called *bammy chips*, but are 'not made by Quashie'.

A kind of fritter was formerly favoured under the name *ackra cakes*. These are of black-eye peas, husked, pounded, seasoned, and fried in hot fat. The word is African: compare Yoruba *akara*, 'a cake' or 'a dish consisting of beans, palm oil, pepper, and onions'. But much better known among fritters is the *stamp-and-go*, which Sullivan described in 1893 as 'rough cakes made with corn meal and flour, . . . salt-fish and a little butter and lard . . . fresh pepper is freely used. . . . The country people as they travel stop at the way-side shops and buy these with a slice of bread for a trifle. Hence the name'. This explanation is generally accepted, and seems appropriate enough until one discovers that there was an English seamen's phrase of precisely the same form, which meant 'An order given to sailors for the performance of certain duties . . . to step out at the capstan, or with hawsers, topsail-halyards, &c., generally to the fife or fiddle'.[17] As early as 1833 we find *stamp-and-go* used (in *Tom Cringle's Log*) as the name for a boat. In short, it must have struck people's fancy and have spread beyond the limited meaning. Like many other nautical word or phrase, this was brought ashore in Jamaica and put to a new use.

These codfish fritters, cheap and easy to make, have been accorded a number of jocular names: *poor-man's fritters*, *macadam* (they are flat and tough as pavement), and *john stagger-back* (from one's action upon biting them — a name also applied to certain hard sweets), and *bragadap*, which apparently means 'tough' (it is applied to other things: rope used to hold the oars of fishing boats; renta yam, etc.). The source has not been found. One more name for these fritters, possibly African, is *flaa-flaa*, which appears to emphasize their flatness.

Salt cod has been widely used in this island — one grade, exported from New England under the name of *Jamaica fish* (DAE), was a staple 'salting' for the slaves. When *salt-fish* is spoken of it generally means cod — so in the dish *saltfish and ackee*, for example. An occasional name for saltfish is /bákalo/, from Spanish or Portuguese. OED enters this as *bacalao*; the last citation is 1765, but it is still to be heard in Jamaica. Saltfish fried in flour paste is said to be called /àchibóng/ or /àchibómbo/, but no clear source for it has been found.[18]

There is also a baked dish made of alternate layers of sliced potato and saltfish (or minced meat), called *twice-laid*. Like *stamp-and-go* this is a sailors' expression brought ashore. 'Twice-laid rope' was that made from the yarns of old rope; this was transferred to 'a sea dish made of the salt-fish left from yesterday's dinner, and beaten up with potatoes or yams'.[19] In other words, the fish had been twice laid on the table! The term, obsolete at sea, survives in Jamaica (though this is not a folk dish).

In 1774 Long mentioned *bra-bra* as 'some dish made by the negroes' and *dab-a-dab* as 'an olio of maize, herrings, pepper'. The second does not seem to survive, unless possibly connected with *bragadap*; but *bra-bra* today means 'a dish made up from bits and pieces'.

The Spanish *escabeche*, a pickle for fish, came into West Indian English first as *caveach* (OED), but its present Jamaican form is *scaveeched fish*, usually pronounced /skovíich/. King-fish (or some other) is fried and served cold with pepper, salt, onion, vinegar, and seasoning. Salmagundi is still called *Solomon Gundy* (or simply *Gundy*) in this island — a survival from the eighteenth century. Finally, the Spanish *tamale* is very different here; it is a dish of crabs (pronounced /tumáali/). OED makes this *tomalley*.

One of the earliest West Indian delicacies to be adopted was the sea-turtle, and two parts especially were favoured: 'The Belly is call'd *Callipee* and the Back *Callipach*.' Neither word seems to have been specifically Jamaican, though both were well known in this island, and in one book the creature itself, as well as its flesh, is given the name: 'Turrapine, or Land-Turtles, Callipe, or Sea-Turtles; this last is a great Dish baked with forc'd-meat Balls, and some say it tastes of all sorts of Flesh.'[20]

Another Spanish word of Indian origin, first recorded in its English form in Jamaica, is *jerk*, to prepare pork in the manner of the Quichua Indians. As Sloane wrote in 1707:

> Swine ... running wild in the Country ... are shot or pierced through with lances, cut open, the Bones taken out, and the Flesh is gash'd on the inside into the Skin, fill'd with Salt and expos'd to the Sun, which is call'd Jirking. It is so brought home to their Masters by the Hunters, and eats much as Bacon, if broil'd on Coals. These Hunters are either Blacks or Whites, ... The *Indians* are very exquisite at this Game.

The word is treated here as a participle, though it is probably a rationalised form of *jerkin*, which had been used much earlier. The verb *jerk*, really a back-formation from *jerking*, was later converted to the noun *jerk*. The original 'maroons', before this term got its specifically Jamaican sense, were hog-hunters; the Jamaican Maroons have continued the industry. Lady Nugent alluded to '*jerked* hog, which is the way of dressing it by the Maroons' and so did Dallas. Today one may buy *jerk pork* in the Port Antonio market prepared by the Maroons of Moore Town.

A dish of the past with a jocular name is described by Long as follows:

> The Negroe cooks, who are to dress what is called here a *surprised fowl*, or one which is required to be roasted or boiled with great expedition immediately after it is killed and pluck- ed, pour limejuice down the throat, and at the vent, to make the flesh tender and eatable.

Two other humourous names date from slave days, when snake and rat meat were often eaten. The yellow snake was euphemistically *plantation eel*, and the rat *cane rabbit*. Williams has described another dish, *cowskin*: ' "Cowskin". ... cow or ox hide (the hair of which is first singed off) boiled to a jelly, with yams, cocos, ochro, and other vegetables; a famous mess, of which the little negroes made a most hearty meal.' Tripes are usually called /instral/ (entrails), but were once *cow law-book* — an obvious allusion to the 'leaves' or 'many-plies' of the third stomach of the ruminant. A rich stew now greatly favoured is *curry goat* (i.e., curried), introduced by East Indians; another of their stews is said to be called /mazála/.

Other East Indian dishes that have become somewhat known outside their communities are: /daal an baat/ from Hindustani *dāl* and *bhāt* meaning split peas and boiled rice; *kie-baat*, 'a feed of rice', obviously related; *katarri*, an 'Indian delicacy' of Irish potato or rice and 'other else things' — no doubt from Hindustani *kuthārī*, an earthen vase (in which it is cooked); *tankari*, an 'Indian festival' or a 'dish with calalu, curry' (note the latter two syllables of the word) and other ingredients; *baji*, a vegetable dish, from *bhājī*, greens. None of these is widespread, however.

A few vegetable foods deserve mention. *Rice-and-peas* (that is, beans), a favourite dish, is nicknamed *Jamaica coat-of-arms*. *Plantain chips* and *banana chips* are thin slices of these fruits fried in boiling fat. *Leggins* is a bunch of seasoning (or *season*, as the folk call it) for soup: thyme, skellion, a slice of pumpkin, etc. — sold in every market, and the word very likely from French *légumes*. Lunan, quoting from Long, described a dish of corn: 'The ears are often gathered before they are thoroughly ripe; and, being roasted, form a dish known here by the name of *mutton*.'[21]

Sauces and condiments have always formed a part of the tropical diet. The first, *pimentade*, was made with capsicum or Cayenne pepper, 'Juice of Lemons, and Manioc'. Salt ground with it 'makes the universal Indian Sauce, call'd by some *Cayen-butter*'.[22] Browne identified the pepper as the common *bird pepper* of today; his spelling is *Cayan* butter, and Barham's was *Kyan* butter, which represent the earlier pronunciation of Cayenne, still preserved in folk use: /káian/.

Browne described another,

called *Mandram*, . . . which seldom fails to provoke an appetite in the most languid stomachs. The ingredients are sliced cucumbers, eschalots or onions cut very small, a little lime-juice, and *Madeira* wine, with a few pods of bird or other pepper well mashed and mixed in the liquor.

Later came *poor man's sauce* ('sliced ripe peppers, . . . shallots . . . mustard seed . . . pork or herring pickle . . . boiled twice over'), and *Jamaica hot sauce* ('boil and dice chocho; add vinegar, mustard, curry, sugar, pepper, salt, pimento; bottle it').

The common folk have a number of sauces of their own bearing imaginative, descriptive names. *Dip-and-come-back* or *dip-and-fall-back* is put in a bowl in the middle of the table, and everybody dips into it. It is a highly seasoned concoction of coconut milk and salted fish (shad or herring) boiled down slowly till it becomes quite thick. With it are eaten the bland, starchy foods — yam, coco, breadfruit — to which it gives more flavour. Other names for it are *round-the-road*, because it must be stirred constantly to prevent the oil from separating, and *stop-it-a-pass* or /tápiapáas/ — that is, prevent it from passing to an oily condition. If this sauce is boiled down to a still thicker consistency it becomes *run-down* or *johnny run-down*. Add 'a drop of flour' to *round-the-road* and one has *flum-bub* — a name reminiscent of English *flummery*. Gravy made of half boiled coconut oil is *dippidence* and an old-time name for flour sauce is *lung-plung*, a word of unknown antecedents.

Puddings include *ricey-coco*: rice boiled in coconut cream with spice and sugar. Sullivan wrote, 'The people often eat this for their breakfast,' that is, it may be treated as porridge. Another porridge-like pudding is /músa/, occasionally /múse/, made of cassava or banana flour boiled in coconut milk and sometimes sweetened. The earliest reference to it is Russell's: 'Muse — Cassava in form of a thick paste. African.'[23] This -*e* form would appear to be older.

Jamaica has both *corn pone* and *potato pone*, as in the United States; *sweet-potato pone* is still heard here, though obsolete there. The Spanish *guisada*, something stewed, refers to a considerably different thing here: a tart of grated coconut, brown sugar, and nutmeg. Sullivan spells it *gisada* and it is pronounced /gizáada/. One word for flavourings that still has some currency is *essence*, or /ɛsint/, as it is frequently pronounced.

Of fruit desserts perhaps the best known is *matrimony*, a combination of star-apple and orange spiced and sweetened. Sullivan has called this 'strawberries and cream', but I have found it nowhere else. A mixture of orange and coconut is called, in the same book, *angel's food* — which is very different from other foods so called. *Banana figs* are whole raw dried bananas, having much the consistency of figs. Though unrecorded, the term was probably used two hundred or more years ago. In 1725 Sloane wrote: 'The fruit [plantains] cut long ways and dried in the Sun is thought to be as good as Figs so dried.'

A green coconut in which the meat has barely begun to form is a *water-coconut*, and is full of *coconut water*; this is found in the ODS from 1834, but Williamson mentioned it in 1817. Though this is a clear, colourless liquid, most English and American writers call it *coconut milk*. In Jamaica *coconut milk* is the white liquid squeezed out of the grated meat of the ripe or 'hard' coconut; thickened it becomes *coconut cream*, and both are extensively used in native cookery. A *jelly-coconut* is one in which the nut-meat is partly formed but not yet hard — that is, it is *coconut jelly* and is eaten as fresh fruit.

Introduced from Africa and known under several names is a mixture of parched dry corn beaten fine in a mortar and usually mixed with sugar. The name closest to the African is *asham* or *hasham*: Twi *o-siăm* means parched and ground corn. Probably based on this (by reduplication) is *sham-sham*. And third, *Brown George*, the English name for a kind of coarse bread, has been transferred to this dish — appropriately enough, since the native sugar is brown. If to parched, ground corn you 'add hot water and beat it till it come tight in a mortar', the result is *tight-fit*. Guinea corn parched, heated with sugar, coloured, and rolled into balls is *coction* (cook-sham?) — a good deal like American 'popcorn balls'.

Reminiscent of the days when flour and meal were prepared by hand are the jocular names for manufactured flour: *peel-a'ready* (it had no husk) and *'trip-me-naked*. The latter also meant biscuits, cake, or food made of flour. *Pop-off* is flour, or flour and water mixed to make johnny-cake. In 1893 wheat flour was still being called *English flour*, as distinct from that prepared locally in Jamaica from other ingredients.

An old name for manioc, *yuca*, lasts still for cassava bread, or the 'sweet cassada boiled to eat.' Beneath /mempau/, bread, from Hakka Chinese, lies the Portuguese *pão*. Fancy breads include *crown bread* — from the shape, and *show bread* — probably transferred from church usage (shewbread). 'Baking powder helps to *float* things,' as one cook told me — that is, it makes them rise.

o

A very hard biscuit or flat bread is known as /gáta/ or /gráta/
— which suggests French *gateau*. Uncle Newton mentions *jackass
biscuit* or Jackass corn as 'a famous hard biscuit. . . . Like the
jackass it was faithful, long-serving and tough'. Heavy flour
cakes, baked or fried, are *plunkas* — evidently 'plunkers'.

But the two best known native cakes are the *bulla* and the *toto*,
both more or less round and flat. The first is lyrically described
by Uncle Newton:

> A bulla was a cake made by humble people from the
> cheapest grade of flour called 'cake flour' with a worthwhile
> addition of locally made 'wet' sugar (molasses) and a pinch of
> 'drinking soda'. Of a circumference of five inches, a thickness
> of threequarter inch, a colour near to dark brown and a taste
> bordering on that of the famed 'nectar and ambrosia', it was
> something that had an instant and constant appeal to small
> boys, big girls, poor women and hungry men.

Slightly better than the *bulla* are the *butter-dough* and *Michael*;
the *Joe Louis* or *Uncle Joe* is much larger — made of 'one pound
of sugar, one pound of flour'. It is a recent, admiring name. The
wheeler gets its name from its circular shape. The *toto* differs
chiefly in containing grated coconut; it is somewhat smaller and
finer than the bulla. This name is probably African: compare
Fante *tŏtŏe*, roasted. Another coconut biscuit, for its depend-
ability, is known as the *cartman's bible* (he swears by it).

Of confections the native favourite is probably the cake made
of sugar and coconut, of which there are two kinds, depending
on whether the coconut is cut into small bits or grated. It is
cooked in 'wet sugar' till it 'holds together', then spoonfuls are
dropped on something flat to cool and harden. The first kind are
cut cakes, *cut brute* (in allusion to the 'brute' sugar — from French
brut, unrefined), *chopped devil*, or perhaps most often *coconut drops*.
Uncle Newton furnishes yet another name: 'There we sat
with . . . some "pick-me-roun" or "coconut drops" (you know
coconut and sugar cakes by that name, don't you?)' — which
comes from the children's method of eating by picking the bits
of coconut out of the sugar base. The second kind are *grater cakes*
or *grater brute*. Some reserve *grater cake* for one made with white
sugar in a flat pan, then cut into rectangles.

Other sugar cakes include the *wangla*, formerly made with

sesame seeds (wangla), more recently with peanuts, in which case it is also called the *pinda cake*.

Native-made sugar and sugar concoctions have a number of folk names. *New* or *wet sugar* is freshly made, and as the second name suggests, has a lot of molasses in it. If somewhat firmer, it is *pan sugar*, an older name which refers to the evaporating pans in the sugar mills. (Today, because it is put in large pans for sale, the association has shifted.) As Long explained,

> The syrup in the tache, or last clarifier, adheres in a thick crust to the rim, somewhat resembling brown sugar-candy. This is taken off, and passes under the name of pan-sugar. . . . The ladies of this island eat large quantities of it.

Lady Nugent gave witness to this: 'Some pan sugar also from Mrs Lewis. The new sugar is excellent, drank in cold water; and I like the pan sugar of all things.' The drink that pleased the Governor's lady is still a favourite among the peasants under the name of *sugar-and-water*, or as Louise Bennett spells it to show the pronunciation, *sugan-wata*. It is also jocularly referred to as *black-wash*.

When the sugar is boiled dry it may be made into balls or (more commonly) poured into tins to solidify. Taken out of the tins this becomes *head sugar* — a single one is a *sugar head*. Sugar syrup boiled too much until it becomes /glaami/ (elastic) or /straani/ (full of strands), is given the self-explanatory name of *tie-teeth*; also *John Baillie*, though this term is applied as well to 'pulled pink and white peppermint sticks'. The gentleman honoured by this use of his name was the author of *The Jamaica Distiller's Directory*. Tie-teeth sugar is made into a kind of candy, called, for its toughness, *stagger-back*, *iron-cunny*, and more recently, in admiration of Mr Bustamante, *Busta backbone*. A very similar thing is coconut boiled with sugar till it burns: *monkey iron*.

Albion sugar is named for the well known Albion estate, where 'vacuum-pan sugar was first made . . . somewhere about 1870'.[24] It was at first a light brown colour, but now the shops sell both *brown Albion* and *white Albion*. Granulated sugar is popularly *grain sugar*. Muscovado sugar has achieved the local name of *coolie-foot*, from the fact that East Indians working barefoot in the mill would step into the sugar that was spilt on the floor. This was then sold at an especially low price.

Among cheap sweets one may mention the *farthing bump*:

> Me haffe gi' har wan farden bump
> Fe my-sen up har t'roat.

Also the *paradise plum*, a red and yellow lozenge. Among jams one must notice *docey*, made most often with guavas, but also other fruits. As the pronunciation /duosi/ shows, it is from Portuguese *doce*, but recent writers, taking it to be from Spanish *dulce*, have compromised with *dolce*. So Sullivan; also Stafford:

> Grenadilla and orange and guava
> For dolces and rose-marmalade.

The word appears to be falling into disuse, or else its earlier meaning is being obscured: one person identified it with 'grater cake'; one other pronounced it /dozi/ and identified it with dip-and-fall-back. Another concoction — a kind of jam made with peanuts and cashew nuts was called *specia* forty years ago (from Spanish, meaning spice).

The folk regularly call the yolk of an egg the *red*, as they do many other things that are yellow or orange coloured. (This seems to be an inheritance from Africa: in Twi, *fàmm* means either red or yellow.) Russell recorded 'bogro-sal — Coarse mine-salt. African'. This is still known in a few places. Curiously, with these Africanisms turns up the Celtic *bonny*, in the United States known as *bonny-clabber*. In Jamaica it takes adjective form: 'Spoiled milk get bonny.' As for *clabber*, it becomes *clab-up*: peas soup, thick and heavy from overboiling; *clabubs*: coconut half boiled down — what is known as *run-down* in St Thomas and Portland. The phonetically altered form *plabba* means similarly the 'remains from boiled coconut oil; custard', hence a 'mix-up', hence 'a stew, a quarrel'. It is curious indeed to find the same culinary metaphor in such widely separated forms and places.

Drinks

Two things in the tropics led to the development of many kinds of drinks: the warmth, and the accessibility of sugar cane and other sweet fruits. The American word *beverage* came into being owing to these circumstances: it meant sugar or molasses mixed with water, and perhaps flavoured with a little limejuice, and still does in this island among the folk. Its specifically Jamaican equivalent was *cool-drink* (none of the dictionaries enters this though it has a quite specific sense), which included both the fermented and the unfermented. This term probably goes back to 1727, certainly to 1756: at the first date we find, 'They have of their own a small cool sort called Mobby, and another very good made with Sorrel and Citron Water for Drams;' at the second date, 'What people commonly call, Sorrel Cool-drink, in *America*: . . . is a small diluting liquor, that is much used in all our sugar-colonies, and reckoned very refreshing in those sultry climates.' Long also described:

> the *cool drink*, prepared here by many of the free Negroe and Mulatta women, who vend it cheap to the soldiers. It is made with a mixture of sugar, guiacum chips, and ginger, infused together in hot water, and afterwards worked into a ferment with a piece of fresh gathered chaw-stick; which, by the quality of fixed air contained in it, soon excites a considerable froth, and imparts a slight bitter, of a very agreeable flavour. This drink, when cool and depurated, is racy and pleasant, extremely wholesome, and, if taken in too large quantities, intoxicates in some degree, but without causing any ill effect to the constitution.

Moreton, in 1790, made it a synonym of *mobby*; Sullivan identified it with *beverage*.

Of unfermented drinks there were: *sugar drink*, which Sloane described as 'made with Sugar-Canes bruised in a Mortar, or Hand-Mill, and then boil'd with water, and wrought in a Cask: it is clear like water'; *banana drink* and *plantain drink*, the latter known before in Barbados, the former apparently Jamaican:

> Bonano and Plantain Drinks are severally made by mashing of either of these ripe Fruits with water, till it comes to be pretty well mix'd with the Fruits, then they let it stand in a Trough, twelve hours, and draw it off.

China-root was also used: 'To make *China*-Drink. Take four or five handfuls of the Root. . . . It is of a red Colour, and a very pleasant Drink.' It was the regular practice on sugar estates during crop to let the slaves drink all they wanted of the *cane liquor* — that is, the juice of the canes — as it was squeezed out. This term too is first recorded in Jamaica.

From only one source (though a good one) we read of *sum*:

> They also draw a liquor from this tree [the coconut], either
> by cutting the branches that bear the fruit (to which they
> fasten vessels to receive the liquor), or by boring the body and
> plugging it, after which they let out the liquor when and how
> they think fit; this liquor they call *sum*. It tastes like new
> sweet wine; this they sometimes boil up into a grain like sugar,
> which they call *jagra*.[25]

But many drinks were fermented. As Barclay wrote (1826):
'The cane juice . . . is frequently mixed with bruised ginger and
chaw-stick . . . , and let stand till in a state of fermentation. This
the negroes call "*setting liquor for cool drink*".' Among those who
made sugar there grew up a phrase which amused Lady Nugent:
' "I must go home and cool coppers." I thought really he was
going home, to have all the large brass pans emptied to cool,
that I had seen the sugar boiling in . . . ; but I found he meant
that he must go home, and be abstemious, after so much feasting.' But its usual meaning was simply to have a cooling drink.[26]
A similar phrase puzzled Tom Cringle:

> An agent for a number of proprietors . . . rather posed me,
> by asking me during dinner, if I would take anything in the
> *long way* with him, which he explained by saying he would be
> glad to take a glass of small beer with me.

This is certainly connected with the modern difference between
a long drink and a short one, probably referring originally to the
size of the glass.

Sorrel drink, mentioned above, was named for the plant.
Because the sorrel ripens at that season, it is a Christmas drink
— appropriately, a clear, bright red liquid which is mixed with
ginger and drunk unfermented or fermented. It may be strengthened with rum or wine.

Cashew wine is mentioned only by Sloane: '*Acajou* wine, made
of the Fruit so called, is very strong, keeps not long, and causes
vomiting; 'tis reckoned a good remedy in the Dropsie.' *Mobbie*,
already referred to, was originally made with sweet potatoes —
the word is from Carib *mabi*, batata; it was known in Barbados
before, so is not a Jamaicanism in this sense. However, a new
sense developed here as it became a synonym of *cool drink*:
'mauby . . . A fermented liquor made of sugar, water, and

ginger, and lignumvitae.' *Perino* was another, 'the wholesomest of all cool Drinks,'[27] made of cassada bread. Though mentioned in several works (in Barbados first) the dictionaries have missed it. Barham wrote that the Virginia Indians 'make a drink which ferments, and is called *mobby*, or *jetici*, which they fuddle and get drunk with, as they do with potatoe mobby in Jamaica'. Some sweet potatoes are still called *jetici* in this island: this term must have been widespread.

The product of the first stage in distilling rum went under two names: 'singlings, or low wines, as it is termed in Jamaica.' The latter has continued in use. A kind of 'shrub' was called *santa*: 'they [Negroes dancing] were regaled with punch and santa.' 'The effects of the Santa, began to subdue and disperse them.' Patterson also wrote of *porter cup*, 'an excellent and refreshing beverage, made of Madeira wine, Port, and other ingredients, and which I commend to the notice of any traveller.' Today, a mixture of gin and wine is nicknamed among the folk, *steel bottom*.

Two rather more exotic names turn up earlier in Jamaican accounts than elsewhere. One is *cawvaw*, which seems to represent *kava*, the Polynesian intoxicating drink — no doubt brought in by sailors. 'Molossus Drink is called *Cawvaw*. Upon drinking the Molossus Drink of Penils, or very bad Sugar, the Belly-ach came to Barbados.'[28] Barham described the other: 'The liquor [drawn from the coconut tree] ... distilled ... makes a spirit called *orraqua*, or *rack*, which far exceeds that made from rice; and these trees being called in some places *toddie*, it is therefore called toddie-rack.' Neither *rack* nor *toddy-rack* has survived.

Though the word *rum* is not Jamaican (nor *kill-devil*, its earlier name), there are a number of by-names for it, some imported, others local. *Daru*, used among East Indians, is simply the Hindustani *dārū*, strong liquor. *Malawa*, reported from Portland, is African: wine or spirits.[29] In 1868 Russell reported *ga-ge* as an African name for rum, but its source has not been traced. *Cowneck* is new white proof rum; *crab* (/kraab/) rum is estate rum — that is, bought directly at the source of manufacture; *kubu-kubu* is stolen 'factory' rum. A general, jocular name is *puncheon-water*,[30] and a common name for white proof rum in Lucea, *rude-to-parents* — which bears its own social comment.

Drinks made with rum included *locus-ale* (now obsolete);

Sloane's is the last record of it found: 'Locust-Ale is Cane-Juice clarified, mix'd with Rum.' *Pimento dram* is a liqueur with a rum base in which allspice berries have been steeped. *Honey dram* has the 'ingredients . . . honey, water, chewstick, ginger, and rum. When mixed, the dram is put in the sun to ripen'.

One who drinks rum excessively is, in popular slang, a *rummer* or *rummarian*; or a *rum-bumpa* or *bumpa* — that is, one who has a *rum-bump* — a swelling of the throat attributed to too much rum drinking. A drunken sot is also called a *soakapee*.

Of simpler, non-alcoholic drinks one may mention, as apparently Jamaican, *dandy-shandy*, *frisco*, and *snowball*. Uncle Newton writes of the first two: 'rivers of aerated waters like dandy-shandy and cream-soda' and 'patties, candies, fudge, frisco, ginger beer, syrup and sherbet'. *Shandy* may well have been transferred from *shandy-gaff* for its coupling with *dandy* — at least, the two are surely related. *Frisco* is less likely to have anything to do with San Francisco than with the Spanish *refresco*, a cool drink: it is composed of milk, ice, egg, and flavouring shaken up together. As for the *snowball*, this is no more than a glass of shaved ice with strongly sweetened syrup poured over, but the snowball carts, painted in lively colours and enhanced with imaginative topical names, are a characteristic sight in the streets.

Smoking

A few words related to smoking are clearly Jamaicanisms. Sloane wrote in 1707, 'Tobacco . . . is of several sorts . . : that with the broad leaves is call'd Bulls Face.' The dictionaries record this only once: 1800, *bull-face*. (DAE, DA). Locally grown tobacco is traditionally made into thick twists for easy handling. As long ago as 1803, Dallas wrote:

> The leaves were dried and prepared for use by the men, who twisted them into a kind of rope, of about the third of an inch in diameter, which they rolled up in balls, and carried out in the same manner to the different estates for sale.

Nowadays it is more often seen in a coil — or *wheel*, as one man called it, and is popularly known as *jackass-rope* or, euphemistically, *donkey-rope*; also *twist tobacco*. A cigar is jocularly a *bark-wood*, as if made from the barkwood of a tree, like native rope.

A short-stemmed tobacco pipe is a /jongka/, since the adjective *junka* (related to the verb *junk*, chop into pieces) simply means short. Williams, describing an escaped slave, wrote (1826): 'He and his companions sit . . . and smoke their jonkas, or pipes about two inches long, until the evening closes in.' This seems to have some currency still; so, apparently has *cachimba*, ultimately an African word though it probably came in via American Spanish *cachimbo*, a tobacco pipe.

The smoking of *ganja* (Hindustani *gānjā*, the hemp plant) has become common among certain classes in Jamaica in the past two decades. Most often a pipe is used — a *chillum*, which, like the plant, comes from India, where this word (Hindustani *chilam*) refers to the part of a hookah that contains the burning tobacco. Popularly this is also pronounced /chĭlóng/. A *ganja stick* is used too, and a smoke of ganja, or ganja cigarette is a *spliff* — a word apparently suggesting stimulation or inebriation (compare United States slang *spifflicated*, drunk). A smoke of ganja is also a *tampi* but the source or connections of this word have not been traced. One may remark in passing that the spelling 'ganga', which some writers seem to favour, violates both etymology and English orthography: *g* before *a* is always 'hard'. The only acceptable spelling is *ganja*.

Gambling

Jamaica has not added many gambling terms to the vocabulary, but has preserved some traditional ones. The *main*, the point one is trying to match in dice play, has been in use since the sixteenth century, and still is here. *Sweat-table*, a gambling table with a marked oilcloth cover on which dice are thrown, is a reflection of the United States *sweat-cloth*, which, however, is now archaic. In card playing, *wappy* is very much the same as the *main* in dice: a card with the same number, thrown by a second person. (Could this be connected with the verb *wap*, OED: 'to throw quickly or with violence', this being a familiarised name for a card 'wapped'?)

A *liges* (pronounced /laigz/) is a chance, or a piece of luck. One might hear, for example, 'I get a liges,' or 'I tekin a liges off a sweepstake ticket'. Since *bag* and *hag* are often pronounced /biag, haig/, this word probably represents *lag*, an old term used in playing such games as marbles: the player who said 'I'll play lag' got the last chance — therefore the best. In this way *lag* could easily come to imply a good chance, which is close to its meaning here. *Liges* also means 'special privilege'.

A gambling game intoduced by the Chinese and carried on surreptitiously is *peaka peow*. It does not get into print very often, but a calypso song of about 1948, *Big Mattie from New London*, has the line, 'Me win Peaka Peow de odder day.' Another game is known as *drop-pan* from the method of play. One buys from a book of tickets (/tai shiin/ is the Chinese name by which this generally goes) numbered from 1 to 36, each ticket representing something — for example, a part of the body. Later the tickets are dropped in a pan to see which wins. A *rake* is a 'hunch' — a sign or token that guides one in buying a drop-pan ticket. The person who feels he has got this token may say, 'I ketch de rake.'

Money

Jamaica has adopted or developed a number of names and nicknames for coins and paper money. The first two appear in an account of 1740:

> Great Quantities of *Spanish* Coin have been returned from this Island, the Planters not reserving a Bit for their own Use, except Pistorines, nick-nam'd by them Don *Patinho's* Money.[31]

This is the earliest known example of *pistareen* as an English word. The spelling is unrecorded; so also Stewart's spelling *pesterines*, of some years later (1808). (He gave its value as 1s. 3d.) As for Don Patinho, he is unmentioned in other Jamaican accounts, so the nickname alluding to him must have been short-lived; since Portuguese *patinho* means a simpleton, this perhaps signified 'fool's money'.

Though not a Jamaican addition to the language, *bit* was earlier in use than *pistareen*. Sloane mentioned the 'Bitt, or Real', indicating its value, but this has changed in the course of time: in 1808 and 1835 it was valued at 7½d. — five-eighths of a shilling; today its value has fallen to 4½d. — three-eighths of a shilling.

Stewart also listed 'tenpenny and five penny pieces; the latter is the smallest coin in use, there being no copper coin in circulation'. This five penny piece became the *fippance*, *fipenny*, or *fip* — in another pronunciation *fuppance* or *fups* — of today, though for it, too, the value has fallen: it means threepence, the smallest silver coin at present. Williams wrote in 1826: 'Me bet you fippance me mek you go' — which accurately records the pronunciation. In Pennsylvania seventy-five years ago a *fip* was half a *bit*, but the Jamaican coins have not been worth so much. The two words are often combined as *bit-an'-fippance*, which adds up to 7½d. — the value of the former bit!

A *four-bit* is 1s. 6d. (four times 4½d.) — so in the well known song 'One Solja Man', 'Him give me one cockeye fourbit.' This is also called a *bob-tenner*, since a *tenner* is 6d. This word is no doubt an abbreviation of *tenpenny* piece (to which Stewart referred), and as the fippance became worth 3d.' the tenner would become 6d. (English *tanner* is also a possible source.)

An archaic word, hardly used any more, is *feeco*, probably of Spanish origin — compare *ficha*, which had some currency in the United States as a 'piece of five' or 2½ cents. In Jamaica it means a penny, or a cent.

Still quite current as a word for a shilling is *mac*, the abbreviation of *macaroni*. Again Stewart is our source: 'The silver coins are dollars (6s. 8d.), half dollars, and quarter dollars, or maccaronies as they are here popularly called.' A current example is, 'Ef dem summons me, mek me pay few mac,' and it also takes the familiarised form *maxie*. Combinations are *mac-an-truppance*, and a *two-mac* (florin), also called a *two-bob*.

Coming to the copper coins one finds *tup* or *tuppy*, *quattie*, and *gill*, all of long standing. The *tup*, of course, is an abbreviation of *twopence*, but nowadays means the same as *quattie*: 1½d. The latter word is clearly the abbreviation of *quarter* — the quarter of a sixpence. *Gill* (pronounced /jil/) is half a quattie (¾d.), but how it came to be is unknown. On the analogy of measurements of quantity, *gill* and *quart* the gill of money should be one eighth of a *quattie*. Perhaps *gill* was simply taken as suggesting a small quantity. The possibilities are complicated, however, by there being *big gill* and *little gill* among Jamaican measures!

A penny is called a *brass* — on the analogy of English *copper* (Jamaican pence are made of an alloy resembling brass), perhaps with some influence from *brass farthing*? The farthing is a /náagin/ or *Chinaman* — the latter either in allusion to its size or to the proverbial frugality and careful money dealings of the Chinese shopkeepers.

A pound note is, slangily, a *coco-leaf* — compare the U.S. 'lettuce' and 'kale'. From 1835 comes an interesting citation about the kind of currency that preceded the government bank-notes of today:

> There is no paper money, with the exception of island checks, and drafts on Kingston merchants, and other respon-sible individuals, which are common payments in the country parts, and denominated '*town orders*'.

Small change is given the very characteristic nickname *mash-mash*; or it may be *breeze*, as in the phrase 'One poun' an' breeze'. The sense must be guessed at — perhaps it is little bits that the breeze might blow away.

A common word for a small amount of money given as a tip or otherwise is a *raise* — in use since at least 1912. This has no doubt developed from the verb: to *raise* money. A *bite* means the same: 'Gi' 'im a bite, no, sa?' (Give him a small amount of money, won't you, Sir?) — or else the opportunity to earn some money.

Trade

The common folk phrase for buying and selling is /ton han/ (turn hand) — perhaps developed from the English phrase to 'turn one's hand' to some activity, but possibly of local for-mation: to 'turn' goods from one person's hand to another's. In fairly common use for 'business' is *cuento*, no doubt from Spanish *cuenta*, counting, account. But it should be noted that Portu-guese *conta*, account, reckoning, was borrowed in Africa into Fante as *akṓntàd*, and this may very possibly have been brought to Jamaica and have been a reinforcing or facilitating factor in the acquisition of *cuento*.

From French *grand-marché* must have come the former in-stitution of *grand-market*, an especially big buying-and-selling that took place on December twenty-fourth. Another word reported for a market is *shambry*, of origin unknown.

One English and two Spanish words are used to mean some-thing that is added for good measure when a sale is made. The first, and most current today, is *mek-up*, used both as a noun and as an exclamatory phrase: 'Gi me mek-up,' or simply 'Mek-up!' More frequent in the past was /bráata/. Some spell it *broughta*, as if it had some relation to English *brought*; McKay spelt it *brater* (which Jekyll misunderstood as 'brother'):

> No two bit o' brater
> Wid shopkeeper Marter.

The word was recorded in 1877 by the American lexicographer Bartlett, and Mathews offers the etymology 'British dial. *brot(t)*, scraps, fragments, a small quantity' (DA). But it is none of these things: it is merely from the American Spanish *barata*, a bargain. Santamaria records this use in Colombia and Mexico.

The third word is *nyapa*, ultimately from American Indian, but proximately American Spanish *ñapa*. (It is cognate with American *lagniappe*, which passed through one further stage — the French — in coming to English.)

During the Second World War, *marry* acquired a special meaning: it referred to the shopkeepers' practice of selling such desired articles as soap and rice, which were in short supply, only with other, more plentiful articles.

The word *manifac* (from *manufacture*) is a folk verb in Jamaica, meaning to prepare a product for use or sale: 'Ginger is hard to manifac.'

A *banju sale* is a public sale of used articles — probably African: Ewe *gbandyo* means an auction, and *gb-* was always reduced to *b-*.

To buy or sell on credit is to *trust* — a word apparently obsolete elsewhere, but flourishing still in Jamaica. Louise Bennett gives the words of a candyseller speaking of a customer she must dun:

> Ef she wen good she hooden want
> Fe trus' me li candy.

One who does not pay his debts easily is called a *hard-pay man*.

In slavery days there were a number of terms more or less commercial — now obsolete, but of some historical interest. *Vendue* is known as a name for a sale of slaves, but in Jamaica it was also the building in which such a sale took place: 'Above eight hundred . . . were seated on the floor of the two spacious galleries of a large building called the vendue.' Similarly, *vendue room*: 'At the hour of sale, Marly entered the vendue room.'[32] *Privilege* developed a special meaning; as Stewart wrote (1792), it signified 'choice election: for it is now the practice, to estimate and proportion the privilege, to the extent of the demand'. That is, four-fifths of a cargo of new slaves, the best, were 'the privilege', and lots were drawn for them by the prospective buyers. From after the treaty with Cudjoe till at least 1828, *mile-money* was the sum paid to apprehenders of runaway slaves, assessed according to the number of miles they were brought back: 'The sum of ten shillings, and no more, besides mile-money, at the rate of one shilling per mile for the first five miles, and sixpence per mile afterwards.'[33]

Perhaps not Jamaican, though found only in a book about this island, is the phrase *Dutch account*, meaning one confused or perhaps deliberately falsified:

Old Marly, therefore, would not venture the fruits of his industry into such hands, supposing, that when he returned, he would find a Dutch account of his crops.

Chapter Ten

DOMESTIC AND SOCIAL LIFE II

Crime and Punishment

THE USE of the whip in slave days — a universal practice —
has left its trace in Jamaican words. The naval *cat-o'-nine-tails*, or
cat came ashore; it is still used in Jamaican penitentiaries.
McKay described it as 'the tamarind switch or its equivalent,
used for flogging prisoners in Jamaica: cat . . . is employed as
noun and verb'. Till the end of the seventeenth century the
manatee strap was used. There was also the *long whip* or *cowskin*,
now a *cow-cod*,[1] and this has produced the verb to *cod*, meaning
simply to whip or beat:

> Sometime she fetch me aise a box
> Sometime she cod me back![2]

This long whip, when cracked, made a report like a gun. Cracking it was therefore called *firing* the whip — and the report was
used as 'a signal for work to stop', or for some similar purpose.
When a gang was working in the fields, says *Marly*, 'The whip
was sometimes fired behind them to keep them in line, but
seldom did any require to be touched with it.'

Quoting from 'Mr *Barham* in MS' (a1725), Sloane described
the plant called *lance-wood*: 'Of the Succors of it are made, what
are call'd in Jamaica Ground Switches for whipping the
Negroes, when ty'd up for their Offences.'

The *Jamaica ebony* was frequently used to inflict punishment.
As Marsden wrote in 1788: 'He used to give them the further
discipline of *ebonies*, which is something like our birch with
short prickles.' Somewhat later, illustrating a synonymous
phrase *the licks*, this description was elaborated:

> This ebony bush . . . contains a very small but sharp species
> of prickle; it is tied up in bundles like a birch rod. In some
> cases, after the punishment is inflicted with the whip, the
> licks, as they call them, are also inflicted with this ebony bush.

Another phrase is associated:

> This is a very common course in Jamaica; after . . . lashes with the whip, then to use the tamarind switches; the common expression is, 'beating out the bruised blood'.

Finally, there was the practice of *pickling* — rubbing salt into the wounds made by the whip, which, though painful, prevented infection.[3]

As might be expected, several words or phrases were used euphemistically, which gave them special meanings. One of these was to *hide*:

> He gave strict orders to the watchmen to hide every slave which they might find breaking the corn or canes; *i.e.* to chop and murder them, and bury them secretly.[4]

This was also called *doing over*. A slave punished on the treadmill was said to *dance the mill* — and indeed if he did not move his legs fast, they easily became bruised or broken.

Other words for flogging are *key-hauling* — an alteration of the nautical *keel-hauling* — and *duma* (/dúma/). By transfer of meaning a *deal-board* becomes a caning. A *bulla* apparently means a hard blow, in the following:

> De police-man gi her one big
> Bulla an run her weh!

A heavy blow, fit for a horse or donkey, is a *beast-lick*.

From the eighteenth century comes the word *beau-stick*:

> In broils, or disputes [among the Negroes], the beautic, or cudgel, is wielded with dexterity, but the contest is not very obstinately maintained; a little blood spilt soon terminates it.[5]

Such a contest would now be called *stick-licking*. The favourite cudgel, however, the *coco-macka* of today, has been known for a long time in the West Indies. The earliest description comes from 1826: 'the soldiers use the coco macac (a species of heavy jointed cane).' Here the reference is to Haiti, but the name is used elsewhere in the Antilles. In Jamaica it is not usually a cane but the tough wood of the macaw palm. In a 'calypso' tune come the lines,

> Sweetie Charlie a go bus' Mattie head
> Wid im coco-macka.

The echoic words *pam-pam*, *plam-plam*, meaning a quarrel, a flogging, dismissal from a job, seem very likely to be of African origin: *pam'*, in Twi, means to chase away, dismiss, expel, and *pam' pàm* to persecute.

In slave days, and especially during the Maroon wars, a kind of 'passport' was necessary to prove one's identity or the legitimacy of one's business. From 1740 we find: 'All Negroes must have written tickets, which they call *Talkee*, *Talkee*, before they are suffer'd to pass.' Thus *ticket* became the official term, used in the laws as late as 1788.

In Jamaica *manumission* acquired a concrete sense: 'An instrument in writing used by masters in giving freedom to their slaves.' This was known among the latter as a *free paper*, a term seemingly applied also to the Act of Emancipation when that was passed.

> On Sunday, December 24, Steven James, a slave on Chatham estate, Trelawny, went to Mr Knibb, at Falmouth, and informed him that the people were saying, 'Free-paper was come out, and they would not work after Christmas.'[6]

Out of this has grown the proverbial expression *free-paper burn*, meaning that one's time of freedom is over — one must return to work.

Steal is the common word in most of the English-speaking world: *thieve* (pronounced /tiif/ by the folk) is the common one in Jamaica. It also has an iterated form meaning to steal repeatedly or habitually, and an emphatic combination:

> A tiefin-tief like dat deh tief
> Mus tief-tief till him dead.

Tiefenness (thievingness) appears in the same poem. Nicknames for a thief are a *finger-light*, *ulu*, and especially *patta-cat* — a patta being a thatched shelter for cooking, or a kitchen shelf.

Trickery or 'confidence games' aimed at separating the innocent from their money or other possessions have contributed a number of interesting words. To *scuffle* someone is to cheat him: a *scuffler* is a thief. No doubt this is connected with the old word *scuffle-hunter*, a thief who hung about wharves. *Jinnal* means tricky, or a crafty person (adjective or noun). There is a common phrase, 'Chief in town, jinnal mus' dive,' *chief* meaning a gull or potential victim. The origin of this word is uncertain,

P

but it probably comes from *general*, and the association with
chief makes this plausible.

A *radge* (/raj/) is the same as a jinnal and also a puzzling word.
It could be a cant form of *rogue*, or a short form of *Roger*, which
has several cant meanings — among them, a thief-taker (OED).
The word *roguing* is very commonly used in Jamaica to mean dishonest, scoundrelly. And there is *rogueness*, too, for roguery. The
better known term for a *radge* is a *sam fie* or confidence man,
pronounced /samfai/ or /sanfai/. Usually working with an ac-
complice he waits in Kingston for newcomers from the country
whom he pretends he will help. He often professes to the magic
powers of Obeah, plays the old trick of making money multiply,
and in the end *sams* the bumpkin. The origin of this word is
difficult to discover. Possibly it may be connected with Twi *sàm*,
one meaning of which is to entangle, throw down, prostrate.
But this leaves the second element unexplained. Beside *chief*, a
gullible person is a *cuffee* (from the old day-name) or a /kúnu-
mùnu/, spelt *conoo-monoo* by Reid.

Cheating tricks go under the names of *chicaney* (no doubt connected with *chicane* or *chicanery*), a *brain* or *brains* ('Anancy . . .
study a brain fe work pon Ticks'), and a *roongoos, gungus*, or
rungles. What the last of these can be is a puzzle. There is a word
runkle, the Scots form of *wrinkle*, one of the senses of which is 'a
trick', current in the eighteenth century,[7] which might well have
come to Jamaica. Yet the association of this word with 'magic'
and even obeah suggests an African origin as more likely. Perhaps the connection is with *guzu* (obeah).

To cheat or deceive someone is to *play* him *out*, which is clearly
connected with one Standard sense of *play*.[8] An old expression is
to *jiggy-fu* — perhaps an Africanism.[9] *Gwoyou* means to 'bluff' or
fool a person, and *maringle* may be connected with *rungles* (just
discussed) or, more likely, it is a form of *mariggle*, which appears
in the name of a tricky fish (*John Mariggle*) and elsewhere.
Mariggle itself probably is an excerpted part of the formula used
in propounding *riddles* (which the folk regularly pronounce
/rigl/). This was once a favourite entertainment, and began
with the phrase, 'Riggle me riggle; answer dis riggle and perhaps
not.' The sense of puzzlement and deceptiveness associated with
riddles could easily be carried over to deliberate deception
practiced upon another.

McKay mentions a phrase current in 1912 — the *big-tree boys* — which referred to 'a certain big tree in Kingston . . . the resort of idlers and vicious characters'. No doubt this was the large banyan formerly in Victoria Park; the phrase was one of many that designated ruffians and criminals. One such current today is *gangalee*, which seems based on *gang*; another, /raabáaba/ means specifically 'an alias-man' (sometimes merely an alias) and more generally a coarse, rough-spoken person. Considering the many uses of *raw* in Jamaica, it may be present again as the first element of this word. The second is very doubtful; possibly a form of *brother* (cf. *baba-lad*). A /fáiakìti/ is an 'outlaw', a 'fiery, brazen, outrageous' person. The first element may well be the English word *fire*; the second, however, is more likely African: compare the Twi word *kìtikiti*, meaning 'turbulent or violent commotion; tumult'. The vitality of the folk speech may be judged by its latest acquisition (heard in 1955): the bands of gamins who run about Kingston streets stealing and committing petty crimes are /máamàa/ boys — in allusion to the *Mau-mau* of Kenya!

Law enforcement produced a number of words in early days which survive only in part. In 1826 Williams referred to a bailiff as a *marshalman* — a special Jamaican sense. Of the effects of the 'priority act' which forced a money-lender to bring action immediately against a debtor, Long wrote as follows:

> Another bad effect . . . of this law . . . is the custom which many desperate debtors have fallen upon, of standing marshal, as it is called. After a series of persecution[s] on the part of the creditor, iniquity in the officer, subterfuge and evasion in the debtor, the latter is driven at length to his intrenchments. He converts his house (literally speaking) into a castle, prepared to withstand a regular siege, and forms a garrison of armed slaves. Many have held out in this manner till their plantation has been entirely ruined for want of culture, and themselves reduced to a starving condition.

Neither of these expressions survives. The old-time folk word *mashalah*, which recalls a time of slave riots, probably represents *martial law*.

Surprisingly enough, the dictionaries do not have the term

slave-court, though this was an established institution. In the 1817
Act for the Subsistence . . . we find:

> And it is hereby declared, That at every court of quarter-
> sessions, held in each and every parish or precinct within this
> island, the justices there assembled shall and may, after the
> usual business of the said court shall be done, form themselves
> into a court, for the purpose of inquiring into, hearing, and
> determining, all manner of offences for which any slave or
> slaves are liable to be punished with death, or transportation,
> or confinement to hard labour, as aforesaid, and shall open
> the said court by proclamation, declaring the same to be a
> slave-court for such purpose.

A piece of old-time lawyers'-jargon, referring to the proceedings at a trial, comes from 1835:

> The parties now meet for the first time in battle array; all
> their forces mustered, and every manoeuvre practised to gain
> information as to the probable result: This is called 'ear-
> wigging'. (Senior).

At least one title of office is particularly Jamaican, that of
Custos. It is an abbreviation of *custos rotulorum*, of course, but the
office is different here: the Custos is the head of the magistracy
of the parish whom the Governor may consult on matters of local
policy. In the simple form we find this term first used in 1738 in
the Articles of Pacification: 'They shall apply first to the custos,
or any other magistrate.'[10] 'Custos' is sometimes used locally
as a term of respect even for one not holding the office.

Before the modern police came into being there was 'the
watch' — apparently in Kingston called the *nightly-watch*. The
Ordinances of Kingston (1828) refer to 'the town-guard or
nightly-watch, in the said city and parish'. One present-day
nickname for the police, introduced by the *Rastafarians*, is *babylon*
(/bábilan/); *corporal*, however, was long ago reduced and
familiarised to /káapi/. Uncle Newton writes of 'Constable
Cambridge who told us . . . "stop your gambling (strong word,
Corpi!) and your indecent actions." '

Because the policeman's trousers have broad red stripes down
the sides, he has become a *red-seam* or *woodpecker*. (The recently
added force of special police have become '*blue-stripes*'.) The
motorised police are nicknamed *flying saucers*, having come in at

the time of the 'flying saucer' excitement. A widespread term is *pan-head*, which refers to the policeman's round metal badge, considered to resemble a pan-cover. He is also a *dog-driver* (a *dog* being a man who gets into trouble). In the popular formula the victim says, 'I'm your dog, sir,' and the policeman replies, 'I know that!'

To have someone arrested is to *bring* him *up*, an archaism still current in Jamaica: 'Now because o' you dem gone bring me up.' Handcuffs are called *Maggie* (through some association with Black Maria?); the police wagon, from its colour, is also called a *johncrow jacket*. *Eleven steps* symbolises the courthouse in such expressions as, 'tek im up lebm tep,' or 'Me haffe wear me blue-boot go up lebm tep' — that is, to go to court, stand trial. The phrase *tep-tep*, meaning trouble, is perhaps based on this.

A first arrest is jocularly a *wet-foot*; a year's sentence in prison is a *quart*, six months in prison, a *pint*. From the practice of the judge's wearing a black cap when pronouncing sentence of death comes the verb to *black-cap*. At a theatre in Kingston in 1951, watching a moving picture in which a man was threatened with the death sentence, I heard a member of the audience groan, 'Im gwine black-cap im!'

Courtship and Family Relations

Among the Jamaican folk there are many expressions for sweethearts, mistresses and lovers, in casual or serious relationships which lead sometimes to marriage, but very often to an informal living together without either marriage or promiscuity. A sweetheart of either sex is a *stucky* (/stóki/); a *stoshy* (/stúoshi/) is usually a young man. *Stucky* suggests the Americanism of being 'stuck on' someone; *stoshy* is certainly based on *stoshus*, 'high class', which has been discussed.

Most words of this kind, however, seem to be in iterated form, composed of the kind of sounds that accompany the nuzzling and pouting caresses of lovers: *bibi, tutu, lulu, dudu*, and *dundus, putu* and *putus, boso* — all of which mean a darling, favourite (some applicable to children). Certain of these are probably of African[11] source but they could be local creations almost anywhere: they are a sort of amorous baby-talk. *Dundus* is primarily 'a term of affection used by an older person to a young boy or girl' — yet it would appear to be what we have in the song 'Big Sambo Gal':

> Gal you want fe come kill me fe Dundus

— since the young man is humourously afraid of his girl's cooking and fussing over him.

Dude is sometimes used, and may be the Americanism for a dressed up man, though it definitely means a lover in the song of the girl who is roasting a coco in expectation of a visit:

> Posen me roas' i' an' de Dude no come?

Bona, a term of affection (as in the song 'Mada Cantinny') could be from any of several sources — French *bonne*, Scots *bonnie*, or from some such African source as Twi *mpãnã, mpĕnã*, lover, sweetheart. (Initial *mp-* of African words became *p-* or *b-* when adopted into English.) It is perhaps from this word *bona* as a basis that the 'stretched' forms *boonoonoos, boonoonoonoos*, and by analogy *boolooloops* and *floolooloops* are made. *Boonoonoos* is primarily 'a term of endearment', and so means 'pretty or beautiful'; but it also has the sense of very pleasant, lovely, as in Louise Bennett's verse, 'Yes, me had a boonoonoos time.'

It stretches one syllable farther sometimes, as when Uncle Newton writes of a wedding day, 'Oh it was a day of joy and glory; Horatio would describe it as a "boonoonoonoose" day.' And Louise Bennett too;

> We mus answer de call
> To de gran' and great exciting
> Boonoonoonoose Red Cross Ball!

But *boolooloops* seems to remain a term of affection in:

> De ongle ting ah want me lickle
> Boolooloops, is yuh!

The verb *friend* means to take someone as a sexual companion without marriage, and is a converted form of the noun *friend* used in this limited context. As Kerr has written:

> While dancing he spoke to her asking if she would be a friend of his. She said if he wanted to friend her he would have to go to her mother and ask her.

This kind of arrangement is known as *friending*, and is, according to Moore, 'the most informal and variable of the three types of conjugal relations (the other two being formal church-performed marriage and common-law marriage).'

A number of euphemisms exist for the sexual act, probably the quaintest (and quite widespread) being *rudeness*. In the words of Rosita Forbes, ' "Will you do me a rudeness?" is an invitation to pass an entertaining but not restful night.' In the popular songs are several more: *fan*, in 'Fan Me solja Man' and *tumble down* in 'Mattie Walla' may be mentioned.

To *while* is to go out courting but may also mean to 'run up and down with different women'. It would seem to be a specific use of Standard 'while away one's time'. Courting of a more formal sort is still described by the terms to *sit up* or to *walk out*, both of older English origin, and preserved dialectally elsewhere.

Two interesting usages come from the Maroons, one of long ago, the other current. To *kill hog* was based on the custom that the parents of a girl would kill a hog and make a feast for the neighbours as a means of formally announcing that she had reached marriageable age. But 'Although this feast was intended by the family as a signal to the young men for making an offer, the girl herself usually preferred a state of celibacy for some years after it was publicly known *that she had killed hog*'.[12] The other usage is that of *bride* applying to 'either of the parties to a marriage' — 'the two brides' would be, in Standard terms, bride and groom.

Family is used not only as a noun, but as a quasi-adjective equivalent to 'related, akin': 'Me and him is family'; 'Flying ants are family to duck ants.' *Fe we* means 'of our family or kin'. As Beckwith has written: 'Care must be taken in throwing out water at night to warn the family spirits who may be near. "Mind yourselves, me family," or "good people", they cry, or, "Anybody fe we move".

Since formal marriage among the Jamaican folk is not frequent, and friending and other less stable arrangements are common, the relationships of children to parents and to each other become rather complicated. As Dunham has written, 'Yard-children [are] those children who live with their father, rather than away from him in the household of their unmarried mother, the latter being called "illegitimates".' Offspring produced before a marriage are *outside* children, Kerr tells of one such situation: 'May has allowed her outside daughter, born before she married William, to build a house on the land.' And Louise Bennett gets some amusement out of the elaborations of family relationship in the lines:

> Leah fadah outside darter son
> Wey dem call knock-knee Joe.

A child born last in a family is referred to by McKay as the *lasty*, pronounced /láasi/. In mixtures of colour the attempt to have lighter-coloured children than oneself is called *raising the colour*.[13]

Terms of Address

Most terms of address begin as literal references to some relationship between people but quickly become conventionalised as titles of respect or intimacy. As Edwards wrote long ago:

> In addressing such of their fellow-servants as are any ways advanced in years, they prefix to their names the appellation of Parent, as *Ta* Quaco, and *Ma* Quasheba; *Ta* and *Ma*, signifying Father and Mother, by which designation they mean to convey not only the idea of filial reverence, but also that of esteem and fondness.

The old customs have changed much, but are not altogether forgotten. The prevailing form seems to have been *tata*, however, even earlier than *ta*. Moreton prints a song, supposedly sung by a slave, in which there is the line, 'Since dem tief me from me tatta,'[14] and it was applied also to the master, according to Barclay, 'little negro children running to meet their master . . . and vociferating the endearing expression Tata come, Tata come.' *Tata* is still used within the intimate folk circle.

Similar is the term *nana*; in Twi *nãnã* means a grandparent of either sex, but Jamaican *nana* simply means 'granny'. From this have sprung associated uses as a 'term of address to an older woman', and — probably the commonest application today — to mean 'nursemaid'. (Here it comes into competition with the English *nanny*, of entirely different source.) Also current as an

affectionate term for a grandmother or other older woman is
gang-gang, which corresponds strikingly with French *gan-gan*.
Interestingly enough, a *granny* is not the grandparent, among
the folk, but the grandchild. This is true, at least, among the
Accompong Maroons; the more widespread term is *gran-pickny*.

Dunham found 'datter' used in Accompong as a 'term of
address for a woman of one's own age or younger' — an archaic
usage in these days. The ordinary forms of *mama* and *papa* for
one's parents are /múma/ and /púpa/, and these are sometimes
used as terms of address. More often, however, Mother, in the
form *Mada*, is the common title of respect for middle-aged to
older women, particularly those having some special position in
the community, such as herb-healers and religious officers. (The
corresponding masculine title would probably be *Mass* — discussed below.)

Brother and *Sister* take a number of forms in this use. Russell
reported *Brara* and *Breda* in 1868; the latter is still current and is
a common form in Anancy stories, where it alternates with *Bra*.
Dunham found both *Ba* and *Baba* used as terms of 'intimate
address for a man of one's own age'. Like the others, these may
be from English *brother*, but quite possibly they have another
source: in Hausa *baba* means father.

Sister is reduced in various ways: McKay recorded *S'er* and
Bennett often uses *Sta* — the latter as a term of address among
equals. *Uncle*, for an older man, is common also in the southern
United States, not specifically Jamaican. *Cousin* is of the same
kind, used for 'intimate address (not signifying any actual
relationship)', and the OED comments, 'now esp. in Cornwall.'
It is sometimes reduced in pronunciation to *Co-u*. Dunham also
reported *Godbrother* as a 'term of intimate address for a man of
one's own age', but this is certainly not common.

Master, in addition to the Standard *Mister*, has a number of
folk forms. The traditional folk pronunciation is /máasa/; in
earlier accounts one finds *Macky Massa*, which was the exclamation accompanying a curtsy, *macky* being simply a greeting (Twi
makyɛ̃, 'Good Morning!'). This seems to have developed the
further sense, especially in exclamations, of 'esteemed, merciful'
(already discussed); and the phrase has later become by simple
phonetic change and probably reinforced by 'backra', *bucky
massa*. Uncle Newton depicts a frightened small boy begging for

mercy in the words, 'Do sir! I won't do it again. Do bucki massa!' This has an old-fashioned or countrified air, and so has the 'marsa' reported by Dunham as a 'term of intimate address for a man of one's own age'. The more current form is simply /maas/, as in Bennett's verses:

> So me cotchin' wid Mass U, Miss Q,
> Sta P., an Cousin B.

As an exclamation in which *Massa* probably refers to God, there used to be *Massa-tenky*! But this phrase (and more commonly its inverse form, *tenky-massa*) also means a gift. *Mushé* is an old-fashioned title applied usually 'to an Oriental', or a Syrian. This is undoubtedly from French *Monsieur*, which was also borrowed in this form into the Hausa language. It may have come thence to Jamaica, or directly — probably the latter.

For women, *Mistress* is still current as a formal term of respect. *Missis* and *Mam* are less formal, but used politely or to one's superior; and Mam may be further reduced to *ma*: 'Wa kine a nize dat mah?' *Miss*, prefixed to names, is very common among the folk in the friendly familiarity of equals. In the same sort of situation one finds *me chile* or *me son*:

> Noe bothar watch de other gal,
> Noe pay her any mine me-chile.

and 'Tings a 'appen fas' dese days me son!' No difference of generations is necessary.

But by far the most common of these casual terms of address is *man*, which turns up in every other sentence of conversations — 'Yes man!' — 'No man!' — 'Come on, no, man?' It is decidedly not emphatic — an unstressed appendage, in fact, to something more emphatic. It is used without regard to sex or age. In the past, *beau* (paralleled in the southern United States) apparently had much the same force: 'You must not talk in that fashion, beau.'

Greetings and Exclamations

The greeting 'how do you do' has been 'howdy' here as in the other American colonies. As Foulks has written, 'The labourers ... meet ... and the noisy *how d'ye* good humouredly goes round.' But another form came into early use among the folk,

'How you do?' and still flourishes. It is a characteristically Jamaican greeting.

An old-time way of saying 'good morning' was *malembe*. After the greeting 'How you do', a common answer is *poco-poco* (from Spanish) meaning 'not too bad'; or *rough an crusty*, which says the same with equal restraint. Nowadays a very common greeting or acknowledgment of a greeting, often when people are passing each other, is *all right!* Ways of saying 'goodbye' are *day-day* and *coobite*, the latter in three syllables, /kubáiti/, which is clearly a local descendant of *goodbye t'ye*. Both are considered 'old time' expressions. The second, as a noun, is preserved in the proverb, 'Two time cobite, someting want'n' — that is, if someone says goodbye twice, there's something he wants. The similar 'thank ye' has become *tanky* or *tenky*, as in the saying, 'Good me do a tenky me get' — I do good and get 'thank ye,' which is used with heavy irony if the speaker feels that he ought to get more than mere thanks, or if he has been rebuffed rather than thanked.

A number of expressions occur mainly as a part of conversation. The American 'grunts' that are usually spelt *uh-huh* for 'yes' and *unh-unh* for 'no' have Jamaican counterparts. These spellings do not clearly show the nasal element which is regularly present, nor that the syllables begin with glottal closures, and that the pitch of the voice usually rises for 'yes' and falls for 'no'. The same factors are found in Jamaica, but the basic vowel is not central: it is front and usually high. The spelling in the following example represents the norm:

Eee-Hee Missis, is me same one
Sidung yah all de time.

Phonetically this would be [ʔi'hĩ] with some rise of pitch; 'no' would be ['ʔĩ,ʔĩ] with fall of pitch. I have also heard [ʔɛ̃'hɛ̃] for 'yes'. Incidentally, English 'eh?' falls into the same pattern, that of 'an interjectional interrogative particle . . . inviting assent' as in, 'Yuh mussa feel sweet wid yuh wing dem *ee*, Bredda Wasp.' And the murmur with which one fills the gap while trying to recall something, follows too: it is [ĩ:m].

The grunts are usually considered to be of American Indian origin — as *ugh*, an exclamation of assent, certainly is. Yet the striking fact is that the Jamaican ones correspond very closely to

those of Twi, *ɛhɛ̃ɛ̃* implying affirmation, assent, 'yes!', and *ɛ́hɛ̃ɛ̃*
the contrary, 'no!' The rising pitch comes at the end of the first,
at the beginning of the second, which also corresponds. Could it
be that these grunts came to America from Africa?

Yes and *no* are also taken into the folk speech, the latter having
one pronunciation, /noa/, that has become a sign of the old-
fashioned or countrified. On the other hand, /no/, very short
and always interrogative, is extremely common: 'Come on,
no?' — 'You like it, no?' — 'Is a pretty frock, no?' — virtually
the equivalent of Standard 'won't you?' — 'don't you?' —
'don't you agree?' The most likely source of this is Portuguese,
with reinforcement from Spanish, both having the same locution; but it is paralleled in other languages.

However it is *no*, the regular negative particle equivalent to
Standard *not*,[15] that appears in the phrase *No mus*? expressing the
acceptance of a situation, or its rightness. This might be rendered
'Mustn't that be so?' or even, 'What else can you expect?' Once
I saw a garage attendant in Christiana burn his hand on the
manifold of a car which had just been running. The other
mechanic remarked, 'No mus' hot, man?' — mustn't you expect it to be hot under the circumstances?

A similar conversational phrase is *Wa' fe do*? — what's to be
done? —

> I is weary of dis worl'.
> But whey fe do, Cousin Mary . . . ?

And there is the much more lively *Wa mek*? — what's the reason?
what's going on? what are you doing? In Bennett's lines,

> Sometime me want ask a question
> Wich part, wa meck, why or who.

This may well translate an African phrase: compare the Ibo
gɛ nɛ mɛrɛ? — literally, what makes? why?

Harrock and *harrocky* — forms of *hark* and *hark-ye* — are now
considered very old-fashioned; but *mark you* is preserved as a
part of the speech-making tradition. Frequently used to punctu-
ate conversation in the same way (though only among the folk)
is *yaw* (/yaa/) or *yaw sah* — literally meaning 'you hear?', but no
longer strictly interrogative; it is about equivalent to 'you
know' dropped into a train of talk — 'truly'. Another word is

/ya/ — 'you hear?' — tagged with interrogative pitch to the end of a command, warning, or the like; 'Fine youself home befo' ten o'clock, ya?'

Commands and other exclamatory phrases include *kirrout* (evidently from *clear out*!); *bamo*, go, and *benaca*, come here (both obviously from Spanish: *vamos, ven acá*); and *challa*, go quickly (from Hindustani *chalo*, begone, come away). These seem to be relatively recent acquisitions. Whereas Standard usually adds the adverb in come *here*, come *along*, come *on*, and the like, one hears simply *Come!* as the usual command among the folk. *Bankiti* (all right! O.K!) 'used by sugar estate workers and others when given an order to carry out'.[16], is probably African.

When about to throw or hand something suddenly to another, one may warn him with 'Su!' — which is equivalent to 'Here! Catch!' A signal used in threatening or inviting a fight, in sport or seriously, is *feh*. One of the parties says, 'Say "feh" an' I knock you!' The other, if he wants to fight, says 'Feh!' — and battle is joined.[17] A shout used by the hill people is *edoh-edoh!*, as in the song 'House an' Lan'. All three of these are African.

Expressions of indifference are *calash* or *calashte* and *poroo-poroo* (now obsolete) and *caudry*, I don't care, or *no care, no mine*. *Poloo-poloo*, according to Russell, shows 'unfeelingness', but it seems very close to *poroo-poroo*. The word *do!* is used pleadingly as in Standard, but in Jamaica it has also, in fact more frequently, a negative sense, meaning 'Please don't!', and comes before rather than after the imperative. Uncle Newton illustrates it well: see the citation just given for *bucky massa*.

Other typical expressions are 'Po me bwoy!' (or 'Po me gal!') — cries of self-pity (with strong stress on each syllable).

Some interjections seem to have fallen out of use in the course of time. 'Babwa!', an expression of wonder, was soon condemned even among the folk as a vulgar Guinea expression. As Russell remarked, 'The interjection *babwa* is used only on estates and their vicinity, and is of African origin. Settlers in the mountainous parts would consider it disgraceful to be heard using such a word.'[18] 'Kie! Admiration, satisfaction,' also recorded by Russell, was probably the same as the 'Ki' of American Negroes, but one does not hear it today. *Tajo*, an exclamation of pleasure and encouragement while dancing, has been found recorded only in 1790: 'O! laud, O! tajo, tajo tajo!'

Others are now 'old time' or countrified, as when *oh* becomes *a-oh-a* (stress on *oh*). Bennett spelt it *a-oah* in the speech of a country-woman, and I heard it in 1952 in St Ann from a speaker who had just understood something. *Hi!* shows surprise or astonishment; as Williams recorded it, 'Hi! da for me bible book'.[19] A very common and long-standing interjection, now less used, is /wáai/, usually with *oh* or some other word added. In 1826: 'and make de buckra man cry *woio*'; 1868: 'Woy me dead!'; 1950: 'Whai, bwoy!'; and in a song, 'Whai oh! Judy drownded'. This exclamation usually indicates great trouble — fear, grief, pain; but I have heard it often as a burst of amusement followed by gusts of laughter.

One that must have come in early, and is still often heard, is /ku/ (or /ko/), which may be an interjection but quite as often a verb meaning 'look', as in the following: 'Ko 'pon you' jam samplatta nose' — Look at your damned nose, flat as a sandal!

— But whenever Dumpah hears it,
  'Qui Yah!' shouts he in amazement.
— Coo pan de invite wi jes been get.
— Koo Bra Rat! (Look at Brother Rat!)
— Massi me massa! Koo yah lawd
  Miss Katy lissen noh. . . .

One is tempted to see the origin of this in *look!*, yet the loss of /lu/ from a stressed syllable would be unparalleled. It seems more plausible to connect it with *ki!* or some other African form, though no good candidate has been found.

Chambre wrote in 1858:

The servants . . . contented themselves with exclaiming, 'Aye! Aye!' as they never fail to do whenever anything occurs to excite their astonishment.

Like many others, this is probably African,[20] but might possibly be from Spanish, French, or some other language. I heard it in Hanover in 1952 from a man who felt sudden fear that the car he was riding in was going to be struck by another: '/áaaai/!'

Yet another expression of surprise, but without concern, is spelt by Louise Bennett *eh! eh!* Like the grunt for *no*, this has glottal closures before the vowels, and pitch falling from a high start, but it is *not* nasalised: phonetically, [ˀɛˀɛ].

By far the commonest of Jamaican interjections (and it goes most of the way up the social scale) is usually spelt *cho*! It almost always begins the phrase, and shows impatience, scepticism, mild scorn, or the like. I once thought it represented English *tcha*!, but the OED records this only from 1844 and 1887, whereas *cho* was already in folk use in Jamaica by 1830: 'Cha! said the Negro . . . I say *cha*, master attorney, when you say I want to be free.'[21] Modern instances hardly require illustration, but a typical one is, 'De ole ooman sey "cho Anancy dat shouldn't worry yuh".' It seems most probable that this is African. Another form, /chot/, may be heard as an occasional variant.

A number of other exclamatory phrases have English elements, but are old-fashioned even in Jamaica. Russell recorded *Me mada*!, *Me fada*!, *La-a-a-a-a-a-a-a-a*! and *Lack-lack-lack*! If the last is not from *alack*, it may represent *lawk*, a minced form of *Lord* that is still to be heard: in Christiana /laak a masi/; in Hanover /o laak man/; in Moneague /laaks/ — all these were recorded in 1952. McKay had 'S'ep me King' and there are many other variations. An old expression of surprise is 'Massanayga oooo!' *What a way*, a common beginning of exclamatory sentences, means 'how very much' or the like, as in 'Wat a way dem musa shame!'

Some exclamations showing anger, scorn, insult, are: /ráatid/ — already discussed, and probably representing *wrothèd*; /túfa/ — of which Jekyll says, 'tuffa, with Italian *u* imitates spitting, a sign of contempt;' *caca*, which Moreton used in 1790: 'Kackkaw foa you!'[22] To make an asseveration very strong, *God* or *Jesus* is frequently used in modifying position: 'Not one Jesus penny more!' 'Not one God piece of food!' — exactly parallel to Standard *damned*.

Some exclamations are used only as calls to animals, as /kaa kaa/ to urge cattle on: 'and the *ca ca* 'ing, like so many rooks, of the children driving the mules and oxen in the mills,'[23] and /ko/ to horses or mules,[24] /kuuy/ to donkeys. Though 'whoa' is commoner, I have heard the *brrr*! of north-west Europe used to stop a horse (St James). Perhaps this was brought to Jamaica by the German settlers of Seaford Town. Fowls are not told to 'shoo' but *shi*! or *shi-shi*!. Anancy puns on *sh*! (the signal to be quiet) and *shi*! in the following: 'Is who yuh dah tell fe quiat, noh sh-sh me, afta me noh fowl.' When one wants a bird to settle or 'pitch' in a certain spot, one exclaims *em-bo*!

Echoisms

The imitation of sounds in the form or near-form of words is found everywhere. Some Jamaican folk examples were listed by Russell in 1868:

> A lick him *ply* wid de trap [strap].
> Him knock me *bap* wid him fis.
> I hit him wid de horse wip *swi, swi*;
> De gun make *bow*.
> de rock stone knock *dong* 'pan de tank battam
> De trap [trap] fly *bram*, an' cut off de puss foot.
> Him tumble in de pan [pond], *bash*;
> De wood fall down *pongo-rong*.

Bap, of this list, or *baps* is still to be heard for any sudden noise of striking, and has come to suggest a stroke that hits the place intended, therefore one that is just right. The difference between a sharp blow and something tumbling is well suggested in the sentence, 'I hit him biff! and he fall down briggadim.'[25] Other kinds of noises associated with movement are echoed in Louise Bennett's lines:

> Wat a debil of a bump-an-bore,
> Rig-jug an palam-pam!

A well-known word suggesting an unimpressive fall — a *boos* (pronounced /bus/) — has come to mean a disappointment.

Words that suggest a sudden swift, smooth action are *flips*, *flups*, and *swips*, as in the following:

> She linga, an de good good man
> Jus 'flips' outa her han!

'I drink it off *flups*!'; *swips*, 'to pass swiftly'; and 'to swips off a drink'.

Others are far more specific or limited in what they imitate, and are closer to being conventional words. The sound of meal (or other food) frying with water is *shwuwa* or *shuwa* — and strikingly enough, there is a word for this in Kongo *shiaw-shia* 'to splutter in cooking'.[26] A way of whistling in two tones with the fingers half closed in the palm is called *tuttu-watta*. One of the most expressive is to *voon-vap*, or play the organ badly: the two syllables suggest very well the alternation of full tones and panting ones that an inexpert player produces.

Chapter Eleven

RELIGION, BELIEF, SUPERSTITION

VIRTUALLY all the Christian churches and sects are represented in Jamaica, though none is officially established. Christianity is certainly the predominant religion. Yet, as a byproduct of the historical situation, many elements of Christianity, both doctrinal and ritual, have overflowed the bounds of any of the Christian churches and become mingled quite inextricably with the remains of African cultist practices, brought over by the slaves and still having a considerable hold on the folk more than a century after emancipation. It is quite impossible to draw sharp lines of distinction among the multiplicity of mixtures already produced and still continuing. *Obeah* and *myal* were once distinct: now they are not; Christianity and paganism were once separate: now the Bible is read at ceremonies otherwise largely devoted to the worship of 'ancestral spirits'; the former *enthusiasm* of Protestant sects has become interfused with possession by zombies, and Catholic medallions are valued as good *guards* (amulets) against obeah. Such distinctions as we can make among the numerous terms we shall, knowing that not all the actual complexities will be represented.

Names for the chief churches are the standard ones — Church of England, Baptist, Methodist, Presbyterian, and so on. However, Father Joseph J. Williams has reported that 'The first priest to become well known throughout the Jamaican "bush" was a Frenchman, and the Catholic Church came to be known in consequence as the French Church'. (In the folk mind, *French* is associated with Haiti, rather than with France, as will appear in some other terms.)

Since the movement for emancipation was most strongly led by the Baptists and Methodists, the bitterness of the Jamaican planters and the English anti-abolitionists produced the derisive name *the Saints* for Wilberforce and his following. This word appeared first in a Jamaican source: 'Every thing is attributed, right or wrong, to the *Saints* (as they are called) in England, and their interference with the concerns of the proprietors in Jamaica has certainly excited a feeling of the greatest indignation.'[1] An account follows of a 'half-mad' runaway slave 'whose head had been turned by the Methodists' — 'He and his companions sit around the effigy of Saint Wilberforce, as they call it. . . .' The same kind of feeling is expressed about a servant who has turned Methodist: 'Mr Mathews cautioned me, at parting, against the sanchy, as he called my valet; adding, that however well he might serve me, a saint was like a mule.' The nickname *sanchy*, found only here, presumably means *saint*, or *sanctified*. (Because of the date it cannot be the same as the later *sankey*.)

The Baptists' part in emancipation has left behind only a couple of local terms, now historical:

> On many of the revolted estates hundreds of 'Baptist tickets'* were found; while the rebellion was publicly distinguished by the negroes as 'The Baptist War'. *The uninitiated may not understand what is meant by a 'Baptist Ticket'. It is a printed card, . . . Every negro attached to the congregation has a fresh ticket given to him once a month. The members are obliged to present these tickets to the Baptist minister every Sunday, who, on the receipt of a macaroni, (one shilling and eightpence currency,) fills up one of the blank spaces; thus certifying the attendance of the negro at the chapel, and the presentation of the offering. Should two or three Sundays pass, and the production of the ticket be neglected, the slave, so offending, is expelled from the congregation.[2]

The Negroes were said to attach great importance to these tickets. Instead of to *christen*, the old verb to *christian* remained in use till after 1781: 'Quashee . . . got himself christianed, and changed his name to James Reeder.'[3]

The leadership of Baptists and Methodists before emancipation continued after and has added at least two more words. First, *wesley* for a Methodist meeting or, later on other gatherings at which hymn singing or some other Methodist practice was followed: McKay wrote of the *Wesly horn* with which people were called to these meetings. Second, *sankey* (after the American evangelist singer who, with Moody, made a great stir at the end of the past century) meaning a book of religious songs, or a

single song. Beckwith has reported the words of a religious
enthusiast: 'And I dreamt that I saw an angel, and he bids me
get a Bible and a Sankey and a rod with a double fold. . . .' But
the latter meaning is far the more current, and does not apply to
Methodist songs alone, but even to pocomania ones. It has also
made its way into a derisive proverb which evokes a lively picture of loud singing: 'Ebry donkey hab him sankey.'

The local cults not allied to Christian churches (though often
naming themselves after them) fall into three general classes:
Revival, Pocomania, and African or Cumina.⁴ Among the first,
the best known cult was *Bedwardism*, after their leader Bedward.
This man, winning a personal following, and founding what he
called the Jamaica Baptist Free Church (though it was not
actually connected with the Baptist Church), laid the corner-
stone of his building at August Town, St Andrew, in 1894. This
'became the established home of "Bedwardism", with "camps"
for affiliated congregations in other parts of the island'. The Hope
River near by was the 'healing stream' in which the 'Prophet of
August Town' dipped his followers. 'Bedward was ordained
Bishop of this church with the title of Shepherd, and there
were . . . "station guards" and "Mothers", after the Revivalist
pattern.' The climax of the movement came in 1920 when Bedward announced that he was God, and would fly to heaven on
December thirty-first. Great turmoil was occasioned, thousands
of the faithful coming from all parts of the island to ascend with
Bedward, having sold all their possessions to give the money to
him. When the event did not occur, even after some postpone-
ments, and the leader had to be put into the asylum for the
insane, the movement abated somewhat. But it was typical of the
Revivalist type of sect, modelled on the Christian churches in
many ways, but following the personal inspiration of a local
'prophet'. A group of this kind currently in Morant Bay is called
Flenkee, but many have far more impressive names.

The *Pocomania* cults — called /poko/ for short — mingle re-
vivalism with elements of obeah and myalism. The first form of
the word that I have found in print is Beckwith's *pukkumerian*,
which probably represents a real pronunciation, though the
explanation she offers is quite fanciful. 'The name is used in
derision, say the followers of this cult; for they are really Revivalists like the rest. "Pick-them-here" I venture to suggest as the

etymology of the appellation; that is, "Dig here for the buried obeah," because of the claim this cult makes to prophetic powers in detecting buried obeah.' The word is usually understood to-day as if it were of Spanish origin, 'pocomania' meaning something like 'mild madness'. But this is by no means likely. Though Spanish *poco* is well known in Jamaica, and pronounced like this, there is no evidence for 'pocomania' as a Spanish word. It may well be a folk-etymology (like the name Ocho Rios) made up by a speaker of English who knew some Spanish and jumped to a conclusion. I suspect the word to be African; it would certainly bear further investigation.[5]

It has appeared also as *pocomanism*. Moore writes that another name for the cult is 'Black Israelites' and that the pocomania or poco groups are 'looked upon with disfavour by all the other cult groups', who consider this devil worship.

The third general group of cultists, the *African* or *Cumina* (terms used in the lowlands of St Thomas around Morant Bay, and elsewhere), frankly seek possession by 'ancestral spirits', to which end they have elaborate ceremonies with drumming, dancing, and singing. Moore defines *Cumina* as 'A ceremonial memorial dance for the dead the first of which may be held within the first year, often on the first anniversary of the death of the individual. . . . Public *cumina* dances begin usually at sun-down Friday and last till sundown Saturday'. Others are held on the occasions of entombment, betrothal, birth, and nine-night (after a funeral). *Cumina* is undoubtedly an African word: Turner has Kimbundu (Angola) *Kumona*, to see; possession. It has also been reported as *cumuna* and *crumuna*.

The cults have a considerable array of titles for their officers, in which they follow much the same patterns. The Revivalists, for example, have various kinds of *shepherds* and *shepherdesses* (or *mothers*). Highest are the *crowned shepherd* and *shepherdess*; a *cutting shepherd* 'determines whether there is any evil influence coming into a meeting' and if so, cuts it out, using candles or other lights to 'control' the spirits; a *hunting shepherd* 'has the duty, principally, to hunt out every part of the yard', meeting both good and bad spirits; a *rambling shepherd* is a diviner with 'special knowledge of the spirit world', who 'foresees events in the future as well as events about to happen in the ceremony'; a *warrior shepherd* (sometimes called *captain*) is an 'officer of military aspect, whose duty is to 'war the bounds' or 'protect the area being used for the service'; a *water shepherd* must 'see that there is pure water available at all times'; and, finally, a *wheeling shepherd* wheels like a dervish round and round the ceremonial circle, sometimes with a glass of holy water on his head which he does not spill; he is in general charge of the services of a revivalist band. There are a *wheeling mother* and all the other 'mothers' corresponding to the various 'shepherds'.

Subordinate officers attached to these, called *workers*, are *hunter man* and *hunting woman*, *warrior man* and *warrior woman* (who carries a wooden sword), and the similar series of both men and women, cutting, rambling, and spying. A *shepherd boy* is attached to the *wheeling shepherd*, and a *water boy* to the *water shepherd*. Initiates are given the offices of *co-worker*, *bearer*, or *post-holder* — those who hold the central post — and also *bell-ringer*. The highest rank among Revivalists is *Father*: 'This high office may be reached only by a crowned shepherd, who, after serving for a considerable period of time, becomes so respected by his own and other bands that he is advanced to the calling of Father.'

But these usages, even so elaborated, are not fixed; there are local variations. Beckwith reported in 1929: 'The women who . . . become active Revivalists are called mammies, the men, soldiers. They are led by a "captain" and a principal mammy, often called shepherd and shepherdess, who in turn may be directed by a head captain and mammy for a large district.' And there are such offices as *Bible pointer*, 'the woman who reads the psalms at a Revival ceremony' and sometimes a *dove* or *queen dove*; also *acting governess* and *crowned governess*.

The Pocomanians follow most of these usages. According to Beckwith, 'The Pukkumerian leaders are called "governors" or "shepherds". Each shepherd has attached to himself a good-looking young woman (not his wife) who acts as his confederate under the name of "governess" or sometimes "shepherdess". The two have a secret code of speech which the spirits are supposed to speak when they appear at a meeting, the words spoken in frenzy by one being interpreted by the other.'

The African or Cumina groups have a *Queen* or *Mother of the Cumina* who is the female singer. She is 'also referred to as the "black and white girl" ' and is 'either a relative or appointed by the family holding the Cumina. The master of ceremonies . . .

wears a black and white cord around his neck, which is the badge of his office. A number of times during a ceremony the female singer will wear his black and white cord. . . . The qualifications for a Mother of Cumina are predicated upon a knowledge of folk songs and a great deal of strength to withstand the strong zombies who come close and sometimes enter to possess her. . . She is the chief assistant to the master of ceremonies'.

Songs sung at these ceremonies are known as *bilah*; Moore says they are in 'a dialect which is primarily English', whereas 'the Jamaica country songs are in a language referred to, in this area, as African'. He has given one at length, *Tange lange Jenny*, which is a mixture of the folk English, some genuinely African words, and a good deal of free sound-play that is not identifiable as either.

The tribal 'African gods' have many names: Moore lists sixty-two 'earthbound gods' including such as *Macoo*, who 'causes the possessed zombie to climb up poles and trees backwards', *Kanuba*, *Kish*, and so on; and thirty-nine 'sky gods' such as *Oto* or *King Zombie*. And *Zombie*, as used by this cult, he defines as follows: 'A zombie is a god, or an ancestor who was once possessed by a god or other ancestral zombie, or a living being who has been possessed by one of these.' The 'sky gods' who guard the 'four corners of the earth' are called the 'four watchmen' and are similar in function to the Revivalists' 'Four Evangelists'. The names of these 'gods' are a strange hodgepodge of ordinary ones like Jimmie, Brownie, Dorothy, with Biblical ones such as Ezekiel, Uriah, Leah, and the 'African' ones already listed.

Members of the *African* cults in lowland St Thomas are considered quite distinct from the Maroons in the mountains of St Thomas and Portland. Moore mentions in passing a few of the Maroon terms: *shref-shref*, spirit; *jah*, a god; *gangfrara*, a zombie. (One may notice that *Jah* is the form of *Jehovah* used in the English Bible from 1539 through 1758.)

Returning to the Revivalists' words connected with their ceremonies: a spirit investing a possessed person at a meeting is the *old man*, and the meeting itself is a *working* (i.e., of the spirit). Workings may also be private: faith meetings, divinations, ceremonies to protect against evil and to 'take things off people' — which, as will be seen, refers to obeah. The Revival, Revival

Zion, Pocomania, and Cumina ceremonies are conducted in a temporary building known as a *dancing booth*. To achieve possession by the spirit, the dancers go through a peculiar activity on which Beckwith reported as follows:

> Once Margaret Williston began to breathe with a short sharp intake that sounded like the bark of a dog, an exercise which is called 'trooping' and which, if persisted in, will produce in the worker that semiconscious condition so favorable to the communications of spirits, and hence so coveted at a really successful Revivalist meeting.

Moore calls it *trumping*: 'the process of sucking in the breath audibly as the body straightens from a bent position to an upright position while taking a hopping, walking step. Labouring is the term used to describe this same process as it becomes more emphatic and actually develops into an involuntary action.' Hence the phrase, to *trump and labour*, often applied to this phase of the ceremony. (Moore gives *groaning* as a synonym.) Those who are trumping 'dance, always counter-clockwise, around the altar at Revival meetings. . . . If the spirits come, and keep a cult member trumping under possession until high noon, they call this "reaching the sun dial" '.

Two phrases connected with the activities of the shepherds come straight out of the vocabulary of the agricultural labourer: *cutting and clearing* (as the cutting shepherd moves about 'cutting off evil and clearing it away'), and *chopping down* (when a shepherd causes a possessed person to fall to the ground). If the latter happens too often, 'it proves that the man has not the strength ever to become a warrior. A crowned warrior could not be chopped down by a shepherd.'

Dancing is widely known as *jumping*. Among the cults it means dancing under possession. People who dance when not really possessed are derisively said to *dry jump* — so the Revivalists remark of the Pocomanians, for example. Bennett describes a heavy woman trying to get on to a moving train:

> Se' po Miss Hayes outside da gwa'n
> Like she dah jump poco.

No doubt on the analogy of *preachment*, the word *teachment* is used for the 'teaching' derived from possession at a Revival ceremony.

One is *two-minded* when confused, as happened, for example, when the Mother in a Pocomania ceremony, 'because of the presence of a white man,' sang the wrong song. She had a 'mixed spirit' — afterwards she became *one-minded*.[6]

The Cumina groups use many of these terms but have others of their own. At their marriage ceremony, for example, the drums are invoked, sprayed with rum, and tuned; they are then *set*, which means to take them to the dancing floor, 'feed rum to the gods and other zombies, and chalk the ring on the floor of the booth.' The various gods and zombies are then *greeted* — that is, 'drummed into the heads of the drums.' When the rhythmic beating on the rim of the drum increases in tempo, which 'indicates the presence of zombies in the drum', it is said to be *hot*. The gods are then fed and the dance proceeds. When 'the principal zombies and ancestors come into the drum, then stand along the four walls of the house and watch the "setting" ', this is called the *lining of the walls*. 'The rite of drumming sky and earthbound gods through the body of a goat preparatory to sacrificing it' is called *purification*.

Drumming is so important a part of Cumina that the drummer must rise through stages to the honour of playing the lead drum. 'Drummers begin on the *banda* . . . [A certain man] played the *banda* at Cumina dances for six years before he was permitted to "mount" the playing drum.' To *mount* the drum means to sit astride it; it lies on its side and is played with the hands.

The altar in Revival ceremonies may be somewhat like that in a Christian church: a *table* as it is called — which word, by extension, refers also to a service. There are various *mourning tables*, the first 'at any time during the first three months after death' and others at three month periods thereafter; a *memorial table* comes usually two and a half years after burial; a *healing table* is intended to cure someone; a *cutting and clearing table* to 'set up a power to get away from trouble'; an *uplifting table* 'to seek the promotion of understanding and prophecy'; and (sixth) a *crowning table*, which is 'essentially a service of ordination'.

The Pocomanians use the *table* but combine it with a *ground altar*, which is a level circle marked on the earth at least thirty-six feet across, with a triangular stone in the centre called the *power key*. Around the power key there are actually three concentric circles scratched into the earth, the innermost representing

God the Father, the other two the Son and Holy Ghost. In these circles are placed candles, flowers, fruits and by Revivalists a Bible. The area around the outermost circle is known as *the world*: there the trumping and labouring is done. Pocomanians sacrifice a chicken and pour the blood upon, around, and under the *power key* stone, place a black cloth over it, and a white cloth over the black.

Similar to the *power key* is the *power stone* used in Pocomania services, which may be 'placed on the "altar" or table, and covered with a black cloth having a white cross on it'. *Key* means the object which serves as a 'control point through which spiritual powers can come'. It may be 'a stone, a shepherd's crook, a cloth, or a specially dedicated churchyard'. (The crook is also called a *swivel* or *jack*.)

The *smashing of the first altar* is 'the point, in Revival and Pocomania ceremonies, at the end of the first half of the service when "food and drink from the altar are offered to all those in attendance" (Revival) or when the careful arrangement of fruits and candles is kicked out of place and some fruits are hurled in hostile manner into the audience (Pocomania). The latter calls on evil spirits, e.g. Lucifer'. This diabolical appeal is the feature which separates Pocomania most clearly from Revival. It furnishes the further term *second table*: that part of the 'Pocomania service, when the table with a Bible and lantern are set over the Key in the center of the ground altar, the Bible is removed, and the shepherd invokes fallen angels, and trumping and possessions follow'.[7]

Kerr has reported seeing at a balm-yard what was there called a *seal* — very similar to the ground altar. 'The seal is a circle of stamped out red earth with a rope around it. Mother Evangeline says she often goes and works on the seal and draws visions there. It is consecrated.' And Beckwith recorded *prayer key*, which seems to be much like a *power key*; a man at a meeting says, 'I feel to pray, and there isn't any chance to pray at the time, and I bow to squeeze the prayer-key.'

It should be evident from these usages that among many of the Jamaican folk the line between religion and superstition can hardly be drawn. Superstition, the belief in magic, witchcraft, the active intervention of ghostly or diabolic forces in the world of nature and the lives of men is surprisingly strong. It is of

African origin but goes up the social scale much farther than one would expect. *Obeah*, the Jamaican form of sorcery or 'black magic', was once counterbalanced by *myal*, or 'white magic', a healing cult. Obeah employed its powers against people; myal claimed to counteract those powers. But the earliest instance we have of the latter word (from Long's *History*, 1774) shows that the obeah-men had already made myalism a part of their practice, and corrupted it. As Long wrote:

> Not long since, some of these execrable wretches in Jamaica [sc. obeah-men] introduced what they called the *myal dance*, and established a kind of society, into which they invited all they could. The lure hung out was, that every Negroe, initiated into the myal society, would be invulnerable by the white men; and, although they might in appearance be slain, the obeah-man could, at his pleasure, restore the body to life.

And Edwards a few years later:

> *Obia*-men or women . . . is now become in Jamaica the general term to denote those Africans who in that island practise witchcraft or sorcery, comprehending also the class of what are called Myal-men, or those who, by means of a narcotick potion . . . which occasions a trance or profound sleep of a certain duration, endeavour to convince the deluded spectators of their power to re-animate dead bodies.

The spelling *obeah* was Long's and has continued to be the standard one, though *obea* was formerly used and *obi* also. Banbury adopted Long's etymology which went back to 'a Hebrew term (Ob) the name of an ancient idol'. This cannot be supported today, however. The word refers rather to the collection of 'things' with which the obeah-man works his charms, for which the OED gives Efik *ubio*. Twi has *bayi*, witchcraft, sorcery; and *ɔ-bayifó*, witch, wizard — literally 'witchcraft-person' — or *obeah-man*. This noun has been in use since 1784; *obeah-woman* was first recorded in 1803; *obeahism* appears in 1836.[8] As a verb, *obeah* has been recorded since before 1818; two contemporary examples are, 'A obeah dem obeah de man, as a man tek sick,' and Bennett's humourous commentary on the trouble one can have from an old automobile:

> Is betta smady obeah yuh
> Dan sell yuh a ole car!

The *obeah* itself is known as the obeah-man's *things*, sometimes his *bush*, because it frequently contains herbs medicinal or poisonous. 'The Obi is usually composed of a variety of materials; viz. blood, feathers, parrots' beaks, dogs' teeth, alligators' teeth, broken bottles, grave dirt, rum, and egg-shells'[9] — so goes an early description. These materials are essential to the magic. Banbury tells of the fate of one obeah-man: 'Another obeahman with whom he had a quarrel, had burnt his "things", which made him mad. It is the common opinion that when this is done, an obeahman becomes good for nothing. He could never "work" after that, and generally gets out of his head.' Someone who has obtained obeah 'things' and sets out for home 'must not stop on the way, look behind, or speak to any one, nor allow rain to wet him on the way, as this would either tend to destroy the efficacy of the "bush", as it is sometimes called, or obeah might 'turn upon' the person carrying it, and do him material injury'. From this comes another name for the obeah-man: *bush-man*, or *bush-doctor*.[10]

Virtually equivalent to *obeah* too is the word /gúzu/. The first record of it was Russell's: *gaso*, but Beckwith spelt *goozoo*: 'you may say "working goozoo" as well as "working obeah".' It has also been reported in the form *gunzoo*. The source is probably from Twi, which has several related phrases containing *gu so*, and meaning 'to conjure', 'to do against', and so on.

The obeah-man has long been known as a *professor*; Edwards wrote in 1794, 'It is very difficult for the White proprietor to distinguish the *Obeah professor* from any other Negro upon his plantation.' This term is still in use. Much more modern, however, are *science man, scientist,* and *scientific man.* He is also a *magic-man*, or (from his use of those instruments in conjuring) a *knives-and-scissors-man*. An admirer of Mr Bustamante expressed his awe in the phrase, 'Busta seem to be a scientific man.'

Another name for an obeah-woman is *French Woman.* 'Parkes says the "French women" have the most wisdom of all and are the most to be feared,' according to Beckwith, and she refers to 'one who occupied . . . a house backing upon the Kingston race course' and predicted winning horses. 'Betting was high, and even white men have acknowledged their indebtedness to the mysterious powers of the "French woman".' (This suggests an influence from Haiti or Martinique, where voodoo is vigorously practised.)

Though the source of the word *myal* (or *mial*) is not certain, it is very probably African.[11] One reads of a recrudescence of myalism after emancipation in which the myal-men were also known as *angel-men*:

> The great mial procession about the year 1842 . . . took its rise at Newman Hall estate in Saint James, and went through that parish, Westmoreland and Hanover, increasing as it went until it consisted of hundreds of deluded fanatics. They went by the name of 'Mial people'; they were also called *Angel men*. They declared that the world was to be at an end: Christ was coming and God had sent them to pull all the obeahs and catch the shadows that were spellbound at the cotton trees.

Russell defined myal as 'Excitement bordering on madness'. The word seems to have acquired a specialised sense today, however:´ 'dancing with a spirit in a trance', or, at a cumina ceremony, 'the possession dance of a dancing zombie' (Moore).

The myal-man is also '*foyeyed*—or *four-eyed*', as Banbury had it, because he 'can see spirits'. Beckwith interpreted this, rather, as *fore-eyed*; but I am inclined to follow Banbury.

Obeah was used from early days to prevent praedial larceny. *Puntees* were 'hung in the trees and grounds as charms to keep off thieves'. And in 1825 De la Beche wrote,

> The negroes still continue to place watchmen (as they call them), in their provision grounds, though the practice is by no means so general as formerly, these are commonly composed of pieces of the wood-ant's nest, the roots of a particular grass, grave dirt, bunches of feathers, &c., either singly or together. Some people even make small boxes, resembling the coffins of infants. . . . These various 'watchmen' have ceased to be much attended to by the habitual plunderers of provision grounds.

The words *work* and *working* refer not only to the presumably good spirits of the Revivalist, but to the obeah-man's bad powers. In Banbury's words, 'the obeahman is retained as well as the lawyer' by a man in legal difficulties, 'and at times he not only "works" at home on the case, but goes into Court with his client for the purpose, it is called, of "stopping" the mouths of the prosecutor and his witnesses and of influencing the Judge and jury.' But the most characteristic word of this kind is *put*, with its antonym *pull*. They appear together in the Myalist song (from about 1842):

> Obeah pain hot, oh!
> Me wi' pull he, oh! . . .
> Lord, we come fe pull he oh,
> A no we put he, oh!

In short, the obeah-man has *put* obeah on someone, and the myal-man says he will *pull* it. But both functions became absorbed by the former: 'An *obeahman* can always "pull" as well as "put", cure as well as kill. And there is the phrase "dem *put him so*", used of a man who has been put into the power of obeah, in which state he is not responsible for his actions, and will do anything wicked.' An obeah-man was therefore a *puller*. *Put off* and *take off* have recently been reported as equivalents of *pull*. An older word was to *set* obeah for someone — as if setting a trap. Edwards has told how it worked:

> When a Negro is robbed of a fowl or a hog, he applies directly to the Obeah man or woman; it is then made known among his fellow Blacks, that *Obi is set* for the thief; and as soon as the latter hears the dreadful news, his terrified imagination begins to work . . . he presently falls into a decline. . . .

After the obeah has been pulled, it may be *killed*. Banbury described this as putting the object that caused the disease into a basin, and throwing lime juice and ashes over it.

Other phrases, some euphemistic, mean to employ obeah. One is, *to go away for* someone — that is, to seek out an obeahman to employ against him. Bennett has the lines:

> Soh dem gu weh fe har an' de po' chile
> Goh step ovah dem obeah jeng-jeng.

Jeng-jeng refers to the obeah 'things' that have been *set* against the girl: she steps over them, and the charm becomes active. Smith refers to an 'Obeah stick, wid magic tings cut all round it' — some other piece of the paraphernalia of sorcery.

To *burn wangla* for someone implies obeah practice against him. As Banbury explained it: 'Sometimes application is made for the purpose of punishing thieves. A curious custom is connected with this, which prevailed in the western parts of the island formerly, and we believe to some extent still. It is called "Burning wanglo". The seed of this plant is procured, and with pepper and salt is burned on the road where the thief is known to travel over night. This has the effect, the people believe, of "catching" the thief. . . . Such a dread was entertained of the potent effects of this grain when used in this way, that very often the thief restored overnight what he had stolen.'

Obeah is also used in affairs of love. 'To bring about an influence over the mind of anyone, in order to gain some advantage from, or over him . . . is called "turning his eyes". . . . Females among the superstitious use this sort of *incantation* to prevent their *sweethearts* . . . leaving them for other women.' For the similar purpose of winning a lover to a woman, 'the obeahman gives what is called in English "*a love potion*", but in Jamaica, "*tempting powder*", which is a very *nauseous* draught and at times may prove *dangerous*. . . .' In other words, it is sometimes used to injure or kill. There was a notorious obeah-woman at Llandovery once: 'By means of a "peace cup and spoon" she says she dropped off all the fingers and toes of a woman who had stolen from her.'

Father Williams records a curious phrase, used about the country people's misunderstanding of the Catholic priest's use of candles: they think that he is using powerful obeah by *lighting a candle on them.* 'This process is thus described: "Fadder take pin and Fadder take candle, and him stick der pin in der candle; and him light der candle on you. Der candle him burn and him burn and him burn. And you waste and you waste and you waste. And when der flame touch dat pin — you die." '

Obeah is reflected in most departments of the folk life, when not overtly, covertly through the persistence of older spiritualistic notions — the belief in *duppies*, *shadows*, and so on. The distinction was once clearly made between these two terms, following the West African concept of the multiple soul: the soul within the body and the shadow outside it. At death the soul goes to heaven, but the shadow lingers near the corpse. Unless it is laid, it becomes a *duppy*, as one man explained it. But the two words have now become confounded; *duppy* is the usual one, and when *shadow* is used it means very much the same.

Before the distinction was obscured it was thought that a person's shadow could be taken away from him while living. 'It is believed' as Banbury put it, 'that after the shadow of anyone is taken he is never healthy; and if it be not caught, he must pine away until he dies. The shadow when taken is carried and nailed to the cotton tree.' From this developed the terms *shadow-catcher* and *shadow-catching*. Of an early trial Barclay wrote: 'One of the witnesses, a Negro belonging to the same estate, was asked — "do you know the prisoner to be an obeah-man?" *"Ees, massa, shadow-catcher, true."* "What do you mean by a shadow-catcher?" *"Him ha coffin,* (a little coffin produced,) *him set for catch dem shadow."* "What shadow do you mean?" *"When him set obeah for summary* (somebody), *him catch dem shadow and dem go dead."* '

But *shadow-catching* also meant exactly the opposite procedure of getting a spirit away again and restoring it to its owner. This ceremony, invariably performed at night, was described by Banbury as follows:

> The person suspected of having lost his shadow was taken to the cotton tree where it was spell bound, or to which it was 'nailed', as the people expressed it. The mialmen were accompanied thither by a large concourse of people. The victim was dressed all in white, with a white kerchief about his head. Eggs and fowls were taken along with cooked food to the cotton tree. The mialmen paraded up and down before the tree, with white cloths over their shoulders, singing and dancing; and all the people joining in the chorus. Alternately the cotton tree was pelted with eggs, and the necks of fowls [w]rung off, and their bodies cast at it. This was done to *propitiate* the 'deaths', or 'duppies' that had the shadow enthralled at the tree, the song and dancing proceeded more vigorously as the shadow began to make signs of leaving the tree. A white basin, with water to receive it, was held up; after they had sung, yelled and danced to their hearts' content, they all of a sudden caught up the person, and ran home, with him, affirming that the shadow was caught, covered up in a basin. Upon reaching home a cloth was wet in the water, and applied to the head of the patient and the shadow was said to be restored. This is the process of shadow-catching, for this piece of work they exacted six dollars, and were always readily paid.

For the covered basin of this account, a 'shet pan' is used today.[12] Not only shadows may be caught, apparently, but living people. In the case of a lost child: 'Delay is incurred in looking out an obeah, or mial man to "*catch*" the child, believing that it could not be found without such aid, being hidden by the duppies.'

Our earliest Jamaican citation for duppy is Long's: *duppies*; the singular is usually *duppy*, sometimes *duppie*; Russell made it *duppe*. Banbury offered the quite fantastic explanation: 'The word duppy appears to be a corruption of *doorpeep* (something peering through the keyhole).' It is African, of course, from some such form as Bube *dupe*, ghost.

Those who believe in duppies — which includes the greater part of the folk and many others above them — make little if any distinction from 'ghost', except that the duppy is usually invisible even when manifesting its presence. Either by its own impulsion or because it has been *put* by an obeah-man, it may cause *spirit-sickness*: 'when a person is troubled with the wrong kind of spirit, and a "working" by an obeah man is necessary to . . . "take it off"; or else drugs, especially "incense from the doctor-shop". Cumina dancing is used for spirit-sickness' (Moore). Beckwith recounts the cure of a sick man as she heard it from an eyewitness (showing a new application of 'catching'): 'They rescued Walker and took him away to Good Hope. And they got a smart man called duppy-catcher and he put him [the duppy] in a bottle, and when we saw the bottle we saw a sort of fly in the bottle. And Walker got better.'

When a spirit or *death* (or *dead*) touches a living person, it is said to *put the hand on* or *knock* him or her — usually with inimical intent: 'A negro woman . . . fancied her mother's ghost had appeared to her, and warned her of her death, and that whenever she attempted to take any nourishment, the spirit would wash its hands in the broth, gruel, or whatever else it might be; — her expression was, that her mother had "put her hand upon her".' 'The "deaths" are believed capable of returning for any relative or friend, or any one who injured them in life. This they effect by "putting hand" upon them, or "knocking" them. Persons taking in suddenly with convulsive fits are thought to be knocked by duppies, especially children and young infants.'[13]

When duppies communicate during sleep they are said to

R

dream to a person or simply *dream* him. 'When you sick ... and can't get better, and when you may have a dead, he come and dream you; say such-and-such a place trouble you. Then you must look after it.' The duppy may *blow breeze* (or *wind*) on you, which is usually bad, but can be good. 'When good spirit come, he carry a good breeze; but when sick spirit comes, evil spirit bring a high breeze. You can tell by looking at the person.' Baptism is 'a protection of the child against "bad wind" '. 'And so de duppy blow good breeze.'

Duppies work through plants, animals, and birds as well. At least half a dozen plants have duppy names (duppy pumpkin, duppy soursop, and others discussed below). One of the best known superstitions is that the pawpaw tree, if planted near a house, will *reduce you* — that is, sap the strength of the dwellers. There is the superstition of the *talking cow*, which gives an omen of death by lowing sadly. 'Sometimes Negroes will cut out a cow's tongue and leave the animal to die unsuspected of its owner, and it is possible that this practice has some connection with the fear of the "talking cow".'[14] This is also called a *wishing cow*, with a little difference: 'When a cow bawl six, seven, eight time a night, mean someone gwine dead — de cow is wishing dat someone die.' Several birds are looked upon superstitiously, especially the ground dove and gimme-me-bit. It is believed that if you kill spiders and trouble birds' nests, your hands will shake. Louise Bennett has an amusing poem about a clumsy girl who breaks things:

> De gal musa gingle bud nes'
> Meck she start mash up me funicha.

Word-magic is also believed in, as when one exclaims *buzu*! in a game to give bad luck to an opponent and good to oneself. Beckwith has reported '*tan deh* (stand there) as the 'formula of an obeah exorcist or duppy-catcher' used to immobilise the duppy. But she also reports that 'Throughout Manchester there is a belief that a thief who enters a man's field can be made to stay and work until the owner comes and gives him a flogging. The art is called "stand there" and depends upon impersonating the presence of a duppy'. *Tan-deh* is also 'any illness believed to be inflicted by an obeah-man' — he has told it to stay upon the victim, therefore it is hard to cure. One of the signs of the possession of spirit power is supposed to be the gift of tongues — the ability to 'cut unknown tongue' (discussed above with *cut*). Of one obeah-man Beckwith wrote, 'When anyone goes to him who he says has a duppy, he gets into great power, jumps and speaks tongues.' To be *in a power* has become a common phrase for any kind of exhilaration, as if it came from spirits. Here is a humourous application of it from a story: 'Wen de gal dem hear Anancy song de whole a dem run out an crowd roun him. Anancy was eena powah.'

Since duppies are harmful more often than not, one generally seeks to protect oneself against them or drive them away — *drive* or *run* duppy are the usual phrases. Amulets have always been used for this purpose: an early word for such a thing was *ahpetti*, found in print only in 1826, but apparently still known. It is probably connected with Twi 'o-peyi, a certain *amulet'*. Much better known is *amba*. Banbury has explained that 'The "amber" was a talisman by which they pretended to divine. Both the mial and obeahman use it. Anything through which they look at the obeah, either in the ground or skin, is called an "amber", the name is not confined strictly to the substance so called'. He includes a song from about 1842 in which a myalman speaks cajolingly to his amulet to get it to help him, 'Amba do' know me, oh!' This word probably does come from *amber*; elsewhere we read that it was originally an amber bead hung round the neck by a string. Its electromagnetic power when rubbed was no doubt a great part of its 'magic'.

Beckwith also reported *jiggey* (or *jigger*) as a fetish used in the myal dance: the amba was accompanied by 'a second talisman' consisting of 'a bunch of herbs called "jiggey"', probably the same as in Monk Lewis's description'. The expression to *jiggy-fu* someone, to deceive and make a fool of him, no doubt alludes to this object.

But the most current term for a talisman is a *guard* (/gyaad/), (not found in print before 1929). Moore defines it as 'Anything which protects from evil spirits — e.g., crucifixes, rings, charm-medals'; they are often worn round the neck. Widows and widowers frequently wear them: 'Before the coffin is carried out of the yard a bereaved wife or husband should put on a "guard" of a large square of black cloth with a white cross marked upon it with chalk, and should wear this for four or five months.'

Also: 'A person born with a caul has this power to see duppies without their harming him, although some say the faculty can be removed by wrapping up a piece of the caul in black ribbon and keeping it as a "guard".'

A favourite guard today is called an *obi-ring* or *power-ring*. Father Williams found reference to the first in 1934: a signet ring with a hole drilled in it for the reception of the charm or 'medicine'. And Moore describes power-rings as 'the ordinary metal finger rings consecrated by an obeah man, or blessed by Roman Catholic priests, to serve as guards against harmful spirits'. Another kind of guard is the *dealing stick*: Williams reports how a man was imposed on by being sold such an object to keep in his shop against the duppies who were troubling him.

The worst kinds of duppies are supposed to be those of Coolies and babies. Both are alluded to in Bennett's verses:

> Big noise eena Cudelia yard,
> Bra Charles and Sista Clem
> Dah jump and kick an gwan like
> Coolie-duppy deh pon dem! . . .

And,
> For ef dem set a nine-day baby
> Ghose fe teck yuh life,
> Yuh can go a Madda Banna balm. . . .

Moore gives the word *eidon* for 'baby duppies who died before christening', which are dangerous because 'they can never be identified and have no human knowledge'.

Other words for duppies or ghosts include *fraid*, used repeatedly by Uncle Newton. 'Gaining on them, he noticed that the small "fraid" was over-taking the bigger one, so he shouted: RUN BIG FRAID: LITTLE FRAID AFTER YOU!' *Jumbee*, as Beckwith has remarked, is more common in other parts of the West Indies than in Jamaica; yet it has some use here. One description of Anancy says, 'an' him was half man an' half spider — a sort of jumbe man.' The word is African.[15] One other term reported for a ghost is *nookoo*.

In 1774 Long pointed out a distinction which is no longer made: 'They firmly believe in the apparition of spectres. Those of deceased friends are *duppies*; others, of more hostile and tremendous aspect, . . . are called *bugaboos*.' *Bagabu* (which is simply English *bugaboo*) now means a caterpillar or worm, and *duppy* includes the monstrous and terrible spirits as well. Some of these are animal: *rolling calf*, which Banbury first reported: 'ROLLEN (roaring) CALVES . . . evil spirits in the shape of animals, which travel about at nights, and are often seen by the people.' A 1952 description is this: 'rollin calf is a *demon*, not a ghost; look like hog; cohabit with hog or pig; eat out hog food; have eyes like fire itself; travel around in darkness, have a chain trailin' behind. Can't counteract motor car. If you're traveling with light, you have the advantage; if without light, it have the advantage.' And Jekyll has reported: ' "Shopkeeper and butcher," so goes local tradition, "tief too much and when they dead they turn Rolling Calf." '

The *three-foot-horse* is a similar apparition: 'Have one front leg and two back; shape like coffin, and a little man sit on it: don't turn till they get to a cross-roads; have fire travels with it; will kill on sight. If you crawl under wire you're safe, but if you jump over, he can too, and eat you.' And, 'If im buck you up a night, im blow bad breeze pon you.'

Another duppy is *whistling cowboy*, probably the same as *whooping boy*, who 'rides Three-foot Horse, whooping like a human being and dancing on the twigs in the woods'. There are several witches and other supernatural beings, human or partly so. The /kinóul/ (skin-owl) will 'get out of their skin, go and suck people's blood'. Beckwith reports having read about *Long-bubby Susan*, though she has heard no mention of her, 'unless Susan is to be identified with Old Hige.' She 'is characterised by breasts which touch the ground and which she throws over her shoulders when attacked.'

Of all these, Old Hige is certainly the best known (*hige* means *hag*). As Banbury writes, she

> delights in human blood, especially that of new-born infants. In days gone by the '*Old Suck*' (as she was also designated on account of her imagined propensity) was to be seen enveloped in a flame of fire, wending her way late at nights through the 'nigger house', or along the high road . . . infants just born were guarded with the utmost care from the voracious creature of blood. This has given rise to the foolish notion, still generally practiced . . . of keeping up the ninth night after the birth of an infant. This night is thought the most

critical, as on it the *old hag* uses her utmost endeavour to get at the babe . . . a constant watch is kept up by the anxious mother, the midwife, and her friends . . . knives and forks, and sometimes the bible, are placed at the head of the infant. . . . The locked jaw was always believed an invariable sign of the suck of an old hag. . . . The strangest thing in connection with this superstition is, that it was believed to be the living that acted the part of the 'old hige'. Women who were addicted to it had the power of divesting themselves of their skins, and with their raw bodies issued out at nights, in quest of blood.

It seems clear that *kin-owl* and *old hige* are one and the same.

Banbury tells the story of an old hige whose husband, while she was out one night, put salt and pepper into her skin; when she came back, she could not put it on again. This explains the phrase, 'Pepper and salt to your mammy', said to ward off misfortune as a bird of ill omen flies by at night.

There are spirits connected with water, both of sea and rivers. The earliest reference found is from 1830, to 'the water spirit — the diving duppie'.[16] Banbury has a full account of the *rubba Missis*: 'She is believed to inhabit every fountainhead of an inexhaustible and considerable stream of water in Jamaica. For this reason the sources of such streams were worshipped, and sacrifices offered. . . .' She sat and combed her long black hair, appeared always at noon, but disappeared when someone approached. He feels that this superstition took its rise from the story of the mermaid or water nymph of England. Beckwith referred to *fair maid* as the old term; both *river maid* and *river mumma* are now current. Apparently there is a similar belief about the sea: Jekyll referred to the *sea-mammy*, and a present-day St Andrew man says, 'In Hope River, near Gordon Town, there's a big blue hole where people drown. When the water is low you have to pay the River Mumma, as fishermen pay the sea — throw money in.' Revivalists have adapted the former myalist worship of the river mother: during storm or rain the *River Maid* comes into their ceremonies and 'may become the most important officer, superseding others'. She is never harmed by water. Her assistants are the *water shepherd, water shepherdess, water boy*, and *water girl* (Moore).

Belief in the evil eye — or something very much like it — is

strong. Everybody has a *magnet*, the power of personal mag-
netism, which manifests itself through the eye. It may be too
strong for another person and do him harm — in which case the
first is said to *overlook* the second. Newborn babies are especially
likely to be overlooked. 'If overlooking takes place the baby's
clothes must be burnt, and some of the ashes made into tea for
him. . . . After his bath crosses are marked with blue on his back
and on the soles of his feet to prevent overlooking.'[17] This sense
of *overlook* appears to be English: the first instance of it found by
the OED was from the *Merchant of Venice* (III. ii. 15), meaning
to bewitch; but it has taken on local characteristics in Jamaica.
And, curiously enough, the almost contrary sense, to protect
from supernatural harm, is found in the name of the overlook
bean (see below). It may be, of course, that the bean is thought
of as overlooking the thief rather than the plantain ground. As
might be expected, in Jamaica the belief in luck is strong. *Good-
lucked*, *bad-lucked*, and *bad-lucky* (all three-syllable words) have
been recorded. *Luck* is also an adjective, as in the following: 'If
the mother gets twins, they are very luck and very strong. The
zombies love them.'

Partly superstitious, partly an inheritance of real knowledge
of curative herbs, is the institution of the *balm* or *balm-yard*. The
balm-yard today is known by a display of flags (especially a
white one on a tall pole) and banners. There is at least one
building used as a dwelling by the balm man or woman, where
treatment is given; and if, as often happens, some cult is connected, a meeting shed with altar or *table*, and benches for the
participants. The mixture of herb healing, drug-healing, and
myalist-obeah healing may vary from place to place, and the
last, being illegal, is sure to be surreptitious. But it may be
counted on as one component. At first glance the word *balm*
seems certainly English; it is familiar enough to the folk through
Biblical use and the names of patent medicines. Yet one cannot
be sure: Twi *abam'* is the name of a fetish, and refers to the fetish
practices at the birth of twins. This or some similar African word
may well have been absorbed into the English *balm*.

The old-time genuine herb-healing depended on *teas, fever
baths*, and other remedies made from the native 'bush'. Kirkland
has listed the components of a 'bush bath' recently made for
him having twenty-three herbs in it. The balm-yard has taken

over some of this lore but has transformed it by the addition of
'healing oils' from the 'doctor shop', some of which have real
names out of the pharmacopoeia: frankincense, myrrh, oil of
origanum, cassia, juniper, assafoetida, and so on, while others
have names betraying a superstitious or pseudo-Christian
origin: *oil of Virgin Mary, oil of compellance, oil of Calvary, oil of life,
oil of mek-you-walk, oil of rumba, oil of cat-o'-nine, oil of carry-on, oil of
turn-back, oil of conquer, must powder*, and *dead-man oil*.[18] In short,
the imagination of the balmist and the credulity of the patient
set the only limits in this field. The chemist or druggist sells
harmless oddments to those who demand them under whatever
name, and they are prescribed according to the need. Bennett
has a verse about a woman who resorts to balm oil to keep a
man from leaving her:

> For tropence ile-a-stay-wid-me
> Jus rub eena him head
> An him an her couldn' part at all
> So till one a dem dead.

We end this account with words relating to ceremonies connected with birth and death. Still honoured to some extent is the
African institution of the *navel-string tree, birth tree* or *natal tree.*
'The mother must guard it [the umbilical cord] carefully and,
from three days to a year from the time of birth, must bury it in
the ground and plant a young tree over the spot, which hence-
forth becomes the property of the child and is called his "navel-
string tree".'[19] Dunham's account differs slightly in detail:
'Birth tree — a tree given to a Maroon child at his birth, and at
which his navel-cord and afterbirth are buried in token of his
possession. The tree is his for life, and to will to his survivors.' To
Moore it is the *natal tree.*

Burial ceremonies traditionally last nine nights. On the first,
usually, is held the wake or *set-up* (i.e., sit-up). Moore has
recorded a full native description of the *making-up* (preparation)
of the corpse for burial. The *death-water* or *dead-water* is that used
to wash the corpse ceremonially before burial: 'it must not be
poured down the drain, but out in the yard, and it's bad luck to
step over it.'

The morning after the set-up comes the funeral, and ceremonies of hymn-singing, scriptural reading and the like must

continue for eight more nights. 'Unless this is done properly, the soul won't find rest — the spirit may become restless, roam at will, and make trouble.' *Nine-night* means the ninth night after the death, at which time 'the spirit of the dead person will wander back to its home to be "entertained before being definitely consigned to the world of duppies" '. At the grave there may be a definite attempt to make the spirit stay down. Beckwith has written: 'In the Santa Cruz Mountains they build a bonfire, about which the men and boys play games while the women and girls stand by watching the sport. The occasion is called the "Backinny" or "Back in i' [the grave]", as I believe.'[20]

The nine-night finishes the burial ceremonies with an evening of lively singing, dancing, *ring play* or games — even gambling. (Some of these are described in the next chapter.) To the end of this lengthy series of ceremonies the name *crop-over* (which properly refers to the sugar-making season) is often transferred. One of the hymns noted by Beckwith referred to the land of the dead as *Lomas land* — an unexplained word. A legacy is a /krebe/, sometimes spelt *crebay*.

The final part of a burial was what Long knew as the *covering* but is today called the *tombing*. According to Long it came a month after the death; if a wife had died, the widower would at that time hold the ceremony:

'A fowl is dressed at his house, with some messes of good broth, and he proceeds, accompanied by his friends, to the grave. Then begins a song, purporting, that the deceased is now in enjoyment of compleat felicity; and that they are assembled to rejoice at her state of bliss, and perform the last offices of duty and friendship. They then lay a considerable heap of earth over the grave, which is called *covering it*, and the meeting concludes with eating their collation, drinking, dancing and vociferation.'

The period of waiting is somewhat longer today but the essential activity continues of covering the grave with additional earth, and, 'if the family is wealthy enough or the ghost one to be feared in the community, with masonry' — hence the new word *tombing*. Today also, 'if the bereaved person has money, he will hold a "tomb dance" in the evening for his friends and kill a goat or hog for the feast.'

Chapter Twelve

JOHN CANOE: OTHER ENTERTAINMENTS

THE *John Canoe* dancing, recently revived, has had a complex development, and the meaning of the name is uncertain. To understand what it may mean and what it cannot mean, one must go into its history and examine the various explanations that have been offered.

The first account of Christmas dancing by the slaves is that of Sloane (1725). Though he does not mention the word John Canoe, he does observe that the principal dancers would 'tie cows' tails to their rumps', as part of their costume. The word, in fact, has not been found earlier than 1774, when it appeared in Long's account, with a description that is worth quoting at some length:

> In the towns, during Christmas holidays, they have several tall robust fellows dressed up in grotesque habits, and a pair of ox-horns on their head, sprouting from the top of a horrid sort of vizor, or mask, which about the mouth is rendered very terrific with large boar-tusks. The masquerader, carrying a wooden sword in his hand, is followed with a numerous croud of drunken women, who refresh him frequently with a sup of aniseed-water, whilst he dances at every door, bellowing out John Connú! with great vehemence; so that, what with the liquor and the exercise, most of them are thrown into dangerous fevers; and some examples have happened of their dying. This dance is probably an honourable memorial of John Conny, a celebrated cabocero at *Tres Puntas*, in Axim, on the Guiney coast; who flourished about the year 1720. He bore great authority among the Negros of that district. When the Prussians deserted Fort Brandenburgh, they left it to his charge; and he gallantly held it for a long time against the Dutch, to whom it was afterwards ceded by the Prussian monarch. He is mentioned with encomium by many of our voyage-writers.

In 1769, several new masks appeared; the Ebos, the Papaws, &c. having their respective Connús, male and female, who were dressed in a very laughable style.

Long's spelling is significant: it represents accurately the present-day pronunciation of the word among the folk who make the celebration: /jòngkonú/, which suggests that this pronunciation is traditional and has continued unchanged, regardless of what spellings for it may have been attempted. Long has divided it into two words, the form of a man's name — yet several other writers spell it as a single word.[1] What Long says about John Conny is true enough, but he offers no evidence of a connection between that chieftain and the Jamaican slaves; and meantime a serious difficulty lies in the difference between John Conny (/jónkóni/, or in Jamaican folk pronunciation /jánkáni/) and /jòngkonú/. *John Conny*, it is true, is the white man's version of the chief's name; 'Conny' looks very much like the Prussian or Dutch word for 'king' (König, Koning), probably taken as an equivalent of Portuguese *caboçero*. In any case, there is a greater discrepancy in sounds and accentuation between *John Connú* and *John Conny* than appears at first glance. However possible the circumstantial connection may be, the difference in pronunciations still leaves a serious doubt that this can be the source of our word.

The second explanation is that of Williams (1826), whose description runs in part as follows: 'First came eight or ten young girls marching before a man dressed up in a mask with a grey beard and long flowing hair, who carried the model of a house on his head. This house is called the Jonkanoo, and the bearer of it is generally chosen for his superior activity in dancing. . . . The girls also danced. . . . All this ceremony is certainly a commemoration of the deluge. The custom is African and religious, although the purpose is forgotten. Some writer, whose name I forget, says that the house is an emblem of Noah's ark, and that Jonkanoo means the sacred boat or the sacred dove — *caken* meaning sacred, and *jona* a dove, in Hebrew or Samaritan: but as I have no pretension to etymology, I leave this subject to the literati.'

Williams's spelling, though in one word, is also true to present pronunciation. But what is striking is that in the more than fifty

years since Long's account, a new element has entered the celebration. The principal dancer now bears a 'house' on his head —
indeed, it is the house which is said to be the 'Jonkanoo'; but this
may be a transfer — all other accounts give the name to the
dancer. As to the house, the first mention of anything of the sort
was that of Monk Lewis, who had seen a procession at Black
River (1816): 'The John-Canoe is a Merry-Andrew dressed in a
striped doublet, and bearing upon his head a kind of paste-
board house-boat, filled with puppets, some sailors, others
soldiers, others again slaves at work on a plantation, &c.' He
described in detail the *sets* of dancers, which after Long's time
had become attached to the John Canoe celebration.

The 'houseboat' or 'house', in short, was not a part of the
original John Canoe, and cannot explain the name. Only one
account, of those found, mentions a canoe, that in *Marly* (1828):
'John very prudently carried a small imitation of a canoe into
which he and his wife, with their attendants expected the dona-
tions of onlookers to be deposited.' Whatever the house may
stand for, it is quite clear that when it does assume the shape of a
boat this is a *result* of the name, not its source. Williams's Hebrew
etymology, as he himself seemed aware, is quite preposterous.
But even if it were not, it would be beside the point since *John
Canoe* preceded the 'Noah's ark' (if that is what it was).[2] It has
nothing to do with a canoe or any kind of boat; its form is due
to folk-etymology, and only after it had taken that form did the
dancer begin to be dressed to represent it. We may note, too,
that the Jamaican folk pronounce *canoe* /kúnu/, which does not
suit the pronunciation of /jòngkunú/.

A third explanation comes from Belisario (1837): 'The term
John-Canoe has had many derivations applied to it, amongst
others, that it has arisen from the circumstance of negroes
having formerly carried a house in a boat or canoe; but it is
perhaps more consistent to regard it, as a corruption of *Gens
inconnus*, signifying, "unknown folks", from their always wearing
masks. We are strengthened in this opinion, by the frequent
occurrence of foreign appellations, being attached to the various
grades of people of colour, fruits, &c. in this Island.' This is an
ingenious and therefore attractive suggestion; yet upon examination it collapses. Belisario himself pointed out that *French
Set-Girls* had come in from Santo Domingo to Jamaica in 1794;

evidently he thought that John Canoe — which had by his time become attached to the *sets* — was from the same source. But it had been in Jamaica at least twenty years before the sets came, and there is no evidence whatever for French influence. Furthermore, the pronunciation is wrong. *John Canoe* might possibly have been produced by *gens connus*, but hardly by *gens inconnus*. A couple of sources have *Johnny Canoe*,[3] but these are not early enough to be significant; they simply show the form being familiarised. In short, quite apart from the history, the pronunciation would tend to prove exactly the opposite of Belisario's proposal.

The only recent explanation is that of the Dictionary of Americanisms, which obviously rests on inadequate knowledge. It gives only one citation — 1861, which is far too late but evidently the only one its editor had. The etymology proposed is 'App. related to Twi ... *agyanka*, orphan, child bereft of its father'. The citation tells of children rising early on Christmas morning to see the 'Johnkannaus', and says that the companies went about begging for contributions. But there is no evidence whatever — no more than in Jamaica — that these were solicited on behalf of children. In short, the connection with *agyanka* and orphans is a guess, no more. Recognition that the word is originally African is the only step forward that this explanation makes.

Any etymology proposed for *John Canoe* must recognise that the dancer so named was always the central figure in the celebration — the *leading* dancer, grotesquely dressed, wearing a mask or some other disguising but distinctive headdress, who, with his train of followers, leapt about acrobatically and fearsomely as they wound their way through the village collecting contributions. The most likely source is the Ewe language, in which *dzonɔ* means a magician or sorcerer, and *kúnu* means something terrible or deadly, a cause of death; *dzoŋkɔ* is also a name by which a sorcerer calls himself, and *-nu* means a man — thus, 'sorcerer-man', or 'witch-doctor'.

It must also be recognised that the celebration changed considerably in course of time. At first it was clearly African; later on elements of European origin were added (*sets* from French carnival celebrations, *horse-head* and others from English mumming and morris-dancing). At first there was only John Canoe;

after the sets and mumming came in, they and John Canoe ran parallel for a time — as when Monk Lewis saw them. Then John Canoe began to decline: both De la Beche and Bickell (1825) speak of this; the latter explains that 'most of those who had become Christians were ashamed to join in it'. By Tom Cringle's day (1833) the sets had absorbed John Canoe: his part was no longer separate but had become merely the grotesque element in the whole. Insofar as the tradition has been kept up, however, it is the folk who have preserved it, with the original elements and the name, despite the accretion of a considerable number of non-African elements.

The names of many characters have formed a part of the terminology of this celebration. The first reference found to the *blues* and the *reds* as rival sets is from 1808, in Stewart's description. 'On new year's day it was customary for the negro girls of the towns . . . to exhibit themselves in all the pride of gaudy splendor, under the denomination of *blues* and *reds*. . . . These girls were wont to be decked out with much taste, sometimes at the expense of their white or brown mistresses, who took pride in showing them off. . . . The most comely young negresses were selected, and such as had a fine and tutored voice; they paraded through the streets two and two, in the most exact order, uniform in their dress, and nearly of the same stature and age. They were accompanied by instrumental music; but they usually sung together. . . .' The colours of the sets refer to the Red and Blue naval squadrons. Stewart was also first to mention the *queen* as the leader of the set.

Barclay and De la Beche tell of a new element: part of a play of *Richard III*. 'The Joncanoe-men . . . were the two heroes, and fought not for a kingdom but a queen, whom the victor carried off in triumph. Richard calling out "A horse! a horse!" &c. was laughable enough.' The king and his opponent did a sword dance — a feature of English mumming, as De la Beche remarked.

Monk Lewis wrote of *John Crayfish* as a rival to John Canoe — apparently a parallel figure, but mentioned only on this occasion. When Tom Cringle saw the celebration it had become combined with the trade companies. The butchers, gardeners, workhouse people and others, appropriately costumed, reminded him of 'morrice dancers' and 'the May day boys in London'; he referred to 'the John Canoe or Jack Pudding'. Among their musicians were *gumbi-men* and *horn-blowers*.

Belisario's account, with its excellent illustrations, is duly famous. Indeed, part of the misunderstanding of John Canoe has come from its being known largely through this account, which is late (1837) and shows the celebration at its most highly developed stage. The African characters were then *house John-Canoe*, whose house in this case was 'an evident attempt (however humble) at West Indian architecture'; the *jaw-bone John-Canoe*, who played on the instrument known as a *jawbone*; *koo-koo*, a character who begged, and whose name was derived from an imitation of the rumbling stomach of one who is hungry. There were set-girls, the Queen, and another leading woman called the *Maam*. Belisario has given the complete order of the set-girls, from the 'Four Grand Masters' down to the 'Jack-in-the-Green'. Besides these, 'There is another Set, denominated "House-Keepers", who never *dance* in their progress through the streets.' *House-keeper* was a euphemism for the coloured mistress of a white man.

Many characters have become traditional, but there is much local variation. We may give two modern examples. A group that Kerr saw about 1950 was composed, besides John Canoe himself, of a *Queen*, *Queen's daughter*, *Queen's grandchild* (the 'Royalty' of the sets), a *Champion*, and *Warwick* (the villain) with breastplate and two swords (legacy of the mummers), *Satan* dancing alone (one aspect of John Canoe?), a *Wild Indian* and *Indian Girl* (evidently 'Americans', as introduced with the sets) then the satiric characters with allusion to current conditions: the *Sailor* dancing with the *Whore Girl* (who 'dance vulgar all the time'); the *Messenger Boy* who danced with the Queen, her daughter, and the Whore Girl, and also did a homosexual dance; the *Doctor* and *Dispenser*; the *Jockey*, and *Pitchy-Patchy*, who maintained order with a cattle-whip and kept the audience from crowding the dancers.

Another group, the following year in Hanover, first crowned the *King* and *Queen*; the *Warriors* in 'skin-fit clothes' with 'ancient sword' fought; then the *Doctor* danced with the *Matron* and *Nurse*; then the *Drunkard*; then two men in women's clothing did a Quadrille; the *Jockey* kept the crowd in check with the aid of the *Wild Indian* and two other men in front of the procession.

The *Captain* collected the contributions. The *John Canoe* wore a frame of bamboo 'shape like a man' (the descendant of the house). *Horse-head* (descendant of the mummers' *hobby-horse*) had 'opening and closing jaw — snaps at people, and they feed it'. *Bull* (usually called *Cow-head*) was a man with cow-horns over a mask, 'tie with rope around waist' (the original figure of John Canoe). The identity of this masked man must be kept secret; if you try to identify him you may be struck.

Uncle Newton writes an excellent description of what 'Jan Cunnoo' meant to a child — unfortunately too long to include. But among other participants he mentions the 'Satanic host, some with tusks, some with the heads of donkeys and horses but with the feet of men'. They not only go 'shouting, drumming, hurraying' — but singing hymns — a strange mingling indeed!

Our final citation is from a letter to the *Gleaner* in 1951 complaining because the newspaper is trying to revive John Canoe. The writer refers to ' "Juncunoo" commonly called "horse-head" ', and objects to reviving it because it had become 'demoralising and the dances were vulgar'. The police in his district had at last succeeded in suppressing it. 'Many people were taken to court for dancing horse-head, it was so vulgar.'

John Canoe is now a thorough mixture that takes many forms, some of them obviously debased. But at the centre is still the figure of a masked dancer who makes the procession, prancing wildly and shouting, in a traditional African dance. Bowditch's famous description of his reception in 1817 by the King of the Ashanti, may be recalled. The English visitor saw 'Captains of warriors' who 'wore rams' horns on their heads . . . leopards' tails down their backs,' and 'horses' tails at their belts' dancing processionally past; flag-bearers 'plunging and springing from side to side with a passion of enthusiasm'. The bands were principally of drums, horns, and flutes . . . jawbones of human victims were hung on the drums. People of various offices wore their insignia of office; and there were fetish men, of whom 'some danced by with irresistible buffoonery, some with a gesture and carriage of defiance'. Despite the vicissitudes which it has met, the John Canoe dance celebration must have sprung from such roots as these.

Musical Instruments

Modern instruments have almost displaced the traditional, locally made ones of a former time, with their mostly African names and lineage. But some old names linger in partial use or memory, and there are others coined in Jamaica of European components.

Horns have always been important — the *abeng*, for example, which Clerk described as a 'cow horn blown not from the end but from a mouth hole on the concave side. The hole at the small end is stopped with the thumb, which gives a variation of about a tone'. This word, clearly African, is still remembered at Accompong and elsewhere.[4] Horns were greatly favoured by the Maroons; as Dallas wrote, 'They communicated with one another by means of horns; and when these could scarcely be heard by other people, they distinguished the orders that the sounds conveyed. It is very remarkable, that the Maroons had a particular call upon the horn for each individual, by which he was summoned from a distance, as easily as he would have been spoken to by name, had he been near.' With *abeng* Beckwith recorded *kiake* as a synonym (which no one else has mentioned) and her informant said he knew 'a third and secret name' which, however, 'he would not divulge.'[5]

In one of his *Songs* McKay has the lines,

Refreshing breezes fan me as I wake,
And down the valley sounds the wesly horn.

To *wesly* he adds the note, 'Word of uncertain origin. The wesly horn sounds when any work in common is to be undertaken.' As was noted in the preceding chapter, *wesly*, or *Wesly* (named for the Wesleyans) at first referred to a religious singing-meeting, but was transferred to a 'sing' accompanying a communal work-party. The horn had also been used commonly in slave days as a signal to begin or cease work on the sugar estates.

Aketta, said to be a name for a bugle, is probably connected with Twi *kète*, a flute or pipe. An old instrument, the *balafou*, referred to only once in our sources, was evidently similar to the xylophone. 'The Africans struck up a song of welcome, accompanying it with the tones of the balafou.' The final 'u' may be

S

a typographical inversion of 'n' — at least, in Creole French the form of the word is *balafon*.

One kind of flute has been known locally from early days. As Beckford described it in 1790:

> The Caramantee-flutes are made from the porous branches of the trumpet-tree, are about a yard in length, and of nearly the thickness of the upper part of a Bassoon: they have generally three holes at the bottom; are held, in point of direction, like the haut-boy; and while the right hand stops the holes, in the left is shaken, by one of the party, a hollow ball that is filled with pebbles.

Lady Nugent wrote as if she had heard them, and added one surprising detail: 'The Coromantee flute is a long black reed, has a plaintive and melancholy sound, and is played with the nose.' Today this would be known as a *Maroon flute*; they are said to be blown still at Glengoff.

Several crude stringed instruments were made by the slaves. One was the *benta*, a name soon converted through folk etymology to *bender*. In Beckford's description:

> The bender is an instrument upon which the Whydaw negroes, I believe, in particular excel. It is made of a bent stick, the ends of which are restrained in this direction by a slip of dried grass; the upper part of which is gently compressed between the lips, and to which the breath gives a soft and pleasing vibration; and the other end is graduated by a slender stick that beats upon the nerve, if I may so express it, and confines the natural acuteness of the sound, and thus together produce a trembling, a querulous, and a delightful harmony.

Several writers notice this instrument; Russell spelt it *benta*, which best corresponds to its source, Twi *ɔ-bentá*.

The African instrument most widely adopted in America, the *banjo*, was first mentioned in a Jamaican source: 'They have other musical Instruments, as a *Bangil*, not much unlike our Lute in any Thing but the Musick.' If the *l* is not a misprint for *e* or some other letter, this word must have been pronounced /banjil/; Monk Lewis later spelt *banjee*, which seems to represent the same form. But there was another form, the one from which our present word derives. Beckford spelt it *bonjour* (the *r* presumably unpronounced): 'a bonjour, originally taken, perhaps, from a French word, as many have found their way by corruption among the negroes.' But this surmise, which obviously influenced Beckford's spelling, is mistaken.

There were several other spellings yet to come: in 1823, 'the banja, . . . an imperfect kind of violoncello, played upon with the finger, like a guitar'; in 1826 the 'bonja', and in the plural, 'bonjaws'. Not till 1841 did *banjo* appear, and then in an American source. This word used to be thought to come from *bandore*; the evidence at hand today, however, makes it quite certain that (as Russell declared) it is from an African word.

A curious alternative name for the banjo has been recorded only by Long: 'Their *merry-wang* is a favourite instrument, a rustic guitar, of four strings. It is made with a calibash; a slice of which being taken off, a dried bladder, or skin, is spread across the largest section; and this is fastened to a handle, which they take great pains in ornamenting with a sort of rude carved work, and ribbands.' *Merry-wang* may well be a folk-etymology based on West Indian French *maringouin*, a large mosquito, alluding to the humming sound made by the instrument. (Hawaiian *ukelele* means 'flea'.) Or perhaps it is to be connected with the dance named *merengue*.[7] This instrument was also called a *strum-strum*.[8]

Besides these there was one very much larger which Sloane described but did not name — evidently what is today a *toombah* or *tambu*. Sloane wrote of two types of stringed instruments: gourds with necks, strung with horsehair (no doubt the banjo), and 'a hollow'd timber covered with Parchment', having a bow for its neck, the strings tied longer or shorter. The recent description by Clerk is fuller:

> Today . . . the Maroons . . . use a drum; and a Toombah, a large piece of the Trumpet Tree, hollowed out, and three strings stretched across, and pieces of metal in place of shells, strung on each side. The Toombah is a variety of the banjo, guitar, and tambourine, and may probably be the Tabor of the Arawaks.

The word *tabor* can hardly be the source of *toombah* (if that was what Clerk intended); *tabor* had become an English word long before the discovery of America. *Toombah* is undoubtedly cognate with *tumba*, or else a loan-word from Cuba, in the eastern part of which a *tumba* is a drum, and a dance, of African origin. The large hollowed resonance-chamber of the Jamaican *toombah* covered with skin gives it some similarity to a drum, and permits the transfer of the name to it.

Another word, *tambu*, is said to mean among the Maroons 'a rumba box; a Cuban drum; or when many come together'. From a second source comes '*tambus*, holidays'.[9] Despite the difference in form, *tambu* seems to be closely related to *tumba*: it refers to a similar instrument (note the associations with the Jamaican Maroons and with Cuba); and from this basic sense it has been extended to mean a gathering of people on festive occasions — i.e., holidays — through the use of the musical instrument at such times. I suspect not only that some onomatopoetic African word underlies *tumba*, which has its Spanish form from Cuba, but that *tambu* represents French *tambour*, drum — in short, that the African name for the instrument has been adapted to various European languages in the Caribbean islands. (On the other hand, *tumba* and *tambu* could be simple metathetic forms.)

As for the *rumba-box* just mentioned, it is a descendant of the African *zanza*, simulating the tones of a bass viol by means of four pieces of metal of different gauges attached to a box (the resonance chamber), which vibrate when they are plucked with the fingers, and are tuned to correspond to the strings. It cannot produce much of a tune, but is used for background chording and rhythm such as calypso songs require.

Jekyll referred to a local term (not reported otherwise): 'the "rubbing" of the fiddle, as they [the country people] call it . . . "Rubbing" a fiddle conveys the exact idea of the way they play it. Holding it not up to the chin, but resting it on the biceps, they rub a short bow backwards and forwards across the strings.'

Several instruments do not depend on percussion so much as on scraping or shaking. Leslie mentioned the *rookaw*, 'which is two sticks jagged' that are rubbed together to give a rhythmic rattling. The modern descendant of this is the *scraper*, 'a corrugated stick across which is rubbed a plain stick', or the *grater*, 'a stick with many notches used for percussion'.[10] A favourite instrument of the same sort was the *jawbone*: 'the jawbone of an animal, from which is produced a harsh and disagreeable sound'. Usually it was that of a horse, with the teeth loose in the sockets,[11] over which a stick was rattled — a macabre kind of music!

A strange device for producing resonant tones, yet not a true percussion instrument, was also mentioned by Leslie under the name of 'a *Jenkoving*, which is a Way of clapping their Hands on the Mouth of two Jars'. No clue to the source of this word has been found, though presumably it is African.

Drums have been and still are the most important instrument, and their playing the most highly developed. Some are played with sticks, some with fingers; and usually there is a large or bass drum furnishing a steady beat in the background while a small higher pitched drum furnishes the 'tune' or rhythm.

The earliest name had two seemingly related forms, referring perhaps to different instruments, but descriptions do not always correspond. Forms and names both no doubt varied from tribe to tribe. If there were indeed two different drums, the *goombah* or *goombay* was the larger and deeper-pitched, the *gumbi* the smaller. Long's description is the earliest:

> The *goombah* . . . is a hollow block of wood, covered with sheepskin stripped of its hair. The musician holds a little stick, of about six inches in length, sharpened at one end like the blade of a knife, in each hand. With one hand he rakes it over a notched piece of wood, fixed across the instrument, the whole length, and crosses with the other alternately, using both with a brisk motion; whilst a second performer beats with all his might on the sheep-skin, or tabor.

This instrument obviously combined a scraper with the drum part.

Beckford, shortly after, distinguished the 'gomba' from an ordinary drum as being played with the hands; Moreton saw a crude one: 'An herring-barrel, or tub, with sheep-skins substituted for the heads, in imitation of a drum, called a gumbay.' And Belisario: 'The small square wooden frame, over which a goat's skin is tightly strained, is termed a "Gumbay", "Box", or "Bench-drum" ' (played with the hands). This corresponds very closely to the 'Gumbé (pronounced gumbay)', which Miss Roberts saw: a small, square, stool-like drum with a goatskin head held taut by pressure of an inner frame wedged up from below, and played with the hands. Miss Beckwith, who worked with her, saw 'gombay' drums of different patterns in various part of Jamaica, but all had in common this manner of playing.

Clerk is alone in making a triple distinction between 'Gumbie, Goombah, and Goombay'. It seems likely that he took local variations as generic differences, and that there were at most two kinds: a hand-played drum as distinct from those played with a stick or sticks.

Other related words are *gombayer*, and *gumbi-man*; and *gombay* seems to have acquired a broadened meaning: 'Three drums, one playing drum and two bandas, played together are referred to as *gomba*.' The form *kumby* has also been reported,[1a] and a very black person, presumably by association with the African drum-name, is a *goomby*.

The *Eboe drum* appears to have been one of the larger sort. As Williams wrote: 'They again assembled on the lawn before the house with their gombays, bonjaws, and an ebo drum, made of a hollow tree, with a piece of sheepskin stretched over it.'

An early word for the smaller kind was the *dundo*, described as a 'complete tabor'. This word too is African: from Ngombe *ndundu*. The *cotta* or *cotter* must have been a drum or drum-like instrument: 'a cotter, upon which they beat with sticks' as Beckford wrote 'the very children, so soon as they are able to walk, at the first sound of the cotter . . . put their little elbows in motion — their feet shortly follow. . .'. And Williams: 'An incessant hammering was kept up on the gombay, and the cotta (a Windsor chair taken from the piazza to serve as a secondary drum).' Though *cotta* itself does not seem to be used any more — unless it is represented by 'the kitty-katty, or any flat piece of board on which they beat with two sticks' — *cotta stick* is still current for a 'percussion stick or *clapper*, used in cumina' or 'African' religious cults. Moore writes of 'a clapper, or catatic, which is a flat stick beat against the center post of the dancing booth'. (*Catatic* simply represents the folk pronunciation of *cotta stick*.)

Another drum described by Beckwith was the *bon*, probably the same as Moore's *banda*. In Beckwith's words, 'The Myal Man in the cockpits . . . claimed that two drums are required for the dance, a big drum called *bon* or *panya*, played with sticks, and a *gombay* played with the fingers.' I take *bon* and *banda* to represent English *band* and *bander*; for *panya* I have no clue, though it usually means *Spaniard* or *Spanish*.

Kerr has written: 'The name of the Bass drum is Kynando, that of the other, Plain Case. Kynando has a ring round it called a Kagga and is made of breadfruit wood. Plain Case is made of trumpet wood.' 'Plain case' is merely a rendering of *playing case*, also called the *playing drum* or *lead drum* (which 'leads' the rhythm). Other names for these smaller, treble drums are *rattlin drum*, *rattler*, *rackle drum*, and *tittle drum*. Uncle Newton's description suggests the contrasting sounds of big and small drums: 'Right in with the big drums, the tittle drums, the fifes. . . . In the distance we heard it: "Bam . . . Bam". "Ti . . . ti . . . ti . . . tittle!" '

Finally there is the rattle, called a *shaka*, *shakey*, or *shaker*, which both the American Indians and the Africans used. The first word is very likely African, the latter two probably also, with adaptation to English patterns.[18] Stewart described them as 'a kind of rattles, being small calabashes filled with. . . . Indian shot, or with the seed of the wild liquorice'. Belisario was first to mention *shaka*; it is still current. Beckwith recorded *shakeys*, and Moore *shaker*.

Celebrations, Entertainments, Games

Words for the religious celebrations of the cults have already been dealt with; folk entertainments such as the *birth-night party*, the wake or *set-up*, the *nine-night*, are the chief ones. On such occasions there is sure to be singing and eating, usually also dancing and games. The older word for an entertainment at which dancing was a chief feature was *play*. De la Beche has written,

> Negroes in giving dances or plays sometimes go to great expense. . . . The dance, or play, as it is sometimes called, commences about eight o'clock . . . and . . . continues to daybreak with scarcely any intermission, those of the old school preferring the goombay and African dances, and those of the new fiddles, reels, &c.

This word was apparently applied to a wake also; in *Tom Cringle* we find, 'The following night there was to be a grand play or wake in the negro houses, over the head cooper, who had died in the morning.'

Nowadays, people in St Mary who keep up the old customs *jump dinky* or *dinky minny* all nine nights after a funeral. ' "Dinkies" are the ninth night celebrations after a funeral, when at midnight the mourners abandon themselves to gaiety and the occasion becomes a festive affair.' (This word — if it is the same word — has had a curious extension of meaning: in Hanover a *dinky* is a machine used to thresh rice — perhaps from the bouncing motion of the flails?)

Seasonal celebrations of past days were traditionally those of Christmas and Easter: *Christmas* still implies 'holiday time' in folk use: 'A savin' fe de Christmas' — I'm saving to have a good holiday at Christmas time. Two hundred years ago Sloane listed the holidays allowed to the slaves: 'They have *Saturdays* in the Afternoon, and *Sundays*, with *Christmas* Holidays, *Easter* call'd little or *Pigganinny*, *Christmas*, and some other great Feasts allow'd them for the Culture of their own Plantations.'

On the sugar estates the big celebration was *crop-over* (see Chapter V). There were at one time maypole dances, at which the spike of the *coratoe* or American aloe was used, from which that plant acquired the name of *maypole*. There were carnival activities, called *maskins*;[14] *set dances* and the *John Canoe* processions (see above). With the end of slavery came the celebration of the eve of Emancipation Day (1 August), now known as *bringing in the August Morning*.

Gatherings for entertainment not necessarily connected with a ceremony or celebration furnish such words as *muckashandy*, *bowsorow*, and *ring-ding*. Judging by the latter part, *muckashandy* was probably borrowed from the north of England or Scotland. It means a masquerade, and is much the same as a *bowsorow* (pronounced /bòusaróu/) — a 'dress-up' country dance or masking, like that connected with John Canoe. This word is on the edge of being converted by folk-etymology into *bounce-around*, yet it is probably in origin African.[15] *Ring-ding* is a general term for noisy hilarity:

> Soldier da go way tomorrow,
> The last of the ring ding tomorrow.

The most general word for a gathering for entertainment is a *met* — 'a meeting, a ball' as Jekyll defined it, or 'a fair'. This word is less used today than formerly; in even more restricted

use is *tambu*, just discussed among the musical instruments. As
for a feast, one jocular word is an *eating-match* (recorded in
1868); and *combancha* has also been reported. A *sallo* is 'sort of a
met', and according to another source, 'a dance'. These are no
doubt connected with Mandinka (Gambia) *salo*, 'a feast' — in
short, at such meetings, there was both dancing and feasting,
no very sharp distinction being drawn. *Zella*, which is said to
mean 'celebration of ninth-night in form of pocomania' may
well be the same word in slightly altered form and meaning.

Williams has described a *love-dance* as it occurred in 1826:

> They divided themselves into parties to dance, some before
> the gombays, in a ring, to perform a bolèro or a sort of love-
> dance as it is called, where the gentlemen occasionally wiped
> the perspiration off the shining faces of their black beauties,
> who, in turn, performed the same service to the minstrel.

An outdoor popular dance today may be a *bruckins* or a *bram*,
though these are not quite identical. In a calypso tune we find,

> When Big Mattie dance inna London Town
> Whether brukins, mento or Samba
> Parisian gal haffi sit dung tight
> An' grudge de gal from New London.

Bruckins of course means *breakings* in Standard, and is probably
the Jamaican version of American *breakdown*, 'a noisy, rollicking
dance of rustic origin', which goes back to at least 1819, and included the forms *Ethiopian breakdown* and *Negro breakdown* (DA).
If the dance was not of Negro origin, it was certainly favoured
by the Negroes in America, and evidently in Jamaica too. A
bram is not much different but is said to be 'rather higher class
than a "brukins" '.[16] As to the origin of *bram*, I take it to be
ultimately a metathesis of *barn*, and, like *bruckins*, to be connected
with American folk-dancing. In the United States the *barn dance*
was more formal, a 'military Schottische', or the like. Since *barn*
is hardly used in Jamaica in its ordinary sense, it could easily
have been altered. (Metathesis is a very common feature of the
folk speech.)

Another kind of dance party is described by Murray: ' "Moonshine Darlins" are dances held out-of-doors when the moon is
full. Anyone can join in the fun, whether invited or not, and
refreshments are brought by those participating.'

As for individual dance steps, we find several mentioned by Miss Roberts, a student of Jamaican folk music and dance: 'The flutist played various tunes known to the people as *sha-shas* (pronounced shay-shays), catch-me-times, mentos, reels, lanciers, two-steps, and others. Many of these dance tunes are presumably taken from Scottish airs or from old English dance music.' Of these the *shay-shay* is one of the best known. McKay simply described it as a 'barbecue song and dance' — that is, where the barbecue is used as the dance floor. Beckwith is more explicit: it is 'that erotic dance to jazz music which is supposed to have originated in Africa but which DeLisser thinks derived from a Spanish dance called *mento, bamboula,* or *chica* and which "consists of slow movements of the body, . . . the dancer never allows the upper part of the body to move as she writhes or shuffles over the ground". The name DeLisser would derive from the French *chassé*. The shay-shay is danced with a single partner and always to song'. This derivation is the accepted one: compare the American *sashay,* which is the metathesis of *chassé*; yet this is not the same kind of dance or step, and it is very possible that some African word lies beneath *shay-shay*.

Others too identify the *shay-shay* with the *mento*, but I cannot verify DeLisser's 'Spanish' derivation of the latter. The *mento* also has a song accompaniment — to some the song seems the primary thing. *Catch-me-time* has been found nowhere else. *Lanciers* no doubt represents *lancer*, preserved late and in this altered form in Jamaica.

The motions described for the *shay-shay* have been characteristic of African dancing since it was first observed by Europeans. To *wind* was the early word for twisting and turning the hips, and *hipsaw* for oscillating the hips back and forth. In 1790 Moreton recorded a song supposedly sung by a slave as she demonstrated the dance with gusto before her master:

> Hipsaw! my deaa! You no shake like a-me!
> You no wind like a-me!
> Hipsaw! my deaa! You no do like a-me!
> You no jig like a-me! you no twist like a-me!
> Hipsaw! my deaa! . . .[17]

The DA has 'HIPSESAW, lower class dance', with quotations from 1830 and 1832; our citation shows that this is *hip-saw*, and that it was known some forty years earlier in Jamaica. Though the oscillation of this dance may have suggested English *saw*, the primary source of this syllable is surely Twi *sàw*, to dance, to shake.

Other dances or dance steps include *yanga*, which is from *nyanga* (probably through Spanish *ñanga*), an African dance. It has been found only as a verb: 'See yah de music sweet yuh se'! All de fowl dem start fe yanga an merenge roun' de room.' And 'Me kean yanga weel him tun im dung'. In this second citation is the extremely common phrase to *wheel and turn*; in the first, another dance is named which came to Jamaica from a Spanish source. In Puerto Rico it is *merengue*, 'a dance which was introduced into the country in 1842 in substitution for the Spanish *contradanza*.'

Other names for dances have come in via Spanish. The *canga*, or *lacanga*, as the latter form suggests, may be one of these; yet *congo* has been current in American English since at least 1803 for 'A kind of dance performed originally by Negroes but later by white people', and this would be pronounced *canga* by the Jamaican folk. In short, this word may have come directly or indirectly, or both ways.

An older African dance that was more a demonstration of acrobatic prowess than a social pleasure was the *calimbe* or *calembe*. Beckwith has written, 'At a wake. . . . They "dance calimbe" in an antic caper upon a pair of sticks held horizontally by two other players.' The word is now considered 'old time' but has been taken over by the Pocomanians, who may give it a new lease of life. The source has not been traced, but in Venezuela *calembe* means rags or tatters, and is recognised as an African word.[18] Also 'old fashion' is *shim-sham*, 'a wild African dance'. *Buru* is a word with several current related meanings, all condemnatory: a wild dance, sometimes indecent; a low-down dancing place; religious fanaticism (as in Pocomania); and a *buru-man* is a Pocomania dancer. The source would seem to be African, for example Twi *buru*, filthiness, sluttishness; Yoruba *buru*, wicked.

Other words for dance steps include *spotting* (reported from Westmoreland as 'a very pretty clog' executed by a servant girl); *riding* is a step used in many ring games, 'a peculiar shuffling step . . . one flat foot, one toe, without moving the feet from the ground, and turning slowly.'[19] A *rest dance* is the kind of inactive dance, mostly a hug, which is often done today. The regular folk word for a drummer or other musician playing for a dance is *music-man*, recorded since 1833.

As to 'sings' the best known is certainly the *jamma*, a song sung by a group working together in the field: a *digging-sing*. When yam holes are being dug, for example, a leader called a *bomma* sings the words of the jamma, the diggers coming in on a short refrain called the *bobbin* — and so they keep digging rhythmically together. As Una Wilson has put it, 'A jamma is not a poetical production by any means . . . the charm . . . lies in the tune, the voice of the bomma, and the rhythmic swing of the workers.' The subject of the songs is topical and local, and they are partly extemporised by the bomma. I have recorded one which told of the coming of war: airplanes flying over and the necessity of gathering old iron. Another told of a doctor who had stolen somebody's sweetheart, and another of a man who bought red cloth because he feared duppies under the bed. The earliest Jamaican work song I have found — clearly a jamma, though the word is not given — comes from 1790 among the several kinds of songs which Moreton recorded:

[Bomma:]	[Bobbin:]
If me want for go in a Ebo,	Me can't go there!
Since dem tief me from a Guinea,	Me can't go there!
If me want for go in a Congo,	Me can't go there!
Since dem tief me from my tatta,	Me can't go there!
If me want for go in a Kingston,	Me can't go there!
Since massa gone in a England,	Me can't go there!

Jamma is certainly African and must have been in use for a long time, yet surprisingly it is not found in print before 1926 (not even by Jekyll) when Roberts uses the form *jamal songs*, and calls them topical or comic. (There may be some mistake here, though the jamma is indeed often humorous.) One indication of the importance of this kind of song comes from the proverbial saying in Hanover: to 'tek out yam widout jamma' implies the unheard-of or the impossible.

Bomma, like *jamma*, is very likely African, meaning either to shout, sing out, or join together — as this leading singer unites the group.[20] But *bobbin* is from the old English word *bob*, 'the refrain or burden of a song', put into participial form. When the bomma wants to end the song he shouts *black water*! or *Bog Walk*! These two exclamations are variant forms, obviously, and both look very much like folk etymologies. (Possibly they are alterations of the nautical command 'Back water!'.)

Besides digging songs, Jekyll lists ring tunes and dancing tunes. Many are similar to the jammas; some are of European (usually English) origin; but the majority are local. The ring tunes are for adults' dances as well as children's games: the *ring play* which is a regular part of nine-night celebration. Of these the best known is probably *roll rock-stone*, or *bruck rock-stone*, beginning 'Me go da Galloway road'. Twelve players sit in a circle; the leader sings the song and the others join the chorus while passing around within the circle from player to player stones about the size of a brick. The penalty for missing the rhythm and not keeping the stones passing is to have one's fingers 'mashed' — which explains the often repeated phrase, 'galang bwoy, finger mash, no cry!' In Jekyll's version it is a dance rather than a game, and the 'stones' are partners who keep moving from the ring to the centre and back.

The leader of the dances used to be known as *Jigga Nanny*, with *jigger*, one who jigs, and *nanny* in the sense of leader, as the probable components. The song *Ball Gawn Roun'* preserves the line, 'Jigga Nanny show me how de ball gawn roun'.' Beckwith writes of *Kromanti songs* of the Maroons, including the jawbone, new war songs, and old war songs. *Jawbone* no doubt refers to the practice among the Ashanti of making trophies of the lower jawbones of slain enemies, attaching them to their drums, and so on. (But note the musical instrument by this name.)

Entertainments of a more sedentary kind include the telling of riddles and stories. The riddles traditionally begin with a local variant of a formula derived from England: *Riggle me riggle me ree, answer me dis riggle an' perhaps not* was one form of this.[21] The word to *clear* a riddle may be used to mean *solve*.

Best known of all are the *Anancy* or *Nancy stories*. These very numerous fables are named for their hero, the spider who, like other animals in the stories, assumes human characteristics from time to time. The tales come from the Gold Coast: Twi *anànse* means spider; *ntikŭma*, his son, has become *Tacooma* in Jamaica and *kɔnnɔre*, his wife, has become *Crooky*. Anansi's character is proverbial: he is *craven* (greedy), he can't bear to see anyone get ahead of him, and since he cannot win by strength, he depends on guile. Almost never beaten, he is made responsible (as in *Just So Stories*) for the way many things are in the world: why wasps sting, why dogs' bellies are hollow, and so on — 'Is Anancy mek it!'

Anancy is supposed to be tongue-tied, or to lisp; but, as Jekyll pointed out, he talks *Bungo talk* — the lowest level of the dialect, with the most Africanisms, least approaching 'high English'. He says /yiki/ for *little*; he cannot pronounce *r*. He has a falsetto whine. If the story is well told, one knows at once when Anancy begins to speak!

Most of the animals in the tales are found in Jamaica, but not *Asono* or *Asoonoo*, who began as an elephant (Akan *e-sono*) but has become increasingly vaguer in the folk mind till he is now merely the type of hugeness (a fat man, a big dumpling, may be designated so). *Bredda Monkey* must come from Africa; *Bredda Tiga* must represent the leopard and *Bredda Raabit* the hare. Some human characters are mixed in the stories: King, Queen, and so on. *Oman Prim* (woman) is 'a person of rank'. *Mada Cantinny* is a character whose name was 'only known to the animals she fostered'. 'Nancy story' now applies to any folk tale.

Anansi stories begin with 'Once upon a time', or 'One time', the usual formula, and end with one from a nursery rhyme, *Jack Mandora, me no choose none.* Jekyll gave this as *Jack Mantora* and explained it as a formula of excusal: the storyteller is not directing the moral of the tale at any individual in the audience (but he whom the shoe fits may put it on!). An elaborate story has been manufactured to explain the meaning as Dora, the daughter of Jackman. But in fact it is reduced from 'Jack Manory, I'll tell you a story . . . And now my story's done.'

One may mention in passing the terms *live story* and *dead story*, recorded by Beckwith, which mean accounts of things one has seen oneself and can vouch for, as against those one has merely heard of and therefore properly doubts.

As for children's games, most are from Europe, some of local invention: Beckwith has published some sixty-six, with local variants and music. Uncle Newton writes of *puss-puss, tickle-me moonshine baby*, and *zuzu wapp*. *Moonshine baby* is played when the

moon is full: children bring bits of broken crockery to a barbecue; one girl, the 'baby', lies down quite still on the barbecue
and the others outline her with the bits of crockery, which reflect the moonlight. The amusement comes from the players'
remarks while making the figure of the 'moonshine baby', and
filling in the outline afterwards with more mosaic bits.

Zuzu Wapp is a ring game with singing. The leading boy,
Zuzu Wapp, chooses a girl and puts her in the ring. While he
'goes to town' (circles the ring) singing of all the things he will
buy her, other boys enter and try to win the girl with caresses.
From time to time Zuzu Wapp breaks into the ring and chases
the other boys with a belt; whichever one he strikes becomes
Zuzu Wapp, and the game is repeated.[22] *Wapp* apparently
represents *whop*.

Other flogging games are *Master* and *Master and his Cock*. *Hide
and whoop* may be played in the water or on land and is a
catching-game. The person who is 'it' is always, in Jamaica, the
watchman or *watchy*. In this game he turns his back while the
players whoop and dive, then he tries to catch one. To get a rest
a player shouts *five* (that is, five seconds of freedom). To play on
both sides in a game is to *jacka*.

A somersault, in Jamaica, is a *puppa-lick*, from the position a
boy gets into when his father whips him. Banbury recorded
'cutting papa-licks' in 1895; McKay spelt it *pupperlicks*; Bennett
has, to 'kick pupa lick'. Also reported are *kin-cat* and *kin-oba* —
compare the American 'skin the cat' for a somersault performed
on a bar. A pickaback ride is a *donkey-ride*. *Tomfariah* is a way of
riding on two poles.

When children are leaving each other, for instance after
school, they play *last lick*: one hits the other, shouts *last lick*!, and
runs. The one hit tries to hit back and have last lick. This easily
becomes a contest rather than a parting. As Uncle Newton has
indicated, it need not be played with the hands only: 'Stones
were among my best friends. . . . For giving 'last licks' to speedy
school mates, I found them ideal.' The schoolboy trick, the bent
pin placed on a seat, is called a *flying horse* from its effect on the
sitter. *Monkey-face*, for a grimace, has survived in Jamaica and
Barbados though apparently obsolete elsewhere.

A spinning-top is always a *gig* — again a preservation.[23] Kerr
seems to have heard it used not for the top but a game played

with tops. A top homemade from an avocado 'pear-stone' is
known as a *ving-vang* — clearly an echoism. Rolling hoops is
running wheels. A toy 'windmill', as a real one, is called a *breeze
mill*. Kites are usually hexagonal with the top section bowed; on
the string that forms this bow a lunette of paper is pasted, which
buzzes magnificently when the kite is aloft: it is called a *tongue* or
singer. Up the kite string one sends rounds of paper with a hole
at the centre, called *messengers*; they are slipped on at the bottom
of the string and go sailing up it to the kite.

A swing is, echoically, a *zing-zang* or *swing-sang*.[24] A hard
wooden ball used by boys in playing a kind of cricket, is a *kendeh*.
In the shops one can buy packets of sweets that contain a small
toy: these are *lucky packets*. To one of Louise Bennett's characters
the word was *lucky box*; she insults another woman in the
lines:

> Yuh face look like a sey
> Yuh draw it outa lucky box.

Fee-fee (with first syllable stressed) is the echoic name for a
whistle of almost any kind, from those made with a blade of
grass between the fingers to 'a noise-maker blown by a deflating
balloon attached to a squealer'. This has become the name of a
plant too, because one can whistle with the flower.

Jamaican boys have some of their own terms for marble play
as well as many standard ones. For example, the large marble,
or taw, is sometimes a *gulge*.[25] Instead of marbles various native
seeds are used such as the *nickal* (Standard *nicker* — Bonduca).
Grey nickals are common, yellow ones are not; therefore a
yellow one is a *tenny*, worth ten grey ones. A red *horse-eye* is a
foury, worth four grey nickals. Much preferred to marbles, however, are cashew nuts (in the husks). The game is called
/kúshu/ when they are used, and they have the advantage that
at the end of the season one can have a big 'roast' and enjoy
one's winnings more inwardly than one can with marbles. Uncle
Newton has written,

> At Bartons and at Four Paths, the popular cashew games
> were 'knock-and-go-along', 'standing', 'Chink-up' and 'back-
> on-the-hand'. At Chapelton we bigger ones did not play those
> childish games. We played 'bank' ... 'Bank' was an enjoyable

thing. The banker dug a shallow hole in a bank of the road. Standing to one side of it and with some 3 or 4 dozen cashews around him and in sight of all, he would yell: 'Come this way, cashew players! Two 'pon one! Two 'pon one!' Victims would pour in. Each one would stand on the opposite side of the road, pitch (that is, throw) up his cashews one by one and collect two cashews for everyone of his which settled in the hole. Seldom did any settle.

To take away all of an opponent's cashews is to *dry* him.

Two marble games not mentioned in other sources are /brok-nek/ (break-neck) and /bongs-an-spaan/ (bounce and span). In the first a line is drawn and marbles placed along it; the player who can roll his marble closest to the line without going over (breaking his neck), wins all. The second is for two players only. One throws his marble and the other tries to throw his within a span of it. If he succeeds he is paid one; if he fails he pays one; and the players take turns throwing first. This is ideal for getting (slowly) home from school.

Fireworks have some special names. A 'sparkler' becomes in Jamaica a *starlight*. Fire-crackers (more often called *squibs* or *scribs*) are also *clappers*. When a squib does not explode it is broken in two and the powder lighted — this is to /tosh di klapaz/ (tush the clappers).

The game of tit-tat-toe is pronounced *tee-taa-toe*, and when a game is drawn it is said to be a *duppy* game. (One may compare the midwest American expression: the game is 'cat and rat', and a drawn game is 'one for the rat'.) One game played with common pins is called *heads or tails*. One player places two pins side by side, covering the ends. The other must guess whether they are 'heads' (the heads and points together) or 'tails' (pointing in opposite directions). If right, he gets a pin; if wrong, he pays one.

Rather hard to classify are *sagwa* and *poppy-show*. *Sagwa* is 'an amusement' — 'a medicine show — act on stage, paint face, snake-charming, sell ointment'. Here the sense must be much changed, since the probable African source word meant a place where people gathered to drink or where a king or chief held a public reception.[26] *Poppy-show* probably comes not from *puppet-show* but the older form *poppet-show*. The word is used in Jamaica to mean 'a ridiculous show or exhibition — one that fails or is disappointing because it is badly done', or simply the kind of exhibition an individual may make of himself through clownish behaviour, 'stupid talking', or the like. The folk pronunciation is /pàpishúo/.

Chapter Thirteen

WILD ANIMALS

THE TRADITIONAL Jamaican Alphabet begins, 'A is for Asono, him bery big man,' and Asono is remembered, as we have seen, in the Anancy stories. But his identity is no longer clear to the folk; he is big, he is impressive; he is even supernatural. But the fact that Asono was the elephant (as Russell wrote in 1868) has nearly been forgotten. In short, this is one of the many African legacies which have grown dim in Jamaican memory. Somewhat in the same case is the monkey, not native to this island therefore never known in the wild state. It is remembered through tales and proverbs chiefly — for example the saying about 'getting around' people: 'Monkey know which tree fe climb.'

Among the first native wild animals to be noticed was the hutia: 'Here's an Indian Coney, called Raccones, that is good Meat, but of a distastful shape, being something like an overgrown Rat' — so we read in 1683. 'Raccoon' was a misapplication here; yet as late as 1823 we find the word applied again to the cony: 'They [rats] are of a much larger size than the European rat, especially that kind of them called by the negroes *racoons*.' One wonders whether Stewart got this information at first hand, and whether he did not mistake 'coney' (today pronounced /kúoni/) for 'coon', the common American abbreviation of *raccoon*. At least, if *raccoon* or *coon* were words indeed once used in Jamaica they have entirely disappeared, whereas the other term, *Indian coney*, or simply *cony*, is still the current one. Browne reported both 'The large brown *Indian* Coney' and 'The small *Indian* Coney'. Though considered destructive to crops, and though hunted with dogs, some still survive. Another name for them is *grazy* or *gracy* — unrecorded and of unknown origin.

The word *mouse* early took on an African-like form in the folk speech, becoming /musmus/. It remains so in stories (Smith spelt it *moos-moos*). *Rat* was similarly transformed into *ratta*, which is preserved in many songs and still to be heard in talk. Three kinds are recognised in the island: the *black, brown,* and *white-belly* rat, and because of their pestiferous effect on sugarcane some interesting history attaches to them. The *black* is the European rat, thought to have been introduced by the Spaniards. Of the *brown* Gosse wrote: 'The negroes are said to distinguish it by the name of the *George* rat. This name is a curious coincidence with the historic scandal that, under the name of the *Hanoverian* Rat, assigns a similar introduction to the ship that brought the Brunswick family to the British shores.'

Reference to the *George rat* has not been found elsewhere, and the name is apparently forgotten today; *brown rat* is the current one. *White-belly rat,* not mentioned in the dictionaries, is no doubt a local term; it is the same as the *cane* or *cane-piece rat,* of which Sloane wrote, 'The Cane-Rats are numerous, of a gray colour, cheap, large, and very good Victuals,' and Long elaborated:

> The larger [field-rat] is of a light-ash, or greyish colour, on the back, and other parts, except the belly, which is intirely white. This subsists almost wholly upon the sugar-cane, and therefore generally termed the *cane-rat*; from the nature of its food the flesh acquires a luscious and very delicate flavour . . . when roasted.

The cane-rat was later identified by Gosse with the *Charles Price rat,* despite earlier accounts that seem to treat them as different animals. Long, for example, wrote, 'The largest is commonly called the *Charles-price* rat, and obtained its name from having been first observed here about the time when the late Sir Charles Price, Baronet, returned hither from Europe. . . . They are no other than the water-rat of Europe . . . amphibious, and found in holes on the banks of rivers and the sides of ponds.' Long was probably depending on Browne, who had been the first to mention the name: 'CASTOR 1; . . . Water-Rat, commonly called Price's Rat.'

On the other hand, two later accounts credit Sir Charles Price, a well-known Jamaican planter and Speaker of the Assembly, with having brought a large variety of rat from the Mosquito shore 'for the purpose of destroying the small ones, which they did very effectually; but the newcomers have proved so numerous, and even more troublesome that their predecessors'.[1]

Charlie Price or *Charl Price* are the present folk forms of this name, but there is still disagreement about which animal is so called. Perhaps the term has never been applied consistently; one inclines, however, to follow Gosse, who was a capable naturalist.

The sequel to this story is better known: to combat all kinds of rats the mongoose was introduced from India in 1872. Though it is regularly *mongoose*, occasionally one hears it called the *Espeut* (/espyuut/), in honour (like *Charlie Price*) of the man who brought it in.[2]

Bats are regularly *rat-bat* among the Jamaican folk. They do not appear to recognise any special varieties. Gosse was the first to mention the several kinds: the *mastiff, monk, naseberry, owl-faced*, and *red hairy-tailed* bat, which names seem to have been his own coinages.

A toad becomes *toady* — possibly by Scots influence, though the diminutive and familiarising suffix *-y* has always been a favourite among the Jamaican folk. If Scots, this is a preservation; but it may be of local formation. There are no bull frogs in Jamaica, despite the fact that *Bufo marinus* is called *bullfrog*; actually, he is a toad.

Sharks and barracoutas have 'waiting-boys' at sea: on land the snake has one too, the skink, called in Jamaica *snake waitin'-boy*. One country-man described it as a 'plain thing, black — head resemble snake — have legs, but jus' wiggle-wiggle an' run gone', and he explained the name by saying, 'anywe' him de, snake don' lef' far.' (Wherever he is, the snake is not far off.) It is not always distinguished from the similar galliwasp.

This word *galliwasp* is one of the most puzzling that we encounter; its meaning and origin are by no means clear. Though the earliest dictionary citation is from 1725, it was used at least forty-two years earlier:

> In some parts of the North [of Jamaica] there's little ugly Creatures, called by the English Gallivaches, whose bite is Mortal to Dogs, Goats, &c.[3]

Sloane spelt it *galliwasp* and identified it as the great skink. Dancer (1801) made it the 'Gally Asp, a large species of Lizard';

Stewart wrote a few years later, 'The gallow-wasp is an ugly . . . animal;' Jekyll had *gallawoss*, and Lynn and Grant spell both *gally-wasp* and *galliwasp*, also recording *gully asp* and *yellow wasp* as variants.

One modern dictionary considers that 'galley-wasp' first referred to an insect infesting the galleys of ships, then was transferred to this lizard-like animal — which is hardly convincing. There is no evidence to connect the word either with ships or with wasps, and such a transfer lacks plausibility. The earliest form ends in *-vache*, the French word for cow, perhaps by accident, perhaps by some folk-etymologising on the part of the writer. If he was representing a name he had heard, it could be either *-vash* or *-vatch*. *Galli-* is an element also of *gallinipper* (a large mosquito or similar insect with a painful sting); and there is the *galley-worm*, so named because its numerous legs look like the oars of a galley as it moves along. The association with other such insects may have led to the change of *-vache* to *-wasp*; but since the creature is nothing whatever like a wasp (unless the supposed sting was alluded to), others have tried to make it an asp, which comes closer to its actual shape. Further alterations are still being made: the usual folk form today is /gyalawás/, but it has also been recorded as /gàlangwás/ (go-'long-wasp). The explanation that seems to me most likely is that this name goes back to some native Indian word, which was roughly rendered into English at first, then later folk-etymologised to *galliwasp*. Students of Caribbean Indian languages should take up the chase at this point!

As for lizards, they are numerous and have many local names. *Iguana* is not a Jamaicanism though the word has been in use here all along. The common form is /gwáana/ in the name *green guana*, also called *big green-lizard*. There is a *small green-lizard* too, 'sometimes designated the "chamelion lizard".' Well known from early days was the *ground lizard*, of which Browne distinguished a large spotted and a small variety. Because its range is limited and it is very common around Kingston, it is sometimes called the *Kingston lizard*.

The noise it makes and its creeping motion have given an unpleasant reputation to the *croaking lizard* (first mentioned by Senior). Lynn and Grant distinguish between the ordinary and the *white croaking lizard*. In folk pronunciation one hears /krókin/,

/krókng/, and /klókin/ *lizard*; also *croaker*, and it is said that, 'When crokin' lizard bawl, sign of rain comin'.' Both *croak* and *cluck*, of course, are onomatopoetic (so is the Malay *gecko*, which has been taken as the family name). A striking parallel is *ke-ke*, another name reported for it in Jamaica; and one may perhaps note that in Twi *kekáw* means to bark, cry, scream, or howl.

A number of names listed early but apparently no longer current are Sloane's *grey lizard*; Browne's *leather-coat*; Senior's *wood lizard*, which 'has a sleeky skin, like the common snake, and slips about in search of food'; and Gosse's *Venus* and *zebra lizards*. Current names include the *cricket lizard* (from the sound it makes); *bush lizard*; *blue-tail lizard*; *skellion lizard* (from the colour); and the widely known *coffee lizard*.

Finally, there are some very tiny lizards from an inch to two inches long, called the *Polly* or *Pauly*. Sloane was the first to describe these under the name of *woodslave* (current still in Barbados and the Cayman Islands, though little known any more in Jamaica). Sloane wrote: 'I saw one of these Spiders eat a small Lizard call'd a Woodslave, which was half out and half in his Mouth. . . . The Wood Slave . . . is about an inch long . . . brown above, with white spots like Stars . . . a white belly and reddish brown tail;' it 'lodges in old rotten Timber', and though said to be venomous, is not. Senior called it the *baby lizard*; it is also *lucky lizard* today.

Current folk pronunciations are /pali/ and /paali/, the latter being spelt both *Pawli* and *Pauly*. The earliest use of a name like these is that of Gosse, who lists *Eyed Pallette-tip* and *Ringtailed Pallette-tip* lizards. It therefore seems probable that *Polly* and *Pauly* are abbreviations of *pallette*, with the personalisations so common in Jamaican folk names. And what does *pallette-tip* mean? Evidently the word is Gosse's own; he uses it in reference to the flat, palette-like process on each toe of these little lizards which he takes as characterising them.

Other names for the Polly are *Charley lizard* and *squeechy*. One variety is also called a *water lizard*. Among general terms for lizards one finds *house lizard* and *common lizard*. The male is sometimes called a *cock*, and the fan-like process which the lizard spreads and folds at his throat is his *gill*.[4]

Snakes are not numerous and are named chiefly for their colour. First to be noticed was the *yellow snake*, which, according to

Sloane, had a 'somewhat poisonous but not fatal bite' — a bad and quite unjustified reputation. For this Lynn and Grant also give *nanka* — clearly an African name[5] — and remark that natives of Jamaica erroneously call the young of the yellow snake *red switchy-tail*.

Next to be noticed was 'AMPHISBENA I . . . The Silver Snake'. The Latin betrays the source of its present name, recorded by Gosse: 'From the uniform thickness of both extremities, and its power of moving backward or forward with equal facility, they designate [it] as the Two-headed Snake.' Today it is commonly called *worm snake*.

Stewart first mentioned the *brown snake* in 1823, Gosse the *zebra snake* in 1851, Wood the *grey snake* in 1863, and Lynn and Grant the *black snake* in 1940. Gosse had two other names: *pardaline* and *spotted-chinned snake*, evidently his own; modern names are *thunder* and *wood snake*. We have no record of folk usage for any of these.

From earliest days the turtles and tortoises have been valued and hunted among the islands, therefore their names are less localised than those for other animals. Early writers adopted Spanish *hicotea* (from Indian *jicotea*) and Englished it as *hicatee* or *hecatee* (one misprints it as *hickerie*), which was very soon discarded in favour of *land turtle*, the name that has lasted till today. (Neither word is a Jamaicanism, but both were used longer here than elsewhere. Though the hicatee is a terrapin, it is not so called in Jamaica.)

The sea turtles include the *loggerhead*, *hawksbill*, and *green*. Sloane has given the following description:

> Turtle, (Tortoises) are of several sorts, those of the Sea call'd green Turtle from their Fats being of that colour, feed on Conches or Shell-fish, are very good Victuals, and sustain a great many, especially of the poorer sort of the Island. They are brought in Sloops . . . in which forty Sloops . . . are always imployed. They are . . . brought and put into Pens, or Palisadoed places in the Harbour of *Port-Royal*, whence they are taken and killed as occasion requires. . . . There is a sort of Loggerhead Turtle or Tortoise at *Jamaica*, very little differing from the common sort, only in every part less, and having the Brest of a yellowish white colour.

Both terms are common today. The latter is understood to

mean that the animal has a large head but is stupid — like the loggerhead bird. *Hawksbill* has been altered by the Jamaican fishermen. The Standard 'hawk's' should have produced /haaks/; instead it has produced /haks/ as if it meant 'ox-bill' or 'axe-bill'. These three names were first recorded in Barbados by Ligon but are included because of their local forms and their importance in this island. The hawksbill is also called a /kài-wáama/ — compare British Guianese *kaiwana*.

Finally there are the *mulatto* and *yellow-bill* turtles, which resemble the hawksbill (both names evidently based on features of colour); and the leather-back or trunk turtle is known, from its prominent dorsal ridges, as the *three-keel* — an accurate and appropriate designation.

Spiders, Insects, Worms

One form of life that thrives in Jamaica far too well for human comfort is that of the spiders, insects, and worms. But, having made their presence felt, they have earned a number of names, usually interesting, sometimes remarkable.

Of spiders the really important word is *anancy*, or *nancy*, which refers to the tribe in general, but specifically is the name of the hero of so many folk stories: *Anancy*, the spider that may take human shape and characteristics. The word is African, as we have seen, and there are the *ground* and *black anancy*. *Anancy* usually refers to harmless ones, in contrast to *spider*, which is poisonous. 'Spider webs of any kind' are called *anancy rope*. The word *cobweb* has acquired among the folk the sense of the 'black stuff [that] gathers on spiderwebs', and is pronounced /kábob/ or /kábog/. Another name for it is *natta-bige*, of which the second part means *bag* clearly enough, but the first may either be distantly connected with *atter*, an old word for a spider, or possibly *annatto*, regularly pronounced /náta/, from some resemblance to annatto bags, which the loops of cobweb heavily covered with soot might well suggest.

Ground-anancy seems to be a name for the black spider with a red spot under its abdomen (called the 'black widow' in the United States) as well as the 'brown widow' variety in Jamaica that is not quite so poisonous. The first name on record for this was Browne's *red-arsed spider*: 'This insect is frequent in the woods, and its nip or bite said to be very venomous.' Somewhat later this was euphemised to *red-tailed spider*, and still later to *black spider*, the commonest name today. *Black-anancy* is said to be different from the black spider, but in what way is not made clear.

Two other spiders mentioned by Browne were the *black jumper* and *grey jumper*: the first is 'very frequent in the country parts of *Jamaica*, especially in the parish of *St Mary's*. It is a very remarkable jumper'; the second 'is an elegant, active, little spider; but seldom spins a web, depending chiefly on its agility in catching its prey'; it is frequent around Kingston. Browne was also first to adopt *tarantula* as an English word (1756) and to mention the *crab-spider* — both for specimens he had found in Jamaica. The crab spider is also called *banana spider*. A present-day folk word is *open-web spider*, apparently used to contrast the class that make elaborate wheel-like webs with those that make tunnels, such as the black spider.

Ants and termites are both numerous and various. The termites were first known as *wood lice*, a name now out of use; later *white ants*, which still has some use though the common terms are *wood-ants* and *duck-ants*. *Wood-ants* may be a Jamaican-ism in this sense: as long ago as 1725 Sloane described a spider which 'spreads some few Threads in Lieu of a Web, and catches in it Wood Ants, &c.' — and it still has this meaning for many of the folk. On the other hand some say that *wood ants* are 'black; nest inside wood; have a strong smell' — which evidently describes a real ant, the *stinking ant*.

Duck-ants is unquestionably a Jamaicanism, first put in print it would seem by Senior: 'Another terrible plague is the "duck ant", or wood ant . . . it is flat, has feet, and emits a very offensive smell.' These insects make large, bulging, blackish nests of macerated wood, a characteristic sight on the trees; in early days they were used in feeding poultry: 'These Poultry are all fed on *Indian* or *Guinea* Corn, and Ants Nests brought from the Woods, which these Fowls pick up and destroy mightily.' Despite this association with poultry the name probably comes from the appearance of the creature, which is white and has a waddling gait.

The earliest folk name for wood-ants, according to Long, was *bug-a-bug*. Today the folk make a distinction between those which live in trees and those which live in houses, furniture,

etc. — the dry-wood termite — though they seem to apply
wood-ants and *duck-ants* to both. The head of the termite is black,
which is supposed to explain one name: *nigger-head*;[6] but this
would apply even better to the appearance of the nests. The
adults have wings; they come out in swarms during the rainy
season, shed their wings, and start a new life cycle. This explains
the names *flying-ants* and *rain fly*. The dry-wood termites leave a
characteristic 'dust' of fecal pellets, called *chi-chi*, a word which
seems to suggest the fineness of this dust. Some apply it to the
insects themselves.

Among the real ants two have colour names: the red and the
black. The dictionaries list *red ants* but not *black ants*, yet the
latter were noted in 1740: 'There are large *black Ants*, which
build on high Trees, and others on the Ground; they destroy
other Vermin.' And again in 1835: 'The common *"black ant"* is a
terrible plague, finding its way into everything eatable.'[7] Another kind of black ant (mentioned above) is the *stinking ant*.
(One man called it /kotúon/, evidently *cut-stone*, without being
able to explain this name; it is a tree-living ant.)

Two, at least, have African tribal names: *Congo Peggy* and
Cromanty. The former dates from at least 1868 (Russell), and is
still so called and identified as red ants. *Congo*, even so, may be
the result of folk etymology: in Twi *ŋkaŋka* is a termite, and in
Okwawu *kàŋkaŋ* is 'a kind of big ant'; some such African word
may have been converted into *Congo*. *Peggy* presumably is one
of those personifications in which the folk so often indulge toward all forms of animal and even plant life. The *Cromanty* ant
preserves the reputation for fierceness that the Koromantyn
or Coromantee slaves once had: it is a 'big size black ant; live in
ground; have a claw, send liquid poison in you'.

Another with a personal name is *Tom Raffles*, first noticed in
1790: 'An ant, which is known by the name of Tom Raffles: . . .
in some places so excessive is their number, and so destructive
their rapacity, that when they have not rats to encounter, they
will attack the poultry; and have been even known to blind, by
their numbers and perseverance, . . . the eyes . . . of negro
children.'[8] The name comes from that of the St Thomas planter,
Thomas Raffles, who in 1762 introduced this ant from Cuba to
prey on young rats. McKay has recorded the name as Tom
Rafflin and identified them with *mad-ants*, as do some people

today; others say they are large and black, though 'not as big as *kap-kap*'. *Mad-ants*, also called *crazy-ants*, 'run like mad but don't bite'. The *kap-kap* takes its name from the noise it makes with its mandibles: it is big, black, lives in the ground, and 'claps its mouth'. Another named onomatopoetically is the /pr-o-pr-o/: the size of red ants but black, and living in rotten wood.

A name recorded in 1740, and still current (though not in the dictionaries) is *sugar ant*: 'There is also a very small sort, called the Sugar-Ant; they are very troublesome in Houses, by running over Victuals and whatever is uncover'd, but inoffensive else.'⁹ These tiny insects, also called *running ants*, appear remarkably as if from nowhere the moment anything sweet is present. Similar to them in colour (reddish) and size are the *pepper-ants* or *burn-ants*, so called because their 'sting burn like pepper'. On the other hand, *biting* or *stinging ants* are black and live in the ground. (They are sometimes called *fire ants*.)

Another has an ironic name, *pity-me-little*, that seems to beg for mercy: it means 'pity little me'. But though small this ant stings very sharply. In one man's description it is 'red with black eyes; it sting you one place a thousand times'.

Browne listed, 'FORMICA I ... The Lion-Ant ... greenish blue head, brownish behind.' The OED says the lion-ant is the same as the ant-lion, but this is a mistake, both here and in its own citation for 1774. *Lion-ant* does not seem to be used any more; the ant-lion (*Myrmeleon*) is called *nanny* or *turkle* in Jamaica.

The usual folk pronunciation of *ants* is /hans/ or /hants/. Russell recorded *hanen*, but it must have been a different word — indeed, it was surely connected with Twi *hãnĩ*, a black ant. Thus we have another coincidence of form and meaning between the English and African; *ants* or *hants* today has absorbed the former *hanen*.

Names for flies include many found elsewhere, but one that is specifically Jamaican is *pepper-fly*. In Long's explanation, 'If it happens to fall upon the tunicle of the eye, [it] gives a very disagreeable smarting pain, resembling what is caused by pepper.' It is still widely current.

A name no longer used of insects (today it applies to a kind of chicken) was *Jack Spaniard*. Scott wrote of 'horses fretting and jumping all the time ... if the Jack Spaniards or gadflies be rife'.

Probably the most characteristic, though its name is some-what of a puzzle, is the *gingy fly* (as it is spelt), usually pronoun-ced /ginggi/, sometimes /jinji/. It is quite small, with a bluish cast (therefore also called *blue fly*), and annoying: it buzzes persistently and lays its eggs in sores. The name is said to come from the sound it makes, but the form *jinji* would seem rather to connect it with the *junjo fly*, which is also blue and which comes where there is anything sour (*junjo* is the folk name for any fungus), and with the *sour fly*, which does the same. Its egg-laying habits recall the *maggot-fly*, 'a black sort with red head', also known as *bugu-bugu* fly (probably made up from the word *bug*, in reference to the maggots).

The smallest fly is the *mini-mini*,[10] a word also used for any glittering speck — such as the 'stars' one sees when given a blow on the head — and which describes the appearance of these tiny insects very well. Other flies include the *Congo fly*, which is black; *horn fly*; *yam fly*, which appears 'when negro yam in season'; *money fly*, which is bluish, bores wood, and 'when they fly out you're going to get money'; *stable fly*; and *buck fly*, which 'catch you in eye when you driving or riding — a lot flying together in Lent'. The last name may be based on the sense of *meet, come upon*, which is the usual meaning of *buck up*.

Mosquitoes and their tribe are not lacking, though no great annoyance nowadays. Their earliest name was *merrywings*, of which Ogilby wrote: 'In some parts of the Countrey there are also a sort of stinging Flies, call'd *Muschilli* and *Merrywings*, but the English Quarters are little infested by them.' The name was explained in 1683: 'They are called Mery-wings, from their Noise,'[11] which evidently influenced the editors of the OED to accept the name as a combination of *merry* and *wings*: 'app. with reference to the rapid beating of the wings' — one of their rare lapses, for the word is a palpable folk-etymology. It is ultimately a Tupí-Guaraní word which came into French as *maringouin* and Spanish as *maringuín*, and from one or both of these to English. Sloane identified the 'merrywing' as the common mosquito. The word has long been out of use in Jamaica, but still means a midge in Barbados.

Another old name, generally American but first recorded in a Jamaican source, was *gallinipper*, so called 'from their Biting'.[12] Browne also listed the 'Loggerhead *Muskeeto*' — larger than others and with a sharp bite, but 'unactive' and therefore easily killed. Sloane mentioned yet one more: 'Culex niger minor. A Bottle-Arse. . . . This Fly is very small, no larger than a Pin's head, the Body is very black, the Wings grey, the other Parts scarce perceivable.' Another writer elaborated: 'Bottle-Arses is a small Fly with a large Breech; they are chiefly in the Country; they will suck the Blood where they fasten till they are full.' This name alone of the three survives today, though in an obscured form: its folk pronunciation is /batlas/ or /baklas/, but the composition of the word has been forgotten. The worm-like larva of the mosquito was called *tadpole* by Long, and today is a *kick-foot* or *jump-up* from its wriggling motion in water.

Jamaica has been known for its fireflies; almost every early writer has remarked on them. There are two distinct kinds: those with the intermittent light at the 'tail' and those with steadily shining 'eyes', the latter much larger. The earliest name, *candle-fly*, evidently included both: 'There are two sorts, which are not only innocent but beautiful by Night, casting Beams of Light like Sparks of Fire thro' the Air; they are called *Candle-Flies*.'[13] Though still known, this word is considered 'old time'. Candle-fly Peak in the Blue Mountains probably owes its name to these insects.

Two other inclusive names are *winky* (or *winker*) and (far more common) *blinky*. To make the distinction between the two kinds, one may refer to their contrary size: *big winky* and *little blinkie*. The big one is also *peeny* or *peeny-wauly*, an unexplained word, though *wauly* may refer to its shining 'eyes'.[14] Another name, *moony*, certainly does. Still another, /kape/, is supposed to refer to the sound it makes, a sort of click. At the east end of the island one finds a variety of related forms: /kitibú/, /kikibú/, /kichibú/, /chichibú/, /tichibú/; the most common might be spelt *kitibu*. These names sound as if they might be ultimately African — for example Twi *Kétee*, bright, and *bu* from Fanti *būbū*, insect.

An account of these fireflies from 1838 says: 'There are several varieties: the bottle-fly is the largest. . . . There is another, a smaller kind . . . alternately shewing and withholding their light, which is feeble in comparison with that of the bottle-fly.' This term has been found nowhere else, and is not current today: one wonders whether there may not have been some confusion with candlefly (and perhaps bottle-arse). There has certainly been some confusion about the *stranger fly*, or *stranger*; some identify it with the small firefly, others not. It is supposed to indicate that a stranger is coming: 'if it fly high, a gentleman; if it fly low, a lady.'

A very similar belief is found with the *newsmonger* (or *newsvunga, newsbunga, newsbug*), a large grayish beetle, first mentioned in 1756 (Browne). When one comes, you knock it down; if it falls on its back it brings bad news. Others say you must spit on it and make a wish: if it flies (as it always does!) that means good news.

Beetles in general are called *hard-back*. One of the best known is the *tumble-turd*, an eighteenth-century American word for which the dictionaries have citations no later than 1754. Yet it is still very much alive in Jamaica as *tumble-tud*; also *tumble-bug*; and one man called it a *hog-vunga*, a curious name whose second element is apparently taken to mean *bug* (compare *newsvunga*).

Other beetles early mentioned here include Sloane's *tortoise fly* (from its highly rounded back), *stag fly* (named for its horns), and *musk fly* (from its smell); and Browne's *wood-digger, monk beetle*, and *Jamaica clock* or *black dor*. The present-day *wood-clock*, perhaps one of these, is said to 'bore cotton tree; start at six and keep on till four in the morning'.

The *June-bug* or *screwy*, which 'sings at night, saws limbs off cotton tree and gungu', seems to be the same as the *fiddler bug* or *fiddler beetle*. The *July fifer* is probably the cicada.

Russell recorded *granke* as 'The cock-roach. African' but the word has been found nowhere else and is unexplained. The largest Jamaican cockroach is the *drummer* 'which makes a noise at night by knocking its head against the woodwork of houses'. Fortunately it is only two to three inches long.

Browne's name for the praying mantis was 'The *Spanish-Horse*', now obsolete. Today it is not always distinguished by name from the *stick-insect*: both seem to be called by the generally American name *devil's riding-horse*, with several Jamaican variants: *devil-horse, devil horse-whip, duppy ridin' horse, god-horse*, and *primenta horse*, the last indicating that these insects are found commonly on pimento trees.

The last of the 'bugs' are *banana borer, cashew bug*, and *soldier bug* or *cotton stainer*, whose names are self-explanatory. The cricket is called a *mango bug* because it comes at the season when mangoes are ripening. The 'lady-bug' or ladybird is known to the Jamaican folk as *my-lady*, *day peeny*, and *policeman* (from the supposed similarity to the police costume: dark blue with a red stripe). The *Easter bug* is named for its season and is similar to the May bug; the *night-baby* may be the cicada: its name refers to its 'crying' by night. The stink-bug is also a *bishop*, evidently from its shape which resembles an alb or cope, or, reversed, a mitre.

The green stink-bug is frequently called *Mary Grudgeful*; but this name is quite generally applied to cutworms also and to the *sweet-potato bug*. And *Grandy Mary* is the inch-long black worm with many white legs that rolls itself up in a spiral when touched.

In slave days the newly imported slaves often had Guinea worms in their skins. It was the custom at first to extract these by gradually rolling them around a small stick, taking a turn each day. Sloane, citing Barham, called them *negro-worms*, and wrote: 'A Cataplasme made of the green Leaves, Cassada-flower, and a little Oil . . . if apply'd with a green Leaf to the part, where Negro-worms lye, it softens and brings the Worm out.' Referring to the former method of extraction they were also called *ring-worms*. These are now happily no more, and the words are obsolete.

The Indians of the Caribbean considered certain grubs a delicacy. As Sloane reported: 'Great Esteem was set on a sort of *Cossi*, or Timber-Worms, call'd Cotton-Tree-Worms, by the Negros and Indians.' These were better known by the name of *macaccas*. Browne referred to them: 'When it [the silk-cotton tree] falls, it becomes a nest for Macaccas, and other insects . . . LUCANUS I . . . large caterpillars, commonly called Macaccas;' and he remarked on their being a delicacy. Today the word is spelt *macaca* and the meaning extended to almost any white grub,[15] but the folk pronunciations are varied: /makáko/, /makúku/, /makakú/, /makwákwa/, and /makóngo/; the worms are said to be no longer eaten. The word came through Spanish but probably goes back to Angola (Friederici).

Other words for grubs include *apeke* (three syllables) and *parched-corn* (they are light brown dotted with dark brown). A pupa is sometimes held in the palm of the hand, in a sort of game, and the player chants 'Suzy, Suzy, show me town'; the pupa then twists and turns and supposedly points itself towards town. From this chant it has the names *show-me-town* or *show-me-show-me*, and /jìji-wáina/ from its 'winding' or twisting. The first part of this word may be African.[16]

A quaint name for the caterpillar is *gormandiser*; and there is the *orange dog*, which feeds on orange leaves and has a face like a bulldog. But /bàgabú/ is the common name for caterpillars (or *catchapilla* as one woman said it), worms in general, and even lice. Russell, in 1868, spelt this *bagabo* and considered it 'African'; but it is simply the English word *bugaboo* (which, by the way, is the source of *bug*, applied in America to insects in general). It is true that Fanti *bũbũ* means insect, and that Jamaican *bubo*, 'worm' may very well come from it; but this is quite different from *bagabu*. The web spun by caterpillars on the back of cassava leaves is called *god-cotton* or *pain-a-ears* from its use as a remedy for earache.

The Jamaican folk preserve the Spanish form of *centipede*: they pronounce /sàntapíi/. The commonest name, however, is *forty-leg*, an English provincialism still alive in this island.

The dragonfly is most frequently called *needle-case* (from the resemblance of its body to that object), but also *water-dipper* (from the way it dives toward the water and comes up again), and *needle-pointer*.

Butterflies are not much attended to by the folk. Beckwith reported *but-but* as a local (probably humourous) name; and they are sometimes called *bat* — *green bat, yellow bat*, and so on. But *bat* or *night-bat* is usually reserved for the far more impressive moths that fly at dusk and by night, some of which are very large, which beat on windows and around lights, while the smaller ones fly into lamp flames. (The real bat is always a *rat-bat*.)

This similarity of moth and bat was noticed as long ago as 1740: 'There are several sorts of *Butterflies* as in *England*, and one great sort which has in the upper part of his Wings small Sinews like the *English* Batt.'[17] Shortly after, Browne gave *mosquito hawk* (which in the southern United States means a dragonfly) as a name for these moths: 'PHALAENA I . . . The *Muskeeto* Hawk. . . . It is never abroad but in the earlier hours of the night, when the Muskeeto's are most troublesome, which gave rise to its common appellation; most people imagining that it feeds on these insects.' Among those who accepted the belief was Marsden, who

u

wrote that mosquitoes 'have a rooted enemy in an insect about the size of a bat, called the musquitoe-hawk'.

The *lamp-bat* or *lamp-fly* is smaller; it 'outs' lamps at night by flying into the flame. The large moth that sucks the nectar of flowers at dusk as the humming-bird does by day is called a *night doctor-bird*. (Some of these moths are actually larger than humming-birds.)

There is little to be said of bees. A stingless variety was reported from 1764 as *Spanish bees*, and *Italian bees* are imported.[18] The bumble bee has become a *bungo bee*, evidently from its size and black colour, perhaps also its clumsiness. Wasps have a number of names, however. First, the general or collective term is *wass-wass*, and there are both the paper-nest kind (or *biting wasp*) and mud-nest kind (*night wasp, house wasp*). Browne evidently intended the latter by his term *Free-Mason* wasp; he was also the first to mention *Grave-Digger* as the name for the wasp that seals spiders or worms in with its grubs as food for them when they develop. Finally, the *Eddy wasp* was named in honour of Mr W. H. Edwards, Government Entomologist, who introduced it in 1930 to combat the citrus black fly.

The Standard word *chigoe* is regularly /chiga/ or /jiga/ in Jamaican use. Stewart has the strange spelling *chigise*: 'An insect called a *chigise*;' he must have heard a plural used as singular, a common enough usage in the folk speech. Some also say *Congo chigger*; they badly infest the feet of country people who always go barefoot. Both *chink* and (less often) *chinch* are heard for the bedbug; Browne also mentioned a 'small green Wood-Chink'.

There are *silver ticks* (large ones on cattle), also called *constab ticks* by cattle men in the St Ann hills (from their being striped — the usual reference to the policeman's striped trousers); *pimento ticks*; *fowl ticks*; and the tiny, flat, red tick called *flatty-cut*. And as for lice, there are *fowl* and *pigeon* lice and the so-called *grass lice*, which are really young cow ticks. Perhaps it was these that Sloane long ago described under the name 'Patata Louse'.

The fungal galls on turnips and cabbages are known as *finger and toe* or 'anbury' — evidently *hand-berry*. Leaf galls are said to be called *animal fruits* by children in St Ann and St James, which accurately enough expresses the part played by insects in their formation.

Chapter Fourteen

BIRDS

SINCE THIS is an account of bird names and not of birds, the reader must not expect to find any mention of standard names unless they began as Jamaicanisms. If a bird is found only in Jamaica, all its names are pertinent; if it is found elsewhere too, or includes this island in its migrations, only the Jamaican names are dealt with. Most of these are, necessarily, folk terms: it is our good fortune that many students of Jamaican birds have been careful to record them. Some names are obsolete; some died aborning, offered by naturalists perhaps but never generally adopted. The presentation here is not by ornithological classes but in the sort of groupings that the folk observer might make, beginning with sea birds.

In the folk pronunciation *pelican* has become /pílikin/. When adapted toward the Standard this becomes /pílikan/. But almost as common is the alternative name *ol'-Joe*, with its variant *Joe-bird*. The usual name for the frigate bird is *man-o'-war*, a word first recorded in Barbados. Jamaican fishermen also call it *scissors* from the way it manipulates its long, forked tail, like scissors opening and closing, to balance itself while soaring.

The sooty tern, whose eggs are collected on the Pedro and Morant Cays and sold in Kingston as *booby eggs*, was once known as the *egg-bird*. (Gosse called it the *dusky booby*, and the royal tern *white egg-bird* — names not found elsewhere.) Gulls are sometimes called *white-bird* by the fishermen; and 'some say *sea-gulf*' — a vague kind of folk-etymology. *Noddy* is occasionally pronounced /náadi/.

Undomesticated ducks of any kind are generally called *wild-duck* among the folk. Of these, the *white-bellied duck* seems to have been mentioned only in early Jamaican sources; it is not known today. Gosse listed the *Blue Mountain duck* and said that it burrows into the earth; but he failed to identify it. It was

probably not a duck but a petrel, and is no longer found here.[1]
A curious name in this group is *duckanteal*, evidently made by
converting duck-and-teal into a single word. The country
people insist that this is one bird, not two, and that it looks like a
duck. Unusual though it is, this combination is paralleled on the
Atlantic coast of the United States by the old word *duckinmallard*,
composed of duck-and-mallard (DAE). English *diving dapper*
(or *didapper*) is found in Jamaica in the forms 'divin' dapper' and
'divin' hopper', the two rhyming: /dapa/ and /hapa/. The
second is no doubt a folk-etymological alteration of the first,
alluding to the suddenness with which these birds dive.

A number of wading birds are found near the sea in river
estuaries and mangrove swamps. The night herons go by the
name of *quok* or *water partridge*. *Quok* is onomatopoetic, of course;
it recalls the similar American name *qua-bird*, also applied to
these species. *Water partridge* describes the habit and appearance.
This latter term was used by Gosse, but he identified the bird as
the *red rail* (apparently the Virginia rail). Perhaps the name has
been used for both.

The same may be true of *clucking-hen*, one of the first Jamaican
bird names to be recorded, dating as it does from 1679.[2] Early
writers mentioned it without identification until 1840: 'The
Jamaica Heron — Clucking hen — by some called Qua bird.'
Judging by this it was the same as the *quok*, yet Gosse shortly
after took it to be a rail, and the folk today seem to call more
than one bird by this name. Indeed, the application of folk
names is by no means precise.

For yet another bird, not clearly identified, Gosse recorded as
folk names *cacky-quaw* (i.e., *cocky-*), *Johnny-ho*, and *Kitty-go*; it was
in all likelihood a rail, perhaps the qua-bird. The names follow
a common pattern: the cry of the bird is imitated and personalised. From its habit of frequenting mangrove swamps, the
clapper rail is known as *mangro-hen* and has been since at least
1843.[3]

The stilt has the Jamaican names *black-back*, *cock-soldier*,
soldier, and *crack-pot soldier*. *Soldier* no doubt refers to its posture;
the pots which it cracks — could they be fish-pots?

An interesting example of folk-etymology combined with
personalisation may be seen in the conversion of the scientific
name *Jacana spinosa* into a more familiar form: 'Near Black

River ... people call them "Jack Spence".' Another local
name for this bird is *lily-trotter* because it 'has long splayed toes
to enable it to walk easily upon pond vegetation and water lily
pads'.[4] *Pond coot, queen of birds* (from the brilliant coloration), and
river chink have also been reported[5] for the Jacana, but the last
seems doubtful. In the folk speech a *chink* is a bedbug, which
hardly applies here, nor can 'chink' very well represent the
sound made by this bird. I suggest that *river-chick* is more likely,
chick being a common element in folk names.

One distinctive Jamaicanism is *gaulin*, pronounced /gaalin/
by the folk, evidently a preservation of Scots *gawlin*, a water
bird (see EDD), perhaps influenced in Jamaica by Spanish
gallina, hen. *Blue gaulin* is usually applied to the adult of the little
blue heron, and *white gaulin* to the immature birds. When the
great blue heron and the snowy egret put in an appearance,
however, they are *gaulins* too. (Sloane's other name for the blue
gaulin was *black gaulin*, and Gosse called the snowy egret *black
legged gaulin* — terms not found elsewhere.) Sloane's spelling
actually was *gaulding*; another current form is *gawlin*.

The little green heron is sometimes called *green gaulin*, but
more often *crab-catcher*. (Gosse's name was *red-necked gaulin*,
which nobody else seems to have used.) Last of the herons, the
Louisiana heron, is 'often known in Jamaica as Switching Neck'[6]
because of the sinuous movements of its neck.

A series of names for the smaller wading birds — in several
cases his own coinages — was presented by Gosse, but none
seem to have been adopted. They are listed here simply for the
record. For the 'little yellow bittern', probably the little yellow
rail of today, he gave *tortoiseshell bird*; for the killdeer, *tilderee* and
tell-tale; for the sandpipers, *little, spotted*, and *bar-tailed*; and for
similar birds *yellow-shanks* and *bar-flanked gambet*.[7]

In the folk speech *snite* seems to be preferred to *snipe*, and
plover appears as /plóba/. Sloane remarked that 'The Grey-
Plover' was 'so called in Jamaica by the inhabitants'. Evidently
he took it to be a local word; however, it was already in English
use by 1674. Last of the water birds, the kingfisher, is known as
fisherman bird.

Names for game birds, especially doves and pigeons, which
are numerous and relatively easy to distinguish, mostly refer to
their habits or appearance. Smallest, and one of the most famil-

iar, is the *ground dove*, so called from its habit of feeding on the ground. The OED lists the name from Antigua, 1792, but it appeared in a Jamaican source well over a hundred years earlier when Trapham wrote of 'Pigeons, of various sorts, Turtle Doves, Ground Doves, Parrats . . .' (1679). It is regarded superstitiously (among others) as a *duppy bird*. As Uncle Newton has written, 'Of course we were careful not to shoot "Duppy Birds". I nearly shot one one day . . . if I had shot that bird I would have died . . . He said that all Ground Doves were "Duppy Birds".'

Next in size is the *pea-dove*, said to feed on peas; the name has been in use since at least 1840.[8] An earlier name apparently was *ear-dove*, which Sloane recorded with the explanation, 'it had two Spots of each side of the Neck of a dark Colour, whence the name of Ear-Dove.' A present-day folk name is *Mary coat blue*, which is what the bird is supposed to be saying when it coos. The *long-tailed peadove* or *paloma* is simply the American mourning dove. *Paloma*, the Spanish word for 'dove', may have been applied by Jamaicans who had known the bird in some Spanish speaking area before seeing it in Jamaica, where it has become common only recently.

Descriptive names include *bald-pate*, *blue-belly*, *blue-foot*, *blue pigeon*, *white-belly* (or *white-breast*), *white-wing*, and *ring-tail*; *barble dove* and *mountain witch* are less obviously so. *Bald-pate* refers to the conspicuous white top of the head; it is the common term, in use before 1713.[9] One countryman made it *bald-plate* not a surprising alteration considering that *pate* is hardly understood by the folk. In an early account one dove is referred to without further identification as a 'blew-belly'. This may have referred to the bald-pate, which is blue except for the head (but note *blue-dove* below). *Blue-belly* probably was meant to contrast with the next.

White-belly or *white bellied dove* has also been current since at least 1713.[10] (Stewart added the probably euphemistic equivalent *white-breast*, not recorded elsewhere.) This bird is found only in Jamaica and Grand Cayman. The *white-wing* is sometimes confused with it but is not the same — it is, in fact, closer to the peadove. *White-wing* too seems to be a Jamaicanism, found here in 1840: 'White-wing pigeon', and 1847: 'whitewing dove'; and it is still current throughout the island. Another but less widespread name for it is *lapwing*, though of course in England this designates not a dove but a plover.

Perhaps the most interesting in this group of names is *mountain witch*, first recorded in 1823.[11] According to Gosse, the 'moans, heard . . . while the bird is rarely seen, have . . . given it the name of Mountain Witch'. But other characteristics are probably responsible too: as Lady Taylor has written, 'When disturbed it does not take readily to the wing, but waddles rapidly away stopping at intervals and looking back at its pursuer with a curious bobbing gesture. Eventually it disappears into the forest undergrowth. The head is grey with the feathers on the nape lengthened so that it almost looks as though the bird were wearing a grey wig.'

This bird is found only in Jamaica; a common alternative name is *blue dove* or *blue pigeon*; some writers also call it *crested quail-dove*, as distinct from *ruddy quail-dove*, a close relative. The distinction is not always made by the folk, but the ruddiness of the latter and the fullness of the feathers at its neck have given it the name of *partridge*, earlier *mountain partridge*, *partridge pigeon*, and *partridge dove*.

Sloane is the only writer to give the form *ring-tailed pigeon*; all others have simply *ring-tail*, and so it regularly is in current usage. In Sloane's day an alternative name was *mountain pigeon*; *mountain dove*, still in use, no doubt refers to the same bird. Finally there is the *barble dove* (/baabl dov/), evidently a folk form of *barbary dove*;[12] it is small, whitish, with a black mark at the throat, and is tame and caged.

An early account mentions the *Spanish pheasant* but does not describe it — one can only guess what it may have been. One small game bird today is called a *dodging quail* from its habit of hiding in the grass to avoid the hunter.

The American bobolink migrates to Jamaica where it has had the names *ortolan*, *butter bird*, *October bird*, *October pink*, *pink*, and *rice bird*. The first is not a Jamaicanism; it was always rather literary and is now hardly to be found. Next was *pink*, dating from 1740 and still widely used. It has nothing to do with the colour: like bobolink it imitates the bird's cry. *Butter-bird*, another early local name (1790), is now the most common. It refers to the fatness of these birds, prized by the epicure. The next two names allude to their arrival in October: *October bird* dates from at least 1793; *October pink* is from 1847. Only Gosse has reported *rice bird*: it may well be his translation of the Latin species name *oryzivorus*, rice-eater.

The Jamaican thrushes (there are only two) have a surprising array of names, usually referring to their conspicuous eyes and hopping walk. One is the *glass-eye*, otherwise known as *shine-eye* and *fish-eye*, the eye being whitish and glassy against the brown of its head. *Glass-eye* and *fish-eye* have been in use since at least 1842, *shine-eye* since 1847.[13] The latter is used attributively too: *shine-eye jumper*. The *shine-eye* is also said to be called *long-day bird* from its cry, which sounds like 'long day coom!'. (The *shine-eye blackbird* or *shine-eye Barbados* is the kling-kling, discussed below.)

Names for the second thrush fall into groups: first, *hopping dick*, *jumping dick* (or *jumper*), *mountain dick*, or *mountain cock*; second, *tricking-chick*, *chick-man-chick*, or *chip-man-chip*; and third, *twopenny chick*, or *tapna-chick*. The earliest mention of them was in 1740: 'The Mountain-Cock or Tricking-Chick, which digs up their Corn.' *Mountain cock* is still in use, but *tricking-chick* has evidently been converted into the other forms grouped with it. As we have noted, the combination *tr* is difficult for the folk and often becomes *ch*, as here. *Trickin' chick* would thus turn into *chickin' chick* (though this is unrecorded) and so into *chick-man-chick* and (with substitution of *p* for *k*) *chip-man-chip*; Uncle Newton also gives the form *chick-ma-chick*, and Taylor *chick-me-chick*.

Mountain cock was either converted into *mountain dick*, or served as a model for it. The latter is not recorded before 1847 (and then with a mistaken identification); it is identified at present with *chick-man-chick*, or else applied to the female of the *Jamaican becard*, while *mountain judy* is applied to the male. (According to Gosse, *Judy* was the same as *mountain dick*.) *Dick*, of course, is a common English element (as in dicky-bird, etc.) which, once introduced, was taken up by the folk and used in forming the newer names *hopping dick* and *jumping dick*. As these imply, the bird has a characteristic way of moving; it is also known as *red-foot jumper* or *red-foot jumping-dick* from its conspicuously orange coloured legs. By contrast the glass-eye or shine-eye is sometimes a *black-foot jumping-dick*.

Two-penny chick was first recorded in 1774: 'Black-bird. This is commonly called here the *two-penny* chick.' As to its· being a 'black-bird', this is not far wrong: it is indeed quite dark. 'Two-penny', judging by the present form 'tapna-', must have been pronounced 'tup'ny'. One cannot but wonder whether this element and *tricking* may not have had a similar origin though they seem clearly enough separated now. 'Tup'ny' was probably applied in its common disparaging sense.

Related to these is a bird found only in Jamaica, the *solitaire*. This is a book name; the folk do not use it. Their names are *whistler* and *glass-eye*. And the folk name for the Elaenia is *Sarah bird*.

The woodpecker is generally called *red-head* among the populace, but also *woodpicker*. In books this is the *Jamaican Woodpecker*; the American yellow-bellied sapsucker, when it comes to this island, is known as *Spanish woodpecker* — 'Spanish', as a colour word, having its usual folk sense of yellow. When Sloane wrote of the *yellow woodpecker* he probably meant this bird.

The two Jamaican parrots are *yellow-bill* and *black-bill parrot*. *Parrot* tends to be pronounced /pórot/ among the folk, though /párat/ and /páarat/ are common too. The parakeet is better known because it flies in flocks, is noisy, and destroys field crops; however, it seems to have acquired no new names. One alternative pronunciation is /pàrakíi/.

Among the smaller birds are the king-birds, known as /pichíeri/ in Jamaica. This is onomatopoetic, of course, representing 'that ceaseless shriek, . . . very similar to the words *pecheery-pecheery, pe-cheer-ry*, from which they receive their name'. Gosse's spelling was *petchary*, which the OED adopted (mistakenly placing the accent on the first syllable, however). Other attempts to represent this cry account for the variant spellings *pecheere, pecheree, pitcheary, petchery* or *petcherry*; also the considerably different *pepeeret* and *pippari*.[14] One may note that the same bird is called *pitirre* in Puerto Rico, which suggests that some Indian word perhaps preceded both the English and Spanish versions.

Various 'pecharies' (sometimes they are flycatchers) are recognised among the folk. The usual one (which Gosse called *gray petchary*) is contrasted with the *loggerhead* or *loggerhead petchary*. (Gosse also listed *red* and *common petchary*.) *Loggerhead* refers to two things: the largeness of head produced by this bird's black crest, and its supposed stupidity. As Sloane put it, 'They . . . let Men come so near them that they knock them down with sticks, whence they have the Name of Loggerheads.' Another reference to the crest is found in the more recent name *cottahead*, a *cotta* being a pad used in carrying loads on the head. Other local names are *September petchary* and *Cuban petchary*. Presumably the first refers to the fact that the petchary migrate southward about the end of September; the latter may refer to *Tyrannus cubensis*.

A common name applied to the loggerhead and to some smaller flycatchers is *Tom-fool* or *Tom-fool petchary* because of their refusal to fly away when threatened. This seems at first sight an entirely English name, yet it may be another example of coincidental reinforcement: the Fante noun *ɔ-tám* means a simple, silly fellow, and the adjective *tám* silly. One or both of these may well have strengthened the English name, leading to its adoption or preservation among the folk (who pronounce *Tom* /tam/). *Little Tom-fool* is applied to the somewhat smaller Sad Flycatcher and Antillean Pewee. *Loggerhead fooly* combines both elements.

Sloane referred to '*The Singing Bird, Mock Bird,* or *Nightingale*' for the bird still called the *Jamaica nightingale* 'because it sings at night'. (It is simply the American mocking-bird.) Its song is said to go as follows: 'See me foot, see me foot, see me foot — pain, pain, pain, pain — doctor gi' me liniment — no better, no better, no better!'

In the early eighteenth century, *Spanish nightingale* appears to have referred to an oriole, perhaps the Baltimore, more likely the Jamaican: 'Icterus minor nidum suspendens . . . *The Watchy Picket*, or Spanish *Nightingale. The* American *Hang-nest.*'[15] Here again *Spanish* evidently implies yellow or orange. The first name is unrecorded in the dictionaries but also seems definitely Jamaican: *watchy* means 'watchman', and reinforces the sense of *picket*. If these names were once used in this island, however, they have since disappeared. Today the oriole is known as *banana bird* (discussed below with *banana quit*).

Another bird mentioned early (1740) but without identification was the *watchicraca*: 'Among the curious are . . . Cardinal Birds, Bill-Birds, Watchicracas, Canary Birds. . . .'[16] Perhaps *watchy* had the same sense here; *craca* was presumably onomatopoetic. (The *bill-bird* is also unrecorded elsewhere and unidentified.)

There are two common blackbirds, quite distinct though their names are occasionally confused. The first, allied to the cuckoos, has a heavy, curved beak and a long flat tail, and is simply *blackbird*; its proclivity for eating the ticks off cattle is responsible for its genus name and for the occasional folk name *tick-bird*. Long early recorded the similar name *tick-eater*, and Browne *Savanna blackbird*. Its dull black colour, clumsiness, and the ugly beak have also earned it the nickname *old slut*.

The other, a grackle with a sharp, straight beak, is generally called *kling-kling*, sometimes *tin-tin*, *ting-ting*, or *ting-ling*. Though he does not use any of these words, Long's description makes their source very clear: 'Their note is something like the creaking of an inn-keeper's sign in a high wind, or the handle of a grind-stone; at other times it more resembles the gentle squeak which may be formed by means of a comb and paper. They vary frequently both the key and the tone, making altogether a very whimsical kind of concert.'

Gosse regularly called this the 'tinkling grackle', probably his personal rationalisation of the onomatopoetic names, though it has had some acceptance since. However, he confused its scientific name and identified it with the *Barbados blackbird*. This, indeed, is the only term that has been confused. It was earliest applied to the kling-kling, but Long identified it with the *tick-eater*,[17] and some now call the heavy-billed blackbird so.

Another black bird (allied, however, to the orioles) is the *wild-pine sergeant*, which gets its food in the epiphytic plants called 'wild pines' that grow on the branches of large trees in the hills. It is found only in Jamaica.

Other birds related to the cuckoo are the *black-eared* or *mangrove cuckoo*, which frequents mangrove trees, and the *yellowbilled cuckoo* or *May bird*, which was thought to come in the month of May. These four are book terms; the folk name for both birds is *rain-bird*, evidently a favourite since it is applied to at least two other species as well. The *old man*, *old man bird*, or *hunter* was the first to be so called; as Sloane wrote it, '*An Old-Man*, or, *a Raine-Bird*. . . . They are call'd Old-Men from the light brown, or grey Colour. . . . It makes a Noise generally before Rain, whence it had its name of Rain Bird.' (By analogy the *lizard-cuckoo* is the *old-woman bird*.)

Most recently, *rain-bird* — occasionally *weather-bird* — has come to be applied to swallows and their like because they fly low in swarms before rain. As for swallows otherwise, Gosse used the names *golden, great blue*, and *cave swallow* for Jamaican birds, but they have not been adopted. His too seem to be *palm swift, black swift*, and *ringed gowrie* — indeed, *gowrie* is hardly to be found elsewhere.

There are two 'crows' — a true one, the *jabbering crow*, and a vulture, the *Johncrow*. The first has had a variety of names; first '*A Chattering Crow*, or *A Cacao-walk*',[18] which, as Sloane wrote, 'frequents the Mountains, where it loves to be always making a chattering Noise, different from that of any of the European Crowes.' Neither name was reported again; the second is no doubt a folk-etymology of the sound made by the bird — one that would appeal to the whimsical imagination at a time when 'cocoa-walks' were being cultivated everywhere. The next to appear was *gabbling crow*, which continued in use for some time — at least, Gosse put it down again in 1847. From 1740 comes a curious form, *javaline crow*, evidently a variant of either 'gabbling' or 'jabbering', perhaps even influenced by the word 'jabbling' which was then in use. It is worth noting that the commonest folk pronunciation today is /jáblin krúo/. Perhaps the writer of 'javaline', having heard this, assumed that the folk *b* represented a Standard *v* here as it does so often. *Jabbering crow* was first recorded by Gosse. Meantime, Long had set down an amusing nickname: 'Their strange, noisy gabble of guttural sounds, which imitate some human languages, and are thought to have much the confused vociferation of a parcel of Welsh folks exercising their lungs and tongues at a grand scolding-match; hence these birds have been nick-named the Welshmen.' This bit of English humour has not survived.

It is quite impossible to know whether the folk pronunciation just given comes from *gabbling* with change of *g* to *j* (which sometimes happens), or from *jabbering* with change of *r* to *l* (a very common occurrence). At least, *jabbering crow* has become the Standard form. The bird is found only in Jamaica, in the western parts.

The *Johncrow* (pronounced by the folk /jángkro/) was at first known as a *carrion crow*, a generally West Indian name which Sloane and Long also used. Edwards wrote of 'The rav'ning Gallinazo . . . The Turkey vulture, vulgarly called the carrion crow'. As late as 1826 we find the present Johncrow Mountains still designated as the *Carrion Crow hills*. In short, the name Johncrow, now nearly universal, had evidently not yet come into use. It is from that very year, 1826, that our first record comes, when Williams wrote of 'the dead carcass of a mule, on which a score of john-crows were holding an inquest . . . Abdallah told me that they were called john-crows or carrion-crows till lately; but now, he said, they were called amen-preachers, because they finished everything, and eat it all up'. The third was no more than a nickname, unrecorded elsewhere; however, it witnesses the resentment that was felt against the anti-slavery ministers. *Johncrow* had evidently seen some use already; it soon displaced the other names and became the regular one.

The story now often told to explain its origin may be found in Gardner's history: a certain Irish clergyman, the Rev. John Crow, succeeded Mr Spere at Port Royal, and, in 1689, preached an extremely unpopular sermon in which he exhorted John Coad (and others who had been transported to Jamaica as prisoners with him) to submit without complaint to their unjust masters. So far the facts; the rest is legend: In contempt they named the bird *John Crow*, its black plumage and bald red head reminding them of the time-serving preacher.

It should be noted that Gardner does not record the legend, nor have I found any early account of it; its currency is recent and it has every appearance of a late invention. The greatest objection is that we must assume a period of over one hundred and thirty years to have elapsed between the giving of the name and the first record of it. Since this is one of the best known birds in the island — one that has been a subject of legislation and one that most writers have taken notice of — it is hard to believe that *John Crow* can have been its name for so long without anyone's mentioning it. As with such stories, this was very likely made up after the fact — indeed, quite some time after.

It is probably significant that the American term 'Jim Crow' came into being at almost the same time as *johncrow*. In 1828 Thomas D. Rice copyrighted a song in which the chief character was a Negro entertainer named Jim Crow, including the lines, 'My name's Jim Crow, Weel about, and turn about, And do jis so.' *Jim Crow* was applied to the dance performed with this song, to the stage presentation, and ultimately to any Negro; and to 'jump Jim Crow' was to perform the dance. Most of these things are paralleled in Jamaica: to *jump* means to dance, especially a vigourous or jigging dance; to *wheel and turn* is a traditional movement in folk dancing; and *johncrow* is sometimes applied to the Negro in allusion to his complexion, as in the proverb, 'Every johncrow t'ink him pickny white.' (The young turkey vulture is white but soon becomes black.) My suspicion is that the popularity of the American 'Jim Crow' helped the parallel creation, Jamaican *johncrow*, to rise into prominence. Applied to the 'carrion crow' as a nickname, it must have established itself rapidly until it superseded all its competitors.

Occasionally there is an albino crow: it may be called *johncrow parson* or *johncrow headman* in allusion to its being white.

Jamaican owl names include screech-owl, generally pronounced by the folk /krìchúol/, and the name appears to be applied to the white or brown owl indiscriminately. Browne's 'Mountain-Owl' may have been the former, which is found in the mountains as well as the lowlands; and Gosse's 'dusky eared-owl' is no doubt the same as the present-day *horny-owl* — other names, evidently, for the brown owl.

Sometimes confused with the brown owl is the goat-sucker or night-jar, whose proper Jamaican name, *patu*, is then transferred to the owl. Sloane's 'Wood Owle', judging by his description, was this goat-sucker. *Patu* is an African word (Twi *patu*, owl) and is pronounced by the folk as /patu/; the spellings *patoo* and *patto* therefore represent it more accurately than Gosse's *potoo*, which the OED and some writers have adopted. A peculiar form with an added *k* has been in existence since at least 1879: *patook*. One countryman explained this by saying the claws are like a pot-hook, another seemed to think it was the beak; in either case the form seems folk-etymological. (Gosse also wrote of a 'white-headed potoo', but it has not been mentioned elsewhere.) This bird has become in Jamaica a symbol of the unbeautiful: the proverbial comparison is 'ugly no patu'.

The closely related nighthawk has the echoic folk name *gi-me-me-bit*. Gosse was first to record something like this: he gave

its name as *piramidig*, and said the cry 'sounds like *gi' me a bit*'. I
have not heard *piramidig* among the folk; it may well have been
Gosse's personal interpretation.

Humming birds of any kind are popularly called *doctor-bird*.
The name refers primarily to the way these birds lance the
flowers with their long bills, entering them head first or pricking
a hole at the base to get at the nectar. But since *doctor* also applies
to an obeah-man, and since it is common knowledge that 'docta-
bud a cunny bud, hard bud fe dead' — that is, a tricky bird,
and hard to kill — there are superstitious overtones to the name.
Another evidence of this is the name *god-bud*, in use since at
least 1868. (*Grugudo*, also reported, may be connected with
gru-gru.)

When *doctor-bird* is applied specifically, as it sometimes is, it
means the *long-tailed, long-tail, scissors-tail, streamer-tailed* or
streamer-tail humming bird, which in the male has two long scallop-
edged tail feathers that cross when it sits at rest, and stream out
behind when it flies. Oldest of these names is *long-tailed humming-
bird*, which goes back to 1713[19] and is still in use. (In the song
Chi-chi-bud-O!, the *long-tail* is no doubt this bird.) *Doctor-bird*
was first recorded in 1826, but misapplied to the tody or robin.[20]
Scissors-tail was current in St Andrew about 1910–20, and
streamer-tailed in print by 1929.

The other humming-birds are the *mango*, and the *vervain* or
bee, all 'book' names. *Vervain*, given by Gosse, has been adopted
by ornithologists.

As was just pointed out, the *tody*, from its size and colouring, is
sometimes mistaken for a humming-bird — indeed, Sloane
called it the 'Green Sparrow, or Green-humming Bird', terms
which have not survived. To Gosse it was the *green tody*, and it
had become *robin* by 1894; but the present-day name among the
folk is regularly *robin red-breas'* in allusion to the scarlet patch at
the throat.

Among small birds one finds a number called *quits* — the
grass quit, banana quit, blue quit, soursop quit, and so on. As Gosse
pointed out, it is applied 'without much discrimination' to
creepers, finches, and others; and 'it is probably an African
designation'. This probability still holds though no specific
African source has been determined. The OED also suggests that
quit may be imitative of the sound made by these birds; perhaps

this was so in the beginning, though it would not apply to all the birds called quits today. However the word originated, it now refers more directly to size than to any other feature.

Best known is probably the *grass-quit*, at first (and still) called *grass-bird*. It is a finch, and there are two kinds: *black-faced* and *yellow-faced grass-quit*, both names introduced by Gosse. (His *bay-sided grass-quit*, however, has not been adopted.)

The *banana quit* is a black-and-yellow honey creeper, easily known by its curved beak and the whitish streak on each side of the head above the eye. This name goes back to 1847 at least; others are *beeny* (or *beany*), *beeny bird*, *beeny quit*, and *little beeny*, in which 'beeny' seems to mean 'small' but may mean 'banana'; also *Bessie bird*, *Bessie quit*, *Bessie guba*, or *Bessie gupa*. Its earliest name appears to have been *banana bird*, found first in 1713. But today *banana bird* is pretty consistently limited to the Jamaica oriole, along with the other names *banana Katy*, *Aunty Katy*, and *Ma Katy*. *Katy* itself may well be a form of *quit*, personalised as so many names of non-human things are among the folk.

The *orange quit* is similar to the honey creepers and fairly easy to recognise: it is dark blue except for reddish-orange patches at the throat and under the tail. Most of its names were first recorded by Gosse: *orange quit*, *orange bird*, *soursop bird*, all referring to fruits that it favours; *feather-tongue* to the furrowed, rough-edged tongue with which it sucks up nectar; and *blue-quit* for the predominant colour. More specifically it is the *long-mouthed blue-quit*; and other names are *blue baize*, *blue baige* (with a *j* sound), *blue-swee*, *obeahman cunny*, and *obeahman bluebird*. *Baige* is a form of *baize*, once a very common cloth, here suggesting colour; *swee* (as in *swee-swee* below) is an imitation of the cry, here made almost a generic term;[21] *cunny* is cunning, and with *obeahman* suggests the great cleverness of this bird, for it is very hard to catch. *Sweden* — related to *swee*? — includes both kinds of blue quits, the long- and short-mouthed. This last, the *short-mouth blue-quit* is really a tanager, also called the *cho-cho bird* or *cho-cho quit* from its fondness for the young shoots of that plant. Probably the earliest name to be applied to the blue-quit was *plantain bird*,[22] but the identification is not certain. *Banana yoky* may also be one of its names.

As Taylor has written, the long-mouthed blue-quit 'among

trees or in a poor light . . . looks almost black and might be confused with the Jamaica Bullfinch except for the shape of the
beak'. Evidently Gosse fell into this confusion when he identified
the *orange bird* with the 'Mountain bulfinch' or 'cashew bird'.
'Bullfinch' is not much used among the folk; they generally call
the Jamaica Bullfinch *black sparrow*; also *cock sparrow* and *cotton-
tree sparrow*. It was perhaps this bird that Browne called the
mountain sparrow, but since he took it to be a native of Jamaica, it
may have been the yellow-backed finch. *Coffee-bird* appears to be
yet another name for it, due to its often building in coffee
bushes.

Cashew bird, today, applies to the spindalis or *goldfinch*, which
the folk pronounce also /guolfrinch/ and /guulfrinj/. Its other
names are *mark-head* (from the striped black-and-white head);
silver head; and *yam-cutter* (because it cuts the young sprouts of
yam plants).

Another finch is the *tichicro*. Both the name, which is onomatopoetic, and the explanation come from Gosse: the call is
'cro-cro-tichicro'. This is a small and unimpressive bird, suggestions which are carried over when the name is applied to
human beings: a 'chichi-crow' is a 'small or undersized person'.
These two forms are surely related, but whether one is the source
of the other or they represent independent imitations of the
bird's call it is impossible to say. Its earliest name was *savanna
bird* — not exclusively Jamaican. It is called *grass pink* too; and
perhaps this is the bird called *grass dodger*: it makes only short
flights from clump to clump of grass. Taylor records *Grasshopper
Sparrow* as another name for it, which refers to this same habit of
'grass-hopping'.

Two well-known vireos have imitative names, the *John-chewit*
and the *sewi-sewi*. The first is pronounced by the folk /jàntuwít/,
/jànchuwít/, /jànchúit/, /jànchúwi/ or /jàntuhít/. In short, the
spelling given, and McKay's *john-tuhit* and Carley's *john-to-whit*
are accurate enough. Reid also reports *tweet-to-whit*. One more
name given by Browne and Long was *whip-tom-kelly*; Browne
applied it to the oriole, Long to a flycatcher.[23] But Gosse challenged its use for the flycatcher, declaring that he had never
heard it at all in Jamaica. It certainly does not seem to
exist today — which would justify Gosse's doubt of its
genuineness.

x

The *sewi-sewi* or *swee-swee* (pronounced /síwisíwi/ or /swíi-swíi/) is the Jamaica vireo; this name too was first recorded by Gosse. 'Swee' and 'sewee' are interesting reflections of folk pronunciation. This distinctive part of the bird's call has a rising pitch which, in speech, would be represented by increased emphasis on the second part: se-*wee*. As has been pointed out, the folk have difficulty with *s*, generally dropping it before *p*, *t*, and *k*, or inserting a vowel between it and the consonant as in *su-mall*, small, *si-norin*, snoring. Here *swee* and *sewee* are alternating forms which illustrate the latter pattern.

Because its song is loud in proportion to its size, this bird is also called *big-voice*; and still other names are *check-check* (from some chequered colour effect — perhaps the whitish bars on the wing), and *little furuh*, in contrast with a larger vireo which is *big furuh*. *Furuh* appears to be a folk alteration of *vireo*, but clear evidence is lacking.

An insect-eating bird conspicuously striped — the black-and-white warbler — has acquired Jamaican names from these and other characteristics: *ants-picker* (also *ants bird, ant bird, ant-eater*), *stripe-holland* (because it is like striped Holland cloth, once widely used in the island), *worm quit*, and *Christmas bird* (from its supposed appearance at that season — actually it comes earlier). According to Taylor, *chip-chip bird* is applied generally to the warblers; a variant is *chip*.

Another warbler, the American ovenbird, gets its Jamaican name from its curious way of flipping its tail as it walks: *kick-up*, *Bessy* (or *Betsy*) *kickup, Bessy shake-up*, and *Mary shakewell*. From its habit of accompanying the white-belly dove, it is also *white-belly maid*. Gosse was the first to record *Bessy Kick-up* (applying it however to the water thrush or river pink; he also gave *land kick-up* for the 'gold-crowned thrush').

Gosse called the Cape May warbler a *spotted creeper*, but this name has not been adopted. The American redstart 'has the habit of fluttering about in the upper branches of large trees, looking with its fanned-out tail almost like a brilliant butterfly. For this reason in Jamaica it is often called the Butterfly Bird'.[24]

A handful of names remain over, found in books or in oral use though the birds were not clearly identified: *chamba beezer*, 'reddish; black under throat';[25] *limey* or *lime blossom*, 'comes out after rain; belly resembles a ripe lime; wings black;' *shacka bird*, 'eats the seeds of the shacka bush (rattle-weed); is like goldfinch but smaller;' and *blue-foot*, mentioned in the song 'Chi-chi-bud-O!'. These are recorded here in the hope that the identification may be made later.

Chapter Fifteen

FISH

JAMAICAN fish names are of two chief kinds: those given early and found in the accounts of adventurers and travellers, many of which have since become standard; and those given locally by Jamaican fishermen, which vary from place to place and overlap in usage so that the same fish may have several names, or a single name may be applied to different fish. As in the preceding chapter, we deal here with names; there is no attempt to mention all the fish that may be found in or near the island, but only those names which are in some sense Jamaican.

We may begin with the bigger fish. Largest is said to be the *ocean* or *black-fin* shark; the tiger-shark is known also as *ground-shark* or *white shark*; the 'ordinary shark' is sometimes called a *glass-eye shark*. One early record that mentions what is now the hammer-head or shovel-nosed shark, spells the latter 'shevil-nosed'[1] — a form not noticed in dictionaries though it may well be the original one. *Shevel*, in the eighteenth century, meant distorted, twisted — the expressions *shevil-gabbit*, *shevel-mouthed* show how it was used to describe human faces. The probability is that this shark was first called *shevel-nosed*, which then became *shovel-nosed* by folk-etymology. *Shevel* is now obsolete but the other word has remained current, for this shark is known too as *shovel-head*, *shovel-beak*, and *shovel-mouth*. From the shape of its head it is also *horn-shark*. The commonest of these fish would seem to be the nurse (pronounced /nos/, /nors/), sand shark, or *cutter*, because it breaks holes in the fish pots.[2] In fact, *cutting fish* or *cutter* is applied generally to all that exhibit this annoying trait: sharks, barracouta, large snappers, and so on. (What is sometimes called a *puppy shark*, evidently from some resemblance it bears to the nurse, is more properly a *puppy fish*, as Cockrell was the first to note.) Another name is *bobo*, which could be Spanish or African, in either case meaning stupid, or dull.[3]

Barracuda is standard outside Jamaica, but here the name is regularly pronounced /barakúuta/ and spelt *barracouta*, which is closer to the source form. Early evidence comes from 1756: 'The Paracuta, and Paracute', and 1790: 'baracooter'. One local name is simply the abbreviation *barra*.

Very similar is the *snit*, today pronounced both /snit/ and /sinit/. Browne recorded this as *sinnet*, from which *snit* is evidently reduced. *Snook* has also acquired a disyllabic form in the folk speech: /sunúk/ or /sinúk/. One sub-type is the *lantern-jaw snook*.

The names of skates and rays have also suffered alteration. The first is usually /kiit/ or /kiet/, though one also hears /skiit/. One variety is the *hog-nose skeet*. *Thornback* appears first in a Jamaican source; today the fishermen call it /tonbak/, evidently interpreting it as *turn-back*.[4] *Whipray* regularly becomes /wipri/, occasionally /ripri/; and *sting-ray* is /tinggri/. The whip-ray is also widely called a *numb-fish* because as the fishermen put it, it has 'a poison bone on its tail' — 'after it jook you it cramp you'. One small kind of ray is a *juna* (/juuna/), a word that has not been traced. For the torpedo or electric ray Cockrell recorded *trembler*.

In 1756 Browne noted that the saw-fish was 'commonly called the Sword-fish in *Jamaica*', and this is true today; yet *saw-fish* has also been and still is in use. An early name for it that has not survived was *sea-unicorn*.

The earliest example of *tarpon* hitherto known was from 1685. We find it six years before in Jamaica, however, as *tarpum*.[5] The fishermen today most often metathesise this: /trapóng/, but /tárapong/ or /tárapom/ may also be heard, forms that have been long established, to judge by earlier spellings: *tropon*, and *trapong*. Two other names for this fish are /sábilo/ and /bóulin/.[6]

One of the largest fish, which may weigh several hundred pounds, is the *Jew-fish*, a name which Trapham was again the first to record. He considered it one of the most delicious and desirable — 'nourishing and restaurative, without the usual hazard of surfeiting entailed thereon: It never affecting the stomach fulsomely, but dissolves into spermatick nourishment readily, our *Botargo* Treasurer.' Folk etymology (as with the *Jew plum* that became a *June plum*) had already converted this to *June-fish* by the end of the nineteenth century, and that is the only form by which Jamaican fishermen know it today.

Porpoise has undergone changes in both form and application. It is pronounced /paapas/ as one would expect, but also /pampas/, with a surprising intrusive *m*. Yet the latter has been in existence over 200 years, since Sloane recorded *pampus* in 1725, and apparently, like *porpoise*, referring to the cetacean. (On the other hand, Cockrell identified the Jamaican 'porpoise' differently;⁷ evidently there has been some confusion in the application of the name.)

A number of fish that possess strange properties have received appropriately descriptive names. The well known porcupine fish (locally pronounced as /prákyupain, pákrapain/) is more often *hedgehog fish*, which fisherman today pronounce /íejàg/. Covered all over with sharp spines, especially when it distends itself, it is also called *macca fish*, but most commonly *soursop fish*, a name first recorded by Cockrell. (Some make a distinction: The hedgehog larger, the soursop smaller.) One other name is *cutacoo* — that is, a thatch bag or basket — in allusion to its way of swelling up.

Another that inflates itself is the *bottle-fish*, so called throughout the island. Browne recorded this, and made the porcupine fish, by contrast, the *prickly bottle-fish*. Thomson referred to it as the *smooth bottle-fish*. Local names today are *puff-fish* or *puff-gut*, *toad-fish* or *toady*, and /jéje/, which Smith spelt *jejea*.

One whose peculiar box-like shape has earned it several names was first described by Browne:

OSTRACION 5 . . . The trunck-fish . . . OSTRACION 6 . . . The Cuckold-fish. . . . The two species are so like each other that they can be distinguished only by the horns that shoot from above the eyes of the latter; they are also furnished each with two other horns that rise from the posterior angles of the trunk.

This distinction is still recognised by the fishermen, who call the first *sheep-head*, 'trunkfish without horn', and the second *horn-head, horny-money*, or *cow-fish. Cuckold-fish* lasted at least to Cockrell's time: he heard it as *cockle-fish*, which suggests that the joke behind the name (as with 'cuckold's increase' peas) had been lost. When this fish is taken out of water and set upon its flattish bottom, it rocks slightly forward and back like a rocking-horse. From this, and perhaps also in allusion to the horns, come the names *cunny-buck* or *cunnibo* and *buck-buck* (in Jamaica, *buck* means butt). Finally, it is called *box-fish* and *scuttle*. (*Trunk-fish*, though not a Jamaicanism, is widely used here for both the horned and hornless varieties.)

The trumpet-fish, first called a *trumpeter* in Jamaica, keeps both these names today (the latter more current), and in addition *trumpet, flute, fifer*, and *piper*. These all allude to the peculiarly elongated mouth with a round opening in the tip. But *piper* is applied too to the *gar-fish* (also *long gar* or *long-jaw gar-fish*). And this name in Jamaica has generally become by folk-etymology *guard-fish*. As long ago as 1851 the alternative name *long-jaw* had already been established; and it is also called *top-jaw piper* and /jángho/ *piper* — the last being of unknown source. From the prominent long, sharp beak, the marlin is today associated with this among Jamaica fishermen under the name *ocean piper*. (*Balaho* is yet another alternative for *piper*, but it is found in the U.S. too.)[8]

Several kinds of eels are recognised. Cockrell recorded *deep water eel* as a name for the conger eel, and one variety is called the *green eel* or *green congry*. But the characteristic thing is the reduction of the name 'conger-eel' to *congreel* and especially *congry*. The only historical dictionary to recognise this is the DA, which gives one citation from 1884 and notes, 'Local variant of conger-eel; *Obs.*' Yet the term is anything but obsolete in Jamaica — indeed, it is the commonest form.

A general distinction is made between *river eel* and *sea eel*; one of the latter bears the name of *mud-hook* because it is said to push its tail through the meshes of a fish-pot and hook it to the bottom of the sea. The moray eel has become universally pronounced as the /mori/; similar to it is the *spotted snake-eel*.

Skin-fish — a term not in the dictionaries — includes any having a thick or stiff skin that must be stripped off before they are eaten: *turbot, old-wife, tobacco fish*, and their like — a large group. *Turbot*, pronounced /torbit/, is not the same as the European fish. Particular varieties are *puppy turbot* (smaller, and 'use dem fe feed dog'), *police turbot* (because it has 'red stripe and two macka at the tail'), and *tobacco turbot* (from the shape and colour). The last is also called *tobacco fish* or *tobacco old-wife*; and *Spanish old-wife* in St James and St Mary: *Spanish* refers here to the yellow tail and the yellow colour which this fish imparts to water in which it is cooked.

There are other kinds of old-wives (or alewives): *rainbow old-wife* and *silver old-wife* (the latter first mentioned in 1826); and the *silver old-wife*, so called at Negril, is also known at Kingston as the *sheepshead alewife* (some calling it *silver jack* too). Cockrell is the only writer to mention *old wench* as a synonym of *old-wife*; it does not seem to be used today. In 1725 Sloane identified the old-wife with the *cunny-fish* (i.e., *cony-fish*).

The turbot is known occasionally as a *goat-fish*; or a *go-far* (pronounced /gò-fór/) because 'it could share to a lot of people'; sometimes as a *mingo*; frequently as a *nigga-fish* or *nayga-fish*. The latter names suggest colour: I take *mingo* to be an application of the personal name. Of the same family are the *Bessy Cockburn*, *high-forehead*, and *Bessy Corca* or *Fanny Corca* (pronounced /káaka/). All of these refer to the 'cocked-up' shape of the fish's forehead.

The *sea-galliwasp*, so called because it resembles the galliwasp in shape, was noticed first by Ray: 'The SEANFISH or SEA GALLEY WASP' in his list obtained from Sloane; and Sloane himself a few years later repeated this in changed spelling: 'The Sein-Fish, or Sea Gally-Wasp. This was about fourteen inches long, in the middle five Inches round, and tapering at both Ends.'[9] Simplified to *gallawass*, this name is still the most current. *Seine-fish* lasts today in the form *san-fish* (as if it meant *sand-fish*); whereas *seine-fish* means to the fishermen 'fish catch in net'. In short, this is hardly a synonym for *sea-galliwasp* any more. The same fish is called *ten-pounder* and *John Mariddle*; but *John Mariggle* is the commoner form. As this name implies (*mariggle* meaning *trick*), this fish is 'tricky; jump and try to shake out hook'. Cockrell identified it with the bony fish, but fishermen today insist that they are different: bony-fish is 'rounder' than John Mariggle, and has a 'pointed head'. (The Jamaican bony-fish, in any case, is not the same as the American menhaden.)

One fish that is 'shape like bony-fish', and 'very scarce' is the *rolling-pin*; another like it, 'yellowish, poor, with stripes around' is a *German*. The flying fish has become a *sea angel*. Long seems to have been the only writer to mention a *bracket flounder*; and the name is now out of use.

Cockrell set down as a *lion-fish* one of those which today would be called *poison-grouper* or *stinging grouper* (pronounced /grupa/). The grouper is first mentioned in a Jamaican source, spelt

'Groopers',[10] and there are not only the poisonous kind which 'jook you' and 'cramp you up', but also *rock grouper, day grouper,* and *dago. Rock-fish* seems to be an alternative name for rock grouper.

Sea-bat appeared earliest in a Jamaican source, and has become the standard name: 'LOPHIUS 2 . . . The Sea-Batt.' The folk know it, but since, to them, bats are *rat-bats,* the fish has become a *sea rat-bat* too.

Leaving these and coming to the common food fish, we find, as with the staple vegetables, that all kinds of small variations in colour, shape, habit and the like are noticed in a multitude of names. Among the kingfish there are said to be the *crossbar* and the /gàú/, the first having stripes while the second is plain. Another name for the *crossbar kingfish* is *queenfish* (it has a pointed mouth and softer flesh); and sometimes it is called *crossbar mackerel.* The meaning of *ga-oo* has not been found.

Similar to mackerel is the *yellow-coat;* the *red-coat* is 'deep pink' and 'shape like bony-fish'. A local name for bonito is *Joe Clark,* after a St Elizabeth man. The *cutlass fish* is usually simply *cutlass,* occasionally *machete.*

Surprisingly enough, *jack* is not cited in the dictionaries as the name of a fish before 1883. Yet we find it in Jamaica in 1697.[11] Names for the jack based on colour are: *silver, yellow* or *butter, yellow-tail, green, green-back, burn-fin, black,* and *amber jack.* The last of these is also called *ocean jack,* and very similar, though smaller is the *tamarind* jack (/tambrin/), which probably means that it is underfed (since *tambrin season* is the time of year when foodstuffs are short). Reference to other striking features may be seen in *round-head, swine-head, point-nose, pig-nose, goggle-eye, horse-eye, crab-eye, mule* or *mule-back, wire-back, hard-bone,* and *streamers jack,* the last referring to a hair-like process on the fin.

Pampido jack — evidently a form of 'pompadour' — refers to the shape of the dorsal fin; but there may well be some confusion with *pompano. Leather-coat* jack has a thin, silvery, tough skin; and like it is *alewife jack,* another name for *silver jack.* Gosse listed without explanation the 'Buntung jack' — evidently intended to spell the folk pronunciation of *burn-tongue;* but it has not been reported since. A common Jamaican form of *skip-jack* is *kip* or *kips jack.* As *ground jack* probably refers to a habit of swimming close to the bottom, so *mud jack* is caught over muddy bottoms. The *pilot jack* 'lead the troop'. Another name for the goggle-eye is *bang-bang* — the iteration implying a quantity; it is probably connected with Cockrell's record of *bang* for one kind of sprat.[12] *Whiting* often takes the form *whitening* (/waitnin/), which we may compare with such other folk forms as *huntning, fishning, icening*; or it may become /waitn/. Another kind of whiting was called the *sunshine* by Cockrell.

Interesting because it appears in so many forms is *cavally*, which the folk may pronounce in half-a-dozen different ways: /kubáali/ or /kubáalo/, /kúbaali/, /kóvaali/, /kòváli/, /kóvali/, and /kobálo/. It is an old name: the OED attests it from 1634; we find the form *cavalles* in 1820, and *covally jack* in 1892. Cockrell recorded *cobbler fish* for today's *cobbler jack* — obviously folk-etymological forms of the same name: from *coballo* to *cobbler* is no long step.[13]

One of the earliest to be named was the *silver fish* (1679); Sloane later described it, and Cockrell identified it as the *macca-back* or *shad*. All three terms are still in use though small local distinctions are made among them. *Macca-back shad*, which combines these elements, is the most common. It refers to the prominent dorsal spines: 'have four bone in back' as one fisherman put it. Other shads are the *Spanish, fireside*, and *deep-water shad*, meaning that they are respectively yellow or orange coloured, marked with black, and caught well out from the shore.

A curious thing has happened with the name *stone-bass*, first recorded by Trapham in 1679, and in 1725 by Sloane. Some time afterward, in the folk speech, *bass* must have been taken to be plural, and therefore was reduced in the usual way to /baa/, understood as *bar*. Thereafter we find a new form, *stone bar*, as Cockrell and Smith record it. But *stone-bass shad* continues too, and one fisherman made it *stone-balls*.

Of sprats the best known (because it is considered poisonous) is the *yellow-billed* or *yellow-bill sprat*, first mentioned in 1801 (Dancer). In 1820 Thomson wrote, 'The yellow-billed sprat in particular is to be dreaded, producing convulsions and sudden death.' This name is still in use; other sprats are the *black-bill, black-back, blue-back, jack sprat* (the young jack), and *herring sprat*.[14] Of the same group is the *white-bill* or *pincers* — so Cockrell recorded the names; today the latter is pronounced /pinshaz/ by the fishermen, which looks very much like an -n- form of *pilcher* (pilchard). If this is so, Cockrell was mishearing or misinterpreting the name; and we are certain that *pilcher* was current from the first, since Trapham's list contained it.

For more than two hundred years the 'Mountain or Hogsnout Mullet' has had a reputation as a delicacy. Writing of a dinner engagement, Lady Nugent remarked, 'There was a new fish, the Mountain Mullet, very small, but excellent.'[15] The alternative name has now become *hog-nose mullet*, and there is also the *thick-lipped mountain mullet*. These fall into the general class of *river* or *stream mullet* along with *black-eye*, *glass-eye*, *marble-head*, and *cork-head mullet*. Widely known too, but thought of as sea fish, are what Gosse wrote of as the 'King-mullets, . . . called also Queen-mullets'. Only the latter name appears to be used today, but it is widespread. Considered to be very much like queen mullet is the *goat fish*, so called because it has a 'beard' (a barbel). The *cape mullet*, also known as *jump mullet*, (though as one fisherman remarked, 'every mullet jump') is a sea fish too. *Roe-mullet* and *red-eye mullet* have not been identified.

Largest of the mullets and considered excellent eating is the *calipeva*, whose name has taken a variety of forms. It comes ultimately from Tupí through Brazilian Portuguese *carapeba*, with the common substitution of *l* for *r*. The first appearance in English is found in Browne: 'MUGIL 2 . . . The Calapaver, or Coromai'; the second term has not been found elsewhere. Spellings which it has had down through the years are: 1774 *calipever*; 1790, *calapavre*; 1808, *calapavor*; 1858, *calipiva*; 1893, *calepeaver*[16] — which shows that the variants of today have been present all along. The 'educated' forms now are /kǽlipíivǝ/ or /kǽlipéevǝ/; the folk pronunciation makes further alterations: /kyàlifíeva/ *mullet*. The fine flesh of this fish once earned it the kitchen name of *Jamaica salmon*, now apparently out of use. Among the fishermen, however, there is a fish still called salmon, which grows 'up to thirty pounds', goes into fishpots and is a 'heavy puller'; it 'favour yellow-tail but much bigger', has a soft head, and is 'very good to eat'. I have not identified this fish, but the description does not properly fit the calipeva.

One of the chief classes of food fish is that of the *snapper*, which name itself appears earliest in Trapham's account of Jamaica. Those named for colour are *red*, *black*, *grey*, *yellow-tail*, *red-tail*, and

red-belly snapper. Those named for some other striking characteristic or fancied resemblance include the *dog-teeth* (from the
prominent canine teeth) — which is the same as *schoolmaster*,
old-shoe, *sha-shwa*, *heavy-lead*, or *butt snapper*. (*Sha-shwa* is the sound
made in imitation of the hissing of something being fried in
water; *heavy-lead* presumably means heavy as lead.) Smith has
recorded two other names for the *dog-teeth*: *bad bottom* and *grey
snapper*, and others identify it variously. (*Bad bottom* means that
the fish is caught over bad sea bottoms.)

Lantern-jaw snapper, except for its jaw, is much like *pot-snapper*
(which is usually caught in pots); and Cockrell identified this
with *rounder*, *red*, and *mutton snapper*. The *plum-head* may be named
for its colour: it is 'pale pink right through'; the *moonshine* or
shiny-moon snapper is also pink, but has big, glassy eyes.

Other snappers yet are named for some association or habit
of living: *mangro* is found near mangrove trees, *reef* out by the
reefs, *mud snapper* over muddy bottoms. *Running snapper* (which
means that it runs in schools) is another name for the *red-belly*.
The *burn-fin* whose under fin looks as if it had been charred, is
widely known as /bon-fin/. Only Sloane has mentioned the
fresh-water snapper, which remains unidentified.

Two fish generally classed with the snappers are the *silk* and
satin, not always distinguished in the popular mind, though the
satin is generally thought of as bigger, longer, rounder than the
silk and of a different colour. *Satin* snapper is not in the dictionaries; *silk* is recorded as 'a Bermudan fish' from 1876. It appeared
in a Jamaican source, however, some fifty-two years earlier,[17]
and by 1863 it had even developed another Jamaican form, *silt-
snapper*, by the common substitution of *t* for *k*. Both forms are to be
heard today though *silk* is the common one. There are also the
black silk (the *black snapper* of Kingston) and the *sun-silk*, which is
red.

Malantang, not found in the dictionaries or other published
sources, is a name used all over southeastern Jamaica for the
blenny family. The origin of the name is unknown.

The grunts and drummers, large classes that are not clearly
separated in folk use, derive their names from the noises they
make when taken out of the water. Both appeared first (as did so
many others) in Trapham's list, antedating other records by
several decades. With them too is the only record of the *grash*

fish, whose name is apparently of like meaning: to *grash* was to *gnash* in Elizabethan and Jacobean times.

Colour names are, earliest, *gray grunt, silver grunt, red mouth* or *dark grunt*. The *red-mouth* is also called *red grunt* today, and Smith finds it used in St Mary for what is called *guinea-hen grunt* in St James and *white grunt* in Negril. The last is a common name; *guinea-hen* is not, and neither is *guinea-corn grunt*. The *yellow* was reported by Cockrell, and Smith found it also called 'Myri', which I take to be *miry grunt* (compare *mud* snapper).[18] Closely related is the *yellow-striped grunt*. Fairly common names too are *black* and *cashaw* (/kásha/) *grunt*.

Physical features distinguish the *thick-lip* and *sweet-lip* grunts; *pork* grunt (which resembles the pork-fish); *old-witch* grunt (considered very ugly); and *nanny-eye* grunt (with eyes like a goat). Habits of life characterise the *white-water* (caught where the waves break), *grass* (found over grassy bottoms), and *southward* grunts (pronounced /sódad/). The last is so called in Old Harbour because it comes from the southward 'when you have weather' — that is, storms; but it is the same as *white* grunt. *Bermudian* grunt is thought to have some connection with Bermuda; *bow* grunt is unexplained.

Margaret grunt and *bastard Margaret* were names recorded by Cockrell; only the former appears to survive. Since the use of personal names is common for both fauna and flora in Jamaica, *Margaret* is not at all surprising. Nevertheless the likelihood is that behind it lies the name of an English port: the OED records *Margate-fish* for 'a pearly-white fish' in the Gulf of Mexico, known since 1734 at least. Here no doubt is the ancestor of Margaret: folk-etymology is responsible for this sea-change.

The bream, called /brim/ by Jamaican fishermen, is usually identified with the grunt, but the word is also used attributively: *brim grunt*. One fisherman distinguishes between *grass* brim and *stone* brim according to the environment they favour. Cockrell listed *governor bream*. Closely associated with these is the *Caesar* grunt — so writers seem to spell the name, though with what authority one wonders. It is true that it is pronounced /siiza/, which permits this spelling and the implied interpretation; but *seizer* or some other spelling would be equally possible. In short, the origin of this name is unknown, the fishermen offer no explanation, and the implications of 'Caesar' are unsupported.

The *bottle caesar* is the same as *amber-jack caesar* — a fish longer, rounder, and thicker than the others.

The *porgy* is considered a grunt, and sometimes called *porgy grunt*. Though Trapham has the earlier form *porgo*, Sloane is the first to list the 'Pargie' — a spelling which shows that the present folk pronunciation /paagi/ is more etymological than the standard spelling with *o*. There are *black* and *white* porgy.

Similar too are the *robins*, of which Jamaican kinds are the *round robin* (said to be called *mutton owl* in the books), and *Moco robin*. Cockrell spelt this 'mucco' but offered no explanation. The spelling adopted here is that of the African tribe, also spelt 'Mocho' in early records, which appears frequently in this island (compare *Moco John*, a name for the mountain bauhinia tree).

Last are the *chub grunt* or *chub*, said to be called *squab* in Westmoreland; *Polly grunt*, with crosswise stripes (associated with the Polly lizard?); and what Smith records as *Goolia's grunt*, which probably means *gold(y)-ears* (or *gould(y)-ears* — compare *Mary Gould* for the marigold flower, and the *gold-ears* parrot fish).

The drummers include *black* and *white*; *hard-head, flat-head, mash-mouth, beard, long-teeth*; *river, stone, day, moonshine* (with a round head), and *cast-net* drummer (caught with a casting-net). The *croaking* or *craking* drummer, 'very noisy', is said to be the same as *mongalar* drummer. This name was first recorded, and in this spelling, by Cockrell. Today it is pronounced by the fishermen /mongólo/ or /mongéla/, which better supports Beckwith's spelling *mungala*, and suggests as a possible source the African tribal name *Mongala*.

Cockrell also recorded *Jew harp drummer* but without explanation. Perhaps it refers to shape or to some marking on the fish. The *obeahman drummer* is said to 'have two stone in im head'; if he enters a pot first, no other fish will go in. Other names for this fish are *mule* and *swallow-fish*. Besides, there is the *swallow-tail* or *old-maid drummer*. And finally there is the *kay drummer*, as Smith spelt it, at the Palisadoes; which probably should have been *cay* in reference to the many cays nearby. Perhaps *kile* (or *skile) drummer* of St Thomas, which is many-coloured and has spines, is a form of the same name; if not it may represent *coil*, though evidence is lacking.

Of all the Jamaican fish, it is the parrot that has gathered to itself by far the largest assortment of names, evidently because it has so many colour variations and other differing characteristics. These colours, and the shape of its mouth, were responsible to begin with for its name, first found in Trapham and explained by Sloane.[19] The colour names are: *red-belly* (or *red*), *pink, black, grey, purple, green, blue, mouse-colour, guinea-hen* (that is, speckled), *rainbow*, and by a recent humourous political reference, the *PNP parrot* (the People's National Party signifying 'all colours' — the same as the *rainbow*). Of these only the *blue* and *green* seem to have been noticed in books. Like the *blue* is the *blue roan*; there are also the *blue peter* (from the naval flag?), the *blue-jean* (an alteration of *blue roan*?), and *blue tumpa* ('blue all the way through', and presumably short). The /grógro/ parrot is darkish — that may be what *gro-gro* means.[20]

From physical characteristics come the names *bottle-nose, bottle-mouth* (probably the same), *bridle-mouth* (from some markings on the face), *cock-teeth* (its teeth come out of the mouth and are twisted), *rat-teeth, hog-teeth, dirty-face, puppy-mouth, blue-bill, black-bill, gold-ears, sleepy-head* (it 'snores'), /snáathed/ (it leaves big lumps of slime in the pot — the name may mean *snot-*, possibly *snort-head*), *gold-tail, moon-tail,* and /gyàlan-búo/ (it has a yellow 'bow' across the head, from mouth to lower jaw). This is a curious name; neither part is altogether clear. The first may represent *gallant* or French or Spanish *galón* (from which came English *galloon*, a piece of trimming); the second part may be *bow*, as of ribbon, or *beau*, meaning the same as the noun *gallant*. The most plausible seems to me *gallant-bow*, with *gallant* as an adjective or attributive noun; but *galon-bow* or *gallant-beau* are possibilities. The *jambo* parrot may have some connection.

Some parrots show their unpleasant characteristics in their names. The *okro* is slimy; the *gutu* is brownish and 'let out pus from gut', so the fish peddlers will not buy it; the *poop-stink* does not smell bad but is dark and soft, therefore unattractive; the *slipper-grass* is also slippery and dark. As long ago as 1851 Gosse mentioned two types of *gutu*: 'sand gootoo' and 'eatable gootoo'. A similar fish is known as *pangra* or *fowl-roost*, both grey and black kinds, which 'have mess in belly'; it is also called *pot-cover* from its shape and colour. Beside *okro parrot* are found *okro poll* and *okro paty, okro fish,* and — again in reference to its sliminess — *hard-to-take-up*. There is also the *blue-head paty*; but no source or very clear meaning for *paty* has been found.

A few parrots are named for their habitat: *grassy-ground, grass,* and *bank* parrot, which stays on the banks far out from shore. *Mackenzie* parrot, or *Mr Mac,* is unexplained; to some it is the same as *squab* (or *quab*).

The *hog-fish* and *Spanish hog-fish,* members of this family, are named for their snout-like mouth; the latter is 'Spanish' because bright yellow below, for which reason it is also *banana fish* or *banana Cudjo.* According to Cockrell, the hog-fish was also called *pig-fish* and *boar-fish.*

Another associated group includes the *Welshman, congatony,* and *squirrel.* The first name, an Americanism, which refers to the black colour of the fish (like the clothing favoured by the Welsh), has become converted among the Jamaican folk to *wenchman,* though occasionally one hears other pronunciations.[21] Different kinds are the *white* or *horse-eye, bull-head* (/búled/), *deep-water, switchy-tail,* and *poor Joe* (pronounced /púojùo/) *wenchman.* An alternative for *po' Joe* is *wenchman daddy* or *puppa.*

Congatony is so common a name that its absence from all records is quite surprising. It is always pronounced /kàng-gatúoni/, and very probably represents *Congo Tony,* another allusion, like *Welshman,* to the blackness of this fish. Some say it is the same as *pooky, squirrel, deep-water wenchman,* and *Tommy. Round-head congatony* is yet another name for *deep-water wenchman.* If there is any difference between *wenchman* and *pooky* it is that the first is bigger, rounder, and swims in deep water, the second in shallow water. And if *pooky* also refers to the blackness of the fish, it may well be connected with the *Pooka* or *Puck* of Celtic folklore, brought to Jamaica by Welshmen, Irishmen, or Scots.

It is evident that there is a great deal of overlapping in the application of the names in this group: *pooky, bully, squirrel-fish,* and *bull-head pooky, bull-head squirrel-fish, chub.* There are simple squirrel-fish as well as the *white, mare-tail,* and *chub* squirrel, *Tom* squirrel (probably the same as *Tommy*), and *sow-mouth* squirrel (which recalls the hog-fish).

Several other fish are felt by the fishermen to be similar to the foregoing, for example the *hind,* so named because it is dappled like a deer. This name is obviously English, not Jamaican; in this island it generally takes the form /hainz/. There are the *rock-hinds,* dark and speckled; *brown hinds*; and *butter-hinds,* also dappled but yellower. This is one of the *butterfish,* and there are others. Very similar are *rock fish* and *rock butter-fish*, also known as *grass hamlet*. This is pronounced variously as /hamblit/, /amblit/, /mamlit/, and so on, and it is felt to be the 'same specie' as butter hind, and also 'like grouper'. Smaller than *hamlet* but of the same type is *Juba* — yet another which bears a personal name.

Then there are *deadie*, *dolly*, or *black dolly*; *obeahman* or *Christmas*; and the *blue-gal* or *army-girl*. The names of these smaller, strikingly coloured fish are not consistently applied, and there is much duplication. For example, *bat-fish* turns up again for the fish just named, and it is said to be the same as the *pork-fish*. *Soap fish* is 'very sipple' and if you rub it it will make suds.

Doctor-fish is found first in Monk Lewis's *Journal* with the explanation that the Jamaican fishermen still give:

> No one on board had ever seen this kind of fish till then; its name is the 'Doctor Fish' . . . said to be so named from a sharp, movable spine like a lancet on each side of the tail.

Browne recorded it simply as 'the Doctor'. It is in wide use today; there are *yellow*, *blue* or *macca-back*, *black*, *woman*, *brush-tail*, and *mercy-rye* doctor-fish — the last unexplained, said to be 'the Kingston name for *man doctor-fish*'.

Other brightly coloured fish, notably the Chaetodons, have a considerable repertory of names. The *Spanish angel-fish*, like the *Spanish hog-fish*, is yellow; it is evidently the same as Cockrell's *horizontal angel-fish*. The *mademoiselle* of the United States — here /mamzel/ — has the local names *pretty*, *Miss Pretty*, *Nancy Pretty*, *none-so-pretty*, *Milady*, *pangra* or *pangro*, and *Rolling Calf* (the monster of superstition). *Banana Cudjo*, mentioned above, is also *banana fish*, *banana Katy* (transferred from the common bird), and *policeman*. It is identified by some with *Nancy Pretty* and *Spanish hog-fish*. In Browne's day the butterfly fish was called *sea-butterfly*, but today it is *bat-fish* (butterflies, and especially moths, usually being called bats in Jamaica), or *pork-fish*. The *Portuguese* listed by Browne was probably the same as today's *Portugee* (pronounced /pùotagíi/) or *Portugee hog-fish*.

Another type of *Miss Pretty* is known also as *bastard blue roan*; and very close to this is *berry*, *old runner*, or *picker*. Cockrell listed the *rock beauty*; the *butter-bun* is green with a 'pretty spot on the side like a button'; *sheephead* (not the trunkfish) is a 'small, flat, blue' fish with a 'white streak'. *Yellowtail* is of two varieties,

maiden (small) and *drop* (large). A popular proverb referring to
people who go up in the world and suddenly begin to be fine
seems to be an allusion to this brightly coloured fish: 'You ever
see cock-a-benny turn yellowtail?' If cock-a-benny is also a fish
it can hardly be from Scots *cockie-bendie*, since it is presumably
something plain or low that suddenly becomes elevated or
beautified. Twi *akakabén-ne*, meaning 'he acts in a wayward,
wilful, stubborn manner', is a possible but not very likely source.
My suspicion is that this fish is the *caca-belly*, which is similar to
the grunt; it has a dark under-belly and therefore contrasts
sharply with the gay yellowtail.

Though *pilot fish* has been recorded since 1634, the first
appearance of *pilot* in print seems to be 1823. As Stewart wrote
then:

> It is remarkable that a little fish, called by the seamen the
> pilot-fish, usually attends this monster [the shark], and often
> swims close to his mouth, as if conscious of no danger. It is
> said that this attendant directs the shark to his prey, . . . and
> hence obtains the name of pilot; but this is merely hypo-
> thetical.

Jamaican fishermen call it both *pilot-fish* and *pilot*, but their own
special name is *shark waitin'-boy*, which takes the imagination
back to the days of the plantocracy when gentlemen of great
consequence went nowhere without the attendance of servant-
boys dressed in bright livery. So these little fish swim about the
big fish — sharks and barracouta too, in the latter case being
barracouta waitin'-boy or *barracouta slave*. Another name for the
pilot is *Baltimore cricketer* — from its stripes? The *caca pilot* is said
to have 'clothes like chain-gang man'; it 'goes after caca' (dung).

Considered similar to these are the smaller, less colourful fish
known as *blackie, black pig, sand blackie, Sammy blackie, old man*, or
pig fish. Other small, dark fish that live in sand are the Gobies:
sand fish, suck-stone, or *rock-sucker*, so called because of the ventral
sucking disc with which they are said to 'suck on to a stone'. The
last is also known as *mud fish* or *okro fish*. (Another related *mud fish*
is identified with the *sand-shark*.)[22] The sucking disc is called a
suck by the fishermen, and the suctoria of the octopus are *suctures*.
Incidentally, Trapham's list has the earliest record of *mud-fish* as
a New World fish, though without identification.

Yet another small mud-fish, from its colour called *nayga-man*, is very similar to the *God-a-me* or *bungoby* which are caught in great numbers when the rivers 'come down' after rain, and sold by the calabash or on strings; they are also dried, salted, and fried. 'God-a-me' is supposed to be the exclamation of the fish when one raises the rock under which it is hiding.[23] *Bungoby* was first mentioned by Barclay as 'a small fish 3″–4″ long found in lagoons'. Sometimes it is *bangaby*, *bogoby*, or *banga*, names probably of African origin.[24] Further names for these or their like are *choby*, *yeary-yeary* (explained as 'minnows' by McKay),[25] *tumtum*, *cuss-eye* (with large black eyes surrounded by gold), and most common of all *ticky-ticky*. In fact, this goes back to 1774, though the dictionaries do not enter it; and Gosse identified at least one kind. He took the name, like English *stickleback*, to refer to the spines on the fish's back — in other words, 'stickysticky'; but this is very doubtful. One fisherman currently explains it as 'thicky-thicky' because the fish swim in thick schools — which is more convincing, since *ticky-ticky* is also applied to 'ruinate' lands which are no longer cultivated and have run back to *thicket*. In striking coincidence with this, however, is the Ewe *tikitiki*, crowding, thronging — perhaps the deepest root of this word. *Ticky-ticky* now includes any kind of 'fine' (very small) fish: silver fish, small shad, or fry in general. Among kinds of fry we may note *hard-head* or *loggerhead fry*, and *trapong* (tarpon) *fry*.

The *borambay*, reported by Smith from the mouth of the South Negril River, may be another form of *bungoby*. Last of this group is *poison fish*. Among 'small and useless' fish are included the *pigfoot* or *pigtoe*, the *pick-a-bait* (explained as 'pick of baits'), and the *bait-picker* of Negril, called *winsor* at Whitehouse.

A few miscellaneous names remain: *geroom* (for Jerome?), first mentioned by Sloane in 1713 and again in 1725 as a large herring with small scales and a long, sharp snout. But these are the only references found. Cockrell called the *deepwater cod* a *browned nose*, and he, too, is the only writer to mention *grubber broad-head* and *sea fiddler*.[26]

Other Marine Creatures

What is called a *lobster* in Jamaica is really a crayfish, and so it has been for some time. As Williams wrote about the Jamaican native in 1826: 'He eats soldiers and crawfish, which he calls lobsters.' It probably was so even earlier, since Sloane wrote of the 'Sea Lobster . . . Locusta marina vulgaris dorso spinoso'. Fishermen today, beside the 'real' one, recognise different varieties as *queen* ('flat, with short toes, no tall horns; not pretty'); *guinea-hen* or *guinea-chick* (small and speckled); *patu* (very ugly, like the patu bird) or *cockroach lobster* (from its flat, roach-like shape), also called the *sea-roach*; *lobster mumma* (that is, lobster's mother — like the cockroach lobster); *pagro* or *black-hog lobster* (from its resemblance to the fish of that name); and *tetla*, a deepwater lobster, red, spotted, and pretty, though the meaning of this name has not been found.

Crayfish is in general use for the river creatures, but one hears them called *river lobster* too, just as *sea-crayfish* is sometimes applied to the true lobster with claws. The larger river crayfish is *mountain crayfish*; the next size smaller is *ol'-'oman*, or *shrimps*, pronounced regularly /srimps/, occasionally /swimps/, also /srints/. Fresh-water shrimps caught in the rivers, parched, and used in soup, are *janga* (/jangga/) — printed usually as *jonga* though I have never heard it said so. Other names for these are *jumping chary* (with long joints), *buck-toe* (from the shape, like a toe that sticks up), and *majoe*, of which McKay wrote: 'Sunbeams . . . send their search-rays 'neath the time-worn log, And drive the sleeping majoes from their lair.' He goes on to explain, 'Pronounce the *ma* as in French — fresh-water shrimps, which live in the hill-side brooklets.' One may perhaps surmise some connection between the names *ol'-'oman* and *majoe*, since the herb 'majoe bitters' was said to be named for a famous old woman skilled with medicinal plants.

Names for crabs go chiefly by colour, habit, shape, and size. They are also thought of as *land crabs* (black, white, and box-shaped), or *sea crabs* (all the rest). Best known of all, and considered a delicacy since early days, is the *black* or *mountain crab* (names which Browne was first to record) or *Jamaica crab*.[27] These live in holes on hard land, and annually, in March or April, they 'run' — that is, stopping for nothing they descend to the sea in droves to 'wash spawn' or lay their eggs. Another land crab, 'The white crab, as it is called (although rather purple than white) used principally by the negroes but by the white people also, is larger and more resembles in taste the lobster of this country. These are amphibious' (Barclay).

Browne was also the first to record the names *oyster crab* (it lives in the shell of the mangrove oyster) and *mangrove crab* (evidently the same). Both now seem out of use. The *water crab* is large, 'a sea crab; brown like shoes'; the *thunder crab*, if it catches you, 'won't let go till it thunders' — a reputation shared by the *queen crab*. This is the prettiest, a sea crab with a hard red shell, smooth and spotted; *red crab* appears to be the same as *queen*. The *pound crab* is also a sea crab: 'round; pretty colours, red and white'.

The only historical dictionary to list *soldier* as a name for the hermit crab is the DAE, but its last citation (1834) implies that the term is out of use. This it decidedly is not; it is the regular word in Jamaica. There is said to be a *sea-soldier* too, 'same as land soldier, but would die on land.'

Largest of the crabs is said to be the *bungoby*, a name which is used also for a fish (see above). The *coco* or *jackass crab* 'has a rough back and toes', and is reddish; *bailo* (pronounced /bíelo/) seems to be the same crab. The *sea-anancy* has 'long, thin, cranky' legs — it is the spider crab, of course. The *deaf-ears* crab has a 'small body, one big claw', while *tailor-scissors* has a flat shell, pointed at the sides, and a 'very sharp claw'. The *tafu crab* is caught in pots: it has one big claw that is edible but the rest is used for bait. (The meaning of *tafu* has not been found.) Of the *dago crab* also, only the claws are eaten for 'the back will drunk you'. Named for its pale colour is *ghost crab*; the *mumby crab* is used for bait: it has a soft back, hair on feet and back, and lives in holes in the swamp.

Pampy crab, a 'man crab, big, white', reminds one of the pampy pig, smallest of a litter. In the mangroves is found the *ticklebro*, 'Small, red, with white claw'. The *sananana crab* is pale yellow. These names remain unexplained.

Of shellfish, the best known are the so-called *tree-oysters* that grow on mangrove roots, a name first recorded by Sloane. Browne also wrote of the *yellow onion-peel oyster* and *cap oyster* (presumably named for its shape); the *knife-handle shell* (for its shape); the 'small green Nerite, commonly called the green Peashell'; the similar *bloody-gum* (so called for the two small 'teeth' at the mouth of the shell with red markings at their base); the *white-gum* (without colour at the teeth); the 'pointed arching *Limpets* commonly called Phrygian-Caps'; the 'rugged *Phrygian-*

Cap Limpet'; and finally the 'SIPHONIUM . . . Worm-tube'. None of these names seems to survive today, nor do Sloane's *Barbados limpet* and *Jamaica button shell*.²⁸ Apparently they were book terms never adopted in common usage.

Living folk names, however, are not lacking. Whelks remain in the older pronunciation /wilks/ throughout the island; periwinkles also appear as /pèrríngkl/ and the very ancient /pìniwíngkl/. A very small blue snail is a *sea-thimble*, and the *crown shell* is also named from its shape. The *busu* is a small fresh-water whelk; Beckwith writes, 'bossu, out of which is composed a favorite soup.' This shellfish has become among the folk the symbol of one who retires into his shell, a *kukru busu*.²⁹ The chiton has been dubbed *sea-beef*, which seems to be an application of an old nautical joke, sea-beef being fish or something other than real beef.

Among the folk *conch* is pronounced /kongk/ and there are names for several varieties: the *queen* (a beautiful one), a *broadleaf* (which has a flaring pink mouth), *thick-lip*, *round*, and *rolling conchs*. The *tobacco conch* is from three to five inches long, and twisted like the local tobacco. *Bone-danger* is a very spiny shell that must not be stepped on. The pinna is called *fan shell* or *Chinese oyster*.

The cast 'shells' of sea eggs, according to Long, were called *echini stones* or *hedgehog stones*, and the flatter ones with star-shaped markings *star-stones*; Browne called this the 'Sea-Plate, or flat Sea-Egg'. None of these has survived. Today the folk reserve the term *sea-egg* for the light-coloured ones and call the very dark ones with long spines *sea-needle*; sea-eggs with short, thick prongs they call *borer*. The star-fish, in general folk speech, is a *sea-star*. Sloane used *sea-rose* for one kind of coral.³⁰

The octopus is regularly known in Jamaica as a *sea-cat*, a term apparently taken from Dutch *zeekat*. The OED has only one citation for this (1601), defines it as cuttlefish or squid, and labels it *Obs.* Yet in Chambre's account we find, in reference to a drowned man:

> The most probable seemed to be that he had been seized on the stomach by a sea-cat, which prevented his rising again to the surface. I was told that the extremities of the legs of this strange fish have much the same formation as those of the fly; for they have the power of fixing themselves by them to a rock.

Thus *sea-cat* has been far from obsolete in Jamaica; transferred to the octopus it is in folk use throughout the island; it is also used in Barbados. Occasionally one hears *sea-puss* — a further adaptation to local habits. Squid becomes *squib* or *squibs*; and the squid or cuttlefish is also a *crips* (crisp), which refers to its being, as one fisherman put it, 'like jelly but firm'.

The jellyfish is occasionally *sea-jelly*, regularly *bladder* or *sea-bladder* (pronounced /blada/, sometimes /bloda, bloba/). When applied specifically, *sea-bladder* means the Portuguese man-o'-war, which the fishermen make *man-o'-war bladder*. The stinging jellyfish is a *sea-sting* or *sea-scratch*, but the latter term is also applied to the sea-nettle, whose regular name is *sea-cowitch*, and an occasional one *sea-wasp* — all of these referring, of course, to the itching or irritation it produces on the skin.

The sea-cucumber is a *sea-banana* or *sea-prick*. Since Browne's day the fish louse has been called a *sea-cockroach*, and still is (or simply *sea-roach*); it sucks on to the mouth or gill of jack, mackerel, wenchman, and other fish. Occasionally it is a *sea-ticks*.

The sea-centipede (pronounced like the land creature, /sàntapíi/) is more commonly known in Jamaica as *sea-scorpion* or *sea forty-leg*. Something similar to it but 'broader in back' (it is a sea mantis) is called *shrimp maamy*. It is said to have an unfortunate property, for, 'if it sting you on Friday, you gone!'

Chapter Sixteen

PLANTS

THE NUMBER of plants and plant-names in Jamaica is so huge (it runs into the thousands) that a full list would require a volume in itself. The present account must therefore be limited to only the most characteristic — those which illustrate tendencies of the language. *Daisy, almond, buttercup, pear* and the like are generally omitted; what is different about them is botanical rather than linguistic: an old name has been transferred without change to a new plant. Many names created by botanists found no use outside their books; numerous importations from foreign sources gained no real currency; all these must be left aside.

Nevertheless the early printed sources dare not be neglected, especially as we often discover in them the first record of folk names and of scores of others later adopted as standard throughout the English-speaking world. Jamaica was fortunate in attracting early the attention of botanists, and they had their reward, for this island is remarkable for the variety of its plants: new species are still being discovered. From the end of the seventeenth century, when Sir Hans Sloane published his *Catalogus plantarum quae in insula Jamaica sponte proveniunt* (1696), there is a series of distinguished names — Barham, Browne, Titford, Lunan, McFadyen, and later on Swartz, Grisebach, Fawcett and Rendle — associated with this study.

Even before the botanists there were the adventurers, whose descriptions are full of the excitement of discovery. They found a sea swarming with fish, manatee, tortoise; savannas alive with wild cattle, forests echoing and flashing with flocks of birds. The earth was rich with strange, delicious fruits whose very names were an experience upon the palate. 'There are great plenty of . . . Fruits . . . as Guavars, Mammees, Alumee-Supotas, Suppotillias, Avocatas, Cashues, Prickle-Aples, Prickle-Pears,

334

Grapes, Sower-Sops, Custard-Aples, Dildowes, and many others' — so wrote Richard Blome in 1672 in his *Description of the Island of Jamaica*. To these adventurers we owe some of our earliest records of names.

The historical dictionaries have documented well the nomenclature of plants, but for those of tropical America they would have benefited by going more often to Jamaican sources. From books accessible to them I have collected some hundreds of plant names which they do not include at all.[1] For hundreds more I have found uses anterior to the earliest they cite, and many later than the latest they cite. These names, recorded here first or here only, are true Jamaicanisms, especially those — by far the majority — which have continued in use till today.

The other true Jamaicanisms are the folk names, many never printed before though they are on the people's lips and in their lives every day. These present the difficulty of overlapping usage. Many a name is applied to several different plants: many a plant has several names in various parts of the island or even in the same community. Our treatment here cannot be exhaustive; we give only the chief names and the plants to which they are applied.

Earliest to be recorded were names of native plants (as in Sloane's *Catalogus*) and a few imported ones which had value as sources of food — *cassava, guava, cashew*; as condiments — *annatto, pimento*; as medicines — *oil nuts, cinchona bark*; as dyestuffs — *logwood, fustic*; as timber — *cedar, bullet-wood*. When plantations increased, many new plants were brought in and naturalised — *canes, cotton, indigo*. Then with slavery came foodstuffs that the slaves were used to — *plantains, yams, yampees*; later on *breadfruit, ackees, mangoes* as an addition to their diet. The languages from which these names were taken are, in order, the American Indian, Spanish and Portuguese, French, English, African, and East Indian, with sprinklings of others. Names were adopted and invented at first by the whites, but the slaves brought a number of African ones with them, and since their establishment in Jamaica the negroes have created an almost unending variety of local names. Mangoes, for example, brought from India in 1792, have already acquired over fifty folk names for different varieties.

'Bread Kind'

The standard form today for the name of the manioc root of the Arawak and other Indians is *cassava*, but among the Jamaican folk it more often takes the older form *cassada*. The first full description is found in 1740:

> Cassada, of which there is three sorts, first, the sweet they eat the Root roasted: secondly, the bitter Cassada, the juice of which is Poison, . . . the third sort is the wild Cassada, the Leaves of which are boil'd and eaten with Oil for the Gripes, the water it is boil'd in is drank after it, the Seeds the Birds eat.

Barham remarked, rightly enough, that

> there is another plant, called wild cassada, and is known by no other name by the people in Jamaica, but for what reason I cannot tell, it being in no respect like the other cassada; they grow wild in every savanna.

Sloane describes it as 'ricinus minor', which would class it with the castor oil plant; he says it has a leaf like stavesacre. It was probably the plant now also called *belly-ache weed*. The name *wild cassava* has been transferred as well to the *starch bean*, because the roots of both are used to make starch.

Used too for starch is bitter cassava, which, if properly prepared, is safe to eat. Sweet cassava, which Sloane also called *white cassada*, is eaten as a vegetable and made into *bammy cakes* and *lace cakes*. Cassava liquor — once known as *casareep* and the basis of the traditional *pepperpot* soup — is not however favoured in the Jamaican dish.

Some local names for cassavas are descriptive: *blue-bud* or *bluebird*, *blue-top*, *black-stick* (that is, black-stemmed), *white-stick*, *cotton*, and *bunch-a-key* (because of the way the roots cluster about the rootstock). Others are associated with people who introduced them, or the places where they are grown: *Bobby Hanson, Louisa, Marly hill*; and *agricultural cassada* is a new variety introduced by government agriculturists.

The original potato to come to the attention of Europeans was the 'sweet potato' of today — *batatas* as the Spanish called it, borrowing the native Arawak name. Since the Irish potato has never thriven widely in this island, Jamaicans still think first of the sweet potato when the word is used without a modifier.

Only Sloane has recorded *red potatoes* for these, apparently translating the French *patates rouges*; but a former name that had wide currency was *Spanish potatoes*.

Long was first to record the term *potato slip*, now the common one for the vine or a piece of the vine used for planting; he seems to mean the yellow variety. The Irish potato, a quite different plant, was early called the 'Irish or English *batata*'. These, now at last locally produced, are hawked in the streets of Kingston and its suburbs to the lusty cry of 'Irish! Irish!', but the sweet potato is the one which, grown everywhere for centuries, has acquired all kinds of local names.

Of these the descriptive include *blue-bud* or *bluebird*, *brass cannon* (from the shape and colour), *pigeon neck* (from the shape where the root joins the vine), *yellow coby* (referring to the colour of coby wood?), *red-white*, *dog-blood* and *dog-liver*, *yellow-belly*, *dragon* (probably by association with the shrub called *dragon*, which has dark red leaves), *punkin* (from either colour or shape), *scissors-tail* (from the shape of the leaf), *bunch-a-key* or *bunchy*, *giant*, *full-pot* (i.e., which *fills* the pot), *flour-barrel* (large, of plentiful yield), *flog-all* (because it beats every other), *pickny-mumma* (i.e., nursing mother, from its milky quality or its generous giving of sustenance).

Those that refer to a place of origin (or supposed origin) are *Maryland*, *Costa Rica*, *Prison Farm*, and *St Thomas*; and those associated with people are *Mary Dougal*, *Marshal*, *Liddy*, *Bobby Brown*, *Burke*, *Mother Edwards*, *Mother Thomas*, *John Barnet*, *Jane Denis*, *Charley*, *R.M.*, *Lewis Daley*, *Sarey*, *Seely*, and *Whittaker*. *Chinee sweet potato* seems to be a misnomer for *Chinee yam*. *Pang* was said to be from the name of a Chinese. *Police* is a round potato 'with peg-peg all over'.

The third of the plants which provide staple foods in Jamaica is the *coco* root: the same as the *taro* or *kalo* of Polynesia, which seems to have been its place of origin. Brought to America by the Portuguese, the plant was adopted very widely, so that names probably related to *taro* are found even in the Indian languages: Tupí, Guaraní, Arawak, and Carib,[2] the Jamaican form being *taya*. The dictionaries do not list this; only the OED enters Browne's form *tannier*, which is decidedly the less common, since *taya* is found in almost all other sources[3] and is still the chief spoken form. Beckford called it the *Eboe toyer*, associating it with one group of slaves. *Taya*, then, was the earliest general name for the plant in Jamaica, as in the Caribbean generally. Today it has become restricted to the variety of coco with a yellow 'head' (the rootstock); it is usually fed to pigs, whence also called *hog-taya*. Because it flourishes beside the water, some call it *river-coco*.

The second name to become current in Jamaica was *eddo*, which is surely African: Fante *ɛdwó(w)* means yam, and *ndwo(w)* means root; Bima *edja* is a Colocasia. From some such form our word no doubt derives, given by the slaves who grew it as a favourite food. *Eddo* appeared first in 1725 (Sloane):

> Tayas or Eddos, are eaten in *Jamaica*, and cause a Heat in the Throat, call'd commonly there scratching the Throat, and this when well boil'd.

This uncomfortable property led to another name:

> The old roots are generally called *Scratch Coccos*, from a little pungency with which they are always impregnated; and the young ones that shoot round the top, *Edyes*.[4]

Today *scratch-coco* is probably as common a term as *taya* for the wild plant that pigs eat, but *eddo* is fast going out of use.

Though *coco* was latest it has since become decidedly the most general of these terms. It first appeared in the combination *ground-cocoa* (to differentiate it from tree-borne products called 'cocoa'), in 1740:

> There is also the Ground-cocoa, which grows like Potatoes, with a broad Leaf, in the shape of a Heart; this is called Callaloe, and is a pleasant Sauce to salt Meat.[5]

This is an important citation for it shows that both the root and the leaf were eaten from early days. In uncombined form, the word was first recorded in 1756:

> The purple cocco, and Tannier. The tops of this plant commonly used to feed the hogs; but the root is more valuable.

Following this spelling, the OED enters the word under 'cocco'; yet it is, and has probably always been /kuoko/ or /koko/ in the folk pronunciation. The spelling *coco* was used certainly as early as 1788, probably earlier.

Local names are simply descriptive: *blue, white-stalk, green-stalk, ribbon* (from the colour of the leaves and stems), *white, purple, black, horse-foot, yam-finger* (from the shape), and *maranga* (which is probably from the same African source as the Cuban and Porto Rican *malanga*).

Others are a sort of nicknames implying superior hardness: *commander, duke,* or *lef'-man* (because it does not disintegrate in the pot). *Too-good* is self-descriptive; *pickny-mumma,* a generous provider; *seven-months* is a particularly early variety — harder cocos take twelve months or so to mature. Those named for places are: *Bourbon* (the former name of Reunion Island — one of the first fine varieties introduced), and the corruptions of this as *baboon* and *bamboo; St Kitts, San Blas,* and *Surinam.* Those named for people are *Jeremy, Minty, Sally,* and *My-Lady; Black Jack* is another name for *Bourbon.*

A well known coarse coco, the same or similar to the *eddo,* is the /bádu/; and finally there is the *dasheen,* with a large 'head' that is eaten, rather than the tubers. It is supposed to come from the French *de Chine,* implying origin in the Orient, doubtless Indo-China. The origin of *badu* is probably the Hausa *bădo,* a white water-lily whose root is eaten.

Coco itself is possibly a folk form of some original also represented in the botanical name *Colocasia,* ultimately from the Egyptian name of a water-lily. Reversing the order of things that one might expect, cocos were taken from Jamaica to Africa (1843) and their name with them, so that we find Akem *kóokó* or *koókó,* derived from the Jamaican word.

One small kind of 'coco' is widely used as a pot-herb under the name of *Indian kale,* in Spanish America commonly called *yautía.* The name was first recorded by Sloane: 'Indian Caile, or Tajas the lesser.' Like 'ground cocoa' mentioned above, this is thought of as a type of *calalu* — indeed, some country men call it *sipple* (that is, slippery) *calalu.*

The tuber depended upon most of all as a foodstuff, however, is *yam.* This word is now known to have been brought by the Portuguese, with the plant, from Africa to the new world: it is ultimately from Senegalese *nyami,* to eat, through Portuguese *inhame.* Since the earliest recorded use in English is from Barbados, *yam* itself is not a Jamaicanism; but there are many local names. A number are from Africa, the commonest being *afu,* probably from Twi *afuw*, plantation, cultivated ground. Williams considered the word 'a simplified form of *nkamfo*, the Ashanti name for the same yellow yam'; but this is actually represented not by *afu* but by *camphor* yam, in which the African word is obviously affected by folk-etymology.[6]

There are two varieties — *red afu*, a dark yellow, and *white afu*, a pale yellow, and it is also known throughout the island as *yellow yam*. Other African names are not as widespread, and are dying out. Williams writes, 'in the Jamaica bush a very superior species of white yam is called fufu yam'; in Ewe, *fufu* means yam or cassava. *Bayere* (pronounced /baiyíeri/), from Twi *bàyére*, is something like yellow yam. *Crongoe* which according to Barclay 'roasted would bear comparison with the best Irish potatoes, [and] grows wild in the fields that have been thrown out of cultivation', is now *crunjo* — apparently from a tribal name. It is also called *Guinea yam*, and is like white yam but somewhat harder. *Depa* is an older name for negro yam.[7]

Pumpun or *pumpum* yam appears first in print in 1929: ' "Pompon" which bears "big and round" '; Williams also mentioned it: 'A yam that has developed spherically and not in the usual elongated form is known as pumpun yam, a reduplicated form of the Ashanti word *pun*, primarily meaning to become swelled or distended.'

Probably also African is /taa/ yam, 'a white yellow-yam' that is 'harder than yellow'. And we can be certain of *akam* (or *hakam*) for in Twi we find '*akam*, a species of *wild yam*, eaten in times of famine'. Russell recorded it in 1868 among the Jamaican words borrowed from Africa: '*aham* — a creeping plant', and it is widely known today. The part eaten is not a tuber like cultivated yams but resembles large yam-seeds growing on the vine, the size of a fist and shaped somewhat like an Irish potato.

Another wild yam is *himba*, which grows in the high woods and is edible. The source has not been traced, but it is most likely African. A native Jamaican name for wild yam, or *bitter yam*, is *Bitter-Jessie*, combining the descriptive with the personal name such as cassavas and sweet potatoes have. This yam bears a tuber and has yellow flesh. Two other names for wild yams — not common ones — are reported as *boxen* or *buxen*, and *gashy*. The sources are unknown, but probably African.[8]

Other descriptive names are *blue-vine* or *macca* yam, also called *mozella.* This is something of a puzzle; Beckwith spells it *Mar-zella*, as if it were a personal name, but the only pronunciation I have heard is /mozéla/. It grows very large, sometimes a hundred pounds, with white or pale yellow flesh. There is also *green-leaf* yam. And referring to the eating qualities, there are *flour*, *hard*, *white*, and *sweet* yam, all with white flesh but of different textures: Also, flour yam is a single long tuber, white yam has 'plenty foot', and sweet yam is the smallest, though not as small as *yampi*. *Seed yam* has apparently had a special application in Jamaica since Barham's time. As he wrote, 'Two sorts of white, one of which is called the seed-yam, which is extraordinary white, and makes an admirable fine flour;' today it is applied to any white yam which bears seeds.

An early pair of names that seem at first descriptive are *backra* and *negro* yam, but they refer actually to the quality. As Long wrote in 1774,

Negroe-yam . . . White-yam . . . Both these plants are cultivated here universally for food; but the former, which is of a yellowish colour, is coarse, frequently stringy, and not so much in esteem as the second, vulgarly called by the Negroes, *bochara-yam*.

Today *negro yam* refers to a white yam, but it is hard, in contrast to the so-called *white yam*. *Backra*, in short, did not refer to colour but implied the best quality; and the same contrast was made for calalu and pines.

Snake yam is a long, slender yam; *pingwing* yam is like Negro yam, but softer; its name implies that the vine has prickles (like pinguin) — compare macca yam. *Madam sit-down* (pronounced /sidong/) is a 'white Portland yam' with a 'big round bottom'.

Proper names applied to yams are *Barbados*, *Trinidad*, *St Vincent*, and *St Lucia* for their places of origin. Barbados is white, has 'a heap of foot', and is much like St Lucia. Trinidad and St Vincent grow virtually wild in bush or forest land and look like white yam. St Vincent is soft, purple-white, and gives an early crop; it also keeps long in the earth, 'propagates itself by seed so that one planting will sometimes perpetuate itself for fifteen years,' and is therefore called *come-here-fe-help-we* or *come-to-help-us*.

Renta — a widely known name — has been variously identified with St Lucia, Barbados, and Trinidad yams; it is white, soft, and floury, with a hairy exterior. I have no clue to its meaning; there seems to be no African connection. It could possibly represent the English word *renter* — indeed, one countryman declares that if you 'just tease up the surface [of the ground] and put it in, it rents the earth', making space for itself. St Vincent or renta, being soft, needs little chewing and is nicknamed *sucky-swallow*. *Lucea* yam is grown in the region around Lucea, in Hanover (also called /taa/ yam by one man). Finally there is *Pa Will* or *Puppa Will*.

Yampi is nothing but a variety of yam, smaller and finer. The OED puts the word in with *yam* (though it is certainly different) and dates it 1796 without a supporting quotation. We find it in Jamaican sources in 1811: 'A very delicious species is small, purple outside, very white within, and called the Yampea or Yampoy.' The word is African: compare Vai *dʒambi* 'the wild yam'. *Yampi* is the name all over the island though some call it also *India* or *Indian yam*, some *Portland yam* (a pinkish-white variety), some *moonshine yam* (a dark purple variety, also known as *Red St Vincent*); and there is a small white variety with a shiny skin called *Chinee*.

Last of the starch foods widely used is the breadfruit, though this name is not Jamaican. Broughton tells us that '347 plants of the breadfruit' arrived on 5 February, 1793, on H.M.S. Providence, brought from 'Otaheite' and 'were distributed through the Island'. (However, Beckford wrote of them in 1790 as if they had already been introduced.) Varieties are known today as the *Congo* breadfruit, which has a rough skin and is not as good as *finey*, a floury, white one; *St Kitts*, also fine; and *whiteheart*. There are *Sukey* and *St Kitts Sukey* too. For the breadfruit a number of nicknames have been created which seem to be hypocoristic alterations based on one syllable or another: /breshe/, /brambra/ (the biggest and easiest to roast), /bacha/ or /baajam/, /bufu/ or /bufut/, and /buku/ — the last definitely a children's word: 'Ripe buku no good fe pickny.'

A breadfruit is jocularly a *jackass*. As Russell wrote, 'To pad, or saddle a jackass (culinary business) is to roast it, but to ride it and gallop it is to eat it with no bad apetite [sic].' A half 'full' breadfruit is a *quashie*; and a *monkey breadfruit* is a variety with a prickly skin, also called *prickly breadfruit*.

Other Vegetables

The *akee* (or *ackee*), though now an important food tree, is a relatively late comer to Jamaica — as its name is to the dictionaries: the earliest dated citation is 1829. However, in the description of the 'Exotic Plants Cultivated in the Botanic Garden' of Mr East, in Liguanea (1794), we find among the new genera, 'The Akee. Africa. Dr Tho. Clarke, 1778 . . . This plant was brought here in a Slave Ship from the Coast of Africa, and now grows very luxuriant. . . . I do not know that it has hitherto been described.' Thus the word came into English in Jamaica. In 1801 Lady Nugent spelled it *acqui*. It is from Kru *ā-kee*. The only local name found was *butter-akee*, for a white-pod variety.

Many kinds of beans thrive in Jamaica and names for them even more, but, as in the southern United States, they are more commonly called peas than beans. Probably the most remarkable language development is that which the *Bonavist pea* has undergone. The earliest dictionary citation is from 1682 but we find it twenty-seven years earlier in a Jamaican account: 'Sugar Canes, . . . Bonanoes, Bonavist, Plantans. . . .' Folk etymology begins very soon to transform the word: the OED lists *bonny-vis* (1750) and the DAE has *bonniviss* (1800), 'pronounced bonnybess'. In 1740 we find *Bonnavest-Pea*; in 1912 *Bannabees*; in 1929 Beckwith quotes the proverb, 'Time nebber too long fe Bannabis bear bean,' and explains the word as meaning 'Banner bean', apparently not having identified it as the Bonavist pea.[9] Present-day folk pronunciations take two chief forms: /bánavis/ and /bánabis/, and several cultivators (compare Beckwith's explanation) 'corrected' it to *banner beans*. One man even spoke of *banna wiss* in allusion to its being a vine (withe). Indeed, *banna* seems to be another word for vine to some Jamaicans (compare the *hog-meat* vine, also called *hog-banna* by at least one man). These beans have many colours, often mixed — black, white, red. The *white* and *red bonavist* are mentioned by Sloane as early as 1696. From the long time they take to cook they are widely known as *broke-pot*; a small variety is *pig-tail* peas. Marsden's form, 'The bean called Barrowby' is probably a misprinting of this name — with *r*'s for *n*'s — though his description fits the *gungu pea* better.

Gungu peas is the universal Jamaican form of *Congo peas*. It

z

must have been in use a long time before it was first recorded in 1893: *goongoo*. Later writers spell *goongo* and *gungu*, the last coming closest to the actual pronunciation /gúnggu/. Another name is *pigeon peas*, first found in Jamaica (1696), though used widely through the Caribbean today. 'They are so called from pigeons greedily feeding upon them,' according to Barham. Beckwith identifies these as red kidney beans — a mistake that no Jamaican would make.

There are other, less common names for the gungu. First, *Angola pea* — listed by Long and Lunan, though no longer current here if ever it was. Lunan wrote that it

> lasts from 5 to 7 years in good soil, whence it has derived the name of seven-year-pea . . . they . . . continue in bearing for several months of the year, about Christmas; and therefore sometimes called in Jamaica the *Christmas pea*.

Seven-year-pea no longer seems to be current, but *Christmas pea* is said to be used in St Catherine for *Jerusalem pea*. In the Island generally, *Jerusalem peas* are a very small, dark brown or black bean that grows in a long pod. Finally, the gungu pea is also called the *no-eye pea*, from the inconspicuousness of its hilum.

The other favourite bean in Jamaica is *red peas*. The DAE traces this back to 1805, but we find it here 109 years before. In early days they were called *calavances* or *caravances*, from Spanish *garbanzos*, which was itself adopted as *garvancos* and *gravances* by Sloane, and *garavonzas* as late as 1727. The OED traces *carauances* back to 1634 but does not have *calavances* before 1829; yet Sloane used it in 1696 and Nevill spelled *calavanseys* in 1697. These forms are no longer in use.

Since the beans vary considerably in colour and somewhat in size, folk names for the many varieties sometimes seem contradictory: *red peas*, *black-eye peas* or *lady-peas*, *crab-eye peas* (whitish with black markings, like the eyes of crabs), also called *mix* or *mixture* peas from their colour; *Black Betty*, *Red Miss Kelly* (reduced sometimes to *Skelly peas*), *cow peas*, *Chinee cow peas*, *China peas* — all are identified as varieties of *Vigna unguiculata*. As the Latin name suggest, the pods have a point like a small claw; evidently this looked more like a horn to the unknown humorist who gave them their oldest English name: *cuckold's increase*. This later became *cockle's increase*, spoiling the joke. It is now out of use.[10]

Yet others are *cockstone peas* — obsolete according to the OED, but very much alive in Jamaica to this day; *year bean* (for its long season of bearing?); *beef bean* (large and brown; eaten with beef); *blazes Jane* (for its excellence); *Emma bean* (a large variety); *Caroline peas* (like black-eye but smaller — which makes them quite different from Carolina peas of the U.S.); *Nelson ball* peas ('the grain is round') and *round-red*; and *yam-bank* peas (planted on the yam-hills).

Sloane also mentioned the *great bean, red-spotted bean,* and 'Surinam pease, or Rouncivals', but only the last seems to have survived — as *rounciful,* 'an old-time name'. Titford wrote of *parsley peas* as black with a white spot, the 'ulinga' of Malabar, used in Jamaica as a cure for headache. *White bean* or *white pea* is also often called *sugar beans,* recorded in Jamaica 131 years earlier than elsewhere. Browne gave the alternative name *Jamaica bean* — evidently the same as Sloane's *Jamaica Pease* — but neither has survived.

Some nicknames used by the folk are: *full-mouth,* known since 1868, 'a large kind of beans'; *full-pot* beans, which *fills* the pot; and *sorrow-for-poor* beans (sorry-for-the-poor, like the come-fe-help-we yam). There is also the *starch bean, yam bean,* or *wild starch,* which bears both a bean and a tuber somewhat like yam, used to make starch. And finally there is the *overlook bean* or *pea* which, planted at the edge of a 'ground', reputedly protects it from thieves. Other names for this are *horse bean, jack bean,* and *sword bean.*

Sometimes referred to as 'peason' and 'beans', though they are neither, are the seeds of sesame, most commonly called /wánggla/ today — and this seems to have been the early form of the name too, though the OED and others list it under *vangloe.* Sloane may have meant this: 'Another kind of Peason called Wandos'; Barham certainly did, though his form is metathesised:

Oily Pulse, Which is called *zesamum,* or *sesamum Africanum.* The first time I saw this plant, it was growing in a negro's plantation ... their seed vessels, full of small white seeds, which the negroes call *soonga,* or *wolongo,* which is much like the sago sold in shops, but very oily.

Long introduces the *v*- form, corrects the *w*- form, and adds a third name: 'Vanglo, Wongala, or Oil-plant. — Sesamum orientale.' Dancer was first to spell *vangloe* (1801), but Williamson puts the *w*- form first: 'The wangla, or vangla', and discusses its use in cakes, and medicinally. Roughley adds the spelling *wangola*. The *w*- forms are more etymological: Kongo *wangila* means sesame. Wangla seeds are burned in some Obeah practices.

A plant with many names, native to America, is *calalu*, first borrowed into English in Jamaica: Sloane recorded it in 1696, 'Cararu Brasiliensibus . . . Culilu, or Caterpillars.' The furry flowering tips were no doubt responsible for the latter name, but it has not survived. *Calalu*, on the other hand, has flourished; in Jamaican sources we find it spelled *culilu, caleloe, colalue, colilu, calalue, callaloo*; and it is usually pronounced /kalalú/, sometimes /kololú/. An early account remarked that there are 'Callaloe of three Sorts, Top-a-top, or the Cocoa-Callaloe; another Sort grows like Brocoli, and eats like Spinage; and the Mountain-Callaloe'.[11]

The first of these is obviously the *coco* type, the second the Jamaican *spinach* of today, the third the *poke-weed* type. *Top-a-top* has been found only here, and is not in use today, but *coco-calalu* is — apparently the same as *riverside* or *River Canaan calalu*, a wild coco whose leaves are chiefly fed to hogs. The kind used for human consumption is *Indian kale*.

The spinach type includes *garden* or *green* calalu; *broad-leaf* or *English*, sometimes called *Coolie* calalu because the East Indians cultivate it; and (perhaps the same plant) *backra* calalu, meaning the best quality. Uncultivated varieties (*wild* calalu) include *red* or *red-stick, small-leaved, tall*, and *ground* calalu (which grows low); and the *prickly* or *duppy* calalu, the latter implying that duppies are responsible for the prickles. *Spanish* calalu includes two plants. All these are of the genus *Amaranthus*.

The poke-weed type was recorded in Jamaica by Browne and Dancer as *pork-weed* too (in the folk speech *poke* and *pork* are pronounced identically: /púok/) — perhaps the plant was cooked with pork, or thought to be. It is best known, however, as *jokotu* calalu. This word was first mentioned by Long, 'Mountain Calalue, Pokeweed, Surinam or Juckata Calalue'; Dancer spelled it both *jacatoo* and *jucato*; and it is pronounced today

/jòkotó/ or /jùkutú/. Though the source has not been found it is probably African.[12]

Mountain calalu was recorded as early as 1740, but neither this term nor *Surinam* has survived. *Kreng-kreng* calalu has not been identified, but by its name it must be stalky, and is said to be mucilaginous 'like okro' when cooked. Of *branched* calalu Browne wrote:

> The plant is very common in the low lands of *Jamaica*, and grows frequently in the grass pieces; . . . equally common in *Europe*, and of a virose heavy smell and very narcotic quality in these cold climates, [it] is void of both in *Jamaica*, where it is daily used for food.

But Long writes of its being given in a cold infusion during Myal ceremonies, 'which, after the agitation of dancing, threw the party into a profound sleep' — and so led to the pretence of resurrecting the dead. This plant is also known as *black nightshade* (which is tantamount to a translation of its botanical name, *Solanum nigrum*), and, the best known folk name, *guma*. Lunan was first to record this: '*gooma* or *goomer* calalu'. It is valued for laxative and other medicinal properties, wherefore the saying, 'Ol' 'oman swear fe guma, an' guma swear fe ol' 'oman.' Though the source has not been found, it is certainly African. *Guma* and *jokotu* calalu both appear to be called *pickny-mumma* (nursing mother), and *guma* is similarly named *sucky-baby*.

The word calalu is applied not only to these specific plants, and sometimes to a thick soup made with them, but may be a general word meaning soup greens, or just greens. One country-man referred to cabbage as a type of calalu, and another called purslane *pussley calalu*. (In Cuba and Porto Rico *calalu* is a cooked dish of mixed, pickled greens.)

Both kinds of 'pepper' — *Piper* and *Capsicum* — are well represented in Jamaica. The large capsicum was first known from its shape as *cod pepper, bell pepper* or *Indian bell pepper*, and *great pepper*. The familiar *bird pepper* is recorded in the dictionaries only from 1785, yet Sloane put it into his *Catalogus* eighty-nine years before, and we also find it in 1740, with others: 'Bonnet-Pepper, Hen-Pepper and Bird-Pepper, all used in Soops or Pickles'. *Bonnet* is no doubt the present-day *Scotch bonnet*, shaped like a tam-o'-shanter, and yellow. Titford added *pigeon pepper*, and

Long *Barbary* and *coral* pepper (otherwise unrecorded, though the latter is still in use). Cayenne pepper (still pronounced in the older way, /káian/, by the folk) has received the nicknames *burn-to-hell*, *devil-hell*, and *devil-damnation*. Other names refer to shape: *cherry-pepper*, *olive pepper*, *finger*, *long-finger*, *lady-finger*, *nipple*, *forked*, and *lif'-coat* (because it looks like a woman lifting her coat). *Goat-pepper* dates back to 1740; apparently it was a general term to Barham, so called 'for they smell rank like a ram-goat'. Finally, there was 'Purple or Sore Throat Pepper', mentioned only by Titford; it is used to cure sore throat.

Of the genus *Piper* probably the best known is *pepper-elder*, valued for soups, for 'jerk-meat', as a carminative, and for teas and baths. It is the same as *jointer* or *joint-wood*, which names refer to the conspicuous jointed stems. In contrast to *jointer* is *black jointer* or *black-joint*; but one man gave the name *white jointer* for the first, which has evidently come in to make the distinction clearer. The earliest name of pepper-elder seems to have been *Spanish elder*. Another related plant is *jointy benna*. (The plant usually called *rat ears* is sometimes also *pepper-elder*.)

Though *pimento* (allspice) is not a kind of pepper, being related to the laurels, it was for a long time called Jamaica-pepper because the dried berry looked so much like a peppercorn. The OED has only one citation for it: 1660. In 1662 Stubbe described it as

> that most delicate of Spices, call'd usually in England
> Pepper of Jamaica, by the Spaniards Pepper of Xamaica. . . .
> It is commonly call'd in Jamaica, Pimienta: which name
> they took from the Spaniards.

Actually they took both. *Jamaica pepper* remained in English use as late as 1782, but Jamaicans themselves began to call it *pimento* from the first, and that is its only name in the island today (though botanically outrageous, since pimiento is properly capsicum). Stubbe's description is lyrical, but too long to quote.

In this sense, then, *pimento* goes back to 1662. It is also spelt *piemente* and *pimento* in the seventeenth century, and *piemento* in the eighteenth. In the present folk pronunciation, an *r* is curiously intruded, and it regularly becomes /priménta/.

An early name for *annatto* was *achiots*, of which the first English examples come from Jamaica: 'Achiotl (as it is called by

Hernandez) or Achiote, as it is usually called (Mr Gage calls it Achiotte)'; 'Tamerinds, Vinillos, Achiots or Anetto, which is like to prove a good Commodity'; and it was still in use as late as 1683 in the Laws of Jamaica. But *annatto* had begun to displace it (as just cited) by 1672 and is now the only name used. In folk pronunciation it is regularly aphetized to /náta/. *Achiote* is from Nahuatl and *annatto* from Cariban; both came into English via Spanish.

Okro is another word borrowed in the West Indies, and apparently in Jamaica. Trapham wrote in 1679, 'As a food easy of digestion may well be admitted likewise the young Ocra.' Sloane mentioned also in 1696 the *long okra*, a name still in use. Browne was first to spell 'the Okro plant' and 'Musk Okro', which reflect the chief folk pronunciation of today. Dancer spelled 'ochra' and 'musk ochrow'. This latter plant has also been known as *musk seed* and *wild okro*, but there is no evidence that the folk have ever used forms with *musk*. Their present names include *goat-horn* (from the shape), *bungo* or *Coolie* (stout, green, and ribbed; cultivated by East Indians), and *Chinee* (short, whitish, with ribs), *Christmas* (comes in about Christmas time), and *lady-finger* okro (long and smooth).

Because the okro has a mucilaginous nature its name has been transferred to several other plants. The triangular cactus which climbs like a vine all over walls and trees is called *sipple okro* (that is, slippery or slimy), *wall okro*, *god-okro*, and *dindi-okro*, the last two names implying a supernatural growth. Browne listed one kind of *Sida* as 'Bastard Ochro', which is the same or a similar plant to today's *slippery-okro* shrub. The okro plant was brought from Africa, and so was its name, though the exact source is uncertain.

The plant commonly called *sorrel* today, used at Christmas time to make a bright red drink, has had several variations. Sloane called it *French Sorrel*, and Barham identified it a little later. An account of 1740 mentioned 'two sorts of Sorrels, white and red, of both which they make Jellies and marmalade, and a cool drink'. In 1750 we find it called *Jamaica sorrel*, and in 1814 *Indian sorrel* with the comment, 'this species . . . is thoroughly green . . . there is a variation . . . commonly called red-sorrel.' The name was apparently transferred from the European *Rumex*, because this too has a pleasant acidity: 'sorrel' is related to the word *sour*. Only the simple forms of the name are common today.

Garden egg has already been commented upon, but before it became the general term there were others: *brown-jolly, bolangena* or *valanghanna*, and *egg fruit* (to say nothing of *mad apples*, which was apparently the very first name this vegetable had in English). *Brown-jolly* is a folk etymology of *brinjal*, the Anglo-Indian name. *Bolangena* must have come through Spanish or Portuguese (compare American Spanish *berengena*), which would easily follow from Browne's statement that the plant 'was first imported into Jamaica by the Jews'. Sloane, who first recorded *valanghanna*, said that it was so called 'in Jamaica by the vulgar' — that is, the folk pronunciation. It too is clearly from Spanish; indeed Titford records, as another form of the Spanish name, *balankuna*, which is very close to this. *Egg fruit* appears to be generally American, but the earliest record found is from Jamaica. Of all these varied names, however (and excepting the recently introduced *eggplant*), the only survivor is *garden-egg*.[13]

Then there is the succulent *chocho*, a name which has come from the native Brazilian, via Portuguese *chuchu*. Its Spanish name, *chayote*, from the Nahuatl *chaiotl*, has a Cuban form *chote*, from which a secondary Jamaican form probably derives. Browne was the first to record it (1756); Beckford had it as *chota* (1790), a form similar to the Cuban; but all other writers have *cho-cho*, and that is virtually the only name it bears today. Chochos are *white* and *green*, the latter also called *green-gage* chocho by one countryman.

Fruits

Among fruits, as among vegetables, one finds a large variety of local names for the major, more marketable ones — those which are important as foodstuffs: bananas, plantains, canes, pines (pineapples), and mangoes. Among the canes there are colour names: *black, white, blue*, and *giant purple* cane; *ribbon* and *stripe* or *striped* cane go back at least to 1811 — 'The *riband* or *striped cane* is no longer cultivated by judicious planters' — and is still being grown; *crawfish* cane is also striped.

Shape rules in *elephant-foot* and *goat-foot*, *goat-knee* or *goat-shank*; the last is said to be called *toad-eye* in Westmoreland. Place of origin accounts for *Albion* (a famous Jamaican estate),

B.H. (Barbados Hybrid), *Cuban, Java* or *P.O.J.* (Pride of Java), and *Bourbon* or *Otaheite. Bourbon* was in Jamaica by 1811; and Lunan wrote of 'the introduction of the Bourbon or Otaheite cane, which was brought here in the year 1796, and has since been generally cultivated. This cane is of a much larger size than any other'.

Personal names, not identified, are found in *William Burke, Bullington,* and *Cabana* or *Cavana.* Special properties are alluded to in *drop-trash* or *trash-meself* ('trash' is the dry leaves), *wanderer* (tough and straight), *woman* (black and soft), *lady-fancy* (whitish with dark stripes), *governor* ('yellow striped'), *prima* (/praima/), *yuba* ('switchy and tough'), and *nursery* cane. Newly developed varieties are usually numbered — for example, *ninety-five* cane. *Salango* (from the Malayan place name *Selangor*), one of the many strains brought from the orient to the sugar islands, illustrates the lengths to which folk-etymology can go: one man said that it gives the largest yield, and therefore means 'so long go'.

Bananas named for their appearance include *bumpy* (a small, chunky variety), *frog* (sometimes considered a plantain), *old nayger* (short and thick), *red, smoky* (dark brown but otherwise like the apple banana), and the stout-fingered *robusta.* Flavour and other qualities are reflected in *apple* or *honey* (the smallest), *fig* (very small), *plum* (small), *stainy* and *black stainy* (which is darker; both have a 'stain' or discolouring juice in the skin) and *sulphur* (with a strong taste and its bunch sticking up or out instead of hanging down). Place of origin is alluded to in *West Indies* (the same as *red*), *Cuban* (the same as *fig*), *Martinique* (and its altered forms *Manchinic, mancha, bancha*). In McKay's lines we read,

> She look 'pon de Manchinic tree
> Not a piece of mancha fe eat,

and he explains in a note, 'Martinique, the best variety of Banana. Hence mancha for banana.' In addition to these there are *Jacob* (short and fat), *Whitehouse* (the same as *frog*), *Gros Michel* a French variety that was the great favourite before Panama disease began its attack, and which has been Jamaicanized as /gruos míchel/ or /gràs máikal/.

Before the modern export trade in bananas the plantain was far more important in Jamaica, being a staple food of the slaves as it had been in Africa. The local names are mostly descriptive; Sloane mentioned some as early as 1725:

> The greatest Sort which is rank, is called Horse-Plantain. The larger Pleasant-Plantain. The least Sort called Maiden-Plantain, is reckon'd the most pleasant of any.

The first and third names are still in general use: *horse plantain* has not as many fruits, but they are the largest; *maiden plantain* has smaller fruits, but a great many. *Giant* bears as many as eighteen hands to the bunch; *smoke* is the same as *giant*, but for the colour; *mackerel* has flattened fruits, and *tiger* plantain is 'spreckle-spreckle — have spots all over the skin'.

Names indicating origin are *Cuban* (short, stout and clumsy), and *French* (short, yellowish even when green) or *papoose*. One puzzling name was given in the forms /singkuma/ and /fiekuma/ — apparently the same despite the variation. It is very probably African, from Hausa *sunk'umā*, huge, swollen.

The West Indian fruit that probably had the most enviable early reputation in Europe was the pineapple (always 'pine' in Jamaica). Accounts are full of its praises — for example one written two years after the British occupation: 'Fruits . . . Pyne, the best that ever was eat, in season almost all the year long.' But name of varieties do not seem to have been recorded before 1740, when we find:

> The *Pine Apple* or *Ananias* [sic], is a very rich and delicious fruit . . . There are three Sorts of them; the Cabbage, the Orange, and the Sugar-Loaf; the last is the best esteem'd.

The first two names have been found nowhere else, and do not survive, but the third flourishes still: it is now also abbreviated to *sugar* pine or *sweet* pine.

Next to be noticed were 'The Black Pine-Apple', 'The Queen Pine-Apple', and the *Ripley* pine: 'At Mr John Ripley's near Kingston I saw eight Acres of land under Pine Apple, which he sells there at a Bitt apiece;' also, 'a particular sort are ripe when quite black and are reckoned to have the finest flavour, . . . this is the Ripley Pine.'[14] Long was the first to give anything like a full list, He added 'the bog-walk pine' — evidently one associated with Bog Walk, St Catherine — 'of a compressed form and deep green coat' and another 'with a yellow coat'; the 'smooth-

leaved or king pine'; and the 'smaller green or yellow pyramidal, or Montserrat'. None of these seems to be in use today,
nor are the two which Marsden recorded in 1788: 'the Buckra,
or White People's Pine ... And a ... sort called the Negro
Pine, which is the worst of all.' Current folk names are *bull* or
bull-head — from some fancied resemblance; *cheese* — which
may refer to a colour or consistency of the flesh; and *cowboy* pine
— round and stout with a flat head, though the reason for the
name is unexplained.

Because the mango takes very many shapes, sizes, and colours
— the very features which strike the eye — the number of their
local names is very high. We list them in brief; by shape: *long,
round-point, kidney, cow-foot, bull-stone, apple*; by colour and general
appearance: *black* or *green-skin, cherry-cheek, liver-spot, lime, coal,
parrot, robin, rose, plummy, paper-skin*, and *mackerel*; by taste or
smell: *chinch, burn-tongue, salt-fish, turpentine, sweet*, and *Mary
syrup*; by texture and quality in eating: *beef* or *beefy, cheese, hard,
duckanoo, hairy* or *stringy, yam, pint-o-water*, and *big-and-so-so*; by
source: *East Indian, Bombay, Lucea* (which Uncle Newton describes as 'the last word in mango-merriment. Large, fleshy,
sugary, yielding and everything!') and *St Julian*, as Jamaicans
rather grandly call the Trinidadian *Julian* or *Julie*.

In addition there are miscellaneous names: *Christmas*, for its
season of ripening; *garden gate*, a very tough variety; *hog*, which
like hog plums, attracts worms and is therefore not fit for human
consumption; *Mary Gould*, possibly a colour name; *milk*, because
a white juice comes out when it is green; *pass*, for reasons unknown; *puke*, said to be emetic; *Sophie*; *come-see*; *today-and-
tomorrow*, said to 'ripen on one side today, on the other tomorrow'; and *number-eleven*, the original tree of which, so numbered when it was first brought to the island, did survive although most of the other plants died. By no means all the names
for mangoes have been collected; most of these are very local,
and more are being created constantly.

The *cashew* has already been mentioned. There is also the
'genip', as the dictionaries spell it, though it is regularly *guinep*
(pronounced /ginep/, sometimes /genep/) in Jamaica. This form
shows a simple metathesis of the vowels (possibly also with the
folk-etymological influence of *Guinea*, which enters into many
names: Guinea yam, pepper, grass, hen, etc.). Whatever the

cause, the change may be traced from 1756 *genip*, 1790 *canipes*, 1811 *cunep*, 1893 *guinep*, 1927 *ginep*: the present form dates from the early nineteenth century.[15] The OED records only the first of these forms, and gives a pronunciation based on etymology that was long ago abandoned in this island. The ultimate source is Tupí-Guaraní, the Brazilian *genipe* (*Genipa americana*); but the name has been transferred to *Melicocca bijuga* in Jamaica, and in Porto Rico where it is *quenepo*. Another name once was *honey-berry*; this has not survived.

Though the name *coco-plum* was not first borrowed in Jamaica, it has had some history here. Early spellings were *coquer* plum and *cocoa* plum. This plant is unconnected either with the coco-palm or cacao, however. *Coco* here goes back to Arawak *ikaku*, which came through American Spanish *jicaco* or *hicaco*, forms now used in Cuba and Porto Rico.

The names of citrus fruits are surprisingly few. *Forbidden fruit*, in size between a shaddock and a grapefruit, was recorded in 1756 and explained in 1893: 'It is called "forbidden fruit" because of three brownish marks on the outside peel, supposed to be Eve's finger marks as she plucked the fruit.' Both the name and its meaning are evidently being forgotten by the folk, which has led to changes in its form. One countryman called it /fibini/, and another *fast-breedin'* fruit.

On the other hand, the pronunciation /sivl/ for the *Seville* orange is not an alteration made in Jamaica but a preservation: it was so pronounced in England through the seventeenth century. Since *sour orange* is the same fruit, one hears /sibl/, the folk form, used to mean *sour*: 'It sibl fi true!' Another folk pronunciation, generally used, is *stangerine* with the initial *s-* from over-correction. The first record of *grapefruit* is from Jamaica.

Trees of genus *Anona* have been mentioned from early days, but surprisingly, the OED missed *custard-apple* entirely, and the OEDS has it only from 1819. Yet Ligon listed it more than a century before among the fruits of Barbados, and Blome found it in Jamaica in 1672.[16] Though the OED has *sour-sop* only from 1696, it was already here in 1679. *Sweet-sop* is listed from a Jamaican source. *Cherimoya* came into English elsewhere, but the tree was brought to this island in 1786. Sullivan spelt it *cherry-moyer* — evidently associating it with the cherry — and the popular pronunciation is /cherimaia/, which, by folk-etymology, sometimes becomes *Jeremiah*. Other forms that I have heard are /cheri-miilya/ and /cheriminya/ — but applied to quite different fruit.

As for *naseberry*, this — or at least its latter part — is a Standard English folk-etymology from American Spanish *níspero*. It too appears to have been borrowed in Jamaica, anglicised by 1679 as *nasburies* and by 1696 as *naseberry*. Nevertheless the Spanish pronunciation of the first vowel continued: in 1801 *neeseberry*, and this prevails among the folk today. *Starapple* too came first into the language here.[17]

When *pear* is used without qualification, the *avocado* or *alligator* pear is meant; both these words are originally Jamaicanisms. Though the OED cites the first from 1697, we find it in English form in 1657: 'Avocatas, a wholesome pleasant fruit; in season in August'. As for the second (OED 1763), Sloane recorded in 1696 'the Avocado or Alligator Pear-tree'.

Avocado can hardly have turned into *alligator*; if these two names are related it must be through a common source. The first is a Spanish folk-etymology of Nahuatl *ahuacatl*. If the second is also from this Indian word it must have developed some such form as that given by Marsden: 'The Alicada, or, as the negroes call it, Alligator Pear,' the last again showing folk-etymology. But since this change had already come about by Sloane's time, as we have seen, it may be a quite independent development — compare *alligator apple*. These pears have two shapes, one with a decided neck, the other without. It is the former, because of the neck, that is now considered the 'alligator' pear (also called *long-neck* pear), which seems to prove the metaphor behind the folk-etymology. The *butter* pear is so called because it was once used as a substitute for butter (and once called 'Midshipman's butter') and also because the 'flesh is red' (that is, orange-yellow). Pears are also classified as *white* and *black* (that is, green- or dark-skinned).

The *jackfruit*, according to Broughton, was brought to Jamaica in 1782 by Lord Rodney from the East Indies. It then had the Portuguese name *jaca tree*. However this was soon converted to *jaack tree*, and its fruit to the *jackfruit*. The latter is now the name of both fruit and tree.

A word which the historical dictionaries have failed to record, though adopted in English for over two and a half centuries, is *bichy* or *bissy*, another name for the kola nut. Sloane found in the fields of 'Dom. Bourden' beyond Guanaboa 'The Bichy Tree'. In his later edition he wrote: 'It is called Bichy by the Coromantin Negro's, and is both eaten and used for Physick in Pains of the Belly. . . . The Seed brought in a *Guinea* Ship from that country, was here planted by Mr Goffe.' The word is indeed African: Twi *bisé*, cola nut, also the tree, Akyan *besé*; and the seed is now used in Jamaica 'for malaria, high blood pressure', and as an antidote for poison; it is pronounced /bisi/, sometimes /bizi/.

Other early references to it are plentiful; 1740: 'the *Besse* or Negroe Fruit, so call'd from their Fondness of it'; 1774: 'Biche, or Bissy'; 1814: 'The negroes in Jamaica call it *bichy* or *colu*.' (Incidentally, the dictionaries do not record the form *colu*.)

One of the first fruits to be noticed and praised, though nowadays neglected, is the *mammee* or *mammee-apple* (*Mammea americana*), often confused with the similar fruits *mammee-sapota* (*Achras zapota*) and *sapodilla* (*Sapota achras*). All three names are ultimately Indian; they came into English via Spanish, and are first recorded in descriptions of Jamaica. We read that the 'Mamesapole, tastes like Marmalet', and from a later writer, that 'the fruit is of an oval shape, with . . . a very luscious, sweet, yellow pulp, called American marmalade'.[18] These names have produced folk-etymological forms: *mammee* is /maami/ among the folk, which means mother. *Sapota* very early turned into *supporter*: by 1740 we find 'Mamme Suppotta' in print, and the present folk interpretation still bears this out: the fruit, one is told, supports the people.

There was another use: '*Mamme-Gum* the Negroe Doctors use for the Chigoes;' and today *Mammee bark*, considered poisonous, is used against lice in animals. But *sapodilla* was displaced by its synonym *naseberry*, or *neeseberry*, and today is applied to the tree as a timber tree, not to the fruits.

Other fruits named earlier in Jamaican sources than elsewhere are: *Alligator apple*, also called *cork wood*, *turtle apple*, and *cow apple*; *Barbados cherry* and *Barbados gooseberry*; *breadnut*, now pronounced generally by the folk /brénot/; *clammy-cherry*, formerly called the *turkey-berry-tree*; *cloven-berry*; *garlic pear-tree*; *Otaheite apple*; and many another.

Timber Trees

Jamaican timbers were sought after from early days, and many names were borrowed or invented in the island. Only the most notable can be mentioned.

Alligator wood — from its strong musky smell also called *musk wood* — was first noted by Sloane in 1696. Another tree well known for its odour was at first called simply *cedar*, later *Jamaica cedar*, but also *Barbados, Honduras, Spanish,* or *West Indian cedar.* One Westmoreland variety is identified from the town as *Bluefields cedar*, sometimes pronounced /brúfil/.

Then there is *bascedar* or *bass cedar*, which the dictionaries have missed though it has been in print for over a century. The first element of this name probably represents *bast* (as it does in American *basswood*) in reference to the use of the inner bark in making rope. It is not the same as *bastard cedar*, though that name is also a Jamaicanism.

Cockroach wood or *chink-wood* is so called because of its 'rank smell'; and the *locust* tree, from the shape and odour of its pods, has gained the eloquent nickname of *stinking-toe.* This locust is not to be confused with the *locus* or *locus-berry* (also *lotus tree* and *locust-berry*), which is quite a different tree. Some call it *hog-berry* too.

The West Indian *birch* tree is interesting for what has become of the pronunciation and for the great variety of its names. Among the folk, it has followed the same track as *word, bird,* and so on, becoming /boch/; this has further changed to /boj/, and then has been combined into *budge-wood, budge-gum,* and *budgy-gum.* As the last names suggest, it is resinous; the resin is considered of medicinal value, wherefore the other (now obsolete) names *balsam-tree, turpentine tree,* and *incense tree.* Its smooth, coppery, peeled appearance has led to the further names *red birch* and *mulatto wood* or *malatta tree.*[19]

Another tree noted for its medicinal gum was first called *hog-doctor* or *boar-tree*, but also *hog gum* and *boar-gum, boar-wood* or *doctor-wood,* and *cho-cho-wood.* From 1740 comes the following explanation of the name:

> The *Hog-Gum*, when it first comes from the Tree, is as yellow as Bees Wax, but it changes its Colour. They use it in green Wounds. . . . The Virtues of it were first discover'd by the

wild Hogs, who roll'd themselves in it when wounded until they were cured.

The name has apparently been transferred to other genera.

Jamaica cannot lay claim to the first use of *lignum vitae*, yet this island was an early, important source of the tree and of its gum (Guiacum), and the name has gone through an interesting local development. We find 'Lignum-vit-Trees' and 'Lignum vitee' in the seventeenth century; today, after the substitution of several sounds, the folk pronunciation is /nìngkambáiti/! A former name, which seems to have lasted longer in Jamaica than elsewhere was *pockwood*. It is explained by Long: 'The gum is . . . in demand for its virtues in venereal taints.'

A number of trees are named from the use made of the wood. *Torch-wood* has had two distinct applications. Sloane called one kind 'Dildoe-Tree the Lesser, or Torch-Wood' and reported it was used by the Indians in fishing at night for mullet. This is elsewhere called *torch-cactus*. The second *torchwood* — also widely known as *candlewood* — includes different sorts of *Amyris* and similar plants. *Candlewood* was first recorded in Jamaica; in the folk speech it is /kantu/, which Russell listed as African — quite correctly, since Twi *ɔ-kãntõ* means candlewood. From its pleasant-smelling resin it is sometimes *rose-wood*; from its easy burning, *lightwood*; from the effect of the resin on woodcutters, *burn-eye* or *blind-eye*; and for unknown reasons *beyaca* (pronounced /bíiaka, béyaka, béyuka/). This word has not been traced. One more name that may belong to this group is *crablight*, presumably meaning the wood used for a torch when hunting crabs, but it appears only once without identification. (On the other hand it may be the same as *crabwood*.)

Yokewood is well known in Jamaica,; this is simply *oakwood*, with *y-* prefixed as in *yeyes* for eyes and *years* for ears. In St Thomas this tree is identified with the *mastwood* of Portland. *Spanish oak* is also known as *mastwood* — in other words, the usage overlaps and is probably confused. The third tree is certainly not fit to make the mast of even a small boat, though the first may be. Perhaps the trees have been associated because the flowers are somewhat alike.

Live fence-posts are greatly favoured in Jamaica and a considerable number of trees are used for them — in fact, the general terms have almost displaced some individual ones.

Grow-stake, growing-stake, grow-stick, growing-stick, quick-stick and *grow-quick* include several different trees, but especially *Gliricidia sepium* and *Erythrina velutina,* and it is the specific names of these two that the general names most often replace. Specific names of the first are *maranga* or *marang, St Vincent, Moses-weed*; specific names of the second are *mortelle, never-dead* or *never-die, Spanish machete,* and *sword-rose* or *sword-tree.* Both these plants burst into flower before the leaves appear, which explains such names as *Moses-weed, mortelle* (a lopped form of French *immortelle*), *never-dead* and *never-die*; but whether these are translations or renamings one can only guess. The flower of the latter is scarlet and shaped like a diminutive 'open guard' machete, wherefore the last three names.

As to *maranga* and *marang,* they seem to come from *moringa,* a tree with some similar characteristics. In 1814 Lunan wrote, 'Being of quick growth, this pretty little tree is frequently planted in Jamaica for fences and along garden walks, and is generally known by the name of *moringa.*' *St Vincent* is no doubt associated with the Caribbean island of that name, presumably as the place of origin.

Many trees are named for the nature of their wood, its colour, appearance, or some other striking characteristic. Among these are *beefwood* or *herring-wood,* which the folk think of as male and female varieties of the same tree. Actually they are different species. The 'male' (*Pisonia fragrans*) is *man beefwood* or *cock herring-wood* because it is harder or coarser than the 'female' (*Pisonia obtusata*), which is *woman beefwood, loblolly beefwood,* or *lob-lob beefwood.* 'Loblolly' in fact (a soft porridge or pap that once was staple sailors' fare and was also served to slaves on the plantations) has come to be applied to several soft woods. Browne listed *loblolly-wood* in 1756, remarking that it was 'soft and useless, from whence its name'; also 'Loblolly Whitewood, or white Sweetwood'. *Lobby-lobby, laba-laba,* or *lab-lab sweetwood* apparently are folk variants of loblolly (but *lobby-lobby* is also identified with the *jackass-ears tree,* which has, on the contrary, a hard timber good for logs).

Though the cogs of sugar mills are no longer made of *cogwood,* and though the word did not originate in Jamaica, it is by no means obsolete here. A well-known tree, it goes also by the names *greenheart* and (from its hardness) *break-ax,* 'pronounced

2A

/brókàks/. The latter is probably translated from some African name; in Hausa, for example, some hardwood trees are called *kariye gatari*, which means precisely this.[20] In St Catherine and St Ann *break-ax* is also applied to the tree known as *puss-head* in St Thomas (from the appearance of the fruit) and *comb-wood* in Trelawny and Manchester.

Prickly-yellow is not originally Jamaican: Ligon reported it first from Barbados. Nevertheless it appeared in early use here and has undergone some interesting changes. *Prickly yalla* is very common, and there is *prickelalla*; folk-etymology has further altered it to *pretty-yellow* or *prettyalla*. An old name for this tree was *Hercules* or *Yellow-hercules* — chiefly used by botanists.

Another hardwood that has many types is the *bully-tree*, as it was called at first, now *bullet tree*. This too was first recorded in Barbados: Ligon explained *bully* as referring to the fruit, which is 'like a Bullace'. Barham elaborated: 'This is so called by the Jamaicans, for its fruit, when ripe, is as black as a bully or damson, but in shape of a Lucca olive.' Whether the *t* of *tree* was captured by the preceding word, or by some other cause, the form *bullet* had already developed by 1740, and by 1774 we find Long explaining, 'the window shutters are of bullet-tree-wood (so called, because an inch board of it is bullet-proof).' And Titford, somewhat later, writing of the mammee-sapota:

> A variety of this, called the Bully-tree, grows very tall, and is the hardest timber in Jamaica: from its straight, thick trunk, it is best fitted for main rollers of sugar mills, and a single trunk, for that purpose, fifteen inches diameter, delivered at the mill is worth fifty pounds and upwards.

In short, folk-etymology is responsible for the metamorphosis of *bully* to *bullet*.

In the countryside different species are called *cherry* or *red*, *black*, *white*, and *neeseberry bullet*. The *red-and-white bullet* of St Ann is *redgut* in St Elizabeth and Trelawny. There is *San Domingo bullet* too, or *Bob Cook*, which is 'near to galimeta'. The OED has *galimeta* only from 1756, but Long also referred to the use of its bark for medicine, and it is well known today as /gyalimenta/, with an intrusive *n*, perhaps on the analogy of 'primenta'.

The first appearance of *fiddlewood* is Jamaican (1696): Sloane found the tree in the fields near 'St Jago' and described it. Much later Lunan wrote that 'From its durable quality the French

gave it the name of *fidelle* [faithful] wood, which we have corrupted to fiddle'. This is pure romance, either invented by
Lunan or accepted uncritically from some amateur etymologist;
for there is no such name as *bois fidèle* in French — indeed, this
tree is known in that language as *bois côtelet*. The genus name
Citharexylon means in Greek *cithara wood*, and in Cuba and Porto
Rico it is called *palo guitarra*. If Lunan had consulted Sloane he
would have found the correct explanation: the wood was used
for making 'citharae & pandurae'.

As to the different kinds, Barham mentioned *white fiddlewood*;
Browne listed *black-heart, green-heart,* and *long-spiked fiddlewood*;
Titford added *oval-leaved fiddlewood*; and there is also *yellow fiddlewood*. One variety is named *old-woman's bitter*, in allusion to its
medicinal use.

Another tree named and valued for the colour of the wood is
gold-spoon or *golden-spoon*, though the identification varies. It is
said to be the same as *Bluefields cedar* in St Elizabeth, and *May-
day mahogany* in St Ann.

Glasswood is brittle: chips fly off it like glass when it is cut. It is
said to be the same as *drumwood*, but this term is applied to other
trees too, one of which is *parrotwood*. These latter two refer to the
softness and hollowness of the trees, in which parrots make holes
and nest. *Grazy-wood* gets its name for a similar reason: because
the grazy or Indian cony frequently lives in the hollows.

Coby-wood is the Jamaican version of the *caoba* (earlier, *caobana*)
of Central America and the other Greater Antilles, an Island-
Arawak word. In the Spanish settlements it is applied to several
different trees, and in Jamaica also to several, but chiefly to
Matayba apetala. Other forms of the name are *cob-Anancy* and
cobynancy, which probably preserve the earlier Spanish form. It
is also called *bastard mahogany, Cromanty* or *Cromanty bullet, wanika,*
and *pampandam*. The first recalls one of its Spanish names, the
second and third the African tribe; Wanika is from a personal
name evidently implying toughness; the last is unexplained.[21]

Another untraced name is *yacca*, used in Jamaica for over a
century to refer to various species of *Podocarpus*. (This genus name
has recently been abbreviated, at least among foresters, to *podo*.)
And there is *oda* or *woda*, attested in various parts of the island,
though the word has not been found in print. All agree that it is
good to make wattles, since it splits easily and is pliable.

The *Santa Maria* tree was one of those early noticed, and it is still well known. In Cuba and Puerto Rico it is *Palo Maria*. An account of 1740 stated, 'There is also a tree call'd Sancta Maria, or bastard Mammee; . . . The *Spaniards* pull off their hats whenever they see the Tree.' And Long explained further:

> The Spaniards, when it is just gathered, put it into cases made of the hollow joints of the Trumpet Tree, and call it the *admirable balsam*; but it is for some extraordinary virtues discovered in it, that they have honoured the tree with a consecration to the Virgin Mary, and christened it after her name.

Today the folk pronounce it /sàntamaráia/, but often abbreviate it to *santa*, and 'there's *red santa* and *white santa*'.

Ramoon is from 1740: 'The Ramoon Tree Leaves are Food for their Horses, and fattens them.' And from 1826: 'In cases of drought, the cattle are fed with the leaves of the bread-nut tree and the ramoon, as well as with those of the bascedar.'[22] The word is borrowed from Spanish *Ramón*, used in Cuba and Porto Rico, but is now pronounced by the Jamaican folk /ráamúun/. Other names which have undergone striking alterations on the lips of the folk include *Spanish Elm*: /pànchalám, pànchálan, pànchaláng/ and *Spanish Oak*: /panchúok/. The reduction of *sp* to *p* is regular here; what happens to 'elm' however is more generally colonial — compare the 'ellum' of American dialects, where the combination *lm* also proves difficult to say and is eased by the insertion of an epenthetic vowel between. *Spanish elm* was an early Jamaicanism; the tree was once also called *princewood*. *Spanish oak* is newer, and is not in the dictionaries.[23]

The *trumpet tree* has been known from early days, and probably derives through Spanish: one of its names in Central America is *trompeta*, a reference, no doubt, to its long hollow stems, often used to make flutes and similar instruments. Sloane was first to record this name, which is still the general one, though *snakewood* (unexplained) also has some currency.

The tree now known as *lace-bark* apparently acquired this name in Jamaica. It had been *lagetto* earlier, a Spanish name Englished here in this and other forms. As Sloane wrote in 1725,

> *Lageto* . . . What is most strange in this Tree is, that the inward Bark is made up of about twelve Coats, Layers, or

Tunicles, appearing white and solid, which if cut off for some Length, cleared of its outward Cuticula, or Bark, and extended by the Fingers, the Filaments or Threads thereof . . . form a Web not unlike Gause, Lace, or thin Muslin.

Here is an anticipation (and an explanation) of the later name. An occasional variant of *lace-bark* is *white-bark*.

The *bitter damson,* by a simple substitution of *l* for *n*, has become *bitter damsel* today among the folk. But since *damsel* is not a folk word, it is not at all certain that the name of the tree carries any such suggestions as it would in Standard use. Other more or less folk-etymological forms that it takes are *bitter dandison, bitter dampas, bitter dan*; also *damsel berry, mountain damson,* and *stavewood,* the latter two hardly used by the folk.

If *damsel* is a mere phonetic accident, *maiden plum* had its name more honestly from its pretty appearance. Sloane was first to mention it: 'The Maiden Plumb-tree', and to refer to its red, sweetish fruit. But it was not long until the name produced a folklorish explanation: 'There is a Tree which they call the Maiden Plumb Tree, which has a beautiful Leaf, but never bears Fruit.' Lunan reported later that because *mountain pride,* when not in flower, is so much like it, it also is called *maiden plum.* Today it is used for live fence-posts, and children eat the fruits.

The *woman's tongue* tree has its name from the large, flat beans which rattle in the wind; similarly the *woman-mouth* fern: 'when it burn, it pop.' *Spathodia campanulata* is an example of a tree which is now spreading rapidly and acquiring local names as it goes. One of these, heard in Manchester, is *water-man,* 'because it draws up much water from the earth.' The inner parts of the flowers gather water too; children pick them and squirt the water at each other.

Palms

Several palm trees have characteristically Jamaican names. *Macaw* has already been discussed as the source of *macca*; the common name today for both tree and fruit is *macca-fat,* implying that it was once a source of oil. As Long wrote, the 'Great Macaw Tree . . . yields . . . palm oil'. Dancer was the first to use the present form: 'Mackaw Fat or Oil of the Guiney Palm', though he identified the tree as 'Elais Guiniensis'. A little later Titford wrote, 'Macaw Palm, *Cocos butyracea* . . . an oil or butter prepared from it is in constant use among the Indians in their food . . . The Great Macaw Tree, *C. Aculeata.*' Today the macca-fat palm is identified as *Acrocomia* species, whereas *Elais guineensis* is called by its African name, *abbays* (or *abbeys*), pronounced /abe/ or /habe/. The first record of this name is from 1811:

> Abbays . . . The fruit of a species of palm, called oily palm, . . . They have a fibrous, yellow, oily pulp over the stone, and when boiled are pleasant and wholesome.[24]

A smaller but very spiny palm, apparently peculiar to Jamaica, is the *prickly pole*, first mentioned in 1696, and described in 1740: 'The *Prickly-Pole* bears a pleasant Fruit or hard Berry, which they roast, tho' it is not so big as a Hazel Nut.' As late as 1828 it was a subject of legislation: 'No fence of penguins or prickly poles shall be made . . . within the said city.'

Almost without exception, and from early days, writers have noticed the various kinds of cabbage palms (with some confusions). The general name refers, of course, to the fact that the heart leaves were often cut out and eaten. Our first citation has the single word: 'Of Limon, Orange, Coco, Cabage, Palmeeto . . . there are great plenty.' This is a reference to Santo Domingo, but the same was true of Jamaica, as Hickeringill witnessed six years later: 'All sorts of fruit-bearing Trees, as Orange-trees, a sort of Cabbage trees, rag'd with berries, &c.'

This tree is the *Roystonea*, known today by the folk as *cabbage* or *wild cabbage, cabbage-skin, mountain cabbage, mountain palm*, and *bunka, banga*, or *bangra*.[25] The last, with its varied forms, is puzzling, but is probably to be connected with *bonga* or *bunga*, which means in the Tagalog language of the Philippines the Areca palm and its fruit. This word had been adopted into Spanish by 1609, and was then presumably applied to similar trees in Spanish America. The sheaths of the cabbage palm branches are flattened and used as mats in Jamaica under the name of *buba mat, buba kin* (skin), or *buna kin*, the first word evidently designating the tree. Children also use these sheaths as sleighs, sitting in them and sliding down steep hills. Here also should be mentioned the name *kanda*, loosely applied to the thatch palm, to palm boughs, and to the cabbage-skin or buba mat; though it has not been traced, it is probably a reminiscence of some African form.

The cabbage palm is sometimes confused with the *cabbage-bark tree*, which is not a palm at all. It has long been used as a medicine against worms (therefore also known as the *worm-bark* tree), a valuable one in slavery days. Thomson wrote of it:

> There is a prevalent but erroneous idea, that there are two kinds of cabbage bark, red and white, and that the latter is poisonous: the difference which certainly does exist arises merely from the local situation of the tree: This is well known to carpenters.

This tree was known earliest as *angelyn-tree* (from Portuguese *angelim*), but this did not gain much acceptance in Jamaica. No more did another early name which only Lunan recorded: 'This tree ... is called sometimes the *bilge-water tree*, from its disagreeable smell.' Today it is *cabbage-bark*, *cabbage-wood*, *bastard cabbage*, or *wormwood tree* and is still valued as an anthelmintic. There are even some superstitious beliefs connected with its gathering: wood from the east side of the tree is considered best, 'where the morning sun strikes it;' or 'when moon is full, peel bark and give children for worms'; or 'chip the side that turn to the sun during full moon'.

Palms used for thatch are so numerous in Jamaica that the word *thatch* has almost become synonymous with both tree and leaf, the latter used widely to weave baskets, hats, and other articles. Two main kinds are distinguished according to the shape of the leaf: *long thatch*, which is feather shaped, and *round thatch*, which is fan shaped. *Long-thatch* is used to roof native houses, the edge being plaited for greater neatness. One kind of *round-thatch* is also called *fan-thatch* or *fan-broom* (brooms are made from it); it has small leaves and no trunk, and the heart leaves are used to make jippi-jappa hats. *Broad*, *bull-head* or *bull thatch* has much larger leaves. *Short thatch* is the name of various others, apparently equivalent to round thatch (but whether the leaf or the trunk is short is uncertain). Finally there is *silver thatch*, from which comes *silver straw*.

Cactuses, Agaves, etc.

The first cactus that should be mentioned is the *dildo*, a name apparently used in Jamaica as early as anywhere else (perhaps earliest) and still in current use, though the last OED citation is from 1756 — two hundred years ago. Sloane listed both 'The larger Dildo tree' with red fruit and 'Dildo Tree the lesser or Torchwood' with yellow fruit. Both kinds are still distinguished. Barham seemed to consider the name peculiarly Jamaican: 'Some merry person gave it the name of dildo; but in other places it is called flambeau, torchwood, or prickle-candle, it being in the shape of four candles joined together.'

The other widely known cactus is *tuna*: 'Toona or Cochineal Plant. The natives esteem this most highly' — so Sullivan wrote in 1893, and it is still true. Tuna is said to be 'good for inflammation, wash hair, tie on forehead for headache'. *Cochineal* cactus is now regularly pronounced by the folk /kànchaniíl/ with an intrusive *n*, and still identified with tuna. But as one countryman said, though 'some say conchaneal, the usual name is *swipple-pole*' — that is, slippery-pole — which refers to the soapy juice that makes it useful for washing hair. One kind of tuna with large prickles is called /plímpla/ — the *pimploe* of Barbados. *Tuna* comes through American Spanish from the Taino language; *plimploe* has travelled a much rougher road: the first *l* is intrusive, probably by assimilation to the second; *pimploe* in turn is a reduced form of *pin-pillow*, an old name for a pincushion, which the spiny leaves of this cactus were thought to resemble.

The *Melocactus communis*, often called *Pope's head*, and by translation of the botanical name *melon thistle*, was earlier the *Turk's-head* or *Turks' cap* in Jamaica, though *Pope-head* appears to be the folk form today. Two other names have been reported: *cow-ears* (which, from the shape, would suit tuna excellently, but hardly suits this at all), and *roast pork* (which does not seem particularly apt either).

A number of climbing cactuses are treated below with vines or withes, since the folk think of them together. Here we may mention *Jerusalem candlestick*, which has a prickly pentagonal or round green stem, 'like fingers scattered all over the tree.' (This should not be confused with *Jerusalem thorn*, known in Jamaica since at least 1756.)

Other plants with prickly leaves include the agaves, aloes, yuccas, and such. Best known is the *curratow* or *curato*, variously pronounced and spelt.[26] This word comes through French *carata* from American Spanish *caraguata*, and ultimately from Guaraní. Though not entered in the historical dictionaries it has had a long history in Jamaica. Sloane first listed it as *Curaca*; a spelling which suggests mistaken associations with Curaçao, evidently shared by Browne: 'AGAVE I . . . Coratoe, or Curaça. There are but few plants more common than this in Jamaica.' Yet in 1740 the following had appeared:

> The *Corito* bears a thick Leaf about five Foot long; they use it after it is beaten to a Mash to scower their Pewter with. The Negroes are very careful how the juice falls upon them, for where it touches the Skin it raises Blisters.

Barham spelt it *currato* and guessed the source: 'I take this name to be a corruption of *caragua*, for so it is called in Brazil.' Gosse spelt *keratto*, and Thomson used it attributively: *coratoe-juice*.

Beside many medicinal and domestic uses, the whole plant also serves for live fence, the leaves for thread, rope, and whips, and the long stalk to kindle fire. A man from Bull Savanna remarked: '*Carito* is the correct name, but we call it *maypole*;' and so it is also in the Kingston area. Though this name is not attested in print till recently it must have existed from the seventeenth century, for Barham wrote, 'The top of it, in May, is garnished with fine yellow flowers for three feet down: The people in Jamaica gather them for May-poles.' Nowadays they also serve as Christmas trees.

Best known of the aloes is Sempervivum, which, however, has generally had the form *sempervive* here, as when first recorded by Sloane. Sullivan's spelling, *semprevivy*, represented the educated pronunciation very well. Among the folk this has undergone most surprising metamorphoses through phonetic change and folk-etymology: /singkl-baibl, singgl-baibl, sintl-baibl/, and so on. The element 'bible' may be due to some association with healing, since the plant is highly thought of for medicine.

Superficially similar to these, though really kin to the pineapple, is the *pinguin*, pronounced by the folk /pingwing/, and until recently often spelt *penguin*. The source is unknown — possibly some American Indian word, or there may be a connection with American Spanish *piño*, pineapple. (One dictionary suggests as the source Latin *pinguis*, fat; but as this plant has neither oily properties nor fleshy leaves, the suggestion is doubtful.) Its most notable use was as a live fence: 'penguin-fence', or 'penguin hedges'; and one author writes of 'a double ditch, penguined over'.

For the related plants that grow on the branches of trees, the general term is *wild pine*, which dates from at least 1696. *Tree-pine* too is occasionally heard, and sometimes *toad-trash*, because these epiphytes hold water in the curve of their leaves, in which tree frogs live.

Sansevieria has acquired the local names *lion tongue* or *dog tongue*, and *donkey-ears*.

Ferns

Not many ferns have acquired specific folk names; in general they are merely 'ferm' — a recently developed pronunciation, judging by the presence of *r*. Older pronunciations either lack the *r* — as /fyaan/ — or retain it as Standard English does between vowels — /fiirin/. And there is the curious form /féril/ with *l* substituted for the final *n*.

Markin' fern is any kind which has coloured spores under the leaf, that will mark one's skin if pressed or slapped upon it: *silver* or *white-back fern*, and *gold fern*. Others are distinguished by the stem, as *white-stick fern*. The larger ones, especially tree ferns, are associated with palms through the word *thatch*, as *black-thatch*, 'common name for the tallest and stateliest of the tree ferns'; *crab-thatch*, which grows in low swampy grounds and shelters the crabs, and *nanny-thatch*, presumably associated with goats. Similarly there are *hog-grass*, a fern which grows very thickly and in which wild hogs hide, and *mongoose fern*.

Macca or *prickly fern* is probably the same as black-thatch. *Hard fern* is applied differently in the Blue Mountains and Tre-lawny. *Tiger fern* has a striped look, and *fish-tail fern* has a divided tip. *Cow-tongue fern* has a single, flat frond with a rough back. *Woman-mouth fern* has already been mentioned. One countryman referred to the common fern as *lace plant*, but this name is also used for *wild thyme*. In early days the tree fern was called *fern-tree*, a term which appears to have been first employed in Jamaica.[27]

Grasses

Names for grasses have been applied rather confusedly to species that are superficially alike; there has been much misidentification. One may mention first the *Bahama grass*, a term in use in Jamaica before 1808 when Stewart described it as 'a plant which spreads rapidly, and forms a smooth and beautiful sward'. It is pronounced /bahéima/ by many educated Jamaicans; the folk drop the *h* and say /bíema/. In the names of plants we find that Barbados, Bahamas, and Bermuda are often confused; accordingly this is sometimes called *Bermuda grass*.

Guinea grass appears to have entered the language here: its first occurrence is in a Jamaican source. *Scotch grass* was here long before: Sloane saw it growing at 'Wague water' before 1696, and explained the name as referring to a part of the island of Barbados, called Scotland, whence it was brought. Though some call this *Dutch grass* today, the names were certainly not synonymous to Sloane, who described *Scotch grass* as 'Gramen paniceum maximum, spica divisa, aristio armatum', and *Dutch grass* as 'Gramen dactylon procumbens crassum & viridius culmo reclinato'. In addition to the present confusion of the names, *Dutch* is sometimes altered to *dutchess grass*. *Pard grass* (in the folk pronunciation /pára/) is identified with both of these.

Browne mentioned *savanna grass* in 1756 without identification, the first record of this name. It is now applied to *Panicum molle*, which some call *Dutch grass* too. The folk pronunciation is /subána/, which may therefore not represent *savanna* but the Cuban *súrbana*, a wild grass. *Common-grass* — which grows on the commons — is yet another name for the same or a similar type.

Lemon grass was first recorded in 1801:

This plant (Genus unknown, as I have never seen it in flower) was introduced only three or four years ago, but is now common in the gardens. It makes a grateful Infusion like Baume.[28]

It is the same as *fever grass*, a Jamaican name: 'Fever grass is a fragrant smelling lemony grass; it is excellent in fever just boiled and sweetened.'

A number of grasses bear proper names: *Seymour, Napier, Wynne* (the same as *John*), and *John Taylor* grass, all supposed to be for the men who introduced them. Only *Napier grass* seems to be known outside Jamaica, but I have not discovered who Mr Napier was; the first honours Sir George Seymour-Seymour;

Mr Wynne is said to have been a former owner of Brokenhurst estate in Manchester; John Shekell is said to have introduced the same plant to Chester Vale in the Blue Mountains, where it is therefore *John grass*. Mr Taylor is unidentified.

Other local names include *piano grass* (said on good authority to have been accidentally introduced as the packing material of a piano; when thrown away, it took root and has spread widely)[29] *pimento grass* (because it grows freely in pimento walks); *burr* or *prickle grass*; *cutting grass* (from the sharp, saw-toothed edge); *fowl-toe grass* (because the blossom looks like a chicken's foot); *moth grass* (the same as *cus-cus* grass, because the aromatic roots are 'put in tin-case' to 'keep moth from cutting clothes'); *sour grass*; *corn grass* (from its resemblance to the leaf of maize); and *white-head, lily*, or *star grass* (because the blades each have a white bar across the green, and they ray out from a central stem). Some plants are also called 'grass' though they are not: *skellion grass* (some kind of wild Allium), *water grass* (*Commelina*) and the fern mentioned above as *hog-grass*.

Vines

The general word for trailing or climbing plants in Jamaica is not *vines* but the old one *withes*, pronounced /wis/ among the folk and often spelt *wiss*; the collective form is *wiss-wiss*. These are very numerous and include all kinds of plants; they are useful in so many ways — for tying bundles, building, basketry, as fodder, and so on — that they have acquired a large array of local names.

One that has long been in use to feed pigs is *hogmeat*, recorded in 1756 and still the most common term. But there are several alternatives: *wild potato-slip, hog-slip, wild-slip, hog-string* (apparently a modernisation of the older *hogmeat ti-tie*), *hog-banna*, and *wild potato*. *Slip* and *potato* refer to large tuberous roots that these vines have; *banna* seems to be from 'banna-bis' (see Bonavist above) and to mean 'vine'. Barham mentioned too, without identifying them, 'what we call hog or red-pop in Jamaica' — in which case 'pop' refers to the blossoms that pop open (as in other names). On the other hand, certain plants are called *poison hogmeat*, and if this was one, 'pop' might have meant 'burst' — compare *horse-burst*, the name of another poisonous plant.[30]

Sloane also mentioned *hogweed*, which continued in the lists for species of *Boerhaavia* as late as 1811, when Titford identified it with *hogmeat*. *Hogweed* now appears to have died out.

A smaller Ipomea is that called /núoyu/, /núoyo/, or /yúoyo/. It has a leaf 'like sorasee, all in points', and the 'ripe pods burst like akee'. The source is French *noyeau*, though this does not represent the pronunciation nearly as well as Asprey and Thornton's *know-you*.

A most decorative vine is that which was called, at first, *red-bead vine* and *wild liquorice*, alluding to the scarlet seeds which the dried pods display, and the odour of the leaves. The former name has not survived, though Lady Nugent knew both: 'In the hedges we saw clusters of the red (Liquorice) beads, sold in the jewellers' shops in England.' They are still called /likrish/, however. The black spot on the red seed looks like an eye and suggests the colours of the johncrow, which accounts for the currently more common names *johncrow bead*, *johncrow eye*, and *crab-eye*. This vine must not be confused with the bush, also smelling of licorice, called 'Wild Liquorice or Sweet-weed', 'Liquorish-weed', *sweet broom-weed*, *sweet-broom*, and *fine-leaf sweetweed*; nor with the trees that produce scarlet seeds without black spots. Of the best known of these Lunan wrote, 'In Jamaica, where it has been pretty generally cultivated, . . . it has been called *Circassian pea-tree*, from the beauty of the pea, of which necklaces are made.' This has also been called the *Lady Coote bean*, after the wife of Sir Eyre Coote, who was Lieutenant-Governor of Jamaica from 1806-8. Today it is known to the folk as *red-bead tree* or *johncrow bead*. Another *red-bead tree* is the *Sophora monospermum*, a native of Jamaica, whose seed does have a black spot.

Returning to 'wiss', we find another named with the word 'johncrow' but this time for no clear reason: *johncrow packer* (it is used to tie bundles of firewood), which is probably the same as *johncrow weed* and *guaco-* or *quaco-bush*. Though botanical sources have *guaco-*, (from Spanish *guaco*, ultimately a Carib word), this name element is quite as often pronounced /kwaako/ by the folk; perhaps they connect it with the personal name Quaco.

The *supple-jack*, as Barham wrote, 'is a withe so called, which is full of round knobs at every five or six inches distance' — which explains why the word became a synonym for a cane or

whip. It is now pronounced by the folk /subljak/ or /sobljak/.
Though it is a 'hard-nature wiss' that makes good walking-
sticks, if you 'roast it in fire, mek it more swipple'. When young
it is called *Toby-wiss* and is used to 'tie beast, tie up bundle of
wood'. The last name is unexplained.

One kind of Clematis is known as *pudding-withe* (folk pronunciation: /pudnwis/). In England the corresponding plant
was 'traveller's joy, honesty, or virgin's bower', but it early
acquired a Jamaican name. Barham wrote, 'We never make any
use of it but to tie rails with, and it is commonly called pudding-
withe, being soft and pappy whilst green.'

There is another *pudd'n wiss*, however, with a great many
local names: it is also *soldier wiss*, *snake wiss* (from the way it runs
along walls), *snake bush*, *Mary wiss*, *Mary bush*, *wall-saddle*, *saddle
weed* (it 'rides the wall'), *scratch wiss*, *yaws bush* (it is used against
skin diseases and others), and it has also been reported as *wild
yam*.

Snake wiss is applied sometimes to yet another plant, a small
climbing cactus that is nearly round in cross-section, known too
as *green wiss*. Though the dictionaries and other sources fail to
note this, it would seem to have been the earliest application in
Jamaica. Sloane (1696) has 'Green With', which he describes as
a slender, round, climbing cereus, saturated with a succulent
green juice. Again (1707) he tells of a woman who 'went into
the Country after she had lost the use of her Limbs. She re-
covered them in some measure, by degrees, with the help of the
Green With, and some Salves, and came to her perfect Health'.
Barham also knew this application of the term, and it is still so
called and used medicinally: 'bake it, 'queeze out water, mix
with rum, and rub on for pain.' (*Green withe* was identified as a
kind of vanilla later.)[31]

This round cactus shares two names with a similar but triangular climbing cactus: both are called *dindi okro* or *wall okro*;
only the triangular is *sipple okro*. 'Okro' refers to the mucilaginous juice, as does 'sipple'; 'dindi' (probably a form of *jumby*)
suggests a miraculous quality — as in the *god*-names below. The
triangular cactus was first called by Sloane 'Prickly With', and
Barham added, 'which some call prickly pear withe. In the
centre of the green succulent part there is a strong wire withe,
which planters use, and is very lasting.' The 'wire withe' is now

known as *puss-gut*. Yet another name is *god-okro* which refers to the plant's way of growing up in trees, apparently without touching the earth, which seems miraculous — compare *god-bush* (mistletoe) and *god-tree* (wild fig), which do the same. *God-bush*, 'as the negroes call it,' goes back at least to 1851, and is current still; *god-tree* goes back to 1756 but appears to be out of use today.[32]

Because of the unusual shape of the leaf, various similar passion-flower vines are known to the folk as *bat-bush*, *bat-wing*, *goat-foot wiss*, *duck-foot wiss*; because of their fruit, which looks edible but is not, *duppy-punkin*; and from their climbing habit, *cassada rider*. Another, called *bull-hoof* or *bull-hough* in the books, is no longer so named; the names are now applied to trees (see below).

A famous vine with a bean pod often three feet or more long, and beans large enough to be used as money-purses, is the *cacoon*, formerly often called *cocoon*. So Sloane and Browne spelt it, but the folk pronunciation, /kàakúun/, is probably closer to the original form (as it so often is). Sloane's description includes, as the name of this plant in Malabar, 'Perim-kaku-valli', from the second element of which *cacoon* probably comes. In any case, any association with 'cocoons' is mistaken. A former name of this vine was *mafootoo withe*.[33] It is this that the Maroons used to disguise themselves when in ambush.

Another *cacoon* is the *antidote*, of which Sullivan has written, 'This is a bean, which can be procured at most "doctor shops" (chemists). It is scraped and put into a bottle. ... It is used after bites or stings of spiders, scorpions, wasps, centipedes ... rubbed well into the bitten place.' Browne was first to record it, as 'antidote cocoon', and it is widely known and valued today. This bean closely resembles the 'purse cacoon' though the plant is entirely different: it is the Brazilian *nhandiroba*, and Long has described it at length. Barham also noted that the Negroes called these beans *sabo*.[34]

A vine that has long furnished ribs for baskets is *basket wiss*. In the days when cane fields were manured by hand labour Browne wrote: 'The Basket-Withe ... is generally used for dung-baskets about the country.' (There is a proverb which recalls this too: Old basket no good fe nutt'n but fe ca dutty.) A variant today is *basket hook* (discussed below).

Very similar is *hoop wiss* or *cooper wiss*, on which coopers once depended: 'The Hoop Withe . . . The stalk is very tough and flexile, and often made into hoops, when there is a scarcity of those imported from Europe or North-America.' The most interesting thing is the transformation of *hoop* into *hook* among the folk. One finds *wild hook, hook wiss, cooper hook, hook vine,* and *basket hook* (already mentioned) — seldom *hoop*. Indeed, *hook* has almost become a generic term (like *banna*) meaning vine. The exchange of *k* and *t* is very common; here is a phonetically similar exchange of *k* and *p*.

A number of vines share the general term *coco-wiss* because of their large, arum-like leaves. These include *five-finger* and *seven-finger*, named for the way the leaves are divided, and *mile-walk*, which refers to the great distance the vine grows away from its roots. Coco-wiss is also called *wiss-maami* (withes' mother), but the reason is uncertain. From some of these tree-climbing vines long roots hang down, sometimes thirty or forty feet; these are called *wicker-wiss*: the roots are boiled, stripped, and used to make wicker furniture. *House-wiss* is used in tying thatch when a house is roofed.

One of the vines most sought after from earliest days for its medicinal value was 'China root', or 'China' as it was often called. In itself this is not a Jamaicanism, but Jamaican folk speakers preserve as their regular pronunciation the eighteenth-century form 'Chaney' (/chíeni/) in *chaney-wiss* and other names. In fact, today they identify this plant with coco-wiss, five-finger, seven-finger, and wicker-wiss. Dancer recorded as alternative names 'Bastard Sarsaparilla or Wild Yam', and it is said now that 'Chaney-root mos' like yam'. Other species of Smilax are *brial wiss* (which looks like an alteration of *briar*) and *blood wiss* (said to be the same as sarsaparilla).

The wild grape vine has been called *water-wiss* since the seventeenth century; Sloane listed 'Wild vine or Water-with', and later explained:

> This vine growing on dry Hills in the Woods where no Water is to be met with, its trunc if cut into two or three Yard long, Pieces, and held by either End to the Mouth, there issues out of it so plentifully, a limpid, innocent and refreshing Water or Sap as gives new life to the droughthy Traveller.

Browne also called it *Jamaica grape-vine* and Titford *Indian Vine*, but *water-wiss* is still the folk name and the use described by Sloane is well known.

Other withes are: *teeth wiss* (a remedy for toothache); *cow-gut wiss* (from its toughness); and a number for their colour: *black*, *white*, and *red wiss; milk wiss* (its white sap is made into a rubbery substance); *crab wiss* (unexplained); *velvet wiss* (from the texture of the back of the leaf). This has been more often called *velvet leaf*, its original name, and sometimes *white-back*.

There are many other vines whose names do not include *wiss*. Very well known is that called /sórasi/. As Barham wrote, 'Cerasee ... Is the name that negroes and some others give to a plant growing in great plenty in Jamaica.' And in another, quite independent early account: 'The Sourasea, or Ladies-slipper, grows on a small Wire, and has a small pale Blossom which bears a yellow Pod, which opens upon its being incloased in one's Hand, and has a Seed like a Melon Seed.' Lunan identi-fied two kinds: '*smooth-leaved* cerasee, or male balsam-apple', and 'the hairy cerasee'. Sullivan repeated this spelling and added 'or sorasee'. *Cerasee* (though the dictionaries have missed it) may now be considered the established spelling, yet it represents neither the actual pronunciation nor the source. Furthermore, its form implies a Latin origin, as if there were some connection with the cherry, or possibly with wax (*cerasus, cera*); but since it was from the beginning a word used by the Negroes one should look rather to some African source.[35] One other name for cerasee is *ganah*.

The *strainer* vine has been noticed since 1814, when Lunan wrote, 'This has been called the *strainer vine*, because the re-ticulated part of the fruit is sometimes separated from the pulpy, and made punch strainers of.' This is still the common name but it is also called *quash-quash* and *purril* (/poril/).

Though 'cowhage' and its folk-etymological form 'cow-itch' are not Jamaicanisms, the latter has had a vigourous existence in the island, entering into many combinations: *cowitch cherry*, *cowitch bush*, and so on. *Cowitch* refers both to the plant and to the fine, stinging hairs with which the pods are covered — and by extension to almost anything similarly irritating. In 1740 we find: 'The *Horse-ey'd Bean* has a rough Pod upon which the Cow-Itch grows; the Bean is round and black like a large Eye.' This is

2B

a closely related vine; its fruit is the 'Horse-eye Bean', sometimes called *donkey-eye*, and formerly *ox-eye*.

Bushes and Weeds

The folk names for bushes and weeds are very numerous and varied, with local usage frequently overlapping. We sort them here according to the characteristics on which the names are based: some are descriptive of colour, the shape of the leaf, or some other outward feature; some take note of a property, medicinal, poisonous, or the like; some show various other properties, and the uses to which they are put. We summarise these rapidly.

Names based on colour include: *red-head* and *white-head* (from the flowers); *white-back* (applied to several plants whose leaves are whitish underneath); *Joseph's coat* (several plants); *dragon-blood* or simply *dragon* (with conspicuous red leaves in a tuft at the top, which makes it useful to mark boundaries).[36] Those showing resemblance to animals include: *fowl-bone* (because the stalks look like chicken bones); *goat-foot potato* (from the shape of the leaves — the same as *seaside potato*); *cow-foot* or *cow-hough* (from the shape of the leaves); *johncrow nose-hole* or *johncrow blow-nose* (from its red holes, much like the nostrils of the turkey-vulture); *rat-ears* (from the shape of the leaf — it is also called *man-to-man, consumption weed, pepper-elder, ratta temper, silver bush,* and *shiny bush*, which are discussed elsewhere). Other resemblances are marked in *jockey-saddle*; *old man's beard* (first recorded in Jamaica, though now used elsewhere); and *stone-beard* (because it hangs from rocks).[37] Manner or habit of growth accounts for: *stand-'pon-rock* (another name for *water-grass*); *one-blow* (it 'blows' only one flower at a time); *shine-a'-night* (another name for *man-heart*); *look-up* (from the way it displays its leaves); *rattle-weed, shacka-bush* and *duppy peas* (from the noise of the dry pods in the wind); *duppy gun* (the tiny pods burst violently when moistened — or *trick-weed*, though earlier names were *spirit-leaf* or *spirit-weed*, and *menow-weed*, unexplained);[38] *devil's horse-whip, devil's riding-whip, devil's backbone, old-woman's razor,* or *hug-me-close* (from the sharp burrs on the flowering stalk — also *colic weed* for one of its medicinal uses).

The second group of names, based on healing or other properties, includes: *headache weed* ('rub it up and inhale for a fit' —

the same as *guinea-hen weed*); *headache bush* (at first called *headache weed*, though a different plant from that above); *mirasmy bush* (considered good for marasmus, a common complaint of Jamaican babies — also known by the descriptive names *rice bitters*, *seed-under-leaf*, *carry-me-seed*, referring to the grain-like balls that grow along the leaf stem); the former *yaw-weed* (more commonly called today *strong-back* — also *red gal*, *duppy poison*, and *yellow ginger*, which refers to the orange-coloured root). More recently, *yaw-weed* has been applied to another plant, and *strong-back* to at least four others. Sometimes the first is designated as *woman strong-back* to distinguish it from *man-back* (both supposed to strengthen the back).

Others named for ailments are: *smallpox bush*; *asthma bush*; and *bellyache bush*. The last refers to the 'dry bellyache', a disease of high mortality in early days. Sloane recorded in 1696 'Belly-ach weed', and Barham added another name: 'The plant is so called from curing the belly-ache or cholic with costiveness, which was first made known in Jamaica by Papaw negroes, and therefore commonly called Papaw weed; by this name I knew it.' The change from *weed* to *bush* is due to the folk preference for the latter. Other names for the same plant are *wild cassada* and *cassada marble*.

In addition there are: *fresh-cut* (which is put on fresh cuts); *stone-bruise* (good for bruises, fistulas, etc); *self-heal*; *all-heal*; *cure-for-all*; *heal-an'-draw* (which draws infection out — also called *white-back* and *kema weed*, an unexplained name); *man-heart* (good for the heart — also known as *button weed*, *mongoose grass* or *mongoose weed*, and *wild mint* — which, however, is used of other plants as well). Another herb supposedly good for the heart is *search-my-heart*, often pronounced /saach-mi-haat/ by the folk.

An interesting name is /simikantrak/ — *see-me-contract* as Beckwith renders it; and it has other variant forms including the bizarre *sinner-contract*. The plant is a well known vermifuge, also called *worm-weed*, *worm-grass*, and *stinkin'-weed*. Asprey and Thornton derive the name from Latin *semen contra*, but, as a folk term, it is unlikely to have come directly: more probably it passed through Spanish *semencontra*. Beckwith said it was 'Kromanti talk' — that is, a Maroon word, as it is today. Since the first Maroons were slaves of the Spaniards at the time of the English conquest, this may be one of the earliest Jamaicanisms.

Much valued against colds is *leaf-of-life* (also called *tree-of-life* though it is only a low shrub); so also is *man-to-man* (an obscure name). There are many stomachics: *bitter-weed* is both general and specific; and one finds both *old man* and *old woman bitter-bush*. *Nedge-weed* is a curious formation: the plant is used as a remedy when one's teeth are *on edge*.[39]

Castor oil is usually a product bought at the 'doctor shop' or chemist's. The plant which produces it goes more often by its old name *oil-nut* among the Jamaican peasantry. *Oil-nut tree* lasted longer in Jamaica than elsewhere, and so did its product, *nut-oil*. Russell indicated the folk pronunciation (/ail/) in 1868: 'Eil-nut, Oil nut, castor oil'. Another strong cathartic is fittingly called *pull-coat*, referring to its effect on the bowels.

Various poisonous plants have been alluded to from the earliest days of the colony. *Dumb-cane* (called *poison-cane* by Ligon in his History of Barbados) is not and hardly resembles a cane, yet the name has clung since at least 1679, when Trapham described it:

> There grows almost everywhere in moist and boggish places, a large and remarkable plant called generally the dumb Cane, and that not improperly. For it similates in its large and high joynted Stalk that of a Sugar Cane ... the leaf of this is much other than the flag of the Sugar Cane. . . . The Epithet of dumb is remarkably added thereto, for as much as who so toucheth it with his Tongue becomes dumb and unable to speak for two or three hours: But then without any prejudice the part returns to its former use and volubility.

Today it serves as a rat poison and as an 'antidote — put on poisonous cut'. A cultivated variety with speckled green leaves is called *lucky lily* or *money lily* because money planted at its roots is supposed to increase.

Even better known to early legend was the *manchineel* (a tree, not a bush; and the word is not a Jamaicanism) whose poisonous properties were highly exaggerated. Today this is locally called *swell-hand*, from the effect of the milky sap on the skin.

The present-day *cockroach poison* (also known as *cockroach berry, bush, macca*, and *weed*) is probably the same as Browne's 'Love Apple, and Cock-roch Apple. The plant is a native of Jamaica. . . . The smell of the apples is said to kill the Cockroches'.

One kind of 'nightshade' — or 'night-sage' as the folk frequently have it — is called impressively *Madam fate*. It is supposed to be 'poisonous certain times of year'; and according to
Beckwith it is used to induce indolence. Another name for it is
horse-burst or *horse-poison*, because of its violent effect on horses
that eat it. In Cuba and Puerto Rico it is called *revienta-caballo* —
that is, burst-horse; the Jamaican name is probably a translation.

The third large group includes names referring to any other
properties and uses of plants. Several are domestic, as, *chewstick*, earlier *chaw-stick*, of which Browne wrote, 'The Chaw-
stick . . . is generally kept to rub and clean the teeth, . . . [and]
is frequently used to ferment, and give a flavour to . . . cool
drinks.' Both these uses, and the name, are still current. *Broom-
weed* is applied to several similar plants; as Barham wrote, it 'is
so called by the negroes in Jamaica, . . . because they make a
broom with it, . . . but it hath no resemblance to the English
broom, being of the mallow kind'. *Porter-bush* 'makes draught
porter'; it is the same as *wild hops*, so called because of its flowers
(though it is a bush, not a vine). This name was reported by
Sloane in 1696 and is still current, yet it has been neglected by
the dictionaries.

Qualities in the plants are expressed in a number of names, as,
iron-weed, which is difficult to uproot. Some identify it with
packy-weed (or *packy-bush*), formerly *calabash broom*, others with
dog-tongue, so called from the shape of the leaf and the way it
hangs down. The latter seems to be the same as Lunan's *iron-
shrub*, which is thought to 'have iron' in it; when used as a tea-
bush, therefore, it 'mek strong back'. *Fasten-man-coat* (or *fasten-
'pon-coat*?) has burrs (its old-time name is *rocky-burr*) which stick
to one's clothes. *Fat-bush*, a large-leaved malvaceous shrub, has
'fat' in it — a mucilaginous juice.

Plants whose seeds are used in playing games are the two
kinds of *nicker*, now regularly pronounced /níkal/ by the folk,
with a substitution of *l* for *r*. Sloane mentioned both in 1696:
'The yellow Nickar Tree . . . The Ash-colour'd Nickar Tree';
and Barham wrote, 'There are two sorts of these trees which are
called nickers, the boys playing with the cone or fruit as they do
with marbles.' This use is still made of them; the yellow, being
rarer, are worth ten of the grey. 'Nicker' is of English origin,

simply meaning marble, but these seeds were once called /wári/, which is the name of an African game (Twi *ware*, Fanti *ɔware*) 'played with small balls or globules passed into the holes of an oblong draught-board or table'. Another former name for nickers was *Bezoar nuts*.

Supposedly supernatural or miraculous properties have produced some names: *god-okro* has already been mentioned; there is *god-bush* too, the mistletoe (or *twistletoe*, as one man called it) which never touches the earth, wherefore it is also *scorn-the-ground* (pronounced /kàanigróng/) or *scorn-the-earth*. *God-tree*, found in the books for the Indian fig, was apparently first used in Jamaica, where a small fig may grow over another tree until it entirely swallows it up. An early popular name for such a strangling plant was *Scotchman* or *Scotch attorney*: in *Tom Cringle's Log* it is 'a Scotchman hugging a Creole'; the OED defines it as 'a West Indian name for various species of *Clusia*'. The folk pronunciation today is /kachman/.

Another plant with a supposedly magical property is *spirit-weed* or *myal-weed*. These names refer to religious practices in which the myal-man used the plant to 'bring back to life' a celebrant whom he had previously 'killed' with a narcotic draught. This plant does indeed have a pungent aromatic odour, from which it is also called *fit-weed* or *fit-bush*, and *goat-root*; *snake-weed* and *snake-root* may also allude to cultist use.

Beckwith has reported the curious name *temper-bush* for a plant with a valuable property: 'If a man is angry with you, rub up "temper bush" (*Amyris*) and box him with it, and his mind will become friendly toward you.' It sounds like a dangerous cure!

One may mention here the sensitive Mimosa, which probably has more variant names than any other plant: *shame-lady*, *shame-ol'-lady*, *shame-brown-lady*, *shame-me-darlin*, *shame-me-dog*, *shamy-bush*, *shamy*, *shamer-weed*, *shamer-macca*, and perhaps most commonly *shamer*. It shuts its leaves together the moment it is touched — wherefore also *shut-weed* — but opens them again in a few minutes, wherefore *dead-an'-wake*; and because its prickles shackle one's feet, *sheckle-weed*. McKay has the evocative lines:

> De cowitch under which we hab fe 'toop,
> De shamar lyin' t'ick like pumpkin soup,
> Is killin' somet'ing for a naygur man.

A number of plant names show relations of various kinds to birds or animals: *fatten-barrow* (a kind of 'calalu' fed to pigs); *horse-bath* (pronounced /haas-baat/ — used to scrub horses), also known as *chigger-nit* or *chigger-nut* (because used to kill chiggers); and similarly *dog-flea-weed*.

The *turkey-blossom* was at first so called because, as Browne explained, 'This plant... is now very common about Kingston... The fowls are observed to feed much on the blossoms... when it grows wild, and [it] is thought to heighten the flavour, as well as to contribute to the fattening of them.' A little later Titford called it *turkey weed*, and wrote that it 'covers the road side from within about four miles from Kingston, where the negroes bring baskets to gather it when in flower, to feed turkies and other poultry, who are extremely fond of it. I do not recollect to have met with it in any other place'. These accounts explain one of the current names, *Kingston buttercup* (or *Kingston flower*); it grows all around the Kingston racecourse, wherefore it is *racecourse macca*; and a smaller, related species is *police macca*; possibly the burrs are thought of as punitive. *Turkey blossom* now appears to be out of use; so is another old name, *kill-buckra*, of which Chambre wrote, 'There is a plant resembling a daisy, which appears in great abundance after the rains, and the flower is yellow; the negroes call it "Kill Buckra", probably from sickness prevailing at that season.'

Guinea-hen weed, known since 1696, is said to be similarly named because these birds like it so much: Its harsh smell and taste give it uses in folk medicine as *headache weed* and *strong man's weed*. *Mongoose weed* (mentioned above) is yet another, but the reason for this name is unknown.

Ram-goat dashalong (or *ram-goat rational, rashicali, regular,* or *national*) refers in its first part to the strong odour of the plant. But the second part, whatever it may once have meant, is now much confused. *National* obviously echoes *rational* without understanding; *rashicali* looks like a fanciful derivative; *rational* and *regular* seem to have some meaning in common, perhaps referring to a presumed medicinal property: as Asprey and Thornton write, 'the leaves of this species, boiled to make tea, are a favourite beverage and cold remedy in all parts of Jamaica where the plant can be found.' *Dashalong*, however, by far the commonest of the qualifying words, is a puzzle. Is it a folk-etymology of *rational*? Or is it the original form and *rational* the alteration? And does the plant dash along the roadsides, as one countrywoman declared, or was this an explanation manufactured on the spot to avoid disappointing me? (Incidentally, this must not be confused with *ram-goat rose*, also called *brown man's fancy*, very commonly planted in gardens.)

The *johncrow bush* has some obscure association with the turkey-vulture; it was once also called *parrot weed* — perhaps these birds fed on the berries. Now its commonest name is *salandine* (i.e., wild Celandine; also pronounced /sàlindáin, sàlidáin/) — a good example of a European name preserved in archaic form and beginning to undergo alteration (loss of the first *n*).

The *glass-eye berry* is 'a Scrophularious shrub' on which the *glass-eye* bird feeds; and the *grass-quit plant* is similarly favoured by the *grass-quit* bird.[40]

One bush or small tree that grows fairly widely has a variety of names referring to its fruit: *hog-apple, pig's apple, duck-apple, monkey berry, jumby chocho*, the last implying that though it looks like a chocho it is not good to eat (as in the many *duppy* names — *duppy pumpkin, duppy soursop*, and so on); for *jumby* is a form of zombie. *Monkey* does not refer to actual animals eating the fruit (as hog, pig, and duck do), but suggests also that this is something like the proper plant but not really good — it imitates it in a ridiculous way as a monkey does a man (compare *monkey fiddle* and other monkey names).

A number of animal associations are found in the alternative names of the *susumba* bush. As Lunan wrote in 1814:

> There are two varieties, both very common in Jamaica, the berries about the size of small cherries, which are eaten by turkies, whence the name turkey berries, they are also known by the names *soushumber, cat-nail, Port-Morant tobacco*, and *macaw bush*. One of the varieties has a yellowish and the other a purplish stalk, and it is not easy otherwise to distinguish them.

Browne had recorded 'turkey berry' in 1756, but this term seems now to be obsolete — no doubt because there are no more wild turkeys. Dancer had 'cat-claw' in 1801: it refers to the sharp, recurved prickles which cover the bush. This is still in use: the two varieties are distinguished as 'cat-claw (with cut leaves) and *low cat-claw* (with smooth leaves)'. *Macaw bush* has become *macca bush*, or *cockspur macca*, but *macca bush* is now generalised too to mean any prickly plant. *Port Morant tobacco* was no doubt a local joke; it has not been found in other sources. The current jocular term is *gully beans* because the bushes grow wild and the berries are used to season a popular 'salt fish' dish. However, the really standard name is *susumba* (which spelling renders its pronunciation most simply). Lunan's spelling we have seen; Beckwith made it *sosuma*; Asprey and Thornton spell *sousumba*, which is much closer. The word is in none of the big dictionaries except F & W, where it is spelt *susumber*, but with the accent erroneously placed on the first syllable (actually it comes on the second). The word is surely of African origin though it has not been traced.[41]

Another very prickly plant whose names have become confused with those of susumba is *fingrigo*. Sloane was the first to mention it, and Barham wrote of it: 'FINGRIGO. I believe some negro gave the name, for it is very full of hooked prickles, like cock-spurs; and some call the plant so, which is well known in Jamaica. . . . The seeds, when dry, stick fast to any thing they touch.' Barham implies that the name refers to fingers; I have found no better explanation. In the course of time the form has changed among the folk to *single-go*, but the verb *finger* has at the same time become *fingle*, which parallels part of this metamorphosis; folk-etymology accounts for the rest: *single*. One informant, evidently unaware of the original form, remarked with some superiority, 'the natives distort it to *singrigo*' — which is, of course, just the contrary of the fact. The order of development has probably been: *fingrigo*, to *singrigo* or *fingle-go*, then to *single-go*. (Long mistakenly spelt it *fringrigo*). *Cockspur* is still in use, and another name is *puss-claw*.

A third plant that once used the name *cat's claw* was otherwise known as *nephritic wood* or *tree*. Of it Barham wrote, 'This tree is so called in Jamaica for its being a sovereign remedy for the stone.' In this case cat's-claw is translated from the Spanish *uña de gato* (represented also in the Latin botanical name).

Many plants derive their names from those of nations, persons, places, and the like. *Irish moss*, for example, or *jelly moss*, which currently designates certain edible seaweeds, has not been proved to be a Jamaicanism but is very probably one. The

OED's only citation is from 1845, yet Sloane wrote in 1707: 'Of Submarine Plants. Those growing in the seas about Jamaica, . . . upon drying there sticks to them a white Substance, chiefly made up of Sea-Salt; and from this Concretion . . . sticking to the Leaves of the Delisk . . . it is that this Plant is made delightful to the Irish Palats.'

Indian shot, however, the local name for the Canna lily, was first recorded here. As Barham explained: 'This is so called from its seed being round, black, and so hard that, blown through a trunk or pith, it will kill small birds.'[42] An uncultivated plant of the same kind is now called *wild shot*.

Several plants are associated with the Maroons — sometimes rather obscurely: *Maroon weed*, *Maroon wiss* (the same as *horse-bath*), *Maroon blister* (a 'vine like yam — have harsh scent', 'rub up leaf, put on forehead for headache'), and so on.

Plants with proper names are numerous. Some have been noted among the grasses, above. Among the earliest on record is *Pickering's herb*, about which Sloane relates a story derived from Barham. 'This is call'd Pickerings Herb, from a Cure upon an Eye of Captain *Pickering*, bruis'd and turn'd out by a Stick with fire at its End. This Cure was effected by a mash, or the Herb bruis'd and applied to the Part.' Barham identified it as 'Self-heal, or Alheal', but of the three names only *self-heal* has survived.

Another such name is *Tom Bontein's bush*, as Dancer first spelt it.[43] But who this man was and why the plant was associated with him are unknown. Other early names for it were *majoe bitter* and *macary bitter*, for which we turn again to Barham:

> This admirable plant hath its name from Majoe, an old negro woman so called, who, with a simple decoction, did wonderful cures in the most stubborn diseases, as the yaws, and in venereal cases. . . . It is also called Macary bitter, from its growing in great plenty in the bay of Macary, and being a very bitter plant.

The first is pronounced as /majo/ today. In support of Barham's explanation it may be noted that the Mende (Sierra Leone) word *majo*, meaning 'the leading woman of the Sande, a female society into which nearly all the girls are initiated' is still given as a personal name among the Gullah Negroes of the United States. *Macary* seems to have disappeared except in the place-name *Maccary Bay* (Clarendon), the same that Barham referred to. We may note again, however, that the Hausa (Nigeria) word *makari* means an antidote, and that a grass of the genus *Digitaria* is *makari* in the same language.

Several names include the word 'Doctor', sometimes no doubt in allusion to an actual physician, but often as a personification of the plants' medicinal qualities. *Hog-doctor* or *doctor-wood* has already been noted; *Dr Long* is a former name for the *nephritic tree*, mentioned above; *Dr Buchanan bush* (pronounced /bó-kanan/), also known as *ballad bush* (or *Ballard?*); *Dr John*, another name for *pepper rod*, which burns the eyes violently if one rubs them after handling it; and *Dr McKatty, McKatty bush, wiss,* or *weed.*

Personal names are also common: *John Charles* (or *John Charlie*), also called *Thompson weed* (was there a John Charles Thompson connected with it? — unfortunately we have found no evidence); *Matilda bush*; *Mary bush*; *Mary Gould* (applied to at least two plants); *Auntie Mag* (also called *red water-grass* and *Rolling-Calf bed*); *Miss Jany bush*; *Miss Ritty*; *Fanny-bush*. Russell mentioned in 1868 'Peggydone, A dangerous creeping prickle', but it does not seem to have survived; nevertheless it looks like a name of this kind, perhaps Peggy Dunn.

The last group of names for 'bush' is rather miscellaneous, but all appear to be more or less certainly of African origin. *Adrue* was known before 1711, the rush 'which the negroes call *adru*', and mentioned by several writers, though the historical dictionaries have missed it. Today it is pronounced /áju/ — one of the words in which *j* alternates with *dr*. Beckwith spelt it *hadrow*: she must have heard it pronounced with the common 'Cockney *h*'. This word is evidently from Ewe *adru*.

One cannot be absolutely sure about *junjo* (pronounced /jónjo/ or /júnju/), a widespread and long established name for mushrooms and fungi in general. The earliest citation found, it is true, is only from 1895, but being in a proverb it surely goes much farther back in folk use: 'You po' fe meat, you nyam jungo' — implying that it is not highly thought of as food. Beckwith remarks that *junjo* 'grows abundantly on the trunks of cotton and fig trees and damp places'. Related forms are the French Creole *džŏdžŏ*, Puerto Rican *ŷŏn'ŷŏn*, and in French West Africa *gügu*, 'champignon', which may well be the source of all these words. One may note also the Mende *dзɔɲa*, 'to affect with mildew'.⁴⁴ Though a clear source for the Jamaican form has not been found it seems altogether likely to be African. Another name for it in Clarendon is *lizard looking-glass*, and elsewhere in the British West Indies it is called *jumby parasol* — which is paralleled in St Lucia by *pawesol jab* and in *Dominica* by *pawesol zöbi*. *Jumby* and *zombie*, forms of the same word, refer no doubt to the plant's growth, somewhat mysterious, therefore presumably under the influence of spirits. But in Jamaica the only really current name is *junjo* — some country people know no other; *mushroom*, when known at all, is considered a 'white people' word.

Behind *apempe, apimpe, mapempe, pempe, pem-pem* there is no doubt a single word of African type of which they are variants, though none has been traced. The uncompounded forms mean one or another of the Euphorbiaceous plants also called *milk-weed* (though this is applied to other genera too in Jamaica). *Apempe* is 'male milkweed'; *pempe* and *mapempe* are milkweed also; *pem-pem* was identified with *red-head*. However, *apimpe grass* and *pempe grass* refer to a real grass.

Nunu bush (used in obeah practice) is mentioned by Louise Bennett:

> Me wrap it up wit noonoo bush,
> Same sweet-barsley yuh know . . .

Timi-timi (also called *fall-down-bush* because it is 'good fe bruise', *dog-blood*, and *blood-berry*) has the familiar reduplicated form, but has not been so clearly traced.

A plant highly favoured as a 'tea bush', 'fever bush', and for cuts and sores is that known as /píaba/ throughout the island. It must have been in use long since, though not found in print before 1905: 'Ah tek dis bush dem call "Piobba" an a bwoil it down an mek some tea, gie 'er.' Asprey and Thornton spell it *piaba*, which exactly represents the pronunciation. The source is unknown, but again it is in all likelihood African.⁴⁵ The closely related plant named *pick-nut* (which sometimes becomes *pig-nut*) furnishes a fine example of phonetic reduction and folk etymology, for it is a worndown form of *spikenard*! This word had already appeared in a Jamaican source by 1679 when the plant was called 'Savanna Weed or Spiknard' (Trapham). By this time the *r* was going or gone, so that the Englishman was saying

something like 'spiknaad' or 'spiknud'; the African lopped off
the *s* from all such words, and learnt 'piknud', which then became rationalised to the present forms. There are neither pigs
nor nuts to be picked, yet these seem to make sense where
'piknud' does not.

Garden Plants

We end this account with a few names of garden flowers
which may be claimed as Jamaicanisms. The *four-o'clock*, now
known everywhere, was first mentioned by Sloane in 1696:
'Admirabilis Peruana rubro flore . . . The Four a Clock Flour'.
Barham explained, 'This plant is so called in Jamaica from its
opening and shutting every four hours, night and day, as they
have observed there.' Nowadays it is understood differently:
that the flowers close at four o'clock in the afternoon. A similar
understanding prevails for the *four-o'clock tree*, which is said to
fold its leaves together at that hour, and the *ten-o'clock*, a small
flower which supposedly opens at ten in the morning.

Once much favoured for hedges was the 'Flour fence of
Barbados. Wild Sena or Spanish Carnations', as Sloane had it.
Barham elaborated:

> Barbadoes Flower Fence. This, I suppose, is so called from
> their fencing in their plantations with this shrub, which is full
> of short, strong prickles; but they are commonly called in
> Jamaica *doodledoes*; . . . The flowers are elegantly mixed with
> red-yellow, and therefore called, by some, Spanish carnation,
> or wild senna.

Like such a plant name as *cockspur*, *doodledoes* no doubt refers to
the prickles. But all these names seem to have disappeared in
the course of time, to be superseded by *Barbados pride*, the usual
one today.

The common garden hibiscus was apparently first called *shoe-
black flower* in this island. Even earlier was *shoe-flower*, of which
Lunan wrote:

> The seeds were first brought by the French to Martinico,
> and hence it is sometimes called the *Martinico rose*. . . . They
> are also put to a use which seems little consistent with their
> elegance and beauty, that of blacking shoes, whence their
> names of *rosae calceolariae* and *shoe-flower*.

Another hibiscus had the name of *changeable rose*, which the dictionaries do not record, though Bryan Edwards wrote of it:

> Commonly called the China rose; but improperly: it is the *hibiscus mutabilis*, or changeable rose. . . . Early in the morning it is of a most perfect and beautiful white; about noon it assumes a rose colour; and becomes of a deep red at night, when it contracts and dies.

The cultivated Daturas are called *bell-flower* and *German trumpet* (pronounced /jáaman/); the wild (the 'thorn-apple') is locally *trimonia*, a reduction of the species name, *stramonium*.

South-sea rose, another name for the Oleander, appeared first in a Jamaican source (1740) and is still in use; but a new name, *breadfruit rose*, has recently made its appearance.[46] There is no similarity whatever to the breadfruit except that of origin; it hardly seems appropriate.

Summary

Among the plant names composed of Standard English elements, or borrowed from foreign languages in the early days of the colony, a large number were short-lived — many did not even find their way into the dictionaries. (Some examples are *Achiots, Pickering's herb, Turkey-berry, Lagetto, Bilge-water tree.*) Others, however, that made their first appearance in Jamaican sources have since become a part of the English language everywhere (as, *Avocado, Cashew, Four o'clock, Anatto, Lace bark, Guinea grass*). Some that died out or were displaced in the Standard language remained alive nevertheless in the folk speech in an archaic form (as *Neeseberry, Salandine, Cayan pepper, Cassada*), or in a thoroughly altered one (as *Nickal, Jeremiah, Pick-nut, Lobby-lobby, Trimonia, Pruam, Single-bible*). A goodly number of the folk forms have become Standard within Jamaica — all ranks of people use them, for in many cases there is no other word (as, *Cho-cho, Guinep, Divi-divi, Gungu peas, Susumba*). And there are some strictly Jamaican terms that were probably not of folk origin (*Garden egg, Number-eleven mango, Strainer vine*, and so on). But by far the greatest number of names are those of the folk, known everywhere in town and countryside to the majority of Jamaicans. Most of them are composed of English elements, though a number of Africanisms (or probable Africanisms) survive. We may summarise these in closing.

The names fall into certain clear types, many of which are usual enough, others unusual. The numbers are approximately as follows (though not all the names counted here have been mentioned in this chapter). Among compound names, the modifying element, and the number of times it appears (excluding those that appear only once or twice) are:

Colour — white 38, black 36, red 27, yellow 17, blue 12, green 9 —

(*White bullet, Black cane, Red ginger*, etc.)

Taste and Smell — sweet 19, bitter 13, stinking 5, sour 5.

Shape and Size — long 12, broad 5, round 5.

Locality — mountain 19, sea(side) 14, water 10, ground 4.

Other property — wild 80, bastard 25, Christmas 13, prickle or prickly 12, duppy 9, poison 9, devil 7, lady 7, milk 6, burn 6, macca 5, beef 5, blood 4, hard 4, iron 4, man 4, woman 4, doctor 4, backra 3, negro 3.

Animal or Bird — hog 18, cow 11, dog 11, horse 10, goat 9, bull 7, johncrow 7, crab 7, monkey 6, donkey 5, snake 5, turtle 5, puss 4, jackass 3, dragon 3.

Nationality — Jamaica 28, Indian 17, Spanish 13, French 11, Chinee 7, Maroon 5, Coolie 4, Cuban 4.

Most of these have the ordinary meanings, but there are local nuances. *Red*, quite often, is what would be orange or even yellow in Standard usage. *Sweet* often implies cultivation; *bitter* sometimes a poisonous quality. *Bastard* is the ordinary word for a wild or 'false' plant that has not the full property of the 'true' one; it is, or was, very widely used. *Prickly* is the more recent, *prickle* the older of the 'white people' forms, while *macca* is the 'black people' word. *Lady* implies a finer, more dainty or delicate variety of a plant. *Milk, beef, blood, iron* suggest respectively that the juice is milky, the texture firm or coarse, the colour red or the plant good for the blood, and the roots or stems tough. *Burn* refers to the effect on the eyes, nose, tongue or skin. *Man* and *woman* designate respectively varieties of the plant that are coarser or finer, stronger or weaker. *Doctor* is curative; *backra* is a choicer quality. *Devil* implies some harmful property, *duppy* usually less harmful, often merely tricky or mysterious. *Christmas* refers to the season at which the plant blooms or bears — appropriately, in slave days, the chief holiday of the entire year.

The animal names may mean that the plant is used to feed or care for the animal, or else that it resembles the animal in some way. The national names imply origin or special varieties. Interestingly, *Indian* refers almost always to American Indians, *Coolie* being reserved for East Indians and implying careful cultivation. *Chinee* usually implies a smaller, finer variety.

But most striking are the phrase names (some of which are translations of similar African ones). *Break-ax, Come-fe-help-we, Pull-coat, Big-family, Fatten-barra, Pickny-mumma, Big-an-so-so, Sarch-me-heart, Shine-a-night, 'Tan-pon-rock, Dead-an-wake, Trash-myself, Heal-i'-an-draw* and many more show this pattern. Another favourite type is made by simply transferring to the plant the name of some individual who introduced it or made it known: *Auntie Mag, Miss Ritty, John Charles, Dr Buchanan, Pa Will, Mary Dougal, Mada Thomas, Bobby Brown*. These, and sundry folk-etymologised forms such as *Fancy Anna* for *Poinciana, Jeremiah* for *Cherimoya*; the familiarised forms like *Jackini* for *Jack-in-the-bush, Julie* for the *St Julian mango*; the hypocoristic names *Ricky-rocky, Lobby-lobby, Timi-timi*, and many more — all these show the underlying anthropocentric view of life still in a flourishing state, a branch from the African past of the Jamaican folk engrafted on the European cultural stock.

Chapter Seventeen

CONCLUSIONS

JAMAICA TALK, as we have seen, is an amalgam of many elements. The attempt must now be made to judge the proportions of each: contributions of various languages, characteristic types of words, the aspects in which it agrees and disagrees with Standard English.

American Indian words have come in from many places and by several routes — often indeed one cannot be sure exactly how. But one thing is certain: the chances of direct adoption by the English or their slaves in Jamaica are very slight. Few if any Indians remained in the island by 1655 and not many came after. Even when the proof is lacking, therefore, it is vastly more likely that Indian words should have come via the Spanish, Portuguese, and occasionally the French, rather than directly.

The early adoptions through Spanish and Portuguese are limited almost wholly to names for plants, animals, or foods. Of these *achiots, callipee, carribi, casareep, hickatee, merry-wings, nyapa,* and *tumaali* are now out of use or virtually so; but the majority are current throughout the island: *barbecue, calalue, calipeva, coratoe, cho-cho, coby*-wood, *galimeta, guinep, guana, guango, jigger, macca, malantang, mammee* and *mammee-sapota, naseberry, pechary, pinguin, taya, tuna, yippi-yappa,* and *yuca.* A few — *avocado, annatto, cashew, cassava,* to *jerk* meat, and *porgie* — have achieved a much wider use as Standard English terms. We know that several of these are from the Quichua or Nahuatl of Central America (as *achiots, avocado, cherry-moya*), others from the Tupí-Guaraní of Brazil (as *cashew, guinep, coratoe*), a number from the Carib or Arawak of the islands or Guianas (as *annatto, macca, coco*-plum, *mobby, cay*). North American Indian words that turn up in Jamaica (as *pone, papoose* plantain), though not Jamaicanisms, testify further to the wide diffusion of these aboriginal terms. As already noted, *cashew* and *coratoe* among others passed not only through Portuguese and Spanish but French; the Tupí-Guaraní words, in the nature of the case, probably came first through Portuguese.

Some that have Indian forms may themselves be loans into the American languages: *taya* and *coco* would seem to be ultimately from India or Indo-China, *bungay* and *yaw* from Africa. *Bammy, tarpon* and a number of others are puzzling with insufficient evidence to back them, but on the face of it seeming unlikely to be anything but Indian. Altogether we can be sure of perhaps two score terms, ultimately Indian, that are Jamaicanisms in one sense or another. (A great many more, of course, are used in this island as part of the general English language: such words as *tobacco, potato, guava, chocolate, mahogany*, and so on.)

Of Spanish and Portuguese words not ultimately Indian there is a much wider range. These languages were the channels through which much of the lore of the New World flowed to the English, later colonisers in this area. Some of the first terms to be adopted had to do with weather and topography (as *bogue, north, salina*); with stock raising or agriculture (*asinego, hato, palenque* or *polink, stancha, takada*); with sugar making and other such trades (*barquadier, capouse, tache*); with slavery and racial mixture (*albino, mustee, mustifino, quarteron, terceron*); with foods and cookery (*baccalow, bolangena, bulla, calavances, callipash, caveach* or *scoveitch, chaklata, docey, frisco, funda, guizada, pimento, sancocho, specia*); with plants and animals (*balahoo, cavally, jack*-fruit *lagetto, palmino, ramoon, Santa Maria, santapee, sapodilla*); others with money and trade (*braata, cuento, Don Patinho's* money, *feeco, pistareen*); and there are recent colloquialisms used pretty much in their Spanish form (*bamo, bobo, bolo, combolo, pasayro, poco-poco, poco-tempo, tanto, wampara*); plus a few miscellaneous others (*brags, caca, machete, Parattee, sampatta* or *sand-platter*). Some terms connected mostly with dancing are ultimately African but come through Spanish: *canga* or *lacanga, cachimba*, perhaps *calembe, mento, merengue, samba, yanga*. *Pine* is a perfectly good English word, but in the sense of 'pineapple' it undoubtedly shows the anterior influence of Spanish *piña*. A number of the Spanish and Portuguese loans are now obsolete: the terms for coins no longer in circulation, those for racial mixtures, the older sugar terms. (*Ratoon, dunder*, and some others are not Jamaicanisms.)

Some have been put into a French form (*barquadier, bogue*), just as others were given a pseudo-Spanish one in early Modern English (*palisado*, *stockado*). *Caca* may be French quite as well as Spanish. A considerable number of words, too, have the sound and form of Spanish or Portuguese though at present they cannot be identified as such. Discounting Indian terms, we find about three score Jamaicanisms that came from these two languages.

The French element was more limited. It was strongest in regard to superior varieties of plants: *Bourbon* cane, coco, cotton, *Martinique* bananas, *St Vincent*, *St Julian*; the *Gros Michel* banana; *dasheen*, *gormandizer*; and perhaps *bahu*. *Red potato* and *in arrow* are probably translations. Other plant names that are French or partly so include *coratoe*, *coco-macca*, *mortelle*; names of foods are *gata*, *leggins*, *munjay* (perhaps), *pimentade*, and the *brute* in *grater* and *cut brute*; miscellaneous others are *grand market*, *mal de stomach*, and perhaps *merry-wings*. A number of terms intimate, familial, or affectionate are probably or certainly French: *beau*, *bowbo*, *bibi*, *dude*, *dudu*, *gang-gang*, *po*. *Mamzelle* and *mushe* have special forms and meanings; *shay-shay* and *tambu* possibly represent African things in a partly French form. Spanish *cimarron* was beheaded and passed through French *marron* before being Englished as *Maroon*.

The Dutch element is negligible. *Sea-cat*, evidently a translation of *Zee-kat*, may have been acquired directly, but *craw-craw* and *crawl* are evidently Dutch *kraauw* and *kraal* brought over from Africa. The only others that can be claimed are *vendue-room* (obsolete) and *marosh* or *morass*. It is clear that the European element is very largely Spanish, which has contributed from the first and continues to do so through contacts within the largely Spanish-speaking Caribbean.

The Oriental influence, having had one century at most in which to make itself felt, is quite limited. Many words the East Indians use among themselves alone; we include here only those which appear to be known to some degree beyond their settlements. They are almost entirely domestic: names of foods (*baji*, *daal* and *baat*, *daru*, *katarri*, *kie-baat*, *tankari*); terms of address or the like (*betty*, *challa*, *mawi*); objects around the home (*chunta*, *dadjaka*, *juta*); and the two basic things for smoking hemp (*ganja* and *chilam*). The annual *hussay* (or /wuse/) festival (Muharram) has made this term generally known.

Chinese words in common use are less than a handful: the gambling game *peaka peow*, and one of its terms, *tie-sheen* are almost all. A kind of sweet potato is said to be called *pang*, a 'Chinaman name', but the evidence is weak; and there is a vegetable somewhat like chard called *pop-chow* or *pot-chow* which one sometimes sees in the markets.

Of non-British influences it is obvious that the African is the largest and most profound; it appears not only in the vocabulary, but has powerfully affected both pronunciation and grammar. We may feel fairly certain of about two hundred and thirty loan-words from various African languages; and if the numerous compounds and derivatives were added, and the large number of untraced terms which are at least quasi-African in form, the total would easily be more than four hundred. Even at its most restricted, the African element in the vocabulary is larger than all the other non-English ones together.

African loans come from most spheres of life but are especially numerous for plants, foods, animal life, utensils, music and dancing, superstition, people and their conditions, and greetings and exclamations. The plant names include *abbeys*, *ackee*, *adrue*, *afu* yam, *akam*, *bayere* yam, *bichy* or *bissy*, *brang-brang*, *camphor* yam, *cantu*, *crang-crang*, *crongoe* yam, probably *depa* yam, *eddo*, *fufu* yam, *guma*, *grang-grang*, *gungu* peas, *jocotu*, *junjo*, *macary* bitter, *mafutu* wiss, *majoe*, *mapempe*, *maranga*, probably *menow*-weed, *pumpun* yam, *soonga*, perhaps *sorasy* and probably *susumba*, *taa* yam *wangla*, *warry*, and *yampee*. (A number of other African plant names such as *okro*, *goober*, and *yam* itself are not Jamaicanisms.)

Foods, drinks, and cookery terms are: *ackra* cakes, *asham* (also called *hasham* or *sham-sham*), *bogro* salt, *duckunu*, *cungoteh*, *flaa-flaa*, *fungee*, *malawa*, *muse*, *ninyam*, *shwuwa* or *shuwa*, *toto*, *tum-tum*. Names for animals and birds include *anancy*, *asono*, *bang*, *bungoby*, probably *busu*, *gingy* fly, possibly *granke*, *gutu*, *hanen*, *janga*, *kitibu*, *majoe*, *mingo*, *mumby* crab, *mungala* drummer, *nanka*, *patu*, *sense* fowl, *yeary-yeary*.

Names for furnishings, utensils and materials are: *abu* earth, *afana*, *bankra*, *bedja* or *bedwa*, *buba* mat, *bungay*, *cachimba*, perhaps *kitty*-up, *cotta*, *cutacoo*, *dutty*, *fro-fro*, *hangra* or *hankra*, *packy*, *padda* or *patta*, *pre-pra*, *tanna* or *tenna*, and *swing-sang* or *zing-zang*.

Musical instruments, song, dance, and entertainment furnish a sizable group of words: *abeng*, *aketta*, *bangil* or *banja*, *benta* or *bender*, perhaps *bomma, bowsorow, buru, calembe, dinky, dundo, gombay* or *gumbi*, probably *balafou, jamma, jenkoving, John Canoe, kynando, mento, merengue, rookaw, saqwa, sallo, samba, shaka*, perhaps *shay-shay, tittle* drum, *tumba*, and *yanga*. As noted already, a number of these passed through Spanish; *shay-shay* may be French.

Matters of belief and superstition have brought in numerous words: *ahpetti, buzu, crumuna* or *cumina, dindi*-okro, *duppy, guzu, jeng-jeng, jegge* or *jiggy, jumby*, probably *mial, nookoo, noonoo, obeah, puntee*, and perhaps *sam. Jumby* was never common; *ahpetti* and puntee are now obsolete; but the others are in vigourous use, especially *duppy* and *obeah*, which have entered into a great many combinations and invaded every part of life.

Words for diseases or abnormal bodily conditions include: *baffan* or *bafwam, bubuafu, buffooto, cocobay, duggy* or *ducky, fennay, kenge*, possibly *montompy, mumu*, and *yaw*; and the similar words that describe people's tendencies of physique or character include *buffro-buffro, bufu-bufu, bugo-bugo, bugu-yaga, chaka-chaka, conga-so, fire-kitty, kukru-busu, nyaams, nyaka-nyaka, nyami-nyami, piangy-piangy, pyaka-pyaka, pyaa-pyaa, takro-takro, timiny, tuku*, and *wenya-wenya*. The large proportion of iterative forms among the last will be noted: they are numerous also among words for the conditions of things, or things as characterised by their conditions: *bungo, chi-chi, mini-mini, pere-pere, puckro(-puckro), putta-putta, ruku-ruku, so-so*, and for physical actions: *busu, congconse, juck, juck-cum-peng, laba-laba, kas-kas, massu, nyam, pam-pam* or *plam-plam, pra-pra, saka-saka, se-se* or *say-say, su-su*.

The only other sorts of things that have given several words to the folk speech are names — the old 'day names' (Chapter VIII) with their newly acquired connotations; tribal names; others such as *Accompong, Crooky, Tacooma*; and terms of address, relationship, or affection such as *backra*, perhaps *bona* and *boso, dundus, nana, tata*, and greetings such as *macky* and *malembe*.

Since interjections and exclamations are outside the framework of syntax and sometimes even employ sounds or combinations not ordinarily found in the repertory of a language, and further because coincidence often produces in these elemental words the same or almost the same forms from quite unrelated sources, it is difficult — sometimes impossible — to know whether certain ones are African, English, from some other

European language, or possibly of multiple source. *Aie* or
/aaaay/ is an example: it is found in many places; *oh* or /oooo/ is
another. Nevertheless the following would appear to be African
or partly so: *babwa, cho, edoh-edoh, ee-hee, eeeem, eh-eh, embo, feh, kie,*
possibly *ku, shi, su, tuffa,* and *waa-yo.* Finally, there are a few
terms of chiefly grammatical force: *a, da, de, de-so, di-de, se* or
say, so, and *unu.*

Some words must continue to be suspected of the multiple
source just mentioned: in them there is a coincidence of form
and meaning that might come from two or more languages. *Se*
is probably Twi, the verb form with relative force, yet it coincides perfectly with English *say* in 'Im tell me *se* im gwine come'.
Similarly *se-se* means 'gossip', as *say-say* could well have been
combined to mean. *Si* means *sit* in Mandinka, but could be
plausibly derived from the English word. *Kas-kas* is often spelt
cuss-cuss and thought to represent *curse* — yet Twi *kasá-kàsa* is
'contention, dispute'. *Dutty* means *dirt,* and would seem clearly
to come from it, yet its real basis is Twi *dòté,* which means the
same. Standard *canoe* is always pronounced /kúnu/ among the
folk — if that is what they are saying, for it might equally well,
perhaps better, be derived from Bambara *kunu,* a boat. *So-so* is
parallelled in form in English, Spanish (*so-so, asi-asi*), Dutch
(*zo-zo*), and other languages; only the special meaning of
'plain, mere' indicates that it is probably none of these alone,
for Yoruba *sho-sho* means 'only'. When only one English first-
person pronoun was made to serve for all cases, it can hardly be
an accident that *me* was taken rather than *I* (or *my*): Twi has *me*
for all cases. Spanish *bobo,* 'fool', coincides with Twi *bɔɔ-bɔɔ,*
'phlegmatic, dull'; which one did Jamaicans take? These are
only the most striking examples of coincidence that suggest a
double or multiple source for a number of forms, or the mutual
reinforcement of African and European ones. The form or the
meaning seems more often to favour primacy of the African
source.

Not only direct loans but loan-translations show the African
contribution. These are more difficult to recognise and to be
sure of. Nevertheless, *break-ax, break-pot,* and their like are
parallel to African forms and turn up also in the Spanish of the
Caribbean area — probably loan-translations there too. *Eye-
water* and *mouth-water* could represent Ibo or Mandinka

expressions for tears and saliva. In Ibo 'eye big' means 'greedy':
in Jamaica it is *big-eye* and *strong-eye*, the latter also having the
sense of domineering. *Wa mek* exactly parallels an Ibo phrase
meaning 'why'. I suspect, though cannot prove, that *door-mouth*,
pickny-mumma, and *make four eyes* are expressions of this kind.
Carry-go-bring-come and others like it exhibit the African pen-
chant for heaping verbs together — in this case to mean 'gossip'.
And while it is quite true that English has many terms for trades
or occupations formed by adding *-man* to a noun (*fireman, milk-
man, seaman*, and so on), the Jamaican *music-man, obeah-man,
samfie-man* and many more may just as well represent such a
suffix as *-fo*, which is used in exactly this way in Twi. (More than
half of all the Africanisms identified appear to be from this
language, and many others from closely related ones.)

As for the English part of the vocabulary, it is overwhelmingly
the largest: of the more than four thousand Jamaicanisms that
this book records, the non-English element, including mixed
compounds, is less than ten per cent; a good ninety per cent are
of English origin, though often altered in form. Nor does this
take account of the still larger body of English words that
Jamaicans use in common with other speakers of the language.

By 'words of English origin' are designated those which came
to the Jamaican folk via the British Isles, whatever the ultimate
source. There was as we have seen a goodly mixture of Welsh,
Irish, and later Scottish settlers with the English; their local
usages have left some trace, though not a very strong one. Of
Welsh there is perhaps nothing distinctive except *taffy* goat, and
possibly the preference for *puss* over *cat*. Of Irish we may best
count *streeler*. The greatest number may be Irish or Scots: *bonny*
and *clabub* or *plabba* (compare the *bonny-clabber* of the eastern
United States), *gawky, kench, lep, crabbit*, perhaps *cutta*-frock, *no
wut* (no worth), *mickle-muckle* and perhaps *mekam-fekam*, the
second half or perhaps all of *peeny-wauly, pooky*, possibly *rungles*,
and the latter part of *muckashandy* and *dandy-shandy*. English
words which lasted longer in the North and in Scotland, whence
they presumably were brought to Jamaica, would include the
comparative *no, no-mo* meaning 'only', possibly *what a way*, and
probably *can* in such combinations as *should can, must can*. Most
indicative of this source however is the ubiquity of *man* (unstressed) appended to almost any kind of statement or question

— 'Yes man!' 'Aa right man!' 'We yu a go man?' 'Mine yuself man!' 'Come on, no man?' 'Laaaad man!' This is most common among the folk, but in familiar conversation it goes very far toward the other end of the scale. Not that it is by any means un-English — 'Cheer up, man!' — except by the much higher frequency than it would have in England.

Not many specifically American usages have come into Jamaica except in the slang of the day that the cinema, radio, and periodicals introduce. There may be some influence from tourists, or (more likely) Jamaicans who have journeyed to the United States for labour or education. So far this has been slight and ephemeral. One might wonder whether the increasing use of *r* in such words as *car* and *cart*, from which it has hitherto been absent both in the folk and Standard speech, might not be owing to American influence. But this is probably the 'spelling-pronunciation' that comes with book-learning, rather than any imitation of the Yankee. In Jamaica, where school-language and book-language carry unquestioned prestige, one may expect spelling-pronunciation to flourish.

On the other hand, because Jamaica was once on a par with other English colonies on the North American continent, there remains today a common Colonial element in which the two agree in differing from Britain. In the United States these words are fast becoming archaic or dialectal, and many are localised in the South; in Jamaica they are mostly folk words, archaic too by contrast with Standard. The chief ones are: *afternoon* (twelve o'clock to about three) and *evening* (about three to six); *beast* (horse or mule); to *break* a crop; *buck* (butt); *buttery* (place under the house for storing ground provisions); *carry* (to conduct someone); *chains* (as a common measure of distance); *chinchy* (mean, small); *dominick* fowl, and indeed *fowl* in preference to *chicken*; *first* (first time); *gap* and *gut* as topographic terms; *great-house*; *johnny-cake* and *pone* (very different from the foods so called in the United States); *pick up* (to tidy); *Solomon Gundy*, usually reduced to *gundy* (from *salmagundi*); *season* (heavy rain); *shift* (undergarment); *stone fence*; *thank-you-ma'am* (dip in a road); *thought* (thwart in a boat); *waiter* (tray); *wait on* (wait for).

Other words from the early period, English in origin rather than American, and still current in Jamaica though obsolete, archaic, or dialectal in England, include: *blow* (to bloom), the *bobbin* of a song, *bread-kind, catch to* (arrive at), *chenks* (small bit), *chimblet* (lamp chimney), *chowy* (chewy), *cobell* (quarrel, disturbance), to *cut* language, *feisty, fleam, gulge, hold one's road, jerkin, lap* (to wrap), the *main* in gambling, *moonshine, pumble-foot, quitter* (pus), *rax* (to torment), *roguing, stand* and *stay* meaning 'be', *tinnen, vial,* and the pronunciation /úman/ for *woman*. These are only the most interesting: the list could easily be lengthened.

It was noted by Long and other early writers that the nautical influence in Jamaica, the long voyage out and the presence of sailors among the settlers, had left an imprint in the vocabulary. One might mention too the island's constant dependence on the navy for defence, the inter-island trade, and fishery. In early sugar-making the head-man or foreman was called the *boatswain of the mill,* and sometimes a slave-driver was *boatswain* too. An estate with a good labour force was *well-handed,* and the contrary kind *bad-handed.* To *rig* and *put the mill about* (as if it were a capstan) meant to set it in operation; and the *cockpit* of the mill was the sunken part in the middle where the grinding was done. *Cookroom,* said to have been favoured over *kitchen,* was a sea word; *twice-laid* and *stamp-and-go* are two nautical phrases that came ashore as nicknames of foods. The east side of the island was regularly known as the *windward* side (and often is still); *aback* may be used of past time. Fishermen naturally preserve many of the sea terms today, but others have come into more general use among the folk: a *weather* for a storm, *weather-time* for the rainy season, *white squall* as a nickname for hunger, *topside* for 'above' (though this could be coincidentally African), and I have heard of someone who wanted to '*launch out* a factory' — that is, start one. The exclamation *black water,* used to stop a song, is very likely from *back water,* the action which stops a rowing boat. From the sailors the slaves adopted *shipmate,* giving it a special meaning of their own: a fellow-slave who had come out from Africa in the same ship as oneself.

As to the types of word-formation in the Jamaican vocabulary, one finds the same as in Standard English, though in somewhat different proportions. Derivatives and compounds form the greatest part in both, while blends, back-formations, and established malapropisms are few. More common than in Standard are metatheses, and much more so folk-etymologies, or reinterpretations along with altered form. Of somewhat greater frequency than in Standard is aphetism, and not with English words alone but with some African ones: *benta, packy, duckanoo, sense,* and so on. It is not true, however, that African loan-words are regularly treated in this way: compare *obeah, abbeys, asham, afu,* and others that might have been beheaded. *Anancy,* the full form, is more common than *Nancy,* the aphetic one.

The folk speech has a special affinity, it would seem, for words involving sound-play of one sort or another. Reduplications or iterations, and onomatopoetic forms, have been discussed (end of Chapters IV and X). There seems definitely to be something analogous to nicknaming by which a word is not kept in its full form but reduced in some way. A breadfuit may become *bufut, bufu, buku,* a banana *bancha, mancha, baajam*; a basket *baasi*; a cousin *co-u*; *namsack* becomes *nambo* or *nambu*; *sword* (a kind of machete) becomes /sou/; the *cunny-buck* fish becomes *cunny-bo*; and *coobla* is probably a reduction of *calabash,* which is what it means. The effect is thoroughly to disguise the source of such words; indeed, a number of the forms that have not been traced are probably due to this kind of familiarising alteration. Of much the same order is the folk liking for the *-y* or *-ie* suffix, both for ordinary words and for names.

Not without its effect on the vocabulary is the personifying tendency which implies a vitalistic view of the world of nature. The man who lives always with the awareness of ancestral spirits close about him, which take on horrible shapes at times, but merely remind him of their presence through the cracking of a stick, the scattering of gravel, the uncanny cry of bird or beast, is the man who gives human-like names to plants and animals who thinks of *man* and *woman* dandelions or beefwood, *duppy* pumpkins and soursops — who calls a rat *Charlie Price* and a worm *Mary Grudgeful.* Among the Jamaican peasantry this is very common and characteristic.

There is also a decided liking for whole phrases compounded into words. More often than not this is jocular in spirit, lightly cynical, grotesque, or in some other way humourous. The *kick-and-buck* water cistern, *lick-an'-'tan-up* mats, the *'oman-be-damn'* cooking pot, *bruck-kitchen* dog, *pity-me-little* ant, and for foods *dip-and-fall-back, round-the-road, pick-me-round. Carry-go-bring-come* as a concise description of gossip or tale-bearing, and *hurry-come-*

up for a parvenu, are certainly expressive enough. Of the more grotesque one may mention *stagger-back* candy, *heng-'pon-nail* and *law-Ma* clothes, *puss-prayers* for an avocado pear. Self-consciously humourous exaggerations are *foot post-hole* for long boots, *floating bullet* for a breadfruit, *johncrow head-man* for a white crow, and *mout'-a-gram* for a chatterbox or source of false news. Some may be parallelled in American frontier expressions, but the number and individuality of the Jamaican examples suggests that they are not mere imitations or colonial archaisms.

So much for vocabulary. As for pronunciation, the only sources of any consequence are the English and African — indeed, anything else is virtually unprovable. In the formation of the folk speech there was a sort of compromise between these two, the influence of each being both positive and negative. It is a commonplace of naïve language-learning, that rather than acquire the unfamiliar sounds of a new tongue, one substitutes the closest thing that already exists in one's own. If Frenchmen say *zis sing* for *this thing*, Englishmen repay them with *tray bong* for *très bon*. So speakers of West African languages trying to learn English in Jamaica already had most of the sounds in their possession, but lacked our two *th* sounds, often *v*, and though many had *r* where some had *l* they seldom used both together as contrasting sounds. As a result, Jamaican folk speech still has *dis ting*, *bery* and *bickle* for *very* and *victuals*, and numerous interchanges of *l* and *r* (*maranga*, *simple-bible*, *maranta*). The difficulty with the *th*'s may have been increased by the fact that many Welsh and Irish speakers were about who themselves stumbled with these English sounds and cannot have furnished perfect models. In any case it is the fact today that even speakers who have crossed the middle of the scale and approach the Standard in many respects often fall short in this.

Meantime, Africans brought in a few sounds of their own that were lacking in English. The palatal nasal *ny* ([ɲ]) is far more frequent in Twi and related West African languages than it is in English, where *new, newt, nuisance* and a very few other words have it, and then only before [u]. (*Onion, union* and the like separate the *n* and *y* into different syllables.) The Jamaican folk, however, have several more words with this sound, mostly African (though a couple come through Spanish, in which *ñ* is very common), and generally before /a/: *nyam, nyaka-nyaka*, etc.

Occasionally too it intrudes into such an English word as *young*, which I have heard pronounced /nyong/.

The greatest difference is not in single sounds, however, but in their combinations. The West African languages have such consonant clusters (in single syllables) as /kp, gb, jw, chw, fw, sr/, which are wanting in English, and /gw, hy, hw/, which are unusual, or in the last case local. Also they frequently have nasals initially before consonants as English does not: /mf, mp, nt, ngw, ngk/ and others. Since English normally reduces unEnglish clusters in borrowed words (Greek *mnemonic*, *pneumonia*, *ctenoid*; German *gneiss*), it is not surprising that *mbakara* became *backra* and *nkamfo camphor yam* in Jamaican folk speech. Other clusters were similarly simplified.

The compromise was from both sides, however. Twi does not have such combinations as /sp, st, sk, sm, sn, shr, ld, rd, nd, lm, rm/ in single syllables, and these the Jamaican folk have found very difficult. One consonant or the other (the first initially, the second finally) is rejected: the *s* in *spider*, *stick*, *skin*; the last sound in *clasp*, *last*, *task*, *bald*, *hand*. Or to make both pronouncible an epenthetic vowel may be inserted between (making *small* and *elm* into *sumall*, *alam*). Or they may be metathesised — *crisp* and *ask* becoming *crips* and *aks* — as in dialects of the British Isles (which, indeed, could have furnished these very words). African *sr* takes the place of English *shr* in *srimp*, *sred*, and of *sl* in *sripple*, from *slippery*. (*Shrimp* also appears as *swimp* and *slippery* as *swipple*, with possible influence from *supple*.)

At the time when Jamaica was being colonised, *r* at the end of a word or before a consonant was being lost in southern Standard English: it is now gone. It continues, however, in the north of England, in Scotland, Wales, Ireland, and the greater part of the United States. In a colony composed as the Jamaican was, there must have been good reasons both for and against the retention of this *r* in the folk speech. That the decision went against it was due, perhaps, to the unconscious weight of African influence: the learners would hardly have adopted a feature that was not always present in the English model and quite absent from their ancestral tongues.

The vowels of Twi corresponded closely enough to those of English so that no borrowing or violent adjustment had to be made. Nevertheless there seems to have been one positive influence from the African: [ʊ, ɔ, ɛ] cannot come at the end of a word in English, but the corresponding sounds can in Twi and Jamaican folk speech. Nor is it only African loan-words that do this; the sound patterns permit it for any kind of word (see Chapter III).

Other differences in vowels are chiefly due to archaism. In lacking the present Standard [ɔ, ɔ:, ɔɪ] as in *bot, bought, boil,* the folk speech merely reflects English literary usage of the seventeenth and eighteenth centuries, when these vowels had all but fallen together with [ɑ, ɑ:, ɑɪ]. The un-Standard vowel of *first, birch, bird,* and so on (/fos, boch, bod/) can hardly be African; it has been widespread in English dialects, whence it also entered United States dialect usage — compare *bust, cuss, wuss.* As to the eccentricities of the mid front and back diphthongs (in *bait* and *boat*) one cannot at present be sure. They might be of English or African source, or perhaps developments that took place within this island.

The effects of West African syllabic structure probably are to be seen, however. English syllables may end with consonants; those of Twi and similar languages almost always end with a vowel though sometimes a nasal. One finds with English words early adopted by the slaves a tendency to add /a/ or /i/ to a syllable that ended in a consonant: *rat* became /rata/, *rock-stone* /rakatuon/, *cunning* /koni/, *death* or *dead* /dedi/, *what* and *that* /wara/ and /dari/. This would hardly be done with words adopted today, but some of the old forms hang on. And quite similar is the very common addition of hypocoristic and familiarising /i/, corresponding to English *-y, -ie* (as in *cooky, Dutchy* pot, *rashy, cauchie, corpy, loney, paly,* and so on) — in part more frequent, one may guess, because it produces words with this African-like syllabic structure. By coincidence the Celtic liking for this suffix must have reinforced it in Jamaica: note the borrowing of *shandy, gawky, pooky, Taffy,* and other such. One final bit of evidence may perhaps be seen in the folk use of *hasty* for *haste, hungry* for *hunger, greedy* for *greed* — a fairly common occurrence.

The peculiarities of intonation, as we have seen (Chapter III), are also to be traced to African influence. Though strongest and most obvious at the folk end of the scale and decreasing to the vanishing point at the other, most of the way their subtle effect may be noticed in the characteristic Jamaican rhythm and lilt, musical and pleasing more often than not. This is a subject that deserves much further study, and more attention than it can be given here.

In the grammar, as in the sounds, there has been a compromise between African and English structures. English inflections were chiefly suffixed (as in plurals), Twi (such as there were) more often prefixed; Jamaican folk speech preserved neither, but lost more, so to speak, from the English side. One African contribution, however, was the adding of a pronoun (-*dem*) to a noun to form the plural (see Chapter IV); another perhaps the interrogative *a*; and certainly the pronoun *unu*.

Twi has only three distinctive parts of speech: noun, pronoun, and verb — no adjectives, adverbs, conjunctions or prepositions as such, no participles, no passive. Nouns and verbs are therefore used as modifiers and conjunctions; nouns of place function as prepositions. Jamaican folk speech of the most conservative kind, least influenced by Standard English, is strikingly parallel to this. It favours such expressions as *duck pickny* rather than *duckling* or *little duck*, *pickny mumma* rather than *nursing mother*; and it has *dis end* for *here*, *dat end* for *there* (or *side* instead of *end*): 'A nebba walk dat end'; 'Plenty mango dis side'. As we have seen, it has no passive, and it carries conversion of the parts of speech much farther even than English does — evidently because the English distinctions were never mastered: the African language had no precedent for them. In short, while there were few positive influences from African grammar, there has been a powerful negative one. The folk speaker who seeks to acquire Standard English has the longest distance to go in respect to the grammar.

At the beginning of this book the question was raised whether Jamaican folk speech is to be considered a dialect or sub-type of English or whether a separate language. We are now in a position to answer. As to the vocabulary there can be little doubt: it is a type of English. The vast majority of the words used are simply English; and of the smaller, specifically Jamaican part, again the greatest number came from the British Isles. Other components European and non-European there are, the African being chief; yet this accounts for but a small portion of the vocabulary, and even among the folk many Africanisms are obsolescent. There may be some recrudescence of them in cumina and other cults, but only in this limited sphere. African words are to Jamaican English somewhat like Indian words in American border speech of seventy-five years ago.

As to pronunciation, the individual sounds of folk speech are pretty close to Standard but rather archaic — somewhat like Canadian French alongside Parisian, they preserve features from the seventeenth century with a certain dialectal cast, reflecting the time and manner of the colonial settlement. Most of the African influence in pronunciation (except as regards rhythm and intonation) has been negative, yet in sum considerable. Differences in syllabication, simplification of consonant clusters, and the admission of new patterns have altered the appearance of the English element. Many an English word comes to sound decidedly un-English, and the words in groups do not pattern according to the expectations of Standard. In its extreme form, therefore, Jamaican folk speech certainly sounds like a different language from English. But to the uninitiate, so do the dialects of Yorkshire or Devon — yet they are closer to English than to anything else.

The biggest difference of the folk speech comes, without question, in grammatical structure. This is certainly not African and emphatically not English. The major complexities of both have been dispensed with, though minor features of both remain. In the absence of inflections, most conjunctions, some auxiliaries and articles, the primary words are left tumbling on top of one another; this, with the emphatic syllabication and the accidentation of pitch makes the folk speech seem abrupt and rather elemental. It gets along with less grammatical complexity than either of its source languages: it has not kept much more than the basic structure common to both.

When linguists speak of languages simplified from European and African as 'Creolised' tongues they refer chiefly to this. Whatever the source of the vocabulary (English, French, Spanish), the same kind of grammatical reduction has taken place throughout the Caribbean. If this makes a separate language, the Creole vernaculars of Haiti, Curaçao, Jamaica are alike in being separate. Jamaican folk speech in this respect is decidedly different from any dialect of England — it has, indeed, been formed in a very different way.

But structure is not everything, and even the marked differences of grammar and sounds are not enough to overbalance the large part of Jamaica folk speech that is English. If it is Creole, it is still English Creole as distinct from Spanish or French Creole. It coexists with English, and the two have more in common than apart.

I cannot leave this subject without a few words of a personal sort. Any speech is as interesting as the people who speak it: it is the most revealing reflection of their lives. In Jamaica it has grown and flourished by preserving things from the past; by developing new and often surprising, amusing, and imaginative meanings; by making a variety of new permutations and combinations, lively, penetrating, and often remarkably apt. It has a character all its own of which none but the least imaginative can remain unaware.

Will education eradicate it? Supposing that it could, I, for one, should hate to see this happen. As Jamaicans prosper and schooling becomes more widely spread, the speech of many will change. But may the new generations not be so dull as to scorn this possession of the folk or try to root it out. If it has not the vitality to survive it will die anyway. But that would be a loss to the human variety of the world without any special gain to counterbalance it.

My own belief is that it will continue for some time to come, coexisting with the Standard, each in its own sphere; that educated Jamaicans, like educated Europeans who value their provincial ties, will continue in a sense to be bilingual; that in acquiring Standard those whose origins are from the folk will not fling away this heritage. Perhaps, indeed, they may become increasingly aware that it is a subject worthy of serious study, and may set about investigating the many problems it poses that still wait to be solved.

BOOKS, PERIODICALS, AND
MANUSCRIPTS CITED

ITEMS are cited by the Author's name or short title, as shown in the first column. When one author has more than one work, or there are different authors of the same name, the date is also given. When the same name and date coincide, short title is also given. Attributions of works to authors made by the Institute of Jamaica are accepted.

Abraham	Abraham, Major B. C., *Dictionary of the Hausa Language*, London (Austin) 1949.
Acts & Laws	*The Acts of Assembly and Laws of Jamaica*, in Institute of Jamaica, *c.* 1695. (346.3)
Act to Repeal	*An Act to Repeal Several Acts . . .*, in Institute of Jamaica, 1788. (326.9)
Attempt	*A Book of the Continuation of Foreign Passages . . . Moreover, An Attempt on the Island of Jamaica*, London (Jenner) 1657.
Asprey	Asprey, G. F. and Thornton, Phyllis, 'Medicinal Plants of Jamaica, Parts I–IV,' reprinted from *West Indian Medical Journal*, Vol. 4, No. 4; Vol. 3, No. 1; Vol. 4, Nos. 2, 3. 1953–5.
Assembly	Jamaica House of Assembly. *The Proceedings of the Governor and Assembly of Jamaica in Regard to the Maroon Negroes . . .*, 1796.
Bailey	Beryl L. Bailey, *Creole Languages of the Caribbean Area*, M.A. Thesis, unpub. (Columbia Univ.) 1953.
Baillie	Baillie, John, *The Jamaica Distiller's Directory*, St Jago de la Vega (Gazette Office) 2nd ed., 1821.
Banbury	Banbury, Rev. (R.) T., *Jamaica Superstitions, or the Obeah Book*, Jamaica (De Souza) 1894.
Barclay	Barclay, Alexander, *A Practical View of the Present State of Slavery in the West Indies*, London (Smith & Elder) 1826.
	Barclay, Alexander, *Remarks on Emigration to Jamaica*, London (Calkin & Budd) 1840.

Bargery   Bargery, Rev. G. P., *A Hausa-English Dictionary*,
               London (Milford) 1934.
Barham   Barham, Dr Henry, *Hortus Americanus . . . particu-
               larly of the Island of Jamaica*. a1725; Kingston
               (Aikman) 1794.
Barrett   Barrett, Mr, *A Reply to the Speech of Dr Lushington . . .
               on the Condition of the Free Coloured people of Jamaica*,
               London (Shackell & Baylis) 1828.
Beckford   Beckford, William, Jr, *Remarks upon the Situation of
               Negroes in Jamaica . . .* , London (Egerton)
               1788.
               Beckford, William, Jr, *A Descriptive Account of the
               Island of Jamaica*. London (Egerton) 1790.
Beckwith   Beckwith, Martha W., 'Folk-Games of Jamaica,'
               Pub. of the Folk-lore Foundation, No. 1, Pough-
               keepsie (Vassar) 1922.
               Beckwith, Martha W., 'Christmas Mummings in
               Jamaica,' *ibid.*, No. 2, Poughkeepsie (Vassar)
               1923.
               Beckwith, Martha W., 'Jamaica Proverbs,' *ibid.*,
               No. 6, Poughkeepsie (Vassar) 1925.
               Beckwith, Martha W., 'Notes on Jamaican Ethno-
               botany,' *ibid.*, No. 8, Poughkeepsie (Vassar) 1927.
               Beckwith, Martha W., 'Jamaica Ananci Stories,'
               Memoirs of the American Folk-lore Soc., Vol. XVII,
               New York 1924.
               Beckwith, Martha W., *Black Roadways; a Study of
               Jamaican Folk Life*, Chapel Hill (Univ. of N.
               Carolina) 1929.
Belisario   Belisario, I. M., *Sketches . . . of the Negro Population
               in the Island of Jamaica*, Kingston (Belisario) 1837.
Bennett   Bennett, Louise, *Dialect Verses*, Kingston (Gleaner)
               1942.
               Bennett, Louise, *Jamaican Humour in Dialect*, King-
               ston (Gleaner) 1943.
               Bennett, Louise, poems printed in the *Star* and other
               Kingston newspapers, 1955.
Bickell   Bickell, the Rev. R., *The West Indies as they are; or a
               real picture of slavery . . .* , London (Hatchard &
               Relfe) 1825.
Blome   Blome, Richard, *A Description of the Island of Jamaica*,
               London (Milbourn) 1672.
               Blome, Richard, *A Description of the Island of Jamaica*,
               London (J. B. for Newman) 1678.

Blome, Richard, *The Present State of His Majesty's Isles and Territories in America*, London (Clark for Newman) 1687.

Bond   Bond, James, *Birds of the West Indies*, Philadelphia (Acad. Nat. Sciences) 1936.

Brassey   Brassey, Lady Annie, *In the Trades*, London (Longmans) 1885 (1887).

Broughton   Broughton, Arthur, *Hortus Eastensis*, St Jago de la Vega (Aikman) 1794.

Browne   Browne, Patrick, *The Civil and Natural History of Jamaica*, London (Osborn & Shipton) 1756.

Calendar   *Calendar of State Papers, Colonial Series V, s.a.* 1655.

Calypso   *Calypso Tunes*, with words; in Institute of Jamaica, 1948? (F 784.4)

Campbell   Campbell, Granville, *Jamaica Folk Songs*, in Institute of Jamaica. (MS 784.4)

Chamberlaine   Chamberlaine, Dr Richard, 'Contributions to Ornithology,' *Companion to the Jamaica Almanack*, 1840, 1842, 1843.

Chambre   Chambre, Major, *Recollections of West-End Life*, London (Hurst & Blackett) 1858. (Vol. II, Chaps. III–IX.)

Christaller   Christaller, the Rev. J. G., *Dictionary of the Asante and Fante Language Called Tshi (Twi)*, Basel (Evangelical Missionary Soc.) 2nd ed., 1933.

Clerk   Clerk, Astley, *The Music and Musical Instruments of Jamaica*, in Institute of Jamaica, 1914. (780.9)

Cockrell   Cockrell, T. D. A., *A Provisional List of the Fishes of Jamaica*.

Collymore   Collymore, Frank C., 'Barbadian Dialect,' *BIM*, V. 17, Dec. 1952.

Courant   *The Weekly Jamaica Courant*, Kingston (Baldwin) 1718–20.

Cruikshank   Cruikshank, J. Graham, *Black Talk, being Notes on Negro Dialect in British Guiana*, Demerara (Argosy) 1916.

Cundall   Cundall, Frank, *Chronological Outlines of Jamaica History, 1492–1926*, Kingston (Govt. Printing Off.) 1927.

Cundall, Frank, 'The Migration from Surinam to Jamaica,' repr. from *Timehri*, VI, Sept. 1919.

Dallas   Dallas, Robert C., *The History of the Maroons . . .*, London (Strahan for Longman & Reese) 1803.

Dalziel   Dalziel, J. M., *A Hausa Botanical Vocabulary*, London
               (T. F. Unwin) 1916.
Dancer   Dancer, Thos., *The Medical Assistant; or Jamaica
               Practice of Physic* . . . , Kingston (Aikman) 1801,
               1819.
Day   Day, C. R., 'Native Musical Instruments . . . ,' in
               Mockler-Ferryman, Capt. A. F., *Up the Niger*,
               London (Philip) 1892.
De la Beche   De la Beche, Sir H. T., *Notes on the Present Condition
               of the Negroes in Jamaica*, London (Cadell) 1825.
DA   Mathews, Mitford M., *A Dictionary of Americanisms*,
               Chicago (University of Chicago) 1951.
DAE   Craigie, Sir William A., *A Dictionary of American
               English*, Chicago (University of Chicago) 1938–44.
Dodd   Dodd, E. A., *Maroon Medicine*, Kingston, 1905.
DOST   Craigie, Sir William A., *Dictionary of the Older Scot-
               tish Tongue*, London (Milford) 1937 —.
Doyley   Doyley, Edward, *A Narrative of the Great Success* . . . ,
               London (Hills & Field) 1658.
Duncan   Duncan, Rev. Peter, *A Narrative of the Wesleyan
               Mission*, London, 1849.
Dunham   Dunham, Katherine, *Journey to Accompong*, New York
               (Holt) 1946.
Earthquake   *A Full Account of the terrible Earthquake at Port-Royal
               in Jamaica, in the year 1692.*
Eclogues   *West-Indian eclogues*, [attrib. to Edw. Rushton],
               1787.
EDD   Wright, Joseph, *English Dialect Dictionary*, Oxford
               (Frowde) 1898–1905.
Edmonds   Edmonds, Mrs. F. S., *One Hundred Jamaica Recipes*,
               Kingston (Gleaner) 1926.
Edwards   Edwards, Bryan, *Poems, written chiefly in the West-
               Indies*, Kingston, 1792.
               Edwards, Bryan, *The History, civil and commercial of
               the British Colonies in the West Indies*, London
               (Stockdale) 2nd ed., 1794.
Egan   Egan, Francis, *West-Indian pot pourri*, 182–, in Insti-
               tute of Jamaica. (MS 784.4)
Ellis   Ellis, A. B., *The Tshi-Speaking Peoples of the Gold
               Coast of West Africa*, London (Chapman & Hall)
               1887.
Evidence   *Evidence and Examinations taken before the Secret Com-
               mittee of Safety*, St Jago de la Vega (Aikman)
               1798.

Eye-Witness   S., J. (an Eye-Witnesse), *A Brief and Perfect Journal of the late Proceedings & Success of the English Army in the West-Indies* . . . , London, 1655.

F & W   Funk and Wagnalls, *New 'Standard' Dictionary*, New York, 1913.

Fawcett   Fawcett, W. and Rendle, A. B., *Flora of Jamaica*, London (British Museum) 1910–36, 7 vols.

Focke   Focke, H. C., *Neger-Engelsch Woordenboek*, Leiden (P. H. van der Heuvel) 1855.

Forbes   Forbes, Duncan, Ll.D., *A Dictionary, Hindustani & English*, London (Allen) 1848.

Forbes   Forbes, Rosita, *Islands in the Sun*, London (Evans) 1949.

Foulks   Foulks, Theodore, *Eighteen Months in Jamaica* . . . , London (Whittaker, Treacher, Arnott) 1833.

Francklyn   Francklyn, G., *Observations occasioned by attempts made in England to effect the Abolition of the Slave Trade*, Kingston (Strupar & Preston) 1788.

Frank   Frank, Harry A., *Roaming through the West Indies*, New York (Century) 1921.

Friederici   Friederici, Georg, *Amerikanistisches Wörterbuch*, Hamburg (Cram, De Gruyter) 1947.

Gardner   Gardner, Wm. James, *A History of Jamaica*, London, 1873

Gazette   *The Jamaica Gazette*, Kingston, 1775.

Glnr list   *The Daily Gleaner*, list of Jamaican Words and Expressions collected in a contest in December, 1943; on deposit at University College of the West Indies, Mona; analysed by Sheila Hugh-Jones.

Gordon   Gordon, Lord Adam, 'Journal of an Officer's travels in America and the West Indies, 1764–5,' in Mereness, N. D., *Travels in the American Colonies*, New York (Macmillan) 1916.

Gosse   Gosse, Ph. H. (and Hill, R.), *The Birds of Jamaica*, London (Van Voorst) 1847.

Gosse, P. H., *A Naturalist's Sojourn in Jamaica*, London (Longman, etc.) 1851.

Greenberg   Greenberg, Joseph H., *Studies in African Linguistic Classification*, New Haven (Compass) 1955.

Hamel   *Hamel, the obeah man*, London (Hunt & Clarke) 1827, 2 vols.

Heaven   Heaven, Violet, *Jamaica Proverbs and John Canoe Alphabet*, Kingston, 1896.

Heaven, Violet, *The Negro Alphabet*, Kingston, 1897.

412   JAMAICA TALK

Hickeringill   Hickeringill, Capt. E., *Jamaica Viewed: with all the Ports* ..., London (Williams ?) 1661. Also ed. 1705.
Higgins   Higgins, Bryan, *Observations and Advices for the Improvement of the Muscavado Sugar and Rum*, St Jago de la Vega (Aikman) 1797–1801, 2 vols.
Hill   Hill, Richard, *On poisonous fishes, and on Fish poisons* (Cundall, *Bibliographia*, Supplement, No. 311) 1868.
Hitchcock   Hitchcock, A. S., *Manual of the Grasses of the West Indies*, USDA Misc. Pub. 234, Washington (U.S.G. Printing Office) 1936.
Hooper   Hooper, E. D. M., *Report upon the Forests of Jamaica*, London, 1886.
Importance   *The Importance of Jamaica to Great Britain Consider'd*, London (Dodd) 1740.
Inst List   List of the plants of Jamaica, on deposit at the Institute of Jamaica.
Intelligencer   *The Intelligencer*, a letter from Jamaica, 30 June, 1664 ..., in Institute of Jamaica. (272.8)
Jacobs   Jacobs, H. P., 'The Settlers of Morant,' *West Indian Review*, Vol. xxix (July 1950), 23–5.
                Jacobs, H. P., Materials on Jamaican Language, on loan to University College of the West Indies, Mona.
James   James, Williams, *A Report of Evidence* ... 1837. [This reference is a duplication: see Williams, James.]
Jekyll   Jekyll, Walter, *Jamaica Song and Story*, the Folk-Lore Society, Vol. LV, 1904; reprinted 1907.
Kelly   Kelly, James, *Voyage to Jamaica*, Belfast, 1838.
Kerr   Kerr, James, *Reasons Why Lucea is more convenient* ..., in Institute of Jamaica (F 387), p. 1750.
Kerr   Kerr, Madeline, *Personality and Conflict in Jamaica*, Liverpool (University Press) 1952.
Kirkpatrick   Kirkpatrick, Oliver, *Country Cousin, by John Canoe*, Kingston (Gleaner) 1941.
Koromantyn   *Koromantyn Slaves; or West-Indian Sketches*, London (Hatchard & Son) 1823.
Laws   *The Laws of Jamaica, Passed by the Assembly*, ..., London (Hills for Harper) 1683; also c. 1695.
                The Laws of Jamaica, Passed by the Assembly, ..., London (H. H. Jun. for Harper) 1684.
Leslie   Leslie, Charles, *A New and Exact Account of Jamaica* ..., Edinburgh (Fleming) 1739.
                Leslie, Charles, *A New History of Jamaica* ..., London (Hodges) 1740, 2nd ed.

Legion   *A Letter from Legion to His Grace the Duke of Richmond,*
                . . . , London (Bagster) 1832.
                *A Second Letter from Legion to His Grace the Duke of
                Richmond,* . . . , London (Bagster) 1833.
Lewis   Lewis, M. G., *Journal of a West India Proprietor* . . . ,
                London, 1834 (1845).
Livingstone   Livingstone, Noel B., *Sketch Pedigrees of Some of the
                Early Settlers in Jamaica,* Kingston, 1909.
Long   Long, Edward, *The History of Jamaica,* . . . , London
                (Lowndes) 1774, 3 vols.
Lunan   Lunan, John, *Hortus Jamaicensis,* . . . , Santiago de la
                Vega (Gazette) 1814.
                Lunan, John, *An Abstract of the Laws of Jamaica
                Relating to Slaves,* Santiago de la Vega (Gazette)
                1819.
Lynn & Grant   Lynn, W. G., and Grant, C., *The Herpetology of
                Jamaica,* Kingston (Institute of Jamaica)
                1940.
Macfadyen   Macfadyen, James, *The Flora of Jamaica,* London
                (Longman, etc.) 1837.
Malaret   Malaret, Augusto, *Diccionario de Americanismos,* Maya-
                guez, Puerto Rico (Carrero) 1925.
Marly   *Marly; or, The Life of a Planter in Jamaica,* Glasgow
                (Griffin) 1828, 2nd ed.
Marsden   Marsden, Peter, *An Account of the Island of Jamaica,*
                Newcastle (Hodgson) 1788.
Mason   Mason, J. Alden, 'The languages of South American
                Indians,' in *Handbook of South American Indians,*
                Smithsonian Inst., Bur. of Amer. Ethnol., Bull.
                143, Vol. 6, part 3, pp. 157–317 Washington
                (USG Pr. Off.) 1950.
Mathison   Mathison, Gilbert, *Notices Respecting Jamaica in 1808,
                1809, 1810,* London (Stockdale) 1811.
McKay   McKay, Claude, *Constab Ballads,* Kingston (Gard-
                ner) 1912.
                McKay, Claude, *Songs of Jamaica,* Kingston (Gard-
                ner) 1912.
                McKay, Claude, *Banana Bottom,* New York (Harper)
                1933.
M'Mahon   M'Mahon, Benjamin, *Jamaica Plantership,* London,
                1839.
M'Neill   M'Neill, Hector, *Observations on the treatment of the
                Negroes in the Island of Jamaica,* London (Robinson)
                1788–9.

Merchant	An English Merchant, *Some Modern Observations Upon Jamaica:* . . . , London, 1727.
Missionaries	The Baptist Missionaries, *Narrative of Recent Events Connected with the Baptist Mission in this Island*, Kingston (Jordon & Osborn) 1833.
Moore	Moore, Joseph Graessle, *Religion of Jamaican Negroes*, Northwestern University Doctoral Dissertation, 1953; unpub.
Moreton	Moreton, J. B., *Manners and Customs in the West India Islands*, London·(Richardson, Gardner & Walker) 1790.
Murray	Murray, Henry Garland, *Manners and Customs of the Country . . . Tom Kittle's Wake*, Kingston (E. Jordon) 1877. Murray, Henry Garland, *Feedin' 'Perrit*, Kingston (M. De Cordova & Co.) 1877.
Murray	Murray, Tom, *Folk Songs of Jamaica*, Oxford (University Press) c. 1953.
NHN	Natural History Society of Jamaica, *Natural History Notes*, Kingston (Mimeographed at Institute of Jamaica) 1941 fwd., Vols. I–IV.
Nevill	Nevill, Vice Admiral, *Journal*, Phillipps MS 8606, copy in West India Library, Institute of Jamaica, 1696-7.
Nugent	Nugent, Lady Maria, *Journal*, 1801-5; ed. Frank Cundall, London (West India Committee) 1907, 1934.
OED	Murray, Sir James A. H. *et al.*, *A New English Dictionary*, Oxford (Clarendon) 1888-1928.
OEDS	Craigie, W. A., and Onions, C. T., *Supplement* [to OED], Oxford (Clarendon) 1933.
Ogilby	Ogilby, John, *America: being the latest, and most accurate description* . . . , London, 1671.
Olivier	Olivier, Lord, *Jamaica, the Blessed Island*, London, 1936.
Ordinances	*The Ordinances of the city and Parish of Kingston*, Kingston (Jamaica Courant) 1828.
Patterson	Patterson, Capt. John, *The Adventures of Capt. John Patterson*, London (Boone) 1837.
Pioneer	*Anancy Stories and Dialect Verse*, Kingston (Pioneer Press) 1950.
Planter	A Jamaica Planter, *Observations upon the African Slave Trade*, London (Law, Faulder, Deighton) 1788.

Present State   *The Present State of Jamaica*, London (Clark for Malthus) 1683.

Proprietor   A Jamaica Proprietor, *Negro Emancipation No Philanthropy*, London (Ridgway) 1830.

Rampini   Rampini, Charles, *Letters from Jamaica*, Edinburgh (Edmonston and Douglas) 1873.

Ray   Ray, John, *Synopsis Methodica Avium & Piscium*, London (Innys) 1713, with list of Jamaican birds from Sir Hans Sloane.

Reid   Reid, V. S., *New Day*, New York (Knopf) 1949.

Renny   Renny, Robert, *An History of Jamaica with Observations on the Climate* . . . , London (Cawthorn) 1807.

Rev. Divine   A Reverend Divine, *The Truest and Largest Account of the Late Earthquake in Jamaica, June the 7th, 1692*, London (Buttler) 1693.

Rivero   Rivero, Luis Howell, *Collection of Fishes from Jamaica*, in Institute of Jamaica, 1936. (597)

Roberts   Roberts, Helen H., 'Possible Survivals of African Song in Jamaica,' *Musical Quarterly*, July 1926.

    Roberts, Helen H., 'Some Drums and Drum Rhythms of Jamaica,' *Natural History*, 24: 241–51, 1924.

Roughley   Roughley, Thomas, *The Jamaican Planter's Guide;* . . . , London (Longman, etc.) 1823.

Russell   Russell, Thomas, *The Etymology of Jamaica Grammar*, Kingston, 1868.

Santamaría   Santamaría, Francisco J., *Diccionario General de Americanismos*, Mexico City (Robredo) 1942, 3 vols.

St Jago   *The St Jago Intelligencer*, St Iago, Jamaica, 1757.

Scott   Scott, Michael, *Tom Cringle's Log*, Edinburgh (Blackwood) 1833.

SND   Grant, William, *The Scottish National Dictionary*, Edinburgh (Riverside) 1931—.

Senior   Senior, Bernard M., *Jamaica as it was, as it is* . . . , Kingston, 1835.

Shooting   *Account of a Shooting Excursion*, Jamaica, 1825.

Slave's Diary   A *Slave's Diary*: 'Father Finlayson' of Penshurst Estate, St Ann; MS in Institute of Jamaica.

Sloane   Sloane, Sir Hans, *Catalogus Plantarum quae in insula Jamaica sponte proveniunt* . . . , London, 1696.

    Sloane, Sir Hans, *A Voyage To the Islands Madera, Barbados*, . . . *and JAMAICA*, . . . , London (B.M.) vol. 1, 1707; vol. 2, 1725.

Smith   Smith, Pamela C., *Chim-chim. Folk stories*, Kingston, 1905.

Smith   Smith, Victoria, *File List of Jamaican Fishes*, compiled 1950–1; in Institute of Jamaica.

Stafford   Stafford, Hurlburt, *The Orange Grove and other poems of the Jamaican Peasantry*, Montego Bay (St James Press) 1927.

State of Ja.   *The State of Jamaica*, Brit. Mus. MS. Egerton 2395, copy in the Institute of Jamaica.

Sterne   Sterne, Henry, *A Statement of the Facts*, . . . , London (Chappell) 1837.

Stewart   Stewart, James, *A Brief Account of the Present State*, in Institute of Jamaica, 1792. (326.9)

Stewart, James, of Trelawny, *An Account of Jamaica and its Inhabitants*. London (Longman, etc.) 1808, 1809.

Stewart, James, *A View of the Past and Present State of the Island of Jamaica*, Edinburgh (Oliver & Boyd) 1823.

Stubbe   Stubbe, Henry, *The Indian nectar . . . chocolata*, London, 1662.

Subsistence   *An Act for the Subsistence . . .* , in Institute of Jamaica, 1817. (326.9)

Sullivan   Sullivan, Caroline, *The Jamaica Cookery Book*, Kingston, 1893.

Taylor   Taylor, F. W., *A Fulani-English Dictionary*, Oxford (Clarendon) 1932.

Taylor   Taylor, Lady R. G., *Introduction to the Birds of Jamaica*, London (Macmillan) 1955.

Thomson   Thomson, James, *A Treatise on the Diseases of Negroes as they occur in the Island of Jamaica*, Kingston (Aikman) 1820.

Titford   Titford, W. J., M. D., *Sketches toward a hortus botanicus Americanus*, London (Stower) 1811.

Trapham   Trapham, Thomas, *A Discourse on the State of Health in the Island of Jamaica*, London (Boulter) 1679.

True Des.   *A True Description of Jamaica*, London, 1657.

Turner   Turner, Lorenzo D., *Africanisms in the Gullah Dialect*, Chicago (University of Chicago) 1949.

U. Newton   Burke, Edmund N., *Stories told by Uncle Newton*, in 6 books, Kingston, 1946–50.

Walker   Walker, Rear-Admiral Sir Hoveden, *Journalls*, October 1712, MS in the Institute of Jamaica.

Ward	Ward, Edward, *A Trip to Jamaica: With a True Character of the People and Island*, London, 1698, 1700.
W2	*Webster's New International Dictionary*, Springfield (Merriam) 1934.
White	White, Charles, *An Enquiry Concerning the Trade, Commerce, and Policy of Jamaica*, St Jago de la Vega (Brett) 1757.
Widow	R., M. ('a Widow'), *A Young Englishman's First Residence . . .*, Ashton (Orme) 1836.
Williams	Williams, Cynric R., *A Tour through the Island of Jamaica . . .*, London (Hunt & Clarke) 1826.
Williams	Williams, James, *A Report of Evidence taken at Brown's Town and St Ann's Bay . . .*, in Institute of Jamaica, 1837. (326.8)
Williams	Williams, Joseph J., *Whence the 'Black Irish' of Jamaica?*, New York (Dial) 1932.
	Williams, Joseph J., *Psychic Phenomena of Jamaica*, New York (Dial) 1934.
	Williams, Joseph J., S. J., 'The Maroons of Jamaica,' in *Anthropological Series*, Boston College Grad. Sch., III. 4, Des. 1938, Chestnut Hill (Boston Coll.) 1938.
Williamson	Williamson, John, *Medical and Miscellaneous Observations relative to the West India Islands*, Edinburgh (Smellie) 1817, 2. vols.
Wilson	Wilson, Una, 'Digging Songs,' from *Daily Gleaner*, Kingston, *c.* 1953.
Wright	Wright, Capt. Lawrence, *Journall, H.M.S. Assistance*, 1687–9; Captain's Journal, 68, P.R.O. series, in MS copy at Institute of Jamaica.
Yellow Fever	*An Essay on the Bilious or Yellow Fever of Jamaica*, Kingston (Daniell) 1750.

INFORMANTS

INFORMANTS are identified by Parish name (abbreviated) and a number; extra informants by Parish abbreviation and 'x'. The latter gave isolated bits of information, therefore are not listed. With the facts given about the Informants, the reader may better judge each response — whether it is perhaps old-fashioned, restricted in usage, sophisticated, naïve, or the like.

Clar 1 — near May Pen, man, about 50, well educated, estate owner.

Clar 2 — Chapelton, man, about 45, well educated, social worker.

Han 1 — Askenish, man, about 45, educated, cultivator, landowner.

Han 2 — Askenish, man, about 45, uneducated, agricultural labourer.

Han 3 — Lucea, man, 65–70, educated, planter, member parochial bd.

Han 4 — Lucea, man, about 25, intermediate education, artisan.

Han 5 — Orange Bay, man, about 35, little education, fisherman.

Kgn 1 — Kingston, man, about 35, some education, fisherman.

Kgn 2 — Kingston, woman, about 40, well educated, secretary.

Man 1 — Christiana, man, 52, intermediate education, ginger grower.

Man 2 — near Sedburgh, man, about 45, some education, ginger grower.

Man 3 — near Old England, woman, about 40, little education, domestic servant.

Port 1 — Prospect, man, about 45, some education, fisherman.

Port 2 — Moore Town, man, about 30, intermediate education, general work.

Port 3 — Port Antonio, woman, about 50, good education, schoolteacher.

StAnd 1 — Barbican, man, about 45, little education, manual labourer.

StAnd 2 — Cross Roads, woman, about 60, little education, domestic servant.

StAnn 1 — Moneague, man, 76, some education, busha on estates.

StAnn 2 — Moneague, man, about 40, intermediate education, forester.

StAnn 3 — near Llandovery, man, about 60, uneducated, fisherman.

StAnn 4 — Mt Pleasant, man, about 35, intermediate education, chauffeur.

StAnn 5 — Mt Pleasant, woman, about 60, well educated, manager.

StC 1 — Harker's Hall, man, 35–40, uneducated, small settler.

StC 2 — Old Harbour, man, about 40, little education, fisherman.

StE 1 — Frenchman's Bay, man, about 65, some education, fisherman.

StE 2 — Frenchman's Bay, man, about 40, intermediate education, planter.

StE 3 — Treasure Beach, woman, about 45, little education, cook.

StE 4 — Quickstep, man, about 65, no education, small settler.

StE 5 — Quickstep, man, about 35, intermediate education, forester.

StJ 1 — Reading, man, about 65, little education, fisherman, cultivator.

StJ 2 — Flagstaff, man, about 50, some education, small settler.

StM 1 — Claremont, woman, about 65, intermediate education, teacher.

StM 2 — near Claremont, man, about 70, little education, small settler.

StM 3 — Port Maria, man, about 35, some education, fisherman.

StM 4 — Grant's Town, man, about 60, little education, small settler.

StT 1 — Morant Bay, woman, about 40, educated, social worker.

StT 2 — Ginger Hall, man, about 65, intermediate education, forester.

StT 3 — Cedar Valley, man, about 45, little education, carpenter.

StT 4 — Morant Bay, man, about 45, little education, fisherman.

Tre 1 — Wait-a-bit, man, about 35, intermediate education, forester.

Tre 2 — Burnt Hill, man, about 50, no education, small settler.

West 1   — South Negril, man, about 40, little education, fisherman.
West 2   — Seaford Town, man, about 70, little education, cultivator.
West 3   — Seaford Town, man, about 45, educated, cultivator,
landowner.
West 4   — Savanna la Mar, woman, about 50, educated, guest-
house owner.

HOW TO USE THE NOTES

THE following abbrevations are used in addition to the conventional ones:

anted — antedates
app — appears, apparently
appl — applied
cit — cited, citation
conn — connected
def — defines, definition
esp — especially
etym — etymology
expl — explained, explanation
gen — generally distributed, in general use
ident — identifies
Inf — Informants (see list)

not 4 D — not found in the OED, OEDS, DAE, or DA
perh — perhaps
postd — postdates
prob — probably
pron — pronunciation, pronounced
quot — quotation, quoted
reg — regular, regularly
resp — respectively (members of a series covered by one note)
sp — spelling, spelt
trans — translated
transf — transferred

Abbreviations for books and informants are with those lists.

Most notes are short; following is a long note and its expansion:

Text: '. . . other sprats are the *black-bill, black-back, blue-back, jack sprat* (the young jack), and *herring sprat*.'[14]

Note: 'Resp Inf Port 1; Thomson 41, Inf StM 3, StJ 1, not 4 D; Smith: *Opisthonema oglinum*, Kgn; Inf Port 1, StAnn 3, StE 1; StM 3, West 1, StE 1, Moore 280: "arransprat", not 4 D.'

Expansion: Information about the five individual names is given, as *Resp* indicates, in the same sequence as the names, with semicolons between groups: *black-bill* and any information about it is from Portland Informant no. 1; *black-back* is mentioned in Thomson, *Diseases of Negroes*, page 41, also by Informants from St Mary (no. 3) and St James (no. 1), and is not treated in any of the four historical dictionaries (see list of books); *blue-back* is given the indicated scientific identification by Victoria Smith in her list of Jamaican fish (see book list), and it was the name she heard in the Kingston area; *jack sprat* was used by Informants from Portland (no. 1), St Ann (no. 3), and St Elizabeth (no. 1); *herring sprat* was used by Informants from St Mary (no. 3), Westmoreland (no. 1), and St Elizabeth (no. 1), and by Joseph G. Moore in his *Religion of Jamaican Negroes*, page 280, who records the form 'arransprat', but *herring sprat* is not in the four historical dictionaries.

421

NOTES

CHAPTER ONE

1. Titford, xiii. 2. Sullivan, 65.

CHAPTER TWO

1. A chronology of Jamaica states that 'several planters' from New England and Bermuda came in 1657; in 1658 there were said to be 250 from Bermuda and 'some Quakers' from Barbados. Again, in 1664, Sir Thomas Modiford brought in a group from Barbados. Since this book was completed, Dr. R. B. LePage has made another attempt to study carefully the sources of Jamaica's population and the language types represented: *Creole Language Studies* I (1959), Macmillan.
2. Copy in the West India Library, Institute of Jamaica.
3. From Kelly, 68-9. 4. Importance, 15.
5. Op. cit, I. 492, II. 372-3, 384.
6. St Jago, 14 May, 1757, etc.; *Courant*, 10 Feb., 13 July, 5 Aug., 1718; 8 Apr., 1719; 5 June, 1720; *Gazette*, 25 Mar., 1775; Bickell, 38-46; Senior, 34; McKay, *Ballads*, 13.
7. Bongo, Crongoe, Madagascar are exceptions; the first two from far inland, the third surprising considering how far away Madagascar was — yet there were certainly some Negroes called 'Madagass' (see Chap. VI). Hittoe and Sumino have not been traced. All these are numerically small.
8. Kelly, 21. 9. 1790 Moreton, 116; also 131.
10. 1858 Chambre, II. 129. 11. Olivier, 293-4.
12. Erickson, E. L., 'The Introduction of East India Coolies into the B.W.I.', *Journal of Modern History*, VI. 128.

CHAPTER THREE

1. See Chap. II, p. 12, and note 2.
2. See Chap. II, pp. 22, 23.
3. *Book* and *boil* actually do not end in *t*, but *foot* and *Hoyt* do; the contrast that matters is in the vowel nucleus. See Appendix I.
4. But not always; they may be substituted for the vowels most like them in Standard, thus: *say* /se/, *you* /yu/, *go* /go/, the lax vowel in each case taking the place of a tense vowel or diphthong.
5. Stewart, 259; this means *path*, not *pass*.

CHAPTER FOUR

1. Christaller; see also Turner, 223-4. 2. Greenberg, 29.
3. There may be confusion here with *lots of*.
4. *Paradise Lost*, III. 438. 5. 1942 Bennett, 42. 6. Moreton, 156.
7. Belisario, plate 8. 8. Clerk. 9. Pioneer, 72.
10. 1912 McKay, 76. 11. Turner, 227; cf. Twi *mo*, he, she.

12. Resp. Russell, 16; Informants StM 2, StM 4, StT 4; Pioneer, 60; U. Newton V. 22; 1955 Bennett, *Me Dream*.
13. Resp. 1912 McKay, *Songs* 38; U. Newton, II. 38.
14. There is also a preposition *a*, formed from *at* but meaning *to*: Go *a* Kingston; and another, formed from and meaning *of*: One *a* dem wrong.
15. Turner, 213.   16. Christaller, 433.
17. From Miss Phyllis Caws, Institute of Jamaica.
18. 1929 Beckwith, 100; the introductory impersonal is lacking here.
19. 1839 McMahon, 58.
20. OED conj² 'Scots and dial'; see also English *na*, Scots *no*, OED: 'mair ... no I will tell yow' — more *than*. Williams, 190; Banbury, 39.
21. Moreton, 125.   22. Turner, 210.   23. *Ibid.*, 212.
24. Louise Bennett in *Pioneer*, 61.   25. Turner, 210.

CHAPTER FIVE

1. Friederici questions African origin and thinks it Amer. Ind.; the name of the boat is probably from that of the tree it is made of.
2. OED sb¹ 2, last quot 1596.   3. Frank, 416, 414.
4. Present State, 10; not 4 D.
5. Moore, 133, etc.; OED resp. 1795–1890, 1553–1818, but considered Jamaican-isms from characteristic use here.
6. Jekyll, 77; also Russell, 5; *Pioneer*, 66; Inf Han 4, etc.; not 4 D.
7. 1826 Barclay, 224; not 4 D.
8. Russell, 6; also Banbury, 7, *bancra*; 1734 Williams, 36, *bonkra*.
9. Resp. 1929 Beckwith, 48; Dunham, 93; also Inf Tre 2; not 4 D.
10. Russell, 5; Glnr list, 12 cits; Inf Tre 2.
11. Avis, *Amer Speech Mag*, Apr. 1955.
12. 1808 Stewart, 232; in ed. 1823, 269, spelt *croocas*.   13. Dodd, 30.
14. Russell, 5.   15. 1942 Bennett, 11.   16. U. Newton, VI. 32.
17. Possibly connected with /bikl/ (victuals).
18. Long, I. 450; 1790 Beckford, I. 172; OED has *stool* from 1790, *stole* from 1807.
19. Resp. 1778 Beckford, 46; Roughley, 99; De la Beche, 6; Roughley, 102; Marly, 93.
20. Bickell, 50; not 4 D.   21. Resp Mathison, 75; Roughley, 217; not 4 D.
22. 1790 Beckford, I. 51; OED, 1833.   23. Barclay 10.
24. p. 341; this phrase also shows the nautical influence noted by Long; *boatswain* was often used for 'foreman' — cf. 1837 James 7.
25. Ligon, OED cit.; Browne, 131; spelt *teach*, 1788 Marsden, 26, etc.; *teache*, 1803 Dallas, I. xcvi; *taitch*, ibid., II. 347, etc.; *tack*, 1790 Moreton, 71; none of these forms is in OED, though the last would support the etymology offered there.
26. Marly, 36, 43; not 4 D.   27. Long, I. 463.
28. Banbury, 30.   29. Browne, 174; not 4 D.
30. Glnr list; none of these three is common.
31. Resp. Sloane, lxx; Browne, 163; Infs St And. 1, West 2; Long, I. 495; OED sb¹ 10c, 1793.
32. 1929 Beckwith, 10; corrected by Miss V. L. McLoskey.
33. Senior, 52; not 4 D.   34. U. Newton, I. 26.   35. Browne, 163.
36. Senior, 53; not 4 D; 1943 Glnr list.   37. Roughley, 405, 407.
38. Blome, 122; Present State, 17; neither in OED.   39. 1943 Glnr list.
40. p. 14; also 1929 Beckwith, 35; U. Newton, V. 26; Inf Man 1, Han 4, etc.
41. Malaret, Santamaría; EDD, *callyvan*.

CHAPTER SIX

1. Cundall, pref. to Nugent, 10.   2. 1912 McKay, 75.
3. Information from Dr David DeCamp.
4. Resp. 1825. Bickell, 49, OED first quot 1828; 1826 Barclay, 329; 1837 James, 14; not 4 D.
5. 1826 Williams, 252.
6. Jacobs interprets 'Saturday him heng' as meaning that it is even worse than Friday; but this does not agree with Saturday's being pay-day, which would put an end to Friday's difficulties.
7. OED 1740.   8. *Jamaica, a Poem*, 11.
9. 1699 Dampier; OED cit.
10. *North*, as a noun, parallels and probably translates Spanish *Norte*; *norther* is *north* with the *-er* suffix showing relationship.
11. Chambre, II. 83.   12. Koromantyn, 123.
13. Clearly from English dial *rubbage*.
14. Resp. U. Newton, III. 11; also Inf Tre 2; U. Newton, I. 11.
15. *Here* acquires a palatal glide /y/ and loses /h/ and /r/, becoming /ya/; *so* may be, English but more likely African: cf. Twi *-sò*, which means something like *thus*.
16. 1955 Bennett, *Back to Africa*.
17. Williamson, I. 37; also Titford, xvi.
18. OED 21c: 'obs'; OEDS has quots only to 1846. Information on the StT usage comes from Dr David DeCamp.
19. 1955 Bennett, *Gawn a Match*.   20. 1955 Bennett, *Sweepstake*.
21. U. Newton, I. 9.   22. Williams, 300.

CHAPTER SEVEN

1. Resp. 1739 Leslie, 328; Beckford, II. 283; Senior, 124.
2. Grant, 29: 'dry cholick'; Beckford, II. 302: 'dry cholic'.
3. 1661 Hickeringill, 80.   4. 1750 Williams, iii. i.
5. Resp McNeill, 35; Dancer, 230; Renny, 205; Thomson, 99; Banbury, 10.
6. Dancer, 232; Thomson, 99; last OED quot 1683, prob a different disease.
7. p. 171; first OED quots 1802 *dirt-eater*, 1817 *dirt-eating*.
8. Resp. 1823 Stewart, 307; Thomson, 24, also 32.
9. Resp. 1789 Reports, 28–9; Dancer, 269; Long, III. 713; not 4 D.
10. 1788–9 McNeill, 8; also 1801 Nugent, 40; only OED quot 1828 this sense.
11. Cf. Twi *fè*, to vomit; *nè* 'to cack'; Fante *fenã*, to trouble, to be troubled, Christaller; Bambara *fono*, to vomit, Turner, 88.
12. 1781 Dancer, 51; not 4 D.
13. From a dial. pronunciation of Sp. *anisado*.
14. Inf Han 4; also in Barbados (Collymore).
15. Both from Glnr list, the latter Man; for third syllable of *montompy* cf. Twi *mpẽ*, matter found sometimes, esp. after a night's sleep, in the corner of the eye (Christaller).
16. Heard as a child: a form of *bugaboo* (which also means caterpillar in Jamaica).
17. Williams, 205; also 1837 James, 11.
18. Chap. XIII; this is another Jamaican preservation.
19. p. 154; by metathesis from *arse*; not 4 D, but see Partridge, *Dictionary of Slang*, s.v. *raspberry tart*.
20. Glnr list both; *lep*, also Inf StAnd 2; EDD *gander*, wander, ramble aimlessly.
21. A possible connection is with Twi *nyãkã-nyãkã*, cut into pieces, to which the sense 'make badly or carelessly' of the Spanish forms could be related.

22. Kerr, 157.
23. Resp. 1868 Russell, 17; 1955 Bennett, *Cricket History*, also *Pioneer* gloss; Dodd 51; ibid., 5; *Pioneer*, 20.
24. With the usual reduction of *sp-* to *p-*: compare also *strand* pron. /straan/.
25. Resp. Moreton, 154; 1895 Banbury, 28; Twi *tùm-tum* is 'imitative of the sound of pounding "fufuu" in a wooden mortar' (Christaller).
26. See OED.   27. p. 195.   28. Marly, 41.
29. 1868 Russell, 17.   30. 1826 Barclay, 325.
31. Greenberg lists related forms from eighteen languages for the noun meaning *animal, meat*, from which the Jamaican verb comes; 18.
32. 1788 Marsden, 49.

CHAPTER EIGHT

1. Importance, 20; this spelling not 4 D.
2. 1826, 92, 95, 320; none in 4 D.
3. Glnr list; Inf StAnd 2; cp. Twi *a-màrátònì, omurdtòni*, borrowed from Portuguese or some other European language.
4. 1740 Importance, 16; but Marsden, 7, 9, gives *mestee* as the offspring of white and quadroon; *castee* is not in 4 D.
5. 1825 Bickell, 111.
6. 1828 Marly, 94, mistakenly identified with *quadroon*, and see also 183; 1833 Foulks, 26.
7. 1739 Leslie, 248.
8. Resp. Moreton, 149, 153; 1826 Williams, 202; 1828 Marly, 63.
9. 1823 Stewart, 261–2; in this sense, only DA, 1828, 1839.
10. Resp. 1823 Roughley, 91; 1835 Senior, 30, 31; 1836 Widow, 245.
11. Etymology worked out by Dr R. B. Le Page.
12. 1707 Sloane, lii; DA first quot 1653.
13. Resp. Moreton, 152; Russell, 6; Stafford, 26.
14. From Port. *mofino*, an unfortunate person, poor, much reduced.
15. 1774 Long, II. 49; first OED quot 1777.
16. Though *Surrey* is one of the three divisions of Jamaica, an African word probably lies behind; cf. Bambara, Songhay, Yoruba *sari*, all denoting foods.
17. Russell, 12.
18. Possibly, though less suiting the sense, from *purposeful*.
19. 1929 Beckwith, 167.   20. Williams, 19; *no worth* is chiefly Scots (EDD).
21. Glnr list; see OED *funk* sb⁴ and SND *funky*.
22. Both Glnr list; cp. *bolo*, a fellow, companion.
23. See EDD senses, 3, 4.   24. Cf. Twi *kasákàsa*, to dispute.
25. *Combolo* may combine various source words: cf. Cuban *cùmbila*, comrade and Amer. Sp. *cumpa, compa*, familiar abbr of *compadre*, companion; also *compañero*, comrade, and *carabela*, a word used among African-born negroes of Cuba for one who was brought from Africa in the same ship (Jamaican slaves called such a person *shipmate*, and it was considered a very strong bond). Cf. also Kimbundu *camba*, comrade.
26. Kerr, 42.
27. Glnr list; Inf StAnd 2; cf. Twi *bɔɔbɔɔ* phlegmatic, dull, sluggish; *mùmu*, deaf-and-dumbness.
28. Similarly, a *buryin'-bessy* attends every wake: 1877 Murray, *Kittle*, 16.
29. Moreton, 157.   30. 1934 Williams, 165.
31. Black River, etc.; cf. Twi *nyámoo*, lean, feeble, meagre, poor.
32. But cf. Fanti *puróu*, to stumble, to knock, throw about, etc.; or Twi *apùrukù*, that which is rough instead of being soft and smooth.

33. Cf. Christaller: Fanti *gyakaa*, confused.
34. 1803 Dallas, II. 226-7.

CHAPTER NINE

1. Importance, 44.
2. It could not be French, which does not pronounce the *t* or have the final vowel.
3. Resp. Ins Tre 2, StE 3; StM 1, StJ 2, West 3; StJ 2.
4. Marsden, 19 *et passim*; not 4 D.   5. Bickell, 9-10.
6. Marly, 104; not 4 D.
7. Mugil *liza* is the calipeva; Sp. *liza*, an ocean fish (etym unknown).
8. Ward, 15; 1873 Rampini, 64: 'For here [in Chapelton], was I not introduced to "pepper-pot" and mountain mullet? Not the Demerara pepper-pot with its evil-smelling and even more evil-tasting Cassareep sauce . . .; but a rich, succulent potage.'
9. Trans from Malaret.   10. Christaller.
11. Resp. ODS, not other 3 D; Leslie, 35.
12. Christaller; Jekyll, erroneously, *fee-fee*, 134; see also Russell, 6; 1934 Williams, 35; Turner, 88.
13. Cf. *bollo*, small bread roll, cake; none of these 4 in 4 D.
14. Glnr list; could this be from Fr. *manger*, to eat?   15. 1929, 21.
16. This is not an adequate etymology, but perhaps accounts for the first part of *bammy*; the second element is unknown.
17. Smyth's *Sailor's Word-book* (1867).
18. The first part may be from Fr. *hachis*; the second is obscure.
19. Smyth op. cit.; OED quot.
20. Importance, 39; other forms: *callapee, calapee*, Trapham, 61, 64; *callepee*, 1707 Sloane, lxxxviii; *callipash, callipee*, Nugent, 121.
21. 1774, 762, quoted in 1814, I. 337; cf. U.S. dial *mutton corn*.
22. 1725 Sloane, 378, 'Mr Barham MS' — i.e., recorded a1725; *pimentade* is from Fr.; neither in 4 D.
23. p. 6; not 4 D; perh ultimately from Arabic *mauzaʰ*, banana; cf. OED *muse* sb⁴.
24. Cundall, in Nugent, 88.   25. 1794 Barham, 132.
26. 1835 Senior, 115; only OED quot 1861.
27. 1707 Sloane, lxii.   28. Ibid.; first OED quot for *kava*: 1817.
29. Turner, 128: Kongo, Kimbundu, etc.: *malavu*.
30. 1896 Murray, *How Quamin Learnt*; 1924 Beckwith, 83.
31. Importance, 69.   32. Resp. Koromantyn, 121; Marly, 180.
33. Resp. Laws, 88; 1788 *Act to Repeal*, 21.

CHAPTER TEN

1. *Cowskin* not specifically Jamaican; *cow-cod*, Inf StT 2; also specifically a bull's-pizzle whip.
2. 1955 Bennett, *Me Dream*.
3. Resp 1833 Letter from Legion, 27; ibid., 22; ibid., 27.
4. 1790 Moreton, 84.   5. 1792 Stewart, 19.
6. Baptist Missionaries, 26.   7. OED senses, 7, 8.
8. 1912 McKay, *Ballads*; OED sense, 9, but the phrase not 4 D.
9. Glnr list; cf. Twi *gigyé*, to lead astray, decoy, cheat; *fu* is prob from English *fool* — cf. *foo-fool*, foolish.
10. p. xviii; cf. H. P. Jacobs in *Ja. Hist. Review*, II. 1 (Dec. 1949), 67 ff.

11. Cf. Fante, *abɛbɛ*, pet; *adɔdɛ*, a favourite thing, pet; several similar ones exist in French.
12. Dallas, I. 115.   13. Kerr, 96; not 4 D.
14. p. 153; Turner cites forms from Ewe, Kongo, Kimbundu, Bobangi, and Tshiluba, 167.
15. Cf. Scottish *no'*, for *not*.   16. Glnr list and H. P. Jacobs.
17. Cf. Twi *sud*, to set, place, put; Twi *fɛ̀, fɛ̀ɛ̀*, interj., a challenge to fight and its answer (Christaller).
18. pp. 21–2; see also Chap. II above; cf. Twi *bɔbɔ́ɔ́o*, interj.
19. Cf. Twi *dò*, interj., what! why! hey! ay! fie! (Christaller); Twi *hɑ́ì*, interj., an expression of fear or astonishment.
20. Cf. Twi *ai, aaì, aìi*, interj., ah! ah me! alas! woe!
21. Cf. Twi *ɛ̀ì, ɛ̀ɛ̀ì*, interj. expressing surprise, astonishment: *indeed!* Hamel, I. 333; cf. Twi *twɛ́aa*, interj. of contempt; Ewe *tsòò*, interj. of astonishment, anger, impatience, disappointment.
22. p. 131; this simply means *dung*, cf. English *cack*, Fr. or Sp. *caca*; Mende, *ka*, waste matter (Turner 102).
23. Scott, II. 370.   24. Cf. Twi *kɔ̀*, to go.   25. H. P. Jacobs.
26. Respelled from Turner, 239.

CHAPTER ELEVEN

1. 1926 Williams, 37.   2. Foulks, 111–12; not 4 D.
3. p1781, Dr Moseley, quoted in 1934 Williams, 120.
4. We depend heavily here upon Moore's useful study.
5. No satisfactory African term has come to hand but /poko/ seems to mean *bad* in the folk speech.
6. Moore, 100.
7. The foregoing account is digested from Moore's study.
8. See OED; *obeah-woman* Dallas, I. 74, first OED quot 1840; also 1934 Williams, 126.
9. Koromantyn, 177.
10. Resp p. 9; Jekyll, 241. When the obeahman deals in herb ('bush') medicines, the word has double applicability.
11. Cf. Ewe *mayɛ́*, evil, and *lɛ́*, to take hold of, grasp.
12. Beckwith spelt this 'sheppon', apparently not identifying it as shut-pan: 1929, 147; cf. Chap. V, note 15.
13. Resp. De la Beche, 31–2; Banbury, 28.   14. 1929 Beckwith, 119.
15. Cf. Turner: Vai *dʒuma*, witchcraft; *zombie* is a related form.
16. Hamel, II. 32.   17. Kerr, 31; this sense not 4 D.
18. Resp Kerr, 139; Inf StE 3; Inf StAnd 1; 1929 Beckwith, 94; Inf StE 3.
19. 1929 Beckwith, 55.
20. *Ibid.*, 83. This guess is certainly wrong; the refrain of the song (which has been recorded by Dr DeCamp) is /baakini tumbe/, African words or a corruption thereof, which were probably taken by Beckwith to mean 'back in the tomb'.

CHAPTER TWELVE

1. De la Beche, Barclay, Williams, Glnr correspondent; see quots below.
2. Beckwith has written that the 'houseboat is reported much later and may be a pattern derived from Mohammedan tomb dances . . .'; 1929, 150.
3. 1801 Nugent, 65–6; Chambre, II. 151; 1923 Beckwith, 5, offers another explanation supposedly from Phillippo: *John Cornu*, which she takes to refer to the horns of the masked dancer; but it turns out to be merely a typographical

error: Phillippo has *John Connu*, taken directly from Long's account; see also F. Wurdimann, *Notes on Cuba* (1844), 83–4.

4. Dunham, 53–4; Christaller: Twi *abέη*, *àbὲη*, horn of animals; musical instrument, etc.; not 4 D.
5. 1929, 194; her form is *abong*, prob a misprint.
6. Possibly connected with Bambara or Mandingo *bala*, xylophone; Turner, 190.
7. Compare *merry-wing*, name for a large mosquito; see next chapter.
8. Importance, 18; OED 'Obs. rare': last quot 1728.
9. Resp Inf StAnd 2; Glnr list; cf. Sp. *tambor*, a dance (used in Cuba).
10. Resp 163; 326, not 4 D; Moore, 172, 137, gloss.
11. Beckford, II. 387, also 1929 Beckwith, 210; Belisario, expl to plate III.
12. Glnr list; cf. Turner, 117: Kongo (Angola) *ηkumbi*, a drum.
13. V. 32, 30; Turner, 238: Bini *titititititi*, imitating the sound of a small drum; cf. Hausa *chàki*, Yoruba *shekere*, a rattle; resp from Dalziel, 13, Turner, 164.
14. Inf StAnd 2; OED has 'masking' for 'The action of performing or taking part in a masquerade' till 1864, but not as the name of the celebration itself.
15. Cf. Hausa *bowsorow*, which refers to cheating [the masks?] and to unkempt things or people.
16. Glnr list; in Barbados, *bram*: small dancing party (Collymore).
17. pp. 156–7.
18. Cp. also Argentinian and Brazilian *candombe*, 'obstreperous negro dance' (trans from Malaret). Cf. also Santamaría, Mendonça.
19. 1929 Beckwith, 214; 1922 Beckwith, 61.
20. Cf. Twi *bom'*, *bomu*, to cry; to join, unite; the root *bɔ* is to strike (Christaller senses, 16, 23). As to *jamma*, it is not only a song but a digging tool, so the saying may have double reference. Note also Twi *edwóm*, a song, hymn, etc.
21. OED v¹ 2a, b; latest quots 1773, 1673, [1841].
22. Sent to me directly by Mr Burke, 'Uncle Newton'; see also U. Newton, I. 3, III. 18, IV. 7.
23. Last OED quot 1765; Collymore; OED sense 1, 'Obs.' — latest quot a 1793.
24. Cf. Turner, 237: *swing-swang*, Gullah.
25. Cf. EDD, *gulch*, a fat person.
26. Twi *sã-gud*, a place of assembly.

CHAPTER THIRTEEN

1. Chambre, II. 120–1; also Marly, 23; Sir Charles Price (1708–72).
2. NHN: W. B. Espeut brought 4 males, 5 females to Spring Garden, Port.
3. Present State, 20.
4. *Gill* is pronounced / gil / ; *cock* lizard is also said in Barbados (Collymore).
5. Cf. Twi *ɔ-nãnkã* , a large horned snake (Christaller); first OED quot for a W.I. snake, 1868; Lynn and Grant identify as *Epicrates subflavus*.
6. NHN; could this be a mistake, the insect for the nest?
7. Importance, 48; Senior, 79.
8. Beckford, I. 56–7; nót 4 D.
9. Importance, 48; this genus is generally called *house ants*.
10. Inf Han 1, StAnd 2; cp. Glnr list: *ninge-ninge*, small flies; also Twi *mmĩmĩnã*, small stinging flies; Efik *nĩηinĩηi*, a small quantity of something (information from Dr Jack Berry).
11. Present State, 20.   12. Ibid.; DAE, DA earliest quot 1709.
13. Importance, 48–9.
14. EDD: Scots *waul*, to gaze wildly, roll the eyes. (Actually these are not the insect's eyes but luminous spots.)

15. NHN: Grub of May or June bug, rhinoceros beetle, parch-corn; not 4 D.
16. Cf. Twi *gyigyi*, be unsteady, vacillate, stagger, be excited (Christaller).
17. Importance, 48.   18. Gordon, 381; not 4 D; NHN; Inf StT 2, Port 2.

CHAPTER FOURTEEN

1. 1847, 437, not 4 D; Bond identifies it as the Black-Capped Petrel.
2. Trapham, 67; also 1727 *Observations*, 18; OED quots 1847, 1860.
3. Chamberlaine, 83; OED first quot 1847; Inf StC 2; Taylor, 63.
4. M. M. Carley in *Sunday Gleaner*, March 1952.   5. Taylor, 74.
6. Ibid., 67; 'switchy-neck' would more accurately represent the folk form of such a name.
7. pp. 330, 343, 348–54; his '*knit, Tringa Canutus*' looks like an error for OED *knot* sb², a Scots name for the yellow-legs.
8. Chamberlaine, 19, OED first quot 1847; Taylor, 92.
9. Sloane, in Ray, 184.   10. Sloane, in Ray, 183; Taylor, 93.
11. Stewart, 78; also Chamberlaine, 19; OED 1847.
12. Infs StT 2, StAnd 1, Han 1; U. Newton, V. 26; not 4 D, but cf. OED, Barbary 'a fancy pigeon' 1834. It is not a native wild dove but an 'escape'.
13. Chamberlaine, 26; *glass-eye* first OED quot 1847; *fish-eye* not 4 D; Taylor, 95.
14. Resp 1840 Chamberlaine, 26; 1843 Same, 77; NHN; Taylor, index; ibid., 3, 14; 1840 Chamberlaine, 26; Glnr list.
15. Sloane, in 1713 Ray, 184, only OED quot; 1725 Sloane, 299–300.
16. Importance 38.   17. *Observations*, 18, not 4 D; II. 893.
18. 1713 in Ray, 181.   19. Sloane, in Ray, 187; only OED quot 1868.
20. Williams, 36; not 4 D.
21. Note, however, that *swi-swi man* is one of the names for an obeah-man.
22. Importance, 38, not 4 D.
23. Gloss; not found elsewhere; Gosse writes ibid.: 'the accent . . . is most energetically on the last syllable', but note forms of the name with *-chu-* accented; p. 476; III. 895.
24. Taylor, 22.
25. Mr W. Adolphe Roberts has just reported (1958) having known *chamba beezer* in southern Manchester in his boyhood as the name of the black-and-white creeper. *Chamba* means 'cut', and refers to the prominent stripes.

CHAPTER FIFTEEN

1. Browne, 458.   2. Only *cutter* is a Jamaicanism; not 4 D; gen.
3. Twi *bɔɔbɔɔ* or (more likely) Sp. *bobo*.
4. 1725 Sloane, II. 277; OED sense 1b, first quot 1731; Inf StC 2.
5. Trapham, 59.
6. Inf StC 2; *sabilo* poss conn with Sp. *sable*, Cuba and P. Rico; *bowlin* perh conn with *bowline*? Neither in 4 D.
7. p. 281, not 4 D; 'Tetrodon testudineus'.
8. P. Rico: *balajú*; Inf StC 2; Smith: *Piper, bally-hoo*.
9. 1713 Ray, 169; 1725 Sloane, 284; Smith: *Galliwasp*, Pedro Bay.
10. 1679 Trapham; OED first quot 1697.
11. Trapham, 59.
12. Not 4 D; cf. Fanti ɛ-baŋ, Twi m̃maŋ, a kind of herring.
13. Cf. Smith's *pompado*; Infs StT 4, StM 3, StC 2; OED has *cobblerfish* without citations and for a different fish; not other 3 D; *cavally*, etc., go back to Sp. *caballa* or Pg. *cavalla*, which themselves derive from *caballo* or *cavallo*, horse; Jamaican forms in -*o* are no doubt influenced by the latter.

14. Resp. Inf Port 1; Thomson 41, Inf StM 3, StJ 1, not 4 D; Smith: *Opisthonema oglinum*, Kgn; Inf Port 1, StAnn 3, StE 1; StM 3, West 1, StE 1, Moore 280: 'arransprat', not 4 D.
15. Browne, 451; 1802, 79; Smith.
16. Resp Long, II. 48; Beckford, I. 234; Stewart, 87; Chambre, II. 73; Sullivan, 8. none of these spellings in 4 D. *Mugil liza.*
17. 1823 Stewart, 81: 'silk'; also Cockrell.
18. Smith, Pt. Antonio; 'Myri' Negril (could this be from the genus name *Myripristes?*).
19. Resp 1679, 66: 'Parret fish' — OED first quot 1712; 1725, 281.
20. But cf. Twi *gɔ̃rɔgɔ̃rɔw*, weak, feeble, languid.
21. Inf Montego Bay: *renchman.*
22. Smith: *Bathygobius soporator*, Kgn.
23. Lewis spells it *god-dammie*, but the accent is actually on the first syllable.
24. No satisfactory source found, but cf. Twi *koóbí*, a species of river fish.
25. 1912 *Ballads*; not OED; cf. Twi *yìri*, (of water) to rise, inundate — perhaps referring to their being caught when the rivers are flooding.
26. In Ray, 159; 1725, 282; neither in 4 D.
27. p. 423; see OED *crab*, DAE *Jamaica crab*.
28. Browne 399–413; not 4 D except *onion-peel*, OED 1898; 1725, 232, not OED; ibid., 229, OEDS ref 1895.
29. Glnr list.
30. II. 49; Browne 394, not 4 D; Infs Port 1, StM 3, StE1; 1696, 2, not 4 D. (*Seaplate* and *sea-star* are still current in Barbados — Collymore).

CHAPTER SIXTEEN

1. In the first 3 letters of the alphabet there are more than 50. Also in the first 3 letters there are 40 antedatings — from 193 years (*clammy cherry*) to 3 years (*Bourbon cane*) — averaging 55 years earlier; and there are 5 postdatings — 197 to 32 years — averaging more than 87 years.
2. Friederici, s.v. *taye.*
3. 1696 Sloane, 62; 1725 Sloane, 367; Browne 332, *tyre* (with r silent); Beckford *toyer*; Dallas, I. 106, *toyaus*; Lunan, I. 212.
4. Browne, 332.
5. Importance, 30; Fawcett and Rendle identify *ground coco* and *wild coco* as *Eulophia alta* — evidently later names.
6. Not 4 D; first record found 1907 Jekyll, 18, *hafoo yam*; also 1927 Stafford, 26; Christaller; 1934, 35; Glnr list; Christaller *ŋkámfó.*
7. Glnr list; cf. Twi *ɔdepá ne*, a type of yam.
8. 1929 Beckwith, 16; 1934, 36; cf. Twi *pumpũŋ*; cf. Twi *ɔ-dé*, yam; Christaller; Russell, 5; Gen; Infs Tre 1, StE 4; cf. Twi *hãmã*, climber, trailing plant; Infs StT 3, Tre 2; StE 4; Glnr list, *gashy* perh from Twi *kwasea* — cf. Christaller *ɔde-kwasea.*
9. DAE; Eye-Witness, 19; Importance, 34; McKay, *Songs*, 15; Beckwith, 19.
10. Browne, 292; Rampini, ref by 1929 Beckwith, 19. *Cockle peas* is still known.
11. p. 49; via Sp. from Guaraní *caaruru*: Malaret, s.v. *caruru*; resp Sloane, Browne, 174; Long, II. 417, Titford, expl to plate XII. 8, Lunan, I. 141, Dunham, 94; Infs StM 1, StAnn 5, etc.; 1740 Importance, 30, 34: resp *Colocasia, Amarantus,* and *Phytolacca.*
12. Cf. Twi *ɔ-dókoto*, growing wild.
13. *Brown jolly*, Browne, 173, Long, III. 772, 854; *bolangena*, Browne, 173, Titford, 53; *valanghanna*, 1725, 377; *balankuna*, Titford, 53; *egg fruit*, 1811 Titford, 53 (DA 1817).

14. Resp Browne 192 (not 4 D); ibid., also Ligon, 1673, 83 — perhaps also in ed. 1657?; 1764 Gordon, 381.
15. Resp. Browne, 210, Moreton, 41, Titford, xv, Sullivan, 79, Stafford, 28.
16. 1773, 11, perh in ed. 1657; 1672 Blome, 25; also, 1696 Sloane, 205.
17. *Sapota achras*; 1657 Attempt, 46 'nispero'; 1679 Trapham, 79, first OED quot 1698; Sloane, 206; Dancer, 364; Gen; 1683 Present State, 21, also Sloane, 206 (OED first quot 1697).
18. Resp. 30 Lunan, I. 388, 1808 Stewart, 93; Lunan, ibid., 'jaack fruit' (OED first quot 1830); 1696, 154; 1725, 61; Inf Port 3; Gen; Inf Port 3; Gen; Importance, 31; Long, III. 855; Lunan, I. 87; Taino *mamey*, Nahuatl, *tzapotl*; State Ja. fol 489, Blome 25, 1696 Sloane 180–1, Barham 93, etc.; Attempt, 46.
19. *Bursera* spp; 1696 Sloane, 167; OED: *West Indian Birch*; resp. Infs StAnd 2, StAnn 2; StM 4, StAnn 4, StE 4; StC 1; 1696 Sloane, 168, *et al.*; Fawcett-Rendle; ibid; Long, II. 128; Inf StAnd.
20. Dalziel, 58; in the Spanish islands and Mexico various trees are also called *quiebra-hacha* (break-ax), and other plants are named *quiebra-arado, -ollas, -piedras, -plato* (break-plow, -pot, -stone, -plate); see Malaret; *Sloanea jamaicensis*; Infs StT 2, StAnn 2; StAnn 2.
21. Friederici: *caóban* — cf. Central Am. and P. Rican *caobana*, an antiquated name for *caoba* (Malaret); in Jamaica (1657 Attempt, 45) this appeared as *cawobena* (not 4 D); *wanika*, cf. 1834 Lewis (1845), 71, and 1877 Murray, *Tom Kittle*, 27.
22. Importance, 54; first OED quot 1756; Williams, 40.
23. Resp. 1740 Importance, 54, OED first quot 1758; 1696 Sloane, 155, Long, 846, OED first quot 'princes wood' 1686.
24. Christaller: Twi *a-bé*, palm tree 'the most common in western Africa'; Infs StAnd 1, StAnn 1, StJ 2; Titford, xvi, also U. Newton, III. 17.
25. Resp. Inf StJ 2; same; Inf Port 2, StM 2; Inf StT 3, StJ 2, StE 4, Importance, 54; Inf StM 2; Inf StT 3, StM 2; Inf Port 2; Same: '*banga macca* is the same as macca-fat palm'; Jekyll, 119 reported *cullabunka* as 'a kind of Palm' — perh the same as this.
26. W2 'Curratow' with first syllable stress; *carato* in present folk use, some stressing first, some second syllable; also minor variants.
27. 1756 Browne, 95, 104; earliest OED quot 1827.
28. Dancer, 361; OED first quot 1837.
29. Infs StT 1, StAnn 4; Inst list.
30. Browne, 329, 'poisoned Hog-meat'; Inf StM 4, etc.; Inst list.
31. Titford, 91; Lunan, I. 339 ff.; OED cites Sloane (1725); Fawcett-Rendle.
32. Resp Gosse, Inf StM 2, 4, StC 1, etc.; Browne, 110, OED first quot 1866.
33. Inf Port 2, StM 4, Tre 2, etc.; Lunan, I. 137: 'mafootoo wythe', poss from Fante *ɛ-mā-futuw*, very luxuriant; but poss also a tribal name.
34. II. 418–9; 1725 Sloane, 372; Barham, 113; *sabo* is perh conn with Twi *asaabó*, kidney (these beans are the colour and nearly the shape of a kidney).
35. Poss the first part is conn with Twi *nsuró*, a climbing vine.
36. Resp. Gen; Man, Asprey; see *white-black fern, velvet leaf*, etc.
37. Resp. Inf Tre 2, Inst list; 1696 Sloane, 77 (OED only quot 1756); Inf Port 2.
38. Resp. Inf StAnd x, StM 4; Inf StAnn 4; 1696 Sloane, 52, etc.; 1699 Sloane, *Phil. Trans*, XXI. 119, Browne, 268; ibid.
39. Inf StAnd 2, StC 1, Inst list; cf. Asprey (*N*)*edge Teeth*.
40. Resp. 1847 Gosse, 142; Inst list.
41. But note Twi *nsúsúaa*, a species of pot-herb, and *mbá* (plur.), the young of plants.
42. a1725 (1794) 76, 1740 Importance, 35 (OED first quot 1760).

43. Resp. 1707, I. 174 (not 4 D); Inst list; 1801, 366; ed. 1819, 386 'Bontein's', 377 'Bontin's' (not 4 D); Asprey.
44. Information from Mr R. W. Thompson, UCWI; R. P. Alexandre, *Mémoires de l'Inst. français d'Afrique Noire*, 34, 1953; Turner, 101; Prof M. Sandmann, UCWI, has recently made a good case for descent of all these forms from Fr. *champignon*, mushroom.
45. Christaller; Twi *apēd*, a certain plant, apparently of pleasant odour; *mbd*, young plants.
46. Importance, 35 (OED first quot 1753); Kingston *Gleaner*, 2 Sept., 1951, in an article on flowers.

Appendix 1

PRONUNCIATION

IN THE list below are given, with key words, the phonetic values of (1) Standard 'Received' English according to Daniel Jones's 1956 notation; (2) Jamaican Folk English; (3) the phonemic spelling used for the latter in this book. The folk speech lacks Standard [ɛə, ɔ, ɔː, ə, əː, ɔi]; when these are adopted into folk texts they may be spelt respectively /ea, oh, oo, uh, oe, oi/.

Key word	Standard Eng.	Ja. Folk Speech	Phonemic Sp.
beat	[iː]	[iː]	/ii/
bit	[i]	[i]	/i/
bait	[ei]	[ie]	/ie/
bet	[e]	[e]	/e/
bare	[ɛə]	—	/ie, e/
bird	[əː] ⎫	[ə]	/o/
butt	[ʌ] ⎭		
bite	[ai] ⎫	[ai]	/ai/
boil	[ɔi] ⎭		
bat	[æ] ⎫	[a]	/a/
bot	[ɔ] ⎭		
boot	[uː]	[uː]	/uu/
book	[u]	[u]	/u/
boat	[ou]	[uo]	/uo/
bought	[ɔː] ⎫	[aː]	/aa/
bard	[ɑː] ⎭		
bout	[au]	[ɐu]	/ou/

Among consonants, only [θ] and [ð] are lacking from the Folk Speech. In the phonemic spelling, /b, p, d, t, v, f, h, m, n, l, r, y, w/ have the usual values. Others differ as follows: /g/ only as in *give*; /j/ only as in *gin, jib, ridge*; /k/ only as in *care, kin*; /z/ only as in *lose zinc*; /s/ only as in *loss, sink*; /ch/ only as in *chin*; /sh/ only as in *chute shin*; /zh/ as in *azure*; /ng/ as in *ring*, or for nasalisation of a preceding vowel: thus /dong/, *down*, may represent [dɐŋ] or [dɛ̃]. *Qu* and *x* are spelt respectively /kw, ks/.

Appendix 11

ANANSI AND KING'S SON

THIS SHORT tale, part of which was analysed in Chapter III for its intonation pattern, is given here in the phonemic writing adopted for this book. It represents the folk speech well, but shows also some imitation of Standard. Note that the song has /dong/ where the story has /doun/; in the first line the writing /oe/ has had to be added where the speaker imitated Standard [ɔː] in *heard*: /oed/.

/Wans apan a taim, Breda Anansi, oed dat King av a Son. Fram di die im baan im didn waak. An Breda Anansi se iing gwain to mek dat Son waak. Nou, iz pik up iz myuuzik man, wich iz tree kakruoch, dat i tuk intu a guodi, an wen ing riich about a aaf mailz, tu di King giet, im straik up di myuuzik man. Nou, a gwain tu staat di myuuzik:

> King oooo, King oooo, kimbembe King,
> King oooo, King oooo, kimbembe King,
> King Son a kom dong, kimbembe King,
> King Son a kom dong, kimbembe King.

Breda King sen out iz sorvant, an wail ing sen out ing sorvant, tu kom doun an si wat myuuzik woz dat, hout der pliein, di sorvant kom an di myuuzik woz suo swiit, dat di sorvant neva ritorn bak. Di myuuzik staatid up agen:

> King oooo, King oooo, kimbembe King,
> King oooo, King oooo, kimbembe King,
> Kingz Waif a kom dong, kimbembe King,
> King Waif a kom dong, kimbembe King,
> Kingkimbembe kimbembe, kingkimbembe kimbembe,
> Kingkimbembe kimbembe, King!

Di Waif kom doun nou, an di Waif neva torn bak. Anansi strike out agen:

> King oooo, King oooo, kimbembe King,
> King oooo, King oooo, kimbembe King,
> King self a kom dong, kimbembe King,
> King self a kom dong, kimbembe King.
> Kingkimbembe kimbembe, kingkimbembe kimbembe,
> Kingkimbembe kimbembe, King!

Di King imself kom doun an lef di puo bwaai dat neva waak fram di die im baan. Ing straik out agen:

> King oooo, King oooo, kimbembe King,
> King oooo, King oooo, kimbembe King,
> King Son a shofl dong, kimbembe King,
> King Son a shofl dong, kimbembe King.

Den a kingkimbembe kimbembe, kingkimbembe kimbembe,
Kingkimbembe kimbembe, kingkimbembe kimbembe, King!

Di Son imself shofl, an staatid tu waak, an kom rait doun wer di adaz iz, and der endid, di hend av dis stuori./

WORD LIST

Brackets around part of an entry indicate that that part is sometimes present, sometimes absent. A few bracketed words are explanatory.

437

blue-gal 327
blue gaulin 299
blue-head paty 325
blue-jean parrot 325
Blue Mountainduck 297–298
blue parrot 325
blue peter (parrot) 325
blue pigeon 300–1
blue quit 309–10
blue roan (parrot) 325
blues and reds 260
blue-stripe 218
blue-swee 310
blue-tail lizard 285
blue-top (cassava) 336
blue tumpa parrot 325
blue-vine yam 340
board slipper 113
boar-fish 326
boar-gum 357
boar-tree, -wood 357
boasify 177
boasy 177
boat 36, 44
boatswain (of the mill) 91, 399, 423
bobbin 274, 399
Bobby Brown sweet-potato 337, 390
Bobby Hanson (cassava) 336
Bob Cook 360
bobo 70, 169, 181, 314, 392, 396
bob-tenner 209
bochara-yam 341
bog 120
bogoby 329
bogro(-bogro) 170
bogro-salt 170, 202, 394
bogue 119–20, 392
Bog Walk! 275
Bog Walk pine 352
boil 33, 35
bolangena 350, 392
bolo 180, 392
Bombay mango 353
bomma 274, 395
bon 268
bona 270, 395
bonavist pea 343
bone 100
bone-danger 332
bongo man 159
bonja(w), bonjour 264–265
bonkra 423
bonnet pepper 347

bonnavest-pea, bonniviss 343
bonny (-clabber) 202, 397
bonny-bess peas, bonny-vis 343
booby egg 297
book 33, 36, 44
book-keeper 164–5
boolooloops 220
boonoonoos, boonoonoo-noos 220
boos 230
boot 33, 35, 99
booty-foot 104
borambay 329
bore 61
borer 332
boso 219, 395
bossu 332
bot 33
bottle-arse 292
bottle caesar 324
bottle-fish 316
bottle-mouth parrot 325
bottle-nose parrot 325
bought 33, 34, 44
boughted 58
bounce 45
bounce-and-span 279
bounce-around 270
Bourbon cane 351, 393
Bourbon coco 339, 393
Bourbon cotton 393
bout (about) 37
bout-bout 71
bow 230
bow-bo 169, 393
bow-foot 139
bowl hat 115
bow grunt 323
bowsorow 270, 395
box drum 267
boxen (yam) 340
box-fish 317
boya 193
bra 223
braata 210–11, 392
bra-bra 179, 195
bracho 103
bracket flounder 318
braga 116
bragadap 119, 195
brags 75, 392
brain(s) 216
bram 230, 271
brambra 342
bram-bram 101
bran 103
branched calalu 347

brang-brang 101, 394
brara 41, 223
brass 209
brass cannon sweet-potato 337
brater 211
breadfruit 190, 335, 342
breadfruit rose 388
bread-kind 190, 399
breadnut 356
breakaway 121
break-axe 359–60, 390, 396
breakfast 188
break (in), breaking 99, 398
break-neck 106, 279
break-pot 343, 396
breast 103
breda, breder 43, 223
breeding-pen 95
breeding vein 133
breeze 111, 210, 248
breeze-mill 77, 278
brennut 39
breshe 122, 342
brial wiss 374
briar 40
brice 134
brichy 134
bride 221
bridle-mouth parrot 325
brim (grunt) 323–4
brindle 40, 175
bring (a) calf out 103
bring-come 63
bringing in the August Morning 270
bringle 175
bring (one) up 219
brinjah 181
brittle 40
broad-leaf calalu 346
broad-leaf conch 332
broad thatch 365
broke (break) 58
broke-pot peas 343
broke-neck 279
broomweed 379
brother 43
broughta 210–11
brown Albion 201
browned nose 329
brown George 199
brown hinds 326
brown jolly 350
brown-man's fancy 382
brown snake 286
brown widow 287

brrr 229
bru-bru 170
bruchy 134
bruck (in) 99
bruckins 271
bruck-kitchen 105, 400
bruck rock-stone 275
bruck stone 75, 79
bruck-tummick 121
brush 98
brush-brush 101
brush-tail doctor-fish 327
buaw 103
bubaka 96
buba kin 364
buba mat 100, 364, 394
bubo 295
bubu 137, 169
bubuafu 169, 395
buccaneer 164
buck 40, 144, 398
buck-buck 316
bucket pan 85
buck fly 291
buckle foot 139
buckle(-hold) 142
buckra 155
buckra calalu 155
buckra-hall, -house 77
buckra pine 155, 353
buckra yam 155
buck-toe 113, 144, 330
buck-up 144
bucky massa 181, 223-4
bud (bird) 34
budge-gum, -wood, budgy-gum, 357
buff-jacket 193
buffooto 181, 395
buffro-buffro 70, 169, 395
buff-teeth 137
buffuto 181, 395
bufu(-bufu) 169, 395
bufu(t) 342, 400
bugaboo 250-1
bug-a-bug 288
buggo-yagga 170
bugo-bugo 179, 395
bugu-bugu (fly) 179, 291
bugu-waga 170
bugu-yaga, -yanga 170, 395
build (up) a squall 112
buku 342, 400
Bull 262
bulla 200, 214
bulldog boot 114
bullet tree 360
bullet-wood 335

bull-face tobacco 206
bullfrog 283
bull(-head) pine 353
bull-head pooky, squirrel-fish 326
bull(-head) thatch 365
bull-head wenchman 326
bull-hoof, -hough 373
bull-stone mango 353
bully 326
bully-tree 360
bumpa 206
bump-an'-bore 230
bumpy banana 351
buna kin 364
bunch 99-100
bunch-a-key (cassava) 336
bunch-a-key (sweet-potato) 337
bunchy (sweet-potato) 337
bungay 74, 392, 394
bungo 158-9, 395
bungo bee 296
bungoby 329, 394
bungoby crab 331
bungo okro 159, 349
bungo talk 42, 276
bunka 364
bunks (bounce) 45
bun-pan (burnt-pan) 86, 115
bu'n-pan hat 115
buntung jack 319
Burke sweet-potato 337
burn 39
burn-ant 290
burn-eye 358
burn-fin jack 319
burn-fin snapper 322
burning to 92
burn-mark 102
burn side 97
burn-to-hell pepper 348
burn-tongue mango 353
burnt-pan 86
burn wangla 244-5
burr grass 370
buru, buru-man 273, 395
bus 75
bush 242
busha 165
bush bath 253
bush-doctor 242
bush fence 97
bush lizard 285
bush-man 242
business 185

busquine 181
bussu 147
Busta backbone 201
busu 332, 394-5
but 33, 34, 36, 44
but-but 295
butleress 166
butter-akee 343
butter-bird 301
butter-bun (fish) 327
butter-dough 200
butter fish 326
butterfly bird 312
butter-hinds 326
butter jack 319
butter pear 355
buttery 398
button weed 377
butty 147
butu 147
buxen (yam) 340
buy 34
buzu 131, 248, 395
buzuyako 82
byute (brute) 42

C

Cabana, Cavana cane 351
cabbage-bark (tree) 365
cabbage (palm, tree) 364
cabbage pine 352
cabbage skin 364
cabbage wood 365
ca ca 229
caca 229, 392-3
cacabay 131
caca-belly 328
caca-nabu 186
cacao-walk 306
caca pilot 328
cachimba 207, 392, 394
cacky-quaw 298
cacoon 373
cadger 167
Caesar grunt 323
cake 43
calaban 105
calabash 83-4, 400
calabash broom 379
Calabash Estate 94
calalu(e) 339-40, 346-7, 391
calapaver, -or, -re 321
calash(te) 227
calavance 344, 392
caleloe 346
calembe, calimbe 273, 392, 395

Coolie calalu 346
Coolie duppy 250
coolie-foot sugar 201
Coolie okro 349
coon(-hat) 115
coop 41
cooper hook, wiss 374
cooy 229
copper 91
copperwood 91
coquer plum 354
coral 45
coral pepper 348
coratoe, corito 270, 367, 391, 393
cork-head mullet 321
cork wood 356
corn 34, 35, 98
corn-beard 98
corn-grass 370
corn-head 98
corn-mouth 98
corn pone 198
corn-puss 105
corn stick 98
corojungo 172
coromai 321
Coromantee 20
Coromantee flute 264
corpi, corpy 218, 403
corpion 37
Costa Rica sweet-potato 337
cot 35
cotch 147–8
cotch-up 189
cotta 83, 268, 394
cottahead (petchary) 304
cotta stick 268
Cottawood 160
cotter 83, 268, 394
cotton cassava 336
cotton-reel 87
cotton stainer 293
cotton-tree sparrow 311
cotton-tree worm 294
co-u 223, 400
could 61
count bunch 99
counter, countra 41
country disease 129
country mark, scar 134
cous-cous 191
cousin 223
covally jack 320
covering 255
cow apple 356
cowboy pine 353
cow-cod 213

cow-ears 366
cow-fish 316
cow-foot 376
cow-foot mango 353
cow-gut wiss 375
cowhage 375
Cow-head 262
cow-hough 376
cowitch (bush) 375
cowitch cherry 375
cow law-book 197
cow-neck 205
co-worker 236
cow pea 344
cowskin 196, 213
cowskin hero 165
cow-tongue fern 368
crab 44, 151
crabbit 175, 397
crab-catcher 299
crab-eye 371
crab-eye pea 344
crab-eye (jack) 319
crablight 358
crab rum 205
crab-spider 288
crab-thatch 368
crab wiss 375
crabwood 358
crab-yawed, -yaws 130–1
crack-pot soldier 298
cra-cra 170
craking drummer 324
cramoojin, cramouchin, cramougin 41, 174
crampify 180
cran-cran, crang-crang 101, 394
crape 37
cratch 37
craven 172, 276
craw-craw 132, 393
crawfish cane 350
crawl 95, 393
crawny 37, 170
crazy ant 290
crebay 255
creole 21, 156, 161–2
creole potato 162
creolian 161
creolise 153
crescent 43
crested quail-dove 301
cricket lizard 285
crips 333, 402
cris(p) 38, 177, 402
croaker 285
croaking drummer 324
croaking lizard 284–5

crocus(-bag) 83, 115
Cromanty ant 289
Cromanty (bullet) 361
Crongoe 159
crongoe yam 340, 394
crooca, crooka 115, 423
Crooky 276, 395
crop-over 90, 255, 270
crop (time) 90
cross-and-pile 117
crossbar (kingfish) 319
crossbar mackerel 319
cross-pass 41, 75
crown bread 199
crowned governess 236
crowned shepherd 235
crowned warrior 238
crowning table 239
crown shell 332
cruchument 172
cruckuss bag 115
cruff(y) 5, 170
crumuna 235, 395
crunge 148
crunjo (yam) 159, 340
cry 151
cry-cry 72, 179
Cuba (Cooba) 157–8
Cuban banana 351
Cuban cane 351
Cuban petchary 304
Cuban plantain 352
Cubbenah 157
cubbitch 174
cubbitch-hole 138, 174
cubbitchness 174
cuckold fish 316
cuckold's increase pea 344–5
Cudjo(e) 157
Cudjo-rubba 132
cuento 210, 392
Cuffee, Cuffy 157–8, 216
Cuffy-routen 132
culilu 346
culu-culu 122
Cumina, cumuna 235–240, 395
cunep 354
cungoteh 192, 394
cunnibo, cunnybo 316, 400
cunny (cunning) 176
cunny-buck 316, 400
cunny-fish 318
cunu-cunu 122
curaca 367
curato 366
cure-for-all 377

curer 93
curmudgeon 41, 174
currato(w) 366–7
curry goat 197
curse 151
cus-cus grass 370
cuss-cuss 180
cuss-eye 329
custard-apple 354
custom 185
custos 218
cut 149–50
cutacoo 81, 316, 394
cutaway 121
cut brute 200, 393
cut cake 200
cut capoose 150
cut cedar board 152
cut English 149, 399
cut-eye 137
cut Grecian 141
cutlass 79–80
cutlass (fish) 319
cut-stone 289
cutta-frock 116, 397
cutter 314
cutting and clearing
    (table) 238–9
cutting grass 370
cutting shepherd 235
cut unknown tongue 249

D
da 58–61, 396
daal an' baat 197, 393
dab-a-dab 195
dadjaka 114, 393
dago 319
dago crab 331
dah 58–9
damsel berry 363
dance the mill 214
dancing booth 238
dandan 116
dandy-shandy 206, 397
dare 61
dari 55, 403
dark grunt 323
daru 205, 393
dasheen 339, 393
dat 40
dat-de 55
dat end 404
day-cut 109
day da cut, light 109
day-day 225
day drummer 324
day grouper 319
day-morning 109

day peeny 294
de (is) 58–61
de (there) 43, 67, 396
de (to) 67
dead (corpse) 247, 403
dead (die) 58, 68, 152
dead-an'-wake 380, 390
dead-flesh 135
deadie 327
dead story 276
deaf-ears crab 331
deal-board 214
dealing stick 250
dead-man oil 254
dead-water 254
death 47, 247, 403
death-water 247
decent 45
deep curve 76
deepwater cod 329
deepwater eel 317
deepwater shad 320
deepwater wenchman
    326
deggeh(-deggeh) 126
dem, -dem 51–2, 54, 404
dem-de 55
dem-ya 55
denky 86
depa yam 340, 394
dere 40
de-so 118, 396
develop, devel up 5
devil-damnation, -hell
    pepper 348
devil horse (-whip) 293,
    376
devil's backbone 376
devil's riding-whip 376
dibidibi 71
dickens 124
did 60
did-deh, di-de 67, 396
digester 85
digging-sing 274
dildo 365–6
dildoe-tree 358
dill(-dill) 104
dimmo 131
dindi okro 349, 372, 395
dinghy 75
dinky (minny) 270, 395
dinner 189
dip-and-come-back, -fall-
    back 198
dippidence 198
dirt 46, 47
dirt-eating 132
dirty-face parrot 325

dis end 404
dis(h)-ya 55
Dispenser 261
divin' hopper 298
division 36
do 227
docey 202, 392
doctor 111, 309
Doctor 261
doctor-bird 309
Dr Buchanan bush 385,
    390
doctoress, doctress 134,
    166
doctor-fish 327
Dr John 385
Dr Long 385
Dr McKatty 385
doctor shop 136, 254
doctor woman 134
doctor-wood 357, 385
dodging quail 301
do-do 151
do-fe-do 187
dog-bline-me 114
dog-blood 386
dog-blood sweet-potato
    337
dog corn-piece 186
dog-driver 219
dog-flea weed 381
dog-liver sweet-potato
    337
dog-teeth snapper 322
dog-tongue 368, 379
do it 42
dokunu 193
dolce 202
dolly 327
dominick fowl 398
done 63, 65
dong 230
donkey ears 368
donkey-eye 376
donkey-ride 277
donkey-rope 206
Don Patinho's money
    208, 392
don't 60
don't-care 177
doodledoo 387
door-mouth 77, 397
do over 214
dove 236
down 38
down to 125
dragon(-blood) 376
dragon (sweet-potato)
    337

draw 42, 64, 154
draw bungy 152
draw down 135
dream (to) 248
dress down 142
drink 42
drink Yallahs water 153
drip 93
drive 63, 143, 249
driver, driveress 163
drop pan 208
drop-trash cane 351
drop yellowtail 328
drummer 293
drum pan 85
drumwood 361
Drunkard 261
drunk(en) 58, 152
dry 42, 279
dry belly-ache, colic 128–
    129
dry jump 238
duckano(o) 193
duckanoo mango 353
duck-ant 288–9
duckanteal 298
duck-apple 382
duck-foot wiss 373
duckonoo 193, 400
duck pickney 404
duckunoo, duckunu 193,
    394
ducky hen 104, 395
dude 220, 393
dudu 219, 393
duffidia 171
dug 58
dugged 58
duggy (fowl)   104, 168,
    395
dugolow 122
duke coco 339
dukunu 193
duma 214
dumbarton 139
dumb-cane 378
dumby 139
dun 65
dunder 93, 392
dunder cistern 94
dundo 268, 395
dundu 81
dundus 171, 219–20, 395
dung 39
duppe, duppie 245, 247
duppy 245–55, 279, 395
duppy bird 300
duppy calalu 346
duppy-conqueror 180

duppy-gun 376
duppy peas 376
duppy poison 377
duppy-punkin 373, 382,
    400
duppy ridin' horse 293
duppy soursop 382,
    400
during the while 108
dusky booby 297
dusky eared-owl 308
Dutch account 212
Dutch(ess) grass 369
Dutchy (-maid, -pot) 85,
    403
dutty 119, 394, 396
dweet 42
dwindle 40
dye 63

E

ear-dove 300
ears 44
ears-corner 138
earthbound god 237
earth-eating 132
ear-wigging 218
Easter bug 294
East Indian mango 353
eating-match 271
Eboe drum 268
Eboe toyer 337
ebony 45, 213–14
echini stone 332
eddo 338, 394
Eddy wasp 296
edoh-edoh 227, 396
edye 338
ee 225
eee-hee 225, 396
ee-m (iim) 225, 396
ef 43
egg-bird 297
egg fruit 350
eh-eh! 228, 396
elephant-foot cane 350
eleven steps 219
elm 402
em-bo 230, 396
Emma bean 345
English calalu 346
English flour 199
enough 37
entrails 46
Espeut 283
essence 198
evening 398
eyed pallette-tip 285
eye water 137, 396

F

faam 43
facetiness, facety 178
facey 178
fadge 149
faiakiti 217
fall-down-bush 386
fall rain 112
family 221
fan 151, 221
fan-broom, -thatch 365
Fancy Anna 6, 390
fandangus 116
Fanny-bush 385
Fanny Corca 318
fan shell 332
farthing bump 202
fass 178
fassy 135
fast 178
fast-breedin' fruit 354
fasten-man-coat, -'pon-
    coat 379
fast-fast 72
fat 154, 172
fat-bush 379
Father 236
fatigue 184
fatten-barrow 381, 390
fattoon 169
favour say 185
fe 66
feather-foot 104
feather-tongue 310
feather up 153
feeco 209, 392
feed-feed 72
fee-fee 6, 71, 278
feel up 143
fegat 58
feh 227, 396
feisty 178, 399
fenky(-fenky) 5, 171, 179
fennay, fenneh 135, 395
fe purpose 67
feril 368
ferm 41, 43, 368
fern 35, 43
fern-tree 368
fe true 67
fever bath 253–4
fever bush 136
fever grass 369
fe-we 221
fe-who 56
fi, fi- 52, 55
fia 39
fiddle 40
fiddler beetle 293

gap 398
garavonza 344
garden 35
garden calalu 346
garden egg 5, 350
garden gate mango 353
Garge 34
garlic pear-tree 356
garvanco 344
gash 113
gashy (yam) 340
gaso 242
gat 35
gata 200, 393
ga-u (kingfish) 319
gaulding 299
gaulin, gawlin 299, 392
gawky 181, 397, 403
G.B. 114
geechy 174
gelop 43
genep, genip 353-4
gentleman's complaint 135
George 34, 131
George rat 282
geow 177
German 318
German trumpet 388
geroom 329
ghost crab 331
giant plantain 352
giant purple cane 350
giant sweet-potato 337
gig 277-8
gill (3/4 d.) 209
gill (of lizard) 285
gimme-me-bit 6, 308-9
ginep 353-4
ginghy 75
gingy fly 291, 394
gisada 198
giving 58
gizaada 198, 392
glass-eye 302-3, 382
glass-eye berry 382
glass-eye mullet 321
glass-eye shark 314
glasswood 361
go 58, 62
goat-fish 318, 321
goat-foot cane 350
goat-foot potato 376
goat-foot wiss 373
goat-horn okro 349
goat-knee cane 350
goat-pepper 348
goat-root 380
goat-shank cane 350

go away for (someone) 244
goblet 41, 85
God 229
God-a-me 329
god-bird 309
Godbrother 223
god-bud 309
god-bush 373, 380
god-cotton 295
god-horse 293
god-okro 349, 373, 380
god-tree 373, 380
go-far 318
goggle-eye (jack) 319
goglet 85
goh 68
going 42
gold-crowned thrush 312
gold-ears parrot 324-5
gold(en) spoon 361
golden swallow 306
gold fern 368
gold-fringe 311
gold-tail parrot 325
gold(y)-ears grunt 324
go-'long-wasp 284
gomba, gombay 267-8, 395
gombayer 268
go-no-mo 118
goodbye t' ye 225
good-lucked, -lucky 253
Goolia's grunt 324
gooma, goomer 347
goombah, goombay, goomby 267-8
go on 42
goongo(o) pea 344
gootoo 325
goozoo 242
Gordon 35
gormandiser 100, 295, 393
got 35
gourdy 84
governess, governor 236
governor bream 323
governor cane 351
grabalicious 173
gracy 281
grain sugar 201
grambay 114
gran-coppa 39, 91
grand 47
grand boiler 91
grand copper 39, 91
grandee 133
grand-market 210, 393

Grandy Mary 294
grang-grang 70, 101, 394
grangi-grangi 101
granke 293, 394
gran-pickny 223
grapefruit 354
grash fish 322-3
grass bird 310
grass brim 323
grass dodger 311
grass gang 89
grass grunt 323
grass hamlet 327
grasshopper sparrow 311
grass lice 296
grass parrot 326
grass-pen 95
grass-piece 96
grass pink 311
grass quit 309-10, 382
grass-quit plant 382
grassy-ground parrot 326
grata 200
grater 152, 266
grater brute, cake 200, 393
gravance 344
grave-digger (wasp) 296
gravilitious 173
gray grunt 323
gray petchary 303
grazy 281
grazy-wood 361
great bean 345
great blue swallow 306
great copper 91
great gang 88
great-house 398
great pepper 347
Grecian 141
greedy 403
green-back jack 319
green bat 295
green calalu 346
green congry 317
green eel 317
green(-gage) chocho 35c
green gaulin 299
green guana 284
greenheart 359
green-heart fiddlewood 361
green-humming bird 309
green jack 319
green-leaf yam 341
green parrot 325
green pea-shell 331
green-plantain porridge 192

green-skin mango 353
green sparrow 309
green-stalk coco 339
green tody 309
green wiss, withe 372
greet 239
grey jumper 288
grey lizard 285
grey parrot 325
grey snake 286
grey snapper 321–2
groaning 238
gro-gro parrot 325
grooper 319
Gros Michel banana 351, 393
gross 122
ground (field) 38, 96
ground (grind) 58
ground altar 239
ground anancy 287
ground basket 81
ground calalu 346
ground-coco 338
ground dove 300
ground-fruit 190
ground-god 118
ground itch 131
ground jack 319
ground lizard 284
ground-shaking 113
ground shark 314
grow(ing)-stake 359
grow-quick 359
grow-stick 359
grubber broadhead 329
grudgeful 176
gru-gru 309
grugudo 309
grupa 318
guaba 40
guaco-bush 371
guana 284
guango 391
guard 232, 249–50
guava 334—5, 392
Guinea bird 18, 156
guinea-chick lobster 330
guinea-corn grunt 323
guinea-corn yaws 130
guinea grass 369
guinea-hen grunt 323
guinea-hen parrot 325
guinea-hen weed 377, 381
Guinea yam 340
guinea-yard 78
guinep 353–4, 391
guizada 198, 392

gulge 278, 399
gully 121
gully asp 284
gully-bean 383
guma 347, 394
gumbay, gumbé 267
gumbesh 104
gumbi 267–8, 395
gumbi-man 261, 268
Gundy 195
gunfire 108
gun foot 116
gungu pea 343–4, 394
gungus 216
gungu walk 97
gunzoo 242
gut 398
gutu (parrot) 325, 394
guzu 216, 242, 395
gwaan 42
gwap, gwat 152
gwine 42, 61–2
gwoyou 216

H

hab 40
hackle 184
hadrow 385
had was to 61
hag 44, 83
hairy cerasee 375
hairy mango 353
hakam 340
half a miles 46
half bunch 99
hamlet 327
hamper 51; 82
hand 99
hand-berry 296
handle 40
hand-middle 138
hand up 101
hanen 290, 394
hang 43
hangra, hankra 82, 394
hanya-huo 181
hard 39
hard-back 293
hard-bone jack 319
hard-bound 134
hard-ears 174–5
hard-eye 174
hard fern 368
hard-head fry 329
hard-head drummer 324
hard mango 353
hard-pay man 211
hard-sock 114
hard-to-take-up 325

hard yam 341
hark-ye 226, 403
harrigan 169
harrock(y) 226, 403
harsh 44
hasham 199, 394
hasty 403
hato 11, 94, 392
haughty 34
haulie 106
hawksbill turtle 286–7
head 51
headache bush 377
headache weed 376–7, 381
head-man 165
head skull 136
heads or tails 279
head sugar 201
heal-an'-draw 377, 390
healing oil 136, 254
healing table 239
hear 29, 46, 47
hearty 34
heave 143
heavy 64
heavy-lead snapper 322
heb 143
hecatee 286
hedgehog fish 316
hedgehog stone 332
hegg 36
help down, up 143
henda 43
heng 43
heng-pon-me 81–2
heng-pon-nail 116
hen-pepper 347
Hercules 360
here 39
herring roll 190
herring sprat 320
herring-wood 359
hi 228
hib 143
hicatee 286, 391
hice 36
hickerie 286
hide 214
hide and whoop 277
hige 83, 184, 251–2
higgler 167
high 36
high-forehead 318
him 29, 53–5
himba 340
hinder 43
hinka-hinka 71, 149
hipsaw 272–3

hither 43, 46
Hitler boot 114
hoganeer(in) 173
hog-apple 382
hog-banna 343, 370
hog-berry 357
hog-doctor (tree) 357, 385
hog-fish 326
hog-grass 368, 370
hog gum 357
hog-hunter 164
hog mango 353
hogmeat (ti-tie) 343, 370-1
hog-nose mullet 321
hog-nose skeet 315
hog-slip 370
hog-snout mullet 321
hog-string 370
hog taya 338
hog-teeth parrot 325
hog-vunga 293
hogweed 371
hold 142
hold (one's) road 4, 143, 399
hole-hole 72
holing gang 89
Holland blind 78
Honduras cedar 357
honey banana 351
honey-berry 354
honeycomb rock 119
honey dram 206
hood 41
hoodias 175-6
hood-i-up 176
hood'n 41
hook 374
hook-point 80
hook vine, wiss 374
hooky (machete) 80
hoop wiss, withe 374
hopping dick 302
horizontal angel-fish 327
horn-blower 261
horn fly 291
horn-head 316
hornman 166
horn-shark 314
horny-owl 308
horny-money 316
horse 44
horse-bath 381, 384
horse bean 345
horse-burst 370, 379
horse-catcher 163
horse-eye (bean) 278, 375-6

horse-eye (jack) 319
horse-eye wenchman 326
horse-foot coco 339
Horse-head 259, 262
horse plantain 352
horse-poison 379
hot 239
hot (hurt) 44, 134
hot-house 134
hough 151
house 36
house John-Canoe 261
housekeeper 167, 261
house lizard 285
house-wasp 296
house wiss 374
how 36, 56-7
how d'ye 224
how much 44, 124
how you do? 225
hug-me-close 376
hungry 139, 403
hunter 305
hunter man 236
hunting 45
hunting shepherd 235
hunting woman 236
huntning 320
hurry-come-up 182, 400
hurt 134
husk 38, 41
hussay 393

I

I 53-4
icening 46, 320
if 43
ignorant 6, 177
iim 225
illegitimate 222
impurence 41
in 42
in a power 249
in arrow 89, 393
incense tree 357
in crop 90
Indian bell pepper 347
Indian Coney 281
Indian Girl 261
Indian Kale 339, 340
Indian shot 384
Indian sorrel 349
Indian vine 375
India(n) yam 342
in (one's) salt 169, 190
interval 89
in the long way 204
into 42
ipi-apa 115

Irish moss 383-4
Irish (potato) 337
iron-cunny 201
iron-shrub, -weed 379
is 59
isle 34
it 38, 53-4
itch 42

J

jaack tree 355
jabbering, jabbling crow 306
jabby 102
jacatoo calalu 346
jack 240
jacka 277
jackass 342
jackass biscuit 200
jackass crab 331
jackass-ears tree 359
jackass-rope 206
jack bean 345
jackfruit 355, 392
jackfruit foot 131
jackini, jack-in-the-bush 390
Jack Mandora, Mantora 276, 395
Jack-Spaniard 104, 290
Jack Spence 299
jack sprat 320
Jacob banana 351
jah 237
jam 146
Jamaica bean 345
Jamaica black dor 293
Jamaica bullfinch 311
Jamaica button-shell 332
Jamaica cedar 357
Jamaica clock 293
Jamaica coat-of-arms 197
Jamaica crab 330
Jamaica ebony 213
Jamaica fish 195
Jamaica grape-vine 375
Jamaica hot sauce 198
Jamaican becard 302
Jamaica nightingale 304
Jamaican woodpecker 303
Jamaica pea 345
Jamaica-pepper 348
Jamaica salmon 321
Jamaica sorrel 349
jamal song 274
jambo parrot 325
jamma 274, 395
Jan Cunnoo 262

kill-devil 205
kill hog 221
kirrout 227
kill-kill 72
kill (obeah) 244
kiln 46
kimbo 139
kin-cat 277
King 261
king mullet 321
king pine 353
Kingston buttercup,
   flower 381
Kingston lizard 284
King Zombie 237
kin-oba 277
kinoul, kin-owl 251–2
kip(s) jack 319
Kish 237
kitchen dresser 77
kitchen-key 182
kitibu 292, 394
kittereen 74
kitty-go 298
kitty-katty 268
kitty-up 78, 394
kling-kling 305
knaum 152
knife-handle shell 331
knives-and-scissors-man
   242
knock 247
knock-and-go-along 278
knot-gut 134
know-you 371
ko 228–9
kobalo 320
konggote, kongkonte 192,
   394
koo 228–9
koo-koo 261
kovaali, kovali 320
krakra 70
krang-krang 70
kratch-kratch 42, 132
kreng-kreng 82
kreng-kreng calalu 347
krichuol 308
Kromanti song 275
ku 228, 396
kubaali, kubaalo 320
kubu-kubu 205
kukru busu 332, 395
kumby 268
kunchin 168
kunu 258, 396
kunu-munu 216
kushu 278
kuuy 229

kwee-kwee 71
ky 37
kya 67
kyalifieva (mullet) 321
kynando 269, 395

L

laaaaaaaaa 229
laan 34
laasi 222
laba-laba 179, 185, 359,
   395
lab-lab sweetwood 359
labouring 238
labrish(er) 179, 185
lacanga 273, 392
lace-bark 362–3
lace-cake 336
lace plant 368
lack-lack-lack 229
ladies-slipper 375
lady-basket 81
Lady Coote bean 371
lady-fancy cane 351
lady-finger okro 349
lady-finger pepper 348
lady-pea 344
lageto, lagetto 362, 392
laigz 207
lamp-bat 296
lamp-fly 296
lamp oil 86
lance-wood 213
lancier 272
land breeze 110
land crab 330
land kick-up 312
landslip 121
land turtle 286
langulala 168
lantern-jaw snapper 322
lantern-jaw snook 315
lap 147, 399
lapwing 300
larta 86
last lick 277
launch out 399
lawk(s) 229
lawma 116, 401
lawn 34
lay-him-straight 117
lead drum 269
leading cattle 103
leaf-of-life 378
learn 34
leather-coat 285
leather-coat jack 319
leave 63
lebbey-lebbey 179

lee 38
leetle 45
lef, left (leave) 58
lef'-man coco 339
leg 139
leggeh-leggeh 122
leggins 197, 393
leggo 170
lemon grass 369
lep 141, 397
let-go 170
Lewis Daley sweet-potato
   337
li' 38
liard 45
libba 40
libwell 180
lice 51
license 38
lick 144
lick-an'-'tan-up 78, 400
lickle-lickle 71–2
licks, the 213
licky-licky 173
Liddy sweet-potato 337
lie 63
lie-an'-story 185
lif'-coat pepper 348
lif'-up 141–3
liges 207–8
light a candle on 245
lighter 34, 74
lightwood 358
light-work people 89
lignum vitae 41, 358
lily grass 370
lily-trotter 299
limba 169
lime blossom 312
lime mango 353
limey 312
lining of the walls 239
lion-ant 290
lion-fish 318
lion-tongue 368
liquorish-weed 371
liquor still 93
little 38, 40
little beeny 126, 310
little blinkie 292
little Christmas 270
little furuh 312
little gill 121–2
little most 125
little Tom-fool 304
liver(-spot) 163
liver-spot mango 353
live story 276
Liza 190

lizard-cuckoo 306
lizard looking-glass 386
lobby-lobby 71, 191, 359, 390
lob-lob 191
lob-lob beefwood 359
loblolly beefwood 359
loblolly whitewood 359
loblolly-wood 359
lobster 329–30
lobster mumma 330
locus(-berry), locust-berry 357
locus(t)-ale 205–6
locust tree 357
log 34
loggerhead fooly 304
loggerhead fry 329
loggerhead mosquito 291
loggerhead (petchary) 303–4
loggerhead turtle 286
logo-logo 122
logwood 335
logwood-chipper 164
logwood walk 97
loiter 34
Lomas land 255
loney 403
long 37
Long-bubby Susan 251
long-day bird 302
long-finger pepper 348
long mango 353
long-mouth(ed) blue quit 310
long-neck pear 355
long okra 349
long out 137
long-saal 190
long-spiked fiddlewood 361
long-tail(ed) humming bird 309
long-tailed peadove 300
long-teeth drummer 324
long thatch 365
long time 107
long whip 213
look 64, 68, 148
look-look 72
looks 52
look-up 376
loss, lost 58
lots 52
lotus tree 357
Louisa (cassava) 336
love-dance 271
low cat-claw 383

lowland-pen 95
low (wine) 93
low-wine butt 94
Lucea mango 353
Lucea yam 342
lucky box, packet 278
lucky lily 378
lucky lizard 285
luggo-luggo 143
lulu 219
lung-plang 198
lungs 47
lurrucks 116

M

Ma 222
maaga 138
Maam 261
maamaa 217
mac 209
macaca, macacca 294
macadam 195
mac-an-truppance 209
macary bitter 384, 394
macaw bush 382–3
macaw palm 363–4
macca 7, 8, 391
macca-back doctor-fish 327
macca-back (shad) 320
macca breadfruit 7
macca bush 383
macca-fat 5, 7, 363–4
macca fern 7, 368
macca fish 316
macca yam 5, 340
macka 7, 8
machete, machetto 79–80, 319, 392
Mackenzie parrot 326
mackerel mango 353
mackerel plantain 352
mack-eye 137
macky (Massa) 181–2, 223, 395
Macoo 237
macooche 191
Mada 223
Mada Cantinny 276
Madagass 159
Madam fate 379
Madam sit-down (yam) 341
mad-ant 289–90
maestifino 162
mafeena, mafino 171
mafootoo, mafutu withe 181, 373, 394
Maggie 219

maggot fly 291
magnet 253
maiden-plantain 352
maiden plum 363
maiden pullet 104
maiden yellowtail 328
main 207, 399
majoe (bitters) 330, 384, 394
makaku, makuku 294
Ma Katy 310
make 43, 141
make four eyes 136–7, 397
make (one) know 183
making-up 254
makla-makla 172
makongo 294
makwakwa 294
malahack 145
mala-mala 70, 144, 146
malantang 322, 391
malatta tree 357
malawa 205, 394
mal d'estomac, mal de stomach 132, 393
malembe 225, 395
mama(-man) 182
mamma yaw 130
mammee(-apple) 356, 391
mammee bark 356
mammee-gum 356
mammee-sapota, -suppotta 356, 391
mammick 146
mammy 236
mammy-supporter 356
mampalo 182
mamzelle (fish) 393
man 224, 397–8
manatee stone 135
manatee strap 213
man-back 377
man beefwood 359
mancha 42, 351, 400
manchineel 378
manchinic 42, 351
man dandelion 6, 400
man doctor-fish 327
mandram 197
mango 335, 353
mango bug 293
mango humming-bird 309
mangro-hen 298
mangro snapper 322
mangrove crab 331
mangrove cuckoo 305

man-heart 376–7
manifac 211
mannersable 179
mannish 178
man-o'-war (bird) 297
man-o'-war bladder 333
mantle-stick 87
man-to-man 376, 378
mantry-maker 167
manumission 215
mapempe 386, 394
marang(a) 359, 401
maranga coco 339, 394
maranta 401
marasme, marasmus 133
marble-head mullet 321
mare-tail squirrel-fish 326
Margaret (fish) 323
mariggle, maringle 216,
318
mark-head 311
marking fern 368
mark work 100
mark you 226
marl hole 75
Marly hill (cassava) 336
Maroon 19–21, 160–1,
164, 393
Maroon blister 161, 384
marooner 164
Maroon flute 264
Maroon lance 161
Maroon pimento 161
Maroon weed, wiss 161,
384
marosh 78, 120, 393
marry 211
marshalman 217
Marshal sweet-potato 337
Martinico rose 387
Martinique banana 351,
393
Mary bush 372, 385
Mary coat blue 300
Mary Dougal sweet-
potato 337, 390
Mary Gould 324, 385
Mary Gould mango 353
Mary Grudgeful 294, 400
Maryland sweet-potato
337
Mary shakewell 312
Mary syrup mango 353
Mary wiss 372
marzella yam 341
mash (mesh) 43
mash (smash) 147
masha, masher 114
mashalah 217

mash-flat 142
mash-mash 210
mash-mouth drummer
324
mash (one's) sore toe 183
mash up 147
masi 43
maskin 270
Mass 223–4
Massa-tenky 224
massu 143, 395
Master (and his Cock)
277
master yaw 130
mastiff bat 283
mastwood 358
matchet 80
Matilda bush 385
matrimony 198
Matron 261
matta-matta 71
mauby 34
mauger, maugre 138
mawi, mawy 163, 393
may 61
May bird 305
May-day mahogany 361
maypole 270, 367
mazala 197
McKatty bush, weed,
wiss 385
me 53–5, 396
meager 138
measure 36
meat-kind 190
me-chile 224
meck-up 138, 210
mecky-mecky 120
meet up 142
me fada 229
mek 43, 141
mekam-fekam 179, 397
mek-up 138, 210
mel, mell 39, 184
melon thistle 366
me mada 229
memorial table 239
mempau 199
menow-weed 376, 394
mento 272, 392, 395
menya-menya 123
mercy 43
mercy-rye   doctor-fish
327
merengue 265, 273, 392,
395
merino 116
merry-wang 265
merrywing 291, 391, 393

meself 57
mesh 43
me-son 224
messenger 278
Messenger Boy 261
met 85, 270
met-pot 85
mial 243, 395
Michael 200
mickle(-muckle) 124, 397
middle cattle 103
middleday 109
might 61
Milady 327
mile-money 212
mile-walk 374
milk mango 353
milkweed 386
milk wiss 375
Mimba 157
min 40
mind 183
mingling pains 133
mingo 318, 394
mini-mini 70, 123, 291,
395
Minty coco 339
mirasmy (baby) 133
mirasmy bush 377
miry grunt 323
Miss Cooba 158
Miss Jany bush 385
Missis 224
Miss Pretty 327
Miss Ritty 385, 390
Mr Mac (parrot) 326
mistletoe 380
mix(ture) pea 344
mobby 34, 203–5, 391
Moco 158
Moco John 158, 324
Moco robin 324
moist 64
molasses cistern 93
money fly 291
money lily 378
mongalar drummer 324
mongoose 283
mongoose fern 368
mongoose grass 377
mongoose weed 377, 381
monk bat 283
monk beetle 293
monkey berry 382
monkey breadfruit 342
monkey-face 138, 277
monkey fiddle 382
monkey iron 201
monkey-jesus 169

montompy 137, 395
Montserrat pine 353
moochu 149
moodoo 171
moon-full 113
moonshine 4, 113, 399
moonshine baby 276–7
moonshine darlin' 271
moonshine drummer 324
moonshine snapper 322
moonshine yam 342
moon-tail parrot 325
moony 292
moos-moos 71, 282
morass 120, 393
mori 317
moringa 359
morosso 120
mortelle 359, 393
Moses-weed 359
mosquito boot 113
mosquito hawk 295–6
moss 47
Mother 234–5
Mother Edwards sweet-potato 337
Mother of the Cumina 236
Mother Thomas (mach-ete) 80, 390
Mother Thomas sweet-potato 337
moth grass 370
mount 239
mountain bulfinch 311
mountain cabbage 364
mountain calalu 346–7
mountain cock 302
mountain crab 330
mountain crayfish 330
mountain damson 363
mountain dick 302
mountain dove 301
mountain Judy 302
mountain mullet 321
mountain owl 308
mountain palm 364
mountain partridge 301
mountain pigeon 301
mountain pride 363
mountain sparrow 311
mountain witch 300–1
mourning table 239
mouse-colour parrot 325
mout-a-gram 180, 401
mout-a-massy 179
mout-have-nutt'n-fe-do 179–80
mouth-water 137, 396
2G

mouty-mouty 71, 179
mozella yam 341
mucco robin 324
much more 125
muckashandy 270, 397
muckle 124
muckumdash 169
mud-fish 328
mud-hook 317
mud jack 319
mud-mud 72
mud snapper 322
muka 153
mulatto 162
mulatto turtle 287
mulatto wood 357
mule(-back) (jack) 319
mule 324
mule-rial 102
mumble 153
mumby (crab) 331, 394
mumu 70, 181, 395
mungala (drummer) 324, 394
munjay 194, 393
musa, muse 198, 394
muschilli 291
mushé 224, 393
mushroom 386
music-man 274, 397
musk fly 293
musk okro 349
musk seed 349
musk wood 357
musmus 281
must 61
must can 61, 397
mustee 162, 392
mustifino, mustiphino 162, 392
must powder 254
mutton 197
mutton owl 324
mutton-snapper 322
myal 323, 241, 243–4
myal-man 243
myal-weed 380
my-lady 294
My-Lady coco 339

N

naadi 297
naagin 209
nambo, nambu 82, 400
namprel 102
namsack 82, 400
nana 3, 166, 222, 395
Nancy Pretty 327
Nancy (spider) 287, 400

Nancy story 275–6
Nanga 159
nanka 286, 394
nanny 102, 222, 290
nanny-eye grunt 323
nanny-thatch 368
Napier grass 369
nasbury, naseberry 355–356, 391
naseberry bat 283
nata 349
natal tree 254
natta-bige 287
navel-string tree 254
nayga 156–7
nayga-fish 318
nayga-man 329
naygur 156–7
nebba 39, 40
neck-back 138
neck-string 138
nedge 137
nedge weed 137, 378
need 61
needle 40
needle-case, -pointer 295
neegrish 157
neeseberry 355–6
neeseberry bullet 360
neger 156
Negro day 109
Negro fruit 356
Negro-ground 96
negro itch 132
negro pine 353
negro-pot 85
negro-worm 294
negro yam 341
neighbour 185
Nelson ball pea 345
nenyam 189
nephritic tree, wood 383, 385
nes(ses) 52
neutral up 183
never 108
never-dead, -die 359
newsbug, newsbunga 293
newsmonger 293
new sugar 201
newsvunga 293
next 125
nickal 278
nickar, nicker 278, 379–380
nigga-fish 318
nigger-head 289
night-baby 294
night-bat 295

panny 85
pan sugar 201
pant 102
pant(s) 51, 116
pan-tub 85
panya 268-9
panya jaw 84
Papaw weed 377
paper-skin mango 353
papishuo 280
papoose plantain 352, 391
paracuta, paracute 315
paradise plum 202
Para grass 369
parakii 303
parangle 116
para-para 116
Paratee, Parattee 160, 392
paraventure 4
parched-corn 294
pardaline snake 286
pargie 324
parrot mango 353
parrot-weed 382
parrot wood 361
parry-cart 75
parsley pea 345
partridge (dove, pigeon) 301
pasa-pasa 122
pasayro 180, 392
pass 41, 75
pass mango 353
pat 34
path 41
patoo, patook 308
patta 77, 394
patta-cat 215
patto 308
patu 36, 169, 308, 394
patu-dowdow 169
patu lobster 330
paty 325
Pauly lizard 285
Pa Will yam 342, 390
pawn (span) 142
pawn (spawn) 37
pawnz-belly, pawnzo 160
payrin 171
peace cup and spoon 245
pea-dove 300
peaka peow 208, 394
pean-pean, pea-piu 177
pear 39, 355
peas 51
peas walk 97
pechary, pecheere, peche-
    ree 6, 37

peckle 37
pecta 37
pedita 41
peel-a'ready 199
peel-head, -neck 104, 136
peeny(-wauly) 292, 397
pee-pee 71, 104
peg 99
Peggydone, Peggy Dunn 385
pempe, pem-pem 386
pen, penn 95, 164
penguin 367-8
penning over 88
penn-keeper 164
People of Colour 21
pepeeret 303
pepper 347-8
pepper and salt to your
    mammy 252
pepper-ant 290
pepper-elder 348, 376
pepper-fly 290
pepperpot 191, 336
pepper rod 385
pere-pere 395
perino 205
person of colour 161
perverse 175
pesterine 208
petchary, -ery, -erry 303-
    304, 391
pettifogging 124
Pheba 157
Phrygian-cap (limpet) 331-2
piaba 386
piangy-piangy, pianji
    (-pianji) 168, 395
piano grass 370
pichieri 303
pick-a-bait 329
pickaninny Christmas 270
pickaninny gang 89
picker 327
Pickering's herb 384
pick grass 89
pickiny 168
pickle 214
pick-me-round 200, 400
pick-mout 180
pick-nut 386
pickny 168
pickny mumma 168, 347,
    390, 397, 404
pickny-mumma coco 339
pickny-mumma sweet-
    potato 337

pick-up 398
picky-picky 173
pider 37
piece 96
piemente, piemento 348
pigeon lice 296
pigeon-neck sweet-potato 337
pigeon pea 344
pigeon pepper 347
pig-fish 326, 328
pigfoot 329
pig-nose (jack) 319
pig-nut 386
pig's apple 382
pigsty fence 97
pig-tail peas 343
pigtoe 329
pilcher 321
pile 35
pilikin 297
pillung 101
pilot (fish) 328
pilot jack 320
pimentade 197, 393
pimento 45, 335, 348, 392
pimento dram 206
pimento grass 370
pimento tick 296
pimento-walk 97
pincers, pinchers 320
pinda cake 201
pine 352-3
pinguin 367-8, 391
pingwing (macca) 7, 69, 97, 367-8
pingwing yam 341
piniwinkle 332
pink 167, 301
pink parrot 325
pin-pillow 366
pint 219
pint-o'-water mango 353
piobba 386
piper 317
pippari 303
piramidig 309
pissibed 6
pistareen 208, 392
pitcheary 303
pitchy-patchy 69, 169
Pitchy-Patchy 261
pity-me-little 290, 400
plabba, plabber 151, 202, 397
plague 43
plain case 269
plam-plam 215, 395

plantain 335, 351–2
plantain bird 310
plantain chips 197
plantain drink 203
plantain walk 96–7
plantation eel 196
plant-cane 88
plaw 151
play 269
playing 180
playing case, drum 269
play (one) out 216
pleasant-plantain 352
pleasuration 187
pleasure 36
pleasureness 187
pleg 43
plenty-plenty 71–2
plimploe 366
plit 37
plum banana 351
plum-head (snapper) 322
plummy mango 353
plunka 114, 200
ply 230
P.N.P. parrot 325
po 85, 393
pockwood 358
poco 234, 238
pocomania, pocomanism
    234–5, 238–40
poco-poco 225, 392
poco-tempo 124, 392
pod 98
podo 361
Poinciana 6, 390
point-nose (jack) 319
poison-cane 378
poison fish 329
poison-grouper 318
poison hogmeat 370
P.O.J. cane 351
poke-weed 346–7
poleen 76, 94
police macca 381
policeman 294, 327
Police sweet-potato 337
police turbot 317
polink 76, 94, 392
poll-head 102
Polly grunt 324
Polly lizard 285
poloo-poloo 227
po me bwoy, gal 227
pommel-foot 140
pompano 319
pon 37
pond coot 299
pone 391, 398

pone pan 86
pongo-rong 230
pooka-pooka 71
pooky 326, 397, 403
poop-stink parrot 325
poor 39
poor Joe wenchman 326
poor-man's fritters 195
poor man's sauce 198
pooroo 186
pop 146
pop-chow 394
pope('s) head 366
pop-off 199
pop-pop 71
poppy-show 279
porcupine (fish) 41, 316
porgo 324
porgy (grunt) 324, 391
pork-fish 327
pork grunt 323
pork-weed 346
poroo-poroo 227
porot 303
porter-bush 379
porter cup 205
Portland yam 342
Port-Morant tobacco
    382–3
Portugee (hog-fish) 327
pose off 153
post-holder 236
pot 34
potato louse 296
potato piece 96
potato slip 337
pot bammy 194
pot-belly 133
pot-chow 394
pot-cover (fish) 325
potoo 308
pot-snapper 322
pot-spoon, -stick 86
potting (sugar) 93
pot-water 191
poultice 45
pound crab 331
power key 239–40
power-ring 250
power shoes 114
power stone 240
pox 102
pran 153
pran-pran 101
pra-pra 70, 149, 395
prayer 44
prayer key 240
preachy-preachy 71
precke, precky 181, 186

pre-pra 86, 394
pressing 76
press-oil 136
prettyalla 360
pretty (fish) 327
pretty-pretty 72, 169
pretty-yellow 360
Price's rat 282
pricke 186
prickelalla 360
prickle 46
prickle grass 370
prickle walk 97
prickly bottle-fish 316
prickly breadfruit 342
prickly calalu 346
prickly fern 368
prickly pear withe 372
prickly pole 364
prickly withe 372
prickly-yalla, -yellow 360
prima cane 351
primenta 348
primenta horse 293
prims (off) 153
princewood 362
Prison Farm sweet-potato
    337
privilege 211–12
professor 242
prong 46
property pony 182
pr-o-pr-o 290
provision ground 96
pruce 34, 37
prusy 178
puchin 168
puckro(-puckro) 171, 395
pudding pan 86
pudding-withe, -wis 372
puff-fish 316
puff-gut 316
puka(-puka) 170
puke mango 353
pukkumerian 234–6
pull 147
pull-coat 378, 390
pull (obeah) 244
puller 244
pull foot 141
pulp 136
pulper 97
pulp eye 136
pumble-foot, pummel
    foot 140, 399
pumpum, pumpun yam
    340, 394
puncheon-water 205
pung 144

punkin (sweet-potato)
337
puntee 243, 395
punyaak 81
puppa-lick, pupperlich
277
Puppa Will yam 342
puppy fish 314
puppy-mouth parrot 325
puppy shark 314
puppy turbot 317
purification 239
purple coco 339
purple parrot 325
purple pepper 348
purpose 175
purril 375
purse cacoon 373
puss 6, 105, 397
puss boot 114
puss-claw 383
pussery 105
puss-gut 373
puss-head 360
pussley calalu 347
puss prayers 401
puss-puss 276
puss shoe 114
put (off) (obeah) 244,
247
put (one's) foot in order
141
put (one) so 244
putta-putta 70, 395
put (the) hand on 247
put the mill about 90,
399
putu(s) 219
pyaa-pyaa 177, 395
pyaka-pyaka 170, 395
pyaw-pyaw 177
pyramidal pine 353

Q

quab 326
qua-bird 298
quabs 180
Quaco 157-8
quaco-bush 371
quail 152
quality 177
quality spell 89
Quamin 157-8
Quao, Quaw 157-8, 171
quart 219
quarter bunch 99
Quarteron 162, 392
Quasheba 157-8
Quashee, Quashie 157

quashie (breadfruit) 342
quash-quash 375
quattie 209
Quawy 158, 171
Queen 260-1
queen-conch 332
queen crab 331
queen dove 236
queen-fish 319
queen lobster 330
queen mullet 321
queen of birds 299
Queen of the Cumina 236
queen pineapple 352
Queen's daughter, grand-
child 261
queeze 37
queng 158
quick-stick 359
quick time 108
quinge-up 148
quint 37
quit 309-10
quitter 4, 135, 399
qui yah 228
quok 298

R

raa-baaba 217
raabit 44, 276
raatid 175, 229
raccoon 281
racecourse macca 381
racial 180
rack 205
rackle drum 269
radge 216
ragga-ragga; raggity 72,
169
raging 44
rain-bird 305-6
rainbow old-wife 318
rainbow parrot 325
rain fly 289
raise 64, 210
raise a kite 183
raise (the colour) 222
rake 208
rale 44
ram 105
rambling shepherd 235
ram-goat 103
ram-goat dashalong,
national, rashicali, ra-
tional, regular 381-2
ram-goat rose 382
ramoon 44, 362, 392
rank 43
rap-house 76

rash(in), rashy 189, 403
rass, rassa 139
rat 34, 47, 402
rat-bat 283
rat book 90
rat-cut 97
rat-ears 348, 376
ration 189
ratoon 392
ratta 282, 402
ratta castle 79
ratta-temper 376
rat-teeth parrot 325
rattler, rattlin drum 269
rattle-weed 376
raw-chaw 69, 170
rax 184, 399
reach 142
reach the sundial 238
ready-money land 96
real 44
really 33
receiver 92
red 202
red afu (yam) 340
red-and-white bullet 360
red ant 289
red-arsed spider 287
red banana 351
red-bead tree 371
red-bead vine 371
red-belly parrot 325
red-belly snapper 322
red birch 357
red bonavist 343
red bullet 360
red calalu 346
red-coat 319
red crab 331
red disease of Guiana 132
red Eboe 163
red-eye mullet 321
red-foot jumper, jumping-
dick 302
red gal 377
red grunt 323
redgut bullet 360
red hairy-tailed bat 283
red-head 376
Red Miss Kelly pea 344
red-mouth grunt 323
red-necked gaulin 299
red-parrot 325
red pea 344
red petchary 303
red potato 337, 393
red rail 298
red St Vincent yam 342
red santa 362

salt-water creole, negro 18, 156
sam 216, 395
samba 168, 392, 395
sambo 163
same like 66
same one 126
same time 67, 108
same way 67
samfie, sanfie (man) 216, 397
Sammy blackie 328
samplatta 113, 392
sananana crab 331
San Blas coco 339
sanchocho 147
sanchy 233
sancocho 191, 392
sand 38
sandal 41
sand blackie, fish 328
sand-gall 121
sand-patta, -platter 113, 392
sanfai 216
san-fish 318
sangkochie 191
sangkoko 147
sankey 233-4
sankutu 147
santa 205, 362
Santa Maria tree 362, 392
santapee, santapii 295, 392
sapodilla 356, 392
Sarah bird 303
Sarey sweet-potato 337
Satan 261
satin (fish) 322
sauly 169
savanna bird 311
savanna blackbird 305
savanna grass 369
savat 40
saw-fish 315
say, say-say 63, 395-6
scaveech(ed fish) 7, 195, 392
schoolmaster snapper 322
science, scientific man, scientist 242
scissor(s) 51
scissors (bird) 297
scissors-tail (humming-bird) 309
scissors-tail sweet-potato 337
scorn-the-earth, -ground 380

Scotch attorney 380
Scotch-bonnet pepper 347
Scotch grass 369
Scotchman (hugging a Creole) 380
scoveitch (fish) 7, 195, 392
scrape 45
scraper 266
scrapses 52
scratch 153-4, 171
scratch-coco 338
scratch-scratch 132
scratch wiss 372
scratchy 171
screbbey 172
screwy 293
scrib 279
scrub dry yaws 183
scuffle(r) 215
scuttle 317
se 63, 396
sea-anancy 331
sea angel 318
sea-banana 333
sea-bat 319
sea-beef 332
sea-bladder 333
sea breeze 110
sea-butterfly 327
sea-cat 332, 393
sea-cockroach 333
sea-cowitch 333
sea crab 330
sea-crayfish 330
sea eel 317
sea-egg 332
sea-fiddler 329
sea forty-leg 333
sea-galliwasp, gally-wasp 318
sea-gulf 297
sea-jelly 333
seal 240
sea-mahmy, -mammy 252
sea-needle 332
sean fish 318
sea-plate 332
sea-prick 333
sea-puss 333
sea rat-bat 319
search-my-heart 377, 390
sea-roach 330, 333
sea-rose 332
sea-scorpion 333
sea-scratch 333
sea-side potato 376

sea-soldier 331
season 197, 398
season (rain) 112
seasoning 128
sea-star 332
sea-sting 333
sea-thimble 332
sea-ticks 333
sea-unicorn 315
sea-wasp 333
second breakfast 189
second cockcrow 109
second gang 88
second table 240
seed 99
seed under leaf 377
seed yam 341
Seely sweet-potato 337
see-me-contract 377
seh 63
seh-sa 185-6
sein(e)-fish 318
seizer 323
self 57, 126
self-heal 377, 384
semencontra 377
sempervive, sempervivum, semprevivy 6, 367
send-go 63
sensay, sense(h) fowl 36, 104, 394, 400
s'ep me King 229
September petchary 304
S'er 223
sese 70, 395
set 111-12, 239, 257-62
set dance 270
setting liquor 204
settle 40
setting stick 105
set-up 254, 269
seven-finger 374
seven-months coco 339
seven-year pea 344
Seville orange 354
sewi-sewi 311-12
sey 63
Seymour grass 369
sey-sey 186
shabers 180
shacka bird 313
shacka-bush 376
shadow 245-7
shadow-catcher, -ing 246
shaka 269, 395
shaker, shakey 269
shaky-shaky 71, 113
shall 61

shall-I 115
shamar 380
shambry 210
shame(-brown)-lady 380
shame-me-darlin, -dog 380
shame-ol'-lady 380
shamer(-macca, -weed) 380
sham-sham 199, 394
shamy(-bush) 380
shandy 403
shan't 61
shark waitin'-boy 166, 328
sha-sha 272
sha-shwa snapper 322
shay-shay 272, 393, 395
she 55
sheckle-weed 380
shed 98
sheep-head 316, 327
sheepshead alewife 318
sheg 184
shekrey 169
shell 87, 100
shell-blow 87, 109
shell copper 91
shell teach 91–2
shepherd 234–6, 238
shepherd boy, shepherd-ess 235–6
sheppon 86
sherrif 184
shet pan 86, 247
shevil-nosed shark 314
shi 70, 229–30, 396
shift 116, 398
shim-sham 273
shine 172
shine-a'-night 376, 390
shine-eye 302
shine-eye Barbados, black-bird 302
shine-eye jumper 302
shiny bush 376
shiny-moon snapper 322
shipmate 156, 399
shi-shi 70, 229–30, 396
shoe-black, shoe flower 387
shoe-patta 114
shoes 46
shooks 184
shoolah 149
shorance 37
shore 39
shortage 45
short-mouth(ed) blue quit 310

short thatch 365
should 61
should can 61, 397
shove 40, 44, 143
shovel-beak, -head, -mouth 314
show belly 133
show bread 199
show-me-show-me, show-me-town 295
shref-shref 237
shrimp maamy 333
shrip-shrap 115
shum-shum 70
shut pan 86
shut-weed 380
shuwa, shwuwa 86, 230, 394
sibl 354
sicky 135
side-bag, -basket 82
silk (fish) 322
silt-snapper 322
silver bush 376
silver fern 368
silver fish 320
silver grunt 323
silver-head 311
silver jack 318–19
silver old-wife 318
silver snake 286
silver straw, thatch 365
silver tick 296
simple-bible 6, 367, 401
since-when 182
sing 58, 274
singe 45
singer 278
singing bird 304
singkuma plantain 352
single-bible 6, 367
single-go, singrigo 383
sinket 121
sinner-contract 377
sintle-bible 367
sipple 151, 171
sipple calalu 339
sipple okro 349, 372
sit up 221
sivl orange 354
skellion 5
skellion grass 370
skellion lizard 285
Skelly pea 344
skile drummer 324
skin 402
skin-fish 317
skin (one's) teeth 137
skin-owl 251–2

skin up (one's) lip 137
skip, skipping 92
skipping gutter, trough 92
sky god 237
slave-court 218
sleepy-head parrot 325
slimmy-like 169
slipper-grass parrot 325
slippery-okro 349
slip-slop 115
s'm'ady 39
small 38, 402
small-leaved calalu 346
small green-lizard 284
smallpox bush 377
small-stock 103
smashing of the first altar 240
s'mody 168
smoke-mill 91
smoke plantain 352
smoky banana 351
smooth 38
smooth bottle-fish 316
smooth-leaved cerasee 375
smooth-leaved pine 353
snake 38, 43
snake bush 372
snake-cap 42
snake-root 380
snake waitin'-boy 283
snake-weed 380
snake wiss 372
snakewood 362
snake yam 341
snapper 321–2
snite 299
snook 38, 315
snoring 38
snort-head, snot-head parrot 325
snowball 206
so (and thus) 65–6, 396
so (even as) 65–6
soakapee 206
soap fish 327
sob 40
soft 38
soggy 45
soldier 236, 298, 331
soldier wiss 372
solitaire 303
Solomon Gundy 195, 398
so long 67
somebody 57, 168
something 57, 168

soonga 345, 394
Sophie mango 353
sorasi, sorasy 375, 394
sore throat pepper 348
sore toe 87
sorrel 45, 349–50
sorrel drink 204
sorrow-for-poor (bean) 365
so-so 126, 395–6
sosuma 383
so tell 125
sourasea 375
sour fly 291
sour grass 370
sour orange 354
soursop 354
soursop bird 310
soursop fish 41, 316
soursop quit 309–10
soushumber, sousumba 382–3
South-sea rose 388
southward grunt 323
sow (machete) 80, 400
sow-mouth squirrel 326
span 142
Spanish angel-fish 327
Spanish bill 80
Spanish calalu 346
Spanish carnation 387
Spanish cedar 357
Spanish elder 348
Spanish elm 5, 43, 362
Spanish hog-fish 326
Spanish-horse 293
Spanish jar 84
Spanish machete 80, 359
Spanish nightingale 304
Spanish oak 358, 362
Spanish old-wife 317
Spanish pheasant 301
Spanish potato 337
Spanish shad 320
Spanish wall 79
Spanish woodpecker 303
specia 202, 392
species, speesh 52, 56
spell 89
sperit 43
spider 287, 402
spikenard 386–7
spinach 346
spinner 194
spirit-leaf 376
spirit-sickness 247
spirit-weed 376, 380
spliff 207
spoil 35

spokes 52
sporter 167
spotted-chinned snake 286
spotted snake-eel 317
spotted creeper 312
spotting 273
spout 45
sprain 63
sprickle-sprickle 71
squab 324, 326
squally 112
squeechy 285
squeeze-eye 163
squeezer 87
squib(s) 333
squirrel(-fish) 326
sred 402
srimps, srints 330, 402
sripple 402
Sta 223
stable fly 291
staff 100
stag fly 293
stagger-back 201, 401
stain, stainy 171
stainy banana 351
stamp-and-go 194–5, 399
stancha 94, 392
stan(d) 34, 60, 140, 399
standing 278
stand marshal 217
stand-'pon-rock 376
starapple 355
starch bean 336, 345
star grass 370
starlight 279
star-stone 332
station guard 234
stavewood 363
stay 60, 140, 399
steel bottom 205
steeper 101
stem 99
sterling 37
stick 402
stick-licking 214
stinging ant 290
stinging grouper 318
sting-ray 315
stinking ant 289
stinking oil 87
stinking-toe 357
stinkin'-weed 377
stirring stick 93
stole 88
stomach evil 132
stone-balls, -bar, -bass 320

stone-beard 376
stone brim 323
stone-bruise 377
stone drummer 324
stone fence 398
stone hole 121
stool 88
stop-it-a-pass 198
stoshus 178
stoshy 219
strain 64
strainer vine 375
stranger (fly) 293
strawn-up 72
strawny 171
streamers jack 319
streamer-tail(ed) humming bird 309
stream mullet 321
streela, streeler 116, 397
striking 92
stringhalt 42
stringy mango 353
stripe(d) cane 350
stripe-holland 312
strive 5
strong 64
strong-back 377
strong-eye 174, 397
strong-man's weed 381
strong-mouth 174
strong-physic 175
strong-yeye 174, 397
strum-strum 265
stucky 219
study (one's) head 184
sty 95
su 227, 396
such-like 47
suck 328
sucko-bolo 179
suck (one's) teeth, tongue 137
suck-stone 328
sucky-baby 347
sucky-swallow yam 342
sucture 328
sugar-and-water 188, 201
sugar ant 290
sugar bean 345
sugar drink 203
sugar head 201
sugar-loaf pine 352
sugar-pot 93
sugar tea 188
Sukey breadfruit 342
sulphur banana 351
sum 204
Sun 158

suna 176–7
sun hot 109
sunshine 320
sun-silk 322
supple 45
supple-jack 371
Surinam coco 339
Surinam pea 345
surprised fowl 196
susumba, susumber 382–383, 394
su-su(-su-su) 70, 186, 395
swallow-fish 324
swallow (one's) spit 137
swallow-tail drummer 324
sweat-table 207
Sweden 310
swee-swee 312
sweet 182–3
sweet broom(-weed) 371
sweet-lip grunt 323
sweet mango 353
sweet-mouth 173
sweet-potato 336–7
sweet-potato bug 294
sweet-potato pone 198
sweet-sop 354
sweet-up 183
sweet-weed 371
sweet yam 341
swell-hand 378
swimps 330, 402
swine-head (jack) 319
swing-sang 278, 394
swipple 171, 402
swipple-pole 366
swips (off) 143, 152, 230
swi, swi 230
switching-neck 299
switchy 171
switchy-tail wenchman 326
swivel 240
sword bean 345
sword (machete) 80, 400
sword-rose, -tree 359
sympathisement 187

T

Ta 222
Taam 44
taa yam 340, 342, 394
table 239, 253
tach, tache 91–2, 392
tack 91
Tacooma 275–6, 395
taffy (goat) 103, 397, 403

tafu crab 331
Taggoram 103
tail 111
tailor-scissors crab 331
tai shiin 208, 394
taitch 91
tajas 339
tajo 227
takada 97, 392
take 29, 43, 148
take off (obeah) 244, 247
take off crop 90
take time 108
take up work 100
takro-takro 170, 395
talk 47
talkee-talkee, talky-talky 71, 215
talking cow 248
tall 122
tallaban, tallala 179
tallawah 178–9
tall calalu 346
tamarind jack 319
tamarind season 109
tambo 106
tambu 265–6, 271, 393
tampi 207
'tan deh 248
tangerine 46
tankari 197, 393
tanky 225
tanky-massa 115
tanna 82, 394
tannier 337–8
'tan-'pon-rock 390
tanto 122, 392
tap 37
tapiapaas 198
tapna-chick 303
tarantula 288
tarpon, tarpum 315, 392
tarra 41
tart 34
task 38
taste 58
tata 222, 395
tatch 91
tatta 222
taya 337–8, 391
tea 188, 253
teach, teache 91
teacheress 166
teachment 238
tear-up-tear-up 72
tee-taa-toe 279
teeth 51
teeth wiss 375
teggereg 180

tegrey 75
tek 29, 43
tek spring 99
tek time 142
tel 43
tell-say 63
tell-tale 299
temper-bush 380
temper lime 92
tenk 43
tempting powder 245
tenky 225
tenky-Massa 224
tenna 82, 394
tenner 209
tenny 278
ten o'clock 387
ten-penny 138
ten-pounder 318
tep 123
tep-tep 219
terceron 162, 392
tetch 91
tetes 180
te-tie 82
tetla lobster 330
thank 43
thank-you-ma'am 74, 398
that 403
thatch 365, 368
thatch hat 115
thatch stick 93
that side 117
there 43
thick-lip conch 332
thick-lip grunt 323
thick-lipped mountain mullet 321
things 242
thirsty 172
this-here 47
this side 117
Thompson weed 385
thorn-apple 388
thornback 315
thoroughbred 41
thought 34, 75, 398
thread-bag 83
three-foot-horse 251
three-keel (turtle) 287
three-quarter 99
three-quarter bunch 99
through 42
throw 62, 143
throw off 153
throw sarcasm, words at the moon 184
thunder crab 331

thunder snake 286
thwart 34, 75, 398
tichibu 292
tichicro 311
tick-bird 305
tick-eater 305
ticket 215
ticklebro 331
tickle-me 276
ticks (stick) 46
ticks (tick) 52
ticky 37
ticky-ticky 329
tie 101
tie-a-leaf 193
tief 63, 148, 215
tiefenness 215
tief-tief 5, 71, 215
tie-leaf 193
tie-sheen 208, 394
tie-teeth 201
tie-tongue 138
tie-up 138
tiger fern 368
tiger plantain 352
tight-fit 199
tilderee 299
tile 34
till 43
timbim 131
timiny 168, 395
timi-timi 386, 390
tin-case 84
ting-ling 305
tinggry 315
ting-ting, tinkling grackle 305
tinnen 4, 172, 399
tin-tin 305
tip-dung 147
tittle drum 269, 395
toad-eye cane 350
toad-fish 316
toad-trash 368
toady 283, 316
tobacco conch 332
tobacco fish 317
tobacco old-wife 317
tobacco turbot 317
Toby-wiss 372
tocks 37
today-and-tomorrow mango 353
toddy-rack 205
tody 309
toe 99
toil 34
tomb dance 255
tombing 255

Tom Bontein's bush 384
tomfariah 277
Tom-fool (petchary) 304
Tommy 326
Tom Raffles (ant) 289
Tom squirrel 326
tongue 38, 278
tongue-cattle 103
tongue-steer 103
ton han 210
too 124
too-good coco 339
took-took 84
toombah 265-6
toona 366
top-a-top 346
to pieces 124
top-side 399
torch 44
torch-cactus 358
torch-wood 44, 358
tortoise fly 293
tortoiseshell bird 299
torture 44
toto 70, 200, 394
tough 64
tout 37
town 38
town order 210
trampooze 141
trapong 315
trapong fry 329
trash 89, 100
trash hat 115
trash house 89
trash-meself cane 351, 390
treat 37
tree 42, 51
tree-of-life 378
tree-oyster 331
tree-pine 368
tremble 43
trembler 315
trespass 176
triangle 41
trickify 176
tricking-chick 302
trick-weed 376
trimble 43
trimonia 388
Trinidad yam 341
trinklet 116
trip 37
,trip-me-naked 199
trooping 238
tropon 315
trouser(s) 51
trump and labour 238

trumpet(er) 317
trumpet tree 362
trumping 238
trunk-fish 316-17
trunk fleet 166
trust 211
truvel 40
tube 76
tub-pan 85
tuff 37
tuffa 229, 396
tuku 168, 395
tumaali 195, 391
tumba 265-6, 395
tumble-bug 293
tumble down 221
tumble-tud 293
tumbozoo 131
tumpa 168
tumpa-foot, -toe 139-40
tumpy 138
tumtum 70, 144, 192-3 329, 394
tumtum mortar 193
tun 64
tuna 366, 391
tung 39
tun-tun 71-2
tup(py) 209
turbot 317
turkey-berry-tree 356
turkey-blossom 381
turkey-rial 102
turkey weed 381
turkle 290
Turk's cap, head 366
turn 39, 99
turn-back 315
turn-bill 80
turned cornmeal 192
turn hand 210
turn (one's) eyes 245
turn-point 80
turn stick 86, 93
turpentine mango 353
turpentine tree 357
turtle apple 356
tush the clappers 279
tuttu-watta 231
tutty 169
tutu 219
tweet-to-whit 311
tweh 123
twice-laid 195, 399
twistletoe 380
twist tobacco 206
two-bob 209
two-headed snake 286
two-mac 209

two-minded 239
two-penny chick 302–3

U

udge 184
ugly 45, 187
ulu 215
unarrowed 90
uncle 223
Uncle Joe 200
unconscionable 176
undertaker('s wind) 111
unknown tongue 249
unmannersable 179
untidy 178
unu 54, 396
up 68
uplifting table 239
upon 37
upstairs 77

V

valk 41
vanglo(e) 345–6
vater 41
vell 41
velvet leaf, wiss 375
vendue (room) 211, 393
Venus lizard 285
vervain humming-bird 309
vex(ed) 40
vial 136, 399
victory 117
victuals 40, 189
ving-vang 278
visit (one's) Indian cousin 117
volunteer 46
voon-vap 231

W

wa 56
waaí-uo 228, 396
waan 60
waang-fu 171
waa-yo 228, 396
wack-a-tack 179
wa' fe do, wa-fi-du 226
wagga-wagga 122
waiter 398
waiting-boy 166
wait on 398
wake 269
walk 58, 96–7
walk and cotch 148
walk-go 63
walking buckra 155–6
walking train 76

walk out 221
wall okro 349, 372
wall-saddle 372
wa mek 226, 397
wampara 80, 392
wanderer cane 351
wangla, wangola 346, 394
wangla (cake) 200–1
wanika 361
want 60
wappy 207
wappen-bappen 79
wara 56
wari 380, 394
warra 41, 56, 403
warrior man, woman 236
warrior shepherd 235
warry 380, 394
Warwick 261
washaway 121
wash-mout' 188
wash-pap 191
wass-wass 51, 71–2
watchicraca 304
watchman 243, 277
watchy 277
watchy picket 304
water boy 236, 252
water-bush 151
water coconut 199
water crab 331
water-dipper 295
water-dry 113
water-fetcher 103
water girl 252
water grass 370, 376
water lizard 285
water-man 363
water partridge 298
water shepherd(ess) 236, 252
water-wash 121
water-wiss, -withe 374–5
watery yaws 130
watlef 189
wat'melon 39
wattle 40
wattle-and-daub 78
wattle-pane 78
we (where) 43
we (we, us, our) 54
weather 111, 399
weather-bird 306
wedd'n-bessy 182
weeding gang 89, 165
wee-wee 71
we-fi-du 115
weh 37

weight 122
well 124
well-handed 399
welshman 306, 326
wen 40, 60
wenchman 326
wenchman daddy, puppa 326
wenya-wenya 169, 395
wera-ke-te 169
were-were 116
weself 57
Wesley (horn) 233, 263
West Indian cedar 357
West Indies banana 351
wet 63
wet-foot 219
wet sugar 201
whai 228
what 38, 56–7, 403
what a way 127, 229, 397
what-left 189
wheel 206
wheel and turn 308
wheeler 200
wheeling mother, shepherd 236
when 56–7
where 43, 56–7
which 56–7
which part 118
while 221
whipray 315
whip-Tom-Kelly 311
whistler 303
whistling cowboy 251
white afu (yam) 340
white Albion 201
white-a-middle 163
white ant 288
white-back 375–7
white-back fern 368
white-bark 363
white bean, pea 345
white-bellied duck 297
white-belly (dove) 300
white-belly maid 312
white-belly rat 282
white-bill 320
white-bird 297
white bonavist 343
white-breast (dove) 300
white bullet 360
white cane 350
white cassada 336
white chocho 350
white coco 339
white crab 330
white croaking lizard 284

white drummer 324
white egg-bird 297
white fiddlewood 361
white flux 134
white gaulin 299
white grunt 323
white-gum 331
white-head 376
white-headed potoo 308
white-head grass 370
white-heart breadfruit
    342
whitehouse banana 351
white jointer 348
white-man 171
whitening 320
white pear 355
white-people's pine 353
white porgy 324
white rain 112
white santa 362
white shark 314
white squall 112, 399
white squirrel-fish 326
white-stalk coco 339
white-stick (cassava) 336
white-stick fern 368
white sweetwood 359
white-water grunt 323
white wenchman 326
white-wing (dove) 300
white wiss 375
white yam 341
whitlow 40
Whittaker sweet-potato
    337
who 56–7
whooping boy 251
Whore Girl 261
why 56–7
wi 60–1
wich 56
wicker-wiss 374
wig 117
wiggle-wiggle 71
wild cabbage 364
wild calalu 346
wild cassada, cassava 336,
    377
wild celandine 382
wild-duck 297
wild hook 374
wild hops 379
Wild Indian 261
wild liquorice 371
wild mint 377
wild okro 349
wild pine 368
wild-pine sergeant 305

wild potato (-slip) 370
wild senna 387
wild shot 384
wild slip 370
wild starch 345
wild thyme 368
wild yam 372, 374
wilk 332
will 38, 60–1
William Burke cane 351
wind 272
windgy 103, 138, 168
windward 118, 399
winji 103
winjy-winjy 71
winker, winky 292
winsor 329
wipri, wipry 52, 315
wire-back (jack) 319
wire withe 372–3
wis, wiss 7, 45, 370–6
wishing cow 248
wiss-maami 374
wiss-wiss 71, 370
wit 40
withe 45, 370–6
woda 361
woio 228
wolongo 345
woman 40, 399
woman-be-damned 86
woman beefwood 359
woman cane 351
woman dandelion 6, 399
woman doctor-fish 327
woman-mouth fern 363,
    368
woman's tongue 363
woman strong-back 377
wongala 346
wood 41
wood-ant 288–9
wood-chink 296
wood-clock 293
wood-digger 293
wooden-foot 139
woodpecker 218
wood lizard 285
wood louse 288
wood owl 308
woodpicker 303
woodslave 285
wood snake 286
word 34
work 242–3
working 237, 243, 247
work (one's) head 184
world, the 240
worm 38, 93

worm-bark 365
worm-grass 377
worm quit 312
worm snake 286
worm-tube 332
worm-weed 377
wormwood tree 365
worserer 64
worth 39
worthless 177
would 61
wouldn't 41
wounded 58
woy 228
wrapper coolie 163
wrap up 183
wring 135
wrong-side 172
wroth(ed) 175
wud 34
Wynne grass 369

Y

-y 87
ya 55, 67
ya(a) 226–7
yabba 85
yacca 361
yagga-yagga 116
yalla-yalla 72
yam (root) 335, 339–42,
    394
yam (nyam) 152
yam bank 100
yam-bank pea 345
yam bean 345
yam-cutter 311
yam field 100
yam-finger coco 339
yam fly 291
yam ground 100
yam head 99
yam hill 100
yam hole 100
yam mango 353
yampee, yampi 335, 341–
    342, 394
yam piece 96
yanga 141, 273, 392, 395
yard 77
yard-child 221
ya-so 66, 118
yaw 92, 392, 395
yaw-bump 99
yaw hospital 130
yaws 104, 129
yaw (sah) 226
yaws bush 372
yaws-children 130